KT-199-953

COLOUR LIBRARY BOOKS

NICE & EASY
COOKBOOK

COLOUR LIBRARY BOOKS

NICE & EASY COOKBOOK

COLOUR LIBRARY BOOKS

CLB 2135

This edition published 1988 by Colour Library Books Ltd,
Godalming Business Centre, Catteshall Lane,
Godalming, Surrey GU7 1XW

Reprinted 1989

© Marshall Cavendish Limited 1988
Prepared by Marshall Cavendish Books Ltd,
58 Old Compton St, London W1V 5PA

All rights reserved. No part of this publication may be
reproduced, stored in a retrieval system or transmitted, in any
form or by any means electronic, mechanical, photocopying,
recording or otherwise, without the permission of the publishers
and the copyright holder.

Printed in Italy

ISBN 0 86283 601 8

Contents

Introduction

The *NICE & EASY COOKBOOK* provides the modern family cook with a comprehensive collection of information and over 500 recipes. It is bang up to date with large sections on microwave cooking and freezing techniques, while the Cook Healthy section keeps pace with current thinking on healthy eating. At the same time it offers ideas for economical family meals and help with traditional cooking skills such as cake making and decorating.

A microwave cooker is ideal, of course, for cooking meals quickly and economically. All the information and recipes you need are provided in the first section of this book to help you make the most of this versatile and increasingly popular cooking method. In addition to main meals, there are recipes for fast midweek snacks, all manner of puddings, cakes and breads, plus a range of recipes for children to cook.

The microwave cooking section is perfectly complemented by the following section on freezing, since a microwave cooker enables you to thaw frozen foods and ready-prepared meals in a fraction of the time usually needed. The freezing section explains all about freezing fresh and cooked foods while the recipes provide ideas for complete meals which can be cooked and stored away in the freezer until required.

You will also find lots of dishes to cook ahead in the One-pot Meals section which is full of recipes for satisfying and nutritious soups, stews and casseroles. Many of the recipes may also be cooked in the microwave and there is plenty of advice on the various other methods of cooking one-pot meals, including pressure cooking and slow cooking.

Healthy eating concerns us all these days and the Cook Healthy section will help you stay on the right track. It comprises some sound nutritional advice followed by a selection of calorie-counted, satisfying and wholesome recipes, including such traditionally forbidden treats as cakes and teabreads.

A meal from a foreign cuisine is a challenge for any cook and makes a welcome change on the family menu. Selections of recipes from two of the most popular, Italian and Chinese, are included in this book. Clear and comprehensive instructions are given and step-by-step photographs help with some of the less familiar techniques. You could try your hand at authentic Italian dishes like Ossobuco or Sicilian Cassata, or sample a Chinese speciality, such as Peking Duck or Prawn Foo-Yung. And if you're keen enough to try a complete Italian or Chinese meal, there are helpful guidelines on planning the menu and buying the ingredients.

Cake making and decorating are traditional crafts of long standing, but they often defeat the amateur. The Cake Craft section in this book is designed to give you the confidence to make even the most elaborately decorated cakes. It includes a collection of fun cakes guaranteed to make any child gasp in amazement. Some of these impressive cakes, such as the Gingerbread House, may look difficult to make, but the recipes take you step by step through the instructions, making it all seem simple. You will find many cakes suitable for a celebration, including a wedding cake to take pride of place on the buffet table, as well as more simple iced tea-time treats and gorgeous gâteaux to serve at a dinner party or other special occasion.

The final section, Party Planner, takes the guesswork out of entertaining and makes it possible to give a party that you can actually enjoy yourself! All types of gatherings are covered — from a child's birthday tea-party to cocktails and canapés for adults, as well as more grand occasions such as wedding receptions and family christenings. The recipes are specially adapted to cater for large numbers, and the colour photographs illustrate just how magnificent a spread you can put on. There are also plenty of ideas for drinks to suit the occasion, including exciting and exotic cocktails and punches to make sure your parties go with a swing.

Every recipe in the book is written in a clear, concise style with numbered steps making them easy to follow, and many techniques are illustrated in step-by-step colour photographs so you can cook with confidence. The inspirational colour pictures of the finished dishes will help you select the recipes you want to cook, and your family and friends cannot help but be impressed by your extensive and varied repertoire.

Microwave
Cookery

Introduction

Whether you cook for a large family or just for one, microwave cookery is fast, simple and economical. The advantages are numerous – whole meals may be prepared in minutes, saving time, energy and washing-up! All you need is an understanding of how your microwave oven works and of the few basic techniques required.

Everything is explained, in simple terms, in this chapter, including what containers to use, how to test when food is cooked and everything else you need to know to cook, thaw or reheat food with confidence. All this, together with the recipes that follow, will ensure that your microwave cookery is successful every time.

Your Microwave

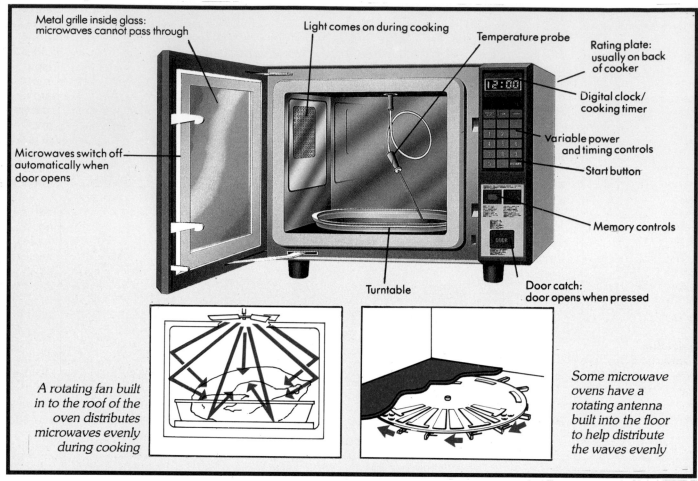

Metal grille inside glass: microwaves cannot pass through

Light comes on during cooking

Temperature probe

Rating plate: usually on back of cooker

Digital clock/ cooking timer

Microwaves switch off automatically when door opens

Variable power and timing controls

Start button

Memory controls

Turntable

Door catch: door opens when pressed

A rotating fan built in to the roof of the oven distributes microwaves evenly during cooking

Some microwave ovens have a rotating antenna built into the floor to help distribute the waves evenly

Whether you have chosen a small, basic microwave or whether you have bought one of the latest electronic models, the first thing you need to know is the power output of your cooker. Most domestic models range from 500 to 700 watts and this should be shown in your handbook or on a plate at the back of the oven. The power output determines how quickly food will defrost, reheat or cook. A 500 watt output will work more slowly than a 600 watt machine. This in turn will take longer than a 650 or 700 watt cooker.

The higher wattage cookers often have variable controls. This means you can control the amount of energy available for use in the oven. So, for instance, instead of trying to cook a casserole, using a tougher cut of meat, at full power, you can cook it at a lower setting, thus giving it longer time to tenderise and develop the flavours. Don't forget we're

talking about minutes rather than hours though!

In our recipes the power settings are given in percentages – 100%, 70%, 50% and 30% – and also as descriptions – high, medium high, medium, and low. Your cooker may have specific terms like Roast, Simmer and so on. Your manual will tell you what percentage each setting is and that's what is important, not the manufacturer's terminology for it.

If your machine has just 'cook' and 'defrost', a recipe calling for less than full power may be cooked using the 'defrost' setting. This may equal up to 50% of the power. Check your handbook and then you can adjust the time for the recipe accordingly. Unless you are following a recipe exactly, specifically designed for your type of cooker, you will have to exercise a little 'trial and error'. The recipes in this book were tested in a

650-700 watt cooker. For a 600 watt oven you will need to add 20 seconds per minute. For a 500 watt machine you will have only 50-70% of the power output so will have to add up to 40 seconds per minute (add a little less then add a few more seconds if necessary). This may sound very complicated but, really, it isn't. The best way to understand it is to read your manufacturer's instructions. Learn the controls and start by cooking very simple things until everything you've read falls into place.

As your confidence grows you will probably want to try out your favourite conventional recipes. Until you become more expert, find a recipe with similar quantities and ingredients and use as a guide. Honestly, what seems baffling at first will become second nature once you are familiar with your oven and with the basic techniques.

Basic Techniques

Cooking in a microwave is simple, quick and efficient. In order to get the best from it though, you need to know how it works.

In a conventional cooker, heat is radiated round the food. It starts cooking the outside then gradually penetrates the food until it is cooked through, giving the traditional brown, cooked appearance to the outside.

In a microwave oven, the microwaves (similar to radio waves) pass into the food to a depth of about 5 cm (2 in) causing the water molecules in the food to vibrate. The heat generated by this vibration carries on cooking the food through to the centre. There is no outside source of heat so the oven and utensils stay cool and the surface of the food will not turn crisp and brown.

There are a few basic techniques to be learned before you start.

Shielding

Microwaves can't pass through metal so as a rule metal utensils and foil are not used (large quantities of metal in the oven, when in use, cause the microwaves to bounce off the surface, known as arcing, which can damage the cooker). Thin strips of foil, however, can be used to protect selected bits of food to prevent overcooking – the ends of chicken or lamb bones or the tail end of a fish for example. The foil should be kept as smooth as possible and be of single thickness. Only shield in this way for part of the cooking time. If reheating more than one food on a plate you may wish to shield the more delicate ones if likely to overcook. Check manufacturer's instructions before using foil.

The other most effective way of protecting foods from overcooking is to mask them with a generous portion of sauce. This can also help prevent meat, vegetables or even a piece of sponge pudding from drying out when being reheated in the microwave.

Standing Time

Food goes on cooking when it is taken out of the microwave oven. The molecules continue to vibrate, generating heat within the food. The standing

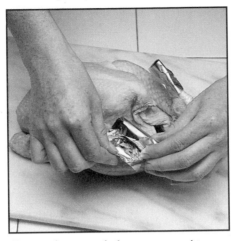

Protect bone ends from overcooking with small pieces of foil

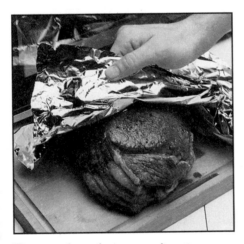

To retain heat during standing time, cover food with foil, shiny side in

Some foods need stirring during cooking to distribute heat evenly

time is therefore an important part of the process. Lots of foods will seem undercooked when first removed from the oven but after the specified standing time will be perfectly cooked.

Roast meat requires this standing time both to tenderise it right through without drying the outside and to make carving easier. Large or dense vegetables or fruit need this, rather than more microwave time, to ensure the outside doesn't become mushy while the inside completes cooking. But for some foods, like thin rashers of bacon, the standing time will be only as long as it takes to transfer it to the table.

If food has been cooked with a covering or lid, leave it covered for the standing time. If uncovered, cover it loosely with foil to help retain the heat. It is always better to cook food for the shortest time suggested in the microwave, leave it to stand then test it. If still slightly undercooked it can always be put back in the oven for a minute or two. If overcooked, nothing can be done to rectify it.

Turning and Stirring

The magnetron which converts everyday electricity into microwaves is situated at the top of the cooker. To ensure they are evenly distributed through the food it is necessary to turn it frequently. Most microwave cookers have a turntable to assist this process but our recipes assume you don't have one so give instructions for turning food manually. If you do have a turntable, you won't need to do this except for joints of meat or poultry that stand high in the oven. They will need turning over once during cooking so that all parts receive the same amount of energy.

Several small dishes being cooked at the same time will need a half turn during cooking so that the food near the centre of the oven receives the same amount of energy as that on the outside.

Small foods like steak or chops and large whole vegetables need some rearranging too and other dishes, like casseroles and sauces will need stirring to distribute the heat evenly. All the recipes in this section will tell you when food needs to be turned or stirred.

Covering

A cling film cover should be pierced to allow steam to escape

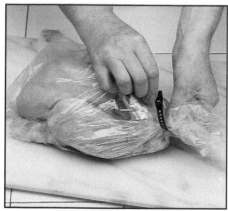

Seal roasting bags with all-plastic ties, string or rubber bands

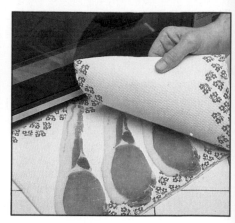

Absorbent paper helps to keep food crisp and prevents fat spattering

Covering

In general, foods which are covered for conventional cooking should always be covered for microwave cooking.

Although there is little evaporation because everything cooks so quickly, a cover keeps steam in which keeps it moist, helps to tenderise it and shortens the cooking time even more. It also helps food cook more evenly and means that only a small quantity of liquid is needed so vegetables, for instance, retain maximum flavour and nutritional value.

A casserole lid can be used to make a loose or tighter fitting cover. On its own it will allow some steam to escape but if your recipe calls for a tighter seal, a sheet of greaseproof paper under the lid will do the trick. An ordinary dinner plate (or tea plate for a small dish) can be used in the same way. Cling film, too, makes a good covering for a dish without a lid but remember to pierce it to prevent 'ballooning'. Use the new type of cling film, made without plasticizers and suitable for microwave cooking.

Roasting and boil-in bags are also very useful. Don't use the metallic ties supplied though.

Absorbent kitchen paper and greaseproof paper can help absorb moisture and stop fat spattering around the oven. Damp absorbent paper can be used to cover fish to 'steam' it.

Browning

To a lot of people, one of the most off-putting things about microwave cooking is the lack of a good, brown exterior to many foods. All the flavour and most of the natural goodness is retained but for a more traditional colour there are lots of remedies.

Savoury foods can most easily be browned using a special microwave browning dish or plate. They have a special coating on the base which absorbs the microwaves and reaches a temperature of 240-330°C (500-600°F). They must be preheated in the microwave for several minutes (*never* in a conventional oven) before use and some manufacturers recommend you place an insulator such as a heatproof, microwave-proof dinner plate between the browning dish and the glass turntable.

Some cookers have a special browning element in them. Follow the manufacturer's instructions for when and how to use them.

Browning

Brown chicken pieces by coating with melted butter, herbs or tomato purée

Glaze poultry pieces with marmalade halfway through cooking to brown

Cover with toasted breadcrumbs, dry stuffing mix or crushed cornflakes

Use a conventional grill for a few minutes at the end of cooking time to brown toppings or crisp outer surfaces. This is also useful for browning meat or poultry prior to microwaving. You can, of course, use a frying pan for this.

There are several special microwave browning agents available in supermarkets but your storecupboard can help too, without the added expense.

Most meats and poultry can be brushed with a mixture of melted butter and paprika, herbs, brown or fruity sauce. Or try equal quantities of water and soy sauce, tomato purée, mushroom ketchup or Worcestershire sauce.

Crumbled stock cubes or dry soup mix also make suitable coatings and, as with conventional cookery, glazes can really enhance the appearance of meat or

Use a preheated browning dish to brown chops and other savoury foods

poultry. Brush with an appropriate preserve halfway through cooking.

Instead of actually colouring the food, you can mask it with a well coloured and flavoured sauce and garnish it attractively. Or try toasted breadcrumbs, crushed nuts, cornflakes or crisps or dry stuffing mix to improve the appearance of chicken pieces and cutlets.

Cakes and Breads Plain sponges and white bread will not brown in a microwave. Plain cakes served 'plain' look awfully anaemic even if the texture is perfect. Dark coloured cakes, such as chocolate, coffee, spiced or rich, fruity ones, will look good naturally. Wholemeal flour and brown sugars will help too.

To cover up a pale specimen, scatter desiccated coconut, chopped nuts, cinnamon or chopped glacé fruits over before cooking. Alternatively sprinkle cakes with a mixture of soft brown sugar and

Disguise a plain sponge cake with a variety of decorations

chopped nuts halfway through cooking.

Icing the cake or even a good dusting of caster or sifted icing sugar will work wonders for a pale exterior too.

As bread won't brown in the microwave it is best to use wholemeal flour for

a good colour. You can also brush loaves and rolls with egg yolk then sprinkle with poppy or sesame seeds, cracked wheat, crushed cornflakes, dried herbs or toasted, crumbled, dried onions.

You can also brown loaves under a conventional grill after cooking but remove the cooking container first as it may not withstand the heat from the grill.

Cooking Containers

One of the most peculiar aspects when first using a microwave cooker is realising you can't use any normal metal baking tins, pots or pans. This is because metal reflects the microwaves so they cannot penetrate the food to cook it. All that unabsorbed energy can cause arcing which can severely damage the cooker. Watch out for metal trim, detachable handles, screws in lids and gold or silver decorations on crockery – even a trademark in metallic lettering could be enough! Don't use foil containers either, unless your manufacturer's instructions say you may and don't try to reheat or thaw foods in foil-lined take-away-style cartons, the microwaves won't be able to get in!

On the plus side you've only got to look around your kitchen to find a whole wealth of suitable cooking containers – some most unlikely ones too!

A wide range of special microwave cookware is now available

Also you will discover that you can often mix and cook in the same bowl or even take something out of the freezer, put it into the microwave, out of the microwave and on to the table – no effort, no mess!

Basically you can use any container that is transparent to microwaves so they pass straight through into the food, leaving the container and oven cool. Natural transfer of heat from the food to the dish will sometimes happen and take care

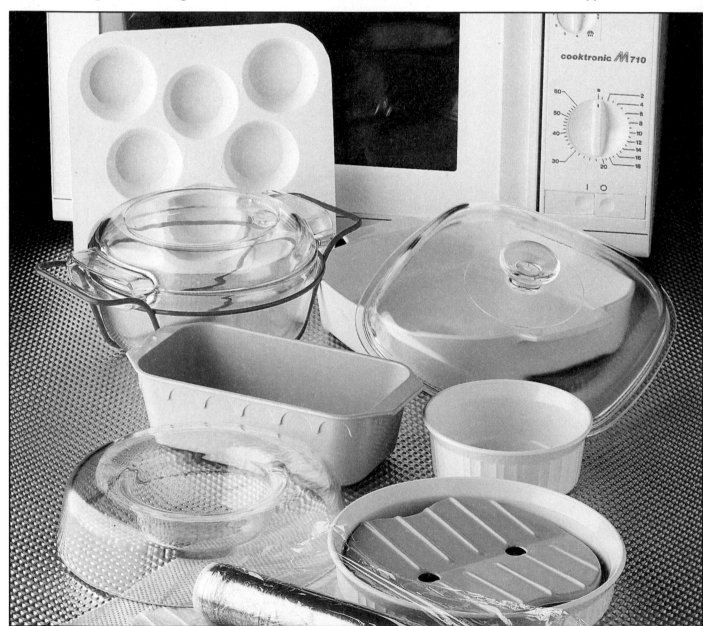

when lifting lids – they may not be hot but the steam that will have built up inside can be scalding.

Glass

Oven-to-table and ceramic glass cookware are usually fine. Attractive enough to serve in as well as for cooking.

Earthenware

Again, good for cooking and serving. Be careful though when using mixtures with a high sugar content – the dish may become too hot.

China

Everyday dinner and tea plates, cereal bowls and even the tea things can be used. Do the 'dish test' (right) if in doubt. It's not advisable to use the finest porcelain – it could get damaged.

Plastic

The best type of plastic to use in the microwave is thermoplastic. This can withstand very high temperatures. In general, food storage containers and supermarket cartons are best used for thawing and reheating small quantities of food only. High proportions of fat and sugar in the food can cause these materials to melt or warp. Do not use melamine as it will scorch.

Don't forget too, cling film, roasting and boil-in bags. If ordinary cling film gets you all in a twist – try microwave cling film which is slightly tougher and will adhere to plastic as well as glass and crockery. Cling film is also good for lining other baking containers where necessary. Don't use ordinary plastic bags, they may melt.

Paper

Paper plates and cups can be used for reheating and serving foods that don't have to get too hot – don't use them for cooking raw foods as they will become too hot and could burn. Absorbent kitchen paper and paper table napkins can be used to sit food on as well as for covering (be careful about coloured napkins though, the colour may run!). Absorbent paper is best used when moisture or fat should be absorbed, not when the final result should be moist and juicy. For this sort of texture, use greaseproof or non-stick baking paper. They are also excellent for lining cake containers.

Waxed paper and cardboard should only be used for thawing; the wax would melt if the food gets hot.

Wood

Not normally used in a conventional cooker but can be used in the microwave for reheating bread, 'ripening' cheese (i.e. melting it very briefly just to soften it) and for very short cooking periods only. Basketware too may be used, just for reheating.

Non-Metallic Racks

Meat and poultry should be placed on a rack so they don't stew in their own juices when they're supposed to be roasting. An upturned plate in a shallow dish will serve the same purpose.

Microwave Plastic

There are more and more specially designed moulds and dishes for microwave use. The more adventurous you become, the more likely you are to want some 'special' utensils.

Shape and Size

The shape and size of the container can make all the difference to the end result. If too small a dish is used, food could

Round dishes or rectangular dishes with rounded corners give best results

bubble over and may take longer than expected to cook because of its density.

If too large a container is used, food may become dry – especially in a recipe where the sauce is too thinly spread over the base of the dish. Round or oval shaped dishes will give the best results, square or rectangular ones have a greater concentration of microwaves at the corners so these areas tend to overcook (so shield with foil – see 'shielding' page 15).

Choose straight-sided containers whenever possible and remember that a shallow dish of food will cook more quickly than a full deep one.

Therefore a casserole is best cooked in a deep dish to give it longer to tenderise.

Ring moulds (non-metallic of course) are ideal for cakes and other foods which cannot be stirred during cooking. The microwaves can penetrate from the centre as well as round the outside for quicker, more even cooking.

THE DISH TEST

Stand half a cup of water in the dish to be tested. Microwave at 100% (high) for 1 minute. If the dish feels cool but the water is hot, the dish is safe to use.

Thawing and Reheating

Thawing Foods

Food can be packed for the freezer in serving dishes best suited to your requirements and extra portions and leftovers can be frozen for use just whenever you need. Don't forget to use containers suitable for your microwave though.

As with conventional cooking, some foods, like vegetables, can be cooked straight from frozen at 100% (high). Fish can be cooked when still partially frozen. Large, dense pieces of meat or poultry, on the other hand, must be completely thawed before cooking. When thawing them, remove from the microwave while still cool to the touch and icy in the centre.

Standing time is as important as when actually cooking to thaw the centre fully. Meat, fish, poultry, casseroles and vegetables should always be covered during thawing. Rolls and bread should be wrapped in kitchen paper but frozen cakes and pies should be left uncovered otherwise the melting ice crystals could make them soggy. Don't thaw for any longer time than necessary or the outside will start to cook. So if you are thawing uneven shaped foods, shield thin parts with narrow strips of foil.

Finally, when thawing several pieces of food, frozen together, like chops, pies or fish fillets, remove from the freezer wrapping as soon as possible, ease apart and continue to thaw in a single layer. This way they will all thaw in the same amount of time.

Reheating

A microwave cooker is ideal for reheating all types of food. The colour, texture and flavour will be retained and so will most of the goodness.

Plated meals can be ready in minutes for members of the family coming in at different times. Arrange foods with the thickest ones around the outside of the plate and quicker heating foods, like small vegetables in the centre. Cover with a tight layer of cling film, pierced to allow steam to escape, or cover with a non-metallic lid or plate.

You can reheat up to three plates at the same time, using specially designed microwave stacking rings or upturned soup plates. Only the top plate will need covering but it is advisable to swap top plate to bottom halfway through heating so that all the plates of food are equally hot.

Some foods, like casseroles or stews, actually benefit from being cooked one day, chilled, then reheated the next. The flavours will develop and meat will become even more tender.

Another fantastic benefit of reheating in a microwave is when weaning a baby. All mums who have fiddled around with a couple of teaspoons of some tasty morsel, trying to get it hot through over a saucepan of simmering water while the baby is screaming for its supper in the background will be able to produce the goods in seconds! The same goes for warming milk — especially in the middle of the night — no more rummaging for the saucepan and then letting the milk boil over while consoling the child. Just into the cup, microwave for a few seconds and back to bed!

When thawing frozen foods, shield thin parts with small pieces of foil to prevent overcooking

Frozen bread slices may be thawed in seconds. Separate them as soon as possible as they thaw

Most foods can be hot through and ready to eat in minutes. A good test is to feel the centre of the base of the container – it should feel hot to the touch where the heat generated in the food has transferred to the dish.

Always cover food when reheating and stir foods like rice, small vegetables or casseroles from time to time to distribute the heat as evenly and quickly as possible.

Bread can be warmed in rapid time. Always wrap in kitchen paper to stop it drying out and don't heat too long – literally 30 seconds or so – or the results will be rather chewy and unappetising instead of warm and soft.

Lastly, don't throw away that cup of cold coffee or tea – reheat it still in its cup. Make one 'instantly' too without having to boil the kettle. Just put the instant coffee or even a tea bag (unless you are a specialist tea maker) in a mug with cold water and microwave for a minute. Then add milk and sugar to taste – and don't forget to remove the tea bag!

Right: *Freeze pre-cooked meals in trays ready for reheating in the microwave*
Below: *Reheat several plates of food at once using microwave stacking rings*

Do's and Don'ts

DO

✔ Make sure your oven is plugged into a normal 13 amp socket, using a properly earthed, fused plug.

✔ Check the oven is at least 10 cm (4 in) out from the wall to ensure adequate ventilation.

✔ Read your oven manufacturer's instructions carefully.

✔ Use your microwave oven fully – to cook fresh food as well as to thaw frozen food and reheat leftovers or convenience foods.

✔ Use everyday kitchenware for cooking, including ovenproof glass and glass ceramic utensils, china and earthenware, plastic, wood, paper and even basketware. Look for labels saying 'microwave safe' or 'suitable for microwave'.

✔ Test your favourite bowl or best china if unsure first (see Cooking Containers, page 18).

✔ Use your microwave to warm up drinks like the toddler's milk or your forgotten cup of tea.

✔ Be careful about timing – seconds can be crucial. It is always better to undercook than to overcook.

✔ Use cling film to keep food moist during cooking and absorbent paper to keep bread or jacket potatoes dry and to stop fat spattering.

✔ Use thin strips of foil to shield parts of food that may overcook (page 15).

✔ Keep the door seal and door surfaces clean or microwaves could escape. Keep oven surfaces clean or cooking time may be lengthened.

A sheet of absorbent paper keeps garlic rolls (page 40) dry during heating

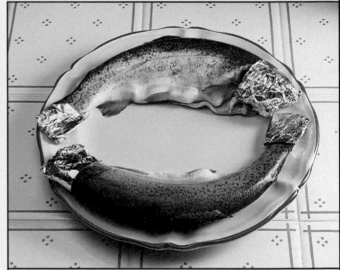

Thin strips of foil will protect parts of food that may overcook

DON'T

✘ Use metal utensils, foil containers or large pieces of foil in the microwave. Also don't use metal ties – use string, rubber bands or all-plastic ties to secure cooking bags.

✘ Cook eggs in the shell or reheat hard-boiled ones – they will explode.

✘ Place cans of food in the oven.

✘ Try to deep-fry foods in your microwave – you cannot control the temperature of the oil or fat.

✘ Dry fruit in the oven.

✘ Attempt to operate the oven when empty – damage may be caused. Keep a small container of water in the oven in case it is switched on accidentally.

✘ Let any thin strips of foil used for shielding touch any part of the interior.

✘ Dry wet clothing or papers in the oven. They could ignite.

✘ Use conventional meat or sugar thermometers inside the oven. They may be used, however, to check the temperature of food after it has been taken out of the oven.

✘ Use the cooker if it is damaged in any way, especially if the door seems faulty.

✘ Attempt to repair the machine yourself – get an approved service engineer to look at it.

Cooking Principles

Remember that the microwaves only penetrate food to a depth of about 5 cm (2 in); the centre of the food is cooked by the generated heat. There are several other important principles to remember as well:

1 If cooking more than one item, the length of time needed will increase. Microwaves make straight for the food – the more there is, the less energy there is to penetrate each item. For example, one rasher of bacon will take 45-60 seconds, two rashers will take almost twice as long.

2 Dense food takes longer to cook. For example, a medium-sized jacket potato will take 4 minutes; a baked apple 1½ minutes. Also a prepared meatloaf weighing 450 g/1 lb will take longer to cook than the same weight of plain minced beef.

3 Thicker food should be placed towards the outside of the dish. For example,

Arrange chicken drumsticks with the thickest parts towards the outside

chicken legs should be placed with bone ends towards the centre. This way the microwaves penetrate the thickest part and the heat will be conducted towards the bone ends to cook them easily. The same applies to vegetables like broccoli. The stems take longer to cook than the heads so should be placed towards the outside of the dish.

4 Food at room temperature will cook more quickly than items straight from the freezer or refrigerator.

5 Most foods will not crisp and brown though meat and poultry will start to colour naturally after about 12 minutes owing to the high fat content. Bacon, too, will crisp on standing after cooking. Bread will become soft, not crusty, on re-heating and, in fact, will become almost rubbery if microwaved for too long!

6 Foods with a high fat or sugar content will become very hot very quickly. Be careful if using plastic containers as they could melt.

7 Spillage in the oven can cause extra cooking time (microwaves don't differentiate between food for eating and that gone to waste!). Wipe the oven clean as soon as possible after use.

8 Add salt after cooking when possible. Salt toughens meat and vegetables by causing a larger moisture loss. (If you're not absolutely sure you have the cooking time right, it is best to season at the end of standing time, just in case you have to cook the food a little longer.)

9 The size and shape of cooking vessel is important. Too large and food may dry up, especially if there is only a thin layer of sauce spread over a wide area. Too small and boiling over may occur. The

All the cleaning a microwave oven needs is a wipe with a damp cloth

food will probably take longer to cook too as it will be more tightly packed. Round or rounded cornered dishes give more even cooking. Square ones tend to overcook at the corners where the microwaves are concentrated.

10 Always tend to undercook rather than overcook until you become really experienced. Microwave cooking is so quick it is no problem to have to cook something for literally a minute or two more to get a perfect result. Overcooking can happen very quickly indeed in a microwave.

Microwave cookware is both practical and colourful

When is it Cooked?

It is difficult to understand that when cooking in a microwave you have to remove the food from the oven before it is completely cooked. This is because the food will carry on cooking during standing time. If food is left in the oven for too long the outside surfaces of the food will toughen and dry.

It is wise to check food regularly as the cooking times are so short. Like conventional ovens, microwave ovens vary slightly so you need to get used to your own. In time you will know exactly when to take foods out and leave them to stand.

When cooking in a conventional oven it is easy to see when food is cooked by its appearance. This is a less reliable test in a microwave oven because food does not brown in the same way and will often appear uncooked when it is ready to be removed from the oven. However, there are various other ways to test when food is cooked. Some of these tests are similar to those you would use if you were cooking food in a conventional oven.

It is always best not to test to see if food is cooked until after the standing time. If it is not quite cooked, food can then be returned to the oven for a minute or two more.

You will also get used to organising your cooking so that the recipe with the longest standing time is cooked first and the one that needs least cooking and standing time is cooked last, so that your planning will be as efficient as your cooking!

Times for thawing and cooking everyday foods in your microwave oven will be given in the manufacturer's handbook.

Meat

When cooked, meat should feel tender when tested with a skewer. Cheaper cuts should be easy to shred with a fork. For a more accurate test, use a microwave thermometer (or a probe if your cooker has one). Insert as you would a conventional thermometer with the point in the centre of the joint, avoiding bone or fat where possible. The joint should be removed from the oven when the thermometer registers a given temperature.

A temperature probe is an accurate guide to when meat is cooked

During standing time the internal temperature of the joint will rise by 10°C (50°F). If you use a probe, the oven will automatically switch off when the meat reaches the pre-set temperature.

Only use conventional thermometers when the joint has been removed from the microwave, never during cooking. The correct internal temperatures will be given in recipes.

Poultry and Game

Whole birds are cooked when the juices run clear when the thickest part of a thigh is pierced with a skewer. Drumsticks should also move freely in their sockets. A thermometer or probe may not give an accurate result because the fat on poultry becomes hot very quickly and there is a large proportion of bone.

Vegetables

The amount of cooking time vegetables need depends on personal taste. The recipes in this book give cooking times for vegetables that are just tender to a fork.

Season vegetables just before serving as salt toughens the fibres.

Rice and Pasta

Both will seem still quite hard and inedible when taken out of the cooker – the standing time gives perfect results every time. When cooked, rice and pasta should feel just tender when pressed between finger and thumb.

Eggs

Eggs cook extremely quickly in the microwave so watch them carefully. They toughen horribly if overcooked and can burst. Always remove eggs from the oven when the whites are still translucent as the yolks cook more quickly than the whites. Remove scrambled eggs when they are still rather runny; as with other foods they will complete cooking during standing time.

Egg-based custards should still be soft in the centre when removed but a knife inserted halfway from the outer edge to the centre should come out clean.

Fish

Fish should be removed when the thinner parts flake easily with a fork or knife but the thicker parts are still slightly translucent. The same applies to shellfish.

When fish is cooked it will flake easily when tested with a knife

Cakes and Sponge Puddings

With visions of collapsed centres when you've opened the door too soon in a conventional oven, it's really difficult to steel yourself to take a cake out of the microwave when it is still damp on top. The damp appearance will disappear during standing time.

Cakes are ruined if overcooked. On removal from the oven a cake should

A cooked cake will pull away easily from the sides of the container

pull away from the sides of the container easily and a wooden cocktail stick inserted in the centre (not through one of the damp spots) should come out clean.

Pastry
Use unsweetened shortcrust pastry and make cooked, unfilled cases. When cooked, the surface will appear dry and puffy. A few brown spots may have appeared, called 'hot spots'. This is where the microwaves have been attracted to the same spots, probably because the fat was not evenly distributed through the dough.

Planning Meals
Once you have fully grasped how your microwave works – the cooking process, standing times and reheating capabilities – and have really got used to using it, you will be able to cook whole meals in it.

As a general rule, cook foods with the longest standing times first so they can complete cooking while you are microwaving the quicker dishes. Remember to wrap or cover foods well for standing.

As foods like casseroles actually benefit from reheating, prepare and cook them in advance. Vegetables, too, can be cooked, then quickly reheated with no loss of flavour or colour and little or no loss of food value.

If you have chosen a recipe with lots of preparation, get this done well ahead ready to cook just before serving.

For a dinner party, the easiest way is to prepare a starter and dessert that are

With the help of your microwave oven, whole meals can be ready to serve in a very short time

served chilled so they can be cooked earlier in the day or even the day before and stored in the refrigerator until required. If you want to serve a hot pudding, choose something that can be cooked or reheated between courses.

Don't forget too that you still have a conventional cooker and your microwave should be used to complement it. For instance, you may find it is much quicker to cook your pasta conventionally while cooking a sauce or main meal to accompany it in the microwave.

Menu Content
Colour, texture and flavour should all be considered when planning a meal. Nutritionally, a main meal should have a portion of protein (meat, fish, eggs, cheese, dried beans or lentils). There should also be some starchy filler (potatoes, rice, pasta or bread), the amount depending on the individual's needs, and a good portion of vegetables for vitamins, minerals and fibre.

The choice of pud depends very much on what has gone before. Most people love their dessert course but are unlikely to be starving hungry at this stage so keep it light, fluffy or fruity.

Main Meals and Vegetables

From simple family fare to extra-special recipes for dinner parties, you'll find something in this chapter to suit every occasion.

Look how cleverly your microwave can work for you: a heart-warming stew but with no steamy kitchen; stuffed fish but with no lingering cooking smells; or succulent roast lamb that won't leave you with a three-hour oven cleaning job! These are just a few of the treats in store. We've also selected some exciting vegetable dishes to complement your chosen main course or to cheer up plainly cooked chops, steaks, sausages or fish. Your microwave oven will enable you to cook satisfying meals in minutes.

Lamb

Lamb stew with dumplings

Serves 4
**12 best end neck of lamb cutlets,
  trimmed (about 1.1 kg/2½ lb
  trimmed)**
salt and pepper
40 g/1½ oz margarine or butter
1 large onion, peeled and chopped
40 g/1½ oz plain flour
600 ml/1 pt boiling chicken stock
4 tomatoes, skinned and chopped
2 sprigs fresh rosemary (optional)
225 g/8 oz frozen mixed vegetables
rosemary sprig, to garnish
For the dumplings
100 g/4 oz self-raising flour
50 g/2 oz shredded beef suet
2 tsps chopped fresh rosemary
about 75 ml/3 fl oz cold water

1 Arrange the cutlets in the base of a
large casserole. Cover with pierced cling
film and microwave at 100% (high) for 9
minutes, rearranging them halfway
through cooking. Drain and season.
2 Place the fat and onion in a 1.7 L/3 pt
bowl and microwave at 100% (high) for
2 minutes. Stir in the flour.
3 Gradually add the stock. Microwave
at 100% (high) for 1-2 minutes, or until
thickened, stirring 2-3 times. Add the
tomatoes, rosemary, seasoning and frozen vegetables and pour over the cutlets.
Cover with pierced cling film and microwave at 50% (medium) for 10 minutes.
4 Meanwhile make the dumplings. Mix
together the flour, suet, rosemary and
season. Add sufficient cold water to
make a soft, but not sticky, dough. Using
floured hands, shape into 8 dumplings.

5 Add the dumplings to the casserole.
Re-cover with pierced cling film and
microwave at 50% (medium) for 6
minutes, remove cover and microwave
at 50% (medium) for 10-12 minutes, or
until the dumplings are set. Garnish with
rosemary and serve.

Roast lamb with orange and mint

Illustrated on pages 26-27

Serves 4
900 g/2 lb fillet end leg of lamb
1 clove garlic, sliced in thin slivers
150 ml/¼ pt fresh orange juice
2 tbls bottled mint sauce
salt and pepper
25 g/1 oz margarine or butter
25 g/1 oz plain flour
300 ml/½ pt hot chicken stock
**cooked broccoli florets and orange
  slices, to garnish**

Above: *Lamb stew with dumplings*

1 Using a sharp knife, score the lamb fat
to make a diamond pattern.

2 Make a few slits in the lamb and press
a sliver of garlic into each one.

Micro-facts

Remove lamb joints from the
microwave at the following
internal temperatures to ensure
correct cooking on standing –
Rare: 54°C/129°F;
Medium: 64°C/147°F;
Well done: 70°C/158°F.

3 Weigh the lamb and calculate the exact cooking time as follows: 9-10 minutes per 450 g/1 lb for rare; 11-12 minutes per 450 g/1 lb for medium; 13-14 minutes per 450 g/1 lb for well done lamb. Place the lamb in a shallow bowl.

4 In a separate bowl, blend the orange juice, mint sauce and seasoning. Spoon mixture over lamb, cover loosely, chill, and leave to marinate for at least 6-8 hours, turning and basting occasionally.

5 Place the lamb dish in the oven and microwave at 100% (high) for 5 minutes. Reduce power to 50% (medium) for the remaining time and cook, turning meat over halfway through, basting occasionally with the marinade.

6 Drain off the marinade juices, and skim off any excess fat. Cover the meat loosely with foil, and leave to stand for 15 minutes, to finish cooking.

7 Place the fat in a jug, and microwave at 100% (high) for 1 minute. Stir in flour, stock and marinade juices. Microwave at 100% (high) for 2-3 minutes, or until thickened, stirring 2-3 times. Season with salt and pepper.

8 Slice the lamb and serve on a bed of rice, if liked. Garnish with broccoli and orange slices. Serve the sauce separately in a sauceboat.

Lamb kidneys in cider

Serves 4
100 g/4 oz button onions
600 g/1¼ lb lamb kidneys without suet
25 g/1 oz margarine or butter
100 g/4 oz small button mushrooms
50 g/2 oz streaky bacon, rinds and bones removed, cut into thin strips
2 tbls plain flour
225 ml/8 fl oz dry cider
1 tbls tomato purée
1 bay leaf
salt and pepper
1 tbls chopped parsley, to garnish
toast triangles, to serve

1 Place the onions in a 1.1 L/ 2 pt bowl with 3 tbls water, cover with pierced cling film and microwave at 100% (high) for 4 minutes. Peel the onions and use a sharp knife to trim the root ends and tops.

2 Rinse the kidneys, drain well and pat them dry on absorbent paper. Skin the kidneys, halve them lengthways and cut out the cores with sharp kitchen scissors.

3 Place the fat in a 2.3 L/4 pt casserole and microwave at 100% (high) for 30 seconds to melt. Add the onions and mushrooms and microwave at 100% (high) for 2 minutes. Add the kidneys and bacon and microwave at 100% (high) for 3 minutes, stirring twice.

4 Stir in the flour. Gradually add the cider and tomato purée, mixing well. Add the bay leaf. Cover with casserole lid or pierced cling film and microwave for 5 minutes, stirring 2-3 times. Season.

5 Transfer the kidneys in their sauce to a warmed serving dish, discard the bay leaf, sprinkle with parsley and serve with toast triangles and a mixed salad.

Left: *Lamb kidneys in cider*

Beef

Meatballs with walnuts

Serves 4-6
1 tbls vegetable oil
100 g/4 oz shelled walnuts,
    chopped
125 ml/4 fl oz milk
2 slices wholemeal bread, crusts
    removed
700 g/1½ lb lean minced beef
1 egg, beaten
grated zest and juice of ½ lemon
salt and pepper
15 g/½ oz margarine or butter
1 tbls plain flour
300 ml/½ pt hot beef stock
2 tbls double cream
walnut halves and lemon twists, to
    garnish
For the noodles
225 g/8 oz egg noodles
1 tbls vegetable oil
1 tsp salt

1 To cook the noodles, place them in a large deep bowl with the oil and salt. Add 1.1 L/2 pt boiling water to cover the noodles. Cover the bowl with pierced cling film and microwave at 100% (high) for 6 minutes. Leave to stand, covered, for 5 minutes, then drain.
2 Place the oil and nuts in a bowl and microwave at 100% (high) for 2-3 minutes. Drain the nuts well.
3 Transfer three-quarters of the nuts to a large bowl. Put the milk in a separate shallow bowl and add the bread. Press the bread down well with a fork to absorb the milk. Break up the soaked bread with the fork and add to the nuts.
4 Add the minced beef, egg, lemon zest and juice and stir thoroughly to mix.

Season to taste with salt and pepper. Divide the mixture into 24 and, using floured hands, shape into balls.
5 Place half the meatballs around the edge of a large round dish, in a single layer, with a gap between each one.
6 Microwave at 100% (high) for 3-4 minutes, rearranging after 2 minutes. Place on absorbent paper. Repeat to cook the remaining meatballs.

Below: *Meatballs with walnuts*

Micro-facts

You may wish to transfer cooked food to your dinner service, but remember that, if it has a metal rim or trim, it must not be put in the microwave as it could damage the oven.

7 Place the fat in a large jug and microwave at 100% (high) for 20-30 seconds to melt. Stir in the flour, gradually mix in the stock, and microwave at 100% (high) for 2 minutes, or until thickened, stirring 2-3 times.

8 Mix all the meatballs together and pour the sauce over the top. Cover with pierced cling film and microwave at 100% (high) for 5 minutes, turning the dish after 3 minutes. Stir in the cream and the remaining chopped walnuts.

9 Arrange noodles around the edge of a serving plate, cover with pierced cling film and microwave for 1 minute to reheat. Pour the meatballs into the centre and garnish with walnuts and lemon.

Beef stroganoff

Serves 4
450 g/1 lb fillet steak, trimmed of fat
salt and pepper
1 tbls vegetable oil
50 g/2 oz butter
1 onion, thinly sliced
250 g/9 oz small button mushrooms, thinly sliced
2-3 tsps French mustard
300 ml/½ pt soured cream
chopped fresh parsley, to garnish

Below: *Beef stroganoff*

1 Lay the meat flat and beat it well with a wooden rolling pin. Cut into 5 mm/¼ in thick slices. Cut each slice across the grain into 5 mm/¼ in wide strips, 2.5-5 cm/1-2 in long. Sprinkle with pepper and set aside.

2 Place the oil and butter in a large bowl and microwave at 100% (high) for 1 minute. Add the onion and meat and microwave at 100% (high) for 8 minutes, stirring after 5 minutes. Add the mushrooms, cover with pierced cling film and microwave at 100% (high) for 2 minutes.

3 Stir in the mustard, season, re-cover and microwave at 100% (high) for a further 4 minutes. Stir in the soured cream, re-cover and microwave at 100% (high) for 1 minute. Leave to stand for 3 minutes.

4 Spoon on to a warmed serving platter, garnish with chopped parsley and serve. Serve with boiled rice, vegetables and a green salad, if liked.

Chicken

Roast chicken with yoghurt

Serves 4-6

1.8 kg/4 lb ovenready chicken, skinned, giblets removed and trussed
1 clove garlic, crushed
2 tbls chopped fresh mint
1 tbls ground cumin
2 tsps sugar
1 tsp ground ginger
1 tsp salt
½ tsp chilli powder
½ tsp ground turmeric
½ tsp ground mixed spice
2 x 150 g/5 oz cartons natural yoghurt
boiled rice, to serve
fresh mint, to garnish

1 Wash the chicken and dry thoroughly with absorbent paper. Score with a sharp knife, then place in a large bowl.
2 Mix together the remaining ingredients, pour over the chicken, cover and leave to marinate in the refrigerator, for at least 8 hours or overnight. Spoon the marinade over occasionally.
3 Place the chicken, breast side down, on a microwave roasting rack or upturned plate in a dish. Pour over the marinade. Cover lightly with greaseproof paper and microwave at 100% (high) for 15 minutes.
4 Turn the chicken over, reduce the oven power to 50% (medium) and microwave for 35-40 minutes or until the juices run clear when the flesh is pierced in the thickest part with a skewer. Give the dish a quarter turn every 10 minutes.

Micro-facts

Although poultry does not brown nicely when cooked in a microwave oven, its appearance can be improved by masking with sauce or by brushing with melted butter before cooking.

Remove the greaseproof paper for the last 20 minutes.
5 Serve on a warm serving dish, on a bed of boiled rice, garnished with fresh mint.

Mediterranean stuffed chicken breasts

Serves 4

50 g/2 oz butter, softened
juice of ½ lemon, strained
salt and pepper
225 g/8 oz peeled prawns, thawed if frozen
4 x 175 g/6 oz chicken breasts, skinned and boned
1 large onion, finely chopped
2 cloves garlic, crushed
1 tbls vegetable oil
400 g/14 oz can tomatoes
1 chicken stock cube
chopped parsley, to garnish

1 Beat the butter with a little lemon juice and salt and pepper. Beat in three-quarters of the prawns, reserving the remainder for garnish.
2 Make a long horizontal slit through each chicken breast to make a pocket. Fill the pocket with the prawn mixture, then secure with wooden cocktail sticks to keep the filling enclosed. Place the stuffed chicken breasts in a large shallow heatproof dish and cover loosely with cling film. Set aside.
3 Put the onion, garlic and oil into a large casserole and mix well. Microwave at 100% (high) for 2 minutes, until the onion softens.
4 Add the tomatoes with their juice, crumble in the stock cube and season with salt and pepper. Cover the dish with cling film rolled back at one edge. Microwave at 100% (high) for 8 minutes, stirring twice during cooking. Remove and set aside.
5 Microwave the chicken breasts at 100% (high) for 7-8 minutes, turning and rearranging them every 2 minutes. Remove, cover and leave to stand for 5 minutes.
6 Microwave the tomato sauce at 100% (high) for 2-3 minutes, or until the sauce is boiling hot.
7 Arrange the chicken breasts on a hot serving dish, then spoon the tomato sauce over them. Garnish with the reserved prawns and chopped parsley and serve immediately.

Chicken with sweetcorn sauce

Serves 4
25 g/1 oz butter
4 x 250 g/9 oz chicken portions,
   thawed if frozen
paprika
salt and pepper
tomato wedges, to garnish
For the sauce
1 small onion, finely chopped
335 g/11.8 oz can sweetcorn,
   drained
25 g/1 oz plain flour
300 ml/½ pt milk
pinch of grated nutmeg
salt and pepper
2 tbls chopped parsley

1 Put the butter in a bowl and microwave at 100% (high) for 20-30 seconds to melt.
2 Wipe the chicken portions with absorbent paper. Arrange in a single layer in a shallow dish with the thickest parts pointing outwards. Brush all over with butter and dust with paprika.
3 Cover the chicken with cling film rolled back at one edge and microwave at 70% (medium-high) for 8 minutes. Rearrange the chicken so the least cooked parts are nearest the outside. Re-cover and microwave for a further 6 minutes or until the chicken is tender and the juices run clear when the thickest part is pierced with a fine skewer.
4 Spoon off 2 tbls of the cooking juices into a 1.1 L/2 pt bowl. Cover the chicken loosely with foil and leave to stand.
5 To make the sauce, add the onion to the bowl and microwave at 100% (high) for 2 minutes until soft.
6 Stir in the sweetcorn and flour, then gradually add the milk and nutmeg until well blended. Microwave at 100% (high) for 5 minutes, stirring 2-3 times, until thick. Season and stir in the parsley.
7 Arrange the chicken on a warmed serving dish. Spoon a little of the sauce over and pour the remainder into a warmed sauceboat. Garnish the chicken with tomato wedges and serve with green beans and potatoes, if liked.
Note: Use your microwave to partially cook potatoes before roasting to a crisp brown finish in your conventional oven.

Left: Roast chicken with yoghurt
Below: Chicken with sweetcorn sauce

Fish

Plaice with creamy mustard sauce

Serves 4
4 large plaice fillets, skinned
6 tbls dry white wine
1 tbls lemon juice
salt and pepper
4 tbls double cream
2 egg yolks
2 tsps French mustard
2 tsps capers
parsley sprigs and lemon slices,
to garnish

1 Roll up the fillets and arrange close together in a shallow dish that will just hold them comfortably in a single layer side-by-side. Mix together the wine, lemon juice and salt and pepper to taste, and sprinkle this mixture over the rolled up fillets.

Micro-facts

Check fish towards the end of the cooking time. Whole fish vary in thickness so an exact cooking time is difficult to specify. It will flake easily when cooked.

Above: *Plaice with creamy mustard sauce.*

2 Cover with pierced cling film and microwave at 100% (high) for 5-6 minutes, or until the fish is tender when tested with the point of a knife.
3 Pour the cooking liquid into a jug and microwave at 100% (high) for 1 minute, or until boiling. In a small bowl, mix together the cream, egg yolks and mustard. Stir a little of the hot cooking liquid into the cream mix, then stir this mixture into the liquid in the jug.
4 Microwave at 100% (high) for 30-45 seconds, until the sauce thickens, stirring several times. Do not boil. Stir in the capers, then taste and adjust the seasoning.
5 Arrange the fish on a warm plate, pour the sauce over and serve at once, garnished with parsley and lemon slices.

Red mullet parcels

Serves 4
4 red mullet (about 225 g/8 oz each)
25 g/1 oz butter
1 tbls lemon juice
1-2 tbls capers
lemon slices and watercress, to
garnish
For the stuffing
40 g/1½ oz margarine or butter
1 onion, finely chopped
175 g/6 oz mushrooms, finely
chopped
25 g/1 oz wholemeal breadcrumbs
2 tbls chopped parsley
salt and pepper

1 To make the stuffing, put the fat and onion into a bowl and microwave at

100% (high) for 2-3 minutes, or until soft. Stir in the remaining ingredients.

2 Stuff each mullet with a quarter of the mushroom mixture. Weigh the stuffed fish together and calculate the cooking time at 3-4 minutes per 450 g/1 lb.

3 Make 2-3 small diagonal slits on both sides of each fish. Cut 4 rectangles of

greaseproof paper, large enough to enclose a fish, and grease lightly. Spread the centre of the paper with butter. Put one fish on each piece of paper and sprinkle with lemon juice. Wrap the head and tail of each mullet in a strip of foil. (Check with your oven manufacturer's

instructions to see if they recommend the use of foil first.)

4 Bring the edges of the paper together to enclose the fish. Fold the edges over once or twice to seal.

5 Arrange the fish parcels head to tail, on a large plate. Microwave at 100% (high) for half the calculated time. Turn the parcels and rearrange. Continue to cook at 100% (high) for the rest of the cooking time, or until just cooked.

6 Unwrap the parcels and slide the fish on to a hot serving plate. Sprinkle with capers, garnish with lemon slices and watercress and serve.

Above: *Red mullet parcels*

Vegetables

Sweet and sour carrots

Illustrated on pages 26-27

Serves 4

450 g/1 lb carrots, thickly sliced
2 tbls vegetable oil
1 onion, sliced
3 celery stalks, sliced
2 tsps cornflour
2 tsps soy sauce
1 tbls light brown soft sugar
1 tbls cider vinegar
2 tsps lemon juice
150 ml/¼ pt hot vegetable stock
salt and pepper
25 g/1 oz blanched almonds,
  halved

1 Place the carrots in a 1.7 L/3 pt bowl with 8 tbls cold water. Cover with pierced cling film and microwave at 100% (high) for 10-12 minutes. Stir halfway through the cooking time.

2 Place the oil, onion and celery in a 1.7 L/3 pt casserole and microwave at 100% (high) for 4 minutes, stirring after 2 minutes.

3 Mix in the cornflour, then add the soy sauce, sugar, vinegar, lemon juice and stock. Microwave at 100% (high) for 2-3 minutes, until boiling, stirring 2-3 times.

4 Add the carrots, cover with pierced cling film and microwave at 100% (high) for 5 minutes. Take care not to overcook the carrots or they will be soggy. Season well. Scatter with almonds and serve immediately as an accompanying dish.

Note: The unusual sweet and sour flavour of these carrots makes them ideal for serving with plainly cooked chicken or pork.

Micro-facts

Vegetables benefit greatly from cooking in a microwave oven. They retain their texture and more of their nutrients and colour than when boiled conventionally.

Mushrooms with garlic peas

Serves 4

8 medium-sized flat mushrooms
50 g/2 oz margarine or butter
2 cloves garlic, crushed
2 tbls chopped parsley
salt and pepper
175 g/6 oz frozen peas

1 Remove the mushroom stalks and chop them finely. Wipe the mushroom caps and place them, gill sides up, around the edge of a plate lined with absorbent paper.

2 Cream the margarine or butter, using a wooden spoon, and mix in the chopped mushroom stalks, garlic, parsley, salt and pepper.

3 Divide the peas equally between the mushroom caps, spooning them on top. Dot with the flavoured butter.

4 Cover with greaseproof paper and microwave at 100% (high) for 2-3 minutes, until heated, rotating the plate once or twice.

5 Transfer the mushrooms to a serving plate and serve immediately. Garnish each stuffed mushroom with a little chopped parsley, if liked.

Below: *Mushrooms with garlic peas*
Right: *Chinese beans and beansprouts*

Spicy vegetables

Illustrated on pages 12-13

Serves 4-6

1 tbls oil
50 g/2 oz margarine or butter
2 cloves garlic, crushed
1 tbls ground coriander
2 tsps ground cumin
3 tbls hot vegetable stock
275 g/10 oz broad beans
350 g/12 oz leeks, sliced
225 g/8 oz broccoli, cut into even-sized florets
1 large red pepper, deseeded and cut into thin strips
pepper
1 tsp lemon juice

1 Put the oil, fat, garlic, coriander and cumin into a 1.7 L/3 pt casserole. Cover with a lid and microwave at 100% (high) for 2 minutes, stirring after 1 minute.
2 Stir in the stock. Add the broad beans, leeks and broccoli, re-cover and microwave at 100% (high) for 5 minutes. Stir in the red pepper, re-cover and microwave at 100% (high) for a further 4-5 minutes, or until the vegetables are tender but still crisp. Stir after 3 minutes.
3 Season with pepper and stir in the lemon juice. Serve immediately.

Chinese beans and beansprouts

Serves 4

2 tbls vegetable oil
1 onion, sliced
250 g/9 oz small French beans
2 tbls water
1 tbls thin soy sauce
1 tbls lemon juice
salt and pepper
50 g/2 oz mushrooms, sliced
250 g/9 oz beansprouts

1 Preheat a large browning dish at 100% (high) for 4-5 minutes, or according to manufacturer's instructions.
2 Add the vegetable oil, onion and beans, stir and cover with the lid. Microwave at 100% (high) for 3 minutes.
3 Add the water, soy sauce, lemon juice and season to taste. Add the mushrooms and beansprouts and mix together. Microwave, uncovered, at 100% (high) for 2-3 minutes, until the vegetables are tender but still crisp. Transfer to a warmed serving dish and serve immediately.

Midweek Meals and Snacks

Quick, easy and absolutely delicious – definitely qualities needed if you want to feed the family in a hurry. From hearty soups and finger foods to fish, pasta and vegetable dishes, the appetising, nutritious recipes in this chapter can be prepared in less than 30 minutes.

They're perfect for TV suppers, snacks round the fire or even for easy eating in the garden – weather permitting! And some would make exciting dinner party starters too.

We're living in the age of 'fast food' and this is the way to do it in style – with the help of your microwave of course!

Soups

Asparagus soup with garlic rolls

Serves 4
450 g/1 lb fresh asparagus,
   trimmed of woody stems
5 large spring onions
1 onion, chopped
50 g/2 oz margarine or butter
600 ml/1 pt hot vegetable
   stock
40 g/1½ oz plain flour
300 ml/½ pt milk
3 tbls double cream
For the rolls
2 granary rolls
50 g/2 oz full fat soft cheese with
   garlic and herbs
1 tbls chopped parsley

1 Cut the asparagus spears into short lengths and set tips aside. Chop the spring onions, keeping the green and

white parts separate. Separate the white parts into rings and reserve.

Micro-facts

Soups actually improve in flavour if made in advance. Cook them in the microwave oven, chill and then reheat quickly in the microwave when required.

Above: *Asparagus soup with garlic rolls*

2 Put the spring onion stems in a 2.3 L/ 4 pt casserole and add the asparagus stalks, onion, fat and half the hot stock. Cover tightly with a lid or pierced cling film and microwave at 100% (high) for 9 minutes. Stir after 5 minutes.
3 Gradually blend the remaining stock with the flour, stirring constantly. Stir in a little of the hot soup then pour the mixture back into the casserole. Microwave at 100% (high) for 2-3 minutes, or until thickened.
4 Allow the soup to cool slightly, then purée in a blender or food processor. Stir in the milk. Put the reserved asparagus tips into a small bowl with 4 tbls water. Cover with pierced cling film and microwave at 100% (high) for 4 minutes. Add the spring onion rings, re-cover and microwave at 100% (high) for 1 minute, then drain.
5 Reheat the soup, covered, at 100% (high) for 1-2 minutes, then stir in the cream. Meanwhile cut the rolls in half and spread with the cheese. Place around the edge of a plate lined with a white paper napkin. Microwave at 100% (high) for 30-60 seconds, to melt the cheese slightly.

6 Serve the soup in individual bowls garnished with asparagus tips and spring onion rings. Serve the rolls sprinkled with parsley.

Corned beef soup

Serves 4
2 tbls vegetable oil
1 large onion, chopped
**250 g/9 oz carrots, cut into 5 mm/
   ¼ in dice**
**450 g/1 lb potatoes, cut into 5 mm/
   ¼ in dice**
700 ml/1¼ pt hot beef stock
200 g/7 oz can corned beef, diced
salt and pepper
chopped parsley, to garnish
grated Parmesan cheese, to serve

1 Place the oil and onion in a 2.3 L/4 pt casserole and microwave at 100% (high) for 2 minutes. Add the carrots and potatoes, cover with a lid or pierced cling film and microwave at 100% (high)

Above: *Corned beef soup*

for 6 minutes, stirring after 3 minutes.
2 Pour on the stock, re-cover and microwave at 100% (high) for 6 minutes, or until the vegetables are just tender.
3 Add the corned beef and season to taste with salt and pepper. Re-cover and microwave at 100% (high) for 2 minutes. Serve at once, sprinkled with a little parsley. Serve with Parmesan cheese.

Vichyssoise

Serves 4
50 g/2 oz butter
**350 g/12 oz leeks, white parts
   only, washed and thinly sliced**
1 large onion, thinly sliced
**50 g/2 oz potatoes, peeled and
   thinly sliced**
850 ml/1½ pt hot chicken stock
salt and pepper
150 ml/¼ pt double cream
snipped chives, to garnish

1 Put the butter into a very large heat-proof mixing bowl or microwave-safe casserole. Microwave at 100% (high) for 5 minutes, stirring frequently, until the butter has melted.
2 Add the leek and onion slices to the butter and mix well. Microwave, uncovered, at 100% (high) for 5 minutes, stirring frequently, until the leeks and onion are soft.
3 Add the potato slices and chicken stock, mix well, then cover with cling film rolled back at one edge and microwave at 100% (high) for 20 minutes, or until the potatoes are soft, stirring every 5 minutes.
4 Allow the soup to cool a little, then purée in an electric blender or food processor until smooth. Season the soup well with salt and pepper, then return to a bowl and leave in the refrigerator for 3-4 hours until chilled.
5 Stir the cream into the chilled soup before serving. Spoon the soup into chilled serving bowls and garnish each with snipped chives.

Fish

Tangy fish fingers

Serves 4
225 g/8 oz long grain rice
600 ml/1 pt boiling salted water
1 tbls vegetable oil
10 fish fingers
For the sauce
2 tbls cornflour
150 ml/¼ pt hot chicken stock
225 g/8 oz can pineapple tit-bits
2 tbls soy sauce
pinch of ground ginger
2 tsps tomato purée
25 g/1 oz light brown soft sugar
1 tbls vinegar
salt and pepper
¼ red pepper, deseeded and diced
2 spring onions, chopped

1 Place the rice in a large deep bowl
with the salted water and oil. Cover with
pierced cling film and microwave at
100% (high) for 10 minutes. Leave to
stand for 5 minutes.
2 To make the sauce, place the
cornflour in a 1.7 L/3 pt casserole. Add a
little stock and blend well, then stir in the
remaining stock. Add the pineapple with
its juice. Stir in the remaining sauce
ingredients.
3 Cover the casserole with cling film
rolled back at one edge and microwave
at 100% (high) for 3-4 minutes, or until
thickened, stirring 2-3 times.
4 Place the fish fingers on a microwave
rack and cook uncovered at 100% (high)
for 4 minutes, rearranging and turning
halfway through the cooking time.
5 Divide the rice between 4 warmed
plates. Cut each fish finger into 3 or 4
and place on top. Spoon sauce over
each portion and serve.

Micro-facts

If you do not possess a ring
mould, it is possible to make one
by standing a tumbler, open end
up, in a round dish. This method
can also be used when baking
cakes.

Haddock mousse

Serves 4-6
300 ml/½ pt milk
1 small onion
1 small carrot
1 bay leaf
6 black peppercorns
350 g/12 oz smoked haddock
25 g/1 oz butter
25 g/1 oz plain flour
salt and pepper
1 sachet powdered gelatine
65 ml/2½ fl oz chicken stock
2 hard-boiled eggs, chopped
1 tbls chopped parsley
finely grated zest of 1 lemon
1-1½ tbls lemon juice
**150 ml/¼ pt double cream,
  lightly whipped**
**watercress and 4 unpeeled prawns,
  to garnish**

1 Place the milk, onion, carrot, bay leaf
and peppercorns in a jug and microwave
at 30% (low) for 10 minutes. Place the

Below: Tangy fish fingers

haddock in a dish with 1 tbls water, cover
and microwave at 100% (high) for
4 minutes until cooked. Skin and flake
with a fork.
2 Place the butter in a bowl and microwave at 100% (high) for 30-45 seconds
to melt. Add the flour, mixing well. Strain
the milk and gradually add to the flour
mixture, stirring continuously. Microwave at 100% (high) for 1-2 minutes,
whisking every 30 seconds until the
sauce is thick and smooth. Season, cover
with wet greaseproof paper and leave to
cool.
3 Soak the gelatine in the chicken stock
in a small bowl for 2 minutes, then
microwave at 100% (high) for 30-45
seconds until the gelatine has dissolved.
Cool slightly, then add to the sauce.
4 Add the flaked haddock, eggs, parsley
and lemon zest and juice to the sauce
and mix well. Fold in the cream, then
pour into an 850 ml/1½ pt ring mould
and leave to set.
5 Dip the mould briefly in hot water,
then turn the haddock ring on to a plate.
Garnish with watercress and unpeeled
prawns and serve with buttered rolls,
toast or crackers.

Scampi paprika

Illustrated on pages 38-39

Serves 4
450 g/1 lb scampi, thawed if frozen
400 g/14 oz can tomatoes
1 large onion, thinly sliced
1 green pepper, deseeded
**   and sliced**
2 tbls vegetable oil
1 tbls paprika
2 cloves garlic, crushed
1 vegetable stock cube
3 tsps cornflour
150 ml/¼ pt soured cream
salt and pepper
chopped parsley, to garnish

1 Make a cut through the back of each scampi and carefully remove the black intestine.
2 Pour the tomatoes into a sieve placed over a small bowl to drain, then roughly chop. Allow the juice to stand for about 10 minutes, until a clear liquid rises to the top, then carefully spoon this liquid off and discard, leaving behind the pure tomato juice.
3 Put the onion, pepper and oil into a large casserole. Microwave at 100% (high) for 5 minutes, until the onion and pepper are soft.
4 Add the paprika and garlic to the onion, crumble in the stock cube and mix well. Microwave at 100% (high) for 2 minutes.

Above: *Haddock mousse*

5 Mix the cornflour to a paste with a little of the strained tomato juice, then add to the remaining juice. Add to the onion and pepper mixture with the tomatoes and stir well. Loosely cover the dish with cling film and microwave at 100% (high) for 3 minutes. Add the scampi and microwave at 100% (high) for a further 2½ minutes, turning the scampi 2 or 3 times.
6 Stir the soured cream into the scampi mixture and season well with salt and pepper. Microwave at 100% (high) for another 1-2 minutes, or until very hot. Sprinkle with parsley and serve with rice and a green salad, if liked.

Ham and Bacon

Bacon and sausage pittas

Serves 4
1 tbls vegetable oil
16 pork cocktail sausages
8 rashers streaky bacon, derinded
   and cut into four
25 g/1 oz margarine or butter
1 tbls French mustard
¼ tsp Worcestershire sauce
4 small tomatoes, halved
4 wholemeal pitta breads
4 lettuce leaves
8 pickled onions

1 Preheat a browning dish at 100% (high) for 4 minutes, or according to manufacturer's instructions. Add the oil and sausages and microwave at 100% (high) for 3-4 minutes, turning often.
2 Place the bacon pieces in a single layer on a plate lined with absorbent paper. Cover with more absorbent

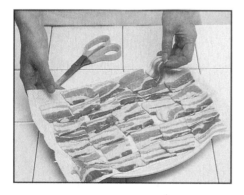

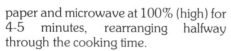

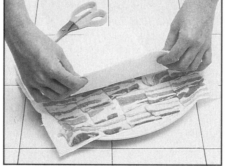

paper and microwave at 100% (high) for 4-5 minutes, rearranging halfway through the cooking time.

Micro-facts

Microwave oranges and lemons at 100% (high) for 30 seconds before squeezing. This will increase the amount of juice you can extract from them.

3 Mix together the fat, mustard and Worcestershire sauce. Place the tomatoes on a plate and dot with some of the flavoured fat. Microwave at 100% (high) for 1-2 minutes.
4 Slit open the pitta breads and line each one with a lettuce leaf. Divide the sausages, bacon, tomatoes and onions into 4 and use to fill the pitta breads.
5 Place the pittas on a large platter, dot the remaining flavoured fat over the fillings, and microwave at 100% (high) for 1-1½ minutes, or until the pitta bread is warm and the fat has melted. Serve immediately.

Ham and orange fricassée

Serves 4

2 x 225 g/8 oz slices ham
4 servings instant potato,
    reconstituted according to pack
    instructions
1 tsp chopped parsley, to
    garnish
For the orange sauce
25 g/1 oz margarine or butter
25 g/1 oz plain flour
300 ml/½ pt milk
finely grated zest and juice of
    1 small orange
salt and pepper
225 g/8 oz frozen peas

1 Cut the ham into 2 cm/¾ in cubes.
2 To make the sauce, place the fat in a 1.7 L/3 pt casserole and microwave at 100% (high) for 30 seconds, or until melted. Stir in the flour.
3 Gradually add the milk, stirring continuously. Microwave at 100% (high) for 3-4 minutes, or until thickened, stirring 2-3 times.
4 Add the orange zest, orange juice and

Left: *Bacon and sausage pittas*
Below: *Ginger gammon steaks*

seasoning. Stir in the ham and peas. Cover the dish with a lid or pierced cling film and microwave at 100% (high) for 4 minutes, to heat through.
5 Put the potato in a bowl and cover with pierced cling film. Microwave at 100% (high) for 1-2 minutes, to reheat.
6 Pipe or spoon the potato around the edge of a large serving dish or 4 individual plates. Arrange the fricassée inside the potato ring. Garnish with chopped parsley and serve at once with carrots, if wished.

Ginger gammon steaks

Serves 4

4 unsmoked gammon steaks
    (about 175 g/6 oz each)
15 g/½ oz margarine or butter
2 onions, thinly sliced
1 tbls cornflour
400 g/14 oz can tomatoes
40-50 g/1½-2 oz stem ginger, cut
    into thin strips
4 tbls ginger syrup
salt and pepper
parsley sprigs, to garnish

Above: *Ham and orange fricassée*

1 With a sharp pair of scissors, snip the fat around the edge of the gammon steaks at 1 cm/½ in intervals to prevent curling.
2 Arrange the steaks as far as possible in a single layer on a large plate. Cover with absorbent paper and microwave at 100% (high) for 8-9 minutes, rearranging the steaks halfway through the cooking time.
3 Place the fat and onions in a 1.1 L/2 pt bowl and microwave at 100% (high) for 2 minutes. In a small bowl mix the cornflour with 2 tbls of the tomato juice from the can to make a smooth paste.
4 Add the tomatoes with the remaining juice and the stem ginger and ginger syrup to the onions. Stir in the cornflour paste, mixing well. Microwave at 100% (high) for 3-4 minutes, or until boiling. Season with salt and pepper.
5 Transfer the gammon steaks to a warmed serving dish, arranging them overlapping slightly, then spoon over the sauce. Garnish with parsley sprigs and serve at once with noodles and courgettes, if liked.

Eggs and Cheese

Dutch fondue

Illustrated on pages 38-39

Serves 4-6
**250 g/9 oz flat mushrooms with
   stalks, finely chopped**
600 ml/1 pt hot chicken stock
4 tbls cornflour
150 ml/¼ pt milk
**250 g/9 oz Gouda cheese, finely
   grated**
1 tbls finely chopped parsley
1 tsp Worcestershire sauce
salt and pepper
**mushroom slices and parsley,
   to garnish**
To serve
**1 small French loaf, cut into
   2.5 cm/1 in cubes**
**450 g/1 lb pork chipolata
   sausages, fried and thickly sliced**
**225 g/8 oz cauliflower florets,
   lightly cooked**
**225 g/8 oz broccoli florets, lightly
   cooked**

1 Place the chopped mushrooms and stock in a 2.3 L/4 pt bowl. Cover with pierced cling film and microwave at 100% (high) for 5 minutes.
2 In a small bowl, blend the cornflour to a smooth paste with a little of the milk. Stir into the mushroom stock, then add the remaining milk. Re-cover and microwave at 100% (high) for 2 minutes, stirring once or twice.
3 Add the grated cheese, 2 tbls at a time, stirring well, until it has melted. Microwave at 50% (medium) for 3 minutes, stirring occasionally.
4 Stir in the parsley and Worcestershire sauce and season to taste. Pour into a

fondue pot or individual bowls, garnish with mushroom slices and parsley and serve at once.
5 Serve the bread cubes, sausages and hot, lightly cooked vegetables in separate bowls and provide fondue forks for dipping.

Scrambled egg savoury

Serves 4
40 g/1½ oz margarine or butter
6 eggs
2 tbls milk
salt and pepper
4 large slices of bread
To garnish
4 strips anchovy (optional)
4 strips pimiento
parsley sprigs

1 Place 15 g/½ oz of the fat in a 1.1 L/2 pt bowl. Microwave at 100% (high) for 20-30 seconds or until melted.
2 Add the eggs, milk and seasoning to the bowl and beat well with a fork. Microwave at 100% (high) for 1½ minutes until beginning to set.

Micro-facts

When cooking eggs conventionally the white cooks first; in the microwave oven the yolk sets first. Stop microwaving before the white is completely set and leave to stand until cooking is complete.

3 Stir the set pieces of egg from the outside to the centre, then cook for a further 1½-2 minutes. The eggs should still be moist and just beginning to set when they are removed from the oven. Leave to stand while preparing the toast.

4 Toast the bread lightly on both sides, and remove the crusts. If wished, cut into circles. Spread with the remaining fat.
5 Pile scrambled egg on the slices of toast, then arrange the anchovies, if using, and pimientos in a lattice pattern on top. Serve at once garnished with parsley sprigs.

Below: *Scrambled egg savoury*

Tomato and egg bakes

Serves 4
4 tomatoes, peeled
1 tsp chopped fresh basil or ½ tsp dried basil
salt and pepper
4 large eggs
basil leaves, to garnish (optional)

1 Dice the tomatoes and divide between 4 individual 150 ml/¼ pt dishes or ramekins.
2 Sprinkle a little basil into each dish, and season to taste with salt and pepper. Mix well.
3 Break 1 egg into each dish on top of the mixture. Prick the yolk of each egg twice with a cocktail stick.
4 Cover each dish with cling film rolled back slightly at one edge. Microwave at 50% (medium) for 6-8 minutes. Rotate the dishes every 2 minutes. Each dish may not cook at the same speed, so remove as cooked.
5 Leave to stand for 1 minute, for whites to finish setting, then serve. Garnish with basil leaves if wished.

Above: *Tomato and egg bakes*

47

Vegetables and Pasta

Stuffed onions

Serves 4
4 large Spanish onions, skinned
chopped parsley, to garnish
For the sauce
1 clove garlic, crushed
25 g/1 oz margarine or butter
400 g/14 oz can chopped tomatoes
2 tbls tomato purée
salt and pepper
For the stuffing
225 g/8 oz liver pâté
2 tbls chopped parsley
To serve
350 g/12 oz small pasta shapes
1 tbls oil

1 Cut a slice from the top of each onion. Using a teaspoon or sharp knife, scoop out the centre, to leave a shell about 5 mm/¼ in thick.

2 To make the sauce, finely chop the scooped out onion flesh and put it in a small bowl. Add the garlic and fat, cover with pierced cling film and microwave at 100% (high) for 3 minutes. Stir in the tomatoes and tomato purée and season to taste. Re-cover and microwave at 100% (high) for 4 minutes, or until bubbling.

3 To make the stuffing, mix the pâté and parsley and spoon into the onion shells. Arrange the stuffed onions in a shallow dish and pour the tomato sauce around them. Cover with pierced cling film and microwave at 100% (high) for 12-14 minutes, or until the onions are soft, turning the dish twice during cooking. Leave to stand, covered, for about 5 minutes.

4 Meanwhile, put the pasta into a large bowl and add the oil and 700 ml/1½ pts boiling water. Cover with pierced cling film and microwave at 100% (high) for 5 minutes, until the pasta is just tender. Leave to stand for 2 minutes, drain and serve. Garnish with parsley.

Micro-facts

Use your microwave to dry excess parsley or other fresh herbs for use in the winter. Lay them between sheets of absorbent paper and microwave until they will crumble. Store in airtight jars.

Tortellini with tomato sauce

Serves 4-6
450 g/1 lb fresh tortellini
1 tsp salt
1 tbls vegetable oil
4 slices processed cheese
For the sauce
400 g/14 oz can peeled tomatoes
1 onion, chopped
few sprigs parsley
40 g/1½ oz margarine
40 g/1½ oz plain flour
1 tbls tomato purée
½ tsp sugar
salt and pepper

1 To make the sauce, place the tomatoes, onion and parsley sprigs in a blender or food processor and purée.

2 Place the margarine in a 1.1 L/2 pt bowl and microwave at 100% (high) for 30 seconds to melt. Stir in the flour. Gradually stir in the puréed mixture, then add the tomato purée and sugar. Season to taste. Microwave at 100% (high) for 2-3 minutes, until thickened, stirring 2-3 times.

3 Place the tortellini in a large bowl with 1.1 L/2 pts boiling water, the salt and oil. Cover with pierced cling film and microwave at 100% (high) for 8 minutes. Leave to stand for 4 minutes, then drain and divide between 4 individual serving dishes.

4 Pour the tomato sauce over the top. Place a cheese slice on top. If wished, cut cheese animals, using biscuit cutters. Place the dishes in the microwave oven and microwave at 100% (high) for 30-45 seconds, or until the cheese has melted. Serve at once.

Left: *Stuffed onions*

Vegetable crumble

Illustrated on pages 12-13

Serves 4
25 g/1 oz margarine
2 leeks, cut into 1 cm/½ in slices
2 large carrots, thickly sliced
1 small red pepper, deseeded and diced
450 g/1 lb courgettes, cut into 1 cm/½ in slices
400 g/14 oz can tomatoes
½ tsp dried basil
salt and pepper
50 g/2 oz pine nuts
2 tsps wine vinegar
For the topping
100 g/4 oz wholemeal flour
¼ tsp salt
40 g/1½ oz margarine
65 g/2½ oz Parmesan cheese, grated

1 Place the margarine in a large bowl and microwave at 100% (high) for 30 seconds to melt.

2 Add the leeks and carrots, cover with cling film, rolled back at one edge, and microwave at 100% (high) for 3 minutes. Add the red pepper and courgettes, re-cover and microwave at 100% (high) for 4-5 minutes until all the vegetables are tender.

3 Add the tomatoes and their juice, the basil and seasoning. Re-cover with cling film and microwave at 100% (high) for 2 minutes.

4 Meanwhile, to make the crumble topping, mix the flour and salt in a bowl. Add the margarine and rub into the flour until it resembles fine breadcrumbs. Stir in 50 g/2 oz of the grated Parmesan cheese and set the crumble aside.

5 Add the nuts and wine vinegar to the vegetables, and transfer to a 1.7 L/3 pt casserole. Sprinkle the crumble evenly over the vegetables and top with the remaining Parmesan cheese. Microwave at 100% (high) for 7-9 minutes. If wished, place the casserole under a preheated grill to brown the crumble topping.

Below: *Tortellini with tomato sauce*

Puddings, Cakes and Breads

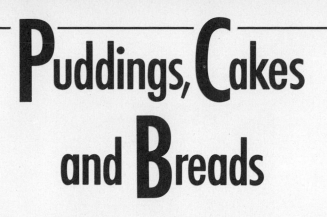

Most of us love puddings but they can often take a long time to cook. Use your microwave to make a steamed pudding in minutes, a cheesecake in a flash or even ice-cream in an instant – well, not quite, you've still got to freeze it!

Baking day can now take on a whole new meaning – like baking hour or two or, at most, baking morning.

Cakes cook so quickly it's almost unbelievable; and so does bread – it will be softer and lighter than you've ever produced before too.

You may want to make cakes for tea, a really comforting nursery-type pudding or a stunning dinner party dessert. There's a wide range to choose from and all will show you just how versatile your microwave can be.

Hot Puddings

Tropical crumble

Serves 4-6

4 oranges, peeled and chopped
4 fresh apricots, stoned and
  chopped
2 large bananas, peeled and sliced
100 g/4 oz fresh pineapple,
  chopped, or canned pineapple
  chunks, drained
single cream or ice-cream, to serve
For the topping
50 g/2 oz plain flour
1/2 tsp ground ginger
25 g/1 oz rolled or porridge oats
25 g/1 oz desiccated coconut
150 g/5 oz dark brown soft sugar
65 g/2½ oz butter

1 First make the topping: sift the flour and ginger into a mixing bowl. Add the oats, coconut and sugar and mix.
2 Cut the butter into pieces, place in a small bowl and microwave at 100% (high) for 50-60 seconds to melt. Stir into the topping mix.

3 Put all the fruit into a deep microwave-proof glass dish, turning the bananas in the juice from the oranges to prevent them discolouring.

Below: *Tropical crumble*

4 Sprinkle the topping evenly over the fruit and press down gently to level the surface. Microwave at 100% (high) for 10-12 minutes, giving the dish a quarter turn every 3 minutes.
5 Serve hot with cream or ice-cream.

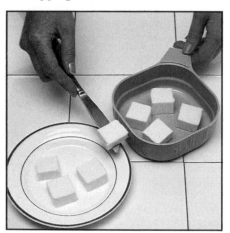

Micro-facts

Steamed puddings take only minutes to cook in the microwave. To reheat, arrange in slices around the edge of a plate, with a glass of water in the centre to help keep the pudding moist.

Date and pecan baked apples

Illustrated on pages 12-13

Serves 4
4 large cooking apples (about 200 g/7 oz each)
25 g/1 oz butter
6 tbls natural unsweetened apple juice
whipped cream, to serve
For the filling
50 g/2 oz dates, stoned and coarsely chopped
15 g/½ oz pecan nuts, chopped
25 g/1 oz light brown soft sugar
½ tsp ground cinnamon

1 Using an apple corer or a small sharp knife, remove the core from each apple. Score the skin around the middle of each apple.
2 To make the filling, mix together the dates, pecan nuts, sugar and cinnamon in a bowl. Use to fill the apple cavities, pressing down firmly with the back of a teaspoon. Dot with butter.
3 Place the apples in a shallow casserole dish, then pour the apple juice around them. Microwave at 100% (high) for 8-9 minutes, or until the apples are soft when

pierced through the centre with a sharp knife.
4 Serve at once, accompanied by whipped cream.

Apricot and nut sponge pudding

Serves 4-6
100 g/4 oz no-need-to-soak dried apricots
100 g/4 oz margarine or butter
100 g/4 oz caster sugar
2 eggs, lightly beaten
few drops of almond essence
175 g/6 oz self-raising flour
pinch of salt
50 g/2 oz shelled walnuts, roughly chopped
3 tbls milk
To serve
4-5 tbls apricot jam
1 tsp lemon juice

1 Grease an 850 ml/1½ pt pudding basin or line with cling film. Wash the

Above: *Apricot and nut sponge pudding*

apricots and cut them in small pieces with scissors.
2 Cream the fat with the sugar until light and fluffy. Add the beaten eggs, a little at a time, beating after each addition. Thoroughly stir in the almond essence.
3 Sift the flour and salt together, then using a metal spoon, lightly fold into the creamed mixture alternately with the apricots and walnuts. Stir in the milk.
4 Spoon the mixture into the prepared pudding basin and smooth the top. Cover with cling film, snipping 2 holes, to allow the steam to escape. Microwave at 100% (high) for 5-6 minutes, giving the basin a half turn after 3 minutes. Leave to stand for 5-10 minutes, before serving.
5 Meanwhile, place the jam in a small bowl with the lemon juice. Stir and microwave at 100% (high) for 45-60 seconds to heat.
6 Turn out the pudding on to a warmed serving plate. Pour the hot apricot jam over the pudding and serve whilst still piping hot.

Surprise meringue pie

Serves 4-6
**175 g/6 oz shortcrust pastry,
thawed if frozen**
For the filling
100 g/4 oz butter
50 g/2 oz light brown soft sugar
**150 ml/5 fl oz can sweetened
condensed milk**
2 large egg yolks
For the meringue
2 large egg whites
100 g/4 oz caster sugar

1 Roll out the pastry and use to line an 18 cm/7 in round pie dish. Finish the edge 5 mm/¼ in above the rim, to allow for shrinkage, and crimp.

2 Prick the sides and the base well. Line the base with a double sheet of absorbent paper. Microwave at 100% (high) for 2 minutes, turning a quarter turn after 1 minute. Remove lining paper and

Micro-facts

Before making meringue, microwave egg whites at 100% (high) for 5-10 seconds per white. Beat immediately with a pinch of salt and you will achieve a greater volume than if using chilled whites.

Above: *Surprise meringue pie*

microwave at 100% (high) for 1-2 minutes, turning as before.

3 Put the butter, sugar and milk in a 1.4 L/2½ pt bowl and microwave at 100% (high) for 4 minutes, stirring every 2 minutes. Beat in the egg yolks and pour into the pastry case.

4 Whisk the egg whites until stiff, whisk in half the sugar and fold in the rest. Swirl meringue over the filling to cover. Microwave at 100% (high) for 2 minutes. Brown the meringue under a preheated grill, if liked.

Ice-cream variety

Serves 6
1 egg
2 egg yolks
75 g/3 oz caster sugar
300 ml/½ pt milk
few drops of vanilla essence
300 ml/½ pt double cream

1 Place the egg and egg yolks in a 1.7 L/3 pt bowl with the sugar and whisk until pale and creamy. Stir in the milk.

2 Microwave at 50% (medium) for 8 minutes, until slightly thickened. Stir every 2 minutes and then 3-4 times in the last minute. Stir in the vanilla essence, cover with cling film and leave to cool completely.

3 Whip the cream until just thick enough to hold its shape. Fold into the custard. Pour into a freezerproof container. Cover and freeze for 1 hour, or until frozen about 1 cm/½ in around the sides.

4 Turn the mixture into a bowl and whisk thoroughly to break up the ice crystals. Return to container, cover and freeze for 1-2 hours, or until firm. Soften at room temperature for 10 minutes before serving. Scoop into individual glasses or dishes to serve.

Note: To flavour the ice-cream, fold one of the following into the custard before freezing, then continue as above:

Hazelnut: Add 100 g/4 oz toasted, skinned and chopped hazelnuts.

Chocolate: Blend 2 tbls cocoa powder with 1 tbls boiling water, cool and add.

Ripple: Swirl 2 tbls sieved raspberries through the mixture after breaking up the ice crystals in stage 4 above. Do not overmix.

Blackcurrant: Drain 2 x 215 g/7½ oz cans blackcurrants, purée in an electric blender or food processor and add.

Peach and rice condé

Serves 4-6

75 g/3 oz round grain rice, rinsed and well drained
3 tbls sugar
800 ml/1½ pts milk
300 ml/½ pt double cream
½ tsp vanilla essence
4 tbls raspberry jam
425 g/15 oz can peach halves, well drained

1 Put the rice, sugar and milk into a large bowl and microwave at 100% (high) for 10 minutes, or until almost boiling, stirring occasionally.

2 Reduce power to 30% (low) and microwave for 60-70 minutes, or until almost all of the milk is absorbed, stirring every 15 minutes. Cover closely with cling film to prevent a skin forming and leave to cool completely.

3 Whip the cream until it forms soft peaks. Fold half into the cold rice with the vanilla essence, spoon into a serving dish and level the surface.

4 Sieve the raspberry jam into a small bowl and microwave at 100% (high) for 30-40 seconds, or until melted.

5 Arrange peach halves, cut side down, on top of the rice, leaving a border around the edge. Brush the peaches with the warmed jam. Pipe rosettes of the remaining cream around the edge of the rice and in the centre. Serve cold.

Below: *Peach and rice condé*

Flans and Teabreads

Oatmeal fruit flan

Serves 4-6
75 g/3 oz plain flour
pinch of salt
75 g/3 oz fine ground oatmeal
75 g/3 oz margarine or butter,
  diced
1-2 tbls water
fresh pouring cream, to serve
For the filling
1 tbls custard powder
1 tbls caster sugar
300 ml/½ pt milk
400 g/14 oz can pear halves,
  drained with juice reserved
212 g/7½ oz can apricot halves,
  drained with juice reserved
2 tsps arrowroot

1 Sift the flour and salt into a bowl. Add the oatmeal and mix with a fork. Rub in the fat. Add just enough water to draw the mixture together to a firm dough and knead lightly until smooth.
2 Roll out on a lightly floured board and use to line a 20 cm/8 in flan dish. Trim the pastry edge to 5 mm/¼ in above the flan dish to allow for shrinkage. Crimp the pastry rim.
3 Prick the sides and base thoroughly, to help crisp the case and stop it from puffing up. Microwave at 100% (high) for 4-6 minutes, turning a quarter turn every 2 minutes. Leave to cool.
4 To make the filling, mix the custard powder and sugar together with a little milk. Gradually blend in the remaining milk and microwave at 100% (high) for 4-5 minutes, until thick and smooth, stirring or whisking every minute.
5 Leave the custard to cool slightly,

then pour into flan case and leave to set.
6 Cut one pear half into thin slices. Put one apricot half in flan centre and surround with pear slices. Arrange pear halves over the slices with apricots around the edge.
7 Combine the reserved juices, measure 150 ml/¼ pt and discard the rest. In a 600 ml/1 pt bowl, blend the arrowroot with a little of the fruit juice and then stir in the rest of the juice. Microwave at 100% (high) for 2 minutes, or until thickened. Spoon over the fruit and refrigerate for 2 hours.
8 Serve the flan chilled, with cream.

Right: *Kiwi fruit and grape cheesecake*
Below: *Oatmeal fruit flan*

Sultana and walnut teabread

Illustrated on pages 50-51

Makes one 22 x 12 cm/8½ x 5 in loaf
75 g/3 oz sultanas
1 tsp bicarbonate of soda
175 g/6 oz light brown soft sugar
grated zest of 1 orange
50 ml/2 fl oz vegetable oil
1 egg
175 g/6 oz plain flour
salt
1 tsp ground cinnamon
½ tsp grated nutmeg
25 g/1 oz chopped walnuts

Micro-facts

When cooking teabreads, pastry and cakes, place the dish on an upturned plate to help avoid localised overcooking. This encourages a more even distribution of microwaves.

50% (medium) for 8 minutes, giving the dish a quarter turn every 2 minutes. Increase the power to 100% (high) and microwave for 2-4 minutes, or until a skewer inserted in the centre comes out clean.

5 Leave to stand for 5-10 minutes before turning the teabread out of the dish. Turn on to a wire rack and leave to cool before serving.

Kiwi fruit and grape cheesecake

Serves 6
225 g/8 oz plain flour
pinch of salt
100 g/4 oz margarine or butter, diced
3-4 tbls milk
For the filling
175 g/6 oz curd cheese
75 g/3 oz caster sugar
2 tsps cornflour
3 eggs
few drops vanilla essence
300 ml/½ pt double cream
To decorate
3 kiwi fruit (Chinese gooseberries), peeled and sliced
black grapes, halved and seeded

1 Sift the flour and salt into a bowl, then rub in the fat. Sprinkle over the milk and mix to a dough.

2 Roll out the pastry on a lightly floured surface and use to line a 23 cm/9 in flan dish. Trim the pastry edges 5 mm/¼ in above the top of the dish to allow for shrinkage. Crimp the pastry rim.

3 Prick the sides and base of the pastry well with a fork. Line the base with a double sheet of absorbent paper, and microwave at 100% (high) for 3 minutes, turning a ¼ turn every minute. Remove paper and microwave at 100% (high) for 1-2 minutes, or until cooked.

4 Beat the cheese, sugar and cornflour together. Mix in the eggs, vanilla and cream. Microwave at 100% (high) for 4-5 minutes, or until thickened, blending with a wire whisk every minute. Do not overcook or the mixture will separate. If necessary reduce power to 50% (medium) after 3 minutes, for greater control.

5 Pour the cheese filling into the pastry case. Draw a palette knife back and forth over the surface. Chill for at least 2 hours. Decorate with kiwi fruit slices and grapes just before serving.

1 Mix the sultanas, bicarbonate of soda and 175 ml/6 fl oz boiling water in a bowl and leave to stand for 10 minutes, to plump the sultanas.

2 Mix the sugar, orange zest, oil and egg together until smooth and add the sultana mixture. Gradually stir in the remaining ingredients.

3 Line base of a 22 x 12 cm/8½ x 5 in loaf dish with greaseproof paper, then spread the mixture evenly over it.

4 Place the dish on an inverted saucer in the centre of the oven and microwave at

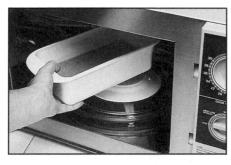

Large Cakes

Mocha gâteau

Makes 6-8 slices
75 g/3 oz butter
100 g/4 oz caster sugar
4 large eggs, separated
1 tbls milk
150 g/5 oz plain dessert chocolate,
  broken into pieces
90 g/3½ oz plain flour, sifted
To finish
25 g/1 oz cornflour
150 g/5 oz light brown soft sugar
300 ml/½ pt milk
1½ tbls instant coffee granules
250 g/9 oz butter
50 g/2 oz chopped nuts
100 g/4 oz plain dessert chocolate
icing sugar
6-8 coffee beans

1 Beat the butter with half the caster sugar until light and fluffy. Beat in the yolks one by one, add the milk. Place the chocolate in a small bowl and microwave at 100% (high) for 1-1½ minutes, stirring after 1 minute, to melt. Stir into the cake mix.
2 Whisk the egg whites until stiff, then whisk in the remaining sugar. Fold into the chocolate mix, then fold in the flour. Pour into a greased 20 cm/8 in cake or soufflé dish lined with non-stick baking paper.
3 Place in the oven on top of an up-turned plate and microwave at 100% (high) for 7-8 minutes, turning the dish every 1½-2 minutes. When cooked, the cake will shrink away from the sides of the dish. Leave the cake to stand in the dish for 5 minutes before turning out on to a wire rack. Peel off paper and leave to cool.

Micro-facts

Cakes have moist spots on top when cooked but will dry on standing. They will not brown like conventionally baked cakes but will shrink away from the sides of the dish when cooked.

4 To make the icing, blend the cornflour and sugar to a paste with 4 tbls milk. Place the remaining milk in a jug with the coffee and microwave at 100% (high) for 2-3 minutes, or until boiling. Add to the cornflour mixture, stir and microwave at

Above: *Mocha gâteau*

100% (high) for 1 minute or until thickened. Cover with wet greaseproof paper and leave until cold.
5 Beat the butter until creamy. Gradually beat in the coffee mixture. Spoon 8 tbls of the icing into a piping bag fitted with a large star nozzle and reserve for decorating the gâteau.
6 Split the cake into three layers. Use the remaining icing to sandwich the layers together and to coat the top and sides. Press nuts around the sides.
7 Using a potato peeler, shave curls from the chocolate block and arrange on top of the cake. Lay strips of greaseproof paper across the curls. Sift icing sugar thickly on top, then remove the paper. Pipe a border of icing around the top and bottom edges and decorate with coffee beans.

Victoria sandwich cake

Makes 8 slices
175 g/6 oz self-raising flour
pinch of salt
175 g/6 oz butter, softened
175 g/6 oz caster sugar
3 large eggs, lightly beaten
2-3 tbls milk
vegetable oil, for greasing
For the filling
3-4 tbls red jam
**150 ml/¼ pt whipping cream
  (optional)**
caster or icing sugar, for dredging

1 Line the base of a 20 cm/8 in cake dish or soufflé dish with greaseproof paper, then lightly grease the paper.

2 Sift the flour and salt together and set aside. Beat the butter and sugar together until light and creamy. Add the eggs a little at a time, beating thoroughly after each addition. Fold in the sifted flour, about one-third at a time, using a metal spoon. Fold in the milk.

3 Place in prepared dish and microwave at 100% (high) for 5½-6½ minutes, until a skewer inserted in the centre comes out clean. Rotate the dish a quarter turn every 2 minutes.

4 Leave to stand for 10 minutes, then turn out on to a wire rack, remove the lining paper, turn the right way up and leave to cool completely.

5 Split the cake in half. Spread one half with jam. Whip the cream until thick, if using, and spread over the underside of the other half. Sandwich the cakes together and dredge the top with caster or icing sugar.

6 Place on a serving plate, and serve immediately, or within 2 hours.

Note: For variety, try one of the following:

Orange sandwich: sandwich cake together with marmalade and cream. Top with whipped cream and decorate with mandarin orange segments.

Coconut sandwich: sandwich cake together with red cherry jam. Blend 100 g/4 oz sifted icing sugar with 1 tbls warm water and use to ice the top of the cake. Whilst still soft, scatter the top thickly with desiccated coconut. Arrange sliced glacé cherries around the top edge.

Chocolate sandwich: replace 25 g/1 oz of the flour with cocoa powder. Sandwich cake together with jam and cream. To finish the top, sift a little icing sugar over, then pipe a lattice of melted chocolate cake covering.

Right: Victoria sandwich cake

Small Cakes and Rolls

Chocolate caramel slices

Makes 12 slices
175 g/6 oz plain flour
pinch of salt
50 g/2 oz rice flour
150 g/5 oz margarine or butter
50 g/2 oz caster sugar
For the caramel filling
100 g/4 oz margarine
75 g/3 oz caster sugar
1 tbls golden syrup
400 g/14 oz can sweetened condensed milk
For the topping
175 g/6 oz plain or milk dessert chocolate

1 Line a 28 x 18 cm/11 x 7 in non-metallic dish with cling film. Sift the flour into a bowl and add the salt and rice flour. Rub in the fat until it resembles fine breadcrumbs. Stir in the sugar, and knead to form a dough. Press into the prepared dish, and smooth the top with the back of a metal spoon. Prick well.
2 Microwave at 100% (high) for 3-4 minutes, giving the dish a quarter turn every minute. Remove from the oven and leave to cool.
3 To make the caramel, place all the ingredients in a large bowl, to allow room for boiling. Microwave at 100% (high) for 4 minutes, stirring 2-3 times.
4 Microwave at 100% (high) for a further 5 minutes, or until light golden brown. Stir 2-3 times. Watch to make sure it does not boil over.
5 Pour over the cold cooked base and leave to cool.

Micro-facts

When cooking the caramel for the slices, the bowl will get very hot so it is essential to use a bowl which will withstand the high temperature, and don't forget to use oven gloves for handling.

6 Break the chocolate into pieces and place in a bowl. Microwave at 100% (high) for 2½-3½ minutes, or until melted, stirring 2-3 times. Spread over the caramel. Mark into slices and leave to set for a few minutes before removing from the dish.

Wholemeal rolls

Makes 16
350 g/12 oz wholemeal flour
1 tsp salt
100 g/4 oz plain flour, sifted
1 sachet 'easy blend' dried yeast
300 ml/½ pt warm water
2 tbls vegetable oil
beaten egg, to glaze
1 tbls poppy seeds
1 tbls sesame seeds

1 Place the wholemeal flour, salt and plain flour in a large mixing bowl, and microwave at 100% (high) for 30 seconds or until warm. Mix the yeast into the flour, add the water and 1 tbls of oil and mix to a pliable dough.
2 Knead on a lightly floured surface until smooth and elastic, about 5-10 minutes. Return to the bowl, cover with cling film and leave in a warm place until double its size.
3 Knead for 2-3 minutes, then divide into 16 pieces. Shape each piece into a small roll and brush with remaining oil. Place on a greased microwave baking sheet or greased greaseproof paper and leave to rise for 20-30 minutes, until well risen and springy to the touch.
4 Cook in two batches. Microwave the first batch at 100% (high) for 3-3½ minutes, turning over and rearranging halfway through the cooking time. Repeat with the second batch.
5 Brush immediately with a little beaten

Below: *Chocolate caramel slices*

egg and sprinkle with poppy or sesame seeds. For a crisp brown crust, place under a preheated grill for a few minutes, then leave to cool on a wire rack.

Lemon top cakes

Makes 12-14
50 g/2 oz margarine or butter, softened
50 g/2 oz light brown soft sugar
1 egg, lightly beaten
finely grated zest of 1 lemon
50 g/2 oz self-raising flour
¼ tsp baking powder
1 tbls milk
For the icing and decoration
2-4 tbls lemon curd
40 g/1½ oz butter, softened
75 g/3 oz icing sugar, sifted
1 tsp milk
12-14 small lemon jelly slices

1 Cream the fat and sugar together until pale and fluffy. Add the egg a little at a time, beating thoroughly after each addition. Beat in the lemon zest.
2 Sift the flour and baking powder together, and fold into the mixture with the milk, using a metal spoon.

3 Place 6 or 7 double thickness paper cake cases in a circle around the edge of a plate. Half fill the cases with the cake mixture, spreading it as evenly as possible in each case.

Above: *Lemon top cakes*

4 Microwave at 100% (high) for 1½-2 minutes, giving the plate a half turn after 1 minute. Place cakes on a wire rack to cool. Repeat with remaining mix.

5 Spread the tops of the cakes with lemon curd almost to the edge.
6 To mix the icing, beat the butter until soft, then beat in the icing sugar and milk. Place in a piping bag fitted with a star nozzle and pipe a border of stars around the top edge of each cake. Decorate each cake with a lemon jelly. Serve as soon as possible.
Note: If liked, half the cakes may be decorated with blackcurrant jam or orange curd instead of lemon curd.

61

Kids in the Kitchen

Children of all ages can operate a microwave with ease. There is little chance of burning fingers (though warn children of the dangers of steam and heat transference to the containers). The controls are simple to use and the speed with which food cooks means they don't get bored waiting for the end results.

Also being able to see foods rapidly changing composition through the oven's glass door is quite fascinating (and not just for the kids)!

We've planned this chapter to appeal to all age groups – everything from family favourites like kebabs and tacos, simple drinks, and home-made sweets to a great party feast.

Small children will enjoy helping to prepare as well as eat the recipes and older kids, hopefully, will make them for themselves – and for you too!

Family Favourites

Beefy bean tacos

Makes 6
1 tbls vegetable oil
1 onion, finely chopped
225 g/8 oz minced beef
**225 g/8 oz can tomatoes, drained
    and chopped**
2 tbls tomato purée
2 tsps cornflour
225 g/8 oz can baked beans
salt and pepper
6 taco shells
To garnish (optional)
shredded lettuce
grated Cheddar cheese
2 spring onions, chopped

1 Place the oil and onion in a large bowl and microwave at 100% (high) for 2 minutes. Add the beef and microwave at 100% (high) for 4 minutes, stirring at 1 minute intervals to break up the meat.

2 Mix the tomatoes with the tomato purée and cornflour, then add to the mince with the baked beans. Stir. Cover with pierced cling film and microwave at 100% (high) for 4 minutes, or until thickened. Season.
3 Place the taco shells upright in an

Micro-facts

Cheese melts rapidly in the microwave oven and care should be taken not to overcook it. Also remember that bread or rolls will dry if overheated so timing is important.

oblong dish, and fill with bean and beef mixture. Microwave at 100% (high) for 1 minute.
4 Garnish with lettuce, cheese and spring onions if wished. Serve at once.

Kids' kebabs

Illustrated on pages 62-63

Makes 6
**2 x 2.5 cm/1 in slices wholemeal
    bread, crusts removed**
1 tbls Marmite
**225 g/8 oz Gruyère cheese, cut into
    2.5 cm/1 in cubes**
**2.5 cm/1 in slice luncheon meat,
    cut into cubes**

1 Spread the bread slices on both sides with Marmite, then cut into 2.5 cm/1 in cubes.
2 Arrange the pieces of bread, cheese

Below: *Beefy bean tacos*

and luncheon meat on six wooden kebab skewers. Do not place cheese at ends of skewers.
3 Place in a large shallow dish and microwave at 100% (high) for 1 minute. Turn the dish a half turn and microwave for 30-45 seconds, until the cheese begins to melt. Watch carefully. Serve.

Bean-stuffed potatoes

Illustrated on pages 12-13

Serves 4
4 x 225 g/8 oz potatoes, scrubbed
salt and pepper
150 g/5 oz can baked beans
**75 g/3 oz mature Cheddar cheese,
    grated**

1 Prick the potatoes with a fork. Place on absorbent paper in the oven at least 2.5 cm/1 in apart. Microwave at 100% (high) for 15 minutes, turning over and rearranging after 8 minutes.
2 Wrap the potatoes in foil when just tender and stand for 5 minutes, or until soft.
3 Unwrap and remove foil. Cut a cross in the top of each potato and squeeze at the bottom so the cross opens up. Season and place the potatoes on a plate.
4 Place a spoonful of beans in each cavity, and sprinkle with cheese. Microwave at 100% (high) for 2-3 minutes to heat the filling and melt the cheese, rearranging halfway through the cooking time. Serve immediately.

Hot corned beef burgers

Serves 4
200 g/7 oz can corned beef
175 g/6 oz Cheddar cheese
3 tbls sweet pickle
2 tbls mayonnaise
**4 wholemeal or white baps, split in
half**
50 g/2 oz butter

1 Put the corned beef in a bowl and mash it well with a fork. Grate half the cheese and stir into the corned beef with the pickle and mayonnaise.
2 Carefully remove some of the soft centre from each bap half, taking care not to make a hole in the crust. Rub the centre gently between your hands to make fine breadcrumbs. Add to the corned beef mix and stir.
3 Place the butter on a plate and microwave at 100% (high) for 5-10 seconds to soften. Spread on the cut

Above: *Hot corned beef burgers*

sides of the baps. Pile the corned beef mix on to the bottom halves of the baps, pressing it down well with the back of a fork.
4 Cover with top halves and press down gently. Slice the remaining cheese thinly and place on top of the baps. Arrange baps in a circle on a plate lined with absorbent paper and microwave at 100% (high) for 2-3 minutes, until heated through. Serve at once.

65

Party Fare

Cheesy hot dogs

Makes 6

**225 g/8 oz can 6 hot dog sausages,
  drained and slit along one side**
6 bread finger rolls, slit
**2 slices processed cheese, each cut
  into 3 strips**

1 Place the sausages inside the slit bread
rolls. Place in a single layer on a plate
lined with absorbent paper.
2 Microwave at 100% (high) for 1
minute to heat.
3 Rearrange the rolls on the plate and
place a strip of cheese in each sausage
slit. Position with slit uppermost.
4 Microwave at 100% (high) for 45-60
seconds to melt the cheese. Serve hot.

Crowned raspberry jelly

Serves 6

**2 x 135 g/4½ oz tablets raspberry
  jelly**
3 small bananas
1-2 tbls lemon juice
300 ml/½ pt double cream

1 Rinse out a 1.1 L/2 pt metal jelly
mould with cold water, shake off the excess moisture and place it in the refrigerator to chill.
2 Cut 1 jelly tablet into cubes, place in a
1.1 L/2 pt bowl and microwave at 100%
(high) for 30 seconds to dissolve. Stir,
then make up to 600 ml/1 pt with cold
water. Refrigerate until thick but not set.
3 Peel and slice the bananas, toss in

Micro-facts

If the chocolate starts to set before
you have coated all the Banana
pops, reheat it at 50% (medium)
for 15-45 seconds, depending on
the amount left in the bowl.

lemon juice, then fold into the thickened
jelly. Spoon into the chilled mould, and
refrigerate until firm but slightly sticky to
the touch.
4 Meanwhile, melt the other jelly in a
1.1 L/2 pt bowl at 100% (high) for
30 seconds. Stir and add 150 ml/¼ pt
cold water and mix. Whisk the cream

Above: *Crowned raspberry jelly*

into the cool but still liquid jelly and pour
over the banana jelly. Refrigerate until
set.
5 To serve, dip the mould into a bowl of
hot water for 1-2 seconds, then invert on
to a dampened plate.

Chocolate banana pops

Serves 8
2 bananas
**100 g/4 oz plain chocolate, broken
    into squares**
15 g/½ oz margarine or butter
**100 g/4 oz shelled walnuts,
    chopped (optional)**

1 Cut the bananas across into 4 equal
pieces then push a wooden cocktail stick
into the side of each piece of banana.
Wrap in foil and freeze for about 6 hours
or until firm.
2 Put the chocolate squares and fat in a
bowl and microwave at 100% (high) for
2-3 minutes, or until melted, stirring halfway through the cooking time.
3 Remove the bananas from the
freezer. Holding each piece by its stick,

dip into the chocolate mix, and turn it
quickly to coat on all sides. If necessary,
use a spoon to complete this covering,
and to scrape off any excess.
4 Quickly roll each pop in chopped
nuts, if using, then insert the cocktail stick
in a grapefruit or melon. Leave for a few
minutes until set, then serve.

Below: *Chocolate banana pops*

Chocolate Dreams

Honey nut brownies

Makes 16
**50 g/2 oz plain chocolate, broken
  into pieces**
100 g/4 oz butter
175 g/6 oz clear honey
2 eggs
1 tsp vanilla essence
175 g/6 oz plain flour
¾ tsp baking powder
½ tsp salt
3 tbls cocoa powder
50 g/2 oz shelled walnuts, chopped

1 Lightly grease a 20 cm/8 in square glass baking dish. Place the chocolate and butter in a 1.7 L/3 pt mixing bowl and microwave at 100% (high) for 1½-2 minutes to melt. Stir after 1 minute. Add the honey, eggs and vanilla and beat together with a fork.
2 Sift the flour, baking powder, salt and cocoa powder together. Add to the chocolate mix and whisk together. Stir in the walnuts and 2 tbls warm water.
3 Pour the mixture into the baking dish. Place tiny triangles of foil over the corners of the dish to prevent overcooking, keeping the foil as smooth as possible. Check your oven instructions first to see that small pieces of foil may be used.

Micro-facts

Watch milk-based drinks when heating as they will easily boil over. If wished, return the hot chocolate to the microwave and heat for a few seconds to plump the marshmallows.

4 Microwave at 100% (high) for 5-7 minutes or until the top is nearly dry, rotating the dish a quarter turn every

1½ minutes. Cool for 10-15 minutes. Cut into squares and serve cold.

Hot marshmallow chocolate

Illustrated on pages 62-63

Serves 4
**50 g/2 oz plain chocolate, broken
  into pieces**
600 ml/1 pt milk
9 white marshmallows

1 Place the chocolate in a large jug. Heat at 100% (high) for 2-2½ minutes, or until melted.
2 Gradually stir in the milk and microwave at 100% (high) for 4 minutes. Chop 5 marshmallows and whisk into the chocolate, until they have melted. Microwave at 100% (high) for 1 minute.
3 Pour into 4 warmed glasses or mugs and serve topped with a marshmallow.

Above: *Honey nut brownies*
Right: *Yummy chocolate cake*

Yummy chocolate cake

Makes 8-10 slices
100 g/4 oz margarine
200 g/7 oz self-raising flour
2 tbls cocoa powder
pinch of salt
225 g/8 oz caster sugar
2 large eggs
5 tbls evaporated milk
5 tbls water
1 tsp vanilla essence
For the filling and topping
225 g/8 oz icing sugar
**40 g/1½ oz drinking chocolate
  powder**
65 g/2½ oz margarine
3 tbls milk
1 tsp vanilla essence
**2 tubes sugar-coated chocolate
  buttons**

1 Lightly grease a 20 cm/8 in soufflé or cake dish and line the base with grease-proof paper, then grease the paper.

2 Cut the margarine into pieces and place in a small bowl. Microwave at 100% (high) for 1-1½ minutes to melt.

3 Sift the flour, cocoa and salt into a large bowl. Stir in the sugar, then make a well in the centre. Beat the eggs with the milk, water and vanilla, then add to the dry ingredients together with the margarine and beat until blended.

4 Spoon the mixture into the prepared dish, then microwave at 100% (high) for 5-7 minutes or until a skewer inserted in the centre comes out clean. Rotate the dish a quarter turn every 2 minutes.

5 Cool the cake for a few minutes, then turn out on to a wire rack, and peel off the lining paper. Turn the cake the right way up and leave to cool.

6 To make the filling and topping, sift the icing sugar and drinking chocolate into a bowl. Place the margarine, milk and vanilla essence in a small bowl and microwave at 100% (high) for 45-60 seconds to melt. Beat into the sugar mix. Leave for 15-30 minutes to thicken.

7 Split the cake in half and spread one half with the chocolate mix. Place the other half on top and spread with remaining mixture. Decorate the top with sugar-coated chocolate buttons. Leave for 30 minutes to firm before cutting.

Sweet Treats

Cherry nougat

Makes 45 pieces
225 g/8 oz granulated sugar
6 tbls liquid glucose
2 tbls golden syrup
1½ tbls water
1 egg white
½ tsp vanilla essence
50 g/2 oz butter, diced
25 g/1 oz whole blanched almonds, toasted
50 g/2 oz glacé cherries, quartered

1 Place the sugar, glucose and syrup in a large bowl with the water. Microwave at 100% (high) for 5 minutes. Make sure the sugar has dissolved completely before the mixture begins to boil. Watch very carefully.

Micro-facts

When testing to see if the boiled mixture has reached the soft ball stage, do not continue to microwave while testing as mixtures can overcook very quickly.

Above: *Cherry nougat*

2 Boil the mixture for 6-8 minutes at 100% (high) until it reaches the 'hard ball' stage. To test for this, drop a little of the mixture into a saucer of cold water. When gathered up between finger and thumb the mixture should form a hard ball. Start testing after 5 minutes of cooking time.
3 Beat the egg white until stiff, then pour a quarter of the hot syrup on to the white in a thin stream, beating all the time. Continue to beat until the mixture cools slightly and holds its shape.
4 Return the remaining syrup to the oven. Microwave at 100% (high) for 1-3 minutes until the hard crack stage is reached (when a little of the mixture dropped into a saucer of cold water forms brittle threads). Pour this mixture in a thin stream over the egg white mixture, beating until thick.
5 Add the vanilla and butter and beat again until thick. Stir in the almonds and cherries. Pour into an 18 cm/7 in square tin lined with non-stick paper to set and cool. Chill thoroughly.
6 When firm, turn the nougat out on to a board, remove the paper and cut the nougat into oblong pieces. Wrap in cellophane and store in the refrigerator. Prettily wrapped and packed, nougat makes an ideal gift.

Lime and lemonade

Makes about 1.7 L/3 pts
3 tbls water
finely grated zest of 1 lime
finely grated zest of 1 lemon
juice of 3 limes
juice of 3 lemons
175 g/6 oz sugar
lemon slices, to decorate

1 Place all the ingredients in a large jug and mix well. Microwave at 100% (high) for 4 minutes, stirring 2-3 times.
2 Cool, then chill. Dilute drink with 1.4 L/ 2½ pts of iced water or to taste, and serve in tall tumblers decorated with lemon slices.

Peanut brittle

Makes about 450 g/1 lb
225 g/8 oz sugar
6 tbls golden syrup
200 g/7 oz unsalted peanuts, skinned
7 g/¼ oz butter
½ tsp vanilla essence
1 tsp baking powder
vegetable oil for greasing

1 Brush a 33 x 23 cm/13 x 9 in shallow baking tin thoroughly with oil. Place the sugar and syrup in a large heatproof bowl. Mix well and cook at 100% (high) for 4 minutes. Add the peanuts and stir well to blend.
2 Cook at 100% (high) for 4-5 minutes, or until light brown. Add the butter and vanilla, mix well and microwave at 100% (high) for 1-2 minutes. Add the baking powder and gently stir until light and foamy.
3 Pour into the prepared tin to form a thin, even layer. Leave to cool for 30 minutes, then mark into squares with a sharp knife.
4 Leave to cool completely, then tip out of the tin and break into squares. Store in an airtight container until required.

Right: *Coconut ice, Lime and lemonade, Peanut brittle*

Coconut ice

Makes 450 g/1 lb
150 ml/¼ pt milk
450 g/1 lb caster sugar
125 g/4 oz desiccated coconut
**few drops of cochineal or yellow
    food colouring**

1 In a very large bowl, mix together the milk and sugar. Microwave at 100% (high) for 2 minutes to dissolve the sugar. Stir 2-3 times.
2 Microwave at 100% (high) for approximately 6 minutes more, or until the soft ball stage occurs. To test for this, drop a little of the mix into a saucer of cold water. When gathered up between finger and thumb it should form a soft ball. Stir *every* 2 minutes, and start testing after 4 minutes.
3 Stir in the coconut and continue stirring until the mixture turns cloudy. Grease a 15 cm/6 in square tin and spread half the mixture into this.

4 Tint the remaining mixture a pale pink with cochineal or pale yellow with food colouring and spread over the white mixture.
5 When cool, mark into squares. When cold, cut into neat pieces and store in an airtight tin.

Freezer
Meals

Introduction

When you've got a family you seem to be forever planning or cooking meals. But if you own a freezer you need never have that headache again.

You don't have to rely on convenience foods either. With a little careful planning and a lot of help from us you can get the best from fresh foods too. Preserving the pick of the crops to use all year round; creating memorable dishes from simple, everyday foods; sweet and savoury batch-cooking and some sumptuous ideas for every kind of special occasion meal as well.

Owning a Freezer

Frozen food is one of the great boons of modern-day living. Providing you freeze the right things and do the job properly, freezing food preserves its colour, texture and goodness.

If you own a freezer you can save time and money by making fewer shopping trips; buying in bulk when the opportunity arises; cooking in larger quantities so there need only be one lot of preparation; freezing home-grown produce for use all-year-round and preserving leftovers and extra portions that would otherwise be thrown away.

You don't have to have a large family either to make it worthwhile as there are several different types of freezer to choose from. Don't fall into the trap of thinking you need only a tiny one – most people find, once they've got a freezer, they could fill it twice over!

As a guide, allow 56 litres (2 cubic feet) of freezing space per person so, if you live on your own, a small table-top model or fridge-freezer would be fine, but for most families it's advisable to get a bigger model. There are large upright freezers which hold the food on shelves or in pull-out baskets. It's easy to see what is inside them and to load and unload them. They take up less space than most chest freezers but are slightly dearer to run and need defrosting more often. Check, too, you can reach the top shelf easily.

Chest freezers take up a lot of space but are cheaper and more economical to run than upright models. More food can be packed in but check before you buy that you can reach the bottom of the cabinet. You also need to keep a record of exactly where you store each type of food – and stick to it – or you could spend hours rummaging around getting frost-bite!

If storing a chest freezer in a garage or outhouse, check it has a lock to deter possible thieves and it's also a good idea to have a freezer alarm fitted to give you immediate warning if anything goes wrong – like a power failure.

Talking of power failure, it's worth thinking ahead about what to do in an emergency. If you have a reasonably-sized, well-stocked freezer, the contents could be worth a considerable sum.

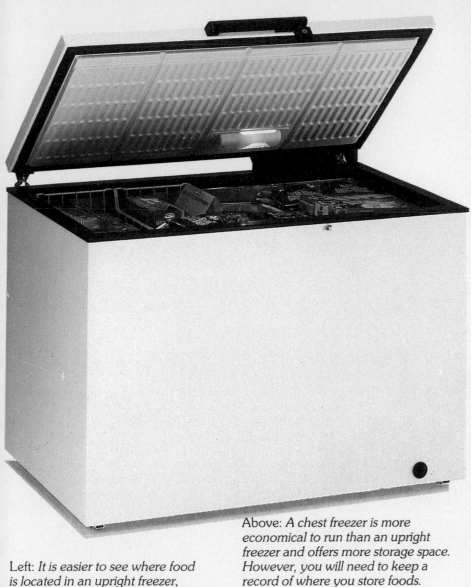

Left: *It is easier to see where food is located in an upright freezer, and loading and unloading are very simple.*

Above: *A chest freezer is more economical to run than an upright freezer and offers more storage space. However, you will need to keep a record of where you store foods.*

Above: *A table-top freezer is ideal if you only need to store small quantities of fresh, pre-cooked or commercially frozen foods*

Therefore consider an insurance policy – but read the small print as some companies make all sorts of exclusion clauses. For example, they may not pay up if theft occurs from an unlocked freezer.

In the event of a power cut – don't panic. Contents of all freezers, if left undisturbed, will stay undamaged for about 36 hours – chest freezers even longer. Cover the cabinet with a rug or blanket though, to give extra insulation (leaving pipes and condenser free).

All freezers must carry this star symbol:

This indicates that the freezer can freeze down fresh food. An appliance with three stars or less can store ready-frozen foods only.

✳ – for one week
✳✳ – for two weeks
✳✳✳ – for up to three months

The Fast Freeze Switch

This is a very important part of your freezer. It works by overriding the thermostat, allowing the temperature inside to fall well below −18° C/0° F, the normal storage temperature. The faster food is frozen the better, because the ice crystals formed in the food are then much smaller so are less likely to spoil the texture when thawed.

Reducing the temperature when freezing down food also means that food already in the freezer will get colder too, so will be less affected by the higher temperature of foods put in the freezer.

If doing several batch cook-ins for the freezer, or if you are planning to freeze any large quantities of food – a glut of vegetables or a side of meat, for instance – turn the fast freeze switch on about 6 hours before you actually want to freeze the food. Then leave it on for up to 12 or even 24 hours after putting the food in the freezer, depending on the load.

For smaller quantities – one or two pies and a casserole, for example – put the switch on just a couple of hours before freezing and leave it on for up to 4 hours until the food is solid.

Some freezers have a special fast freeze section specifically for holding food for freezing down. The temperature will be the same as the rest of the freezer but it just keeps the unfrozen foods separate from those already frozen. If your freezer doesn't have one of these, it's a good idea to put foods for freezing down against the sides or base of the freezer or on a shelf that carries the evaporator coils as this will be the coldest place.

Packaging and Labelling

Correct packaging is vital when freezing food or it will lose its colour, texture, flavour and nutrients. All air must be excluded from packages too or oxidation will occur. This makes the food smell 'off' and it will deteriorate rapidly.

There are many different types of freezer packaging available and you will soon find you have your own preferences.

Polythene bags: The most popular form of freezer packaging. Use heavy-duty ones specially designed for freezing. Ordinary wrapping bags will split very easily if moved around in the freezer then 'freezer burn' will result (greyish white markings on the exposed surface of the food causing loss of flavour and texture). Also free-flowing foods like peas or beans will end up scattered throughout the freezer!

To remove air from bags, either squeeze with the hands working from the base upwards over filling, or put a twist tie loosely round top, insert a drinking straw and suck out all the air. Quickly tie up tightly.

Boil-in-bags and Roasting bags: Both can withstand freezing temperatures as well as heat. They are therefore ideal for storing stews, soups, sauces, casseroles – anything that can be reheated in the bag. They save on washing-up too!

Freezer film: Extra-strong cling film. It is self-sealing so is useful for wrapping any solid food. Use, too, for sealing tops of puddings, flans or pies and for overwrapping for long-term storage.

Aluminium foil and foil containers: Foil is very versatile. Use for lids, wrapping bread and other solids, protecting sharp bones of meat or poultry before wrapping in freezer film or polythene bags then stockinette, muslin or more foil. Heavy-duty freezer foil is best.

Secure foil with freezer tape (adhesive tape that adheres even at freezing temperatures) if not overwrapping.

Foil containers come in all shapes and sizes from pie plates for dinners-for-one to large containers for casseroles. Use straight from the freezer into the oven. They are re-usable but must never be used in a microwave.

Rigid containers: Made of polythene or other types of plastic with airtight lids. Use for semi-solid and liquid foods in particular and any delicate food that may otherwise get damaged if knocked when stored.

Unless you have a vast store of airtight containers, line them with polythene bags, freeze the food then remove container for use again. Square or rectangular packs take up less space than round ones.

To pre-shape food for efficient storing you can also line such packages as icing sugar cartons or cereal packets with polythene bags, fill, freeze then remove them.

Commercial yoghurt-type cartons with lids can also be used but overwrap in polythene bags or seal lids with freezer tape as they are not airtight. Use for short term storage only.

Toughened glass jars: Instant coffee and other screw-top jars are very useful for storing breadcrumbs, grated cheese and so on.

Most oven-to-tableware can also be

used for freezing foods. Usually, it's best to line dishes with foil before cooking, freeze, then remove container as quickly as possible and wrap frozen food. It can then be returned to its dish for reheating. Liquids expand when frozen so leave a 1-2.5 cm/½-1 in headspace between the food and the lid of any container used for freezing.

Labelling: After sealing your packages securely with twist ties, freezer tape or airtight lids, always label them properly. Everyone thinks "I'll remember that odd-shaped parcel" . . . you never will after a month or so!

State the name of the food, weight, date frozen, number of servings and, if

Above: Coloured labels and tags make it easier to identify frozen food.

necessary, any reheating instructions and any additives necessary like seasoning, thickening or a final ingredient (hard-boiled egg in a kedgeree for instance).

Use a chinagraph or waxed pencil or a special freezer marker pen as others fade in the freezer.

Colour coding is another way of identifying different foods.

Most freezer packaging is sold in different colours or you can use a variety of

Below: Useful items for packaging are foil, polythene bags and cling film.

coloured labels or tags to identify items.

Always use special freezer labels as ordinary ones will not adhere to packaging when frozen.

Finally, it's essential when packing your freezer that you know exactly what you have in there and how long it's been there. A chart stuck on the front of the cabinet is one way but the most efficient method is to keep a record book. Divide book into sections; meat, fish, baked goods, fruit, vegetables etc. List what you have frozen, the quantity (i.e. number of packages), date frozen and where it is in the freezer. Don't forget to make a note when you take a package out too, though, or the system will fail.

Thawing and Refreezing

Food should be frozen as quickly as possible but, ideally, thawed as slowly as possible, preferably in the refrigerator. Thawing is complete only when all the ice crystals have dissolved.

Slow Thawing
Take food out of the freezer and place in the refrigerator. Keep in its wrapping. If unwrapped, meat 'bleeds', losing colour and flavour; fish dries and toughens, and fruit will lose its juice.

Always allow enough time – 450 g/1 lb food can take 6 hours to thaw. The more dense the food, the longer it takes.

Quick Thawing
If you try to speed things up a bit you will definitely sacrifice some flavour and possibly texture of your food (unless you own a microwave oven which will thaw most food rapidly without impairing the quality).

Food thawed at room temperature takes about half the time of slow thawing and you can even submerge the package in a bowl of cold water or hold it under a running tap if you are desperate – but this is definitely not recommended.

Once Thawed – Use
Whether thawed quickly or slowly, as soon as the process is complete don't leave food lying around for longer than absolutely necessary. Freezing food stops any micro-organisms growing in the food but it doesn't actually destroy them. So as soon as they warm up they get cracking on multiplying once more – with a vengeance. It sounds awful but as long as you keep food chilled until ready to cook, cook it immediately or eat it as soon as possible there will be no problem. Talking of bacteria, remember to cook food thoroughly – especially those things known to carry 'nasties' like poultry and pork products. Pre-cooked foods too, like delicatessen meats or prepared meat dishes should be reheated very thoroughly and NEVER simply warmed through.

Cooking from Frozen
There are quite a few foods that can be cooked straight from the freezer.

Meat: small cuts like chops, steaks or even mince can go straight into the pan. Allow a few minutes more cooking time and don't cook too fiercely or the outside will toughen before the inside thaws. When absolutely necessary, whole joints of beef or lamb can be cooked from frozen, providing you have a meat thermometer to ensure the centre is properly cooked. Slow roasting is preferable so the outside doesn't overcook before the inside is thawed. NEVER cook poultry or pork from frozen. Always thaw joints or whole birds slowly and completely in the refrigerator.

Stews and other precooked dishes: pies and casseroles can all be cooked from frozen. Allow extra time and make absolutely sure they are heated right through. Ideally, thaw first as it saves fuel and gives a more satisfactory result.

Fish: steaks, fillets and small whole fish can be cooked from frozen but always thaw large whole fish. Cooking from frozen does impair the flavour and texture of all fish but it is only really noticeable on larger ones.

Fruit: frozen in pies etc. can be heated straight from the freezer. For eating 'as is' though, defrost as gently as pos-

sible to keep in most of the juice. All fruit softens on thawing so many people prefer to eat whole fruits like strawberries while they are still slightly 'iced'.

Vegetables: should always be cooked from frozen (except for corn on the cob). The best food value is obtained by very gently cooking vegetables in a knob of butter in a saucepan so they cook in their natural juices. Alternatively, use the smallest quantity of water necessary for boiling them or many of those carefully preserved nutrients will be thrown away in the cooking water!

Bread and rolls: thaw and reheat in a moderately slow oven or, turning occasionally, under a low grill (for French sticks, rolls and pitta breads).

NB Some recipes give microwave times for cooking from the freezer. These are based on a 650-700 watt cooker. For a 600 watt oven add 20 seconds per

minute. For a 500 watt oven add up to 40 seconds per minute.

Refreezing
Obviously frozen raw meat and so on, used to make casseroles and other prepared cooked dishes, can be frozen after cooking. But, say you have a disaster like a power failure for several days without noticing and much of the contents of your freezer have started to thaw.

As a guide, if the freezer temperature has not risen above 0° C/32° F and the food therefore still contains a lot of ice crystals, it can be refrozen without damage to health. Never take chances though – if in doubt DON'T.

Before attempting to refreeze any foods check smell and appearance. As a general guide, raw meat and poultry should be cooked before refreezing. If already stuffed, don't refreeze, it should be cooked and eaten.

Fish doesn't refreeze well as some of the texture and flavour will be lost. It is best cooked first and preferably masked with a sauce.

Cooked meat and meat dishes should not be refrozen. Eat as soon as possible having reheated them thoroughly first, if necessary.

Fruit and vegetables can be refrozen as can bread and plain cakes but use up fairly quickly. Don't refreeze dairy produce or ice-cream.

Remember, no one advocates refreezing anything from choice ONLY IN AN EMERGENCY!

Below: *Joints of meat, large whole fish and corn on the cob must be thawed before cooking, but chops, all other vegetables and a pre-cooked pie with a raw pastry top can be cooked straight from frozen. Hazelnut meringue cake (page 92) can be frozen before or after decorating with cream.*

Single Dishes for Freezing

When you've got yourself organised it's fantastic to have a good stock of deliciously different dishes in the freezer – like starters to turn everyday meals into special occasions; light meals to pull out and reheat in a hurry and nourishing tasty main courses too; puds to please for special treats and even a selection of simple preserves – try raspberry freezer jam, no boiling or possible burning, just perfect results every time, and in small manageable quantities too.

Starters

Tomato rice soup

Serves 4
700 g/1½ lb fresh tomatoes,
  chopped
1 tbls tomato purée
150 ml/¼ pt water
salt and pepper
To serve:
50 g/2 oz long grain rice
2 tbls single cream
1 tbls finely chopped parsley

1 Put all the ingredients into a large saucepan. Bring to the boil, stirring, then lower the heat, cover and simmer gently for 30 minutes.
2 Pass the contents of the saucepan through a sieve, or leave to cool slightly, then purée in a blender and sieve to remove the tomato skins and pips.

To Freeze: Pour into a rigid container and leave to go cold. Cover and freeze.

Freezer Facts

For a change, freeze pâté in ramekin dishes. Serve as individual portions for snacks and starters as required. Garnish with walnut halves.

To Serve: Bring to the boil over a gentle heat, then add rice, lower the heat, cover and simmer for 15 minutes, or until rice is tender. Pour into individual bowls, swirl with a little cream, sprinkle with chopped parsley and serve.

To Microwave: Remove from container into a large casserole dish, cover and microwave at 100% (high) for 12-15 minutes, or until very hot, breaking apart and stirring several times. Stir in the rice, re-cover and microwave at 100% (high) for 10 minutes. Leave soup to stand for 5 minutes, then serve as above.

Chicken liver pâté

Serves 6-8
100 g/4 oz butter
1 onion, finely chopped
2 cloves garlic, crushed
100 g/4 oz streaky bacon, derinded
  and chopped
450 g/1 lb chicken livers, chopped
1 tbls dry sherry or brandy
pinch of grated nutmeg
salt and pepper
To serve:
bay leaves and walnut halves

1 Melt the butter in a saucepan, add the onion, garlic and bacon. Fry gently for 5 minutes. Add the chicken livers and fry briskly over a high heat for 5-6 minutes, stirring continuously, until the livers are cooked.
2 Cool for about 30 minutes, then blend to a purée in a liquidiser. Stir in the remaining ingredients and season to taste. Mix thoroughly.
3 Transfer the mixture to an 850 ml/1½ pt round, rectangular or oval terrine, lined with greaseproof paper. Leave to set in the refrigerator.
To Freeze: Cover and freeze.

Above: *Chicken liver pâté*
Right: *Tomato rice soup*

To Serve: Allow to thaw for 6 hours or overnight in the refrigerator. Run a knife around the edge of the dish, then invert a serving plate on top of the dish. Hold the mould and plate firmly together and invert them, giving a sharp shake halfway round. Remove greaseproof paper and garnish with walnuts and bay leaves.

Blue cheese soufflés

Illustrated on pages 82-83

Makes 6
50 g/2 oz margarine or butter
50 g/2 oz plain flour
pinch of mustard powder
pinch of cayenne pepper
300 ml/½ pt milk
100 g/4 oz blue cheese, finely diced
2 large eggs, separated
25 g/1 oz white breadcrumbs
1 tbls snipped chives
salt

1 Lightly grease the insides of 6 ramekin dishes. Melt the fat in a saucepan, sprinkle the flour, mustard and cayenne into the pan and stir over a low heat for 2 minutes.
2 Remove from the heat and gradually stir in the milk. Return to the heat and bring to the boil, stirring continuously, until thick and smooth.
3 Remove the pan from the heat and stir in the cheese until melted. Add the egg yolks and beat in. Stir in the breadcrumbs and chives and season with salt.
4 Whisk the egg whites until stiff and fold into the cheese mixture using a figure-of-eight motion with the edge of a spoon to cut through the mixture.
5 Pour the mixture into the prepared ramekin dishes.
To Freeze: Cover dishes with freezer film and freeze immediately.
To Serve: Stand dishes on a baking tray, place in a preheated oven at 220°C/425°F/gas 7 and bake for 25-30 minutes, or until risen, golden and set.

Light Meals

Beef and salami ring

Illustrated on pages 82-83

Serves 4-6
vegetable oil
700 g/1½ lb minced beef
175 g/6 oz salami, derinded and roughly chopped
100 g/4 oz fresh white breadcrumbs
2 eggs, beaten
4 tsps English mustard
2 tbls tomato purée
1 tsp Worcestershire sauce
¼ tsp ground nutmeg
salt and pepper
To serve:
watercress sprigs, small wedges of tomato, sliced celery and red pepper and thick slices of cucumber, quartered

1 Brush a 1.1 L/2 pt ovenproof metal ring mould with oil.
2 In a large bowl, thoroughly mix together all the remaining ingredients.
3 Press the mixture into the prepared ring mould and cover with greased foil. Place on a baking tray and bake in a pre-heated oven at 180°C/350°F/gas 4 for about 1¼ hours, or until the loaf is shrinking from the sides of the mould and the juices run clear when the loaf is pierced with a fine skewer.
To Freeze: Leave the loaf in mould until cold, then open freeze until solid. Turn out and wrap in foil. Seal, label and freeze.
To Serve: Unwrap the loaf, transfer to a serving plate and thaw overnight in the refrigerator. Garnish with watercress sprigs, tomato, celery, pepper and cucumber in the centre and serve cold.

Freezer Facts

Double the quantities and make two pizzas. Serve one immediately and freeze the other. You will need only the same quantity of yeast for a double batch of dough.

Courgette flan

Serves 4
225 g/8 oz shortcrust pastry, defrosted if frozen
3 eggs, beaten
25 g/1 oz margarine or butter
350 g/12 oz courgettes, grated
100 ml/4 fl oz single cream
50 ml/2 fl oz milk
½-1 tsp dried oregano
salt and freshly ground black pepper

1 Roll out the pastry on a floured surface and use to line a 23 cm/9 in flan tin or foil dish. Refrigerate for 30 minutes.
2 Heat the oven to 200° C/400° F/gas 6.
3 Remove the pastry case from the refrigerator, and prick the base in several places with a fork. Line the pastry case with greaseproof paper or foil and weight down with baking beans. Bake in the oven for 10 minutes.
4 Remove the pastry case from oven. Lift out the paper and baking beans. Brush the inside of the pastry case with a little of the beaten egg from the filling.

Lower the oven to 190° C/375° F/gas 5 and return the pastry case to the oven for a further 5 minutes.
5 Meanwhile, melt 25 g/1 oz margarine in a frying-pan, add the courgettes and fry over moderate heat for 3-5 minutes, stirring once or twice, until they begin to soften. Remove the pan from the heat and set aside.
6 In a bowl, beat the eggs, cream and milk together, then add dried oregano to taste. Season the mixture well with salt and pepper.
7 Remove the pastry case from the oven and spoon the courgettes evenly over the base, then pour the egg mixture over them.
8 Place in the oven and bake for 40-45 minutes or until the filling is set and golden brown on top.
To Freeze: Allow the flan to cool quickly, then cover with freezer film. Label and freeze.
To Serve: Remove the freezer film from the flan, then thaw at room temperature for 3 hours. Serve warm or cold. If

Below: Courgette flan

serving warm, place the thawed flan in an oven preheated to 180°C/350°F/gas 4 and reheat for 10-15 minutes. Serve with salad as a light lunch or supper dish. Alternatively, this flan would also make a tasty light starter to serve before a meat course, in which case it will serve six people.

Orange-stuffed onions

Serves 4
4 onions, about 175 g/6 oz each
25 g/1 oz margarine or butter
1 tbls chopped fresh parsley
1 tbls chopped fresh thyme
**100 g/4 oz fresh white
    breadcrumbs**
grated zest and juice of 1 orange
2 tsps Dijon mustard
200 ml/7 fl oz hot chicken stock
To serve:
parsley sprigs
orange twists

1 Peel the onions, then cut a 1 cm/½ in slice from the top of each one.

2 Using a sharp knife and a teaspoon, remove the insides of the onions, to leave a 5 mm/¼ in thick shell. Finely chop half the scooped out onion.

3 Melt the fat in a frying pan, add the chopped onion and fry gently for about 5 minutes, until soft and transparent, stirring occasionally.
4 Remove the pan from the heat and mix in the parsley and thyme. Add the breadcrumbs, orange zest and juice and mustard. Mix together well.
5 Place the stuffing in the onions with a teaspoon, pressing it down tightly. Stand the onions in a casserole, and pour the

Above: *Orange-stuffed onions*

hot stock around them. Cover tightly, and bake in a preheated oven at 180° C/350° F/gas 4 for 1 hour. Cool.
To Freeze: Place in a rigid container with the stock, cover and freeze.
To Serve: Place in a casserole dish, cover and heat in a preheated oven at 180° C/350° F/gas 4 for 45 minutes. Serve garnished with parsley and orange twists.
To Microwave: Unwrap and place in a shallow casserole dish. Microwave at 100% (high) for 5 minutes. Reduce power to 70% (medium-high) and microwave for 10-20 minutes, rearranging twice. Serve as above.

Fish

Cheesy mackerel pancakes

Serves 4
100 g/4 oz plain flour
salt
1 egg
700 ml/1¼ pts milk
3 tbls vegetable oil
25 g/1 oz margarine or butter
25 g/1 oz plain flour
pinch of ground mace
white pepper
100 g/4 oz mature Cheddar cheese, grated
350 g/12 oz smoked mackerel, skinned, boned and flaked
To serve:
lemon slices
parsley

1 Make the pancakes: sift 100 g/4 oz flour and a pinch of salt into a bowl. Make a hollow in the centre and add the egg. Gradually mix in 300 ml/½ pt milk and beat to a smooth batter.
2 Pour the oil into a frying pan, heat, drain off and reserve. Pour in enough

batter to coat the base of the pan and cook for 1 minute until golden, then turn over and cook the other side. Slide out on to a sheet of greaseproof paper.
3 Pour the oil back into the pan, reheat, drain off and reserve, and add more batter. Repeat this process until all the batter has been used. It will make 6 pancakes.
4 Melt the margarine in a saucepan, sprinkle in the flour and stir over a low heat for 1-2 minutes. Remove from the heat and gradually stir in the remaining milk. Add the mace and season. Return to the heat and cook until thickened, stirring continuously.
5 Put two-thirds of the sauce in a bowl and stir in 75 g/3 oz of the cheese. Stir the flaked fish into the remaining sauce in the pan. Lay the pancakes flat and divide the mixture between them, placing it in the centre of the pancakes.
6 Fold the sides over the filling, then roll them up to make parcels. Place side by side in a shallow foil dish and pour the sauce over to cover them. Sprinkle with the remaining cheese.

To Freeze: Allow to go cold, then cover with foil and freeze.
To Serve: Place in an oven preheated to 200° C/400° F/gas 6 and cook for 40-45

Above: *Cheesy mackerel pancakes*

minutes, removing the foil lid after 30 minutes. Serve garnished with lemon slices and parsley.

Fun fish cakes

Serves 4
350 g/12 oz smoked haddock fillet, skinned
150 ml/¼ pt milk
225 g/8 oz potatoes, boiled
25 g/1 oz butter
2 tbls chopped fresh parsley
salt and pepper
3 tbls plain flour
1 egg, beaten
75 g/3 oz golden breadcrumbs
To serve:
oil for deep-frying
2 stuffed olives, halved
parsley sprigs
lemon slices

1 Put the fish in a saucepan with the milk and poach for 10 minutes. Drain, reserving 2 tbls of the liquid.

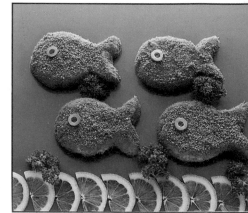

Freezer Facts

The freezer and microwave oven make ideal partners especially where fish is concerned. Prepare fresh fish and freeze; use the microwave to defrost quickly and reheat the fish later.

88

2 Mash the potatoes with the reserved liquid, butter and parsley.

3 Flake the fish, discarding any bones, and mix it thoroughly with the potato. Season with salt and pepper.

4 Divide the mix into 4 and with floured hands shape into flat pear shapes about 2.5 cm/1 in thick. Shape the thinner end of the cakes to form a 'V', like a fish tail.

5 Put the egg in a shallow bowl and spread the breadcrumbs on a plate. Dip the cakes in the egg and then the crumbs to coat thoroughly.

To Freeze: Open freeze on a tray. Pack in a rigid container when frozen and cover. Return to the freezer.

To Serve: Deep-fry from frozen in hot oil at 190° C/375° F for about 6-7 minutes, or until golden and heated through. Serve on a platter. Place olives on one side of the fish to represent eyes. Decorate with parsley sprigs and lemon.

Kipper roulade

Serves 4
225 g/8 oz kipper fillets
2 tbls milk
4 large eggs, separated
½ tsp onion salt
pepper
For the filling
**225 g/8 oz cottage cheese with
    chives**
4 tbls natural yoghurt
salt and pepper
To serve:
sweet paprika
parsley

1 Heat the oven to 200° C/400° F/gas 6. Line a Swiss roll tin 20 x 30 cm/8 x 12 in with greaseproof paper, securing the corners with paper clips if necessary.

2 Poach the kippers in water for 5-6 minutes, cool slightly in the water, then remove and skin. Flake the fish and pound in a bowl using the end of a rolling pin or in a pestle and mortar. Mix to a smooth paste with the milk.

3 In a bowl whisk the egg yolks and onion salt together until thick and pale. Add the fish and lightly combine, until well blended. Add the pepper.

4 Stiffly whisk the egg whites and fold them into the fish mixture. Spoon into the prepared tin, smoothing it into the corners. Cook for about 10 minutes, or until set and golden on the surface.

5 Meanwhile make the filling: mix the cheese, yoghurt and seasoning together.

6 When the roulade is cooked, turn it out on to a sheet of greaseproof paper cut slightly larger than the baking tin. Carefully remove the lining paper, and leave the roulade to cool slightly.

7 Spread the filling over the surface and roll the roulade up like a Swiss roll.

To Freeze: Place in a rigid container, cover and freeze.

To Serve: Allow to thaw at room temperature for 2-3 hours, then place on a baking tray and heat in a preheated oven at 180° C/350° F/gas 4 for 20-25 minutes. Sprinkle with paprika, garnish with parsley and serve.

Tomato fish bake

Illustrated on pages 82-83

Serves 4
700 g/1½ lb cod fillet, skinned
salt and pepper
1 onion, sliced
1 clove garlic, crushed
1 tsp dried mixed herbs
400 g/14 oz can tomatoes
To serve:
½ tsp dried oregano
4 gherkins, sliced into rounds

1 Heat the oven to 200° C/400° F/gas 6. Cut the fish into four portions. Lay the fish in a shallow casserole dish and season well.

2 Add the onion, garlic, mixed herbs and tomatoes with their juice. Cover with the lid or foil and bake for 15 minutes.

To Freeze: Either freeze in the dish or transfer to a foil container. Cover and seal.

To Serve: Thaw for 6-8 hours or overnight in the refrigerator. Heat in a preheated oven at 190° C/375° F/gas 5 for 20 minutes. Transfer to a serving dish if cooked in a foil container. Garnish with oregano sprinkled over the top and gherkin slices.

To Microwave: From frozen, microwave at 50% (medium) for 20-30 minutes, until heated, stirring 3-4 times, gently so that the fish portions are not broken. Keep covered with casserole lid or pierced cling film whilst cooking in the microwave oven. If the fish was frozen in a foil dish transfer to a microwave-safe container first.

Bottom left: *Fun fish cakes*
Below: *Kipper roulade*

Meat

Turkey and mushroom pie

Serves 4
25 g/1 oz butter
100 g/4 oz button mushrooms,
 sliced
1 onion, chopped
25 g/1 oz plain flour
150 ml/¼ pt milk
150 ml/¼ pt chicken stock
350 g/12 oz cooked turkey, cut
 into chunks
salt and pepper
75 g/3 oz frozen peas
225 g/8 oz puff pastry
To serve:
beaten egg to glaze

1 Melt the butter in a heavy-based saucepan and fry the mushrooms and onion for 2-3 minutes.
2 Stir in the flour and cook for 1 minute. Gradually stir in the milk and stock. Bring to the boil, stirring until thickened.
3 Stir in the turkey and season. Stir in the peas and leave to cool.
4 Roll the pastry out slightly larger than the top of an 850 ml/1 ½ pt pie dish. Cut off a long strip of pastry all around the edge. Reserve this and other trimmings.
5 Transfer the pie filling to the dish and place a pie funnel in the centre. Brush the rim of the dish with water, then press the narrow strip of pastry all around the rim. Brush the narrow strip with more water, then place the large piece of pastry on top.
6 Press to seal, then trim, knock up and flute the edge. Roll out the pastry trimmings and use to make leaves.

Freezer Facts

Remember to use a straight-sided casserole dish if lining with foil. If the base is wider than the top you will be unable to remove the frozen casserole.

To Freeze: Open freeze until solid, then wrap in freezer foil and return to the freezer.
To Serve: Unwrap and brush with beaten egg. Bake from frozen at 200° C/400° F/gas 6 for 25-30 minutes, or until pastry is risen, then reduce to 180° C/350° F/gas 4 for a further 20 minutes.

Apricot-stuffed lamb

Serves 6-8
1.8 kg/4 lb shoulder of lamb,
 boned with a pocket for the
 stuffing, and bones reserved
1 tsp ground coriander
salt and pepper
For the stuffing
25 g/1 oz butter
1 onion, finely chopped
50 g/2 oz long grain rice, cooked
100 g/4 oz no-need-to-soak dried
 apricots, chopped
finely grated zest of 1 orange
1 tbls ground coriander
salt and pepper
To serve:
apricot halves
mint sprigs

1 Heat the oven to 200° C/400° F/gas 6. Make the stuffing: place the butter and onion in a pan and cook for 3-4 minutes, until the onion is soft.
2 Add the rice, apricots, orange zest, coriander and salt and pepper to taste.

Below: *Turkey and mushroom pie*

Above: *Apricot-stuffed lamb*

Stir to mix thoroughly, then set aside.

3 Open out the lamb and lay it skin side down on a board. Sprinkle with coriander, salt and pepper. Place the stuffing in the bone cavity, packing it well. Fold the two long sides of the lamb over the stuffing to overlap and form a neat roll. Tie at intervals with fine string.

4 Place the lamb bones in a roasting tin. Set a rack over the bones and place lamb on top. Roast for 30 minutes then lower the heat to 180° C/350° F/gas 4 and roast for a further 1½ hours. Leave to go cold. If wished make a gravy from the pan juices.

To Freeze: Wrap in freezer film and freeze. If you are freezing the gravy, place in a rigid container, cover and freeze.

To Serve: Thaw overnight and serve cold, or wrap in buttered foil and reheat gently at 160° C/325° F/gas 3 for 35-40 minutes. Warm gravy in a saucepan. Garnish with apricot halves and mint sprigs, and serve with courgettes, if liked.

To Microwave: To reheat defrosted joint, place on a roasting rack, cover loosely with greaseproof paper and microwave at 70% (medium-high) for 13-17 minutes. Turn joint over halfway through the reheating time.

Warming beef casserole

Illustrated on pages 82-83

Serves 6
25 g/1 oz butter
2 tbls vegetable oil
900 g/2 lb stewing steak, cut into
    2.5 cm/1 in cubes
175 g/6 oz baby onions, peeled
225 g/8 oz young carrots, cut into
    5 cm/2 in lengths
1 tbls plain flour
1 tbls tomato purée
2 tsps curry paste
1 bay leaf
salt and pepper
175 g/6 oz broad beans
100 g/4 oz sweetcorn kernels
To serve:
chopped fresh parsley

1 Line a freezerproof casserole with freezer foil, double overlapping any seams well. Mould the foil to the dish.
2 Melt the butter and oil in a frying pan, add the meat and fry quickly, until browned on all sides. Transfer the meat from the pan to the casserole.
3 Add the onions and carrots to the frying pan and cook until browned.

4 Stir in the flour, tomato purée and curry paste and cook for 1-2 minutes, stirring well. Add the bay leaf and season with salt and pepper.
5 Pour the mixture over the meat, cover and cook in a preheated oven at 160° C/ 325° F/gas 3 for 1¼-1½ hours.
6 Add the beans and sweetcorn and continue cooking for 30 minutes, or until the meat is tender.

To Freeze: Allow to go cold, freeze until solid. Remove foil parcel by immersing

the casserole in hot water briefly. Overwrap in a polythene bag and return to the freezer.

To Serve: Remove bag and foil from the frozen casserole. Drop it back into the casserole, cover and reheat in a preheated oven at 180° C/350° F/gas 4 for 50-60 minutes, stirring occasionally. Serve sprinkled with chopped fresh parsley.

To Microwave: Place frozen casserole in a microwave-safe casserole, having removed the foil. Cover and microwave for 5 minutes at 100% (high). Break apart with a fork.

Reduce power to 70% (medium-high), re-cover and microwave for 12-16 minutes, or until hot, stirring several times. Serve as above.

Desserts

Hazelnut meringue cake

Illustrated on pages 82-83

Serves 6
pinch of salt
4 egg whites
250 g/9 oz caster sugar
1 tsp malt vinegar
2-3 drops vanilla essence
75 g/3 oz skinned hazelnuts, ground
450 ml/¾ pt double cream, whipped
100 g/4 oz no-need-to-soak dried apricots, finely chopped
icing sugar, for sifting
25 g/1 oz plain chocolate, grated

1 Add the salt to the egg whites, stir and whisk until they stand in stiff peaks.
2 Add the caster sugar to the egg whites 1 tbls at a time, whisking to make sure all the sugar is dissolved.
3 Whisk in the vinegar and vanilla. Fold in the nuts gently.
4 Grease and flour the sides of two 20 cm/8 in loose-bottomed cake tins and line the bases with silicone paper. Alternatively, line two baking trays with silicone paper. Divide the mixture equally between the prepared tins or spread in two 20 cm/8 in rounds on the baking trays.
5 Bake in a preheated oven at 140° C/ 275° F/gas 1 for 50-60 minutes.
6 When the meringues are cooked, gently peel away the paper and cool.
7 Mix two thirds of the cream with the apricots and use to sandwich the meringues together. Pipe remaining cream.
8 Sift icing sugar over the meringue and sprinkle chocolate on top of cream

Freezer Facts

Meringue-based desserts are very fragile, and are best if frozen unwrapped. Place in a rigid container to protect them once frozen. If preferred they can be frozen unfilled.

Above: *Blackcurrant cheesecake*   Below: *Apple strudel*

whirls. If wished this decoration can be left until serving the cake.

To Freeze: Open freeze for 3-4 hours then pack into a rigid container, to protect it. Cover and return to freezer.

To Serve: Allow to thaw at room temperature for at least 5 hours.

Apple strudel

Makes 6-8 Slices
275 g/10 oz plain flour
pinch of salt
1 egg, beaten
150 ml/¼ pt lukewarm water
50 g/2 oz melted butter, for brushing
For the filling
50 g/2 oz butter
75 g/3 oz dry white breadcrumbs
100 g/4 oz caster sugar
½ tsp ground cinnamon
½ tsp ground cloves
grated zest of ½ lemon
75 g/3 oz flaked almonds, chopped
50 g/2 oz sultanas
900 g/2 lb cooking apples, peeled, cored and sliced
To serve:
sifted icing sugar
chilled whipped cream

1 Sift the flour and salt into a large bowl. Add the egg and warm water. Mix until smooth, turn out on to a floured surface and knead and beat until elastic, it will take about 15 minutes. Place in a floured

basin, cover and leave for 15 minutes.
2 Prepare the filling: melt the butter in a small pan, add the breadcrumbs and fry gently until crisp and brown. Set aside. Mix together the sugar, spices, lemon zest, almonds and sultanas in a bowl.
3 Heat the oven to 190° C/375° F/gas 5. Roll the pastry out on a floured cloth and then gently pull from all sides until paper thin and transparent. Do not worry if small holes appear, but take care not to tear the dough.

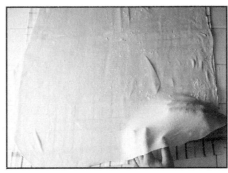

4 Brush with melted butter and trim away the edges to leave a rectangle about 63 x 50 cm/25 x 20 in. Arrange the dough so that a long edge faces you.
5 Scatter the browned breadcrumbs over the pastry. Spread the apples over half the dough, leaving a clear border of 5 cm/2 in from the long edge facing you, and 2.5 cm/1 in from the sides.
6 Sprinkle the sultana mix over the apples. Fold the side edges, and then the long edge nearest you over the apple filling. Using the cloth, roll up the strudel starting with the edge nearest you.

7 Form the rolled up strudel into a horseshoe shape and carefully ease it on to a greased baking tray. Brush with melted butter. Bake for 35-40 minutes, until crisp and golden.
To Freeze: Cool, open freeze, then wrap in foil.
To Serve: Allow to thaw for 2 hours at room temperature, or unwrap and re-heat on a baking tray at 190° C/375° F/gas 5 for 20 minutes. Cut into slices,

dredge with icing sugar and serve with whipped cream.
To Microwave: Once thawed, warm individual slices on a plate lined with absorbent paper for 30-45 seconds at 100% (high).

Blackcurrant cheesecake

Serves 6-8
90 g/3½ oz butter
25 g/1 oz caster sugar
200 g/7 oz muesli or shortbread biscuits, finely crushed
For the filling
450 g/1 lb full-fat soft cheese
75 g/3 oz caster sugar
2 eggs, separated
grated zest of ½ lemon
2-3 drops vanilla essence
150 ml/5 fl oz double cream
1 sachet powdered gelatine
5 tbls water
To serve:
400 g/14 oz can blackcurrant pie filling

1 Grease a deep 23 cm/9 in round cake tin with a loose base.
2 Put the butter into a saucepan and stir over a low heat until melted. Remove from the heat and stir in the sugar and muesli or biscuit crumbs. Press the mixture evenly over the base of the prepared tin. Refrigerate.
3 Put the cheese into a large bowl and beat until softened. Beat in 25 g/1 oz of sugar, the egg yolks, lemon zest, vanilla and cream.
4 Sprinkle the gelatine over the water in a small heatproof bowl. Leave to soak for 5 minutes, then stand the bowl in a pan of barely simmering water for 1-2 minutes, stirring occasionally, until the gelatine has dissolved.
5 Allow the gelatine to cool slightly, then beat into the cheese mixture. Leave in a cool place for about 15 minutes, until about to set.
6 In a clean bowl, whisk the egg whites until standing in stiff peaks, then gradually whisk in the remaining sugar. Fold into the cheese mixture, then turn into the prepared tin and level the surface.
To Freeze: Open freeze until solid. Remove from tin, cover with freezer film and return to the freezer.
To Serve: Thaw for 6-8 hours or overnight in the refrigerator. Top with pie filling and serve.

Preserves

Freezer mincemeat

This mincemeat will only keep for 2-3 weeks if not frozen.

Makes about 2.3 kg/5 lb
700 g/1½ lb peeled, cored and
  grated Cox's apples
50 g/2 oz mixed peel, finely
  chopped
450 g/1 lb raisins
375 g/12 oz currants
225 g/8 oz sultanas
100 g/4 oz shredded suet
50 g/2 oz blanched almonds,
  shredded
grated zest and juice of 2 lemons
½ tsp mixed spice
375 g/12 oz light brown soft sugar
6 tbls brandy or sherry

1 Mix the apples, peel, raisins, currants, sultanas, suet and almonds together. Add the remaining ingredients and mix thoroughly.
2 Leave to stand overnight.
To Freeze: Pack into several rigid containers, cover and freeze.
To Serve: Thaw overnight in the refrigerator and use as required.

Lemon curd

Makes about 900 g/2 lb
finely grated zest and juice of
  4 lemons
150 g/5 oz butter
450 g/1 lb lump sugar
5 eggs, beaten

1 Put the lemon zest and juice in a double saucepan with the butter and heat

Freezer Facts

Glass jars may be used for freezing if made of specially toughened glass that will withstand low temperatures. As a precaution, pack jars in polythene bags or use strong plastic jars.

gently, then add the sugar and stir to dissolve.
2 Strain the beaten egg into the pan. Stir over the heat until the mixture is thick and coats the back of a spoon.
3 Strain the curd into a jug. Cool slightly then pour into 4-6 small containers, leaving a headspace. Cover and leave until cold.
To Freeze: Overwrap with freezer film and freeze.
To Serve: Defrost at room temperature for 1-2 hours. Keep refrigerated once thawed, and use within a few days.

Raspberry freezer jam

Makes about 1.5 kg/3¼ lb
550 g/1¼ lb raspberries
900 g/2 lb caster sugar
125 ml/4 fl oz liquid pectin
2 tbls lemon juice

1 Crush the raspberries in a large bowl, using a wooden spoon. Stir in the sugar and leave to stand for 1 hour, in a warm place. Stir frequently.

2 Add the pectin and lemon juice and stir for 2-3 minutes, until well mixed.
3 Pour into small plastic containers, leaving a headspace. Seal.

Above (left to right): *Freezer mincemeat, Lemon curd, Seville orange marmalade, Raspberry freezer jam*

4 Leave at room temperature for 24 hours.
To Freeze: Label and freeze in containers.
To Serve: Thaw 3-5 hours, depending on the size of the container. Stir well before serving. After thawing, store in freezer containers or transfer to jam jars, label and cover with cling film or cellophane. Keep refrigerated. Use within 7-10 days.

Seville orange marmalade

Makes about 4.5 kg/10 lb
1.6 kg/3½ lb frozen Seville oranges
1.7 L/3 pts water
4 tbls lemon juice
2.7 kg/6 lb preserving sugar

1 Place the frozen oranges and water in a pressure cooker, cover and bring up to 6.8 kg/15 lb (high) pressure. Cook for 20 minutes. Reduce pressure slowly at room temperature.

2 Prick the oranges with a fine skewer to check they are tender. If not, cook for a few minutes more.

3 Lift fruit out of the pan with a draining spoon, cut the oranges in half and remove all the pips. Place the pips back in the pan with the remaining water, return to high pressure and cook for 5 minutes.

4 Thinly slice the orange peel. Place in a preserving pan with the lemon juice and sugar. Strain the liquid from the pressure cooker into the preserving pan and discard the pips.

5 Stir over a low heat until the sugar has dissolved, then boil rapidly until a set is reached. Test after 10 minutes. A set should be obtained when the temperature reaches 105° C/221° F or test with the saucer method. Place a small amount of marmalade on a saucer. When it is cool push it with your finger. The skin should wrinkle if a set has been reached.

6 Pour the marmalade into hot clean jars, cover and label.

Batch Cooking for the Freezer

Here we show you how to make a large quantity of a basic ingredient like minced beef or shortcrust pastry and turn it into several sumptuous dishes for the freezer. It'll save you a lot of time and effort in the long run.

Try and plan an uninterrupted day for a batch bake – well a good part of a day anyway. Remember to wrap all food correctly and to exclude air. Don't freeze until completely cold and label everything, making any necessary notes on how to serve on thawing.

When the day's cooking is lined up ready for freezing you'll feel an enormous sense of satisfaction and that feeling will stay with you every time you open the freezer to take out a ready-made masterpiece.

Beef

Batch cooking minced beef

Order of work:
1 Make Basic beef mix.
2 Divide mix into three.
3 Make Spaghetti bolognese sauce.
4 Make Meatballs.
5 Make Melting beef loaf.
6 Freeze all three dishes according to instructions when cold.

Basic beef mix

450 g/1 lb onions, chopped
75 ml/3 fl oz vegetable oil
1.8 kg/4 lb lean minced beef
salt and pepper

1 Use a large frying pan or 2 smaller ones, and fry the onions in the oil until soft. Remove with a slotted spoon and set aside.
2 Add the mince and fry until browned. Stir in the onions, season and use in the following three recipes, as suggested.

Meatballs

Serves 6
⅓ quantity Basic beef mix
50 g/2 oz white breadcrumbs
2 eggs, lightly beaten
pinch of garlic salt
50 g/2 oz chopped fresh parsley
½ tsp ground cinnamon
flour to coat
To serve:
1 tbls vegetable oil
50 g/2 oz butter
1 onion, sliced

Freezer Facts

It is important to use the fast freeze switch when freezing food, especially large quantities, as when batch cooking. Always use the area in the freezer recommended for fast freezing.

1 Mix the beef with the breadcrumbs, eggs, garlic salt, parsley and cinnamon.
2 Form into balls about 2.5 cm/1 in in diameter, and roll in flour to coat.
To Freeze: Open freeze on a baking tray, then pack in a polythene bag and seal. Return to freezer.
To Serve: Heat the oil and butter in a frying pan and shallow-fry the meatballs for 5-6 minutes. Transfer to a warmed serving dish. Fry the onion and sprinkle over the meatballs. If liked, serve with a salad of cooked sliced potatoes, bacon and onion in a herb vinaigrette dressing.

Below: *Meatballs*

Melting beef loaf

Serves 4-6
⅓ quantity Basic beef mix
50 g/2 oz white breadcrumbs
2 eggs, beaten
1 tsp dried oregano
1 clove garlic, crushed
salt and pepper
175 g/6 oz Mozzarella cheese, sliced
To serve:
50 g/2 oz Mozzarella cheese, sliced
tomato slices, to garnish

1 Line a 20 cm/8 in long loaf tin with freezer film, so that the film is overlapping the tin.

2 Place the beef mix, breadcrumbs, eggs, oregano and garlic in a bowl, season and mix thoroughly.

3 Place one third of the mix in the loaf tin and press across the base to cover.

4 Top with half the cheese slices. Repeat the layers of meat and cheese and

finish with a final layer of meat. Shape the top layer to give a rounded surface.

To Freeze: Freeze in the tin until frozen. Remove and wrap in freezer film. Return to the freezer.

Above: *Melting beef loaf*

To Serve: Remove freezer film and place the loaf in the loaf tin. Cook at 190° C/375° F/gas 5 for 1 hour. Place on a serving plate, arrange sliced Mozzarella on top. Return to the oven for a few minutes to melt. Garnish with tomato slices. If liked, serve with chips and carrots in parsley sauce.

To Microwave: Unwrap loaf and place in a microwave loaf dish. Cover with non-stick paper. Microwave at 100% (high) for 3 minutes. Reduce to 50% (medium) and microwave for 30-40 minutes. Turn a 1/4 turn every 10 minutes. Place on a serving plate, top with cheese slices and microwave at 100% (high) for 2 minutes. Serve as above.

Spaghetti bolognese sauce

Serves 4-6

1 tbls vegetable oil
2 rashers bacon, derinded and chopped
1 carrot, chopped
1 clove garlic, crushed
1 tbls plain flour
1/3 quantity Basic beef mix
2 tbls tomato purée
400 g/14 oz can tomatoes
150 ml/1/4 pt hot beef stock
1/2 tsp sugar
salt and pepper
To serve:
cooked spaghetti
grated Parmesan cheese

1 Place the oil, bacon, carrot and garlic in a pan and cook for 2-3 minutes. Stir in the flour. Add the beef mix, tomato purée, tomatoes with their juice and stock.

2 Bring to the boil and season with sugar, salt and pepper. Leave to simmer for 30 minutes, stirring occasionally, until the meat and vegetables are tender.

To Freeze: Turn into a rigid container, cool, cover and freeze.

To Serve: Thaw for 5-6 hours at room temperature or overnight in the refrigerator. Turn into a saucepan, and reheat gently. Serve with spaghetti, sprinkled with Parmesan cheese.

To Microwave: Cook from frozen in a microwave-safe container. Cover with pierced cling film. Microwave at 100% (high) for 12-15 minutes, or until heated, breaking apart and stirring 4-5 times during cooking. Serve with spaghetti and Parmesan cheese.

Pork

Batch cooking pork fillets

Order of work:
1 Soak 100 g/4 oz black-eyed beans for Bean and pork ragoût overnight in cold water.
2 Prepare Basic pork fillet recipe.
3 Preheat oven to 190° C/375° F/gas 5.
4 Make Prune-stuffed pork and cook for 45 minutes. Cool.
5 Reduce oven to 160° C/325° F/gas 3.
6 Prepare Pork and bean ragoût and place in the oven after cooking the Prune-stuffed pork. Cook for 1 hour, cool.
7 Prepare Pork fillets en croûte and freeze.
8 Freeze Prune-stuffed pork and Pork and bean ragoût, following instructions.

Basic pork fillets recipe

6 pork fillets, weighing about
   350 g/12 oz each
2-3 tbls vegetable oil

1 Slit 4 pork fillets lengthways, and open out to form a flatter shape. Do not

Freezer Facts

When freezing casseroles and stews, try to push the solid ingredients into the sauce to leave a layer of sauce on top, with no food sticking out. Leave a headspace for expansion.

cut right through the fillet. Set aside 2 fillets for Pork en croûte. Beat 2 remaining fillets with a rolling pin to flatten further. Set aside for Prune-stuffed pork.

2 Cut the remaining 2 fillets into strips 2.5 cm/1 in long and 2 cm/¾ in wide.
3 Heat 2 tbls of oil and fry the 2 unflattened fillets, for Pork en croûte, over a moderate heat until lightly browned. Remove from pan and drain on absorbent paper.
4 Add remaining oil, if necessary, and fry the strips of pork for 4-5 minutes, until lightly browned and sealed. Remove with a slotted spoon and drain on absorbent paper.

Above: *Pork fillet en croûte*

Pork fillet en croûte

Serves 4-6
2 pork fillets, cut open and
   browned (see Basic pork fillet
   recipe)
225 g/8 oz puff pastry
50 g/2 oz button mushrooms,
   sliced
For the stuffing
100 g/4 oz fresh white
   breadcrumbs
1 onion, grated
1 tsp dried sage
grated zest and juice of 1 lemon
1 dessert apple, grated
salt and pepper
1 small egg, beaten
To serve:
beaten egg, to glaze
mustard and cress, to garnish

1 Make the stuffing: put the breadcrumbs in a bowl with the onion, sage, lemon zest and apple. Season and mix together with the lemon juice and beaten egg.
2 Roll out the pastry thinly, on a floured board, to make a rectangle measuring 40 x 30 cm/16 x 12 in. Trim the edges and

reserve for decoration. Transfer to a baking tray lined with freezer foil.

3 Place 1 pork fillet in the centre of the pastry. Sprinkle with mushrooms and place the second fillet on top. Spread the stuffing mixture around the sides and top of the fillets.

4 Fold the pastry ends over, then the sides, so that the meat is enclosed in the pastry parcel with the join on top. Seal the edges with water.

5 Decorate the top with pastry leaves made from the trimmings.

To Freeze: Open freeze for 4-5 hours, then enclose in the freezer foil, and remove the baking tray. Return to freezer.

To Serve: Allow to thaw overnight in the refrigerator. Place on a baking tray and brush with beaten egg. Cook in preheated oven at 200° C/400° F/gas 6 for 20 minutes, then at 160° C/325° F/gas 3 for 45 minutes. Serve garnished with mustard and cress.

Above: *Prune-stuffed pork*

Pork and bean ragoût

Serves 4
40 g/1½ oz butter or margarine
1 large onion, chopped
40 g/1½ oz plain flour
600 ml/1 pt chicken stock
4 large carrots, cut into thin slices
thinly pared zest of 1 lemon, cut into strips
100 g/4 oz black-eyed beans, soaked and drained
½ tsp ground coriander
½ tsp ground turmeric
½ tsp ground ginger
salt and pepper
2 pork fillets, cut into strips (see Basic pork fillet recipe)
To serve:
strips of lemon zest and chopped parsley, to garnish

1 Heat oven to 160° C/325° F/gas 3.
2 Heat the fat in a casserole, add the onion and fry gently for 5 minutes, until soft. Sprinkle in the flour and stir over a low heat for 1-2 minutes. Gradually stir in the stock. Bring to the boil and then simmer, stirring until thick.
3 Add the carrots, lemon strips, beans and spices, and season to taste. Bring back to the boil and boil for 10 minutes. Add the pork strips, cover and cook for 1 hour in the oven.

To Freeze: Cool quickly, then pour into a rigid container. Seal and freeze.
To Serve: Defrost overnight in the refrigerator then reheat at 180° C/350° F/

gas 4 for 30-40 minutes, until bubbling. Garnish with lemon strips and parsley.
To Microwave: Place ragoût in a microwave-safe casserole, cover and microwave at 100% (high) for 5 minutes. Reduce power to 70% (medium-high) and cook for 12-16 minutes, or until hot, stirring several times, to distribute the heat. Serve as above.

Prune-stuffed pork

Serves 4-6
275 g/10 oz no-need-to-soak prunes
8 whole almonds
2 pork fillets, cut open and flattened (see Basic pork fillet recipe)
2 tbls vegetable oil
300 ml/½ pt chicken stock
salt and pepper
2 tbls redcurrant jelly
150 ml/¼ pt water
To serve:
10-12 whole almonds, blanched

1 Heat oven to 190° C/375° F/gas 5.
2 Stuff 8 of the prunes with an almond and place on one pork fillet. Place the second fillet on top, then tie the two fillets together with thin string in about four places, enclosing the prunes completely.
3 Heat the oil in a frying pan, add the pork and fry over a high heat, to seal on both sides.
4 Transfer the pork to a roasting tin, add

the stock and season to taste with salt and pepper. Cover the tin with foil and cook in the oven for about 45 minutes, basting occasionally, or until juices run clear when meat is pierced with a skewer.
5 Dissolve the redcurrant jelly in the water over a low heat. Add the remaining prunes and cook gently for 5 minutes until tender.
6 Remove the meat from the pan and leave to cool. Put the tin on the hob and reduce the liquid to about 150 ml/¼ pt by boiling rapidly. Add the prunes and redcurrant liquid. Cool.

To Freeze: Wrap cold meat in freezer film and freeze. Pour sauce with prunes into a rigid container, cover and freeze when cold.
To Serve: Thaw meat and sauce separately in the refrigerator for 8 hours. Wrap meat in foil and reheat at 160° C/325° F/gas 3 for 30-35 minutes. Heat sauce gently in a saucepan.

Remove string from meat and carve into thick slices. Arrange on a warmed serving dish. Garnish with prunes from the sauce and sprinkle almonds in between the prunes. Spoon the sauce around the meat. If wished serve with roast potatoes and French beans.
To Microwave: Reheat meat on a roasting rack, covered loosely with greaseproof paper. Microwave at 70% (medium-high) for 12-15 minutes, turning over halfway through the reheating time. Reheat sauce in a jug, covered with cling film, for 2-3 minutes. Carve and serve as above.

Chicken

Batch cooking chicken

Order of work:
1 Divide chickens into pieces.
2 Prepare and cook Provençal chicken.
3 Prepare and cook Stuffed drumsticks.
4 Prepare and cook Three-spice chicken.
5 Prepare and cook Chicken Tetrazzini.
6 Cool and freeze dishes following individual recipe instructions.

Basic chicken recipe

4 chickens

1 Remove breasts and drumsticks to give 8 of each.
2 Remove the remaining meat from the thighs, wings and carcass, and roughly dice for Three-spice chicken.

Three-spice chicken

Serves 4
2 onions, roughly chopped
100 g/4 oz mushrooms, sliced
3 tbls vegetable oil
stripped chicken meat, diced
1 tsp ground cumin
1 tsp ground coriander
1 tsp ground ginger
1 tbls plain flour
150 ml/¼ pt chicken stock
150 ml/¼ pt single cream
salt and pepper
To serve:
boiled rice
lemon wedges
chopped fresh parsley

Freezer Facts

Freeze bunches of herbs when they are in season. They can be frozen unblanched. Use from frozen and crumble into the desired dish.

Above: *Chicken Tetrazzini*

1 Fry the onions and mushrooms in the oil for 2 minutes. Add the chicken and spices and cook, stirring, for 5 minutes.
2 Stir in the flour, then gradually add the stock, cream and seasoning to taste. Bring to the boil, reduce the heat, cover and simmer for 10 minutes.
To Freeze: Pour into a rigid container. Cool, seal, label and freeze.
To Serve: Thaw overnight in the refrigerator. Re-heat in a saucepan until boiling, then simmer for 3 minutes. Serve on a bed of rice, garnished with lemon and parsley.

Chicken Tetrazzini

Serves 4
4 chicken breasts, cut into bite-sized pieces
500 ml/18 fl oz chicken stock
50 g/2 oz butter
100 g/4 oz whole button mushrooms
50 g/2 oz plain flour
4 tbls dry white wine
150 ml/¼ pt double cream
pinch of grated nutmeg
salt and pepper
150 g/5 oz spaghetti, freshly cooked and covered with cold water until needed
To serve:
25 g/1 oz Parmesan cheese, grated

1 Poach the chicken in a little stock for about 15 minutes, or until tender. Melt the butter in a saucepan, fry the mush-rooms, stirring occasionally, for about 5 minutes. Remove with a slotted spoon.
2 Sprinkle the flour into the butter and stir over a low heat for 1-2 minutes. Gradually stir in the stock and chicken with cooking liquid, and cook, stirring, until the sauce is thickened and smooth. Remove from heat and add the wine and cream gradually. Season with nutmeg, salt and pepper.
3 Drain spaghetti thoroughly then add to the sauce with the mushrooms.
To freeze: Pour the Tetrazzini into a shallow ovenproof dish or foil container about 1.4 L/2½ pt capacity. Cool, cover and freeze.
To Serve: Reheat from frozen at 180° C/350° F/gas 4 for about 1 hour. Stir once or twice during cooking and sprinkle with grated Parmesan cheese halfway through the cooking time.

Stuffed drumsticks

Serves 4
8 drumsticks
25 g/1 oz margarine or butter
100 g/4 oz pâté
2 tbls single cream
2 tsps finely chopped parsley
salt and pepper
2 tbls plain flour
2 tbls vegetable oil
For the sauce
1 tsp plain flour
150 ml/5 fl oz chicken stock
1 tbls soy sauce
1 tsp Worcestershire sauce
3 tomatoes, skinned, deseeded and chopped

1 Heat the oven to 200° C/400° F/gas 6.
2 To prepare the drumsticks for stuffing, use a sharp knife to scrape the bone and push the flesh down to the knuckle end.
3 Place the blade of the knife across the bone at the knuckle end. Bang the knife sharply with a rolling pin to cut the bone, leaving only a small piece of bone inside the flesh.

4 In a bowl mix together the fat, pâté and cream to a smooth paste. Add the parsley and season to taste.

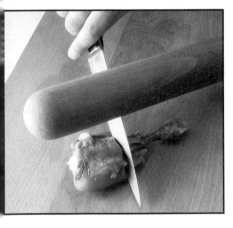

5 Fill the drumsticks with the mix, and sew up the open ends with fine string.
6 Season the flour with salt and pepper, put on a plate and roll drumsticks in it to coat. Heat the oil in a flameproof casserole and fry the drumsticks in a single layer over a moderate heat until golden.
7 Transfer to the oven and cook for about 30-35 minutes, until the chicken is cooked through. Baste once or twice.
8 Make the sauce: remove chicken from casserole and pour off all but 1 tbls fat. Stir in the flour and cook over a low heat for 1-2 minutes, stirring. Gradually stir in the remaining ingredients. Bring to the boil, stirring, then simmer for 2 minutes.
To Freeze: Place drumsticks in a rigid container, remove string, pour sauce over, leave to cool. Cover and freeze.

To Serve: Thaw overnight in the refrigerator. Place in an ovenproof dish or casserole and reheat in a moderate oven preheated to 180° C/350° F/gas 4 for 35-40 minutes.

Provençal chicken

Serves 4
4 chicken breasts, skinned
25 g/1 oz plain flour
salt and pepper
2 tbls vegetable oil
50 g/2 oz margarine or butter
1 clove garlic, crushed
400 g/14 oz can chopped tomatoes
1 tbls tomato purée
½ green pepper, deseeded and diced
½ tsp dried oregano
To serve:
3 spring onions, chopped
1 tbls chopped fresh parsley

1 Place the chicken breasts between 2 sheets of greaseproof paper and, using a rolling pin or mallet, beat them until

Below: *Stuffed drumsticks*

about 1 cm/½ in thick. Pat dry with absorbent paper.
2 Mix the flour, salt and pepper together and coat the escalopes on both sides with the seasoned flour.
3 Heat the oil and fat in a large frying pan. Add the garlic and fry for 1 minute. Add the escalopes and fry over a moderate heat for 3-5 minutes a side. Remove from the pan and drain on absorbent paper.
4 Pour off most of the fat from the pan, add the tomatoes and all the remaining ingredients. Stir, bring to the boil, then simmer for 5 minutes. Season.
To Freeze: Place chicken in a rigid container and pour the sauce over. Cover and freeze.
To Serve: Defrost overnight. Reheat in a shallow, covered casserole at 200° C/400° F/gas 6 for 20-30 minutes. Garnish with spring onions and parsley.
To Microwave: Remove from container and place in a 2.3 L/4 pt casserole, cover. Microwave at 100% (high) for 5 minutes. Reduce to 70% (medium-high) and microwave for 15-20 minutes, or until heated, stirring 3-4 times to break up and rearrange. Serve sprinkled with spring onion and parsley.

Sponge Cake

Batch cooking sponge cake

Order of work:
1 Preheat oven to 180° C/350° F/gas 4.
2 Make Basic sponge mix.
3 Make Chocolate gâteau and cook.
4 Make Cherry castles.
5 After 25 minutes baking, remove Chocolate gâteau and cook Cherry castles. Cool chocolate sponges.
6 Make Sponge puddings and steam.
7 After 15-20 minutes baking, remove Cherry castles and cool.
8 Make filling for Chocolate gâteau, fill when cold and freeze.
9 Finish Cherry castles and freeze.
10 After 1½ hours, remove puddings from steamers and leave to cool. Freeze.

Basic sponge mix

350 g/12 oz plain flour
350 g/12 oz self-raising flour
1 tsp salt
175 g/6 oz butter, softened
350 g/12 oz margarine, softened
500 g/18 oz caster sugar
9 eggs, beaten

1 Heat the oven to 180° C/350° F/gas 4.
2 Place one shelf just above the centre of the oven and one just below.
3 Sift the flours and salt together. In a large mixing bowl cream the butter and margarine together with a mixer or wooden spoon until pale.
4 Beat in the sugar until the mixture is smooth, light and fluffy. Gradually beat in the eggs, taking care to beat well after each addition, to prevent curdling.

Freezer Facts

If you can't cook all the sponge mix immediately, freeze it uncooked in correctly weighed amounts, then thaw and bake as needed.

5 Using a metal spoon, gradually fold in the flours and lightly mix until evenly incorporated.

Ginger and blackcurrant sponge puddings

Makes 2-each serves 4-6
1 kg/2 lb 3 oz Basic sponge mix
1 tsp baking powder
For the blackcurrant pudding
3-4 tbls blackcurrant jam
For the ginger pudding
1 tsp lemon juice
75 g/3 oz stem ginger, chopped
1 tbls ginger syrup (from a jar of stem ginger)
To serve:
4 tbls clear honey
2 tbls ginger syrup
2 tbls lemon juice
75 g/3 oz stem ginger, chopped

1 Place the basic sponge mix in a bowl and sprinkle baking powder over. Fold in gently but thoroughly.
2 Grease two 850 ml/1½ pt pudding bowls or foil pudding basins. Place blackcurrant jam at the base of one. Top with half the sponge mix. Smooth the surface.

3 Mix lemon juice, stem ginger and ginger syrup into the remaining basic sponge mix and place in the second container. Smooth the surface.
4 Cover both containers with greaseproof paper and tie down. Stand each bowl on a trivet in a large pan with boiling water to come halfway up the sides. Cover the pans and steam for 1½ hours, topping up with more water as necessary. Cool.

To Freeze: Replace greaseproof with fresh and cover with foil.
To Serve: Steam or boil for 1 hour. To finish ginger pudding, place honey, ginger syrup and lemon juice in a saucepan, add 4 tbls of water and heat gently.

Below: *Ginger sponge pudding*

Cherry castles

Makes 8-10
**475 g/17 oz (approximately) Basic
   sponge mix**
60 ml/4 tbls cherry jam
50 g/2 oz desiccated coconut
To serve:
glacé cherries and angelica

1 Divide the sponge mixture equally between 8-10 dariole moulds, to half fill
them. Level the tops using the back of a
teaspoon.
2 Bake for 15-20 minutes, or until golden and spring back when touched.

3 Run a knife round the edge of each
mould and turn out on a rack to cool.
Trim off the rounded ends if necessary.
4 Place the jam in a saucepan and
warm. Sprinkle desiccated coconut on a
plate.
5 Brush each cake with jam and roll in
the coconut, to cover, pressing it on
firmly.
To Freeze: Open freeze, then place in a
rigid container or polythene bag.
To Serve: Allow to defrost for 1-2 hours
at room temperature. Decorate with
glacé cherries and angelica.

Turn pudding out on to a serving plate,
pour a little of the sauce over and top
with half the chopped ginger. Mix the
remaining ginger into the sauce and
serve separately.
To Microwave: If frozen in microwave-
safe bowls, the puddings can be reheated in the microwave oven. Microwave at 30% (low) for 10 minutes,
turning a ¼ turn every 3 minutes.
Increase power to 100% (high) and
microwave for 1-1½ minutes. Remove
foil cover from freezing before cooking.

Chocolate gâteau

Serves 8
**750 g/1 lb 10 oz Basic
   sponge mix**
2 tbls evaporated milk
50 g/2 oz cocoa powder
75 g/3 oz flaked almonds, chopped
75 g/3 oz plain chocolate, grated
For the filling
175 g/6 oz margarine or butter
375 g/12 oz icing sugar, sifted
1 tbls cocoa powder
1 tbls coffee and chicory essence
1 tsp dark rum (optional)

1 Grease 2 x 20 cm/8 in round
sandwich tins, then line with greaseproof
paper and grease.
2 Place the sponge mix in a bowl, pour
over the evaporated milk, then sift the
cocoa powder on top. Gently fold in with
a metal spoon, until blended.
3 Divide the mix between the prepared
tins and smooth the surfaces. Bake for
20-25 minutes, until the surface is golden and springy to the touch. Leave to
stand for a few minutes, then turn on to a
wire rack. Carefully peel off the lining

Above: Chocolate gâteau

paper and leave the sponge layers to cool.
4 Make the filling: Beat the fat until
creamy, then gradually beat in the icing
sugar. Dissolve the cocoa in the coffee
essence, then beat into the filling with the
rum, if using.
5 Place about 5 tbls of the filling in a
piping bag fitted with a 1 cm/½ in star
nozzle. Use about half the remaining
filling to sandwich together the sponges.
Spread the rest over the top and sides of
the assembled sponges, to cover.
6 Press almonds on the sides of the
sponge, using a palette knife. Pipe a border around the top edge and sprinkle
chocolate over the top of the sponge.
To Freeze: Open freeze, then pack in a
rigid container.
To Serve: Unpack and thaw at room
temperature for 3-4 hours.

Below: Cherry castles

Pastry

Batch cooking pastry

Order of work:
1 Make Basic pastry mix.
2 Preheat oven to 200° C/400° F/gas 6.
3 Make Cheese and tomato ring and cook for 25-30 minutes. Leave to cool. Reduce oven to 180° C/350° F/gas 4 as soon as the ring is cooked.
4 Meanwhile make Beef pasties, then Almond slices. Cook together in the oven with the pasties above the slices. Check Almond slices after 30 minutes and Beef pasties after 35 minutes.
5 Leave to cool. Wrap and freeze dishes according to individual recipe instructions.

Basic pastry mix

900 g/2 lb plain flour
1½ tsps salt
225 g/8 oz white vegetable cooking fat
225 g/8 oz margarine or butter
about 8 tbls cold water

1 Sift the flour and salt together in a large bowl. Rub the fats into the flour until the mixture resembles fine breadcrumbs.
2 Mix to a firm but pliable dough with cold water.
3 Use as required in the following recipes. Keep well covered with cling film until each batch is required, to prevent it drying out.
4 Arrange two oven shelves, one just above the centre and one just below, in the oven.

Freezer Facts

When batch cooking pastry, roll out trimmings and cut into fancy shapes. Sprinkle with Parmesan cheese and season. Bake at 200° C/400° F/gas 6 for 12-13 minutes until brown. Freeze.

Above: *Beef pasties*

Below: *Cheese and tomato ring*

Beef pasties

Makes 4
500 g/18 oz Basic pastry mix
175 g/6 oz lean minced beef
1 onion, finely chopped
1 tbls Worcestershire sauce
2 tsps tomato purée
1 tbls chopped parsley
½ tsp dried thyme
salt and pepper
**150 g/5 oz can baked beans in
    tomato sauce**
beaten egg, to glaze

1 Roll out the pastry on a lightly floured surface into a large round, then using an 18 cm/7 in plate as a guide, cut out four pastry circles.
2 Mix together the beef, onion, Worcestershire sauce, tomato purée, parsley, thyme and seasoning. Fold in the baked beans carefully. Divide between the rounds of pastry, placing it in the centre of each.
3 Brush the edges of the pastry with beaten egg and press them together over the top of the filling to seal. Flute the

edges. Place the pasties on a greased baking tray and prick the pastry around the top to allow steam to escape.

4 Brush the pasties with beaten egg. Bake in a preheated oven at 180° C/

350° F/gas 4 for 35-40 minutes. Slightly underbake to allow for reheating. Cool on a wire rack.
To Freeze: Open freeze until solid, then pack in a rigid container, separating each with non-stick paper. Seal and freeze.
To Serve: Partially defrost for 30 minutes at room temperature, then reheat at 180° C/350° F/gas 4 for 20-25 minutes. Serve with salad.

Cheese and tomato ring

Serves 4-6
**175 g/6 oz Double Gloucester
    cheese with chives, grated**
2 onions, finely chopped
1 tbls Dijon mustard
salt and pepper
500 g/18 oz Basic pastry mix
**400 g/14 oz can tomatoes, drained
    and chopped**
beaten egg, to glaze
1 tsp poppy seeds
To serve:
bunch of watercress

1 Mix the cheese, onions and mustard together in a bowl and season to taste with salt and pepper.
2 Roll the pastry out on a lightly floured board to make a rectangle about 40 x 28 cm/16 x 11 in. Trim the edges.
3 Spread the tomatoes over the pastry, then carefully spread the cheese and onion mixture on top, bringing it almost to the edges.
4 Brush edges with beaten egg and roll up from one long edge. Seal along the seam firmly.
5 Place seam side down on a greased baking sheet and snip along one edge at 2.5 cm/1 in intervals, taking care not to cut all the way through. Shape into a ring, sealing the ends together securely. Use more beaten egg if necessary.
6 Ease the sections apart and tilt slightly sideways, to show the filling. Brush the surface with beaten egg and sprinkle with poppy seeds. Bake in a preheated oven at 200° C/400° F/gas 6 for 25-30 minutes until light golden brown. Do not overcook, to allow for reheating. Place on a wire rack and leave to cool.
To Freeze: Open freeze, then wrap in freezer foil. Return to the freezer.
To Serve: Partially defrost at room temperature for about 30 minutes, then reheat at 180° C/350° F/gas 4 for 30 minutes. Fill the ring with watercress.

Above: *Almond slices*

Almond slices

Makes 16
**350 g/12 oz Basic pastry mix
    (remaining quantity)**
2 large egg whites
150 g/5 oz ground almonds
150 g/5 oz caster sugar
2-3 drops almond essence
100 g/4 oz plum jam
50 g/2 oz flaked almonds

1 Roll out the pastry on a lightly floured board, to a rectangle about 30 x 20 cm/ 12 x 8 in, and use to line a Swiss roll tin measuring 28 x 18 cm/11 x 7 in. Gently press the pastry over the base and up the sides of the tin, then trim off any surplus.
2 In a clean, dry bowl whisk the egg whites until they stand in stiff peaks. Fold in the ground almonds, caster sugar and almond essence.
3 Spread the jam over the base of the pastry, then carefully cover with the almond mixture. Scatter almonds over the top. Bake in a preheated oven at 180° C/ 350° F/gas 4 for 30-35 minutes, until golden. Cook below the Beef pasties.
4 Leave to cool for 20-30 minutes, then cut into 16 slices and remove from the tin to a wire rack to cool.
To Freeze: Pack in a rigid container with non-stick paper between layers. Cover and freeze.
To Serve: Defrost as many as required for 1-2 hours at room temperature.

Enriched Dough

Batch cooking enriched doughs

Order of work:

1 Make Basic enriched dough mix.
2 Make Plaited fruit loaf and leave to prove for about 1¼ hours.
3 Make Iced tea ring and leave to prove for about 1 hour.
4 Make Nut squares and leave to prove until fruit loaf and tea ring are cooked.
5 About 45 minutes after making the tea ring preheat the oven to 220° C/425° F/ gas 7 for about 15 minutes.
6 Cook the Plaited fruit loaf and tea ring when doubled in size, for about 20 minutes. Place loaf above tea ring.
7 Remove loaf, reduce oven to 180° C/ 350° F/gas 4 and cook the tea ring for a further 10 minutes.
8 Increase oven to 190° C/375° F/gas 5, wait 5 minutes, then cook Nut squares for about 25 minutes.
9 Cool all three items. Ice the tea ring when cold.
10 Pack and freeze according to recipe instructions.

Basic enriched dough mix

1.4 kg/3 lb plain flour
1 tsp salt
1 tsp mixed spice
75 g/3 oz caster sugar
2 sachets 'easy blend' dried yeast
175 g/6 oz margarine or butter, melted
500 ml/18 fl oz lukewarm milk
2 large eggs

Freezer Facts

Remove the iced tea ring from the polythene bag before defrosting. This will prevent the icing from sticking to the bag and possible damage to the decoration.

1 Sieve the flour and salt together. Add the mixed spice, caster sugar and yeast and mix. Make a well in the centre.
2 Add the melted fat, milk and eggs and mix together to a soft dough. If necessary add a little more milk.
3 Turn out on to a floured surface and knead for 5-10 minutes to a smooth dough. Place in a lightly greased bowl. Cover with cling film and leave in a warm place until doubled in size. Divide the dough into three and use as required in the following recipes.

Plaited fruit loaf

Makes 12 slices
⅓ quantity Basic enriched dough mix
75 g/3 oz seedless raisins
75 g/3 oz cut mixed peel
beaten egg, for glazing
½ tsp poppy seeds

1 Take the basic enriched dough mix and work in the raisins and peel.
2 Divide the dough into 3 equal pieces. Using your hands, roll each piece into a sausage shape, about 40 cm/16 in long.

Below: *Iced tea ring*

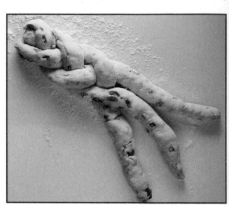

Lay the rolls side by side and plait them from the centre to one end of the loaf, then from the centre to the end.
3 Place the plaited loaf on a greased baking sheet and tuck the ends neatly underneath. Cover with oiled polythene and leave to rise in a warm place for about 1¼ hours, or until the loaf is doubled in bulk.
4 About 15 minutes before the loaf is risen, preheat the oven to 220° C/425° F/ gas 7. Uncover loaf, brush with beaten egg and sprinkle with poppy seeds. Bake for about 20 minutes until well risen and golden.
5 Transfer to a wire rack and leave to cool completely.

To **Freeze:** Wrap in freezer foil or place in a polythene bag and seal. Freeze.

To **Serve:** Defrost, still wrapped, at room temperature for 2-3 hours. To defrost quickly, wrap in foil and place in a pre-heated oven at 180° C/350° F/gas 4 for 15-20 minutes. Slice and serve with butter.

Nut squares

Makes 8
1/3 quantity Basic enriched dough mix
75 g/3 oz sultanas
For the topping
50 g/2 oz caster sugar
2 tbls plain flour
2 tsps ground cinnamon
25 g/1 oz margarine or butter, diced
25 g/1 oz blanched almonds, chopped

1 Take the basic enriched dough mix and knead in the sultanas.

2 Lightly grease a shallow, oblong baking tin about 25 x 15 cm/10 x 6 in. Roll out the dough to the same size as the tin. Place in the tin and press gently over the base and into the corners. Cover with oiled polythene and leave to rise in a warm place for about 1 hour, until the dough is almost doubled in thickness.

3 Heat the oven to 190° C/375° F/gas 5. Make the topping: mix the sugar, flour and cinnamon together. Add the diced fat and rub it in, then stir in the chopped almonds.

Above left: Nut squares
Above right: Plaited fruit loaf

4 Uncover the tin and sprinkle the topping evenly over the dough. Bake in the oven for about 25 minutes, until well risen. Transfer to a wire rack and leave to cool completely.

To **Freeze:** Wrap in a polythene bag, seal and freeze.

To **Serve:** Unwrap and defrost at room temperature for 2 hours. Warm in an oven preheated to 180° C/350° F/gas 4 for 10 minutes, then cut into squares.

Iced tea ring

Makes about 20 slices
1/3 quantity Basic enriched dough mix
3 tbls black cherry jam
caster sugar, for sprinkling
175 g/6 oz almond paste
For the icing
100 g/4 oz icing sugar, sifted
5 tsps lemon juice
25 g/1 oz Brazil nuts, chopped

1 Roll out the basic enriched dough to a 35 x 20 cm/14 x 8 in rectangle and spread with cherry jam.

2 Sprinkle the work surface with caster sugar and roll out the almond paste to the same size as the dough. Place the almond paste on the dough, on top of the layer of jam.

3 Starting from one long side roll up the dough. Dampen the ends with water and

join them together firmly to make a ring. Place on a greased baking tray.

4 Using a sharp knife, cut the ring at regular intervals to within 2 cm/3/4 in of the centre. Working in one direction, turn each cut section slightly on its side.

5 Cover with oiled polythene and leave to rise in a warm place for about 1 hour, or until almost doubled in size. About 15 minutes before the dough is ready, heat the oven to 220° C/425° F/gas 7.

6 Uncover the ring and bake in the oven for 20 minutes, below the fruit plait, then reduce the oven to 180° C/350° F/gas 4 and bake for a further 10 minutes, or until brown. Cool the tea ring on a wire rack.

7 Blend the icing sugar with sufficient lemon juice to give a coating consistency, then spoon over the ring. Decorate with nuts and leave to set.

To **Freeze:** Open freeze, then wrap in a polythene bag. Seal and return to the freezer.

To **Serve:** Remove ring from bag whilst still frozen. Defrost for 2-3 hours at room temperature.

Entertaining from the Freezer

For anybody with a busy lifestyle, entertaining can be an enormous problem. It's not just deciding what to cook but trying to get it all together when you know everyone will be arriving at a certain time. Or, simply, that people turn up unexpectedly and you want to produce an impromptu dinner in style.

In this chapter you will find a menu for every occasion – from a continental dinner party to a picnic. And with the help of our sumptuous recipes you should have the perfect combination ready and waiting to be eaten. There's even a section on Christmas trimmings – the little extras that can so easily be forgotten. So, from now on, you should really be able to entertain with ease.

Sunday Feast

Sunday lunch is a great family time and, when you've got something special to celebrate, here's a lunch to make it a most memorable occasion.

It's well worth preparing fresh best ends of neck of lamb in this way for the freezer. They look so impressive but are very easy to do.

Cheese pots

Serves 6
225 g/8 oz ripe Brie
100 g/4 oz butter
50 g/2 oz cream cheese
1 tsp chopped fresh chives
3 tbls dry white wine
salt and pepper
50 g/2 oz wholemeal bran biscuits, crushed
To serve:
6 prawns
parsley sprigs
herb bread or toast

1 Remove the rind from the cheese, and cream the cheese with half the butter, until light and fluffy. Beat in the cream cheese.
2 Stir in the chives and wine, and season with salt and pepper.
3 Sprinkle the biscuits in the base of 6 small ramekin dishes, top with cheese mix and chill until firm.
4 Melt the remaining butter, leave to stand to allow the sediment to settle. Carefully pour off the pure butter and use to coat the tops of the cheese pots. Leave to set.
To Freeze: Wrap each pot in freezer film, then freeze.
To Serve: Allow to thaw at room temperature for 1-2 hours. Top with a prawn and a sprig of parsley. Serve with herb bread or toast.

Freezer Facts

Freeze any leftover wine in ice-cube trays, and use later. Add to casseroles and sauces for extra flavour.

Guard of Honour with Cumberland sauce

Serves 6
2 best ends neck of lamb, 7-8 cutlets each, chined and about 5 cm/2 in ends of bones trimmed of fat and meat
For the sauce
thinly pared zest of 1 orange and the juice of 2
thinly pared zest of 1 lemon and the juice of 2
350 g/12 oz redcurrant jelly
150 ml/¼ pt red wine
1 tsp made English mustard
To serve:
vegetable oil
salt and pepper
cutlet frills
lemon and orange slices
sprigs of rosemary
vegetables

1 Make the sauce: Put the pared zests into a small saucepan and cover with cold water. Bring to the boil, lower the heat and simmer for 5 minutes until soft. Strain and set aside.
2 Put the orange and lemon juice into a saucepan. Stir in the remaining ingredients, bring to the boil, then simmer for 25-30 minutes, until thickened slightly. Add the softened orange and lemon zests and leave to cool.
3 On a sheet of freezer foil, stand the 2 joints together, with the fatty sides outside and the exposed bones interlocking at the top.
To Freeze: Over-wrap the bones with freezer film. Wrap the joint well with foil and freeze. Place cold sauce in a rigid container, cover and freeze.
To Serve: Allow to thaw, wrapped, in the refrigerator for 6-8 hours. Place in a roasting tin, and unwrap. Brush with oil, season with salt and pepper and cook in preheated oven at 200° C/400° F/gas 6 for about 50 minutes, or until crisp and

Right: Guard of Honour with Cumberland sauce, Cheese pots
Below: Choux ring served with fresh figs

brown. The juices should run clear when the thickest part of the meat is pierced with a skewer. Place cutlet frills on bone ends, place on a serving plate and garnish with orange and lemon slices and rosemary sprigs. Defrost sauce for 3-4 hours and serve cold. Serve with vegetables of your choice.

Choux ring

Serves 6
175 g/6 oz plain flour
pinch of salt
300 ml/½ pt water
100 g/4 oz margarine or butter
4 large eggs, lightly beaten
1 egg, beaten, to glaze
1 tbls blanched almonds
To serve:
300 ml/½ pt double cream, whipped
175-225 g/6-8 oz fresh fruit
icing sugar, to dust

1 Heat the oven to 220° C/425° F/gas 7. Lightly grease a baking tray, and sprinkle with water.
2 Make the pastry: sift the flour and salt together.
3 Pour the water into a heavy based saucepan, add the margarine or butter and heat gently, stirring occasionally, until the fat has melted. Bring to the boil, remove from the heat and tip in the flour. Stir vigorously with a wooden spoon to mix.
4 Return to a low heat, and beat for about 1 minute, or until the paste forms a ball in the centre of the pan.
5 Remove from the heat, cool slightly, then beat in the eggs, a little at a time. Beat until smooth and shiny. Put the paste into a piping bag fitted with a 1 cm/½ in plain nozzle.
6 Pipe a 25 cm/10 in ring on to the prepared baking tray. Pipe another ring inside, touching the first ring, then pipe a third ring on top to cover the join.

7 Carefully brush with beaten egg, then sprinkle with almonds. Bake for about 40 minutes. Transfer to a wire rack and leave to cool.
To Freeze: Open freeze, then place in a polythene bag, seal and return to the freezer.
To Serve: Crisp in a preheated oven at 190° C/375°F/gas 5 for 7-8 minutes.

Cool. Slice the cold ring in half horizontally, then pipe or spoon half the cream into the bottom half of the ring. Top with fruit and cover with the remaining cream. Replace upper half of choux ring. Dust with icing sugar and serve. If preferred, fill the ring with cream only and serve fresh exotic fruits of your choice separately.

Thrifty Dinner Party

If you have friends or family who like to 'pop in' for a meal, or if you want to have an impromptu dinner party that doesn't cost a fortune – here it is!

Below: *Creamy watercress soup, Kebabs served with buttered boiled rice and a mixed salad*

Creamy watercress soup

Serves 4
2 bunches of watercress
1 onion, quartered
600 ml/1 pt chicken stock
1 tsp lemon juice
salt and pepper
To serve:
25 g/1 oz cornflour
300 ml/½ pt milk
pinch of freshly grated nutmeg
watercress sprigs, to garnish

1 Put the watercress into a saucepan. Add the onion, chicken stock, lemon juice and salt and pepper to taste.
2 Bring to the boil, then lower the heat, cover and simmer for 20 minutes. Leave to cool slightly then purée in a blender.
To Freeze: Pour into a rigid container, cool, cover and freeze.
To Serve: Thaw overnight in the refrigerator or for 6-8 hours. Turn into a saucepan and reheat. Mix cornflour to a paste with a little of the milk then stir in the remaining milk. Stir into the soup and bring to the boil, stirring continuously. Simmer for 2 minutes. Add nutmeg and adjust seasoning if necessary. Serve garnished with watercress.
To Microwave: Remove from the freezer container and place in a 1.7 L/ 3 pt casserole, cover and microwave at 70% (medium-high) for 7-10 minutes, stirring 3-4 times to break apart. Increase to 100% (high). Mix cornflour to a paste

Freezer Facts

Unlike solids, it is important to leave a headspace of at least 2.5 cm/1 in when freezing liquids, to allow for expansion. This is because water expands on freezing by about 10%.

with a little of the milk, stir in the remaining milk, add to the soup, cover and cook for 5-7 minutes, stirring every 1-2 minutes, until thickened. Add nutmeg, adjust seasoning and serve.

Kebabs

Serves 4
225 g/8 oz lean minced beef
225 g/8 oz lean minced pork
1 onion, grated
25 g/1 oz fresh white breadcrumbs
½ tsp ground ginger
½ tsp dried thyme
salt and pepper
1 egg, lightly beaten
6 rashers streaky bacon, derinded
6 large no-need-to-soak dried
   apricots, halved
To serve:
225 g/8 oz long-grain rice, freshly
   cooked
sprigs of rosemary, to garnish
For the sauce
3 tbls red wine vinegar
2 tbls dark brown soft sugar
2 tbls tomato ketchup
2 tbls fruit chutney
2 tsps cornflour
2 tsps soy sauce
300 ml/½ pt water
salt and pepper

1 Mix together the meats, onion, breadcrumbs, ginger, thyme and salt and pepper. Add the egg, then mix to combine. Divide into 16 and shape into balls.
2 Cut each bacon rasher in half and wrap around each apricot half. Thread alternately on to 4 skewers allowing 4 balls and 3 bacon rolls per skewer.
To Freeze: Wrap skewers individually in freezer film. Freeze.
To Serve: Unwrap and grill from frozen for about 15 minutes. Make the sauce: Mix all the ingredients together, bring to the boil, stirring continuously and boil for 2 minutes. Serve kebabs on a bed of rice, garnished with rosemary, with the sauce in a sauceboat. Serve with a mixed salad.

Orange and lemon surprise

Serves 4
4 oranges
3 lemons
75 ml/3 fl oz water
150 g/5 oz sugar

Above: *Orange and lemon surprise*

1 Wash the oranges and 2 of the lemons. With a potato peeler, peel the rinds from the 2 lemons, thinly, and put them in a saucepan with the water and sugar. Stir over a low heat until the sugar has dissolved, bring to the boil and boil for 1 minute, without stirring. Leave to cool for 1 hour.
2 Squeeze all the lemons and make the juice up to 150 ml/¼ pt with water, if necessary.
3 Cut the top third off the oranges and carefully squeeze the juice from the bottom two-thirds. Do not split the shells! Strain both lemon and orange juice together. They should measure about 425 ml/15 fl oz.

4 Remove remaining flesh from the orange shells with a teaspoon. Put

orange shells and tops on a tray and freeze.
5 Pour the orange and lemon juice into a large bowl, strain in the sugar syrup and stir well. Freeze for about 2 hours, until it has frozen to a width of 2.5 cm/1 in around the edge.
6 Remove from freezer and stir well with a metal spoon until evenly blended. Return to the freezer until frozen to a firm mushy consistency, about 2 hours. Stir every hour during this freezing process.
To Freeze: Fill the orange shells with the water ice, mounding it up well on top. Replace tops, pressing them on at an angle. Freeze for 1-2 hours, then pack in polythene bags, seal and return to the freezer.
To Serve: Place on individual plates, leave at room temperature for 5 minutes, then serve.

Spanish-Style Supper

What better way to entertain than with mouthwatering continental fare. And as you can have it all prepared well in advance, you'll be able to relax and enjoy the fiesta!

Andalusian gazpacho

Serves 4

2 cloves garlic, crushed
1 green pepper, seeded and chopped
1/2 cucumber, seeded, peeled and chopped
8 tomatoes, skinned and seeded
1 tbls chopped fresh parsley
50 g/2 oz dry white breadcrumbs
2 tbls wine vinegar
2 tbls olive oil
salt and pepper
To serve:
600 ml/1 pt iced water
For the garnish
chopped fresh parsley or small sprigs of mint
2 hard-boiled eggs, chopped
1 onion, finely diced
1 red pepper, seeded and finely diced
12 green and/or black olives, stoned

1 Put all the ingredients in an electric blender and blend at low speed until smooth. If necessary, blend in two batches.
To Freeze: Place in a rigid container, cover and freeze.
To Serve: Place in a large serving bowl and thaw for 2-3 hours. Break up and stir from time to time. When just thawed but still cold, add the iced water, cover and

place in the refrigerator until required. Just before serving add a few ice cubes, if wished and sprinkle with parsley or top with a sprig of mint. Serve accompanied by the remaining garnishes, each in an individual dish.
To Microwave: Remove from container and place in a 1.7 L/3 pt casserole, cover. Microwave at 70% (medium-high) for 7-8 minutes, breaking apart 2-3 times. Leave to stand for 5-10 minutes, then add iced water and finish as above.

Paella Valenciana

Serves 4

3 squid, with backbone and head removed
4 tbls olive oil
1.5 kg/3½ lb chicken, cut into 8
1 onion, chopped
2 cloves garlic, crushed
1 red pepper, seeded and cut into strips
225 g/8 oz tomatoes, skinned and quartered
400 g/14 oz medium grain Spanish or Italian rice
2 pinches saffron threads or ½ tsp turmeric powder soaked in 1 L/1¾ pt boiling hot chicken stock for 30 minutes
salt and pepper
To serve:
12 unpeeled prawns
100 g/4 oz frozen peas
8-12 fresh mussels, cleaned (see right)
1 lemon, cut into wedges

1 Prepare the squid and cut the sac into rings, about 5 mm/¼ in wide.
2 Heat the oil in a paella pan or a large frying pan and add the chicken. Fry for 10-15 minutes, until golden brown on all sides. Remove from the pan and reserve.
3 Add the onion, garlic, pepper and tomatoes and cook for 5 minutes. Stir in

Freezer Facts

Remember to cool food prepared for the freezer as quickly as possible; especially if it contains cooked meat or fish. Do not put hot food into the freezer.

How to clean mussels

1 *To check that mussels are really fresh, tap any open ones on a wooden board. If they do not shut, they should be discarded.*

2 *Use a knife to pull away any 'beards' (pieces of seaweed gripped between the two shells).*

3 *Scrub the mussels under cold running water, then scrape away any encrustations. Soak the mussels in fresh cold water to cover for 2-3 hours, changing the water several times.*

Meanwhile, drain and rinse the mussels, then cook in a covered saucepan with 150 ml/¼ pt boiling water for 5 minutes, shaking the pan occasionally. Discard any which do not open. Top paella with mussels, garnish with lemon wedges and serve.

To Microwave: Place thawed paella in a large casserole dish, cover and microwave at 70% (medium-high) for 8-12 minutes, stirring several times. Add the peas and mussels and stir in. Cover and microwave at 100% (high) for 5 minutes. Add prawns, cover and microwave at 100% (high) for 2 minutes. Discard any mussels which do not open. Serve garnished with lemon wedges.

Valencia chocolate mousse

Serves 4
3 eggs, separated
4 tbls milk
25 g/1 oz caster sugar
15 g/½ oz ground almonds
15 g/½ oz plain flour
50 g/2 oz butter, cut into pieces
grated zest and juice of 1 orange
½ tsp powdered gelatine
200 g/7 oz plain chocolate, broken into pieces
To serve:
150 ml/¼ pt double cream, whipped
50 g/2 oz flaked almonds, lightly browned

the squid and cook for 3 minutes, add the rice and cook for 2 minutes more.
4 Strain the stock into the pan, to remove the saffron threads, and stir well. Season. Cook over a low heat for 15 minutes, until the liquid is nearly absorbed. Only stir if the heat source is uneven. Cool.
To Freeze: Put in a rigid container, cover and freeze.

Above: *Andalusian gazpacho*

To Serve: Allow to thaw overnight in the refrigerator, return to the paella pan and reheat gently, stirring occasionally until hot. Add the prawns and peas, stir and cook gently for 5 minutes.

Below: *Paella Valenciana, Valencia chocolate mousse*

1 Blend the egg yolks and milk together in a bowl over hot water. Stir in the sugar, ground almonds and flour. Heat gently, stirring continuously, until the mixture thickens.
2 Add the pieces of butter, one at a time, stirring between each addition. Add the orange juice, zest and gelatine, mixing well.
3 Add the chocolate piece by piece, stirring until all the chocolate has melted and the mix is smooth. Remove from the heat.
4 Whisk the egg whites until stiff. Place the chocolate mix in a large bowl, and fold in the egg whites. Spoon the mixture into four strong dessert glasses.
To Freeze: Cover with freezer film and freeze.
To Serve: Thaw at room temperature for 1-2 hours. Remove freezer film and top with cream and almonds. Keep in the refrigerator until ready to serve.

Picnic Lunch

Sunny days mean eating out of doors. With these transportable delights in your freezer you'll be able to get up and go as soon as the sun shines!

Cheese, bacon and onion flan

Serves 4
200 g/7 oz streaky bacon, derinded and chopped
175 g/6 oz Cheddar cheese biscuits, finely crushed
90 g/3½ oz butter, melted
1 onion, finely chopped
175 g/6 oz Cheddar cheese, grated
150 ml/5 fl oz soured cream
150 ml/5 fl oz natural yoghurt
4 large eggs, lightly beaten
salt and pepper

1 Fry the bacon in a frying pan until crisp, then remove from the pan, reserving 2 tbls of the fat in the pan. Drain bacon on absorbent paper. Heat oven to 190° C/375° F/gas 5.
2 Combine the biscuit crumbs with the melted butter. Press into the sides and bottom of a 23 cm/9 in flan dish. Sprinkle in the bacon.
3 Add the onion to the frying pan and fry until softened. Combine onion with 150 g/5 oz cheese, soured cream, yoghurt and beaten eggs. Season and spoon into the case. Bake for 30-35 minutes or until cooked.
4 Remove the flan from the oven, sprinkle with remaining cheese and bake for 2-3 minutes more.
To Freeze: Cool, cover with freezer film and freeze.
To Serve: Leave to thaw in the refrigerator overnight.

Freezer Facts

Freeze leftover bread in crumb form. The crumbs remain separate and can be used straight from the freezer for stuffings and sauces. Thaw to coat foods.

Right: *Cheese, bacon and onion flan, Crumbed chicken, Summer rice salad*

To Microwave: Defrost quickly in the microwave oven just before leaving for your picnic, if wished. Microwave on 30% (low) for 10 minutes, turning a ¼ turn every 3 minutes.

Crumbed chicken

Serves 4
8 chicken drumsticks
125 g/4 oz dry white breadcrumbs
2 tbls chopped parsley
2 tbls olive oil
4 tbls apricot jam
1 onion, finely chopped
1 clove garlic, crushed
1 tsp grated ginger
1 tbls cider vinegar
1 tbls soy sauce

1 Heat the oven to 180° C/350° F/gas 4. Rinse and pat the chicken legs dry. Combine the crumbs, parsley and oil. Set aside.
2 Mix the jam with the chopped onion, garlic and ginger. Purée in a blender to mix thoroughly. Add the vinegar and soy sauce.
3 Roll chicken in the apricot mixture and leave for 15-20 minutes. Recoat in apricot mix then roll in the breadcrumb mix, to coat well.
4 Place in a lightly greased baking tin and bake for 45 minutes.
To Freeze: Open freeze, then place in a rigid container. Separate each drumstick with a piece of non-stick paper.
To Serve: Defrost overnight in the refrigerator. If wished they can be frozen uncooked then cooked after defrosting at room temperature for 1 hour. Bake at 180° C/350° F/gas 4 for 1 hour or until juices run clear. Cool. This is best done the evening before the picnic, to allow time for cooling. Only freeze uncooked if fresh, not previously frozen, drumsticks are used.

Summer rice salad

Serves 4
225 g/8 oz long grain rice, cooked
125 ml/4 fl oz vinaigrette dressing
1 small bunch spring onions, sliced
1 green pepper, deseeded and very finely chopped
salt and pepper
¼ tsp mustard powder
To serve:
2-3 tbls thick mayonnaise
1 small bunch of radishes, thinly sliced
5-6 small gherkins, chopped

1 Purée the fruit then sieve into a bowl to remove the pips. Stir in the sugar and lemon juice.
2 Fold in the whipped cream. Spoon

the fool into four plastic sundae glasses or plastic containers.

To Freeze: Cover with freezer film and freeze.
To Serve: Remove from the freezer 3-4 hours before serving. Top with cream. These fools are best transported whilst defrosting, so that they are still chilled when served. Cover to transport and keep upright. Decorate with strawberries.

1 Mix the warm rice with the vinaigrette and cool to room temperature. Leave to go cold.
2 Stir in the onions, peppers, seasoning and mustard.
To Freeze: Place in a rigid container, cover and freeze.
To Serve: Defrost at room temperature for 2 hours. Break up with a fork as soon as possible. Stir in mayonnaise, radishes and gherkins. It will finish defrosting on the way to your picnic.
To Microwave: To defrost quickly, place in a 1.7 L/3 pt casserole and cover. Microwave at 100% (high) for 2 minutes. Break apart, then microwave at 100%

(high) for 1-2 minutes, stir and add the mayonnaise, radishes and gherkins.

Fruit fool

Serves 4
225 g/8 oz raspberries
175 g/6 oz strawberries
50 g/2 oz caster sugar
1 tbls lemon juice
275 ml/1/2 pt double cream, whipped
To serve:
whipped cream
strawberries, to decorate

Dining in Style

Here's an elegant meal for those times when you want something a little bit special. The main course and dessert can be made a long while ahead and kept in the freezer. Frozen whitebait make an appetising and rather unusual starter – quick and easy to prepare too. They may be stored in the freezer for 3-4 months before use. Serve the Braised beef with broccoli and buttered rice.

Whitebait

Serves 6
750 g/1½ lb frozen whitebait, defrosted and dried on absorbent paper
vegetable oil, for deep-frying
75 g/3 oz plain flour
½ tsp salt
pinch of cayenne pepper
watercress and lemon wedges, to garnish

1 Preheat the oven to 130° C/250° F/ gas ½.
2 Heat the oil in a deep-fat frier to 190° C/375° F or until a cube of day-old bread browns in 50 seconds.
3 Put the flour in a large polythene bag and season with salt and cayenne. Make sure the whitebait are completely separate. Add a small batch to the flour mixture and shake until well coated. Repeat until all the fish are coated in the same way.
4 Deep-fry one third of the fish for 2-3 minutes, or until lightly browned. Drain well on absorbent paper, transfer to a hot serving dish and keep hot in the oven. Repeat with the remaining fish and transfer all to the hot serving dish.
5 Garnish with watercress and lemon wedges and serve at once while the whitebait are piping hot.

Freezer Facts

Any summer fruit may be used to make the sauce for the ice-cream. Try strawberries, redcurrants, blackcurrants or blackberries.

Braised beef in port

Serves 6
5 tbls vegetable oil
1.4 kg/3 lb braising steak, trimmed of excess fat and cut into 6 even-sized pieces
1 large onion, sliced
1 green pepper, deseeded and sliced
4 carrots, sliced lengthways
4 celery stalks, chopped
40 g/1½ oz plain flour
425 ml/¾ pint beef stock
150 ml/¼ pint port
3 tbls tomato purée
1 tsp ground allspice
1 tsp dried thyme
salt and pepper
250 g/9 oz button mushrooms, sliced
To serve:
chopped fresh parsley, to garnish
cooked broccoli
buttered boiled rice, garnished with lightly fried onion strips

1 Heat 4 tbls of the oil in a large heavy-based frying pan. Add 2 pieces of steak and fry briskly for 3-5 minutes until browned on both sides. Using a slotted spoon, transfer the steaks to a shallow ovenproof dish large enough to hold the steaks in a single layer. Fry the remaining steaks in the same way and transfer to the dish.
2 Heat the remaining oil in the frying pan, add the onion and fry gently for 5 minutes until soft and lightly coloured. Add the green pepper, carrots and celery and fry for a further minute. Stir in the flour and cook for 1 minute more.
3 Gradually stir in the stock and port, then bring slowly to the boil, stirring constantly. Add the tomato purée, allspice, thyme, and salt and pepper to taste, then

pour over the steaks in the ovenproof dish.
4 Cover the dish tightly with foil and cook in a preheated oven at 160° C/ 325° F/gas 3 for 2½ hours.
5 Add the mushrooms and cook for a further 15 minutes.
To Freeze: Transfer the meat and sauce to a rigid container and leave until cold. Seal, label and freeze.
To Serve: Defrost overnight in the refrigerator and reheat in the oven at 190° C/375° F/gas 5 for 30 minutes or until heated through. Transfer to a warmed shallow serving dish, garnish with chopped parsley and serve hot. Accompany with broccoli and buttered rice garnished with fried onion strips.

Frozen raspberry favourite

Serves 6

300 ml/½ pint double cream
3 tbls kirsch or medium
   sweet sherry
8 ready-made meringue shells
   or nests, roughly broken
   into pieces
50 g/2 oz icing sugar, sifted
450 g/1 lb fresh raspberries or
   frozen raspberries,
   defrosted
vegetable oil, for greasing
To serve:
50 g/ 2 oz fresh raspberries
   or frozen raspberries,
   defrosted

1 Brush the inside of a 450 g/1 lb loaf tin with oil and place in the bottom of the refrigerator. Leave to chill for about 1 hour.

Above: *Frozen raspberry favourite*
Left: *Whitebait, Braised beef in port served with buttered boiled rice and lightly cooked broccoli*

2 Whip the cream until it forms soft peaks, then add the kirsch or sweet sherry and whip again until the mixture has thickened.

3 Using a metal spoon, fold in the meringue pieces and 1 tbls of the icing sugar.

4 Turn the mixture into the chilled greased loaf tin, cover with foil, seal, label and freeze.

5 To make the raspberry sauce, press the raspberries through a sieve into a bowl. Blend in a liquidizer or food processor, until smooth. Stir in the icing sugar and mix well. Pour the raspberry sauce into a rigid container, seal, label and freeze.

To Serve: Defrost the sauce for 2-4 hours at room temperature. Just before serving, remove the ice-cream loaf from the freezer and remove the wrapping. Dip the base of the tin in hot water for 1-2 seconds, then invert on to a serving plate, giving a sharp shake halfway round.

Pour a little of the sauce over the ice-cream loaf and decorate the top with a row of whole raspberries. Serve at once. Pour the remaining sauce into a jug and serve separately.

Christmas Trimmings

We're not going to tell you how to cook your turkey – we're sure you can do that already – but here are those little extras that can make the festive meals extra-special and so easily get forgotten if left to the last minute.

it. Spread the mincemeat on the top to within 1 cm/½ in of the edge. Brush the edges with beaten egg.

3 Fold the remaining pastry in half lengthways. Using a sharp knife, cut diagonal slits right through the pastry, on the folded edge, to within 1 cm/½ in of the raw edge. Carefully lift on to one half of the filling and unfold. Ease into shape to cover the filling. The filling should be just visible through the slits.

4 Firmly press the edges together to seal. Knock up and flute. Brush with glaze, taking care to avoid brushing between the slits. Leave for 30 minutes in the refrigerator to relax.

5 Bake for 20-25 minutes, until risen and golden brown. Cool on a wire rack.

To Freeze: Allow to go cold, place in a polythene bag, seal and freeze.

To Serve: Thaw at room temperature for 3-4 hours. Serve cold or reheat at 160° C/ 325° F/gas 3 for 15 minutes. Serve with cream and brandy butter.

Above: *Mincemeat tart*

Below: *Cranberry potato balls*

Mincemeat tart

Serves 8-10
450 g/1 lb frozen puff pastry, defrosted
450 g/1 lb mincemeat (see page 94)
beaten egg, to glaze
To serve:
single cream
brandy butter (see Freezer Facts)

1 Heat the oven to 200° C/400° F/gas 6. Roll out the pastry to a long rectangle 40 x 25 cm/16 x 10 in. Cut in half crossways to make two rectangles 20 x 25 cm/8 x 10 in.

2 Carefully place one piece on a rinsed baking sheet, using a rolling pin to lift

Freezer Facts

Make brandy butter by beating together 100 g/4 oz unsalted butter and 100 g/4 oz icing sugar until creamy. Gradually beat in 4 tbls brandy and freeze. Serve with Mincemeat tart.

Cranberry potato balls

Serves 4
**450 g/1 lb potatoes, cut
  into chunks**
salt and pepper
25 g/1 oz butter, softened
4 tbls cranberry sauce
1 egg
50 g/2 oz golden breadcrumbs
To serve:
vegetable oil, for deep-frying
parsley sprigs, to garnish

1 Cook the potatoes in boiling salted water for 20 minutes, or until tender. Drain well.
2 Mash the potatoes, then rub through a sieve. Beat in the butter, then season with salt and pepper. Leave to cool, cover and refrigerate for 1 hour.
3 Form the cold potato into 12 balls about the size of table-tennis balls, then press the end of a wooden spoon handle into the centre of each one. Carefully put 1 tsp cranberry sauce into each indentation, then lightly re-shape so that the sauce is covered by potato.
4 Beat the egg in a shallow dish and spread the breadcrumbs on a flat plate. Dip each potato ball in the egg, then roll in the breadcrumbs until evenly coated.
To Freeze: Open freeze and pack in rigid containers. Cover, label and freeze.
To Serve: Thaw the potato balls. Heat the oil to 190° C/375° F, or until a stale bread cube turns golden in 50 seconds. Deep-fry the balls in the oil for 2 minutes, or until golden. Drain well on absorbent paper. Serve garnished with parsley.

Yuletide log

Makes 10 slices
65 g/2½ oz plain flour
40 g/1½ oz cocoa powder
1 tsp instant coffee powder
4 eggs
100 g/4 oz caster sugar
2-3 drops vanilla essence
100 g/4 oz unsalted butter, melted
caster sugar, for dredging
For the filling
150 g/5 oz caster sugar
5 egg yolks
275 g/10 oz unsalted butter
**200 g/7 oz plain chocolate,
  melted**

1 Heat the oven to 230° C/450° F/gas 8.

Above: *Yuletide log*

Line and grease a 36 x 25 cm/14 x 10 in Swiss roll tin.
2 Sift the flour, cocoa and coffee powders together. Place the eggs, sugar and vanilla essence in a bowl and whisk until pale and creamy, and increased 2-3 times in volume.
3 Fold in about ⅓ of the flour and cocoa mix, using a figure-of-eight motion. Pour over ⅓ of the cooled butter and fold in. Repeat twice more with the remaining flour and cocoa mix and melted butter.
4 Pour into prepared tin and lightly ease into the corners with a spatula, lightly smooth the surface. Bake on top of a baking sheet for 8-10 minutes, until well risen and springy to the touch.
5 Meanwhile lay a clean tea-towel on the work surface, cover with a large sheet of greaseproof paper, dredge with caster sugar. Turn the baked sponge on to the paper and carefully peel off the lining paper.
6 Trim the edges with a sharp knife and make a shallow cut along one short side, 1 cm/½ in from the edge. Carefully roll up the cut edge. Place on a wire rack, join side down, to cool.
7 Dissolve sugar in 200 ml/7 fl oz water over a gentle heat, stirring to dissolve,

then boil steadily until it reaches 103-104° C/216-218° F. Pour the hot syrup on to the egg yolks and whisk until a thick mousse is formed.
8 Cream the butter until soft, then beat in the mousse a little at a time. Stir in the cooled, melted chocolate.
9 Unroll the sponge, and spread with about half the filling. Re-roll firmly. Trim one end straight and the other at an angle, to look like a log.

10 Fill a piping bag fitted with a star nozzle with the remaining cream and pipe uneven lines, close together down the length of the cake. Pipe small irregularities in 2-3 places to look like bark. Pipe the ends.
To Freeze: Open freeze then pack in a rigid container and return to the freezer.
To Serve: Thaw at room temperature for 2-3 hours.

Guide to Freezing Everyday Foods

Everyone talks about 'storage times' as if it were a matter of life or death to leave food in your freezer a day longer than recommended. As far as safety goes, you could leave food frozen forever, practically, as long as it stays at a constant temperature of −18° C/0° F.

Food poisoning bacteria cannot multiply when food is frozen – only when you thaw it out. If it was contaminated in the first place, before freezing, the germs will start to multiply again as the food thaws.

So, food *can* be left in the freezer but food value, taste, colour and texture will begin to alter after differing lengths of time. That is why each food has a recommended storage life. After this time it will start to deteriorate, albeit slowly. There are differing opinions about how long storage times should be because everyone's ability to detect the changes varies considerably. Thus any recommendations given here are purely a guide for you.

It is also difficult to give exact storage times because any tests carried out to determine at what stage foods will deteriorate are carried out under ideal conditions. The temperature will stay the same, the food will be in perfect condition and will have been wrapped with maximum care. At home these ideal conditions cannot necessarily be achieved so, to compensate for this, our recommendations are definitely on the conservative side.

Freezing Everyday Foods

Food	Storage Time	Preparation	Thawing and serving
BREAD	6 months	Wrap in foil and seal with freezer tape or wrap in polythene bags. The crusts of 'crusty' loaves tend to 'shell off' after a week.	Thaw in sealed wrapper at room temp. for 3-6 hours. If foil-wrapped, thaw and reheat in a hot oven. Sliced bread can be toasted from frozen.
CAKES	**Iced:** 2 months **Plain:** 3 months **Fruit:** 6 months or more	Wrap plain cakes with freezer film or foil between layers. Roll Swiss rolls in cornflour not caster sugar before wrapping. Ice, if liked, but do not fill with jam as it soaks into cake.	Unwrap iced cakes before thawing. Cream cakes cut better when frozen. Thaw plain cakes wrapped, at room temperature, for 1-2 hours, iced up to 4 hours.
COMMERCIALLY FROZEN FOODS	Up to 3 months	No further preparation needed.	Follow packet directions.
DAIRY PRODUCTS	**Cheese:** 3-6 months	Freeze soft and cream cheeses in blocks. Grate hard cheese first. Do not freeze cottage cheese. Wrap in freezer film or polythene bags.	Thaw blocks in 'fridge. Bring to room temp. for serving. Use grated cheese from frozen.
	Cream: 3 months	Freeze double or whipping cream, not single. Piped rosettes can be open frozen then packed in a single layer in foil.	Thaw cream in 'fridge for 24 hours or at room temp. for 12 hours. Position rosettes for decoration while still frozen.
	Eggs, separated: 8-10 months	Pack in rigid containers. Mix 1 tsp salt or 2 tsps sugar with every 6 yolks. Label carefully. Freeze white separately.	Thaw in 'fridge or at room temp. for 1½ hours. Use as required.
	Yoghurt: 6 weeks	Sweetened, fruit yoghurts freeze well. Do not freeze natural yoghurts. Freeze in retail cartons, overwrap in freezer film.	Thaw for about 1 hour at room temp.

Food	Storage Time	Preparation	Thawing and serving
FATS	**Butter, salted:** 3 months **Butter, unsalted:** 6 months **Margarine:** as butter **Shredded suet:** 6 months	Overwrap in foil.	Thaw in 'fridge for about 4 hours per 225 g/8 oz.
FISH	**White:** 3 months **Oily (eg. salmon):** 2 months **Smoked:** 2-3 months **Shellfish:** 1 month **Caviar:** do not freeze	Must be very fresh. Freeze whole fish unwrapped. Remove from freezer, dip in cold water. Freeze. Repeat until ice glaze is 5 mm/¼ in thick. Wrap in freezer film or foil. Separate steaks or fillets with foil. Overwrap in foil. Cook shellfish before freezing.	Thaw in 'fridge for 24 hours. Thaw in 'fridge or cook from frozen. Partially thaw if coating in batter or egg and crumbs.
FISH DISHES	1-2 months	Prepare as usual. Do not add hard-boiled eggs until reheating.	Thaw in 'fridge or cook from frozen in a moderate oven.
HERBS	Up to 6 months	Freeze in small bunches or chop first. Store in rigid containers.	If whole, crumble while frozen. Use from frozen.
MEAT, raw	**Beef:** 8 months **Lamb:** 6 months **Pork:** 6 months **Minced meat:** 3 months **Offal:** 3 months **Sausages:** 3 months **Cured and smoked meat:** 1-2 months	Protect end of joint bones with foil. Wrap in freezer film then stockinette, muslin or foil and freezer tape. Separate steaks or chops with foil, then wrap in foil or polythene bags.	Most can be cooked from frozen but for large joints best thaw in 'fridge for 6 hours per 450 g/1 lb. If egg and crumb-coating, partially thaw first.
MEAT, cooked	**Casseroles etc:** 2-3 months **Sliced meat in gravy:** 3 months **Plain sliced meat:** 2 months **Meat loaves, pâtés:** 1 month	Prepare and cook in usual way but don't season heavily or use too much garlic or celery. Freeze in rigid containers or freezer/ovenware (see page 78). Turn meat loaves and pâtés out of tin, wrap in foil.	Reheat from frozen in a hot oven for 1 hour then reduce to moderate until hot through. Or heat gently in a saucepan. Best to thaw sliced meats thoroughly first. Also meat loaves and pâtés should thaw slowly, preferably overnight in 'fridge.

Food	Storage Time	Preparation	Thawing and serving
PASTRY, uncooked	3 months	Roll out and shape into pie shells or vol-au-vents. Make pies as usual, do not slit top crust. Freeze uncovered then wrap in freezer film.	Cook shells from frozen back in original dishes. Cook pies from frozen in a hot oven. Slit top crusts when starting to thaw, if liked.
PASTRY, cooked	3 months	Prepare in usual way. Brush edges with egg white before filling. When cold, wrap carefully as easily damaged. Protect top with paper plate if necessary before wrapping.	Thaw at room temp. for up to 4 hours. Reheat in oven if required. Or follow individual recipes.
PIZZAS	2 months	Make base in usual way. Cover with chosen topping. Open freeze then wrap in foil or polythene bags.	Remove packaging. Cook from frozen in a very hot oven for about 30 minutes.
SAUCES, SOUPS, STOCKS	3-6 months	Make as usual. When cold pour into rigid containers. Seal well.	Thaw for 1-2 hours at room temp. or heat from frozen until boiling. Sauces may need extra thickening when reheated.
POULTRY AND GAME	**Chicken:** 12 months **Duck:** 4-5 months **Turkey:** 6 months **Game birds:** 9 months **Giblets:** 2-3 months	Prepare in usual way. Do not stuff. Hang game birds before freezing. Cover ends of bones with foil. Pack in polythene bags. Freeze giblets separately if long-term storage. Joint birds before freezing for quicker cooking.	Thaw completely in 'fridge whenever possible. A small bird should be thawed overnight; up to 1.8 kg/4 lb, up to 12 hours; 1.8-5.5 kg/4-12 lb up to 24 hours; over 5.5 kg/12 lb up to 72 hours. Joints up to 6 hours.
SPONGE PUDDINGS	3 months	Make in usual way. Use foil or polythene basins. Cool then cover with foil and overwrap.	Steam in a steamer, or on an old saucer in a pan, with enough boiling water to come halfway up sides of basin, for about 45 mins-1 hour or until hot through when tested with a skewer.
SWEETS AND DESSERTS	2-3 months	Make in usual way. Ensure dishes are freezer-proof. Line dish with foil, open freeze, remove dish then wrap in polythene bags.	Remove foil lining and return to original dish. Thaw in 'fridge for up to 6 hours or at room temp. for about 2 hours. Decorate as required.

Foods That Cannot Be Frozen

Although most foods can be frozen in one form or another, some just don't take to being kept on ice. Here's a quick guide to foods that are best eaten just the way they are.

Bananas: go black but are okay cooked in a dish like banana bread when totally disguised.

Caviar: goes rather watery and should not be frozen.

Cheese: most freeze well but don't freeze cream or cottage cheese unless well mixed in a filling.

Custard: egg-based custards tend to separate and cornflour ones tend to go lumpy, but canned custard freezes well.

Eggs: don't freeze in the shell or when hard-boiled. Can be frozen separated (see page 124).

Garlic: if used in excess in dishes tends to give a musty flavour when frozen for quite a while.

Gelatine: soufflés and mousses freeze well for a few weeks then may start to separate. Dishes such as pure jellies do not freeze well. Beware too of aspic toppings, they will crack and look very unappetising after a while.

Jam: tends to liquefy in large quantities, e.g. a jam cake filling will soak into the cake.

Potatoes: some varieties go rather leathery unless mashed first. Tiny new ones can be frozen but are rather like canned ones when defrosted.

Mayonnaise: and other egg-based sauces tend to separate.

Salad stuffs: lettuce, cucumber, etc., will go limp if frozen.

Sauces: tend to be runnier when thawed.

Single cream: will separate and become 'grainy'.

Yoghurt: natural ones separate but can be frozen as part of a filling.

Freezing Vegetables

Only freeze top quality produce. Freezers can't work miracles – food will come out only as good as it goes in!

Select vegetables which are just mature. If they are too young they will lack flavour; if too old some toughness or 'woodiness' will occur.

Blanching is essential when preparing vegetables for freezing. This destroys the enzymes present and so preserves colour, flavour and texture. It also helps to retain the vitamin C content.

The same lot of blanching water can be used for six or seven batches of vegetables.

Prepare vegetables in the usual way. Blanch 450 g/1 lb only at a time. A blanching basket makes life easier and is not too expensive to buy. Simply plunge the prepared vegetables into not less than 4 litres/7 pts of rapidly boiling water with 2 tsps salt added. Quickly bring back to the boil and boil for the time stated in the chart on pages 128-129.

Remove immediately from saucepan and plunge into iced water to cool quickly. It should take the same length of time to cool as to blanch. Drain as soon as cool.

It is very important to blanch vegetables for the correct time – no longer – to ensure best results. A kitchen timer or watch with a second hand is really essential. Pack according to chart and freeze.

It is possible to freeze vegetables without blanching but it is not recommended for long term storage.

Although tomatoes are fruit, we have included them in this section as they are used in savoury dishes. Always pack prepared vegetables for the freezer in meal-sized portions. For instance, if you are a family of four and always eat together, pack enough for four people in each bag or container. If you sometimes cook just for two, or often entertain, say, six people, then pack some quantities accordingly.

DO NOT FREEZE chicory, cucumber, endive, lettuce, radishes or kale, except when made into a soup or sauce. Jerusalem artichokes are suitable only if puréed. Garlic in cooked dishes tends to taste musty if frozen for too long as do herbs.

Freezing Runner Beans

1 After blanching, plunge beans in the basket into a pan of ice-cold water.

2 Remove air from bag of beans by sucking it out through a straw.

Freezing Duchesse Potatoes

1 Pipe Duchesse potatoes on to a baking tray for open freezing.

2 Pack frozen potatoes in a foil container, cover and label.

Freezing Tomato Purée

1 Cook peeled, quartered tomatoes in their own juice to form purée.

2 After sieving, pour purée into a rigid container for freezing.

Freezing Vegetables

Food	Storage Time	Preparation	Thawing and cooking
ASPARAGUS	12 months	Grade according to thickness of stem. Trim and scrape stalks. Blanch: thin – 2 mins; thick – 4 mins. Tie in small bundles. Pack in polythene bags.	Plunge, frozen, in boiling, salted water for 3-5 mins.
AUBERGINES	12 months	Peel and thickly slice (about 2.5 cm/1 in) Blanch: 3 mins, open freeze (see Freezing Fruit, page 130). Pack in bags.	Plunge, frozen, in boiling, salted water for 5 mins, or thaw and use for Moussaka etc.
BEANS, French runner broad	12 months	French: top and tail. Blanch: 2-3 mins. Runner: string and slice. Blanch: 2 mins. Broad: shell. Blanch: 3 mins. Pack in bags.	Plunge, frozen, in boiling, salted water for 6-8 mins.
BEETROOT	6-8 months	Use small beets. Cook in boiling salted water until tender. Peel. Pack in bags.	Thaw in refrigerator before use.
BROCCOLI	12 months	Trim leaves and stems. Blanch: thick- 2 mins; thin – 1 min. Pack in rigid containers.	Plunge, frozen, in boiling, salted water for 5-8 mins.
BRUSSELS SPROUTS	12 months	Trim and grade. Blanch: small – 1½ mins; medium – 3 mins. Pack in bags.	Plunge, frozen, in boiling, salted water for 5-8 mins.
CARROTS	12 months	Grade. Scrub or scrape. Slice thickly or dice if large. Blanch: small, whole – 3 mins. Pack in bags.	Plunge, frozen, in boiling, salted water. Cook about 5 mins. Use frozen in stews and casseroles.
CAULIFLOWER	12 months	Break into even florets. Blanch: 3 mins. Pack in bags.	Plunge, frozen, in boiling, salted water for 5-8 mins.
CELERY	12 months	Trim off green. Cut in bite-sized pieces. Blanch: 3 mins. Pack in small quantities in polythene bags.	Use frozen in stews and casseroles.

Food	Storage Time	Preparation	Thawing and cooking
CORN-ON-THE-COB	12 months	Young cobs only. Remove husks and silks. Blanch: 4-6 mins. Pack in bags.	Thaw before cooking. Boil in water for about 5 mins.
COURGETTES	12 months	Cut in 2.5 cm/1 in slices. Blanch: 1 min. Pack in bags.	Plunge, frozen, in boiling, salted water for about 3 mins. Or thaw, then fry in butter.
MARROW	12 months	Peel, if tough. Dice, remove seeds. Blanch: 2 mins. Pack in bags.	Plunge, frozen, in boiling, salted water for about 5 mins.
PARSNIPS	12 months	Trim and peel. Cube or cut in 'fingers'. Blanch: 4 mins. Pack in bags.	Plunge, frozen, in boiling, salted water for about 10 mins. Or thaw then roast.
PEAS	12 months	Pod. Blanch: 1 min. Pack in bags.	Plunge, frozen, in boiling, salted water for about 5 mins.
PEPPERS, RED OR GREEN, raw blanched	6 months 12 months	Freeze whole without blanching or halve, de-seed and blanch 3 mins. Pack in polythene bags.	Use from frozen as required.
POTATOES, **Duchesse** croquettes chips	 3 months 3 months 3 months	Make in usual way. Pipe on to baking trays. Open freeze. Pack in rigid containers. Make in usual way. Toss in browned breadcrumbs. Open freeze. Pack in rigid containers. Prepare potatoes. Partially fry in hot oil for 2 mins. Open freeze, then pack in polythene bags.	Thaw, glaze with beaten egg, if liked. Cook at 200° C/400° F/gas 6 for about 15 mins. Thaw, deep-fry for about 4 mins. Cook from frozen or thawed in hot oil, until golden brown.
SPINACH	12 months	Wash very well. Blanch in small quantities, 2 mins. Press out excess moisture. Pack in bags.	Plunge, frozen, in just 1 cm/½ in boiling, salted water. Cook 5 mins, stir frequently. Drain well.
TOMATOES	12 months	Whole: plunge in boiling water 30 seconds, skin. Purée: skin as above, gently cook until tender in own juice. Blend or sieve. Pack in rigid containers.	Cook from frozen or thaw in refrigerator.
TURNIPS	12 months	Peel. Dice, if large. Blanch: whole – 4 mins, diced – 2 mins.	Plunge, frozen, in boiling, salted water for 10-15 mins.

Freezing Fruit

Like vegetables, only freeze fruit in tip-top condition. Over-ripe produce should be puréed first (great for sauces, desserts and even baby food – if frozen without sugar). These days, as many people are becoming sugar conscious, you may prefer to freeze currants and berries 'free flow' fashion. Simply pick over, wash and dry. Layer in a single layer on a tray or baking sheet lined with greaseproof paper. 'Open freeze' then pack in rigid containers or polythene bags and store in the freezer. If you prefer, coat each piece of fruit with sugar before open freezing on trays.

For those with a sweet tooth you can 'dry sugar pack' the fruit instead. Simply layer in rigid containers with the amount of sugar recommended in the chart on pages 131-132, cover, label and freeze.

Most stone fruits and others which tend to discolour, like apples and pears, are best frozen in syrup. Add lemon juice or ascorbic acid to prevent discoloration, as indicated in the chart on pages 131-132.

The chart tells you the quantity of sugar to water – it depends on the fruit. Make sure before you start the freezing ritual that you have sufficient syrup. It must be used cold so it's best to make it the night before you intend using it and chill overnight.

As a rough guide, you will need 300 ml/½ pint syrup to every 450 g/1 lb fruit.

Simply dissolve the sugar in the water, bring to the boil, leave to cool, lightly covered. When cold pour over fruit, prepared and packed in rigid containers. Prevent pieces of fruit from floating by adding crumpled, damp greaseproof paper. Cover with lids, seal and label before freezing. Make a note of the quantity of fruit in each container either on the label or in a notebook. After thawing, remove fruit from container just before serving so fruit stays immersed in syrup for as long as possible.

DO NOT FREEZE bananas or pomegranates. Avocados also do not freeze well, but can be frozen mashed with a little lemon juice, ready for use in a dip or soup.

Freezing Strawberries

1 *Select strawberries that are not over-ripe, wash carefully and hull.*

2 *Dip strawberries in sugar and arrange in rows for open freezing.*

Freezing Oranges and Lemons

1 *Dry sugar pack orange segments in layers with sugar in a rigid container.*

2 *Squeeze juice from lemons and freeze in ice-cube trays.*

Freezing Peaches

1 *Plunge peaches in boiling water, if necessary, to peel.*

2 *Cover peach halves with cold syrup and freeze.*

Freezing Fruit

Fruit	Storage Time	Preparation	Freezing
APPLES	12 months	Peel, core and slice evenly into a bowl of cold water with 1 tbls lemon juice added to prevent browning.	Blanch for 1 min. in boiling water. Drain, rinse with cold water, drain well. Pack in bags or rigid containers. OR prepare then stew in the minimum amount of water. Sweeten if liked. Mash or purée. Pack as above.
APRICOTS	12 months	Plunge in boiling water for 30 secs. Rinse with cold water. Peel, cut in half, stone.	Pack and cover in cold syrup using 225 g/8 oz sugar to 600 ml/1 pt water.
BLACKBERRIES	12 months	Pick over, removing stalks. Wash and dry if necessary.	Open freeze then pack in bags or rigid containers. OR Dry Sugar Pack using about 100 g/4 oz sugar to every 450 g/1 lb fruit.
CHERRIES	12 months	Wash, drain, remove stalks then stone if liked.	Open freeze then pack in bags or rigid containers. OR Dry Sugar Pack using 100 g/4 oz sugar to 450 g/1 lb fruit.
CURRANTS (red, black or white)	12 months	Top and tail, wash and dry if necessary.	Open freeze then pack in bags or rigid containers. OR for blackcurrants stew in a very little water with 100-175 g/4-6 oz sugar per 450 g/1 lb fruit. Purée if liked. Pack in rigid containers.
GOOSEBERRIES	12 months	Top and tail. Wash and dry if necessary.	Pack in bags or rigid containers. OR stew in a very little water with 100-175 g/4-6 oz sugar to every 450 g/1 lb fruit. OR pack and cover with cold syrup using 450 g/1 lb sugar to 600 ml/1 pt water.
GRAPEFRUIT	12 months	Squeeze juice. OR peel, removing pith, segment.	Pour into ice-cube trays. Freeze then transfer to bags. Dry Sugar Pack using 225 g/8 oz sugar to 450 g/1 lb fruit.

Fruit	Storage Time	Preparation	Freezing
GRAPES	6 months	Leave seedless whole. Skin, halve and de-pip others.	Pack and cover in cold syrup using 225 g/8 oz sugar to 600 ml/1 pint water.
LEMONS and LIMES	12 months	Squeeze juice. OR scrub well.	Pour into ice-cube trays. Freeze then transfer to bags. Freeze whole, in wedges or slices for garnishes and drinks, packed in bags or rigid containers.
MELONS	6 months	Remove seeds, cut flesh into balls or cubes, discarding skin. (They become rather soft after freezing but still taste good in a fruit salad.)	Pack and cover in cold syrup using 225 g/8 oz sugar to 600 ml/1 pt water.
ORANGES	12 months	Scrub whole Seville oranges. Peel, removing pith of sweet oranges. Segment or slice. OR squeeze juice.	Pack in bags ready to use for marmalade when needed. Dry Sugar Pack using 225 g/8 oz sugar to 450 g/1 lb prepared fruit. OR pack and cover with cold syrup using 450 g/1 lb sugar to 600 ml/1 pt water. Pour into ice-cube trays. Freeze then transfer to bags.
PEACHES and NECTARINES	12 months	Skin without plunging in boiling water if possible as flesh is very delicate. Halve, remove stones.	Brush with lemon juice. Pack and cover in cold syrup using 225 g/8 oz sugar to 600 ml/1 pt water. OR purée with 1 tbls lemon juice and 100 g/4 oz sugar to 450 g/1 lb fruit.
PEARS	12 months	Peel, quarter and core if liked.	Poach in syrup using 175 g/6 oz sugar to 600 ml/1 pt water with 1 tbls lemon juice or ¼ tsp ascorbic acid added. OR poach whole in half quantity of syrup with equal amount of wine or cider added for a complete dessert. Cool then pack in rigid containers.
PLUMS, DAMSONS, GREENGAGES	12 months	Skins tend to toughen after freezing. Wash, halve, remove stones.	Pack and cover in cold syrup using 225 g/8 oz sugar to 600 ml/1 pt water with 1 tbls lemon juice or ¼ tsp ascorbic acid added.
RASPBERRIES, STRAWBERRIES, LOGANBERRIES	12 months	Wash and dry carefully if necessary. Remove any stalks.	Open freeze then pack in bags or rigid containers. OR pack straight into rigid containers in small quantities. OR Dry Sugar Pack using 100 g/4 oz sugar to every 450 g/1 lb fruit. OR purée ripe fruit then freeze in rigid containers with or without sugar.
RHUBARB	12 months	Trim and cut into short lengths.	Pack straight into bags. OR blanch in boiling water for 1 min. Drain, rinse in cold water, drain well, then pack and cover with cold syrup using 450 g/1 lb sugar to 600 ml/1 pt water.

Freezer Maintenance

Unless you're lucky enough to have a self-defrosting freezer, you will have to defrost your freezer once or twice a year, or as often as the manufacturer's instructions recommend.

As a guide, when the ice is about 5 mm/¼ in thick it's time to take action. Defrosting is best done on a cold day and when the freezer is low on food (perhaps before you order your next batch of meat, before the garden produce becomes prolific or, in the case of smaller freezers, when you've deliberately 'run down' stocks ready for defrosting). Everyone has their own theory on how best to tackle the job. Here's what we suggest:

Have several large cardboard boxes to hand (the number depending on the amount of food in the freezer). Also find a couple of old blankets or rugs, a lot of old newspapers, and buckets or bowls to collect the ice.

1 Arrange the cardboard boxes, tightly together, in a group.

2 Line each box with several thicknesses of newspaper.

3 Remove packages of food from the freezer and pack close together in the boxes. Use a different box for each type of food. If you have, say, only a few bags of fruit or just a couple of loaves of bread, pack them on top of the food in one of the other boxes. If you have only a small freezer, pack all the contents in one or two boxes, keeping each type of food grouped together.

4 Cover the boxes with more layers of newspaper, then cover the whole lot with blankets or rugs for extra insulation.

5 Switch off the freezer.

6 If your freezer manufacturer's instructions allow it, put bowls of nearly boiling water in the freezer cabinet and leave the door open to help thaw the ice.

7 Scrape the ice from the interior surfaces of the freezer, using a plastic or wooden spatula. NEVER USE METAL TOOLS OR WIRE BRUSHES. Scoop the ice out of the bottom of the freezer into buckets or bowls. As it thaws, you will be able to knock off whole chunks very easily.

8 When empty, wipe out the cabinet with a clean cloth, then wash over with a

A freezer needs defrosting when the ice is about 5 mm/¼ in thick.

solution of 2 tbls bicarbonate of soda to 600 ml/1 pt water, just warm to the touch. This will remove any stale smells. Dry thoroughly.

9 Switch the freezer back on at the coldest setting. Check it is working properly for 15 minutes or so, then return the food packages. Switch to normal setting after 2-3 hours.

Defrosting the freezer provides a good opportunity for a 'sort out'. Use up things that have been in the freezer for some time, such as forgotten portions of leftovers, the odd bread roll or the nearly-finished container of ice-cream. Then, when everything goes back in, all neat

and tidy, you won't be wasting valuable space with bits and pieces.

Fortunately, freezers need very little other maintenance. From time to time the outside of the cabinet should be cleaned with warm, soapy water, rinsed and dried thoroughly. The dust should be removed occasionally from the network of pipes at the back, taking care not to damage them. If your freezer is in a garage or outhouse, polish it with silicone polish from time to time to help protect against damp. Finally, if you have your freezer serviced once a year or so it should stand you in good stead for many years to come.

One-pot Meals

Introduction

Let's face it, whether you're a single person on the go or someone who's looking for a quiet life, cooking for you and your flatmate or a busy mum or dad, everyday cooking can seem like an awesome task. But with our delicious and nutritious choice of all-in-one meals, you can say goodbye to endless preparation and washing up. There are thick and hearty soups, succulent casseroles and stews, main course vegetable dishes and salads and meals with pasta and rice.

Here we tell you all you need to know about cooking one-pot meals, including information on choosing ingredients, equipment and a wealth of suggestions for simple accompaniments.

So whatever the occasion, Sunday lunch, children's tea or Saturday supper, our minimum fuss recipes are bound to please family and friends and keep the cook smiling and as cool as a cucumber!

Cooking One-pot Meals

A one-pot meal is one which is cooked and served from a single pot, although some of the preparation may, but not necessarily, involve the use of one or more saucepans. The food in the pot makes a meal in itself, but a little French bread or salad are popular accompaniments.

Many people think that one-pot meals are all the same: stews, casseroles and other variations on a similar theme. But a soup can make a delicious one-pot meal and so can a pasta or vegetable based dish. Indeed, many one-pot meals involve cooking methods other than stewing or casseroling, such as braising, pot roasting or stir-frying.

Stewing or casseroling both refer to the long, slow method of cooking food in a simmering liquid. With both stewing or casseroling the meat is cut into small pieces and poultry is always jointed. Some authorities think that the difference between the two lies in the fact that stewed food is cooked on top of the cooker, rather than in the oven, as with casseroles (see Pork and pepper stew, page 173), while others believe that the only difference between the two methods is that casseroling refers to the dish in which the food is cooked.

While roasting is suitable for cooking large tender joints of meat or whole birds, pot roasting is an ideal method for cooking smaller and tougher joints. The meat is first browned and then placed on a bed of vegetables in a pan. The dish is cooked, tightly covered, over a gentle heat or in a low oven.

Braising is usually used for smaller cuts of meat, whole birds or poultry joints. The meat is first browned and then placed on a bed of vegetables. A little liquid is added and then the dish is covered tightly and cooked slowly in the oven.

Stir-frying is when finely shredded or thinly sliced ingredients are fried briefly in a little oil over a high heat. The ingredients are quickly turned over and over to ensure even cooking. Vegetables are just tender to the bite and cooking times are kept to a minimum.

Many people ask what is a hotpot? Strictly speaking, it is a casserole that's topped with a layer of crunchy golden potatoes (see Lancashire hotpot, page 171), although the term has been used to describe a number of meat and vegetable dishes with different toppings or indeed without any topping.

Choosing ingredients

No matter how delicious a recipe may sound, the final result is often only as good as its basic ingredients. So when stocking up the larder for one-pot meals, it is wise to look for the best quality food available.

When buying vegetables, aubergines, for example, should be firm, with shiny deep purple skins and no wrinkles. Cabbages shouldn't show any signs of wilting and should have firm heads with closely packed leaves. Cauliflowers should be creamy coloured and firm, with closely packed curds. Look for bright coloured carrots. Maincrop carrots should be tender with no woody core. New carrots should snap easily and have no green tops. Celery should have crisp stalks with no discolouration. Courgettes should be

Below: *All sorts of casserole dishes are suitable for one-pot meals*

smooth and firm. Leeks with withering yellow tops are not suitable buys. Avoid mushrooms which are limp, broken and look 'sweaty', and reject onions which are sprouting; pick those with firm, dry skins.

Choose firm turnips and parsnips, and firm and bright coloured peppers. When picking potatoes, avoid those with sprouts, cuts and soft or green spots. Look out for unblemished tomatoes; avoid 'soft' ones.

With many one-pot meals which call for pot roasting, braising, casseroling or stewing, cheaper cuts of meat are used and the results are extremely satisfying. So the best cuts are not essential by any means. But, as everyone knows, long slow cooking spoils fish! So pick the best available, that is look out for fish with firm flesh, clear and shiny eyes, bright red gills and a clean smell. Steaks, cutlets and fillets should have firm, closely packed flakes. Use fresh fish on the day it is purchased.

Remember, it is essential to avoid goods in cans that are damaged, and that means cans that are dented or those that are bulging or have rusty edges. Do not open cans until ready to use; transfer left-overs to a sealed container and use on the same day.

Useful equipment

Certain items of kitchen equipment are particularly handy when it comes to preparing one-pot meals, and if you cook on a regular basis, it is likely that you will have several or more of these utensils. But for those of you in the process of furnishing your kitchen, in addition to such basic items as measuring scales or a balloon whisk, it would be wise to include the following on your list of essentials.

Wooden spoons, in two or three sizes, for mixing, a slotted spoon for transferring food from the frying pan to the casserole dish or putting it aside, sharp knives for paring and chopping, a knife sharpener, a ladle for serving soup and transferring liquids, and a colander for draining vegetables, rice and pasta are all very useful tools.

So too are an electric blender, food mill and sieve when it comes to making soups; plus kitchen scissors, for snipping chives and derinding bacon.

Heavy based saucepans are a necessity too. Ideally you want one 1.7 L/3 pt pan, one 2.8 L/5 pt or 3.5 L/6 pt pan and one 1.2 L/2 pt milk pan. You will also need a large frying pan with a lid to use for browning meat and vegetables before casseroling and for making a host of one-pot meals, such as Chilli con carne, page 168, or stir-fry dishes, such as Pork chow mein, page 172. A flameproof casserole is also extremely useful, preferably the heavy cast iron kind with an enamelled lining. You may find, as time passes, that you need two sizes, one for serving four people, the other, much larger, for entertaining. The pot should hold the ingredients comfortably. You can prepare the ingredients in the frying pan and then transfer them to an ovenproof casserole, but this increases washing up and preparation time.

The wok

Eventually, you might want to purchase a wok for stir-frying, but this is not an essential piece of equipment. A wok is the traditional Chinese cooking pot. It's round in shape, about 30–35 cm/12–14 in in diameter, with a deep bowl and a dome-shaped lid. A stand is usually supplied to hold the wok at the right height over a gas cooker. (Flat bottomed versions are now available for use on electric or gas cookers.)

The traditional wok is made of carbon steel and is very durable. It must always

Above: *A wok is the ideal utensil for all-in-one stir-fry recipes*

be seasoned before use: wash in hot water, warm over moderate heat, then wipe with a piece of absorbent paper soaked in cooking oil.

The microwave

A microwave oven is also an extremely popular and indeed very useful kitchen appliance, and for this reason we've included microwave instructions for many of our recipes. See pages 14-25 for information on microwave cooking.

The slow cooker

Also useful, but not vital, is an electric slow cooker. This is a self contained cooking pot (also known as a crockpot) with its own electric element that's designed to produce the slow continuous heat needed for casseroles. It is easy to use and economical and can be left unattended quite safely, hence it is ideal for overnight or away-day cooking.

In the slow cooker, a casserole will take anything from 5-8 hours to cook and will come to no harm if left for 10 hours. But you must prepare everything before you go out or retire to bed; and, depending on the model, you may have to allow 20 minutes or more for the pot to heat on HIGH before switching to the low setting for continuous cooking.

Some models can change automatically from one setting to another.

Recipes for conventional cooking methods will have to be adapted for use in the slow cooker, though after practice you can easily devise your own recipes with delicious results. As a rule, one should use less liquid than recommended in ordinary recipes as there is little evaporation; the crockpot is tightly sealed and cooking is so gentle.

When choosing a slow cooker, pick a size that suits your household's needs. A model with a removable pot is preferable to one that is fixed for cleaning and serving meals. Remember always to follow the manufacturer's instructions.

The pressure cooker

Busy cooks might also consider buying a pressure cooker. It cuts down considerably on the amount of time needed for cooking casseroles and as a consequence saves on fuel. However, some cooks do find that vegetables and fruit can easily overcook in the pressure cooker and also that flavour is sacrificed when casseroling cheaper cuts of meat which benefit from long slow cooking.

Pressure cookers have an airtight seal which prevents steam from escaping. As the pan contents are heated on top of the cooker, pressure builds up inside and the liquid can reach a temperature as high as 121° C/250° F (normal cooking temperatures never exceed 100° C/212° F which is boiling point). So cooking time is speeded up considerably.

Most cookers are made of aluminium. Some have a non-stick lining and come with a set of baskets so you can cook different foods at the same time. You should try to buy the largest size you can afford and store comfortably because you can never fill the cooker to maximum capacity. After all the ingredients have been added, the base should not be more than one-half to two-thirds full. The exact amount depends on what you are making. If too full the steam will not have enough room to circulate.

As with the microwave and slow cooker, pressure cooker cooking methods differ from conventional cooking methods, so it is important that you follow the manufacturer's instructions and use recipes specifically designed for the cooker until you are more familiar with how to use it.

Before you do use one of your own adaptations, try to find a similar recipe that's been devised for the pressure cooker (and tested!). Perhaps there is one in your instructions manual. This will give you some idea of the method you should be following. As a rule however,

Above: *Pressure cookers cut down the cooking time of all ingredients*

with whatever you make, you should always use at least 300 ml/½ pt liquid such as water, stock or milk; melted fat or oil should not be part of the extra liquid. After each 15 minutes of cooking time you must add a further 125 ml/¼ pt liquid for the next 15 minutes of cooking time or part thereof. Thickening agents should be added after – not before – cooking and canned soups and sauces should be mixed with 125 ml/¼ pt water before cooking.

Below: *Vegetable hot pot takes about 25 minutes to microwave.*

Serving One-pot Meals

What to serve

Serve our delicious recipes on their own or, to please hearty appetites and provide extra variety, serve them with a very simple accompaniment of your choice. Indeed, the possibilities are almost infinite!

With soups

Garnishes They enhance the appearance, flavour and texture of so many soups. Try pasta with thinnish soups. Break macaroni, tagliatelle or spaghetti into short pieces and add to soups for the last 20 minutes of cooking. But do cook

Below: *Home-made stock will improve the flavour of all soups and stews*

the pasta separately if you don't want the starch to cloud the soup.

Try bread croûtons too. Remove the crusts from slices of white bread and cut the crustless bread into 1 cm/½ in cubes. Toast or, preferably, fry the cubes in a little butter or margarine, until crisp and golden. Drain on absorbent paper and serve separately or sprinkle over the top.

Another particularly savoury garnish for a meat and vegetable soup is a streaky bacon rasher or two, fried until crisp, then chopped or crumbled and sprinkled over.

Suitable vegetable garnishes are lightly fried, thin slices of mushrooms or onion rings, drained and sprinkled over – good for hot soups. For garnishing chilled soups, use strips of cucumber,

carrot or celery. Try diced fruit, such as apple. See Curried apple soup, page 150, for example.

Herbs make wonderfully attractive garnishes. Try snipped chives, chopped mint, parsley or coriander. Paprika looks very pretty sprinkled over a pale coloured soup.

Filling extras Dumplings are a most welcome accompaniment for a meat and vegetable soup, and indeed turn the meal into quite a substantial feast! Mix 100 g/4 oz sifted self-raising flour with 50 g/2 oz shredded suet and a sprinkling of parsley or mixed herbs and salt and pepper. Using a round bladed knife, bind the mixture with sufficient cold water (about 6 tablespoons) to make a soft but not too sticky dough. Knead lightly, then shape into about 16 small

Above: *A hearty beef stew is a real winter warmer*

balls and drop them into the simmering soup for the last 20 minutes or so of the cooking time. The dumplings will float on top. Remember to cover the pot. For a delicious example, see Oxtail dumpling soup, page 150.

Melba toast is a popular extra with soups. Toast thin slices of white bread, then split them through the middle and toast the uncooked surfaces.

With hot or even chilled soups, hot garlic or herb bread is delicious. Cut French bread sticks into slices at an angle, but do not cut right through the loaf. Place the loaf on a piece of foil large enough to wrap well around it, covering the ends. Spread the slices with melted butter and crushed garlic, or creamed butter and crushed garlic. Spread any remaining mixture over the top. Wrap the loaf in foil and then reserve for warming when required in an oven preheated to 425° F/220° C/gas 7 for 15–20 minutes. Quantities depend on how many you have to serve and how much you like the taste of garlic! For herb bread, substitute parsley and chopped chives for the garlic. If liked, sprinkle a little grated Parmesan cheese on top.

Other successful bread alternatives are warmed crusty bread rolls, thick slices of wholemeal bread, or pitta bread.

Try, too, with soups, a mixed green or simple green salad with an oil and vinegar dressing. For the dressing, use three parts oil to one part vinegar, add a dash of French mustard, salt and pepper to taste and mix very well. Or, put all the ingredients together in a screw top jar, cover tightly and shake to blend thoroughly. Mix again just before pouring over and tossing the salad.

Add colour and variety to your salads by adding peeled, chopped and seeded orange or grapefruit, or peeled and sliced avocado. Peeled, cored and chopped pear or apple are delicious additions too. For extra flavour, add a squeeze of lemon to the dressing.

With fish
Salads are perfect partners, as with soups. Add sliced olives and radishes, tomatoes or indeed croûtons and crisply

Below: *Use chicken pieces for quick cooking and easy serving as in Cider pot roast chicken (page 175)*

cooked bacon bits. Try grilled mushrooms or tomatoes or puréed vegetables. Garlic bread is a delicious extra, especially with a fish stew.

With meat and poultry
Try boiled, baked or creamed potatoes or a seasonal vegetable cooked until just tender and tossed with a little butter. Or offer plain boiled rice; with Chilli con carne, page 168, it's perfect. Or serve buttered green or egg noodles; with Pork and pepper stew, page 173, either is ideal.

Toppings These are a wonderful way to add substance to a meat or poultry dish. For beef stews, coat thick slices of bread with mustard on one side and butter on the other. Place the bread, mustard side down, on top of the stew. Push the bread down so the mustard mingles with and flavours the meat juices. Bake for 20 minutes at 200° C/400° F/gas 6 or until a rich brown crust has formed.

A thick crust of mashed potato provides a perfect topping for many meat dishes like Cottage pork pie, page 172. Use other vegetables such as carrot and parsnip or swede in the same way. For a carrot and potato purée use 350 g/12 oz each of carrots and potatoes. Peel and boil them separately in salted water under tender. Drain and return to the heat to dry off any excess moisture. Mash or sieve the vegetables, then mix them together to form a purée. Beat in 25 g/1 oz butter or margarine and about 3 tablespoons of milk. Add salt and pepper to taste, spoon over the meat filling and bake for 20 minutes at 190° C/ 375° F/gas 5.

Try a crumble topping. Rub fat into flour in the proportions of 100 g/4 oz flour to 50 g/2 oz butter. Add seasoning and herbs that will complement the filling. For a crunchier topping, use 50 g/ 2 oz oats in place of 50 g/2 oz flour or add 25 g/1 oz chopped nuts to the basic mix-

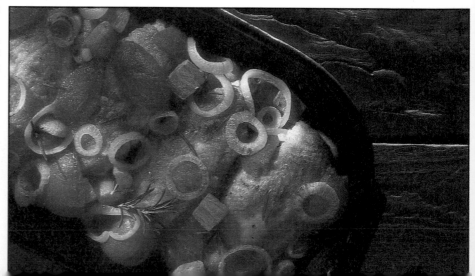

Above: *Pitta bread and a salad are the only accompaniments necessary for some one-pot meals*

ture. Instead of herbs, use 1 tsp grated lemon zest or 25 g/1 oz grated cheese for a different taste. Once the crumble is spooned over the filling, bake for about 30 minutes at 190° C/375° F/gas 5.

Forcemeat balls will cook perfectly well on top of an oven-cooked casserole if the lid is left off so they can become crisp. Mix 100 g/4 oz fresh white bread-crumbs mixed with 50 g/2 oz shredded suet, 1 tbls chopped parsley, 1 tsp grated lemon zest, and salt and pepper to taste. Bind with 1–2 eggs to make a moist mix-ture. Shape into balls, place on top of the casserole and bake for 20 minutes at 190° C/375° F/gas 5.

Scones, cut into rounds or triangles, make scrumptious toppings for cas-seroles. Rub 50 g/2 oz butter into 225 g/8 oz sifted self-raising flour with 1 tsp baking powder, then mix with enough milk (about 150 ml/1/4 pt) to make a soft dough. Roll out to 20 mm/3/4 in thick, cut into shapes and bake on top of the cas-serole for 20 minutes at 220° C/425° F/gas 7.

You can make potato scones by mix-ing 175 g/6 oz mashed potato into the rubbed in mixture. Make cheese scones by adding 50 g/2 oz grated cheese to the rubbed in mixture. Or simply add herbs and seasonings to the basic mixture.

Gnocchi, an Italian dish made with semolina, is particularly good for topping chicken stews. Bring 600 ml/1 pt milk to the boil, season with salt and pepper and add 175 g/6 oz semolina. Stir until the mixture thickens. Remove from the heat and stir in 50 g/2 oz grated cheese and a beaten egg. Turn into a 23 × 23 cm/9 × 9 in greased tin and leave until cold. Cut into squares or triangles and arrange over the oven-baked casserole. Sprinkle with a little more grated cheese and bake for about 30 minutes at 190° C/375° F/gas 5.

And don't forget the dumplings! Use the recipe on pages 141-142, but make larger balls, about 4–8, and place on top of the stew or casserole for the last 20 minutes or so of cooking time. See Rich beef stew with parsley dumplings, page 169, for a mouth-watering example.

With vegetables and salads

As with soups, garlic or herb bread, or thick slices of wholemeal bread and but-ter, or warmed pitta bread – try the wholemeal variety – all make delicious extras. You may, depending on the dish, wish to offer plain boiled white or brown rice or buttered noodles sprinkled with a little parsley. Try cooking the rice in a little chicken or vegetable stock.

With pasta and rice

Do leave out the garlic bread for the sake of your waistline but try a variety of salads. With some dishes, you might like to serve a bowl of grated Parmesan or mature Cheddar cheese for sprinkling.

Recipe notes

When using a recipe, for best results follow either the metric or the imperial measurements as they are not exact equivalents. The recipes have been tested using graded measuring spoons and jugs and measurements are level unless otherwise stated. Use the centre shelf of the oven unless the recipe gives other directions.

Microwave recipes have been tested on 650/700 watt ovens and on full power unless otherwise stated. For a 600 watt model, add 20 seconds per minute to the cooking time. If the recipe says 30 seconds, equivalent cooking time on 600 watt is 40 seconds etc.

143

Soups

Steaming pots of goodness, that's our delicious selection of soups to make a meal. For a light snack on warm days, try Curried apple or Prawn and tomato soup. For chilly winter nights by the fire, serve Oxtail dumpling soup or New England fish chowder. Here are soups to suit all tastes and appetites and they're all so delicious and yet so easy to make.

Creamy vegetable soup

Serves 6
25 g/1 oz butter
2 onions, finely chopped ·
175 g/6 oz carrots, thinly sliced
2 celery stalks, sliced
850 ml/1½ pt chicken stock
1 small green pepper, seeded and
 diced
100 g/4 oz button mushrooms,
 sliced
1 tbls chopped parsley
3 tbls cornflour
300 ml/½ pt milk
3 tbls single cream
salt and freshly ground black
 pepper
bread croûtons, to garnish
 (optional)

1   Melt the butter in a large saucepan, add the onions and fry gently for 5 minutes. Add carrots and celery; cook for 2–3 minutes, stirring occasionally.
2   Add the chicken stock, bring to the boil, then lower the heat, cover and simmer gently for 30 minutes.
3   Add the green pepper, mushrooms and parsley. Cook for 15–20 minutes.
4   In a bowl, blend cornflour with a little of the milk to form a paste. Stir the remaining milk into the pan, then add the cornflour paste. Bring to the boil and simmer for 1 minute, stirring constantly.
5   Remove from heat and stir in cream, then reheat gently. Season to taste.

Below: *Creamy vegetable soup*

6   Pour into warmed soup bowls, garnish, if liked, and serve at once.

To Microwave
Place the butter and onions in a large casserole and cook for 3 minutes. Add the carrots and celery and cook for 2 minutes. Add the hot stock, cover and microwave for 10 minutes. Add the pepper, mushrooms and parsley. Re-cover and cook for 5 minutes. Blend the cornflour and milk together. Add to the soup and cook for 3 minutes, stirring 2–3 times. Finish as above.

Prawn and tomato soup

Illustrated on pages 144-145
Serves 6
450 g/1 lb very ripe tomatoes,
 roughly chopped
2 celery stalks, roughly chopped
1.2 L/2 pt fish stock
salt and freshly ground black
 pepper
225 g/8 oz firm tomatoes
200 g/7 oz pimientos, drained
175 g/6 oz frozen prawns, defrosted
juice of 1 lemon
2–3 tbls finely snipped chives
whole prawns, to garnish (optional)

1   Place the ripe tomatoes and celery in a large pan with the fish stock and salt and pepper. Bring to the boil and simmer for 30 minutes.
2   Meanwhile, blanch, skin and seed the firm tomatoes and cut the flesh into

3 mm/⅛ in dice. Cut the pimientos into 3 mm/⅛ in dice.
3   Drain the prawns, and sprinkle with the lemon juice and salt and pepper.
4   Strain the stock mixture into a clean pan. Add the prawns, tomato and

pimiento and season to taste. Bring to just below boiling point and ladle into 6 individual bowls. Sprinkle with chives and garnish with whole prawns, if liked.

To Microwave
Place the tomatoes and celery in a large casserole with the boiling stock and seasoning. Cover and cook for 15 minutes. Prepare the tomatoes, pimientos and prawns as above. Strain the stock mixture into a clean casserole. Add the prawns, tomato, pimiento and seasoning. Cover and cook for 3 minutes. Serve as above.

Frankfurter and vegetable soup

Serves 4
2 tbls vegetable oil
175 g/6 oz carrots, cut into 1 cm/½
 in dice
1 celery stalk, thinly sliced
250 g/9 oz turnips, cut into 1 cm/½
 in dice
1 onion, chopped
1 clove garlic, crushed (optional)
700 ml/1¼ pt beef stock
400 g/14 oz can chopped tomatoes
salt and freshly ground black
 pepper
50 g/2 oz green cabbage leaves,
 shredded
25 g/1 oz small pasta shapes
100 g/4 oz frankfurters, cut into
 5 mm/¼ in slices
50 g/2 oz Cheddar cheese, grated

1 Heat the oil in a heavy-based saucepan, add the carrots, celery, turnips, onion and garlic, if using, and cook over moderate heat for 7 minutes, stirring.

2 Remove from the heat and stir in the stock and tomatoes. Season to taste with salt and pepper.

3 Return the pan to the heat and bring to the boil. Lower the heat, cover the pan and simmer for 20 minutes.

4 Add the cabbage and pasta, then cover again and simmer for a further 10 minutes until the pasta is soft.

5 Stir in the frankfurters, taste and adjust seasoning, and cook for a further 3 minutes.

6 Ladle into warmed individual bowls or a soup tureen and serve at once. Hand the grated cheese in a separate bowl for sprinkling on top of the soup.

To Microwave
Place the oil, carrots, celery, turnips, onion and garlic, if using, in a casserole and cook for 5 minutes. Add the stock and tomatoes and season to taste. Cover and microwave for 10 minutes. Add the cabbage·and pasta, re-cover and cook for 5 minutes. Add the frankfurters, adjust the seasoning, re-cover and cook for 3 minutes. Serve as above.

Frankfurter and potato soup In place of the turnips, use potatoes; and for sprinkling, serve Parmesan cheese instead of the Cheddar. Croûtons, or fried bread cubes, make a delicious garnish.

Above: *Frankfurter and vegetable soup*

4 Add the cauliflower and simmer for a further 5 minutes. Add the peas and lettuce. Simmer for 3–5 minutes more, until the vegetables are just cooked.

5 To serve, place the lamb chops in individual soup bowls. Spoon the soup and vegetables over and sprinkle with parsley.

To Microwave
Place the hot stock in a large casserole, cover and microwave for 5 minutes or

Below: *Scottish lamb soup*

until boiling. Add the chops, re-cover and cook for 5 minutes. Add the carrots, turnips and spring onions. Re-cover and cook for 8 minutes. Skim off any fat. Add the cauliflower and cook for 5 minutes. Add the peas and lettuce and cook for a further 3 minutes. Serve the soup in individual bowls as above.

Scottish vegetable soup Omit the lamb chops and substitute 2 chopped onions for the spring onions. Garnish with croûtons, or fried bread cubes, and a sprinkling of grated hard cheese. Or hand round a bowl of grated hard cheese separately.

Scottish lamb soup

Serves 6
1.2 L/2 pt chicken stock
6 lamb chops, trimmed of excess fat
6 carrots, diced
4 young turnips, diced
8 spring onions, sliced
salt and freshly ground black pepper
1 cauliflower, broken into florets
350 g/12 oz frozen peas
1 lettuce, shredded
1 tbls chopped parsley

1 Bring the stock to the boil in a large saucepan.

2 Add the chops to the pan. Simmer gently for 10 minutes.

3 Add the carrots, turnips and spring onions to the pan. Season with salt and pepper and simmer for a further 10 minutes. Skim the soup, if necessary, to remove any fat from the surface.

3 Remove the onions from the pork fat and sprinkle over the fish.
4 Discard any fat remaining in the pan. Sprinkle the flour into the pan and stir in the milk, thyme and salt and pepper.
5 Pour the mixture into the casserole, cover and simmer over low heat for 1½ hours without stirring. Season to taste and sprinkle with the pork just before serving.

To Microwave
Preheat a browning dish for 4 minutes. Add the pork and microwave for 4 minutes, stirring twice. Remove and reserve. Add the onions and cook for 3 minutes. Place the potatoes in a large casserole with 4 tbls water. Cover and cook for 5 minutes. Cut the fish into 4 cm/1½ in dice, add to the casserole and top with the onions. Mix the flour with the milk, thyme and seasoning. Pour into the casserole, cover and cook for 20 minutes. Reduce power to Defrost for 30 minutes. Finish as above.

Chilean fish soup

Serves 6
3 tbls oil
2 onions, finely chopped
1 green or red pepper, deseeded and finely chopped
2 carrots, thinly sliced
1 kg/2¼ lb potatoes, quartered
1 bay leaf
¼ tsp dried oregano

Above: *New England fish chowder*

New England fish chowder

Serves 6
200 g/7 oz salt pork, derinded and diced
3 large onions, coarsely chopped
6 small potatoes, diced
1 kg/2¼ lb haddock or cod fillets
2 tbls plain flour
1 L/1¾ pt milk
1 tsp dried thyme
salt and freshly ground black pepper

1 Fry the pork in a large saucepan until golden. Remove the pork with a slotted spoon, drain on absorbent paper and reserve. Brown the onions in the pork fat.
2 Meanwhile, in a flameproof casserole, boil the potatoes for 5 minutes in just enough water to cover them. Cut the fish into 4 cm/1½ in pieces and add to the casserole.

3 Add the fish and simmer gently, uncovered, for about 5 minutes, or until the fish is tender but not breaking up. Remove the bouquet garni, stir in the parsley, then serve.

To Microwave
Place the oil and onions in a large casserole and cook for 6 minutes. Add the tomatoes and juice and bouquet garni. Microwave for 5 minutes, stirring twice. Add the potatoes, olives, capers, tomato juice and hot stock. Cover and cook for 8 minutes. Add the fish, cover and cook for 5 minutes. Finish as above.

Scotch broth

Serves 4–6
25 g/1 oz pearl barley
225 g/8 oz stewing steak, finely diced
1.2 L/2 pt cold water
100 g/4 oz leeks, sliced
250 g/9 oz carrots, diced
250 g/9 oz swede, diced
salt and pepper
50 g/2 oz green cabbage, sliced
2–3 tbls freshly chopped parsley

1 Blanch the barley, then place with the meat in a large saucepan and pour in the water. Bring slowly to the boil, then lower the heat, cover and simmer for 1 hour. Skim off any excess fat.
2 Add the leeks, carrots and swede and season with salt and pepper. Cover and simmer gently for another 1½ hours.
3 Add the cabbage and cook for a further 10 minutes. Skim again to remove any more excess fat. Serve sprinkled with parsley.

Below: Scotch broth

3 parsley sprigs
1.5 L/2½ pt fish stock or water
1.5 kg/3¼ lb cod or haddock fillets, cut into 6 slices
2 tbls chopped fresh coriander, to garnish (optional)

1 Heat the oil in a large flameproof casserole over medium heat and fry the onions until soft but not browned.
2 Add the pepper, carrots, potatoes and herbs. Stir, and cook for 2–3 minutes. Pour in the stock or water, cover and simmer for about 15 minutes until potatoes and carrots are almost tender.
3 Add the fish, cover and simmer for about 10 minutes until the fish is tender. Remove the bay leaf and parsley. Ladle the soup into a warmed tureen, sprinkle with the coriander, if liked, and serve.

Above: Chilean fish soup

300 ml/½ pt tomato juice
600 ml 1 pt vegetable stock
salt and pepper
700 g/1½ lb coley fillets, skinned and cut into 4 cm/1½ in pieces
3 tbls finely chopped fresh parsley

1 Heat the oil in a large saucepan, add the onions and fry gently for 5 minutes. Add the tomatoes, with their juice, and the bouquet garni. Bring to the boil, then simmer for 5 minutes, stirring and breaking up the tomatoes.
2 Add all the remaining ingredients except the parsley and simmer uncovered, for 10–15 minutes, or until the potato is cooked.

Mediterranean fish chowder

Serves 4–6
3 tbls vegetable oil
450 g/1 lb onions, grated
850 g/28 oz can tomatoes
bouquet garni
2 potatoes, cubed
24 black olives, halved and stoned
2 tbls capers, drained

Left: *Mediterranean fish chowder*

Oxtail dumpling soup

Serves 4
600 ml/1 pt packet oxtail soup
 powder
600 ml/1 pt cold water
100 g/4 oz carrot, coarsely grated
100 g/4 oz swede, coarsely grated
For the dumplings
100 g/4 oz self-raising flour
40 g/1½ oz shredded suet
½ tsp mustard powder
¼ tsp dried mixed herbs
100 g/4 oz corned beef, finely
 chopped
salt and freshly ground black
 pepper
about 4 tbls water

1   Make the dumplings: sift the self-raising flour into a bowl and add the shredded suet, mustard powder, herbs and corned beef. Season with salt and pepper, then make a well in the centre of the mixture and add a little water Gradually

Below: Oxtail dumpling soup

work the dry ingredients into the centre until evenly mixed, adding just enough water to form a fairly firm dough. Divide the dough into 12 portions then roll each portion into a ball.

2   Put the soup powder into a wide pan, add the water and bring to the boil, stirring occasionally.

3   Add the coarsely grated carrot and coarsely grated swede then, when the soup is just coming back to the boil, drop the dumplings into it. Lower the heat and simmer, covered, for 18–20 minutes, stirring the soup occasionally to prevent sticking.

4   Carefully spoon the Oxtail dumpling soup into individual warmed bowls and serve at once.

To Microwave

Make the dumplings as above. Mix the soup powder and water together in a casserole and cook for 6 minutes or until boiling, stirring occasionally. Add the coarsely grated carrot and swede, cover and cook for 2 minutes. Add the dumplings, re-cover and cook for 8–10 minutes. Serve as above.

Beef dumpling soup   Use a 425 g/15 oz can beef consommé with 150 ml/¼ pt water in place of the oxtail packet soup and 600 ml/1 pt water. In place of the finely chopped corned beef, use cooked minced beef.

Curried apple soup

Illustrated on pages 144-145
Serves 4

25 g/1 oz butter
1 onion, coarsely chopped
2 dessert apples
850 ml/1½ pt chicken stock
1 tbls curry powder
salt and freshly ground black
 pepper
2 large egg yolks
150 ml/5 fl oz double cream
juice of ½ lemon
16–20 watercress leaves

1   Melt the butter in a large saucepan, add the coarsely chopped onion and fry gently until transparent. Peel, core and slice 1 apple and add to the pan with the chicken stock and curry powder. Bring to the boil, then cover and simmer for 20 minutes.

2   Purée the mixture in an electric blender, then pass it through a sieve into a clean saucepan. Season to taste with salt and pepper. Mix the egg yolks with the cream, add to the soup then stir over a low heat until the soup thickens.

3   Transfer the soup to a serving bowl. Cool, then chill for at least 2 hours.

4   Peel, core and dice the remaining

apple and sprinkle with the lemon juice so that it keeps it colour. Just before serving, stir the diced apple and watercress into the soup.

French onion soup

Illustrated on pages 144-145
Serves 6
40 g/1½ oz butter
3 tbls olive oil
½ tsp caster sugar
**700 g/1½ lb onions, sliced thinly
    into rings**
1.5 L/2½ pt beef stock
For the topping
4 tbls brandy
½ tsp French mustard
**salt and freshly ground black
    pepper**
**6 slices of French bread, each
    3 cm/1¼ in thick**
15–25 g/½–1 oz butter
75 g/3 oz Gruyère cheese, grated

1 In a large saucepan heat the 40 g/
1½ oz butter with the olive oil and caster
sugar. Add the onion rings and cook
over a fairly low heat for 15–20 minutes,
stirring frequently, until the onions are
golden brown.
2 Gradually stir in the beef stock, bring
to the boil, lower the heat, cover the pan
and simmer gently for 1 hour. The soup
should have reduced to about 1.2 L/2 pt
in this time. Meanwhile, heat the oven to
230° C/450° F/gas 8.
3 Stir the brandy and French mustard
into the soup and season to taste with salt
and pepper, if necessary.
4 Toast the slices of French bread and
spread them on one side with butter. Put
a round of toasted French bread in each
of 6 ovenproof soup bowls. Ladle the
onion soup into bowls, wait for a few
seconds while the toast floats up to the
surface, then heap 2 tbls grated Gruyère

cheese on each toast round.
5 Place the bowls of soup in the oven
for 10–15 minutes, until the cheese
is golden brown and bubbling. Serve
immediately.

Autumn soup

Serves 4–6
3 tbls vegetable oil
1 large onion, chopped
2 carrots, cut into 1 cm/½ in dice
**1 small swede, cut into 1 cm/½ in
    dice**
**½ green pepper, seeded and
    thinly sliced**
1 tbls tomato purée
1 L/1¾ pt beef stock
50 g/2 oz red lentils
**salt and freshly ground black
    pepper**
175 g/6 oz pork sausagemeat
25 g/1 oz fresh white breadcrumbs
1 tsp dried rosemary
1 cooking apple
**1 large potato, cut into 1 cm/½ in
    dice**
snipped chives, to garnish

1 Heat the oil in a large flameproof casserole. Add the onion, carrots, swede
and green pepper and fry gently for 3
minutes until the vegetables are soft but
not coloured.
2 Stir in the tomato purée, stock and
lentils, and season to taste.
3 Bring to the boil, then lower the heat,
cover and simmer for 20 minutes until
the vegetables are just tender.

Above: *Autumn soup*

4 Meanwhile, put the sausagemeat,
breadcrumbs and rosemary in a bowl.
Mix thoroughly with your hands, then
shape into 12 small balls.
5 Peel and core the apple, then cut into
1 cm/½ in dice. Add to the soup with the
potato and sausagemeat balls and simmer for a further 25 minutes until all the
vegetables are tender, but not mushy.
Stir occasionally.
6 Serve hot, sprinkled with chives.

To Microwave
Place the oil in a casserole with the prepared onion, carrots, swede and green
pepper and microwave for 4 minutes.
Add the tomato purée, hot stock and
lentils. Season to taste. Cover and
microwave for 10 minutes. Reduce
power to Defrost for 10 minutes. Prepare
the meatballs and apple as above. Add
to the soup with the potato, re-cover and
cook for 10 minutes.

Autumn soup with salami   In place of
the sausagemeat balls, dice 75 g/3 oz
skinned garlic sausage or salami and stir
into the soup 10 minutes before the end
of cooking. Use pearl barley instead of
lentils, but allow at least another 30
minutes cooking time before adding the
sausage or salami.

Fish

Fish dishes are perfect for all-year-round eating as they are not too heavy yet full of flavour. Our choice of meals is made with popular and easily obtainable varieties – haddock, tuna and prawns, to name but a few. Try Sweet and sour tuna for something deliciously different. The kids will love our Fishcake special.

Remember that fish cooks quickly and generally speaking the temperature shouldn't be too high or the cooking time too long. You can tell when the fish is cooked if the fish flakes or falls easily into natural divisions when tested.

Stir in the flour and paprika and cook for a further 3 minutes, stirring the mixture continuously.

3 Add the tomatoes with the wine, dried herbs and bouquet garni and season with salt and pepper.

4 Bring the contents of the casserole to the boil. Stir well, add the fish pieces, cover and cook in the oven for 35–40 minutes, until the fish is just tender. Discard bouquet garni.

5 Heat the remaining butter in a large saucepan and briskly fry the bread slices on both sides until they are crisp and golden brown. Drain the bread on absorbent paper.

6 Stand the bread up round the rim of the casserole. Serve at once.

Kedgeree special

Serves 4–6
450 g/1 lb smoked cod fillets, defrosted if frozen
250 g/9 oz white rice
25 g/1 oz margarine or butter
1 onion, chopped
225 g/8 oz frozen mixed vegetables, defrosted
150 g/5 oz natural yoghurt
juice of ½ lemon
100 g/4 oz can smoked mussels, drained
100 g/4 oz peeled prawns, defrosted if frozen
2 hard-boiled eggs, roughly chopped
2 tbls chopped fresh parsley
salt and freshly ground black pepper
thick lemon wedges, to garnish (optional)

1 Put the cod in a large saucepan, cover with cold water and bring to the boil. Lower the heat, cover and simmer gently for 10 minutes, until the fish flakes easily when pierced with a sharp knife.

2 Remove the fish with a slotted spoon, reserving the poaching liquid in the pan. Leave the fish until cool enough to handle, then flake the flesh into small pieces, discarding any skin and any remaining bones.

3 Make the fish poaching liquid up to 1 L/1¾ pts with water. Bring to the boil, add the rice, cover and simmer for 15 minutes or until tender. Drain in a sieve.

4 Meanwhile, melt the margarine in a separate large saucepan, add the onion and fry gently for 5 minutes until soft

Above: *Cod and courgette casserole*

Making a bouquet garni

Tie herbs in a piece of scalded and dried muslin. Try a combination of thyme, parsley sprigs and bay leaves. Use for any dish in which broken leaves would be undesirable.

Cod and courgette casserole

Serves 4
700 g/1½ lb cod fillet, skinned
75 g/3 oz butter
1 large onion, sliced
350 g/12 oz courgettes, sliced
1 tbls flour
1 tsp paprika
2 large tomatoes, blanched, skinned and sliced
225 ml/8 fl oz dry white wine
½ tsp dried herbs
bouquet garni (see left)
salt and freshly ground black pepper
8 thin slices French bread

1 Heat the oven to 160° C/325° F/ gas 3. Cut the skinned cod fillet into 5 cm/2 in pieces.

2 Melt 25 g/1 oz of the butter in a flameproof casserole, add the onion and courgettes and cook over a moderate heat for 2 minutes, stirring so that the vegetables become thoroughly coated.

and lightly coloured. Stir in the mixed vegetables and cover the pan. Continue cooking over low heat for 5 minutes, shaking the pan from time to time.

5 Add the fish and rice to the vegetables, with the yoghurt, lemon juice, mussels, prawns, eggs and parsley. Season to taste. Taking care not to break up the ingredients, fork through lightly over gentle heat mixed and heated through.

6 Pile the kedgeree into a warmed serving dish, garnish with lemon wedges, if liked, and serve at once.

Creamy cod bake

Illustrated on pages 152-153

Serves 4
700 g/1½ lb cod fillets, defrosted if frozen, skinned and cut into 4 cm/ 1½ in cubes
1 onion, chopped
4 tbls dry white wine
700 g/1½ lb potatoes
salt

25 g/1 oz margarine or butter, melted
freshly ground black pepper
250 g/9 oz smoked bacon rashers, derinded and halved
150 ml/¼ pt single cream
2 tbls grated Parmesan cheese
paprika

1 Put the fish cubes in a shallow dish and sprinkle over the onion. Spoon over the wine and turn the fish carefully to coat. Cover and leave to marinate for 2 hours, turning the fish very carefully from time to time.

2 Heat the oven to 190° C/375° F/gas 5.

3 Put the potatoes in a large saucepan of salted water, bring to the boil, cover and boil gently for about 15 minutes until just tender, but not soft. Drain well and leave to cool slightly.

4 Brush a shallow ovenproof casserole with some of the melted fat. Cut the potatoes into 5 mm/¼ inch slices and arrange them in a single layer in the base of the casserole. Brush the potatoes with remaining fat and season.

5 Using a slotted spoon, remove the fish and onion from the marinade and arrange the fish and chopped onion on top of the potatoes.

6 Arrange the bacon on top of the fish. Bake for 15 minutes, then lower the heat to 180° C/350° F/gas 4.

7 Pour the cream over the top of the casserole, sprinkle with the Parmesan cheese and season the top with a little paprika. Return the casserole to the oven for a further 15–20 minutes, until the topping is golden. Serve hot, straight from the casserole.

To Microwave
Marinate the fish as above. Cut the potatoes in half widthways and place in a dish in a single layer. Add 4 tbls water, cover and microwave for 9–10 minutes. Drain. Arrange in a casserole as above and microwave for 8 minutes. Pour the cream over, sprinkle with grated Parmesan cheese and paprika. Cook for 4 minutes. Place the casserole under a preheated grill to brown.

Below: *Kedgeree special*

Hungarian haddock

Serves 4

700 g/1½ lb haddock fillets, defrosted if frozen, skinned and cut into 2.5 cm/1 in cubes
1 bunch spring onions, finely chopped
150 ml/¼ pt dry cider
450 g/1 lb potatoes, thinly sliced
4 tomatoes, skinned and sliced
25 g/1 oz margarine or butter
salt and freshly ground black pepper
175 g/6 oz streaky bacon rashers, derinded and chopped
300 g/10 oz natural yoghurt
1 tbls cornflour
2 tsp paprika
tomato wedges and sweet paprika, to garnish

1 Put the haddock cubes into a bowl with the spring onions and cider. Stir well, cover and leave to marinate in a cool place for 2 hours.
2 Heat the oven to 190° C/375° F/ gas 5.
3 Arrange sliced potatoes evenly over the base of a large greased ovenproof dish. Cover with tomato slices and dot with the margarine. Season well with salt and pepper. Cover with a lid or foil then bake for about 30 minutes.
4 Using a slotted spoon, remove the haddock and onions from the bowl and spread over the tomatoes. Scatter the bacon on top of the fish and cook un-covered in the oven for a further 15 minutes.
5 In a bowl, combine the yoghurt with the cornflour and paprika. Drain off any excess liquid from the baking dish, then spoon the yoghurt mixture over top. Cover dish and return to the oven for a

further 15 minutes, until the fish and potatoes are tender when pierced with a sharp knife.
6 Garnish with tomato wedges and sprinkle with paprika. Serve immediately, straight from the dish.

To Microwave
Marinate the fish as above. Arrange the potatoes and tomatoes with the fat and seasoning in a large dish as above. Cover and microwave for 9 minutes. Using a slotted spoon, remove the haddock and onions from the bowl and spread over the tomatoes. Scatter the bacon on top. Microwave for 8 minutes. Combine the yoghurt, cornflour and paprika. Drain off excess liquid from the baking dish, then spoon the yoghurt mix over the top. Cover and microwave for 8–10 minutes. Brown under a grill, if wished.

Hungarian cod Substitute cod fillets, cubed and defrosted, if frozen, for the haddock and add a very finely sliced green or red pepper to the potatoes before covering with the tomatoes.

Haddock and pea special

Serves 4

25 g/1 oz margarine or butter
2–3 tbls vegetable oil
850 g/1¾ lb potatoes, diced
2 onions, chopped
225 g/8 oz frozen garden peas, defrosted
salt and freshly ground black pepper
4 haddock steaks, fresh or frozen, each weighing about 150 g/5 oz, skinned
400 g/14 oz can tomatoes
1–2 cloves garlic, crushed (optional)
1 tsp dillweed (optional)
50 g/2 oz Cheddar cheese, grated

1 Heat the margarine and oil in a large frying pan over moderate heat. Add the potatoes and onions, stirring constantly, and fry for 10–15 minutes until light golden and tender. Add the peas.
2 Season the potatoes, onions and peas, then turn into a shallow ovenproof dish, spreading out evenly.
3 Heat the oven to 220° C/425° F/ gas 7.

Left: *Hungarian haddock*

100 g/4 oz peeled prawns, defrosted
   if frozen
a little extra chopped fresh parsley
   and paprika, to garnish

1 Heat the oil in a flameproof casserole, add the bacon and fry gently for 2–3 minutes until the fat runs. Remove the bacon with a slotted spoon and reserve.

2 Add the fish and fry briskly, turning carefully once or twice, for 2 minutes or until lightly browned and opaque. Remove with a slotted spoon and reserve.

3 Return the reserved bacon to the casserole and add the onion and garlic, if using. Cook gently for 5 minutes. Add the potatoes and cook for 1 further minute.

4 Add the tomatoes, stock, parsley, bay leaf, paprika and capers to the casserole. Stir well to mix and season to taste. Bring to the boil, then lower heat, cover and simmer gently for 20 minutes or until the potatoes are tender.

5 Add the cooked fish and prawns to the casserole, stir very carefully and heat gently for 2–3 minutes.

6 Transfer to a warmed deep serving dish, sprinkle with parsley and paprika and serve at once.

Cod stew In place of the haddock use cod (or coley) and substitute drained canned mussels or clams for the prawns. Add 1 tsp dried mixed herbs or basil together with the parsley.

Below: Haddock stew

Above: *Haddock and pea special*

4 Put the fish on the vegetables.

5 Turn the tomatoes with their juice into a bowl, add the garlic and dill, if using, and season. Mash with a fork, to break up the tomatoes.

6 Pour the tomato mixture over the fish, then sprinkle over the cheese.

7 Bake in the oven for 20–30 minutes or until the fish flakes easily when tested with a fork.

To Microwave
Preheat a large browning dish for 8 minutes or according to manufacturer's instructions. Add the fat, oil and potatoes. Microwave for 4 minutes, stirring twice. Add the onions and cook for 4 minutes. Add the peas, season and place in a shallow heatproof dish. Top as above. Microwave for 15 minutes. Place under a preheated grill to brown.

Cod and corn special Substitute cod for the haddock and use frozen sweetcorn instead of the peas. Try thyme in place of dillweed.

Haddock stew

Serves 4
2 tbls vegetable oil
**50 g/2 oz streaky bacon rashers,
   derinded and chopped**
700 g/1½ lb haddock, filleted,
skinned and cut into 2.5 cm/1 in
   cubes
1 onion, chopped
1 clove garlic, crushed (optional)
**450 g/1 lb potatoes, cut into 1 cm/
   ½ in dice**
400 g/14 oz can chopped tomatoes
425 ml/¾ pt chicken stock
2 tbls chopped fresh parsley
1 bay leaf
1 tsp paprika
2 tsp capers
**salt and freshly ground black
   pepper**

Mackerel hotpot

Serves 4
**425 g/15 oz can mackerel, drained
    and flaked**
25 g/1 oz margarine or butter
25 g/1 oz plain flour
300 ml/½ pt milk
1 tbls chopped parsley
1 tbls tomato purée
**salt and freshly ground black
    pepper**
1 packet bacon flavoured crisps

1 Heat the oven to 200° C/400° F/gas 6.
2 Put the mackerel in a 600 ml/1 pt ovenproof dish.
3 Make the sauce: melt the fat in a small saucepan, sprinkle in the flour and stir over low heat for 1–2 minutes until straw coloured. Remove from the heat and gradually stir in the milk. Return to the heat and simmer, stirring, until thick

and smooth. Stir in the parsley and tomato purée. Season to taste with salt and freshly ground black pepper.
4 Pour the sauce over the mackerel and sprinkle the crisps over the top.
5 Bake for 15 minutes. Serve hot straight from the dish.

To Microwave
Place the mackerel in a 600 ml/1 pt heatproof dish. Place the fat in the 900 ml/1½ pt bowl and microwave for 30 seconds to melt. Stir in the flour then gradually add the milk. Microwave for 3 minutes or until thickened, stirring 3—4 times. Stir in the parsley and tomato purée. Season and pour over the mackerel. Microwave for 3 minutes. Sprinkle with crisps, microwave for 30 seconds and serve.

Mackerel cheese hotpot Replace the parsley and tomato purée with 50 g/2 oz grated cheese. Make an alternative topping with thinly sliced parboiled potatoes instead of crisps.

Above: *Mackerel hotpot*

Mackerel pilaff

Illustrated on pages 152-153
Serves 4
25 g/1 oz margarine or butter
1 onion, chopped
**1 red pepper, seeded and cut into
    5 mm/¼ in strips**
250 g/9 oz long-grain brown rice
1 L/1¾ pt boiling chicken stock
**2 mackerel, each weighing about
    450 g/1 lb**
**salt and freshly ground black
    pepper**
**150 g/5 oz courgettes, cut into
    5 mm/¼ in slices**
**25 g/1 oz whole blanched almonds,
    toasted**
**parsley sprigs and lemon slices, to
    garnish (optional)**

1 Melt the margarine in a heavy-based saucepan. Add the onion and red pepper and fry gently for 5 minutes, stirring from time to time.

2 Stir in the rice and cook for 1 minute. Remove from the heat and stir in the stock. Season with salt and pepper, return to the boil, then simmer, covered, for 30 minutes until the rice is tender and nearly all the liquid has been absorbed. Add more boiling stock or water if necessary during cooking.

3 Heat the grill to high. Cover the grill rack with foil. Grill the mackerel for 10–12 minutes on each side, or until the flesh flakes easily.

4 Meanwhile, bring a pan of salted water to the boil and cook the courgettes for 3-4 minutes until just tender. Drain well.

5 Flake the mackerel into large pieces with a fork, removing skin and bones.

6 Drain any liquid from the rice and carefully fork in the courgettes and fish. Heat through for a few seconds.

7 Spoon onto a large serving platter, and sprinkle over the almonds. Garnish with parsley sprigs ands lemon slices, if liked, and serve hot or cold.

To Microwave
Place the fat, onion and red pepper in a large casserole and microwave for 3 minutes. Add the rice and cook for 1 minute. Stir in the hot stock and seasoning. Cover and cook for 20-25 minutes or until nearly all the liquid has been absorbed. Place the mackerel on a roasting rack and microwave for 5-6 minutes. Flake. Place the courgettes in a small bowl with 1 tbls water, cover and cook

for 3 minutes. Drain. Mix the rice, courgettes and fish together.

Herring pilaff Substitute herrings for the mackerel. If the fish is already cooked, grill it for only 1 minute on each side to heat it through. Replace the brown rice with white rice, but remember to allow 15–20 minutes less cooking time.

Fishcake special

Serves 4
**450 g/1 lb potatoes, cut into 2.5 cm/
 1 in cubes**
**salt and freshly ground black
 pepper**
450 g/1 lb plaice fillets, skinned
40 g/1½ oz butter
**175 g/6 oz streaky bacon rashers,
 derinded and chopped**
1 onion, chopped
1 tbls chopped fresh parsley
finely grated zest of ½ lemon
1 tbls vegetable oil
**anchovy fillets and lemon slices,
 to garnish**

1 Bring the potatoes to the boil in a saucepan of salted water. Grease a flameproof plate and arrange the fish fillets on it. Cover with another plate and place on top of the saucepan. Cook for about 20 minutes until the potatoes and fish are tender when pierced with a knife.

2 Meanwhile, melt 15 g/½ oz butter in a 20–23 cm/8–9 in frying pan. Add the

bacon and onion and fry gently, stirring occasionally, for 5 minutes.

3 Drain the potatoes and mash them roughly. Flake the fish and fork it through the potato. Stir the onion and bacon into the potatoes and fish together with the parsley and lemon zest. Season to taste with salt and pepper.

4 Melt half the remaining butter and half the oil in the frying pan. Turn the potato and fish mixture into the pan and, using a fish slice, press down evenly and shape into a round cake. Cook for 8 minutes over moderate heat.

5 Remove from heat. Place a plate on top of the frying pan and invert, holding the pan and plate tightly together, to turn the fishcake on to the plate. Scrape out any bits remaining in the pan.

6 Melt the remaining butter and oil in the pan, then using a fish slice, slide the fishcake back into the pan, browned side uppermost. Cook for a further 8 minutes, then carefully transfer to a warmed serving dish. Arrange the anchovy fillets in a trellis pattern on top and garnish with lemon. Serve hot, cut into wedges.

To Microwave
Place the potatoes in a large casserole. Add 4 tbls water, cover and microwave for 7-8 minutes. Place the fish in a shallow dish, cover with pierced cling film and cook for 3-4 minutes. Place 15 g/½ oz butter and bacon in a bowl and microwave for 3-4 minutes, stirring twice. Mix and finish as above.

Below: *Fishcake special*

Sweet and sour tuna

Serves 4
25 g/1 oz margarine or butter
1 green pepper, seeded and cut into chunks
1 bunch spring onions, chopped
4 tbls soft dark brown sugar
2 tsp cornflour
1 chicken stock cube
350 g/12 oz can pineapple chunks, drained and syrup reserved
2 tbls wine vinegar
2 tbls soy sauce
salt (optional)
2 × 200 g/7 oz cans tuna, drained and cut into chunks

1 Heat the margarine or butter in a saucepan, add the green pepper and chopped spring onions and fry gently for 3-4 minutes until the vegetables are soft but not browned.
2 Put the soft dark brown sugar, cornflour and chicken stock cube into a measuring jug and slowly stir in boiling water up to the 300 ml/½ pt mark. Continue stirring until the ingredients have dissolved. Add the reserved pineapple

Below: Sweet and sour tuna

syrup, vinegar and soy sauce. Season to taste with salt if liked.
3 Pour this liquid into the pan with the green pepper and spring onions and bring to the boil. Lower the heat and simmer the mixture for about 2 minutes, stirring.
4 Add the canned tuna and pineapple chunks and continue to simmer the curry over gentle heat for about 10 minutes. Serve hot.

To Microwave
Place the fat, pepper and spring onions in a casserole and microwave for 3 minutes. Place the sugar, cornflour and stock in a measuring jug and slowly stir in the boiling water up to 300 ml/½ pt mark. Add the pineapple syrup, vinegar and soy sauce. Pour into the casserole and microwave for 2 minutes. Add the tuna and pineapple, cover and cook for 5 minutes.

Sweet and sour pork Substitute 225–350 g/8–12 oz cooked leftover pork, cut into cubes, for the tuna. Try adding 1–2 tbls orange juice to the sauce.
Sweet and sour chicken Substitute 225–350 g/8–12 oz cooked leftover chicken, cut into chunks, for the tuna. Use red instead of green pepper.

Tuna fish curry

Serves 4
300 ml/½ pt milk
50 g/2 oz desiccated coconut
1 tbls vegetable oil
1 onion, sliced
1 green pepper, seeded and sliced
2 cloves garlic, crushed (optional)
2 tsp ground cardamom
1 tsp ground ginger
1 tsp ground turmeric
¼–½ tsp chilli powder
150 ml/¼pt water
2 × 200 g/7 oz cans tuna, drained and forked into chunks
juice of 1 lemon
salt and freshly ground black pepper
2 hard-boiled eggs, sliced, and coriander leaves, to garnish

1 Put the milk and coconut into a saucepan and heat slowly just to simmering point. Remove from the heat, cover and leave for 20 minutes. Strain milk through a fine sieve, pressing coconut with the back of a wooden spoon. Reserve the milk and discard the coconut.
2 Heat the oil in a large heavy-based

saucepan, add onion and green pepper and fry gently for 5 minutes. Add garlic, if using, and spices. Cook, stirring, for 1–2 minutes.

3 Combine the coconut milk with the water and gradually stir into the pan. Bring slowly to the boil, then lower heat and simmer, uncovered, for 5 minutes, stirring occasionally.

4 Stir in the tuna and lemon juice, and season. Cover and simmer very gently for 10–15 minutes. Transfer to a warmed serving dish, garnish and serve with poppadums, if liked.

To Microwave
Place the milk and coconut in a jug and microwave for 5 minutes on Defrost. Cover and leave for 30 minutes. Strain as above. Place the oil, onion and pepper in a casserole and microwave for 3 minutes. Add the garlic and spices, stir and cook for 1 minute. Add the coconut milk and water. Microwave for 3 minutes, stir in the tuna, lemon juice and seasoning. Cover and microwave on Defrost for 8 minutes.

Tomato sardine bake

Serves 4
12 small thin slices of wholemeal bread
40 g/1½ oz butter, softened

115 g/4¼ oz can sardines in tomato sauce
2 tomatoes, skinned and chopped
salt and freshly ground black pepper
75 g/3 oz Cheddar cheese, grated
2 large eggs
150 ml/¼ pt milk
1 tomato, sliced, to garnish

1 Heat the oven to 200° C/400° F/gas 6.
2 Spread the slices of bread with the softened butter.
3 Mash the sardines in their sauce and spread the mixture over the bread. Cut each slice into 4 triangles.
4 Arrange a layer of the bread triangles to cover the base of a very well greased

Above: *Tuna fish curry*

20–23 cm/8–9 in shallow pie dish or baking tin; they should fit neatly but not overlap. Add one-third of the chopped tomato, season with salt and pepper and top with one-quarter of the cheese. Make 2 more layers of bread, tomato, seasoning and cheese and top with a final layer of bread triangles.
5 Whisk the eggs in a bowl with the milk, and salt and pepper. Pour over the layers in the dish and sprinkle the remaining cheese over the top.
6 Bake in the oven, just above the centre, for 25–30 minutes, until crisp and brown on top. Serve hot, garnished with tomato slices.

To Microwave
Prepare and arrange in a 20–23 cm/8–9 in shallow pie dish as above. Microwave for 8 minutes. Place under a pre-heated grill to brown. Serve as above.

Simple sardine bake Use sardines canned in oil, thoroughly drained, instead of sardines in tomato sauce, for a less pronounced tomato flavour. Substitute a can of tomatoes, well drained, for the fresh tomatoes. Use white bread if preferred.

Seafood macaroni bake

Illustrated on pages 152-153
Serves 4
1 lemon
350 g/12 oz haddock fillets, skinned
600 ml/1 pt milk
1 bay leaf
3 whole black peppercorns
salt and freshly ground black pepper
50 g/2 oz margarine or butter
250 g/9 oz mushrooms, thinly sliced
250 g/9 oz short-cut macaroni,
**   boiled, drained and rinsed**
150 g/5 oz jar mussels, drained
40 g/1½ oz plain flour
250 g/9 oz peeled prawns
pinch of grated nutmeg
lemon slices and unpeeled fresh
**   prawns, to garnish (optional)**

1   Squeeze the juice of half the lemon and reserve; slice the other half.
2   Put the haddock in a large frying pan with a lid and pour in enough of the milk to just cover. Add 2 slices of lemon, the bay leaf, peppercorns and a good pinch

of salt. Bring gradually to the boil, then cover and turn off the heat. Leave to stand for 5 minutes, then remove the haddock with a fish slice. Flake the flesh into 4 cm/1½ in pieces, discarding bones. Strain cooking liquid and reserve.
3   Melt 15 g/½ oz fat in the rinsed out frying pan, add the mushrooms and fry for 2–3 minutes. Stir in lemon juice; remove from heat.
4   Heat the oven to 180° C/350° F/gas 4.
5   Put the macaroni into a greased large ovenproof dish with the haddock, mushrooms and mussels. Stir carefully to mix.
6   Melt the remaining fat in a saucepan, sprinkle in the flour and stir over low heat for 1–2 minutes until straw-coloured. Remove from the heat and gradually stir in rest of milk and reserved cooking liquid. Return to the heat and simmer, stirring, until thick and smooth. Remove from heat, stir in the prawns, nutmeg and salt and pepper to taste, then pour over fish mixture. Bake for 20 minutes.
7   Garnish with lemon slices and unpeeled prawns, if liked, and serve hot, straight from the dish.

Above: *Italian fish stew*

Italian fish stew

Serves 4
4 frozen white fish steaks (cod or
**   haddock), each weighing about**
**   150 g/5 oz**
2 tbls olive or vegetable oil
1 onion, finely chopped
1 red pepper, seeded and chopped
2 courgettes, chopped
100 g/4 oz mushrooms, quartered
**   if large**
300 ml/½ pt tomato spaghetti
**   sauce**
1 tsp lemon juice
salt and freshly ground black
**   pepper**
chopped parsley, to garnish

1   Heat the grill to moderate.
2   Brush the frozen fish steaks with oil, then grill for about 15 minutes, turning once, or until cooked through.
3   Meanwhile, heat the remaining oil in a large heavy saucepan. Add the onion,

red pepper and courgettes and fry over moderate heat for 10 minutes until softened. Stir in the mushrooms and fry for a further 3 minutes.

4 Stir in the spaghetti sauce and lemon juice. Season to taste with salt and pepper. Cover the saucepan and simmer.

5 When the fish steaks are ready, place them in the pan in a single layer and spoon over the sauce to coat them. Simmer, uncovered, for 5 minutes.

6 Carefully lift the fish steaks on to a warmed large serving plate and spoon the sauce over and around them. Sprinkle the fish with chopped parsley and serve at once.

To Microwave
Place the fish steaks on a roasting rack and microwave for 8 minutes, rearranging after 4 minutes. Place 1 tbls oil, onion, red pepper and courgettes in a casserole and microwave for 4 minutes, stirring twice. Stir in the mushrooms and cook for 2 minutes. Stir in the spaghetti sauce, lemon juice and seasoning; cover

and cook for 3 minutes. Add the cod and cook for 4 minutes. Serve as above.

Seafood quickie

Serves 4
4 tomatoes, skinned and sliced
450 g/1 lb cod or other white fish fillets, skinned and defrosted if frozen
100 g/4 oz peeled prawns, defrosted if frozen
300 g/10 oz can condensed cream of asparagus soup
15 g/½ oz butter
1 tbls vegetable oil
3 slices white bread, crusts removed and cut into triangles or fish shapes
tomato slices, to garnish (optional)

1 Heat the oven to 190° C/375° F/gas 5.

2 Place the tomatoes in the bottom of a

1.5 L/2½ pt shallow ovenproof dish and arrange the fish on top in a single layer; trim to fit evenly if necessary. Sprinkle the prawns evenly over the surface of the fish and pour the soup over.

3 Cover the dish and bake for 35 minutes. Remove the lid or foil, then continue to bake, uncovered, for a further 10–15 minutes, until the fish pieces are cooked.

4 Meanwhile, melt the butter with the oil in a frying pan. When sizzling, add the bread shapes and fry over high heat for 2–3 minutes, turning once, until golden brown. Drain on absorbent paper.

5 Arrange the fried bread shapes around the edge, garnish and serve.

To Microwave
Place the tomatoes, fish, prawns and soup in a 1.5 L/2½ pt heatproof dish as above. Cover and microwave for 12 minutes. Prepare croûtons as above. Arrange around fish, garnish and serve.

Below: *Seafood quickie*

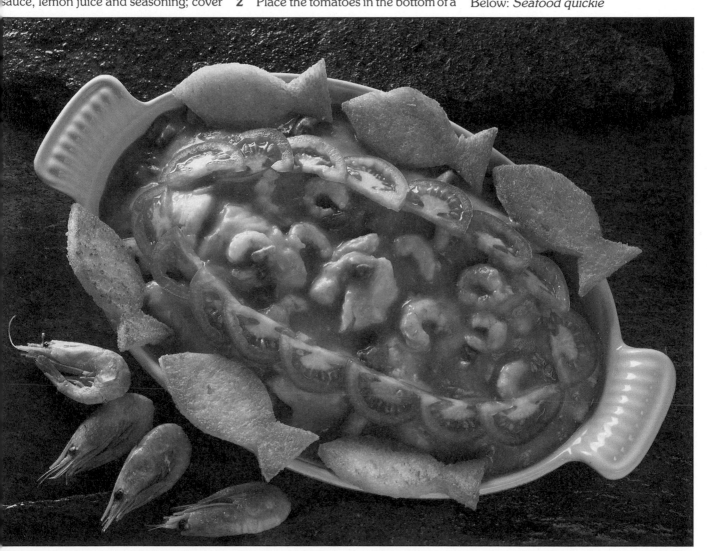

Meat and Poultry

A wonderfully warming choice of casseroles, stews, hotpots and much, much more. There are dishes with an international flavour, such as Pork chow mein or Spicy beef stir-fry, plus some special family favourites such as Lancashire hotpot and Rich beef stew with parsley dumplings. Serve them straight from the dish or for a friendly gathering transfer them to a serving dish and enjoy!

Beef

Roast beef hotpot

Serves 4
700 g/1½ lb potatoes
50 g/2 oz beef dripping
1 large onion, chopped
2 carrots, sliced
1 turnip, sliced
1 parsnip, sliced
**2 large tomatoes, skinned and
  chopped**
50 g/2 oz mushrooms, chopped
**250 g/9 oz cooked roast beef, cut
  into bite-sized pieces**
40 g/1½ oz plain flour
425 ml/¾ pt beef stock
**salt and freshly ground black
  pepper**

1 Heat the oven to 190° C/375° F/gas 5.
2 Parboil the potatoes for 10 minutes, drain and when cool, slice and reserve.
3 Melt 40 g/1½ oz beef dripping in a large flameproof casserole. Add the onion and fry for 5 minutes.
4 Stir in the remaining vegetables, except the potatoes, and fry gently until lightly coloured.
5 Add the meat, sprinkle over the flour, then increase the heat and fry for a further 3 minutes, stirring constantly until the meat is lightly browned on all sides.

Below: *Roast beef hotpot*

6 Stir in the stock, bring to the boil and stir until the mixture thickens. Season with salt and pepper.
7 Arrange the sliced potatoes in layers on the top and sprinkle with salt and pepper.
8 Dot with remaining dripping and cook in the oven for 1 hour until the potatoes are golden brown. Serve hot, straight from the casserole.

To Microwave
Slice the potatoes and place in a casserole with 4 tbls water. Cover and cook for 8–9 minutes. Drain and reserve. Place 40 g/1½ oz dripping and onion in a large casserole and cook for 3 minutes. Add the remaining vegetables, except the potatoes, and cook for 5 minutes, stirring twice. Add the meat and flour, stir and cook for 3 minutes. Stir in the hot stock and seasoning. Cover and cook for 3 minutes, or until boiling, stirring 2–3 times. Top with potato, dot with dripping and cook for 8–10 minutes. Place under a preheated grill to brown.

New England boiled dinner

Serves 8
2 kg/4½ lb salt beef
6 potatoes, halved
1 large swede, cut into 5 cm/2 in dice
10 small pickling onions, peeled
6 carrots, cut into thirds
**1 small head cabbage, cut into
  sixths**

1 In a very large stewing pot, cover the salt beef with about 2.5 cm/1 in of water and bring to the boil. Skim off the foam, then simmer for 3-4 hours, or until the beef is tender when pierced with a fork. Add water as needed to keep the beef covered.
2 About 30 minutes before the beef is done, add the prepared vegetables one type at a time, waiting until the liquid resumes bubbling before adding the next vegetable.
3 Drain the beef and vegetables and place the beef on a large platter and surround it with the vegetables.

Spicy beef stir-fry

Illustrated on pages 164-165
Serves 4
**350 g/12 oz braising steak, trimmed
  and cut into very thin strips**
2 tsp Worcestershire sauce
**salt and freshly ground black
  pepper**
600 ml/1 pt water
1 beef stock cube
1 small red or green pepper
250 g/9 oz courgettes
1 small onion
1 tbls vegetable oil
little soy sauce
**green pepper and onion rings, to
  garnish (optional)**

1 Put the braising steak into a bowl with the Worcestershire sauce and season to taste witrh salt and pepper. Stir well and leave to stand for 10 minutes.
2 Pour the water into a saucepan, add the stock cube, then the meat. Bring to the boil, stirring until the stock cube has dissolved, then lower heat and simmer for about 1 hour or until meat is tender and liquid has almost evaporated. Check the saucepan occasionally to ensure it does not become too dry. If necessary, add a little more water.

3 Meanwhile, prepare vegetables: first seed the pepper and cut into 2.5 cm/1 in strips. Top and tail the courgettes and cut lengthways into thin sticks. Cut the onion in half and slice.

4 Heat oil in a wok or frying pan, add the onion and fry for about 1 minute. Add pepper and fry for a further minute, then add the courgette sticks and stir the mixture well.

5 Stir in the cooked beef and juices. Mix well, cover and cook for 2-3 minutes, then add soy sauce to taste. Transfer to a warmed serving dish, garnish with green pepper and onion rings, if liked, and serve at once.

Beef and olive casserole

Serves 4
15 g/½ oz lard
2 rashers back bacon, derinded
    and chopped
700 g/1½ lb chuck steak, trimmed
    of excess fat and cut into 2.5 cm/
    1 in cubes
1 onion, chopped
2 cloves garlic, crushed (optional)
400 g/14 oz can tomatoes
3 strips orange zest (see right)
juice of 1 small orange
¼ tsp dried thyme
1 bay leaf
salt and freshly ground black
    pepper
75 g/3 oz pimiento-stuffed green
    olives, halved
chopped fresh parsley, to garnish

Stripping orange zest

Carefully peel orange zest using a sharp knife or peeler, then cut into very thin slices.

Below: *New England boiled dinner*

Above: *Beef and olive casserole*

1 Heat the oven to 160° C/325° F/gas 3.

2 Melt the lard in a flameproof casserole, add the bacon and fry for 3–5 minutes over moderate heat, until crisp. Remove the bacon with a slotted spoon and set aside to drain on absorbent paper.

3 Add the beef cubes to the casserole and fry briskly for 3–5 minutes, stirring, until browned on all sides. Remove the beef from the casserole with a slotted spoon and set aside with the bacon.

4 Add the onion to the casserole with the garlic, if using, and cook gently for 5 minutes. Add the beef and bacon and the canned tomatoes with their juice, the orange zest and juice, thyme, bay leaf and salt and pepper. Bring to the boil, stirring, then cover and bake for 1 hour.

5 Add the olives to the casserole and cook for a further 1–1½ hours, until the meat is very tender. Discard the orange zest and bay leaf. Sprinkle with parsley and serve at once.

To Microwave
Place the lard and bacon in a casserole and cook for 2–3 minutes. Remove and reserve. Add the beef and cook for 4 minutes, stirring after 2 minutes. Remove and reserve. Add the onion and garlic, if using and cook for 3 minutes. Add the bacon, beef, tomatoes and juice, orange zest and juice, bay leaf, thyme and seasoning. Cover and microwave for 15 minutes. Add the olives. Reduce the power to Defrost for 1¼-1½ hours or until the meat is tender. Stir 2-3 times. Serve as above.

Beef and aubergine braise

Serves 4
700 g/1½ lb aubergines, cut into 2 cm/¾ in cubes
salt
900 g/2 lb lean beef joint, rolled and tied
3 tbls vegetable oil
3 onions, chopped
1 clove garlic, crushed
1 carrot, thinly sliced
400 g/14 oz can chopped tomatoes
freshly ground black pepper

1   Put the aubergine cubes into a colander, sprinkle with salt, put a plate on top and weight down. Leave to drain for about 30 minutes.
2   Pat the beef dry on absorbent paper. Heat the oil in a large, heavy-based casserole or saucepan. Add beef and fry 2–3 minutes, turning meat once or twice, to brown and seal on all sides. Drain the beef over the pan and set aside.
3   Add the onions and garlic to the pan and fry gently for 5 minutes. Add the carrot, stir well and cook for a further 1 minute.

4   Rinse the aubergines under cold running water, pat dry and add to the pan. Add the chopped tomatoes with their juice, season and stir well. Return the beef to the pan and cover tightly. Cook very gently for about 2½ hours or until the beef is cooked to your liking.
5   Transfer the beef to a warmed serving dish. Carve the beef into neat slices and spoon the vegetables around it. Serve at once.

To Microwave
Prepare the aubergines as above. Place the oil in a large casserole and cook for 1 minute. Add the beef and cook for 4 minutes, turning twice. Drain and set aside. Add the onions and garlic and cook for 3 minutes. Add the carrot and cook for 1 minute. Rinse and dry the aubergines. Add with the tomatoes, juice and seasoning. Stir, then add the beef. Cover and cook for 15 minutes. Reduce power to Defrost for 1–1½ hours or until tender. Baste twice. Serve as above.

Beef and aubergine purée Work the vegetables and juices in a blender or food processor after cooking and serve in a separate serving dish. Or pipe rosettes of purée around the sliced meat.

Above: *Beef and aubergine braise*

Chilli con carne

Illustrated on pages 164-165
Serves 4
2 tbls vegetable oil
1 large onion, chopped
1 clove garlic, crushed
700 g/1½ lb minced beef
1–2 tsp chilli powder or to taste
400 g/14 oz can chopped tomatoes
2 tbls tomato purée
150 ml/¼ pt beef stock
salt and freshly ground black pepper
432 g/15¼ oz can red kidney beans, drained

1   Heat the oil in a large frying pan. Add the onion and garlic and then cook for 5 minutes, stirring occasionally.
2   Add the mince and chilli powder and cook for 5–10 minutes until the meat is well browned, stirring frequently.
3   Stir in the tomatoes with their juice, tomato purée, stock and season to taste. Bring to the boil, then simmer, covered with foil, for 30 minutes.
4   Five minutes before the end of cook-

ing time, gently stir in the kidney beans.
5 Adjust seasoning, then transfer to a warmed serving dish to serve.

To Microwave
Place the oil, onion and garlic in a casserole. Cook for 3 minutes. Add the mince and chilli powder and cook for 5 minutes, stirring twice. Stir in the tomatoes and juice, tomato purée, hot stock and seasoning to taste. Cover and microwave for 10 minutes. Reduce power to Defrost for 10 minutes. Add the beans, re-cover and cook on full power for 3 minutes. Serve.

Extra spicy chilli For an even spicier dish, add a few crushed cumin seeds when seasoning. Use 1 finely chopped chilli pepper instead of the chilli powder.
Mushroom chilli Add about 150 g/5 oz sliced mushrooms when cooking the onions and garlic and serve with soured cream.

Rich beef stew with parsley dumplings

Serves 4
25 g/1 oz plain flour
salt and freshly ground black
  pepper
700 g/1½ lb chuck steak,
  trimmed and cut into 2.5 cm/1 in
  cubes
25 g/1 oz margarine or butter
2 tbls vegetable oil
1 onion, roughly chopped
2 large carrots, thinly sliced
2 celery stalks, thinly sliced
2 tsp tomato purée
2 tsp finely chopped parsley
pinch of cayenne pepper
300 ml/½ pt beef stock
juice of 1 orange
For the dumplings
100 g/4 oz self-raising flour
50 g/2 oz shredded suet
1 tbls finely chopped parsley
about 6 tbls water

1 Put the flour in a polythene bag, season with salt and pepper, then add the meat. Shake the bag vigorously until the meat is well coated.
2 Heat the fat and 1 tbls oil in a large flameproof casserole. Add the meat and fry over brisk heat for about 3 minutes, stirring, until browned on all sides. Fry in

Right: Rich beef stew with parsley dumplings

batches if necessary. Remove from the pan with a slotted spoon and set aside.
3 Heat the remaining oil in the pan, then add the onion, carrots and celery and fry over moderate heat for 3 minutes. Return the meat to the pan, then add the tomato purée, parsley, cayenne pepper, stock, orange juice and salt and pepper.
4 Bring to the boil, stirring and scraping up all the sediment from the sides and bottom of the pan with a wooden spoon. Lower heat, cover and simmer gently for 1½-2 hours until the meat is tender.
5 About 10 minutes before the end of cooking time, prepare the dumplings: sift the flour and a pinch of salt into a bowl and stir in the suet and parsley. With a round-bladed knife, gradually stir in the water to mix to a soft but not sticky dough. Knead the dough lightly, then gently form into 8 balls.
6 Place the dumplings on top of the stew. Cover and simmer gently for about 15 minutes until the dumplings are puffed up.

7 Serve the stew at once, straight from the casserole.

To Microwave
Prepare the meat and flour as above. Place the fat and 1 tbls oil in a large casserole and microwave for 45 seconds. Add the meat, toss and cook for 3–4 minutes, stirring after 2 minutes. Remove and set aside. Add the remaining oil, onion, carrots and celery. Cook for 3 minutes. Add the meat, tomato purée, parsley, cayenne, stock, orange juice and seasoning. Cover and microwave for 10 minutes. Reduce power to Defrost for 1¼–1½ hours or until the meat is tender. Stir twice. Make the dumplings as above. Add to the casserole and microwave for 5–6 minutes on full power.

Special beef stew Replace half the beef stock with red wine. Crush 1 clove garlic with a little salt, then add to the casserole with the vegetables.

Lamb

Lamb chops in tomato rice

Serves 4
15 g/½ oz margarine or butter
2 tbls vegetable oil
4 thick lamb chump chops,
    trimmed
1 onion, chopped
1 celery stalk, chopped
400 g/14 oz can tomatoes, chopped
300 ml/½ pt water
200 g/7 oz long-grain rice
1 tbls chopped fresh basil or
    1 tsp dried basil
salt and freshly ground black
    pepper
basil sprigs, to garnish (optional)

1   Heat the margarine or butter with the oil in a large frying pan. Add the chops and fry over brisk heat for 5–10 minutes, turning once, to brown on both sides. Remove and set aside.

Below: *Lamb chops in tomato rice*

2   Add the onion and celery to the pan and fry gently for 5 minutes. Stir in the tomatoes with their juice, add the water and bring to the boil.
3   Add the rice, basil and salt and pepper to taste and stir well. Return the chops to the pan and cover them with the tomato and rice mixture.
4   Cover the pan and simmer gently for 30-40 minutes or until the chops are cooked through, the rice is tender and all the liquid has been absorbed.
5   Transfer to a warm serving dish, garnish with basil sprigs, if liked.

To Microwave
Preheat a large browning dish for 7 minutes. Add the margarine or butter, oil and chops. Cook for 2 minutes, turn over and cook for 3 minutes. Add the onion and celery and cook for 2 minutes. Stir in the tomatoes and juice and 300 ml/½ pt boiling water. Cover and microwave for 4 minutes. Add the rice, basil and seasoning to taste. Re-cover and cook for 12–15 minutes or until all the liquid has been absorbed.

Pork chops in tomato rice   Substitute pork chops, trimmed of excess fat, for the lamb and use sage instead of basil. You must make sure that the pork chops are thoroughly cooked through.

Lamb and cider pot roast

Illustrated on pages 164-165
Serves 4
25 g/1 oz dripping or lard
1.4 kg/3 lb knuckle end leg of lamb
1 onion stuck with 4 cloves
225 g/8 oz carrots, quartered
    lengthways
225 g/8 oz parsnips, quartered
    lengthways
225 g/8 oz turnips, quartered
225 g/8 oz potatoes, cut into chunks
150 ml/¼ pt cider
150 ml/¼ pt chicken stock
salt and pepper
For the beurre manié (kneaded
    butter)
2 tbls plain flour
25 g/1 oz butter

1   Heat the oven to 160° C/325° F/gas 3.
2   Melt the dripping in a flameproof casserole. Brown the lamb on all sides.
3   Add the vegetables to the casserole, pour in cider and stock. Season to taste.
4   Cover and cook in the oven for 2-2¼ hours or until the lamb is cooked.
5   Transfer the lamb to a warmed serving plate. Using a slotted spoon, lift out all the vegetables and arrange them round the meat, discarding the onion. Keep hot in the oven on lowest setting.
6   Make the beurre manié: blend flour and butter together with a palette knife, then cut the paste into pea-sized pieces.
7   Bring the cooking liquid in the casserole to the boil, then whisk in the pieces of beurre manié. Simmer over low heat, whisking constantly, until the gravy thickens. Pour into a warmed gravy boat.
8   Serve the lamb, cut into slices, with the vegetables and the gravy at once.

Lamb chops with peppers

Serves 4

4 large loin chops, trimmed of
    excess fat
4 tbls vegetable oil
2 onions, thinly sliced
1 garlic clove, chopped (optional)
450 g/1 lb tomatoes, skinned,
    seeded and chopped
2 green peppers, seeded and cut
    into strips
1 red pepper, seeded and cut into
    strips
1 tsp crushed coriander seeds
salt and freshly ground black
    pepper
150 ml/¼ pt dry white wine
1 tbls tomato purée

1   Heat the oil in a large frying pan and brown the loin chops thoroughly on both sides.
2   With all the chops in the pan, lower the heat and add the onions and garlic, if using. Cover and cook for 5 minutes, stirring occasionally.
3   Add the tomatoes, peppers, coriander and seasoning. Cover and cook for 15 minutes or until the chops are cooked.
4   Remove the chops and keep warm. Increase the heat and stir in the wine. Cook rapidly, uncovered, until the liquid is reduced by half, stirring constantly.
5   Stir in the tomato purée and simmer uncovered for 5 minutes. To serve, place the meat on a warmed serving platter and spoon the sauce over.

French spring lamb

Serves 4

25 g/1 oz butter
1 tbls oil
700 g/1½ lb boneless lean shoulder
    lamb, cut into 2.5 cm/1 in cubes
2 tsp sugar
1 tbls plain flour
salt and pepper
425 ml/15 fl oz chicken stock
1 tbls tomato purée
1 clove garlic, crushed
bouquet garni
8 button onions, peeled
8 baby carrots, scraped
12 tiny new potatoes, scraped
150 g/5 oz shelled peas or young
    broad beans

1   Heat the butter and oil in a large flameproof casserole.
2   Fry the meat briskly, in two batches, stirring frequently, until lightly browned. Strain off excess fat and return all the meat to the pan. Sprinkle in the sugar and stir until lightly caramelized.
3   Heat the oven to 150° C/300 ° F/gas 2.
4   Add the flour and season the meat. Lower the heat and stir for a minute or two until the flour is lightly coloured. Add the stock, tomato purée, garlic and bouquet garni and stir until simmering.
5   Cover the casserole tightly; transfer to the oven. Cook for 1 hour.
6   Skim off excess fat, then add the onions, carrots and potatoes, pushing them under the surface of the sauce. Cover and cook for a further 40 minutes.
7   Stir in the peas or broad beans, cover and cook for another 15 minutes or until all the ingredients are tender.
8   Skim off any surface fat, discard the bouquet garni and serve.

Lancashire hotpot

Serves 4

700 g/1½ lb best end neck of lamb,
    chined with rib bones trimmed
700 g/1½ lb potatoes, thinly sliced
6 lamb's kidneys, skinned, halved
    and cored
1 large onion, coarsely chopped
2 carrots, sliced
salt and freshly ground black
    pepper
1 tsp dried thyme
300 ml/½ pt chicken or beef stock
25 g/1 oz butter

Above: *French spring lamb*

1   Heat the oven to 180° C/350° F/gas 4.
2   Cut the lamb into chops, then cut away most of the fat, scraping the bones clean with the knife.
3   Cover the bottom of a well greased medium-sized ovenproof casserole with a layer of potatoes, using one third of the potato slices. Arrange half the chops, kidneys, onion and carrots on top, seasoning between each layer with salt, pepper and thyme. Repeat layering, finishing with a layer of overlapping potato slices.
4   Pour in the stock. Cover the potatoes with a trimmed piece of greased greaseproof paper, fat side down. Cover and bake for 1½ hours.
5   Uncover, remove paper and dot the potatoes with the butter. Return to the oven for 20–30 minutes or until the potatoes are browned and the meat is tender. Serve at once.

Below: *Lancashire hotpot*

Pork

Cottage pork pie

Serves 4
25 g/1 oz margarine or butter
4 tbls milk
700 g/1½ lb potatoes, boiled and
**   mashed**
1 tbls vegetable oil
450 g/1 lb pork fillet, cut into 2 cm/
**   ¾ in pieces**
1 onion, chopped
2 celery stalks, chopped
175 g/6 oz mushrooms, sliced
25 g/1 oz plain flour
150 ml/¼ pt chicken stock
150 ml/¼ pt dry cider
finely grated zest of 1 lemon
2 tbls lemon juice
1 tbls chopped fresh parsley
1 teaspoon dried rosemary
salt and freshly ground black
**   pepper**

1   Heat the oven to 180° C/350° F/gas 4.
2   Beat half the margarine or butter and the milk into the mashed potatoes.
3   Heat the remaining margarine and the oil in a large, heavy-based saucepan, add the pork and fry over brisk heat, stirring, for 2–3 minutes, to seal and brown

Below: *Cottage pork pie*

all over. Remove the pork from the pan with a slotted spoon and drain on absorbent paper. Put in a 1.7 L/3 pt pie dish.
4   Add the onion, celery and mushrooms to the pan and fry gently, stirring, for 2-3 minutes. Sprinkle in the flour and stir for 1-2 minutes. Gradually stir in the stock and cider, then add the lemon zest and juice and the herbs. Bring slowly to the boil, stirring constantly, then season to taste. Pour the mixture over the pork in the pie dish and stir well.
5   Spoon the creamed potato over the top and fork up attractively.
6   Bake for 50 minutes until the meat is tender when pierced with a sharp knife and the topping is lightly browned.

To Microwave
Prepare the potatoes as above. Place the remaining fat and oil in a large casserole and microwave for 30 seconds. Add the pork and cook for 3 minutes. Remove and place in a 1.7 L/3 pt pie dish. Add the onion, celery and mushrooms to the casserole and cook for 3 minutes. Stir in the flour, then gradually add the hot stock, cider, lemon zest and juice, herbs and salt and pepper. Microwave for 3 minutes or until boiling, stirring 2-3 times. Pour over the pork. Top with potato as above. Microwave for 10 minutes. Reduce power to Defrost for 10 minutes. Brown under a preheated grill.

Barbecue pork in pitta pockets

Serves 4
25 g/1 oz butter
2 tbls clear honey
450 g/1 lb boneless pork spare rib,
**   trimmed of excess fat and cut**
**   into 1 cm/½ inch cubes**
1 onion, finely chopped
1 clove garlic, crushed (optional)
150 ml/¼ pint tomato ketchup
150 ml/¼ pint water
2 tsps Worcestershire sauce
2 tsps white wine vinegar
½ tsp sweet paprika
½ tsp chilli powder
salt and freshly ground black
**   pepper**
To serve
4 pitta breads
few lettuce leaves
4 tomatoes, sliced
1 small green pepper, seeded
**   and cut into thin rings**

1   Melt the butter in a large heavy-based frying-pan. Add the honey and pork and fry briskly over fairly high heat, stirring frequently, until the pork is browned on all sides. Add the onion and garlic, if using, lower the heat and fry gently for a further 5 minutes.

25 g/1 oz plain flour
salt
1 tbls paprika
700 g/1½ lb lean boneless stewing
    pork, trimmed and cut into 2.5
    cm/1 in cubes
300 ml/½ pt chicken stock
1 tbls tomato purée
1 tbls clear honey
grated zest and juice of 1 lemon
1 green pepper, seeded and diced
1 red pepper, seeded and diced

1   Heat the margarine or butter and oil in a large flameproof casserole or heavy-based saucepan, add the onion and fry gently for 5 minutes. Remove with a slotted spoon and reserve.

2   Put the flour in a polythene bag, season with salt and add the paprika. Add the cubed pork and shake until it is evenly coated. Reserve any excess flour.

3   Add the pork to the casserole and fry over moderate heat, turning from time to time, for 4–5 minutes until lightly browned.

4   Remove the casserole from the heat. Mix the stock with the tomato purée and honey and gradually stir into the casserole. Stir in the lemon zest and juice, diced peppers, reserved flour and onion.

5   Return the casserole to the heat, bring to the boil, then lower the heat and simmer for 2–3 minutes, stirring all the time.

6   Cover the casserole and simmer very gently for 1½–2 hours or until the pork is cooked and tender when pierced with a sharp knife.

To Microwave

Place the margarine or butter, oil and onion in a large casserole and microwave for 3 minutes. Remove and reserve. Toss the pork with flour, salt and paprika. Add to the casserole and cook for 4 minutes, stirring twice. Mix in the hot stock, tomato purée, honey, lemon zest and juice, peppers and onion. Microwave for 3 minutes or until boiling, stirring 3-4 times. Cover and microwave for 1-1½ hours on Defrost or until the pork is tender. Stir twice.

Pork and pimiento stew   Instead of using a fresh red pepper, add a 175 g/6 oz can of pimientos, drained and diced, about 15 minutes before the end of cooking. For extra spice, add 1 clove garlic, crushed, with the onion.

Above: *Pork and pepper stew*

2   Mix the tomato ketchup and water in a bowl and pour into the pan. Stir in the remaining ingredients, add salt and pepper to taste and bring to the boil.

3   Lower the heat and simmer the meat and sauce, uncovered, for 30 minutes until the pork is tender and the sauce is very thick.

4   Meanwhile, heat the grill to high. Toast the pitta breads very lightly on both sides, then cut in half lengthways and ease them open.

5   To serve, push a lettuce leaf, a few tomato slices and green pepper rings into each pitta half and then spoon a little pork and sauce into each one. Transfer to a warmed serving plate and serve at once.

Pork and pepper stew

Serves 4
25 g/1 oz margarine or butter
2 tbls vegetable oil
1 onion, sliced

Left: *Barbecue pork in pitta pockets*

173

Barley and bacon hotpot

Serves 4
25 g/1 oz margarine or butter
250 g/9 oz streaky bacon, derinded and finely chopped
2 large onions, thinly sliced
250 g/9 oz carrots, thinly sliced
175 g/6 oz celery, chopped
100 g/4 oz mushrooms, thinly sliced
250 g/9 oz pearl barley
600 ml/1 pt chicken stock
4 tbls chopped parsley
salt and pepper

1   Heat the oven to 180° C/350° F/gas 4.
2   Melt the fat in a flameproof casserole. Add the bacon and onions and fry gently for 5 minutes.
3   Stir in the vegetables and pearl barley, then the stock. Bring to the boil. Add the parsley and season.
4   Cover and bake for 1 hour, or until the barley is soft and nearly all the liquid has been absorbed. Serve hot.

To Microwave
Place the margarine or butter, onions and bacon in a large casserole and cook for 5-6 minutes. stirring twice. Stir in the carrots, celery, mushrooms and pearl barley. Add the hot stock, parsley and seasoning. Cover and cook for 8 minutes, or until boiling. Reduce power to Defrost for 35-45 minutes, or until the liquid is absorbed. Serve.

Below: *Barley and bacon hotpot*

Casseroled bacon

Serves 4
900 g/2 lb prime collar joint of bacon
1 tbls French mustard
1 tbls Demerara sugar
2 leeks, sliced
3 carrots, sliced
2 celery stalks, chopped
400 g/14 oz can tomatoes
1 tsp dried mixed herbs
freshly ground black pepper

1   Put the bacon in a large saucepan and cover with cold water. Bring to the boil, then lower the heat and simmer gently for 30 minutes.
2   Heat the oven to 180° C/350° F/gas 4.
3   Drain the bacon and leave until cool enough to handle, then strip off the rind. Mix the mustard with sugar and spread over the fat surface.
4   Put the bacon in a large casserole and arrange the leeks, carrots and celery around it. Pour in the tomatoes with their juice, sprinkle in the herbs and plenty of pepper. Cover tightly and cook in the

Above: *Casseroled bacon*

oven for 45-60 minutes or until the juices run clear when the bacon is pierced with a skewer.
5   Serve the bacon carved into slices, with the vegetables and juices spooned over each portion.

Chicken

Saturday night chicken

Illustrated on pages 164-165
Serves 4
8 chicken drumsticks, skinned
**425 g/15 oz can baked beans in
   tomato sauce**
1 tbls molasses or black treacle
½ tsp mustard powder
75 ml/3 fl oz chicken stock
1 large onion, thinly sliced
**1 small green pepper, seeded and
   roughly chopped**
**salt and freshly ground black
   pepper**
½ tsp paprika, to garnish

1   Heat the oven to 190° C/375° F/gas
5.

2   Place   the   skinned   chicken
drumsticks in a large ovenproof dish.
3   In a bowl, mix together the remaining ingredients and season to taste with
salt and pepper. Mix thoroughly, then
spoon over the chicken drumsticks.

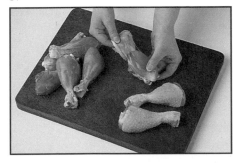

4   Cover and cook in the oven for
1–1¼ hours, stirring occasionally, until
the chicken is tender and the juices run
clear when the meat is pierced in the
thickest part with a fine skewer.

5   Allow to cool for 5 minutes, then
sprinkle with paprika. Serve at once,
while piping hot.

To Microwave
Place the drumsticks in a large casserole
and cover with sauce as above. Cover
and microwave for 10 minutes, stirring
after 5 minutes. Reduce power to Defrost for 10 minutes or until the chicken is
tender and the juices run clear. Serve as
above.

Saturday night chicken special   Serve
with French bread cooked on top of the
chicken: slice half a French loaf into
rounds then spread each with a little
softened butter mixed with herbs. About
15 minutes before the end of the cooking
time for the chicken, uncover the dish
and place the bread, buttered side up,
overlapping around the edge. Return to
oven until golden.

Cider pot roast chicken

Illustrated on page 142
Serves 4
1.7 kg/3½ lb oven-ready chicken
2 tbls plain flour
**salt and freshly ground black
   pepper**
40 g/1½ oz margarine or butter
4-5 carrots, cut into chunks
2 onions, sliced into rings
**450 g/1 lb tomatoes, skinned and
   quartered, or 400 g/14 oz can
   tomatoes, drained**
1 tsp dried rosemary
300 ml/½ pt dry cider

1   Heat the oven to 180° C/350° F/gas
4. Cut up the chicken into four portions.
Season the flour with salt and pepper
and coat the chicken with the seasoned
flour.
2   Melt 25 g/1 oz of the fat in a flameproof casserole, then fry the chicken
pieces over high heat until lightly
browned on all sides. Remove from the
casserole with a slotted spoon and
reserve.
3   Melt the remaining fat in the cas-

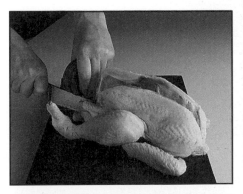

Above: *Cutting a chicken into four portions*

serole and add the carrots and onions.
Fry over moderate heat for 3 minutes,
stirring occasionally.
4   Remove half of the vegetables with a
slotted spoon and reserve. Arrange the
chicken joints over the vegetables remaining in the casserole, then spoon the
reserved vegetables over the chicken.
Add the tomatoes, rosemary, and salt
and pepper to taste. Pour the cider over
the vegetables.
5   Cover the casserole and cook in the
oven for 1 hour, or until the chicken is
tender and cooked through. If you prefer, remove the lid for the last 15 minutes
of cooking time for a 'crusty' top. Serve
hot, straight from the casserole.

Mushroom pot roast chicken Add 225
g/8 oz sliced mushrooms and 4 rashers of
streaky bacon, trimmed and chopped,
when frying the carrots and onions.
Special pot roast chicken Use dry
white wine in place of the dry cider in the
casserole.

Above: *Chicken pilaff*

Chicken pilaff

Serves 4
4 large chicken joints
salt and black pepper
1 tbls vegetable oil
50 g/2 oz butter
1 large onion, peeled and chopped
1 clove garlic, crushed
½ tsp ground cumin
5 cm/2 in piece cinnamon stick,
**   crushed**
6 cardamoms, crushed
6 cloves
250 g/9 oz long-grain rice
600 ml/1 pt chicken stock
½ tsp saffron powder or turmeric
2 bay leaves
50 g/2 oz raisins
50 g/2 oz flaked almonds

1   Wipe the chicken and cut each joint into two pieces. Season lightly. Heat the oil and half the butter in a large saucepan and fry the chicken until browned. Remove the chicken.
2   Fry the onion in the same saucepan for 10 minutes, then add the garlic, ground cumin, cinnamon, cardamoms and cloves, and fry for 2-3 minutes.
3   Return the chicken pieces to the saucepan, cover and cook over a gentle heat for 15 minutes, stirring occasionally.
4   Add the rice, stock, saffron and bay leaves to the chicken; bring to the boil. Cover and cook gently for 10 minutes.
5   Stir in the raisins and cook for a further 5–10 minutes until the rice is tender. Remove bay leaves. Spoon the rice and chicken on to a warm serving dish

and keep warm, until ready to serve.
6   Fry the almonds in the remaining butter for 2-3 minutes; pour over pilaff.

Simple chicken pilaff   If you have difficulty in obtaining spices, omit those listed and substitute 2 tsp curry powder and ½ tsp powdered cinnamon.

Chicken and potato fry

Serves 4
450 g/1 lb potatoes
salt
40 g/1½ oz margarine or butter

1 tbls vegetable oil
2 onions, chopped
1 tsp Worcestershire sauce
250 g/9 oz cooked chicken, diced
pepper
snipped chives, to garnish

1   Boil the potatoes in lightly salted water for 3 minutes. Drain thoroughly and cut into 1 cm/½ in dice.
2   Heat the margarine or butter and oil in a large frying pan. Add onions and potatoes and fry over moderate heat for 10-15 minutes, stirring every 2-3 minutes.
3   Add the Worcestershire sauce and chicken, then season with salt and pepper to taste. Cook for a further 5–10 minutes, again stirring frequently, until the potatoes and onions are just tender and the chicken is heated through.
4   Transfer to a heated serving dish or individual serving bowls, garnish and serve at once.

To Microwave
Dice the potatoes into 1 cm/½ in pieces. Place in a single layer in a casserole. Add 4 tbls water, cover and cook for 5 minutes. Drain. Preheat a large browning dish for 8 minutes. Add the fat, oil, onions and potatoes and microwave for 4 minutes, stirring twice. Add the Worcestershire sauce, chicken and seasoning. Cook for 4 minutes, then serve as above.

Below: *Chicken in the pot*

Pork and potato fry   Use cooked pork in place of the chicken and for additional flavour, add a few rashers of chopped bacon to the frying pan with the onions and potatoes.

If chives are not available, use some finely chopped spring onion tops as a garnish, or 1 tbls of freshly chopped parsley.

Chicken in the pot

Serves 4–6
2.8 L/5 pt chicken stock
2 kg/4½ lb boiling fowl
225 g/8 oz carrots, thickly sliced
225 g/8 oz turnips, thickly sliced
1 leek, trimmed and thickly sliced
salt and freshly ground black
   pepper
6 outer leaves from large green
   cabbage
4 potatoes, thickly sliced
For the stuffing
25 g/1 oz chicken livers
25 g/1 oz butter
75 g/3 oz crumbled stale bread

2 tbls milk
225 g/8 oz smoked gammon, diced
2 cloves garlic, crushed
1 spring onion, finely chopped
2 tbls fresh chopped parsley
pinch each of dried tarragon,
   chervil and ground nutmeg
2 eggs, beaten
salt and pepper

1   Make the stuffing: cook the liver in the butter in a small saucepan over a low heat for about 2 minutes, until browned on all sides but slightly pink inside. Soak the bread in the milk, then chop the liver and mix it with the cooking liquid, the bread, gammon, garlic, spring onion, herbs and nutmeg. Bind the mixture with the eggs and season with salt and pepper. Reserve 150 g/5 oz of the stuffing and put the rest inside the bird. Truss the bird firmly.
2   Bring the stock to the boil in a heavy-based saucepan over a high heat; lower the chicken into it. When the stock boils again, add carrots, turnips and the white part of the leek. Season, then cover and simmer for 1½ hours.
3   Meanwhile, place the cabbage

Above: *Chicken and potato fry*

leaves in a large bowl, pour over boiling water and leave until soft, about 5 minutes. Drain leaves and allow to cool. Place 1 tbls of the reserved stuffing in the centre of each leaf. Fold into square parcels and secure with cocktail sticks.
4   When the chicken has cooked 1½ hours, add the potatoes and cabbage parcels and cook for about 15–20 minutes, until potatoes are tender. Remove chicken and vegetables from pan, and cocktail sticks from cabbage parcels. Serve on warmed plates.

To Microwave
Make the stuffing: put the liver and butter into a small bowl and cook for 1 minute. Finish as above, stuff and truss the bird and put into a large casserole dish. Add the carrots, turnips, leek, hot stock, and seasoning. Cover and microwave for 20 minutes then reduce to Defrost for 20 minutes. Prepare the cabbage parcels as above. Place the potatoes and cabbage around the chicken, re-cover and cook for 10–15 minutes, or until chicken is cooked.

177

Vegetables and Salads

Too often vegetables take second place, while the meat dish takes all the glory. But versatile, flavoursome and economical vegetables make absolutely delicious and filling meals in themselves. Here's a fine choice to prove the truth of these words, using all sorts of imaginative flavourings and ingredients.

Boston baked beans

Serves 8
700 g/1½ lb dried haricot beans,
  soaked overnight
450 g/1 lb salt pork (or bacon), cut
  into 2 pieces
2 Spanish onions, finely chopped
50 g/2 oz butter
2 tsp dry mustard
4 tbls black treacle
4 tbls soft dark brown sugar
salt and pepper
4–6 tbls tomato ketchup

1 Drain the beans and place in a large saucepan. Cover the beans with twice their volume of water and bring to the boil, then simmer for 30–40 minutes, or until tender. Drain, reserving about 600 ml/1 pt of the cooking liquid.
2 Put the pork (or bacon) in another saucepan of cold water and bring to the boil; drain and slash the rind in several places with a sharp knife. Place one of the pieces of salt pork or bacon in a deep casserole.
3 Heat the oven to 140° C/275° F/gas

1. In a medium-sized saucepan, fry the finely chopped onions in the butter until soft and golden. Stir in the dry mustard, treacle, sugar, 1 tsp each of salt and pepper and the reserved cooking liquid. Bring to the boil, stirring. Pour into the beans and mix well, then spoon over the pork in the casserole.
4 Push the remaining piece of pork into the casserole so that the rind remains above the surface. Cover and bake for about 3 hours, stirring every hour, and adding a little boiling water to prevent the beans from drying out too quickly.
5 Stir in the ketchup and serve.

To Microwave

Drain the beans and place in a very large casserole. Add 2.3 L/4 pt boiling water, cover and cook for 15 minutes. Reduce to Defrost for 15 minutes. Drain and reserve 600 ml/1 pt liquid. Place the pork or bacon in a casserole, add 300 ml/½ pt cold water, cover and cook for 10 minutes. Drain and slash the rind. Place the onions and butter in a casserole and cook for 3 minutes. Stir in the mustard, treacle, sugar, seasoning and reserved liquid. Microwave for 5 minutes. Pour over the beans. Add the pork so that one piece remains above the surface. Cover and microwave on Defrost for 1½ hours, stirring twice. Stir in the ketchup and place under a preheated grill to crisp the bacon if wished.

Parsnip and apple layer

Serves 4
salt
700 g/1½ lb parsnips, cut into
  5 mm/¼ in slices
25 g/1 oz margarine or butter
1 onion, finely chopped
450 g/1 lb cooking apples, peeled,
  cored and sliced thinly
½ tsp dried sage
4 tbls vegetable or chicken stock
freshly ground black pepper
100 g/4 oz Cheddar cheese, grated
75–100 g/3–4 oz walnut pieces
walnut halves and parsley, to
  garnish

1 Bring a large pan of salted water to the boil and cook the parsnip slices for 4–5 minutes, until tender. Drain, rinse, then drain again.
2 Heat the oven to 200° C/400° F/gas 6 and grease a shallow ovenproof dish. Melt the fat in a saucepan and fry the onion gently for 5 minutes. Add apple slices, sage and stock. Cook gently, covered, for 5–7 minutes, until the apples are soft. Add salt and pepper to taste and stir to break up the apples.
3 Arrange one-third of the parsnips in the bottom of the prepared dish and season them with salt and pepper. Sprinkle with one-third of the cheese and half the walnut pieces, then spread with half the apple sauce. Repeat layers again, then cover with remaining parsnips and top with the remaining cheese.
4 Bake, uncovered, for 30 minutes

Left: Boston baked beans

Above: *Parsnip and apple layer*

until the cheese is melted but not browned. Garnish with walnut halves and parsley.

Solo savoury suppers

Serves 4

1 tbls vegetable oil
175 g/6 oz streaky bacon rashers, chopped
250 g/9 oz courgettes, cut into 5 mm/¼ in dice
4 large eggs
4 tbls milk
150 ml/¼ pt single cream
salt and freshly ground black pepper
1 tbls grated Parmesan cheese
50 g/2 oz Cheddar cheese, grated
25 g/1 oz fresh white breadcrumbs

1 Heat the oven to 190° C/375° F/gas 5.
2 Heat the oil in a frying pan, add the bacon and fry for 7 minutes until crisp. Remove the bacon with a slotted spoon and put in a bowl. Add the courgettes to the pan and fry, stirring, for 5 minutes until the courgettes are soft. Remove with a slotted spoon and add them to the fried bacon, mixing well together.
3 Spoon mixture into four 300 ml/½ pt ovenproof dishes.
4 Beat the eggs, milk and cream together in a bowl and season to taste

with salt and pepper. Pour the mixture over the bacon and courgettes in the dishes.
5 Bake in the oven for 25–30 minutes until the mixture is just set.
6 Meanwhile, heat the grill to moderate and mix the cheeses and breadcrumbs together in a bowl.
7 Remove the dishes from the oven, sprinkle over the cheese and breadcrumb mixture. Grill for 3 minutes until the topping is golden. Serve at once.

To Microwave
Place the oil and bacon in a casserole and microwave for 3 minutes. Remove the bacon. Add the courgettes and cook for 4 minutes. Mix the courgettes and bacon together and divide between four 300 ml/½ pt heatproof dishes. Top with the egg mix as above. Three quarter cover with cling film. Microwave two at a time for 2½–3 minutes or until just set. Finish as above.

Savoury mushroom supper Substitute chopped mushrooms for the courgettes and use Gruyère or Emmental cheese instead of Cheddar. Use milk instead of cream for a less rich dish.

Right: *Solo savoury suppers*

Above: *Flat leek omelette*

Flat leek omelette

Serves 4
40 g/1½ oz butter
450 g/1 lb leeks, very thinly sliced
salt and pepper
6 eggs
75 g/3 oz Cheddar cheese, grated

1   Melt half the butter in a shallow saucepan. Add the leeks, season well, cover and cook over low heat for 15 minutes, or until soft.
2   Heat the grill to high.
3   Break the eggs into a bowl, season with salt and pepper and beat lightly with a fork.
4   Melt the remaining butter in a large frying pan over high heat, swirling it to cover base of pan.
5   When the butter is really hot, but not brown, quickly add the beaten eggs. Reduce the heat to moderate and allow the edges to set. Using a spatula, gently lift the edges of the omelette and allow the uncooked egg to roll around the edge.
6   Continue until most of the runny egg has been incorporated, leaving a little moist mixture on top.
7   Remove the pan from the heat, spoon the leeks evenly over the top, then sprinkle over the grated cheese. Place the pan under the preheated grill for just long enough to melt the cheese. Run a spatula around the edge of the omelette to loosen it, then cut it into wedges and serve at once.

To Microwave
Place half the butter in a large casserole. Add the leeks, cover and cook for 8 minutes, stirring twice. Lightly beat the eggs and seasoning together. Place the remaining butter in a 25 cm/10 in round dish. Microwave for 30 seconds to melt. Add the eggs, cover with pierced cling film and cook for 2 minutes. Mix with a fork, moving the cooked edges to the centre. Re-cover and cook for 2 minutes, or until nearly set. Spoon over the leeks and sprinkle with cheese. Place under a preheated grill to finish.

Brussels sprouts omelette   Substitute Brussels sprouts for the leeks and add a little grated nutmeg to the vegetables.

Corn and egg nest

Serves 4
8 eggs
25 g/1 oz margarine or butter
100 g/4 oz bacon rashers, derinded and cut into strips
25 g/1 oz plain flour
300 ml/½ pt milk
285 g/10 oz can sweetcorn, drained
1 tsp Worcestershire sauce
salt and freshly ground black pepper
1 small packet potato crisps, crushed
1 tbls finely chopped fresh parsley

1   Put the eggs into a saucepan, cover with cold water and bring to the boil. Simmer for 5 minutes.
2   Meanwhile, heat the grill to high.
3   Run cold water over the eggs and carefully remove the egg shells. Put the hard-boiled eggs into a bowl, cover with warm water and then set the bowl aside until needed.
4   Melt the fat in a small frying pan, add the bacon and fry for 4–5 minutes until lightly browned. Sprinkle in the flour and stir over low heat for 1–2 minutes. Remove from the heat and gradually stir in the milk. Return to the heat and simmer, stirring, until the mixture is thick and smooth.
5   Stir the canned sweetcorn and the Worcestershire sauce into the bacon sauce. Taste and season with salt, if absolutely necessary, and freshly ground black pepper.
6   Spread the sweetcorn mixture in a flameproof serving dish. Dry the eggs on absorbent paper and arrange them in the corn. Sprinkle over the crushed crisps. Put the dish under the grill for a few mi-

1 tbls freshly grated Parmesan cheese

1 Heat the oven to 180° C/350° F/gas 4.

2 Grease a 2 L/3½ pt soufflé or ovenproof dish.

3 Pour the celery soup into a saucepan and warm through gently. Stir in the celery.

4 Remove the soup from the heat and stir in the egg yolks and grated nutmeg. Season to taste with salt and freshly ground black pepper.

5 In a clean, dry bowl whisk the egg whites until they are standing in stiff peaks.

6 Using a metal spoon, fold a spoonful of the stiffly beaten egg whites into the egg yolk and celery mixture and then carefully fold in the remainder of the egg whites.

7 Pour the mixture into the prepared soufflé or ovenproof dish, then bake for 40 minutes.

8 Carefully slide the oven shelf out a little way, sprinkle the grated Parmesan over the soufflé and return it to the oven for a further 5 minutes. Serve the soufflé immediately.

Mushroom soufflé Use a can of condensed mushroom soup and some sliced fresh mushrooms instead of the celery soup and chopped celery. Freshly grated cheddar cheese can be used instead of grated Parmesan. You can, of course, omit the cheese altogether if you like or serve a bowl of grated cheese separately so that guests can help themselves.

Below: *Celery soufflé*

Above: *Corn and egg nest*

Celery soufflé

Serves 4
300 g/10 oz condensed celery soup
3 celery stalks, chopped
3 egg yolks
pinch of grated nutmeg
salt and freshly ground black pepper
4 egg whites

nutes to warm the crisps. Sprinkle parsley over the top and serve at once, straight from the dish.

To Microwave
Prepare the eggs as above. Place the margarine or butter and bacon in a casserole and microwave for 4 minutes, stirring after 2 minutes. Mix in the flour, then gradually stir in the milk. Cook for 3 minutes or until the mixture is thickened, stirring 3–4 times. Stir in the sweetcorn, Worcestershire sauce and seasoning. Finish preparing the Corn and egg nest exactly as above.

Easy eggs in a nest Use canned creamed sweetcorn or a condensed soup like mushroom instead of making the sauce. Add it to the bacon rashers and heat.

Ratatouille

Serves 8
**3 large aubergines, halved
    lengthways**
**3 large courgettes, halved
    lengthways**
150 ml/5 fl oz olive oil
3 large onions, sliced in thin rings
4 tbls tomato purée
4 cloves garlic, chopped
**3 large green or red peppers, seeded
    and cut into thin strips**
**5 large tomatoes, blanched,
    skinned and chopped, or 400 g/
    14 oz can tomatoes, well
    drained**
freshly ground black pepper
pinch of ground coriander
small pinch of cinnamon
pinch of dried basil

1   Cut the aubergines and courgettes across into slices about 20 mm/³⁄₄ in thick. Place them in layers in a colander, sprinkling each layer with salt. Top them with a weighted plate and drain the vegetables for 1 hour.
2   Heat the olive oil gently in a broad, heavy pan over low heat and cook the onions in it for about 15 minutes, then stir in the tomato purée and cook for 3–4 minutes, stirring occasionally.
3   Dry the aubergines and courgettes with absorbent paper and stir them into the pan. Add the garlic and the peppers, shake the pan, cover and simmer for about 20 minutes.
4   Add the tomatoes and the rest of seasoning, stir once or twice and leave to cook for a further 40–45 minutes. Uncover for the final few minutes to let the sauce reduce if the dish seems too liquid. Serve at once.

To Microwave
Prepare the aubergines and courgettes as above. Place the olive oil and onions

in a large casserole and microwave for 5 minutes, stirring twice. Add the tomato purée and cook for 2 minutes. Dry the aubergines and courgettes and add to the casserole. Add the garlic and peppers, cover and cook for 15 minutes, stirring twice. Add the tomatoes, and the rest of the seasoning, re-cover and cook for 5 minutes. Reduce power to Defrost for 15 minutes.

Picnic ratatouille   Cool the ratatouille and chill in the refrigerator. Serve cold at picnics and barbecues with grated Cheddar or Parmesan cheese.

Above: *Celeriac and ham salad*

Celeriac and ham salad

Serves 4
600 g/1¼ lb celeriac
250 g/9 oz cooked ham, diced
150–175 g/5–6 oz radishes, sliced
**1 punnet mustard and cress, to
    garnish**

For the dressing
6 tbls thick bottled mayonnaise
1 tsp French mustard
1 tsp clear honey
salt and pepper

1   Make the dressing: put the mayonnaise into a large bowl, mix in the mustard and honey and season to taste with salt and pepper.
2   Peel the celeriac and grate it coarsely. Stir the celeriac into the dressing with the ham and the sliced radishes until thoroughly coated.
3   Transfer to a serving dish, garnish with mustard and cress and serve at once.

Spicy vegetable kebabs

Serves 6
**1 green and 1 red pepper, each
    seeded and cut into about
    12 squares**
12 button onions
salt
12 button mushrooms
**450 g/1 lb can pineapple cubes,
    drained**
For the sauce
**2 × 150 g/5 oz cartons natural
    yoghurt**
2 cloves garlic, crushed
**5 cm/2 in piece fresh root ginger,
    peeled and grated**
2 tsp garam masala
juice of 1 lemon
pinch of salt

Left: *Ratatouille*

Pasta and salami salad

Serves 4
4 tbls mayonnaise
2 tbls single cream
225 g/8 oz pasta shells, cooked
1 green pepper, seeded and
  shredded
4 spring onions, chopped
4 tomatoes, skinned and chopped
  coarsely
100 g/4 oz sweetcorn, cooked
100 g/4 oz sliced Italian salami,
  quartered
salt and pepper
watercress, to garnish

1   Thin the mayonnaise with the cream.
2   Mix the mayonnaise with all the other ingredients, except the watercress. Transfer to a serving bowl and garnish with sprigs of watercress and serve immediately.

Pasta and ham salad Substitute sliced and chopped ham for the salami. Use red instead of green pepper and add halved pitted black olives.

Below: Pasta and salami salad

Above: *Spicy vegetable kebabs*

1   Make the sauce: put all the sauce ingredients in a bowl, mix well and leave to stand for 30 minutes to allow the flavours to blend.
2   Meanwhile, blanch the peppers and onions: bring a large pan of salted water to the boil, add the peppers and onions and boil for 1 minute. Drain and immediately plunge into cold water to prevent further cooking. Drain well again and pat dry with absorbent paper.
3   Heat the grill to moderate.
4   Divide the peppers, onions, mushrooms and pineapple pieces into six portions and thread them on to six oiled metal kebab skewers, alternating the shapes and colours.
5   Lay the skewers on a baking tray or grill pan and brush with some of the sauce. Grill the kebabs for about 8 minutes, turning them every few minutes, and brushing with more sauce, until vegetables are evenly browned. Serve at once.

Barbecue kebabs Cook the kebabs outside on a barbecue; add three bacon rolls to each skewer for a meaty dish or halved scallops for a fishy one.

Above: *Italian cauliflower*

Italian cauliflower

Serves 4
1 large onion, sliced
1 clove garlic, crushed
3 tbls oil
1 cauliflower, broken into florets
400 g/14 oz can chopped tomatoes
225 g/8 oz salami, roughly chopped
2 tbls chopped fresh or 1 tsp dried
   basil
2 tbls grated Parmesan cheese

1   Fry the onion and garlic in the oil until soft but not browned, about 5 minutes.
2   Add the cauliflower and cook for 1 minute, stirring. Add the tomatoes with their juice, stirring to break up the tomatoes. Bring to the boil, lower the heat, and simmer, covered for 15 minutes, until cauliflower is just tender.
3   Add the salami and cook for a few minutes more to warm through.
4   Transfer the mixture to a warmed serving dish and sprinkle with the basil and Parmesan cheese. Serve at once.

To Microwave
Put the onion, garlic and oil into a 2.3 L/4 pt casserole and microwave for 3 minutes. Stir after 2 minutes. Add the cauliflower, stir, cover and cook for 3 minutes. Add the tomatoes, re-cover and cook for 7 minutes, or until the cauliflower is tender. Stir after 4 minutes. Add the salami, re-cover and cook for 1 minute. Serve as above.

Vegetable hotpot

Serves 4
25 g/1 oz margarine or butter
1 large onion, thinly sliced
250 g/9 oz carrots, sliced
600 ml/1 pt hot chicken or beef
   stock
1 tbls tomato purée
bouquet garni
salt and pepper
250 g/9 oz leeks, sliced
100 g/4 oz parsnips, diced
250 g/9 oz potatoes, cut into chunks
grated Cheddar cheese, to serve

1   Melt the margarine in a large saucepan, add the onion and fry gently for 5 minutes, until soft and lightly coloured. Add the carrots and stir for 1 minute. Pour on the stock, add the tomato purée and bouquet garni and season to taste with salt and pepper. Stir well.
2   Bring to the boil, cover, lower the heat and simmer gently for 10 minutes.
3   Add the leeks and parsnips and cook for a further 10 minutes. Add a little extra boiling water if the sauce seems to be drying out.
4   Add the potatoes to the saucepan, cover and cook for a further 30 minutes, or until all the vegetables are tender.
5   Discard the bouquet garni and serve hot in a warmed serving dish, with the cheese handed round separately.

To Microwave
Place the margarine or butter and onion in a casserole and microwave for 3 minutes. Add the carrots and cook for 1 minute. Add the hot stock, tomato purée, bouquet garni and seasoning to taste. Cover and microwave for 5 minutes. Add the leeks and parsnips, re-cover and cook for 5 minutes. Add the potatoes, cover and cook for 10–15 minutes until tender. Discard bouquet garni and finish as above.

Courgette and tomato bake

Serves 4
450 g/1 lb courgettes, thinly sliced
salt
50 g/2 oz margarine
25 g/1 oz plain flour
300 ml/½ pt milk
75 g/3 oz Cheddar cheese, grated
1 tbls vegetable oil
350 g/12 oz tomatoes, skinned and
   sliced
1 tsp chopped fresh basil
pepper
25 g/1 oz fresh brown breadcrumbs
fresh basil sprig, to garnish
   (optional)

1   Heat the oven to 190° C/375° F/gas 5.
2   Put the courgettes in a colander, sprinkle with salt and leave to drain for 35-40 minutes.
3   Meanwhile, make the sauce: melt half the margarine in a saucepan, sprinkle in the flour and stir over low heat for 1–2 minutes until straw-coloured. Remove from the heat and gradually stir in milk. Return to the heat and simmer, stirring, until it is thick and smooth. Add 50 g/2 oz of the cheese and season with salt and pepper to taste. Set aside.
4   Rinse the courgettes thoroughly under cold running water, then pat dry with a tea-towel.
5   Melt the remaining margarine and the oil in a frying pan, add the courgettes and fry gently, turning frequently, for 10 minutes. Drain on absorbent paper.
6   Arrange half the courgettes in a 1 L/1¾ pt ovenproof dish, cover with half the sliced tomatoes, sprinkle with half the basil and salt, if needed. Add pepper to taste. Spread half the cheese sauce over the tomatoes. Repeat these layers once more.
7   Mix the breadcrumbs with the re-

Above: *Vegetable hotpot*

maining grated Cheddar cheese and sprinkle the mixture evenly over the top of the dish.

8 Bake for 45 minutes until the top is golden. Garnish with a fresh basil sprig, if liked, and serve at once.

To Microwave
Prepare the courgettes as above. Place half the margarine in a jug and microwave for 30 seconds to melt. Stir in the flour, then gradually add the milk. Microwave for 3 minutes or until thickened, stirring 3-4 times. Stir in the cheese and seasoning to taste. Rinse and dry the courgettes. Place the remaining margarine and oil in a casserole and add the courgettes. Cook for 5 minutes and drain. Arrange in a 1 L/1¾ pt heatproof dish as above. Microwave for 10 minutes. Place the dish under a preheated grill to brown. Garnish, if liked, and serve.

Right: *Courgette and tomato bake*

Rice and Pasta

Nutritious and inexpensive, rice and pasta make some of the most satisfying meals for lunch or supper. They're both easy and quick to prepare and mix extremely well with a wide variety of foods. Here's a savoury choice of risottos and pasta dishes with mouth-watering fillings and super sauces, including some new and old favourites.

Egg and bacon spaghetti

Serves 4
4 eggs
75 g/3 oz Parmesan cheese, grated
salt and freshly ground black
  pepper
350 g/12 oz spaghetti
1 tbls olive oil
225 g/8 oz streaky bacon rashers,
  derinded and cut into narrow
  strips
½ dried red chilli pepper (optional)

1 Beat the eggs in a bowl, then stir in two-thirds of the cheese and plenty of pepper. Set aside.
2 Bring a pan of salted water to the boil and cook the spaghetti for about 10 minutes until **al dente** (tender, yet firm to the bite).
3 Meanwhile, heat the oil in a large frying pan and add the bacon strips and chilli pepper, if using. Fry over high heat until the bacon is crisp and beginning to brown. Discard the chilli pepper, if used.
4 Drain the spaghetti well, then add to the frying pan and quickly fork it round to mix with the oil and bacon. Remove the pan from the heat.
5 Pour the egg and cheese mixture over the spaghetti in the pan and quickly fork through. Turn the spaghetti into a warmed serving dish and grind more pepper over the top. Hand the remaining Parmesan cheese separately.

Spinach and mushroom lasagne

Illustrated on pages 188-189
Serves 4
2 tbls vegetable oil
1 onion, finely chopped
100 g/4 oz mushrooms, sliced
450 g/1 lb frozen spinach, defrosted
  and well drained
1–2 tbls lemon juice
¼ tsp grated nutmeg
salt and pepper
225 g/8 oz cottage cheese
100 g/4 oz Cheddar cheese,
  grated
175 g/6 oz green pre-cooked
  lasagne
For the sauce
25 g/1 oz margarine or butter
15 g/½ oz plain flour
225 ml/8 fl oz milk
4–5 tbls grated Parmesan cheese

1 Heat the oil in a heavy-based pan and fry the onion for 3-4 minutes, until soft but not coloured. Add the mushrooms and cook, stirring, for 5 minutes. Add the spinach, lemon juice and nutmeg and season. Simmer for 5-6 minutes, stirring occasionally.
2 Meanwhile, mix the cottage cheese with the grated Cheddar in a bowl; season to taste with pepper.
3 Heat the oven to 190° C/375° F/gas 5. Grease a 19–20 cm/7½-8 in square, shallow ovenproof dish.
4 Make the sauce: melt fat in a small pan, sprinkle in the flour and stir over a low heat for 1–2 minutes, until straw-coloured. Remove from heat and gradually stir in the milk. Return to the heat and simmer. Add the Parmesan cheese and salt and pepper to taste.
5 Put one-half of the lasagne in the prepared dish, spread with half the cottage cheese mixture, then half the spinach mixture. Repeat the layers, ending with the spinach. Spread sauce on top.
6 Bake in oven for 30-35 minutes, until the top is bubbling and golden. Leave to cool slightly before serving.

To Microwave
Place the oil and onion in a casserole and microwave for 3 minutes. Add the mushrooms and cook for 3 minutes. Add the spinach, lemon juice, nutmeg and seasoning. Cover and cook for 5 minutes, stirring twice. Mix the cottage cheese and

Cheddar together and season with pepper. Melt the margarine or butter in a jug for 30 seconds, stir in the flour and gradually add the milk. Microwave for 3–4 minutes, or until thickened, stirring 3–4 times. Add the Parmesan and seasoning. Layer in a 20 cm/8 in square dish as above. Microwave for 10 minutes. Reduce the power to Defrost for 10 minutes. Place under a preheated grill to brown.

Artichoke and bacon lasagne Substitute a 275 g/10 oz can artichoke hearts for half the spinach and put these in the second layer. Add 2–3 rashers chopped smoked bacon to the mushrooms in stage 1.

Cheesy pasta swizzles

Serves 4
salt
1 tsp vegetable oil
250 g/9 oz pasta spirals
25 g/1 oz margarine or butter
1 onion, finely chopped
100 g/4 oz cooked ham, cut into 5
  cm/2 in strips
100 g/4 oz mature Cheddar cheese,
  grated
50 g/2 oz full-fat soft cheese with
  garlic and herbs
1 tbls milk
1 tsp dried marjoram

Noodles napoletana

Serves 4
1 tbls vegetable oil
1 large onion, finely chopped
175 g/6 oz mushrooms
225 g/8 oz back bacon, derinded
  and chopped
3 celery stalks, chopped
1 large clove garlic, crushed
  (optional)
2 tbls tomato purée
175 ml/6 fl oz chicken stock
1 tsp dried oregano
salt and freshly ground black
  pepper
250 g/9 oz ribbon noodles
15 g/½ oz butter
1 tbls grated Parmesan cheese

1 Heat the oil in a frying pan over moderate heat. Add the onion, mushrooms, bacon and celery and fry for 3 minutes, stirring from time to time.
2 Add garlic, if using, tomato purée, stock and oregano to the pan. Season well with salt and pepper, lower the heat and simmer for 5 minutes, stirring from time to time.
3 Cook the noodles in plenty of boiling salted water for 5 minutes or until just tender. Drain and return to the rinsed-out pan, then toss with the butter to coat the noodles evenly.
4 Turn the noodles on to a hot serving dish and spoon the bacon and mushroom mixture over the top. Sprinkle evenly with grated Parmesan cheese and serve at once.

Above: *Cheesy pasta swizzles*

salt and pepper
4 tomatoes, thinly sliced
¼ tsp cayenne pepper or paprika,
  to garnish
1½ tsp finely chopped fresh
  parsley, to garnish

1 Bring a large pan of salted water to the boil, swirl in the oil, then add the pasta. Bring back to the boil and cook for 7–10 minutes, until just tender.
2 Meanwhile, melt the fat in a large saucepan, add the onion and fry gently for 5 minutes until soft.
3 Drain the pasta very thoroughly, then stir into the fat and onion. Add the ham and cook for 1 minute, stirring well until heated through. Remove from the heat and add the cheeses, milk and marjoram. Mix until the cheese melts and coats the pasta. Season to taste.
4 Arrange the tomato slices around the edge of four warmed shallow dishes. Place the pasta and sauce in the centre of each dish. Sprinkle a little cayenne pepper and parsley on top and serve at once.

Left: *Egg and bacon spaghetti*
Right: *Noodles napoletana*

Pasta and ham supper

Serves 4

salt
2 tsp vegetable oil
225 g/8 oz pasta shells
2 × 300 g/10 oz cans condensed
   chicken soup
175 g/6 oz Parma ham, fat removed
   and cut into thin strips
225 g/8 oz frozen peas, defrosted
2 egg yolks
2 tbls snipped chives or chopped
   fresh parsley
pepper

1   Heat the oven to 110° C/225° F/gas
¼. Bring a saucepan of salted water to
the boil, add the vegetable oil and cook
the pasta for about 12 minutes, or until it
is just soft. Drain well and turn into a
warmed serving dish. Cover and keep
warm in the oven.
2   While the pasta is cooking, heat the
chicken soup in a saucepan. Add the
ham strips and the peas. Heat until the
soup is just bubbling.
3   Beat the egg yolks into the contents
of the pan and warm through very gently
without boiling. Stir in half the chives or
parsley and season to taste with pepper.
Spoon the sauce over the pasta and
sprinkle with the remaining herbs.

Below: *Pasta and ham supper*

Pasta and chicken supper Try substituting condensed mushroom soup for
the chicken soup and add shredded
cooked chicken in place of the ham and
drained canned sweetcorn instead of the
peas.

Pork and mushroom risotto

Illustrated on pages 188-189
Serves 4

100 g/4 oz streaky bacon rashers,
   derinded and cut into 1 cm/½ in
   dice
50 g/2 oz margarine or butter
2 onions, chopped
1 clove garlic, crushed (optional)
1 green pepper, seeded and thinly
   sliced
1 red pepper, seeded and thinly
   sliced
100 g/4 oz mushrooms, thinly sliced
350 g/12 oz pork fillet, cut into 2.5
   cm/1 in cubes
300 g/11 oz long-grain rice
about 850 ml/1½ pt hot chicken
   stock
3 large tomatoes, skinned and
   chopped
salt and freshly ground black
   pepper
100 g/4 oz mushrooms, thinly sliced
2 tbls chopped fresh parsley
50 g/2 oz Parmesan cheese, grated

1   Fry the bacon in a large frying pan
with a lid over moderate heat for 3-4
minutes until the fat runs. Remove the
bacon from the pan with a slotted spoon
and set aside.
2   Lower heat and melt the margarine
or butter in the pan. Add the onions and
garlic, if using, and fry gently for 5 minutes
until soft and lightly coloured. Add the

peppers and mushrooms to the pan and
fry, stirring occasionally, for 2 minutes.
Remove the vegetables with a slotted
spoon and reserve with the bacon.
3   Add pork and fry, turning often, for
6–8 minutes until evenly browned on all
sides.
4   Add the rice and stir to coat all the
grains with fat. Stir in the chicken stock.
Return the bacon, onions, peppers and
mushrooms to the pan, add the tomatoes and season with salt and pepper
to taste. Bring to the boil, stir well to mix,
then lower the heat, cover and simmer
very gently for 40 minutes.
5   Taste the rice grains – they should be

Above: *Country risotto*

just tender, but not soft. If necessary, cook for a few minutes longer, adding a little more hot stock if needed.

6 Turn the risotto into a warmed serving dish and sprinkle with the parsley and cheese. Serve at once.

To Microwave

Place the bacon in a large casserole and microwave for 3 minutes. Remove and reserve. Add the fat, onions and garlic and cook for 3 minutes. Add the peppers and cook for 2 minutes. Add the vegetables to the bacon and reserve. Add the pork and cook for 5 minutes, stirring twice. Add the rice and stir. Add the stock, bacon and vegetables. Add the mushrooms, tomatoes and seasoning. Cover and microwave for 15 minutes. Serve as above.

Country risotto

Serves 4
3 tbls vegetable oil
1 large onion, finely chopped
1 clove garlic, crushed (optional)
250 g/9 oz easy-cook long-grain rice
400 g/14 oz can tomatoes
50 g/2oz ham, chopped
100 g/4 oz mushrooms, sliced
½ tsp dried thyme
½ tsp dried oregano
salt and freshly ground black pepper
450–600 ml/¾–1 pt hot ham or chicken stock
25 g/1 oz grated Parmesan cheese, to serve

1 Heat the oil in a large frying pan. Add the onion and garlic, if using, and fry gently for 5 minutes until the onion is soft and lightly coloured, stirring constantly.

2 Add the rice and cook, stirring occasionally, until it begins to brown and swell.

3 Add the tomatoes with their juice, stirring with a wooden spoon to break them up. Add the ham and mushrooms, then sprinkle in the thyme and oregano and season with salt and pepper to taste. Stir in 150 ml/¼ pt stock and simmer, uncovered, over low heat for 15 minutes. Repeat twice more, adding the same amount of stock after 15-minute intervals, stirring well each time stock is added. Test the rice, if it has too much 'bite', add a further 150 ml/¼ pt stock and cook for 10 minutes more.

4 Spoon the risotto into a warmed serving dish, sprinkle with Parmesan and serve at once.

Savoury rice mountain

Serves 4
vegetable oil, for greasing
250 g/9 oz cooked long-grain rice
  (use 75 g/3 oz to give required
  amount)
350 g/12 oz can luncheon meat,
  diced
2 hard-boiled eggs, chopped
200 g/7 oz can sweetcorn, drained
75 g/3 oz frozen peas, cooked
3 tbls thick bottled mayonnaise
salt and pepper
2 tbls snipped chives and grated
  carrot, to garnish
extra mayonnaise, to serve

1 Brush the inside of a 1.2 L/2 pt jelly mould or pudding basin with vegetable oil. Set aside.
2 In a large bowl, toss the rice, luncheon meat, eggs, sweetcorn and peas. Mix in the mayonnaise and season with salt and pepper.
3 Spoon the rice into the prepared mould and then press down firmly. Cover with a plate and weight down. Refrigerate at least 1 hour.
4 Remove the weight and plate from the mould and invert a serving plate on top. Holding mould and plate firmly together, turn them over, then carefully lift off the mould to release the rice. Arrange chives on top and grated carrot around the rice mountain and hand a bowl of mayonnaise separately.

Tuna rice mountain Use a 200 g/7 oz can tuna, drained and flaked, instead of the luncheon meat and add leftover vegetables such as carrots and beans, chopped, to give extra colour and flavour.

Vegetable fried rice

Serves 4
250 g/9 oz long-grain rice
salt
250 g/9 oz carrots, diced
1 parsnip, diced
1 small turnip, diced
2 tbls vegetable oil
1 large onion, chopped
1 clove garlic, crushed (optional)
50 g/2 oz button mushrooms, sliced
2 large tomatoes, skinned and
  sliced
50 g/2 oz frozen peas, defrosted
freshly ground black pepper
2 eggs, lightly beaten
1 tbls chopped fresh parsley
grated Parmesan cheese, to serve

1 Bring a large saucepan of salted water to the boil, add the rice and cover. Lower the heat and simmer for 10 minutes, or until the rice is just tender.
2 Meanwhile, bring another pan of salted water to the boil. Add the carrots, parsnip and turnip and cover. Lower the heat and cook for about 8–10 minutes, or until all the vegetables are barely tender.
3 Drain the cooked root vegetables and reserve. Drain the rice in a colander and rinse well under hot running water to separate the grains. Drain again.
4 Heat the oil in a large non-stick saucepan, add the onion and garlic, if using, and fry gently for 5 minutes, until the onion is soft and lightly coloured.
5 Add the drained root vegetables to the pan, together with the mushrooms, tomatoes, peas and rice. Stir well and season to taste with salt and plenty of pepper. Cover the pan and cook over very low heat for 10 minutes.

6 Stir in the eggs and gently turn the mixture so that the egg cooks. Remove from the heat and turn into a warmed serving dish. Garnish with the parsley and serve at once with the Parmesan cheese.

Meat and vegetables fried rice Add 100 g/4 oz chopped ham or cooked chicken at the beginning of stage 5. Small partly cooked cauliflower florets make a tasty alternative to the root vegetables.

Vegetable biriani

Serves 4–6
2 tbls vegetable oil
1 large onion, chopped
2 cloves garlic, crushed
2 tsp hot curry powder
½ tsp ground cinnamon
½ tsp ground ginger
425 ml/¾ pt water
1 tbls tomato purée
1 large carrot, diced
2 tsp salt
225 g/8 oz long-grain rice
75 g/3 oz seedless raisins
250 g/9 oz sliced runner or French
  beans, fresh or frozen
175 g/6 oz frozen peas

1 Heat the oil in a large saucepan. Add the onion and garlic and fry gently for about 10 minutes until the onion is soft but not browned, stirring frequently.
2 Add the spices to the pan, stir well and cook for a further 2 minutes.
3 Add the water, tomato purée, carrot and salt. Bring to the boil.
4 Add the rice, raisins and fresh or frozen beans, and stir well.
5 Lower the heat, cover and simmer gently for 20 minutes, without stirring.
6 Gently fork in the frozen peas, cover and simmer gently for 5 minutes. Serve hot.

To Microwave
Place the oil, onion and garlic in a large casserole and cook for 3 minutes. Add the spices, stir and cook for 1 minute. Add the water, tomato purée, carrot and salt. Cover and microwave for 10 minutes or until boiling. Add the rice, raisins and beans. Re-cover and microwave for 10 minutes. Add the peas, re-cover and cook for 5 minutes.

Left: *Savoury rice mountain*
Right: *Vegetable biriani*

Spanish rice salad

Serves 4–6

12 stuffed olives, thinly sliced
1 red pepper, seeded and thinly
   sliced
1 green pepper, seeded and thinly
   sliced
1 cooked chorizo sausage, diced
½ Spanish onion, finely chopped
6 tbls olive oil

3 tbls lemon juice or wine vinegar
1 clove garlic, finely chopped
¼ tsp powdered saffron
salt and freshly ground black
   pepper
450 g/1 lb cooked long-grain rice
   (you will need 200-225 g/7–8 oz
   raw rice)
200 g/7 oz can tuna fish, drained
   and flaked

1   In a bowl, combine the stuffed olives,
peppers, sausage and onion.

Above: *Spanish rice salad*

2   Combine the olive oil, lemon juice
and garlic. Add the powdered saffron
and season to taste with salt and pepper.
Mix well and pour over the rice.
3   Add the flaked tuna fish and toss well
with a fork. Correct the seasoning, adding a little more olive oil, lemon juice or
wine vinegar and salt and pepper if
necessary. Sprinkle the olives, peppers,
sausage and onion over the top and fork
in lightly.

Cook Healthy

Introduction

Healthy eating means eating meals that are nutritious as well as delicious and satisfying. Such a diet has lots of exciting variety – it need never be dull or tasteless. The simple guidelines given here show you just how easy it is to cook nutritious and appetizing meals that will appeal to the whole family – and keep them healthy, too. You will find lots of helpful information about what foods provide the nutrients we need and helpful tips on planning meals, as well as about buying and storing fresh foods for maximum goodness.

The recipe chapters that follow are full of ideas for family meals using fresh and natural ingredients. Recipes have been specially chosen for their reduced fat and sugar content, and every one is calorie counted. As well as soups, snacks, main meals, vegetables and salads, there are rice and pasta dishes and, surprisingly enough, recipes for puddings, cakes and breads, proving that it is possible to eat healthy meals without having to give up the foods you enjoy most.

Healthy Eating

What we need to eat

Have a think about what you've eaten and drunk in the last 24 hours. Did you enjoy it, and was it healthy?

It is possible to obtain all the vital substances (or nutrients) which the body needs, such as proteins, carbohydrates, fats, vitamins, minerals, water and even fibre, in one liquid. Such liquids are carefully prepared to contain all these nutrients in just the right amounts to enable someone to survive for months or years without the need to eat at all. Will these liquids be the food of the future providing the perfect diet? It is very unlikely; although they are very useful for sick patients who cannot eat, the rest of us like our food too much! This section is all about eating an equally nutritious diet from the foods available on your supermarket shelves.

The function of food

Food has many functions in our lives and good food and cooking can bring great enjoyment and pleasure. Food not only nourishes us but can do wonders for our sense of well-being. The last good meal you ate probably made you feel well long before it was digested and the nutrients were able to be of any benefit.

Almost all foods contain some nutrients. These are essential substances which the body requires to function properly such as to grow, to produce new body cells, to protect us from illness, etc. The importance of a good diet for good health cannot be over-emphasized. A diet lacking any vital nutrient will sooner or later result in problems.

Check the nutrition chart opposite to see where the vital nutrients can be found and what functions they have. Some foods are listed a number of times in the chart because they contain several different nutrients and are therefore particularly wholesome. Foods which are poor sources of nutrients are sugar and alcohol, and all foods based on them, such as sweets, fizzy drinks and alcoholic drinks.

A nutritious, healthy diet is one which provides adequate amounts of all the nutrients. Since foods contain these substances in different amounts, a golden rule is to go for variety.

Food provides energy

Apart from the nutrients our food supplies, it must also give us energy (or calories). Calories are provided from carbohydrates, fats and proteins. The amount of energy that we require is very much an individual matter; a sports-mad teenager will need far more than an inactive elderly person. Insufficient calories can result in weight loss, tiredness, ill health and lack of growth in youngsters.

On the other hand, excess calories which the body cannot use in other ways will be stored as fat. This fat-accumulating process can easily lead to overweight and obesity. Few people enjoy being overweight and many suffer ill health because of it. It can become a serious problem for some people.

It makes sense to choose foods which contain nutrients as well as energy. Two thousand calories provided from a mixture of healthy foods will be far more beneficial than 2000 calories provided from 550 g/1¼ lb sugar.

What is wrong with our diet?

A healthy diet means eating the correct proportions of each type of food, that is, more of some foods, and less of others. Many learned committees have examined the relationship between diet and health. The verdict seems to be that the average British diet is badly balanced and that this is contributing to many of our health problems.

Our diet contains too much fat, sugar and salt, and insufficient fibre. We are recommended to change to a diet that is high in fibre and low in fats (especially saturated fats – see page 202), sugar and salt. Some of the problems which are thought to be associated with a fatty, sugary, salty diet are obesity, heart disease, diabetes, high blood pressure and strokes, tooth decay, constipation and other bowel problems, and some types of cancer. Many of these problems take some time to develop, but by continuing to eat a badly balanced diet, trouble may be brewing for the future.

To make our diet more balanced we need to eat more starchy foods which are high in carbohydrate, such as bread, cereals, pasta, potatoes and pulses.

Above: *Fresh foods – vegetables and fruits in particular – are the mainstay of a healthy diet. Eat dairy produce in moderation*

Eat less fat

We also need to eat less foods containing fat, both visible fat, such as butter, margarine, oil, fried foods and fatty meat, and the less obvious fats found in foods such as pies, biscuits, cakes, sausages, chocolate, high-fat cheeses and cream. Fats and fatty foods are high in calories since fat is a very rich source of energy.

Fats have many functions in cooking and are used to add flavour and texture to foods. Many people prefer chips and roast potatoes to plain boiled potatoes, and most of us will add a lump of butter to an otherwise fatless jacket potato. Salads are also often preferred when coated in an oily dressing or mayonnaise. In fact, fats can be very tasty and this may be one of the reasons why we eat too much of them. We need to eat *less* fat, not give it up altogether.

Cut down on sugar

Sugar is another problem. Apart from the sugar that is in sweet foods such as sweets, cakes and biscuits, and which we add by the spoonful to drinks and cereals, there is also sugar in many other manufactured foods such as canned vegetables, savoury sauces and peanut butter. Our sugar consumption in Britain is one of the highest per person in the world and many people are unknowingly addicted to it. Sugary foods are so enjoyable it is easy to eat too much of them; again, this may contribute to overweight. Sugar is also the main cause of tooth decay.

Another problem with sugar is that it displaces other foods in the diet. A young child who drinks a glass of fizzy orange instead of, say, milk, will miss out on the protein, calcium and other vitamins and minerals in milk.

Again, we are not being advised to give up sugar altogether, although it would not harm us to do so, but to reduce our present high intake drastically. Incidentally, many foods contain natural sugar, such as fruit, milk and some vegetables. There is no problem with these sugars. It is the sugars and syrups which man has refined which we should be concerned about. Honey is also a refined substance but the work has been done by bees; do not use it as a substitute for other sugars, but enjoy it in moderation.

Use less salt

Concern over salt has arisen because of its association with high blood pressure.

NUTRITION CHART

Nutrients	Sources	Function
Carbohydrates	Bread, cereals, pasta, rice, potatoes, root vegetables, fruits, milk, flour, sugar.	Provide energy. Excess is stored as fat.
Proteins	Meat, poultry, fish, eggs, cheese, milk, pulses, nuts, bread, cereals.	Body growth and repair. Excess is used as energy.
Fats	Butter, margarine, oils, meat, cheese, oily fish, nuts.	Provide energy. Excess stored as fat.
Iron	Meat, offal, pulses, dark green vegetables, bread, cereals, eggs.	Necessary for red blood cells and muscles.
Calcium	Milk, yoghurt, cheese, white bread, fish bones.	Formation of bones and teeth
Phosphorus	Present in nearly all foods.	Needed throughout the body, especially bones and teeth.
Magnesium	Some in most foods, especially vegetables.	Present in bones and all body cells.
Vitamin A	Fish oils, liver, kidney, eggs, milk, dark green and orange fruit and vegetables.	Essential for vision and healthy skin.
Vitamin D	Oily fish, eggs, margarine. Action of sunlight on the skin.	Bone formation.
Vitamin B_1 (Thiamin)	Whole grain cereals, pork, offal, eggs, fortified breakfast cereals.	Release of energy.
Vitamin B_2 (Riboflavin)	Whole grain cereals and breads, milk, liver.	Energy production from food.
Nicotinic acid	Wholemeal bread, liver, potatoes, peas.	Energy production from food.
Pyridoxine (Vitamin B_6)	Meat, fish, eggs, whole grain cereals.	Protein metabolism. Formation of red blood cells.
Vitamin B_{12}	In animal products, especially liver. Also yeast extract.	Formation of cells.
Folic acid	Offal, raw green leafy vegetables, pulses, oranges, bananas.	Formation of cells.
Vitamin C	Fruits and vegetables, especially citrus fruits, potatoes, blackcurrants.	Maintaining healthy tissues.
Vitamin E	Whole grain cereals, vegetable oils, eggs.	As an antioxidant.
Vitamin K	Spinach, cabbage, peas, cereals. It can also be made in the body.	Clotting of the blood.
(Fibre) Not a nutrient but essential in diet.	Whole grain cereals, pulses, fruits and vegetables.	Many functions, mainly smooth functioning of the digestive tract.

Note: There are also other vitamins and minerals which the body requires in small (trace) amounts. They will be supplied from the same sorts of foods as supply the nutrients above.

Some salt occurs naturally in foods such as milk and meat but many people add salt to their food when cooking and eating because they enjoy a salty taste. Again, a great deal of salt is used in food manufacturing. Some foods are obviously salty, but even foods such as bread and biscuits will usually have plenty of salt added to them. It is the sodium (salt is in fact sodium chloride) that seems to be the problem, so look out for other sources of sodium such as sodium bicarbonate (used as a raising agent) and monosodium glutamate (widely used as a flavour enhancer in savoury foods).

Making Changes

Practising what is preached

Your diet may already be high in fibre and low in fat, sugar and salt. If so, that is fine. If you think that your family's diet is not too well balanced, here are some tips to help you to improve it. However, don't try to revolutionize the family's eating overnight; introduce changes gradually.

Please note that the recommendations are meant for the general population. Certain groups such as babies and young children, pregnant women, old people, sick people and certain ethnic groups have very special requirements.

How to eat more fibre
• Use wholemeal bread rather than other types. Eat at least 3 slices per day.
• If you eat breakfast cereals, look for those made with whole grains (read labels) or try porridge or muesli.
• Eat more fruit and vegetables, and try new varieties as well.
• Use wholemeal flour in cooking, or at least a mixture of white and wholemeal.
• Use wholewheat pastas and whole grain (brown) rice.
• Experiment with pulses. They are full of protein and fibre, and good value for money. Use them to add bulk to meat dishes thus increasing fibre and decreasing fat.
• Use whole grain crispbreads, for example, those based on rye.
• It is better to eat whole grains than to add bran to your diet. Adding raw bran may cause problems with digestion.
• Try to include at least one portion of high fibre food at each meal.
• You may need to increase your fluid intake as fibre absorbs fluid in the body. Aim for at least 6 cups of fluid per day.

How to eat less fat
There is much confusion about fats and the various terms used, such as 'saturated fats' and 'unsaturated fats' (including 'polyunsaturated fats'). The difference between them relates to their chemical structure. Saturated fats are thought to be more detrimental than unsaturated fats. Many foods contain a mixture of saturated and unsaturated fats but foods high in saturated fats include meat and meat products, lard, butter and cream, full cream milk, hard cheeses and block margarines and also some types of vegetable oil, such as palm oil and coconut oil, which are often used in the manufacturing of foods.

Foods high in unsaturated and poly-unsaturated fats include oily fish, nuts (except coconut) margarines labelled 'high in polyunsaturates', corn oil, sunflower oil, safflower oil and olive oil.

Although we need to decrease the total amount of fat we eat, make a particular effort to reduce saturated fat.
• Spread butter or margarine thinly on bread, toast or biscuits. Use fewer slices of thickly cut bread, to reduce the surface area for spreading fats.
• Use low fat spreads.

• Do less frying, especially of foods which absorb a lot of fat such as batter, breadcrumbs and vegetables. When you do fry, measure the amount of fat that you add to the pan so that you are aware of how much you are using.
• Buy the leanest meat you can afford; there will be less waste on it anyway.
• Reduce the amount of fatty meat products you buy, such as sausages, burgers and meat pies.
• Trim fat from meat before cooking.
• When cooking mince, cook it by itself and then drain off the fat before adding other ingredients.
• Try to include more poultry and fish in dishes in your regular meal plan.
• Use low fat milks such as semi-skimmed or skimmed, for cooking as well.
• Eat more low fat cheeses such as

Edam, Brie, Feta, Ricotta, curd and cottage, in place of high fat ones such as cream cheese, Cheddar and Stilton.
● Use a strong cheese for cooking such as Parmesan or mature Cheddar.
● If using cream, choose the lowest in fat such as single and soured cream. Whipping cream has less fat than double.
● Try using low fat natural yoghurt in place of cream.
● Be sparing with salad dressings and mayonnaise, look for reduced-fat substitutes, such as low calorie salad cream.
● Reduce the amount of cakes, biscuits and chocolate that you eat. Eat bread or fruit as snacks instead.
● If making pastry, roll it out very thinly. This way you may need to use less.
● Eat more boiled and jacket potatoes, and fewer chips and roast potatoes. Try yoghurt with jacket potatoes instead of butter.
● Watch out for take-away foods, many of them are very high in fat.

How to consume less sugar

One way of reducing sugar is to use an artificial sweetener, such as saccharine or aspartame. The amounts of artificial sweetener commonly consumed have not been found to have an adverse effect but some people may dislike the idea of eating an unnatural substance.
● Do not add sugar to drinks. Either cut it out altogether or reduce the amount you use gradually until you use none.
● Avoid sugary drinks, squashes and 'pops' – either use a low calorie alternative or drink fruit juice or water.
● Do not add sugar to breakfast cereals. Avoid sugar-coated cereals and look for those which contain no sugar.

Pulses (left) provide bulk in the diet, reducing the desire for more fatty foods, while dried fruits (right) make a far healthier snack than sweet foods. Both are excellent sources of fibre

● Reduce sweets and chocolates to a minimum. Try dried fruit as an alternative snack.
● Choose plain or semi-sweet biscuits.
● Keep cakes for special occasions.
● Experiment with using dried fruit for sweetening puddings and baked goods.
● Experiment with reducing sugar in recipes. Some recipes need sugar to give structure, such as meringues and sponges, whereas other recipes use too much sugar unnecessarily.
● Look for fruits canned in natural juices rather than in syrup.
● Reduce the amount of jams, marmalades and syrups spread on bread.
● Avoid particularly sugary snacks and drinks between meals as this is when they do most harm to teeth.
● Read labels on foods and choose an alternative if sugar is listed at or near the top of the list of ingredients.

How to consume less salt
● Add less salt (if any) to your meals.
● Consciously reduce the amount of salt you use in cooking.
● Experiment with using herbs, spices and more freshly ground black pepper in cooking to give flavour.
● Do not automatically add as much salt as a recipe tells you to – be discerning.
● Try making your own bread, you need only add a very little salt.
● Use less salty sauces.
● Make your own stocks and soups. They will be less salty than if you use stock cubes and commercial brands.
● Use fewer processed foods and more fresh foods.

● Look out for products which are labelled 'salt free' or 'low salt'.
● When eating, notice whether the food tastes salty. Remember, salt is supposed to enhance the flavour of food, not to be the taste!

Family Meals

Shopping for foods

In order to be able to put healthy eating into practice, it is obviously vital to choose wisely when shopping. A shopping list may be helpful.

Buying meat, poultry and fish
Look for lean meat. When buying fish and poultry, check that they have not been coated with unwanted additives or had other unnecessary additions, e.g. butter-basted chickens will be higher in fat than other chickens.

Buying fruit and vegetables
Shop frequently for fruits and vegetables and choose those which look fresh and new. Avoid ones which are becoming wrinkled, although if over-ripe fruit is being sold off cheaply, and you can use it up soon, then it may be a useful buy. Look for green vegetables which have a good colour and are not starting to turn yellow. If you are shopping ahead, you may like to choose fruits and vegetables which are slightly under-ripe, e.g. pears, bananas and tomatoes.

Buying packaged goods
If buying packaged goods, check 'sell-by' dates and choose those which will last longest as they will be freshest. Eggs have date marks on their boxes according to the week of packing. The highest week number will be the most recent.

Storing food correctly

It is important to store food correctly. Meat and meat products should be kept in a refrigerator, along with fish and fish products, milk and milk products, and salads. Be careful to separate raw and cooked foods, especially meat, so that bacterial contamination cannot occur. Remember to cover foods such as milk and dairy products so that they do not absorb smells from other foods.

Make sure you know what is in your refrigerator so that you can use foods well before they 'go off' and are wasted. Eggs should not be kept in the refrigera-tor as this will affect their cooking properties.

Keep salads in the refrigerator and all other fresh vegetables in a cool, dark place.

Soft fruit, such as berries, should be kept in the refrigerator and used very soon as they quickly become over-ripe and spoil. Other fruits may be kept in a fruit bowl, but again are better away from direct light.

Convenience foods

There are many hundreds of types of convenience foods available. When considering how they can be used in the diet, you must find out what is in them.

Read the labels
Most foods now have some type of labelling, so read the list of ingredients and try to determine what exactly is in the can, package or box. Some of these foods will be free, or almost free, of any additions and therefore very useful. Other convenience foods seem to contain a long list of chemical ingredients and very few names of foods. They are best avoided.

Many additions are represented by an 'E' number which is given in order to identify exactly which additives have been used. Many 'E' numbers are for additives which are perfectly harmless and are found in nature such as citric acid, chlorophyll (a green colouring) and carotene (a type of vitamin A); there is no problem with these. More concern is centred around the 'E' numbers which are artificially prepared colourings, pre-servatives and flavourings; a very small proportion of people are intolerant or allergic to some of these. There are many books and leaflets available which sort out these 'E' numbers, and suggest which may be suspect to health.

As a general guideline, if an alternative is available to a food containing artificial additives, then it is probably better to choose the more natural product.

When choosing convenience foods, look for foods that resemble fresh foods, e.g. frozen fruits and vegetables (which are very high in vitamin content), canned fish and canned fruits and vegetables, especially those in natural juices.

Many convenience foods, including made up meals, are improving as manu-facturers respond to requests for healthier food. Almost every week new foods appear on the supermarket shelves. Look out for them and decide if they can fit into a healthy eating plan.

Planning meals

When planning meals for the family there will be plenty of points to consider, such as timing of meals and time avail-able to cook them, individual likes and dislikes and finance available. It may seem an additional burden to have to think about producing a balanced, healthy diet but with some thought it can be achieved. You may find it helpful to plan menus in advance – perhaps a 3-week menu to follow. This will save time wondering what to cook each day and be marvellous when your mind is totally blank of ideas. A menu will also

help when you come to sort out shopping and budgeting.

Points to consider when planning menus
- Choose plenty of variety – everyone looks forward to meals if there is an element of surprise.
- Consider how you can put leftovers to good use, for instance making a soup out of the remains of a roast chicken.
- Consider making double quantities and freezing half if you have a freezer.
- Be adventurous with vegetables. Serve a salad as an accompaniment to a main meal sometimes.
- Snack meals, such as a healthy sandwich, can be just as nourishing as cooked meals.
- Be aware of colour and texture; food is far more appetizing if you have variety.

Making existing dishes healthier
One way to plan menus that are healthy would be to write down a list of all the main meals, puddings and snack meals your family eat and then consider how to make them more healthy.
Example: **Macaroni Cheese**
- Use wholewheat macaroni.

Below: *Most vegetable oils contain unsaturated fats. Pictured here from left to right are groundnut oil, blended oil, corn oil, olive oil and sunflower oil*

- Use skimmed milk for the sauce and thicken with cornflour rather than making a sauce containing fat.
- Use strong cheese so that you will need less.
- Garnish with sliced tomato for added vitamin C and colour.
- Serve with frozen peas which are high in vitamin C and full of fibre.

What food should be eaten daily?
If you are not sure what foods to include each day, here is a simple guide:
- Some milk or milk products, e.g. cheese, yoghurt. (Butter and cream do not count as they only contain the fat of the milk.)
- Two helpings of foods high in protein (check with the chart on page 201).
- At least three helpings of fruit and vegetables, including potatoes.
- At least three helpings of starchy foods, preferably whole grain variety.
- Small amount of butter or polyunsaturated margarine.
- If your family enjoy them, include offal and oily fish once a week.

Cooking foods for health

There is no point in buying nutritious foods if they are not going to be prepared in such a way as to maximize nutritional value. This is particularly true with vegetables and fruits.

Tips for preparing and cooking vegetables and fruit
- If possible, use the skins of fruit and vegetables. Most root vegetables, for instance, can be scrubbed with a stiff brush and then cooked in their skins.
- Do not chop up fruits and vegetables too far in advance. Once they are cut they will start to lose vitamin C.
- Cook vegetables as near to the meal time as possible. If they are left to stand, they will lose more vitamins.
- Cook green vegetables in the minimum amount of water. Add the vegetables to boiling water and cook briskly with the pan tightly covered. Do not add bicarbonate of soda – this will totally destroy vitamins. Alternatively, steam vegetables. Use the water that vegetables have been cooked in as stock; it will contain some vitamins.
- Stir-frying with a very little oil is also a good method for cooking vegetables, which helps to retain vitamins.

Tips for preparing and cooking meat
- If you are making a casserole or stew, skim off any fat which rises to the surface. Or, cool the dish overnight and remove the layer of fat before reheating when required.
- Roast meat on a rack in a tin so that the fatty juices will drip away.
- Grilling of meat and meat products is preferable to frying but do not grill under too fierce a heat or the food will become very dry.

A note about overweight
If you are overweight, a balanced healthy diet can help you to lose weight successfully.

Do not attempt to crash diet – it does not help the situation at all as you will probably regain the lost weight as soon as you stop dieting. Also your body is not able to get all the nutrients it requires from a crash diet and your health is likely to suffer. Aim to lose weight slowly, 0.5-1 kg/1-2 lb per week is plenty.

Eat three meals a day and include a helping of starchy high fibre food at each meal. Use low fat foods to provide protein, include plenty of vegetables and 2-3 helpings of fruit each day. Drink plenty of fluids which are low in calories such as coffee, tea, water and low calorie drinks and steer clear of alcohol. Try to keep as active as you can.

How this section can help you

The recipes in this section have been chosen to illustrate some of the many different aspects of healthy eating. All of the dishes are simple to prepare and are based on everyday ingredients. The recipes are nearly all low in fat and sugar with the exception of some of the baking recipes, which should not be eaten every day anyway.

Quite a few of the dishes are for light snack meals, these will be useful if you don't have much time for cooking, but still want to eat healthily from nutritious ingredients.

In conclusion, eating healthily is not about eating a cranky diet which is difficult to follow, but about eating a wide variety of natural wholesome foods prepared and presented to their best advantage. Eating healthily is a pleasure that all the family can enjoy.

Soups and Snacks

Serve nutritious home-made soup as an appetizer before a main course or as a meal in itself. No matter whether a hearty or light soup, if you use fresh wholesome ingredients, it will add valuable nutrients to your diet.

   With the mouthwatering selection of healthy snacks included, there will be no need to rely on convenience foods for your quick meals. These snack ideas will taste fresher with plenty of flavour – plus you will know exactly what they contain. The recipes include pâtés, made from lentils and beans, unusual ideas using eggs and exciting alternatives to sandwiches. Many of these light lunch or supper dishes would make excellent starters, too.

Soups

Chunky soya and vegetable soup

Serves 4

100 g/4 oz soya beans, soaked in
   cold water overnight
1 tbls vegetable oil
50 g/2 oz streaky bacon rashers,
   derinded and chopped
1 large onion, sliced
2 leeks, thickly sliced
50 g/2 oz carrots, thickly sliced
2 celery stalks, thickly sliced
50 g/2 oz turnips, cut into cubes
850 ml/1½ pt chicken stock
1 tbls lemon juice
2 tbls tomato purée
1-2 tsps dried mixed herbs
100 g/4 oz courgettes, thickly
   sliced
a few tender cabbage or spinach
   leaves, finely shredded
salt and freshly ground black
   pepper
2 tsps toasted sesame seeds, to
   garnish (optional)

*Below: Chunky soya and vegetable
soup*

1   Drain the soaked beans, then put
into a saucepan and cover with fresh
cold water. Bring to the boil and boil for
10 minutes, then lower the heat, cover
and simmer for 1½ hours.
2   After the beans have been cooking
for 1 hour 20 minutes, heat the oil in a
separate large saucepan. Add the bacon
and fry gently for 2-3 minutes, then add
the onion and continue cooking for
2 minutes. Add the leeks, carrots, celery
and turnips and cook, stirring, for a
further 2 minutes.
3   Stir in the chicken stock, lemon juice,
tomato purée and herbs.
4   Drain the beans and add to the pan.
Bring to the boil, then lower the heat
slightly, cover the pan and simmer for
1 hour.
5   Add the courgettes and cabbage or
spinach and continue to cook for a further 15 minutes or until the vegetables
and beans are tender. Season to taste
with salt and pepper.
6   Pour into warmed individual soup
bowls and garnish with a sprinkling of
sesame seeds, if liked. Serve at once.
To Serve: Accompany soup with small
bowls of grated cheese and toasted
bread croûtons to sprinkle over.
● 220 kcal/925 kJ per portion

Gardeners' soup

Illustrated on pages 206-207

Serves 6

about 700 g/1½ lb white cabbage,
   tough outer leaves removed
the white part of 6 medium-sized
   leeks
2 tbls vegetable oil
450 g/1 lb potatoes, diced
225 g/8 oz shelled or frozen green
   peas
1 L/1¾ pt stock
1 tbls chopped fresh chervil or 1
   tsp dried chervil
salt and freshly ground black
   pepper
15 g/½ oz butter
1 small firm round lettuce,
   shredded
6 slices of French bread, freshly
   toasted, to serve

1   Cut the cabbage into 6 wedges and
remove the hard core. Very finely slice
the leeks.
2   Heat the oil in a large saucepan over
medium heat, add the cabbage and
leeks and stir well. Cover and cook for
5 minutes, stirring occasionally.

3 Add the potatoes and peas, the stock, dried chervil (if using) and a little seasoning. Bring the mixture back to the boil, cover and cook gently over medium-low heat for 20 minutes or until the cabbage wedges are tender.

4 Melt the butter in a frying-pan over high heat, quickly stir in the lettuce and toss for 30 seconds. Add the lettuce to the soup with fresh chervil (if using) and bring back to the boil. Adjust the seasoning.

5 To serve, place a slice of freshly toasted French bread in each of 6 large warmed soup bowls and pour the soup over. Serve immediately.

- 260 kcal/1092 kJ per portion

Pea soup with cheese toast

Illustrated on pages 206-207

Serves 4
1 tbls dried onion flakes
2 tbls boiling water
540 g/1 lb 3 oz can garden peas
300 ml/½ pt chicken stock
½ tsp dried thyme
3 tbls instant potato powder
1-2 tsps lemon juice
2-3 tbls milk
salt and freshly ground black pepper
1 tbls finely chopped fresh parsley
For the toast
4 small thick slices wholemeal bread
40 g/1½ oz mature Cheddar cheese, grated
2 tbls milk
¼ tsp made English mustard

1 Put the dried onion flakes into a cup, pour over the boiling water and leave to stand for at least 15 minutes.

2 Put the peas with their liquid into a blender with the onion mixture and blend until smooth. Work through a sieve. Put into a saucepan with the stock and thyme and bring to the boil over moderate heat.

3 Lower the heat and sprinkle in the potato powder. Stir for 1-2 minutes then remove from heat and stir in the lemon juice and milk. Season to taste with salt and pepper. Return to the heat and simmer gently while preparing the toast.

4 Heat the grill to high, and toast the bread on both sides.

5 Mix the cheese with the milk and mustard.

6 Spread the cheese mixture on the toast and return to the grill until brown.

7 Sprinkle the parsley into the soup then ladle into warmed individual bowls. Cut each slice of toast into 4 and serve.

- 230 kcal/966 kJ per portion

Thick tomato soup

Illustrated on pages 198-199

Serves 4
3 potatoes, peeled and cubed
2 carrots, cubed
1 large onion, finely chopped
1 garlic clove, crushed
2 tbls vegetable oil
539 g/1 lb 3 oz can tomatoes
300 ml/½ pt hot vegetable or chicken stock
1 tsp dried basil or oregano
1 tsp caster sugar
salt and freshly ground black pepper

1 Gently fry the potatoes, carrots, onion and garlic in the oil for 5 minutes. Add the tomatoes with their juice and half the stock, stirring to break up the tomatoes. Bring to the boil.

2 Add the basil or oregano and sugar and season with salt and pepper. Lower the heat and simmer very gently, covered, for about 20 minutes, until the vegetables are tender.

3 Roughly purée the soup in a blender for a few seconds. Return to the saucepan and add enough stock to give the required consistency; the soup should be quite thick.

Above: *Red lentil soup*

4 Heat through and adjust the seasoning. Serve at once.

To Freeze: Cool the finished soup and freeze in a plastic container for up to 4 months. To reheat, tip into a saucepan and reheat gently from frozen.

- 165 kcal/693 kJ per portion

Red lentil soup

Serves 4
15 g/½ oz butter
1 large onion, chopped
1 stalk celery, chopped
150 g/5 oz dried red lentils
1 L/1¾ pt stock
¼ tsp ground cloves
¼ tsp ground allspice
salt and freshly ground black pepper

1 Melt the butter in a large saucepan and fry the onion and celery lightly for 10 minutes, but do not brown.

2 Add the lentils, stock and spices to the saucepan. Bring to the boil, then reduce the heat and simmer the lentils gently for 30-35 minutes, or until soft.

3 Purée the soup in a blender; reheat, and season to taste with salt and pepper.

- 160 kcal/672 kJ per portion

Split pea soup Use dried split peas instead of red lentils but soak them first in boiling water for 1 hour. Drain. Proceed as above.

Snacks

Lentil pâté

Serves 6
250 g/9 oz split red lentils
600-850 ml/1-1½ pt chicken
  stock
1 onion, finely chopped
4½ tsps tomato purée
2 tsps dried mixed herbs
salt and freshly ground black
  pepper
50 g/2 oz curd cheese
coriander sprigs, to garnish

1 Put the lentils in a large pan, pour in 600 ml/1 pt stock, then add the onion, tomato purée and herbs. Season to taste with salt and pepper.
2 Bring to the boil, then lower the heat slightly, cover and simmer for about 30 minutes, stirring frequently, until the lentils have swollen and the stock has been absorbed. If the lentils begin to dry up and stick to the pan, add the rest of the stock, a little at a time. Remove from the heat and leave to cool for about 30 minutes.
3 Transfer the lentil mixture to a blender and work until smooth, then add the curd cheese, a piece at a time, and work until it is evenly incorporated.
4 Taste the pâté and adjust the seasoning if necessary. Spoon the mixture into an 850 ml/1½ pt serving dish, level the surface and leave until cold.
5 Cover the pâté and refrigerate for at least 2 hours before serving. Garnish with coriander and serve straight from the dish.
To Serve: Accompany with slices of toasted granary or wholemeal bread, tomato wedges and shredded lettuce, this pâté makes a good snack or starter. It is also firm enough to take on picnics – in this case, serve with savoury biscuits or crispbreads.
To Freeze: Pack the pâté into a rigid container and cool completely. Seal, label and freeze for up to 2 months. To serve allow to defrost in the container at room temperature for about 4 hours. Serve as above.
● 145 kcal/609 kJ per portion
Vegetarian pâté Use a meat-free stock made from a vegetable stock cube or vegetable cooking liquid, instead of the chicken stock.

Above: *Lentil pâté*

Herby bean pâté

Illustrated on pages 206-207

Serves 6
2 tbls vegetable oil
1 onion, grated
175 g/6 oz carrots, finely grated
2 x 400 g/14 oz cans cannellini
  beans, well drained
2 eggs, lightly beaten
2 tbls milk
65 g/2½ oz day-old wholemeal
  breadcrumbs
3 tbls finely chopped parsley
1 tbls finely snipped chives
¼ tsp dried basil
¼ tsp dried thyme
salt and freshly ground black
  pepper
oil, for greasing
For the garnish
lettuce leaves
black olives, halved and stoned
sprigs of parsley

1 Heat the oven to 200°C/400°F/gas 6.

Grease an 850 ml/1½ pt soufflé dish, then line the base with greaseproof paper and oil the paper thoroughly.

2 Heat the oil in a frying-pan, add the onion and carrots and fry gently for 5 minutes until the onion is soft and lightly coloured. Set the frying-pan aside.

3 Put the beans in a bowl and mash with a fork, then mix in the eggs. Or, put the beans and eggs in a blender and work until smooth, then transfer to a bowl.

4 Add the onion and carrots to the beans and stir in the remaining ingredients. Mix well and season with salt and pepper.

5 Spoon the mixture into the prepared dish and level the surface. Cover with a lid or foil and bake in the oven for 1¼ hours, until just firm all over. Remove from oven and leave to cool for at least 2 hours.

6 To serve, line a serving plate with lettuce. Run a palette knife around the sides of the pâté and turn out on to the serving plate. Remove the greaseproof paper and garnish with the black olives and sprigs of parsley. Serve at once, cut into slices.

● 190 kcal/798 kJ per portion

Egg and spinach nests

Serves 4

15 g/½ oz butter
250 g/9 oz spinach, stalks and large midribs removed, shredded
salt and freshly ground black pepper
4 eggs
15 g/½ oz grated Parmesan cheese
cayenne, to garnish
oil, for greasing

1 Heat the oven to 190°C/375°F/gas 5. Oil 4 individual ovenproof dishes or ramekins.

2 Melt the butter in a saucepan, add the spinach and cook gently for 8 minutes, or until soft. Season to taste with salt and pepper.

3 Divide the spinach between the prepared dishes. Break 1 egg into each dish on top of the cooked spinach mixture.

4 Place the dishes on a baking sheet and bake in the oven for 10 minutes, until the egg whites begin to set. Remove from the oven and sprinkle a little Parmesan over each egg. Return to the

oven and cook for a further 5 minutes. Sprinkle a little cayenne over each egg and serve at once.

To Serve: Accompany with wholemeal toast for a light lunch or supper.
● 145 kcal/609 kJ per portion

Egg and mushroom nests Place 1 tbls chopped cooked mushrooms in each dish instead of the spinach.

Below: *Egg and spinach nests*

Health Tip

As well as being a good source of iron, spinach is surprisingly rich in fibre. Use it the day you buy it. Try using fresh Parmesan cheese in cooking; it has a stronger taste than the ready-grated variety you buy in cartons.

Kipper and tomato rolls

Makes 6
200 g/7 oz frozen kipper fillets
1 tbls vegetable oil
1 large onion, sliced
200 g/7 oz can tomatoes
1 bay leaf
salt and freshly ground black
pepper
1 tbls cornflour
150 ml/¼ pt water
1 tbls chopped fresh parsley
6 large crusty white or wholemeal
rolls

1 Cook the kippers according to packet instructions.
2 Meanwhile, heat the oil in a frying-pan. Add the onion and fry gently for 5 minutes until soft and lightly coloured.
3 Remove from the heat and stir in the tomatoes, including their juice. Add the bay leaf and seasoning.
4 Heat the oven to 200°C/400°F/gas 6 and cut out 6 pieces of foil large enough to parcel the rolls.
5 In a bowl, blend the cornflour with a little of the water until smooth. Stir in the remainder, then add to the pan.
6 Return to the heat and bring to the boil, stirring constantly and breaking up the tomatoes with a spoon. Simmer, uncovered, over low to moderate heat for 10 minutes, stirring frequently until the sauce is thick. Remove the bay leaf and stir in the parsley.
7 Drain the fish and, when cool enough to handle, skin, bone and flake the flesh. Add the fish to the sauce, taste and adjust the seasoning.
8 Cut off the tops of the rolls and scoop out the centres.

9 Spoon the sauce into the rolls, replace the lids, wrap each one in foil and place on a baking sheet. Bake in the oven for 8-10 minutes, leave to cool for a few minutes, then unwrap and serve.
To Serve: Make a salad of lettuce, sliced cucumber and green pepper.
• 200 kcal/840 kJ per portion

Kipper and tomato loaf Use a French loaf instead of the rolls. Cut the top off the loaf, scoop out the centre and fill with the kipper and tomato mixture. Wrap in foil and heat in the oven for about 10 minutes.
Kipper and tomato vol-au-vents Baked vol-au-vent cases can be filled with the kipper and tomato mixture.

Fruit and cheese kebabs

Serves 4
50 g/2 oz curd cheese
25 g/1 oz seedless raisins,
chopped
2 tbls walnuts or unsalted peanuts,
finely chopped
50 g/2 oz Danish blue cheese
50 g/2 oz smoked cheese
50 g/2 oz Red Leicester or
Cheshire cheese
1 large red-skinned dessert apple
juice of 1 lemon
300 g/11 oz can mandarin orange
segments in natural juice, well
drained, or 2 fresh mandarin
oranges, peeled and divided into
segments
225 g/8 oz can pineapple chunks
in natural juice, well drained
100 g/4 oz black or green grapes
6 lettuce leaves, shredded, to
serve

Below: *Kipper and tomato rolls*

1   Put the curd cheese into a bowl with the raisins and mix well. Roll into 8 small even-sized balls.

2   Spread the chopped nuts out on a flat plate and roll the balls in them. Transfer to a plate and refrigerate while you prepare the other ingredients.

3   Cut the Danish blue cheese into 8 even-sized cubes. Repeat with both the smoked cheese and the Leicester cheese.

4   Quarter and core the apple, but do not peel it. Cut in even-sized slices and immediately squeeze the lemon juice over them to prevent discoloration.

5   On 8 individual skewers, spear 1 curd cheese ball and 1 cube each of Danish blue, smoked and Leicester cheeses, interspersed with apple slices,

mandarin orange segments, pineapple chunks and grapes.

6   Serve 2 skewers per person on a bed of shredded lettuce.

● 270 kcal/1134 kJ per portion

Citrus salad with cheese

Serves 4
1 grapefruit
2 oranges
½ cucumber, sliced
1 onion, sliced into rings
225 g/8 oz can water chestnuts, drained and sliced, or 100 g/4 oz button mushrooms, sliced
100 g/4 oz fresh spinach, washed and thoroughly dried
100 g/4 oz Edam cheese, thinly sliced
1 tbls white wine vinegar
2 tsps sugar
2 tsps soy sauce
few drops hot pepper sauce or Tabasco

1   Peel the grapefruit and oranges and divide into segments over a bowl to catch any juice. Put the fruit into a large bowl and mix in the cucumber, onion rings and water chestnuts or mushrooms.

Above: *Fruit and cheese kebabs*

2   Arrange the spinach on a serving platter, then place the cheese in overlapping slices at the edge.

3   Put the vinegar, sugar, soy sauce and hot pepper sauce into the bowl with the fruit juices and whisk with a fork until well blended. Pour over the grapefruit mixture and toss.

4   Spoon the tossed salad on to the spinach. Refrigerate for 30 minutes, then serve chilled.

To Serve: Accompany this colourful salad with wholemeal bread for a light vegetarian lunch. It also makes an attractive addition to a summer barbecue.

● 155 kcal/651 kJ per portion

Health Tip

Cheese is one of the most versatile sources of protein, but remember that it is high in saturated fats. Choose low fat varieties of cheese such as Edam, whenever possible, or if you want a more distinctive taste, mix cheeses with a stronger flavour, such as the blue cheeses – Danish Blue, Stilton or Roquefort – with milder, low fat types of cheese.

Avocado and shrimp toasties

Serves 2
1 tbls horseradish sauce
2 tbls plus 2 tsps lemon juice
50 g/2 oz peeled shrimps
freshly ground black pepper
1 avocado
4 slices wholemeal bread
watercress, to garnish

1   Heat the grill to high.
2   Put the horseradish sauce and 2 tsps lemon juice in a small saucepan and heat gently. Add the shrimps and heat for a further 2-3 minutes. Season with pepper.
3   Meanwhile, peel, halve and stone the avocado, then slice the flesh thinly. Immediately sprinkle over the 2 tbls lemon juice to prevent the flesh discolouring.

4   Toast the bread on one side only.
5   Arrange slices of avocado on the toasted side of 2 of the slices of bread. Spread half the shrimp mixture over each and then put the other slices of bread on top, toasted side down.
6   Using 2 fish slices, lift the sandwiches into the grill pan and toast the top of each sandwich. Turn over and toast the bottom. Cut in half and serve at once, garnished with watercress.
● 417 kcal/1751 kJ per portion

Sausage and sweetcorn toasties Use a garlic sausage and sweetcorn filling for these toasted sandwiches. For each sandwich, spread the toasted side with 2 tbls sweetcorn relish. Arrange 50 g/ 2 oz sliced garlic sausage on top and sprinkle with 25 g/1 oz grated Cheddar or Stilton cheese.

Above: *Avocado and shrimp toasties*

Below: *Ham and cheese rollers*

Ham and cheese rollers

Serves 4
100 g/4 oz curd cheese
3 spring onions, finely chopped
½ tsp French mustard
few drops of Tabasco
50 g/2 oz button mushrooms, finely chopped
4 long wholemeal bread rolls, halved lengthways
salt and freshly ground black pepper
25 g/1 oz butter
4 large lettuce leaves
4 slices lean cooked ham (total weight 100 g/4 oz)

1   Put the cheese into a bowl with the onions, mustard, Tabasco and mushrooms, and mix all the ingredients together.
2   Scoop out some crumbs from each half of the rolls, crumble them finely with your fingers and stir into the cheese mixture until well coated. Season to taste with a little salt and freshly ground black pepper.
3   Spread butter thinly on each half of the bread rolls and put a lettuce leaf on to each half.

4 Divide the cheese mixture between the 4 ham slices and spoon it in a strip, about 1 cm/½ in from one edge of each slice of ham.

5 Carefully roll up each slice of ham as tightly as possible around the cheese mixture and sandwich a ham roll inside each bread roll.

● 250 kcal/1050 kJ per portion

Chicken or turkey and cheese rollers
Replace the ham slices with pressed chicken or turkey breast slices.

Scrambled smoky

Serves 4
450 g/1 lb smoked haddock fillets,
   defrosted if frozen
150 ml/¼ pt skimmed milk
8 large eggs
salt
cayenne pepper
15 g/½ oz butter
1 tsp Worcestershire sauce
4 large slices wholemeal or white
   bread
parsley, to garnish

Above: *Scrambled smoky*

1 Put the fish in a large saucepan. Reserve 2 tbls milk, mix the rest with a little water and pour sufficient over the fish just to cover it. Cook gently for 15-20 minutes. If using frozen fish, cook according to packet instructions.

2 Drain the fish and flake it into a bowl, discarding any bones or skin.

3 Beat the eggs in a bowl with the reserved milk and season with a little salt and cayenne pepper to taste.

4 Melt the butter in a saucepan or large frying-pan, add the beaten eggs and cook over gentle heat, stirring all the time, until the eggs are just scrambled but still creamy. Stir in the flaked fish and Worcestershire sauce. Taste and adjust the seasoning.

5 Toast the bread lightly, then pile the egg and fish mixture on to the toast. Garnish with parsley and serve at once.

To Serve: Alternatively, the egg and fish mixture can be piled into a warmed serving dish with slices of wholemeal toast, cut into triangles, arranged around the edge of the dish.

This makes a substantial breakfast dish, perfect for a Sunday morning.

● 390 kcal/1638 kJ per portion

Scrambled mushroom smoky Soften 50 g/2 oz sliced button mushrooms in a little butter. Add to the scrambled egg with the flaked fish.

215

Main Meals

The main dish of the day should always include a body building protein food accompanied by vegetables or a salad. Today nutritionists recommend eating less red meat, such as beef, lamb and pork, and using more poultry and fish, as these are lower in fat content. In fact, fish is the perfect convenience food as it is so quick to cook – and it's low in calories too.

The healthy main meals given here show you the best ways to prepare and cook these dishes, retaining all their goodness, flavour and freshness. Liver, rich in iron and the B vitamins, can be found in many different tempting guises.

Fish

Cod and tomatoes in cider

Serves 4
350 g/12 oz tomatoes
850 g/1¾ lb cod fillet, cut into 4
    equal serving pieces, or 4 cod
    steaks, each weighing about
    200 g/7oz
150 ml/¼ pt dry cider
salt and freshly ground black
    pepper
2 tbls chopped parsley
1 tbls chopped fresh thyme,
    or 2 tsps dried thyme
oil, for greasing

1 Heat the oven to 200°C/400°F/gas 6.
2 Cut 1 tomato into 4 slices. Scald, skin and chop the rest.
3 Lightly oil a shallow ovenproof dish. Put the chopped tomatoes into the dish and then place the pieces of cod on top. Pour the cider over.
4 Season the cod and scatter over the herbs. Put a tomato slice on each piece of fish.

5 Bake in the oven for 20 minutes or until cooked through. Serve hot, straight from the dish.
● 155 kcal/651 kJ per portion

Coley and tomatoes in cider For an economical version of the above dish, use coley instead of cod.

Tuna and French bean salad

Serves 4
200 g/7 oz can tuna fish in brine,
    drained and flaked
250 g/9 oz cold cooked French
    beans, cut into 2.5 cm/1 in
    lengths
½ Webb's or iceberg lettuce,
    separated into leaves
2 hard-boiled eggs, quartered
3 firm tomatoes, skinned and
    sliced
1 small onion, sliced into rings
8 black olives
8 green olives

For the garlic dressing
4 tbls olive oil
2 tbls lemon juice
¼ tsp French mustard
½ tsp caster sugar
1 garlic clove, crushed
salt and freshly ground black
    pepper

1 To make the dressing, whisk together the oil, lemon juice, mustard, sugar and garlic in a bowl. Season to taste with salt and pepper.

Left: *Cod and tomatoes in cider*

Sea bass with orange sauce

Serves 4
**4 x 175 g/6 oz skinned and boned
sea bass steaks, with skin and
bones reserved**
1 bay leaf
**salt and freshly ground black
pepper**
2 tbls olive oil
**½ orange, cut into very thin slices,
to garnish**
For the sauce
1 tbls olive oil
50 g/2 oz flour
**150 ml/¼ pt freshly squeezed
orange juice (2-3 oranges)**
juice of ½ lemon
grated zest of 1 orange

1 Simmer the skin and bones of the
sea bass in 200 ml/7 fl oz water with the
bay leaf for 20 minutes. Season, strain
and reserve.
2 Heat the oil in a frying-pan over
medium heat and fry the fish for about
5 minutes per side, or until golden. Drain
the steaks on absorbent paper and transfer them to a hot serving dish and keep
warm in the oven.
3 To make the sauce, heat the oil in a
small saucepan over low heat and stir in
the flour. Gradually add 150 ml/¼ pt of
the fish stock and the orange and lemon
juice, stirring all the time to avoid lumps.
Stir in the orange zest, season to taste
and stir continuously over low heat until
the sauce is smooth.
4 Pour the sauce over the fish steaks
and garnish with orange 'twists'.
● 330 kcal/1386 kJ per portion

Below: *Sea bass with orange sauce*

Above: *Tuna and French bean salad*

2 Put the tuna and beans in a bowl and
pour over half the dressing. Toss until
well coated.
3 Arrange the lettuce in a shallow serving dish and spoon over the tuna and
beans. Arrange the eggs, tomatoes,
onion and olives over the top. Sprinkle
over the remaining dressing.
To Serve: Serve this dish on its own or
with crusty French bread. Served in
smaller portions, it also makes a refreshing starter for 6 people.
● 260 kcal/1092 kJ per portion

Poultry

Paprika chicken with kidney beans

Serves 6

2 tbls vegetable oil
1.5 kg/3½ lb oven-ready chicken,
   thoroughly defrosted if frozen
2 onions, thinly sliced
225 g/8 oz can tomatoes
150 ml/¼ pt chicken stock
1 garlic clove, crushed (optional)
¼ tsp dried mixed herbs
1 bay leaf
2 tbls plain flour
1 tbls sweet paprika
¼ tsp caster sugar
190 g/6½ oz can red pimientos,
   drained and finely sliced, with
   juices reserved
400 g/14 oz can red kidney beans,
   drained
salt and freshly ground black
   pepper
150 g/5 oz natural yoghurt

1   Heat half the oil in a large heavy-based saucepan, add the chicken, breast down, and cook for 3-4 minutes to brown. Remove the chicken to a plate.
2   Heat the remaining oil in the saucepan, add the onions and fry gently for 5 minutes until they are soft and lightly coloured. Stir in the canned tomatoes with their juice, the chicken stock, garlic, if using, and mixed herbs. Add the bay leaf.
3   Bring to the boil and return the chicken to the pan. Cover, lower the heat and simmer gently for about 1 hour or until the chicken is cooked through (the juices run clear when the chicken is pierced in the thickest part with a skewer).
4   Heat the oven to 110°C/225°F/gas ¼. Transfer the chicken to an ovenproof plate and keep warm in the oven. Discard the bay leaf.
5   In a small bowl, blend the flour,

Below: Paprika chicken with kidney beans

paprika and sugar with 4 tbls pimiento juice. Stir the paprika mixture into the liquid in the pan and bring to the boil, stirring, until the sauce thickens. Season to taste with salt and pepper. Add the pimientos and kidney beans and heat through.
6   Cut the chicken into joints and transfer to warmed dinner plates. Pour a little sauce over each serving and top with yoghurt. Hand the remaining sauce separately.
To Serve: Accompany with boiled rice and French beans topped with vegetable margarine.
To Freeze: Freeze this dish before adding the pimientos and kidney beans. Save freezer space by removing the chicken from the bones, then freeze with the sauce in a rigid container for up to 3 months. To serve: defrost overnight at room temperature, then add pimientos and beans and reheat gently on top of the cooker until heated through.
● 520 kcal/2184 kJ per portion

Stir-fried chicken and cashew nuts

Serves 4

1.25 kg/2¾ lb roasting chicken,
   jointed and skinned
2 tbls cornflour
150 ml/¼ pt dry sherry
150 ml/¼ pt stock
2 tbls soy sauce
3 tbls sesame oil
1 garlic clove, finely chopped
1 tbls ground ginger
2 medium-sized onions, finely
   chopped
¼ Chinese cabbage, finely
   shredded
75 g/3 oz unsalted cashew nuts

1   Cut the chicken meat from the bones and then into small, thin slivers. Put the cornflour in a bowl and gradually mix in the sherry, stock and soy sauce.
2   Place the oil and garlic in a wok or a large frying-pan and set it over a low heat until the garlic sizzles and begins to brown. Add the chicken pieces and stir until they brown.

Above: *Stir-fried chicken and cashew nuts*

3   Lower the heat and add the ginger. Mix in the onions and cook for 2 minutes. Mix in the cabbage and nuts and cook for 1 minute more.

4   Stir the cornflour mixture and pour it into the pan. Cook, stirring all the time, until a thick, translucent sauce is formed. Serve.

To Serve: Accompany with boiled brown rice.

● 420 kcal/1764 kJ per portion

Sweet and sour chicken

Serves 6

6 chicken joints (about 200 g/7 oz each)
1 tbls vegetable oil
4 cm/1½ in piece fresh root ginger, grated
1 garlic clove, crushed
1 green pepper, deseeded and cut into fine strips
3 spring onions, green tops only, sliced diagonally
2 tbls light soy sauce
2 tbls white wine vinegar

100 g/4 oz unsweetened pineapple rings in natural juice
1 orange, peel and pith removed
2 tbls orange juice
1 tbls tomato purée
2 tsps cornflour
1 tbls water

1   Grill the chicken joints for about 30 minutes, turning once, until golden brown and tender.

2   Remove the skin from the chicken joints and discard.

3   Heat the oil in a wok or large frying-pan and add the ginger, garlic, green pepper and spring onions. Stir-fry for 3-4 minutes.

4   Add the soy sauce and vinegar to the pan and stir-fry for another 1-2 minutes.

5   Drain the pineapple rings, reserving 4 tbls of the juice. Slice the orange and cut each slice in half. Add the fruit to the pan, together with the orange juice and tomato purée. Stir for 3-4 minutes. Dissolve the cornflour in the water, then add to the pan and continue stirring until the sauce becomes glossy and thickens.

6   Return the chicken joints to the pan, turning them in the sauce several times until thoroughly coated.

7   Transfer to a warmed serving dish and serve immediately with brown bread and vegetables of your choice.

● 220 kcal/1924 kJ per portion

Turkey in honey and ginger

Illustrated on pages 216-217

Serves 4

1 tbls vegetable oil
50 g/2 oz clear honey
2 tbls Dijon mustard
1 tsp ground ginger
salt and freshly ground black pepper
4 turkey breast portions, skinned
watercress, to garnish

1   Heat the oven to 180°C/350°F/gas 4. Heat the oil in a flameproof casserole just large enough to take the turkey portions in a single layer.

2   Stir the honey, mustard and ginger into the oil. Remove from the heat and season to taste with salt and pepper.

3   Arrange the turkey pieces in the mixture in the casserole and turn to coat them well.

4   Bake in the oven for 30 minutes, basting occasionally. Turn the turkey portions and continue to cook for 30 minutes, basting, until tender.

5   Garnish with watercress.

To Serve: Accompany with boiled brown rice.

● 255 kcal/1071 kJ per portion

Liver

Liver and bacon hotpot

Serves 4
2 tbls vegetable oil
450 g/1 lb lamb or pig liver, cut into 16 small slices
2 medium onions, sliced into thin rings
4 lean bacon rashers, derinded
1 cooking apple, peeled, cored and sliced
salt and freshly ground black pepper
few drops of Worcestershire sauce
300 ml/½ pt hot beef stock
1 tsp cornflour
chopped fresh parsley, to garnish

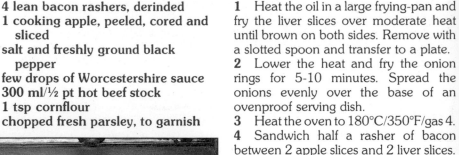
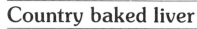

1 Heat the oil in a large frying-pan and fry the liver slices over moderate heat until brown on both sides. Remove with a slotted spoon and transfer to a plate.
2 Lower the heat and fry the onion rings for 5-10 minutes. Spread the onions evenly over the base of an ovenproof serving dish.
3 Heat the oven to 180°C/350°F/gas 4.
4 Sandwich half a rasher of bacon between 2 apple slices and 2 liver slices. Turn the liver sandwiches on their sides and arrange in rows on top of the onions. Sprinkle with salt and pepper.
5 Add a few drops of Worcestershire sauce to the stock. Blend the cornflour to a paste in a small saucepan with a little cold water, then gradually stir in the stock. Bring to the boil, stirring constantly, then lower the heat and simmer gently until thickened. Pour over the liver.
6 Cover and bake in the oven for about 30 minutes. Serve hot, garnished with parsley.
To Serve: Accompany with a choice of vegetables.
● 360 kcal/1512 kJ per portion

Country baked liver

Illustrated on pages 216-217

Serves 4
1 tbls vegetable oil
2 large onions, sliced
2 tsps dried sage
450 g/1 lb lamb liver, sliced
salt and freshly ground black pepper
2 cooking apples, peeled, cored and sliced
150 ml/¼ pt chicken stock
1 tbls chopped fresh parsley

1 Heat the oven to 180°C/350°F/gas 4.
2 Heat the oil in a frying-pan, add the onions and cook gently for about 7 minutes until soft and beginning to brown. Stir in the sage.
3 Using a slotted spoon, transfer one-third of the onions to a 1.75 L/ 3 pt casserole and spread them evenly over the base. Arrange half the liver slices over the onions, season with a little salt

Left: Liver and bacon hotpot

and plenty of pepper, then arrange half the apple slices on top. Arrange half the remaining onions over the liver, then make layers of the remaining liver and apple slices, seasoning well with salt and pepper between each layer. Finish with a layer of onions.

4 Pour over the stock, cover and cook in the oven for about 45 minutes until the liver is tender. Sprinkle with the parsley and serve hot, straight from the casserole.

● 305 kcal/1281 kJ per portion

Liver and onions with sweet and sour sauce

Serves 4
2 tbls vegetable oil
250-350 g/9-12 oz button onions, skinned
450 g/1 lb lamb liver, very thinly sliced
1-2 tbls plain flour, for coating
salt and freshly ground black pepper
3 tbls wine vinegar
4 tbls clear honey
chopped fresh parsley, to garnish

1 Heat the oil in a large frying-pan and fry the onions until they begin to soften.
2 Coat the liver slices in flour, seasoned with salt and pepper. Push the onions to one side of the pan and fry the liver slices lightly for about 2 minutes on both sides. (If there is not room in the pan, remove the onions and keep them warm.)
3 Add the wine vinegar and honey to the liver and onions in the pan. Shake the pan and let the mixture bubble for a minute or so. Sprinkle over the parsley.

Health Tip

Liver of any type is an excellent source of iron and the B group of vitamins. Try to include it in your weekly menus at least once a week. If your family finds the taste too strong – this would apply to pig's liver in particular – try soaking it in milk for about 30 minutes, then draining well before cooking.

4 Serve at once, spooning a little of the syrupy sauce over each portion.
● 380 kcal/1596 kJ per portion

Below: *Liver and onions with sweet and sour sauce*

Meat

Boiled beef and carrots

Serves 6
**1.5 kg/3-3½ lb salted silverside of
    beef, trimmed of fat**
1 bay leaf
6 whole black peppercorns
1 onion, quartered
700 g/1½ lb carrots, quartered
For the parsley sauce
25 g/1 oz cornflour
150 ml/¼ pt skimmed milk
2 tbls finely chopped fresh parsley
**salt and freshly ground black
    pepper**

1   Put the silverside in a very large
saucepan with the bay leaf, peppercorns
and onion. Cover with cold water and
bring slowly to the boil, skimming off any
scum as it rises to the surface. Cover and
simmer gently for 1½ hours.
2   Add the carrots to the pan, cover
again and simmer for a further 30 minutes, or until the carrots are just cooked
and the silverside is tender and flakes
slightly when pierced with the point of a
sharp knife.

Below: *Boiled beef and carrots*

3   Heat the oven to 110°C/225°F/gas ¼.
4   Carve the beef and place on a large
warmed dish and, with a slotted spoon,
arrange the carrots around it. Keep
warm in the oven. Blot off surface fat
from the pan and reserve the stock for
making the parsley sauce.

5   To make the parsley sauce, mix the
cornflour with a little of the milk until
smooth. Place in a saucepan over low
heat with the remainder of the milk and
150 ml/¼ pt of the reserved stock. Bring
to the boil, stirring, simmer until thick
and smooth. Stir in three-quarters of the
parsley and season to taste with salt and
pepper.
6   Remove the boiled beef and carrots
from the oven and serve at once. Hand
the sauce separately in a warmed jug.
Sprinkle with the remaining parsley.
To Serve: Accompany with lightly
boiled cabbage, boiled or mashed
potatoes and English mustard or horseradish sauce.
● 420 kcal/1764 kJ per portion

Pork escalopes
with plums

Illustrated on pages 216-217

Serves 4
250 g/9 oz red plums
2 tbls vegetable oil
1 onion, finely chopped
**150 ml/¼ pt cider or dry white
    wine**
1 tsp ground cinnamon
½ tsp ground coriander
**salt and freshly ground black
    pepper**
**8 pork escalopes, each weighing
    50 g/2 oz**

1 Carefully remove the stones from the plums.
2 To make the sauce, heat half the oil in a pan, add the onion and fry gently for 10 minutes until softened. Pour in the cider and bring to the boil. Add the spices and salt and pepper to taste. Stir well, then lower the heat, cover and cook the sauce gently for 5 minutes.
3 Add the plums to the sauce, cover and simmer very gently for a further 10-15 minutes. Taste and adjust the seasoning.
4 Meanwhile, divide the remaining oil between 2 large frying-pans and heat gently. Add the pork escalopes and cook over high heat for 3 minutes on each side, until browned.
5 To serve, arrange the escalopes on a warmed serving dish and spoon over the sauce. Serve at once.
● 235 kcal/987 kJ per portion

Fruit and nut meat roll

Serves 6
450 g/1 lb finely minced lean beef
250 g/9 oz lean minced pork
2 bunches spring onions, very finely chopped
1 large egg, beaten
salt and freshly ground black pepper
150 ml/¼ pt beef stock
For the stuffing
50 g/2 oz fresh wholemeal breadcrumbs
50 g/2 oz prunes, soaked overnight, stoned and chopped
2 celery stalks, finely chopped
1 medium dessert apple, peeled, cored and grated
50 g/2 oz walnuts, finely chopped
2 tbls dry sherry
1 tsp dried mixed herbs
2 celery stalks, to garnish

1 Heat the oven to 180°C/350°F/gas 4.
2 In a large bowl, mix the meats and spring onions. Add the egg, season well with salt and pepper, then mix thoroughly. Refrigerate while making the stuffing.
3 To make the stuffing, mix all the stuffing ingredients together with salt and pepper to taste.
4 Spoon the meat mixture on to a sheet of greaseproof paper about 37.5 x 30 cm/15 x 12 in, spreading it out as evenly as possible. Place another sheet of greaseproof paper on top and, using a rolling pin, shape the meat into an even

Above: *Fruit and nut meat roll*

rectangle, roughly the same size as the paper. Make straight sides and square up the corners with a palette knife.
5 Remove the top sheet of greaseproof paper. Spoon the stuffing in a straight line close to a short edge of the meat and then start to roll it up like a Swiss roll: lift the lower sheet of greaseproof paper and use it to help you roll the meat. Continue until the meat is completely rolled.

6 Holding the meat roll on the paper, carefully place it in a shallow baking tin. Ease out the paper then pour over the stock. Bake in the oven for about 1-1¼ hours until firm and cooked through, basting frequently. Serve hot, garnished with celery.
To Serve: Accompany with mashed potatoes and a green vegetable or grilled tomatoes. It is also excellent served cold.
● 285 kcal/1197kJ per portion

Prune, onion and nut meat roll Substitute 1 medium finely chopped onion for the celery stalks in the stuffing. Omit the apple.

225

Lamb with pear stuffing

4 Lay the lamb skin side down on a board. Spread the cheese mixture over the lamb, pressing it down with back of a

Above: *Lamb with pear stuffing*

Serves 4
1 tbls vegetable oil
1 small onion, finely chopped
100 g/4 oz curd cheese
50 g/2 oz fresh wholemeal breadcrumbs
1 ripe dessert pear, peeled, cored and chopped
1 tsp chopped fresh tarragon, or ½ tsp dried tarragon
salt and freshly ground black pepper
1 small egg, beaten
1.5 kg/3-3½ lb shoulder of lamb, boned
tarragon sprigs, to garnish

1 Heat the oven to 170°C/325°F/gas 3.
2 Heat the oil in a small frying-pan. Add the onion and fry gently for 5 minutes until soft and lightly coloured.
3 Using a slotted spoon, transfer the onion to a bowl, add the curd cheese and beat well. Stir in the breadcrumbs, pear and tarragon and season to taste. Mix in the egg to bind.

spoon. Roll up the lamb carefully from one short end and tie at intervals with fine string. Weigh the shoulder of lamb

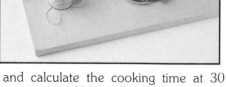

and calculate the cooking time at 30 minutes per 450 g/1 lb plus 30 minutes.
5 Place the lamb on a rack in a roasting tin and roast for the calculated time until the lamb is cooked.
6 Leave the stuffed shoulder of lamb in a warm place for 10 minutes to allow to 'settle' before carving. Transfer the lamb to a warmed serving dish and serve carved into slices, garnished with tarragon sprigs.
● 445 kcal/1869 kJ per portion (lean meat and stuffing only)

Lamb steaks with peppers

Illustrated on pages 216-217

Serves 4
2 tbls vegetable oil
1 onion, sliced
1 green pepper, deseeded and finely chopped
1 red pepper, deseeded and finely chopped
1 garlic clove, finely chopped (optional)
4 lean lamb leg steaks, each weighing about 175 g/6 oz, trimmed of fat
1 tbls plain flour
350 ml/12 fl oz mixed vegetable juice
150 ml/¼ pt water
100 g/4 oz button mushrooms, sliced
2 tbls dried mint
salt and freshly ground black pepper

1 Heat the oven to 190°C/375°F/gas 5.
2 Heat 1 tbls oil in a large flameproof casserole, Add the onion, peppers and garlic, if using, and fry gently for 5 minutes until softened. Remove the vegetables from the casserole with a slotted spoon and set aside, while pre-browning the lamb steaks.
3 Heat the remaining oil in the casserole. Add the lamb steaks and fry briskly for 2 minutes on each side. Transfer the steaks to a plate, using a slotted spoon, and set aside.
4 Sprinkle the flour into the casserole and cook for 1 minute, stirring all the time. Gradually blend in the vegetable juice and water. Bring to the boil, stirring all the time. Return the softened vegetables and lamb steaks to the casserole and stir in the mushrooms and mint. Season to taste with a little salt and pepper.
5 Bring to the boil, then transfer the casserole to the oven and cook for 35 minutes, or until the lamb steaks are tender when pierced with a sharp knife. Serve at once, straight from the casserole.
To Serve: No further vegetable accompaniment is needed with the lamb steaks. Brown rice or wholewheat pasta go particularly well with this dish.
● 395 kcal/1659 kJ per portion

Right: Parcelled pork chops with sage

Parcelled pork chops with sage

Serves 4
1 tbls vegetable oil
4 pork loin chops, trimmed of excess fat
2 courgettes, thinly sliced
100 g/4 oz mushrooms, thinly sliced
4-8 spring onions, finely chopped
salt and freshly ground black pepper
2 tsps dried sage

1 Heat the oven to 190°C/375°F/gas 5.
2 Heat the oil in a frying-pan, add the chops and brown on both sides over brisk heat. Remove from the pan and drain on absorbent paper.
3 Mix together the courgettes, mushrooms and spring onions.
4 Cut out 4 squares of foil each large enough to enclose a chop. Divide the mixed vegetables into 8 portions. Place a portion on each square of foil, and place the chops on top of the vegetables. Season with salt and pepper and sprinkle with the sage. Top with the remaining mixed vegetables.
5 Fold the foil over the chops and vegetables to make neat parcels and place on a baking sheet. Cook in the oven for 45 minutes or until the chops are cooked through (the juices should run clear when pierced with a sharp knife).
6 Serve the chops at once, in the foil parcels.
To Serve: Serving the chops in the baking foil ensures that they come to the table piping hot and all the cooking juices are retained. Have warmed dinner plates ready: each person then turns the contents of the parcel on to the plate.
● 325 kcal/1365 kJ per portion

Parcelled pork chops with thyme
Fresh or dried thyme could be used instead of the sage. With fresh, use about double the quantity.

Vegetables and Salads

Fresh vegetables are most important for our well-being. The various kinds contain a wide variety of vitamins and minerals, and all provide significant amounts of dietary fibre. A balance of raw and cooked vegetables is what to aim for in a diet for health.

Colourful salads are full of different textures, losing none of their goodness if freshly produced, and they are always easy and quick to prepare. Try the tempting new recipes for hot vegetable dishes, which can be served as an accompaniment or as a light lunch or supper. Protein-rich dried beans and pulses offer a whole new range of flavours and ideas when added to vegetable dishes and salads.

Vegetables and Salads

Celeriac and tomato bake

Serves 4

450 g/1 lb celeriac, peeled and sliced
salt
6 large tomatoes, skinned and thinly sliced
½ tsp dried thyme
75 g/3 oz mature Cheddar cheese, grated
freshly ground black pepper
oil, for greasing

1 Heat the oven to 200°C/400°F/gas 6.
2 Put the celeriac in a saucepan of boiling salted water, bring back to the boil and boil for about 5 minutes, until just tender. Drain well.
3 Starting with the celeriac, arrange the slices of celeriac and tomato in layers in a lightly oiled ovenproof dish. Sprinkle each layer with thyme, about one-third

Below: Crunchy-topped swede

of the cheese and salt and pepper to taste. Finish with a layer of celeriac and sprinkle the remaining cheese on top.
4 Bake in the oven for 30 minutes, until the topping is golden brown. Serve hot, straight from the dish.
To Serve: Use as a light lunch or supper dish or, for a change, serve the bake instead of potatoes with a meat-dish.
● 130 kcal/546 kJ per portion

Crunchy-topped swede

Serves 4
1 kg/2 lb swede, cut into even-sized chunks
1 large sprig fresh thyme
75 g/3 oz fresh wholemeal breadcrumbs
2 tbls sesame seeds
25 g/1 oz butter
3 tbls milk
freshly grated nutmeg
salt and freshly ground black pepper

1 Bring a pan of salted water to the boil. Add the swede with the thyme, bring back to the boil, then lower the heat slightly and simmer for 20-30 minutes until the swede is cooked and tender.
2 Meanwhile, mix the breadcrumbs and sesame seeds together. Melt the butter in a frying-pan, add the breadcrumb mixture and fry gently for about 5 minutes until the crumbs are crisp and browned. Remove the pan from the heat.
3 Drain the swede, discarding the thyme, and mash with the milk. Season to taste with nutmeg, salt and pepper, then turn the swede into a deep warmed serving dish.
4 Sprinkle the fried breadcrumb mixture over the mashed swede, brown quickly under a hot grill, if liked, and serve at once, while the dish is still piping hot.
● 175 kcal/735 kJ per portion

Swede and potato layer Instead of using all swede, replace half of it with potato. Either mash together, or mash them separately and arrange in 2 layers in the dish. Continue as above.

Mushrooms in tomato herb sauce

Serves 4
2 tbls olive oil
1 onion, very finely chopped
7 tbls water
juice of ½ lemon
1 garlic clove, crushed (optional)
salt and freshly ground black pepper
2 sprigs fresh thyme, or ½ tsp dried thyme
2 bay leaves
250 g/9 oz tomatoes, skinned, deseeded and chopped
2 tbls chopped fresh parsley
450 g/1 lb button mushrooms

1 Heat half the oil in a saucepan, add the onion and cook over moderate heat for about 5 minutes, until soft and lightly coloured.

1   Top and tail the green beans. Bring a pan of salted water to a brisk boil. Drop in the beans (immersion of green vegetables in boiling water helps to 'set' their brilliant colour); bring to the boil again and simmer until just tender. This will take 3-8 minutes, depending on the age of the beans.

2   Meanwhile, place the olive oil in a small bowl with the tarragon vinegar and salt and pepper to taste. Beat the mixture thoroughly with a fork until it forms an emulsion. Stir in the chopped onion, parsley and garlic.

3   As soon as the beans are cooked, drain them thoroughly in a colander and transfer to a serving dish.

4   Pour the dressing over the steaming beans. Toss thoroughly and taste for seasoning, adding more pepper if necessary. Serve cold.

● 105 kcal/441 kJ per portion

Left: Celeriac and tomato bake
Below: Mushrooms in tomato herb sauce

2   Add all the remaining ingredients, except half the parsley and the mushrooms. Bring to the boil, then lower the heat and simmer very gently for 3-4 minutes, stirring occasionally.

3   Add the mushrooms to the tomato sauce and simmer gently, uncovered, for 15 minutes.

4   Remove from the heat and discard the bay leaves and thyme, if used.

5   Transfer the mixture to a serving dish and garnish with the remaining parsley. Serve the mushrooms warm, cold or chilled, accompanied by crusty wholemeal bread.

To Serve: Mushrooms served this way make an excellent starter or side dish, or serve as part of a mixed hors d'oeuvre, with salads, meat, fish and eggs.

● 85 kcal/357 kJ per portion

Green bean salad

Illustrated on pages 228-229

Serves 6
700 g/1½ lb fresh young green beans
4 tbls olive oil
2 tbls tarragon vinegar
salt and freshly ground black pepper
3 tbls very finely chopped onion
3 tbls very finely chopped parsley
pinch of very finely chopped garlic

6 Cover with cling film and chill in the refrigerator for 30 minutes or until ready to serve.
7 Just before serving, toss the salad again, and garnish with walnut halves.
- 140 kcal/588 kJ per portion for 4
- 95 kcal/399 kJ per portion for 6

Tomato salad

Illustrated on pages 228-229

Serves 4
4-6 ripe tomatoes
2 tbls olive oil
2 tsps wine vinegar
salt and freshly ground black
**   pepper**
2 tbls finely chopped parsley
1-2 garlic cloves, finely chopped

1 Wipe the tomatoes and cut them across into even slices. Arrange them in a serving dish.
2 Mix together the olive oil, wine vinegar and salt and pepper to taste. Pour this dressing over the tomatoes.
3 Sprinkle the salad with finely chopped parsley and garlic to taste.
- 70 kcal/294 kJ per portion

Left: Apricot and bean salad
Below: Broad beans with lettuce and onions

Apricot and bean salad

Serves 4-6
75 g/3 oz dried apricots
1 tsp grated orange zest
salt
450 g/1 lb fresh runner beans,
**   thinly sliced diagonally, or**
**   frozen sliced green beans**
200 g/7 oz can sweetcorn, drained
3 walnuts, shelled and halved, to
**   garnish**

For the dressing
1 tbls orange juice
1 tbls olive oil
1 tsp clear honey
freshly ground black pepper
few drops of lemon juice (optional)

1 Cover the apricots with cold water and leave to stand for 3 hours.
2 Place the apricots and water in a pan and bring to the boil, then cover and simmer for 5-10 minutes until the apricots are just soft. Drain. Cut each apricot lengthways into 3 strips and mix with the orange zest in a salad bowl.

3 Bring a pan of salted water to the boil and add the beans. Simmer for 5 minutes if fresh and 2 minutes if frozen, until the beans are tender but still crunchy.
4 Drain and rinse the beans in cold water and drain well again. Add to the apricots, together with the sweetcorn, and mix.
5 To make the dressing, in a bowl, whisk together the orange juice, olive oil, honey, salt and pepper to taste. Pour the dressing over the salad. Adjust the seasoning and add a few drops of lemon juice if wished.

Broad beans with lettuce and onions

Serves 4
6-8 lettuce leaves
350 g/12 oz frozen broad beans,
  defrosted
½ onion, grated
salt and freshly ground black
  pepper
15 g/½ oz butter
3 tbls chicken stock
vegetable oil, for greasing

1 Heat the oven to 190°C/375°F/gas 5. Lightly oil a small casserole dish.

2 Line the dish with half the lettuce leaves. Spoon the beans and grated onion over the lettuce and season with salt and pepper to taste.

3 Cover with the remaining lettuce leaves, arranging them so that they overlap. Add the butter and pour on the chicken stock.

4 Cover the casserole with a lid and bake in the oven for 40 minutes until the beans are tender. Serve at once.

To Serve: Use this unusual dish as an accompaniment to roast meat or meat casseroles served with baked potatoes: the whole meal can then be cooked in the oven together, to save fuel. For an

Above: *Leeks with walnuts and Chinese leaves*

attractive finish, arrange fresh lettuce leaves on top of the dish.

● 90 kcal/378 kJ per portion

Leeks with walnuts and Chinese leaves

Serves 4-6
250 g/9 oz leeks
2 tbls oil
1 onion, sliced
50 g/2 oz walnut pieces
4 celery stalks, chopped
250 g/9 oz Chinese leaves, sliced
salt and freshly ground black
  pepper
few dashes of soy sauce

1 Top and tail the leeks, then slit them down the centre almost to the base. Fan out the layers under cold running water to rinse off all the dirt. Slice the cleaned leeks into 5 cm/2 in lengths. Heat the oil in a frying-pan, add the leeks and onion and fry gently for 5 minutes until the onion is soft and lightly coloured.

2 Add the walnuts and celery, and fry over moderate heat, stirring, for 3 minutes.

3 Stir the Chinese leaves into the pan and cook for a further 2 minutes until the Chinese leaves begin to soften.

4 Season to taste with salt and pepper, stir in a few dashes of soy sauce and cook for a further minute. Turn into a warmed serving dish and serve at once.

● 160 kcal/672 kJ per portion (4 portions)
● 105 kcal/441 kJ per portion (6 portions)

Cheese and leek supper For a more substantial dish, pour about 300 ml/½ pt cheese sauce over the finished dish. Sprinkle the top with wholemeal breadcrumbs and dot with a little butter. Bake in the oven at 220°C/425°F/gas 7 for 15 minutes until the top is crisp and golden brown.

Grated carrot salad

Illustrated on pages 228-229

Serves 4
450 g/1 lb young carrots, scraped
2 tbls olive oil
2 tsps lemon juice
**salt and freshly ground black
    pepper**
pinch of caster sugar
lettuce leaves, to serve

1 Coarsely grate the carrots. Place them in a bowl with the olive oil and lemon juice and toss well. Season to taste with salt and pepper, add the caster sugar and toss again.

2 Pile the mixture on a lettuce-lined dish and chill until ready to serve.

● 85 kcal/357 kJ per portion

Apple-glazed carrots

Serves 4
450 g/1 lb carrots
salt
1 tsp sugar
15 g/½ oz butter
2 onions, halved and thinly sliced
2 dessert apples
1-2 tbls chopped mint or parsley
freshly ground black pepper
squeeze of lemon juice (optional)

1 Peel or scrape the carrots, then halve them and cut the halves lengthways into sticks. Put the carrot sticks in a pan of cold, lightly salted water and add the sugar. Boil the carrot sticks for 5-7 minutes, until almost tender but still slightly crisp.

2 Meanwhile, melt the butter in a saucepan and fry the onions gently for 5 minutes until soft.

3 Drain the carrots, reserving 4 tbls cooking liquid. Peel, core and slice the apples.

4 Add the drained carrots to the onions with the apples, the reserved cooking liquid, mint or parsley and salt and pepper to taste. Stir in lemon juice, if liked. Transfer to a warmed serving dish and serve.

● 90 kcal/378 kJ per portion

Below: *Apple-glazed carrots*

Pear-glazed carrots Instead of the apples, use ripe dessert pears in this recipe, preparing them in exactly the same way. Either dish would make a delicious accompaniment to pork.

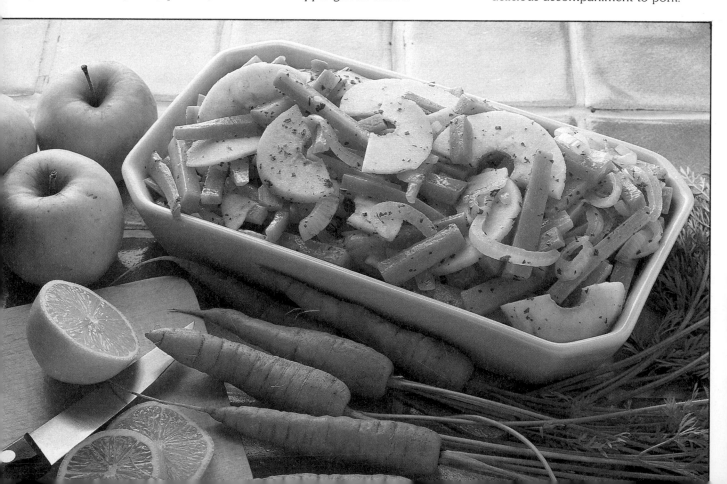

3 Cover and simmer for a further 3 hours, or until the beans are quite tender, but not mushy, and the liquid has thickened slightly.

4 Add the lemon juice and season to taste with salt and pepper. Allow the beans to cool in their liquid for about 2 hours.

5 Transfer the cold beans, plus their liquid, to a serving dish. Serve garnished with chopped parsley.

To Serve: This unusual dish can be served as a vegetable course on its own or accompanied by crusty wholemeal or white bread.

● 235 kcal/987 kJ per portion

Chick-pea salad

Serves 4
100 g/4 oz chick-peas
3 tbls olive oil
1 tbls wine vinegar
**salt and freshly ground black
    pepper**
**450 g/1 lb tomatoes, skinned and
    sliced**
1 medium onion, thinly sliced
**2 tsps freshly chopped basil or
    1 tsp dried basil**

1 Put the chick-peas into a deep bowl, cover with plenty of cold water and leave to soak for 8 hours.

2 Drain the chick-peas, rinse under cold running water, then put them into a saucepan and cover with fresh cold water. Bring to the boil, then reduce the heat and simmer for about 1 hour until tender. Add more water during cooking if necessary.

3 Drain the cooked chick-peas and leave to cool.

4 Put the oil and vinegar into a bowl. Beat together with a fork, then season to taste with salt and pepper. Add the chick-peas and mix gently until well coated with dressing. Take care not to break them up.

5 Lay the tomato and onion slices in a shallow serving dish and sprinkle with the basil and salt and pepper to taste. Spoon the dressed chick-peas over the top and season again with black pepper. Serve cold.

To Serve: This nourishing salad can make a complete light meal, served with soft wholemeal rolls or warm pitta bread.

For a dinner party, serve the salad as a fairly substantial starter, provided the main course is light. It would also be attractive for a buffet party.

To Freeze: Chick-peas freeze well after soaking and cooking. After cooling, freeze in rigid containers for up to 2 months. Before making up the salad, allow several hours for the chick-peas to defrost at room temperature.

● 195 kcal/819 kJ per portion

Above: *Garlic haricot beans*

Garlic haricot beans

Serves 4
2 tbls olive oil
1 onion, chopped
**250 g/9 oz dried haricot beans,
    soaked in cold water for 12
    hours**
2 garlic cloves, crushed
1 bay leaf
pinch of dried sage
1 tbls tomato purée
juice of 1 lemon
**salt and freshly ground black
    pepper**
chopped fresh parsley, to garnish

1 Heat the olive oil in a large frying-pan or shallow saucepan and gently fry the onion for 5 minutes until soft.

2 Drain the soaked beans. Rinse under cold running water and drain again, then add to the frying-pan, together with the garlic, bay leaf, sage and tomato purée. Stir well. Cook over moderate heat for 10 minutes, then add enough boiling water to cover the beans by about 2.5 cm/1 in.

Right: *Chick-pea salad*

1 Slice the chicken in long strips about 5 mm/¼ in wide. Peel the mangoes, then stone and slice them in similar-sized strips.

2 To make the dressing, mix together the chicken stock and lemon juice. Add the vinegar and sugar. Mix well. Add the rest of the dressing ingredients and mix thoroughly.

3 Put the lettuce leaves on a serving plate. Arrange the chicken and mango strips like the petals of a flower, alternating the colours, on the lettuce. Put the tomato wedges in the centre. Pour over the dressing and sprinkle over the chopped coriander leaves just before serving the salad.

● 180 kcal/756 kJ per portion

Turkey and mango salad This salad is ideal for using up leftover turkey. Use turkey or chicken stock to make the dressing.

Cooked lentil salad

Illustrated on pages 228-229

Serves 6

225 g/8 oz continental lentils
1 tbls olive oil
1 Spanish onion, finely chopped
1 garlic clove
1 bay leaf
1 tsp salt
1 tbls wine vinegar
freshly ground black pepper
For the dressing
½ Spanish onion, finely chopped
4 tbls finely chopped parsley
1 tsp made mustard
salt and freshly ground black pepper
3 tbls olive oil
juice of ½ lemon
For the garnish
anchovy fillets
tomato wedges
black olives

1 Soak the lentils overnight in cold water to cover. Drain.

2 Heat 2 tbls olive oil in a saucepan and sauté the onion until transparent. Add the garlic, bay leaf, salt, lentils and 1.4 L/2½ pt water. Bring to the boil and simmer for 30-60 minutes or until just tender. Drain the lentils and leave them to cool.

3 Remove the garlic clove and bay leaf from the lentils, and add the wine vinegar and salt and pepper.

Above: *Carrot, fennel and green pepper salad*

Carrot, fennel and green pepper salad

Serves 4

225 g/8 oz carrots
225 g/8 oz fennel
2 medium-sized green peppers
1 small cooking apple
2 tbls poppy seeds
For the dressing
3 tbls olive oil
1 tbls sherry or white wine vinegar
1 garlic clove, crushed with a pinch of salt
freshly ground black pepper

1 Grate the carrots and chop the fennel. Core, deseed and dice the peppers, and core and chop the apple. Mix them together in a bowl with the poppy seeds.

2 To make the dressing, beat the oil, sherry or vinegar, garlic and pepper together until they emulsify.

3 Fold the dressing into the salad. Leave the tossed salad to stand for 15 minutes before serving.

● 165 kcal/693 kJ per portion

Chicken and mango salad

Serves 6

275 g/10 oz lightly poached boneless chicken breasts, cooking liquid reserved
2 medium-sized ripe mangoes
1 head of Cos or other crisp lettuce
2-3 medium-sized ripe tomatoes, quartered
fresh coriander leaves, roughly chopped, to garnish
For the dressing
2 tbls reserved chicken stock
1 tbls lemon juice
2 tbls red Chinese vinegar or 1½ tbls red wine vinegar
2 tsps sugar
3 tbls peanut or other vegetable oil
1 garlic clove, crushed
1 spring onion, finely chopped
½ tsp ground coriander

4 To make the dressing, place the onion in a bowl with the parsley, mustard and salt and pepper to taste. Mix well, then pour in the olive oil, little by little, beating the mixture continuously, until it thickens. Flavour with lemon juice.
5 Pour the dressing over the lentils and mix thoroughly. Garnish with anchovy fillets, tomato wedges and black olives.
● 210 kcal/882 kJ per portion

Cucumber and pineapple salad

Serves 4
1 medium-sized cucumber
¼ tsp salt
**3 round slices of fresh pineapple,
   5 mm/¼ in thick, peeled and
   cored**
1 small onion, coarsely chopped
juice of ½ lemon
1 tsp sugar
2 dried red chillies, crushed

1 Using a cannelle cutter or the prongs of a fork, score the skin of the cucumber at intervals to give a decorative effect to the slices.

2 Cut the cucumber into thin slices and mix with the salt in a large, shallow bowl. Cut each pineapple round into 8 wedge-shaped pieces.

3 Add the pineapple, onion, lemon juice, sugar and chillies to the cucumber. Mix well. Place in the refrigerator and leave to marinate for 3-4 hours.
4 Arrange alternating concentric circles of pineapple wedges and cucumber slices in a shallow serving dish and serve immediately.
To Serve: This simple salad makes a refreshing and very attractive accompaniment to cold meats and poultry, such as ham or chicken.
● 40 kcal/168 kJ per portion

Pickled carrot salad

Serves 4-6
**4 large carrots, sliced into thin
   matchstick strips**
lettuce leaves, to serve (optional)

Above: *top to bottom, Pickled carrot salad, Cucumber and pineapple salad, Chicken and mango salad*

For the dressing
**1 tbls red Chinese vinegar or red
   wine vinegar**
½ tsp salt
2 tsps sugar

1 Place the carrots in a bowl. To make the dressing, mix the vinegar, salt and sugar with 225 ml/8 fl oz water. Taste and add more salt and sugar if necessary.
2 Stir the dressing into the carrots. Leave to stand for at least 15 minutes.
3 Drain off the dressing and serve the carrots piled on lettuce leaves, if wished, or use them as a garnish for other dishes.
● 40 kcal/168 kJ per portion

Orange and olive platter

Serves 4-6
3 oranges
1 crisp lettuce, shredded
50 g/2 oz black olives
mustard and cress, to garnish
   (optional)
For the dressing
1 small onion, finely chopped
1 tbls chopped fresh parsley
3 tbls vegetable oil
1 tbls wine vinegar
¼ tsp mustard powder
pinch of sugar
salt and freshly ground black
   pepper

1   Using a sharp knife, and cutting in a spiral motion, remove the peel and pith from the oranges. Cut into slices.

2   Arrange the lettuce neatly in a shallow serving dish, then place the orange slices in 2 overlapping lines down the centre of the lettuce.
3   Arrange the olives down the centre of each line of orange slices. Cover and refrigerate until required.
4   Just before serving, make the dressing: put the dressing ingredients into a screw-top jar with salt and pepper to taste. Shake well until blended.
5   Pour the dressing around the salad, garnish with mustard and cress, if liked, and serve at once.
● 140 kcal/588 kJ per portion (4 portions)
● 90 kcal/378 kJ per portion (6 portions)

Orange and watercress platter Instead of arranging the orange slices over a bed of lettuce, use watercress instead.

Left: *top to bottom, Orange and olive platter, Orange and watercress platter, Orange, olive and chicory platter*

Orange, olive and chicory platter Substitute chicory leaves for the lettuce, arranging them like the spokes of a wheel on the serving dish.

Raw beetroot salad

Illustrated on pages 228-229

Serves 4
**2 medium-sized or 1 large raw
    beetroot, about 350 g/12 oz**
1 tart apple, about 175 g/6 oz
2 tsps lemon juice
3 tbls thick yoghurt
pinch of sugar
**salt and freshly ground black
    pepper**
1 tbls finely chopped parsley

1   Scrub the beetroots under running cold water. Drop them into a pan of boiling water for 2 minutes, then drain and peel.
2   Coarsely grate the raw beetroots and the unpeeled apple.
3   Place the grated beetroot and apple in a serving dish with lemon juice to taste, yoghurt and sugar. Toss well and season to taste with salt and pepper.
4   Sprinkle the salad with the chopped parsley and chill until ready to serve.
● 55 kcal/231 kJ per portion

Stuffed tomato salad

Serves 4
250 g/9 oz fennel bulb
175 g/6 oz cucumber
250 g/9 oz radishes
4 large tomatoes
1 tbls chopped fresh parsley

Above: *Stuffed tomato salad*

For the dressing
3 tbls olive oil
2 tsps lemon juice
½ tsp clear honey
½ tsp salt
**generous sprinkling of freshly
    ground black pepper**

1   Trim the fennel and finely chop 1 tbls of the leaves. Reserve the remaining whole fennel leaves for the garnish.
2   Cut the fennel bulb into eighths, then slice thinly. Peel the cucumber, cut it into quarters lengthways, then slice thinly. Cut the radishes into very thin slices.
3   Cut off tops of the tomatoes, then scoop out the flesh and seeds with a teaspoon, taking care not to break the skins.
4   To make the dressing, put all the ingredients into a screw-top jar and shake well to mix thoroughly
5   Put the sliced fennel, cucumber and radishes into a bowl with the parsley and finely chopped fennel leaves. Pour the dressing over the salad and toss the contents thoroughly to mix well.
6   Arrange the tomatoes in individual dishes, and spoon the salad into them. Garnish with the reserved fennel leaves and serve at once.
● 135 kcal/567 kJ per portion

Pineapple and beansprout salad

Serves 4
100 g/4 oz beansprouts
**225 g/8 oz can pineapple rings in
    natural juice**
**7.5 cm/3 in length of cucumber,
    diced**
1 dessert apple
juice of ½ lemon
For the sauce
2 tbls smooth peanut butter
2 tsps soy sauce
juice of ½ lemon

1   Divide the beansprouts between 4 serving plates.
2   Drain the pineapple, reserving the juice, and chop finely. Put in a bowl and set aside.
3   To make the sauce, put the peanut butter in a bowl and beat in the soy sauce and lemon juice to form a thick cream. Add about 2 tbls of reserved pineapple juice. Set aside.
4   Mix the cucumber into the chopped pineapple. Core and dice the apple, toss in the lemon juice and add to the pineapple mixture. Immediately divide this mixture between the 4 plates, piling it on to the beansprouts.
5   Pour the sauce over each salad and serve at once.
● 110 kcal/420 kJ per portion

Below: *Pineapple and beansprout salad*

Rice and Pasta

Rice and pasta dishes make an interesting addition to our weekly menus. Rice and pasta can be used as an accompaniment to a meal instead of potatoes or bread. Alternatively, they can be made into tempting lunch and supper dishes in their own right, by adding a few wholesome ingredients to them; or add cooked rice or pasta to a salad.

Whole-grain rice, known as brown rice, is rich in fibre and other nutrients. Wholewheat pasta is made from the whole part of the wheat grains and provides a delicious flavour and texture – it's high in fibre too. So choose brown rice and wholewheat pasta whenever possible.

Rice

Salmon kedgeree

Serves 4
150 g/5 oz long-grain brown or
  white rice
salt
3 hard-boiled eggs
250 g/8 oz natural yoghurt
2 tsps curry powder
freshly ground black pepper
2 x 200 g/7 oz cans red salmon,
  drained and flaked
sweet paprika, to garnish

1 Cook the rice in plenty of boiling salted water until tender but not mushy (about 40 minutes for brown, 20 minutes for white). Drain and rinse well.
2 Place the rice in a warmed, oiled shallow serving dish, cover and keep warm in a low oven.
3 Chop 1 of the hard-boiled eggs and the white of the others, reserving the yolks.
4 In a small saucepan, warm through the yoghurt over low heat, but do not allow to boil. Stir in the curry powder and pepper to taste, beat with a wooden spoon until smooth. Gently fold in the flaked salmon and chopped egg and warm through. Pour the sauce over the rice and fork it in lightly.
5 Press the reserved egg yolks through a sieve over the top of the kedgeree. Sprinkle with paprika to taste and serve at once.

To Serve: Accompany with a green salad and mango chutney or with ½ cucumber, thinly sliced and dressed with 150 g/5 oz natural yoghurt.
● 385 kcal/1617 kJ per portion

Tuna kedgeree Substitute 2 x 200 g/ 7 oz cans tuna, well drained and flaked, for the salmon.

Brown rice risotto

Illustrated on pages 198-199

Serves 4
1 tbls vegetable oil
1 onion, chopped
1 small green pepper, deseeded
  and chopped
1 small red pepper, deseeded and
  chopped
1 tsp mild chilli powder
250 g/9 oz brown rice
600 ml/1 pt hot vegetable stock
4 tomatoes, blanched, skinned
  and chopped
400 g/14 oz can red kidney beans,
  drained and rinsed under cold
  water
salt and freshly ground black
  pepper

Below: *Salmon kedgeree*

1   Heat the oil in a heavy-based saucepan and fry the onion gently for about 5 minutes, until soft. Add the peppers and cook for 2-3 minutes more.
2   Add the chilli powder and stir for 1 minute, then add the rice and stir until the grains are shiny and coated with oil.
3   Add half the stock, stir once and bring to the boil, then lower the heat and cook very gently until the liquid has been absorbed.
4   Add half the remaining stock and cook until this has been absorbed too. Test the rice. If it is not tender, add more stock and continue cooking until the rice is tender.
5   When the rice is cooked, add the tomatoes and kidney beans. Heat through for 2-3 minutes, stirring gently. Season to taste with salt and pepper and serve at once.
- 370 kcal/1554 kJ per portion

Saffron rice salad

Illustrated on pages 228-229

Serves 4
good pinch of powdered saffron
6 tbls dry white wine
800 ml/1½ pts hot chicken stock
350 g/12 oz long-grain brown or white rice
salt and freshly ground black pepper
90 ml/6 tbls olive oil
2½ tbls white wine vinegar
4 tbls finely chopped parsley
1-2 garlic cloves, finely chopped
¼ tsp dry mustard
350 g/12 oz haddock, cooked and flaked
For the garnish
4 tomatoes, cut into wedges
black olives

1   Mix the saffron with the white wine. Place it in a large saucepan with the hot chicken stock, rice and salt and pepper to taste.
2   Cover the saucepan and simmer for 20-30 minutes until the rice is tender and has absorbed all the liquid. Leave to cool.
3   Make a dressing by whisking together the olive oil, vinegar, parsley, garlic and mustard.
4   Toss the cooked saffron rice and flaked cooked haddock in a bowl with the dressing and season generously with salt and pepper, adding more oil and vinegar if necessary.

5   Garnish the salad with tomato wedges and olives.
- 380 kcal/1596 kJ per portion

Spicy kidney pilaff

Serves 4
8 lamb kidneys
2 tbls vegetable oil
1 onion, chopped
350 g/12 oz brown rice
1 tsp salt
1 tsp ground turmeric
1 tsp ground cumin
1 tsp ground coriander
¼ tsp cayenne
1 bay leaf
150 ml/¼ pt chicken stock
100 g/4 oz frozen peas
lemon wedges, watercress sprigs and cucumber slices, to garnish

1   Halve and skin the kidneys, then snip out the cores with a pair of kitchen scissors.

Above: *Spicy kidney pilaff*

2   Heat the oil in a large saucepan, add the onion and fry gently for 5 minutes until soft and lightly coloured.
3   Cut each kidney half into 4 pieces. Add the kidney pieces to the pan and cook gently, stirring occasionally, for 2 minutes. Add the rice, salt, all the spices and the bay leaf. Pour in the stock, stir and bring to the boil. Cover the pan and cook the kidney and rice mixture gently for 15 minutes.
4   Stir in the peas and cook for a further 5 minutes, or until the rice is tender and all the liquid has been absorbed. Do not stir the pilaff while it is cooking. If the rice is not fully cooked by the time all the liquid is absorbed, add more hot stock or water, 1 tbls at a time, and cook a little longer.
5   Pile the kidney pilaff on to a warmed serving dish, garnish with lemon wedges, watercress and cucumber and serve at once.
- 505 kcal/2100 kJ per portion

Health Tip

Rice is an important part of a healthy diet as it provides bulk, but no fat. Use brown or whole-grain rice in preference to white. The unrefined whole grain provides fibre which is lost in the refining process of white rice.

Pasta

Tagliatelle salad

Serves 4

salt
1 tsp vegetable oil
250 g/9 oz green tagliatelle
200 g/7 oz can tuna in brine,
    drained and flaked
4 hard-boiled eggs, chopped
2 tomatoes, skinned and chopped
45 g/1¾ oz can anchovy fillets,
    drained, soaked in milk for 20
    minutes, drained and chopped
4 celery stalks, chopped
For the herb dressing
3 tbls vegetable oil
1 tbls white wine vinegar
1 tsp lemon juice
1 garlic clove, crushed (optional)
pinch of sugar
1 tsp finely chopped basil
1 tbls finely chopped parsley
salt and freshly ground black
    pepper

1 Bring a large pan of lightly salted water to the boil, swirl in the oil and add the tagliatelle. Bring back to the boil and cook for 10-12 minutes (or according to packet instructions), until tender yet firm to the bite.

2 Meanwhile, to make the herb dressing, put the dressing ingredients into a screw-top jar, adding salt and pepper to taste. Replace the lid firmly and shake the dressing thoroughly until completely blended.

3 Drain the pasta, rinse under cold running water and drain again thoroughly.

4 Put the cooked pasta in a salad bowl. Add the tuna, chopped hard-boiled eggs, tomatoes, anchovies and celery. Pour over the herb dressing and toss the ingredients lightly together. Serve at once.

To Serve: For a more substantial salad, garnish with chopped green pepper, tomato quarters, halved and stoned black olives or pickled walnuts, and a few celery leaves. Serve with warm

Below: *Tagliatelle salad*

244

Above: *Vegetable and pasta stir-fry*

1 Cook the pasta in plenty of boiling, salted water for about 10 minutes until tender. Drain and rinse under cold running water. Drain again.
2 Melt the butter in a non-stick frying-pan and add all the vegetables. Fry them gently for 10 minutes, stirring frequently, until tender.
3 Add the cooked pasta and soy sauce and cook for 2 minutes more, stirring to heat the pasta through. Season lightly with salt and pepper and serve.
● 595 kcal/2500 kJ per portion

Spaghetti with pepper and olives

Serves 4
4 tbls olive oil
1 onion, finely chopped
1 green pepper, deseeded and
    thinly sliced
4 tomatoes, skinned and chopped
salt and freshly ground black
    pepper
100 g/4 oz black olives, stoned
    and halved
400 g/14 oz wholewheat spaghetti
50 g/2 oz Parmesan cheese,
    grated, to serve

1 Heat the oil in a large frying-pan with a lid. Add the onion, green pepper and tomatoes, with salt and pepper to taste, then cover the pan and cook over moderate heat for 20 minutes, stirring from time to time.
2 Add the olives to the tomato and pepper mixture in the frying-pan and cook gently for 5 minutes.
3 Meanwhile, bring a large saucepan of salted water to the boil and cook the spaghetti for about 10 minutes, until *al dente* (tender yet firm to the bite). Drain well.
4 Add the drained spaghetti to the frying-pan and turn gently to coat evenly with the sauce. Transfer to a warmed serving dish and serve, sprinkled with Parmesan cheese.
● 580 kcal/2436 kJ per portion
To Serve: This nutritious lunch or supper dish should really be served with freshly grated Parmesan cheese, but use dried if you cannot get fresh.

Spaghetti with celery and olives
Replace the green pepper with 2 large celery stalks, thinly sliced. The flavour of celery combines well with olives.

Below: *Spaghetti with pepper and olives*

wholemeal rolls. Alternatively, make into 6 individual salads to serve as a dinner-party starter.
● 465 kcal/1953 kJ per portion

Shell pasta salad Replace the tagliatelle with 225 g/8 oz pasta shells, wholewheat preferably. Cook them according to packet instructions – about 10 minutes.

Vegetable and pasta stir-fry

Serves 4
450 g/1 lb wholewheat pasta
    shells
25 g/1 oz butter
1 large onion, sliced
3 celery stalks, cut into strips
2 large carrots, cut into strips
75 g/3 oz green beans, topped and
    tailed
½ red pepper, deseeded and sliced
½ green pepper, deseeded and
    sliced
2 tbls soy sauce
salt and pepper

Spaghetti with courgette sauce

Illustrated on pages 240-241

Serves 4
2 tbls oil
1 onion, chopped
1 garlic clove, finely chopped
1 green pepper, deseeded and thinly sliced
450 g/1 lb courgettes, trimmed and cut into 5 mm/¼ in slices
350 g/12 oz tomatoes, blanched, skinned, deseeded and sliced
1 tsp dried oregano
salt and freshly ground black pepper
350 g/12 oz wholewheat spaghetti
freshly grated Parmesan cheese, to serve

1 To make the sauce, heat the oil in a frying-pan and sauté the onion over moderate heat for 3 minutes, stirring occasionally. Add the garlic, green pepper and courgettes, stir well and sauté for 2 minutes. Cover the pan, lower the heat and simmer for 10 minutes, stirring occasionally.
2 Add the tomatoes, oregano, salt and pepper to taste and cook, uncovered,

over moderate heat for a further 10 minutes. Taste the sauce and add more pepper if necessary.
3 While the sauce is cooking, cook the spaghetti in a large pan of boiling, salted water for 10 minutes, or until tender.
4 Drain the spaghetti and arrange in a warmed serving dish. Top with the sauce and serve hot, with Parmesan cheese.
● 405 kcal/1701 kJ per portion (plus 100 kcal/420 kJ per extra 25 g/1 oz Parmesan)

Pasta with chicken liver sauce

Serves 4
2 tbls vegetable oil
½ onion, thinly sliced
250 g/9 oz frozen chicken livers, defrosted and roughly chopped
25-50 g/1-2 oz plain flour
50 ml/2 fl oz medium-dry sherry
175 g/6 oz mushrooms, sliced
150 ml/¼ pt chicken stock
½ tsp dried thyme
salt and freshly ground black pepper
350 g/12 oz wholewheat or plain pasta spirals
fresh thyme sprigs (optional)

Above: *Pasta with chicken liver sauce*

1 Heat the oil in a saucepan, add the onion and fry gently until soft but not coloured.
2 Toss the chicken livers in the flour to coat them. Add the chicken livers to the pan, raise the heat slightly and cook for 3-4 minutes until browned but still pink inside.
3 Add the sherry to the pan, stirring well to mix, then stir in the mushrooms. Stir in the chicken stock and bring to the boil. Add the thyme and season to taste with salt and pepper. Lower the heat, cover the pan and simmer gently for 12 minutes.
4 Meanwhile, cook the pasta according to packet directions until tender. Drain.
5 Transfer the pasta to a warmed serving dish and spoon over the chicken liver sauce. Top with a sprinkling of fresh thyme sprigs, if using, and serve at once with fresh Parmesan, if liked.
To Freeze: To freeze the chicken liver sauce, cool thoroughly then freeze in a polythene bag for up to 6 weeks. Defrost at room temperature before gently heating through to serve with pasta cooked as above.
● 510 kcal/2142 kJ per portion

Pasta and curd cheese bake

Serves 4
200 g/7 oz wholewheat pasta rings
3 eggs
225 g/8 oz curd cheese
**150 g/5 oz low fat natural
    yoghurt**
100 g/4 oz seedless raisins
¼ tsp salt
¼ tsp ground cinnamon
¼ tsp freshly grated nutmeg
oil, for greasing
For the topping
2 tbls chopped mixed nuts
¼ tsp ground cinnamon

1 Heat the oven to 180°C/350°F/gas 4. Lightly oil a 1 L/2 pt ovenproof dish.

Below: Pasta and curd cheese bake

2 Bring a pan of salted water to the boil and cook the pasta rings for 12 minutes or according to packet instructions until they are cooked but still firm to the bite.
3 Meanwhile, beat the eggs in a bowl, add the curd cheese and yoghurt and beat with a fork until smooth. Mix in the raisins, salt and spices.
4 Drain the cooked pasta rings and return them to the rinsed-out pan. Pour the curd cheese mixture over the pasta and stir in until evenly coated. Transfer the mixture to the prepared dish, sprinkle with the nuts and cinnamon.
5 Bake in the oven, uncovered, for about 30 minutes, until the top is golden and filling has set around the edge but is still creamy in the middle. Serve at once straight from the dish.
To Serve: This wholewheat pasta bake makes a tasty brunch, lunch or supper dish, served with green salad or fruit, such as sliced pears or peaches. This is a traditional Jewish dish, in which potatoes

sometimes take the place of noodles. Jewish cooking includes many semi-sweet dishes like this one, but they are not meant to be served as desserts, despite their sweetness.
● 455 kcal/1911 kJ per portion

Health Tip

Where once it was eschewed for being fattening, pasta is now highly recommended for inclusion in a healthy diet as it contains the good 'bulking' carbohydrates. Always use wholewheat pasta – wholewheat spaghetti, noodles, lasagne and various shapes are widely available, both fresh and dried. It contains twice the fibre of its white counterpart.

Puddings, Cakes and Breads

When keeping to a healthy diet, surprisingly there is no need to go without puddings, breads and cakes altogether. Versatile and refreshing fruit is the ideal ingredient for desserts, being high in fibre and vitamin and mineral-rich. It also contains no more than a trace of fat and is low in calories. Fruit also provides a healthy and natural sweetness.

Bread and cake making have been included in this chapter and, eaten in moderation, home-made wholemeal bread is one of the staples of a healthy diet. The cake recipes given here, such as Wholefood carrot cake and Banana cake, are full of flavoursome and nutritious ingredients. The children will love to make and eat Wholemeal gingerbread men or Sesame and almond flapjacks.

Fresh Fruit Desserts

Sunday fruit salad

Serves 6
450 g/1 lb fresh blackberries
25 g/1 oz caster sugar
150 ml/¼ pt pure apple juice
juice of ½ lemon, strained
250 g/9 oz greengages
250 g/9 oz dessert plums
2 large green dessert apples

1   Put the blackberries into a large bowl and sprinkle over the caster sugar. Cover and leave to stand for at least 1 hour, stirring and turning the berries occasionally.
2   Combine the apple juice and lemon juice in a bowl.
3   Halve the greengages and plums and extract the stones. Add to the fruit juice. Quarter and core the apples but do not peel, then thinly slice them and add to the fruit juice.

4   Mix the fruits gently together in the juice, then add the mixture to the blackberries. Combine gently, then cover and leave for at least 1 hour to allow the flavours to blend well.
To Freeze: Cool completely, then spoon the fruit salad into a freezerproof polythene container. Leave about 1-2.5 cm/½-1 in head room for expansion. Cover, seal, label and freeze for up to 8 months. Defrost in the unopened

Above: *Sunday fruit salad*

container for 8 hours or overnight at room temperature.
● 265 kcal/1100 kJ per portion

Watermelon frappé

Serves 4
1.4 kg/3 lb watermelon
75 g/3 oz caster sugar
finely grated zest and juice of
 1 large orange
finely grated zest of ½ lemon
1 tbls lemon juice

1   Deseed the watermelon by scraping out the seeds with a fork. Peel the fruit and cut it into cubes. Purée the watermelon, in batches, in a blender, or crush to a pulp with a potato masher, then work the pulp through a nylon sieve to form a smooth purée.

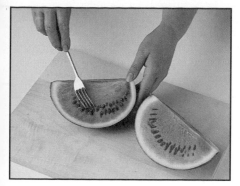

2 Put the sugar in a large bowl with the orange and lemon zest. Slowly stir in the orange and lemon juice. Add the watermelon purée, a little at a time, stirring constantly to dissolve the sugar.

3 Pour the mixture into a 1 L/2 pt rigid polythene container and freeze, uncovered, for about 3 hours, or until the mixture is slushy.

4 Turn the mixture into a large bowl and whisk to break up large ice crystals. Return to the container, cover and freeze for a further 2-3 hours, or until the frappé is firm.

Below: *Watermelon frappé*

To Serve: Transfer to the main part of the refrigerator and leave for 1-1½ hours, until softened. Mash the ice briefly with a fork to break up large lumps, then spoon into dishes and serve at once. This refreshing ice is an ideal dessert after a rich main course. Spoon it into stemmed glass dishes and provide long-handled spoons for easy eating.

To Freeze: Overwrap the container, then return to the freezer for up to 2 months. Serve as above.
- 125 kcal/525 kJ per portion

Gingered fruit cocktails

Illustrated on pages 248-249

Serves 4
3 unpeeled dessert apples, cored and sliced
2 large oranges, peeled and chopped, with pips removed
½ small melon, peeled, deseeded and cubed
150 ml/¼ pt low fat natural yoghurt
8 gingernut biscuits, coarsely crushed

1 Place the prepared fruit in a heavy-based saucepan. Cover and cook gently until the apples and melon are tender but not mushy. Remove from the heat. Leave to cool.

2 Divide the fruit mixture between 4 dessert glasses. Cover each glass with cling film and chill in the refrigerator for 20-30 minutes.

3 To serve, spoon the yoghurt over the fruit and sprinkle the crushed biscuits on top.
- 185 kcal/777 kJ per portion

Health Tip

Full of fibre and natural goodness, fresh fruits are, of course, the ideal ingredients for desserts. Make the most of the soft summer fruits when they are available. When making a fresh fruit salad, use fresh orange juice, rather than a sugar syrup, and benefit from the vitamin C content. A fresh fruit dessert makes the most refreshing finish to a dinner party.

Fresh orange jelly

Serves 4
5 large oranges
50 g/2 oz cube sugar
5 tsps powdered gelatine
1 tbls Cointreau or Grand Marnier
    liqueur (optional)
fresh orange slices, to decorate

1   Chill a 600 ml/1 pt metal mould in the refrigerator. Wash and dry the oranges.
2   Rub the sugar cubes over the orange skins to extract the essence from the zest and place the sugar in a heavy-based saucepan. Add 100 ml/3½ fl oz water and make a syrup by stirring over a low heat until the sugar is completely dissolved. Remove the saucepan from the heat and reserve.

3   Squeeze the juice from the oranges, strain and measure out 350 ml/12 fl oz, making up this quantity with a little water if necessary. Combine the orange juice and sugar syrup, pour into a jelly bag or muslin-lined sieve and leave for about 30 minutes to drip through into a clean bowl.
4   Sprinkle the gelatine over 100 ml/ 3½ fl oz water in a small, heavy-based saucepan and leave to soak for 5 minutes. Place the pan over a low heat for 2-3 minutes until the gelatine is completely dissolved. Remove the pan from the heat and pour the dissolved gelatine in a thin stream on to the strained orange juice, stirring constantly. Stir in the liqueur, if using.
5   Rinse out the chilled mould with cold water and pour in the orange jelly. Cover and leave in the refrigerator for about 8 hours or overnight, until set firm.
6   To turn out the jelly, wring a cloth out in hot water and hold it around the mould for a few seconds, then place a

Above: Fresh orange jelly

chilled, lightly moistened serving plate upside down on top of the mould. Hold the plate and mould firmly and quickly invert them, giving a sharp jerk half-way over. When the mould and plate are completely inverted, give them a firm shake. Carefully unmould.

7   Arrange the orange slices around the base of the jelly just before serving.
● 125 kcal/525 kJ per portion

Tropical fruit salad

Illustrated on pages 198-199

Serves 4
1 medium-size grapefruit, peeled
    and segmented
1 medium-size orange, peeled and
    segmented
1 small pineapple, peeled, cored
    and cubed, or 450 g/1 lb canned
    pineapple cubes, in natural
    juice, drained
14 fresh lichees, peeled, stoned
    and halved, or 450 g/1 lb
    canned lichees, drained and
    halved
1 tsp lemon or lime juice

1   Remove any seeds and white pith from the grapefruit and orange segments and cut them across into halves.
2   In a glass dessert bowl, combine the orange and grapefruit segments with the pineapple and lichees. Add the lemon or lime juice and mix lightly.
3   Chill for at least 2 hours before serving.
● 80 kcal/336 kJ per portion

Puddings

Nutty treacle tart

Serves 6
100 g/4 oz wholemeal flour
50 g/2 oz self-raising flour
pinch of salt
75 g/3 oz butter, diced
a little iced water, to mix
beaten egg or milk, to glaze
For the filling
8 tbls warmed golden syrup
75 g/3 oz fresh brown
  breadcrumbs
grated zest of ½ lemon
50 g/2 oz hazelnuts, toasted,
  skinned and coarsely chopped

1 Sift the flours with the salt into a mixing bowl. Tip the residue of bran left in the sieve into the bowl and stir lightly to mix.
2 Cut the butter into the flour with a palette knife, then rub in the butter with your fingertips until the mixture resembles even-sized breadcrumbs. Gradually stir in just enough iced water to bind the mixture together. Knead briefly until smooth. Wrap in cling film and leave to relax in the bottom of the refrigerator for about 15 minutes.
3 On a lightly floured surface, roll out the dough to a circle about 22 cm/9 in diameter. Line an 18 cm/7 in diameter flan tin, reserving the trimmings. Chill the pastry-lined tin and the trimmings for 15 minutes.
4 Heat the oven to 200°C/400°F/gas 6. Measure the warm syrup into a heavy-based saucepan. Stir in the brown breadcrumbs, lemon zest and chopped hazelnuts.

5 Spread the syrup mixture evenly over the base of the pastry case. Roll out the pastry trimmings thinly and cut into long, narrow strips. Arrange the strips in a lattice over the filling. Neaten the edges, then lightly brush the strips with the beaten egg or milk.
6 Bake in the oven for 30-35 minutes, until the pastry is cooked and the filling a rich dark brown. Serve the treacle tart warm or cold.
● 335 kcal/1407 kJ per portion

Bread and butter pudding

Illustrated on pages 248-249

Serves 4
8 small, thin slices wholemeal
  bread, lightly spread with low
  fat spread and cut in half
50 g/2 oz currants or sultanas
3 eggs
600 ml/1 pt skimmed milk
25 g/1 oz caster sugar
grated rind of ½ lemon
grated nutmeg

1 Heat the oven to 180°C/350°F/gas 4. Grease a rectangular 1 L/2 pt baking dish.
2 Place a single layer of bread slices over the bottom of the dish. Sprinkle over half the currants or sultanas. Add a second layer of bread slices and then sprinkle over the remaining currants or sultanas.
3 Beat the eggs thoroughly then beat in the milk. Finally beat in the sugar and lemon rind. Pour over the bread and sprinkle with nutmeg.
4 Bake in the oven for 30-40 minutes. Serve warm.
● 340 kcal/1428 kJ per portion

Below: Nutty treacle tart

Cakes

Wholefood carrot cake

Makes 16 slices
275 g/10 oz plain wholemeal flour
1 tbls baking powder
2 tsps ground mixed spice
100 g/4 oz shelled Brazil nuts,
  chopped
50 g/2 oz pressed dates, chopped
100 g/4 oz Muscovado sugar
125 ml/4 fl oz sunflower oil
175 ml/6 fl oz unsweetened apple
  juice
350 g/12 oz carrots, grated
extra oil, for greasing
For the decoration
15 whole Brazil nuts
8 whole dried dates, halved and
  stoned
clear honey, for glazing

1   Heat the oven to 180°C/350°F/gas 4.
Oil a deep 18 cm/7 in square cake tin.
Line the sides and base with greaseproof
paper, then oil the lining paper.

2   Put the flour into a large bowl. Sift in
the baking powder and spice and stir
well to mix. Stir in the nuts and dates.
Add the sugar, oil and apple juice and
beat with a wooden spoon until blended.
Stir in the grated carrots and mix again
until thoroughly combined.

3   Turn the mixture into the prepared
cake tin and level the surface. Arrange
the whole Brazil nuts and halved dates in
rows over the top.

4   Bake in the oven for about 1¼
hours, or until a warmed fine skewer
inserted into the centre of the cake
comes out clean. (Cover cake with
greaseproof paper after 30 minutes baking to prevent overbrowning.)

5   Cool the cake for 15 minutes, then
turn out of tin and peel off the lining
paper. Place the cake, the right way up,
on a large wire rack and brush the top
with honey. Leave to cool completely
before cutting.
● 250 kcal/1050 kJ per portion

Below: Wholefood carrot cake

Sesame and almond flapjacks

Illustrated on pages 248-249

Makes 20
175 g/6 oz polyunsaturated
  margarine
75 g/3 oz soft light brown sugar
1 tbls golden syrup
225 g/8 oz rolled oats
25 g/1 oz flaked almonds
3 tbls sesame seeds
oil, for greasing

1   Heat the oven to 180°C/350°F/gas 4.
Oil a 28 x 18 cm/11 x 7 in Swiss roll tin.
2   Put the margarine, sugar and golden
syrup into a medium-sized saucepan and
heat gently until melted. Remove from
the heat. Add the oats, almonds and
2 tbls sesame seeds to the mixture and
stir until all the ingredients are combined.
3   Spread the mixture evenly in the prepared tin. Bake in the oven for 20
minutes.
4   Sprinkle the remaining sesame seeds
over the top of the flapjacks, pressing
them in lightly with the back of a spoon.
Then mark into 20 pieces and leave
them until completely cold before
removing the flapjacks from the tin.
● 150 kcal/630 kJ per portion

Wholemeal gingerbread men

Makes about 15
**225 g/8 oz polyunsaturated
  margarine**
75 g/3 oz sugar
1 tbls set honey
300 g/11 oz wholemeal flour
1½-2 tsps ground ginger
1 tbls milk
currants, to decorate
oil and flour, for greasing

1 Heat the oven to 180°C/350°F/gas 4.
Lightly oil and flour 2 baking sheets.
2 In a large bowl, cream the margarine
with the sugar and honey.
3 Combine the flour and ginger and
gradually beat this into the margarine
mixture. Beat in enough milk to make a
moist dough. Cover the dough and chill
for 15 minutes.
4 Roll out the dough on a floured surface to a thickness of 5 mm/¼ in, rolling

Below: Wholemeal gingerbread men

only a quarter of the dough at a time. Cut
into shapes with a floured gingerbread-
man cutter about 15 cm/6 in long.
5 Place the shapes 2.5 cm/1 in apart
on the prepared baking sheets. Press in
currants for eyes, mouths and buttons.
6 Bake in the oven for 12 minutes or
until they are firm but not coloured.
Allow to cool and harden for 5-10 minutes. Using a fish slice, lift the gingerbread men carefully on to wire racks to
cool.
● 205 kcal/861 kJ per portion

Health Tip

You may be surprised to find cakes
and biscuits included in a 'healthy'
cookery book, but providing you are
careful about the ingredients you use,
they can form part of the diet. Use
wholemeal flour instead of white and
polyunsaturated margarine instead of
butter. Cut down on sugar, using
dried fruit to help provide extra sweetness, and always cut thin slices!

Above: Banana cake

Banana cake

Makes 1 large loaf/15 slices
**100 g/4 oz polyunsaturated
  margarine**
50 g/2 oz sugar
1 tsp vanilla
1 large egg, well beaten
**450 g/1 lb peeled ripe bananas,
  mashed**
100 g/4 oz wholemeal flour
100 g/4 oz white flour
2 tsps baking powder
oil, for greasing

1 Heat the oven to 180°C/350°F/gas 4.
2 Place the margarine and sugar in a
bowl with the vanilla, egg, bananas, flour
and baking powder. Beat well with a
wooden spoon until the mixture is
thoroughly blended.
3 Pour the mixture into an oiled 1 kg/
2 lb loaf tin. Bake in the oven for 1 hour,
or until a skewer inserted in the centre
comes out clean. Turn out on to a wire
rack to cool.
● 140 kcal/588 kJ per portion
To Serve: This deliciously moist and
flavoursome cake is a real tea-time treat,
but could also be served with fruit and
yoghurt for dessert.

Breads

Country loaf

Makes 18 slices
450 g/1 lb granary bread flour
½ tsp salt
7 g/¼ oz sachet easy-blend dried
yeast
300 ml/½ pt hand-hot water
extra granary flour, for dusting
vegetable oil, for greasing

1 Brush a 1 kg/2 lb loaf tin thoroughly with oil, then set aside in a warm place.
2 Put the flour into a warmed large bowl and stir in the salt and yeast. Make a well in the centre, then pour in most of the water. Using a wooden spoon and then your hands, mix to a soft dough, adding the remaining water if the consistency of the dough is too stiff.
3 Turn the dough out on to a lightly floured surface and knead briefly until no longer sticky. Shape the dough into an oblong, then press it out with the heel of your hand until slightly longer and three times wider than the base of the prepared loaf tin.
4 Arrange the dough so that the short end faces you. Fold the top third over the centre section, then bring the bottom third over the 2 layers. Turn the dough over, so the seam is underneath and tuck the ends under. Place the dough in the prepared tin, pressing it well into the corners to give a good shape.
5 Brush the top lightly with water, then sprinkle with flour. Cover with oiled polythene, or place in a large oiled polythene bag and leave to rise in a warm place for 30 minutes, until the dough reaches the top of the tin.
6 About 20 minutes before the dough is ready, heat the oven to 200°C/400°F/gas 6.
7 Uncover the loaf and bake in the oven for 40 minutes. Remove from the oven and run a palette knife around the sides, then turn out of tin.
8 Return loaf, upside down, to oven for a further 5-10 minutes to crisp the base and sides. To test that the loaf is cooked, rap the base with your knuckles: it should sound hollow. Cool completely on a wire rack before cutting.
● 100 kcal/420 kJ per portion

Above: *Country loaf*

Quick wholemeal bread

Illustrated on pages 198-199

Makes 18 slices
700 g/1½ lb stoneground
wholemeal flour
1-1½ tsps salt
1½ tsps soft brown sugar
1 tbls sunflower oil
1½ tbls cracked wheat
15 g/½ oz fresh yeast
about 450 ml/12 fl oz tepid water

1 Sift the flour into a large warm mixing bowl. Stir in the salt and sugar and leave in a warm place for about 5 minutes.
2 Brush a 1 kg/2 lb loaf tin with a little oil. Sprinkle half the cracked wheat over the base and sides and leave the tin in a warm place.
3 Blend the yeast with 150 ml/¼ pt of the tepid water and pour on to the warmed flour mixture. Add the remaining oil and 300 ml/½ pt tepid water and mix by hand to a moist but manageable

dough. If the dough is too stiff, add a little more warm water; if it is too wet, work in extra flour.

4 Turn the dough out on to a lightly floured surface and knead for 1 minute. Place in the warmed tin and press down evenly with your hand. Sprinkle over the remaining cracked wheat and press lightly into the dough.

5 Cover the tin with cling film or a clean, damp cloth; leave in a warm place for 25-35 minutes until the dough has risen just above the top of the tin.

6 About 20 minutes before the dough is ready, heat the oven to 220°C/425°F/gas 7.

7 Uncover the loaf and bake in the oven for 15 minutes. Reduce the oven temperature to 190°C/375°F/gas 5 and bake for a further 25-30 minutes until the bread has shrunk slightly from the sides of the tin.

8 Turn the bread out of the tin and rap the base with your knuckles: if cooked, it should sound hollow. If necessary, return the bread upside-down to the oven and bake for a few minutes more. Then turn it out on to a wire rack to cool.

- 2420 kcal/10164 kJ per loaf
- 135 kcal/564 kJ per slice

Date and walnut loaf

Makes 15 slices
225 g/8 oz wholemeal flour
225 g/8 oz plain flour
4 tsps baking powder
½ tsp ground mixed spice
100 g/4 oz polyunsaturated margarine
50 g/2 oz caster sugar
175 g/6 oz stoned dates, finely chopped
50 g/2 oz walnuts, finely chopped
2 medium-sized eggs, beaten
150 ml/¼ pt skimmed milk
125 ml/4 fl oz black treacle, warmed
oil, for greasing

1 Heat the oven to 180°C/350°F/gas 4. Brush a 1 kg/2 lb loaf tin with oil, then line and oil the base.
2 Sift the flours, baking powder and spice into a large, warmed mixing bowl. Cut in the margarine and rub in until the mixture resembles breadcrumbs.
3 Stir in the sugar, dates and walnuts. Then stir in the beaten eggs. Mix the milk with the warmed black treacle and stir into the other ingredients, a little at a time. If the mixture is too dry, gradually

add extra milk, a spoonful at a time, until a soft dropping consistency is reached.
4 Using a spatula, scrape the mixture into the prepared tin and smooth the top. Bake in the oven for 1 hour 50 minutes, or until a warmed fine skewer inserted into the centre of the loaf comes out clean. Cover with greaseproof paper for the final quarter of the cooking time.
5 Remove from the oven and allow to stand in the tin for 10 minutes. Turn out on to a wire rack, and leave to cool with lining paper in place to retain moisture.

- 245 kcal/1029 kJ per portion

Malt fruit loaf

Illustrated on pages 248-249

Makes 10 slices
50 g/2 oz seedless raisins
50 g/2 oz sultanas
50 g/2 oz light soft brown sugar
100 g/4 oz wheat bran breakfast cereal
1 tbls malt extract
300 ml/½ pt skimmed milk
100 g/4 oz self-raising wholemeal flour
extra malt extract, for glazing
vegetable oil, for greasing

1 Put the raisins, sultanas, sugar, cereal and malt into a large bowl. Pour in the milk and stir well to mix, then cover and leave in a cool place for 1 hour, stirring occasionally.
2 About 20 minutes before the end of standing time, heat the oven to 180°C/350°F/gas 4. Very thoroughly oil a 450 g/1 lb loaf tin, line with greaseproof paper, then oil the paper.
3 Uncover the mixture, sift in the flour and mix with a wooden spoon until thoroughly blended.
4 Turn the mixture into the prepared tin. Bake in the oven for about 1 hour, until risen, browned and just firm to the touch.
5 Leave the loaf to cool in the tin for 5 minutes, then run a palette knife around the sides to loosen it. Turn the loaf out of the tin and carefully peel off the lining paper.
6 Place the loaf on a wire rack and brush the top with malt extract, then leave to cool completely. Wrap the cooled loaf in cling film and store in an airtight container for 24 hours before cutting and serving.

- 125 kcal/525 kJ per portion

Below: Date and walnut loaf

Cook Italian

Introduction

Few countries have as great a variety of cooking as Italy. Food is extremely important to the Italians, and the regional cooking styles vary so much that there is an endless selection of mouth-watering dishes to choose from.

Pasta has a high status in Italy, and it is a healthy, natural food that offers incredible scope for quick, tasty and economical meals. Equally well known are pizzas, which use inexpensive ingredients in a multitude of different toppings. But Italian cooking is much more than just pasta and pizzas.

This section contains over 100 of the most famous, popular and representative Italian dishes, prepared in the authentic way but adapted where necessary to the British kitchen. Buon appetito!

Techniques and Ingredients

Eating is not merely a matter of survival in Italy; it's a pleasure. Italians cook with a combination of love, instinct and skill — and they serve with style.

Italian meals
Italian meals consist of at least three courses: a soup or pasta dish (or, in the north, a risotto), then a main course and then fruit. Simple vegetables or a salad may accompany the main course, served on a separate plate. Sometimes an antipasto precedes the soup or pasta, and for a special occasion a dessert will be served before the fruit. Bread and wine are accompaniments to every meal.

However, there is no reason why you cannot adapt an Italian menu to suit your own requirements. For example, you could serve a substantial pasta dish as a main course, preceded by a soup or antipasto; or a light pasta dish as an accompaniment to a main course, or with a salad for a luncheon.

Equipment
You don't need any special equipment to cook Italian food. However, the Italian kitchen often has the following items which you might like to consider: a box cheese grater, in which the grater forms the lid; a mezzaluna (wooden bowl with a crescent-shaped chopper) for chopping herbs, nuts and tomatoes; a long rolling pin or a pasta machine if you plan to make home-made pasta. A food processor is also a help but not essential.

Cooking techniques
Cooking methods vary considerably, according to the region, as Italian cooking is really a collection of specialized regional dishes. Many dishes take their name from the region where they originated. The recipes in this book represent a cross section of Italy's greatest dishes, and the techniques relating to them are described step-by-step.

Italians treat all their ingredients with respect, to make the most of their flavour and nutritional value. Vegetables, pasta and rice are all cooked al dente, or until they are done but still slightly firm. Ingredients like oil or salt are added to cooked vegetables to enhance their flavour, salads always have a dressing, and wine or vinegar is often added to meat juices.

Meat is not allowed to dry out during cooking, and pot roasting in just a little liquid is a popular technique throughout Italy. Veal, chicken and, especially, pork are sometimes baked in milk to keep them moist; Coriander Pork in Creamy Sauce (page 298) is an example of this. The Italians are also justly famous for their stews, such as Roman Beef Stew (page 297).

Deep frying mixtures of food is popular, and there are several dishes where different meats, fish or vegetables are cooked together in this way. One of the classics is Deep-Fried Fish and Shellfish (page 291).

Nothing is wasted in an Italian kitchen.

Left: Cheese is vitally important in Italian cooking, and there are many different types. Shown here are some of the best known cheeses. **1, 2** Fontina and Bel Paese are both mild, soft-textured cheeses. **3, 4, 5** Gorgonzola, Taleggio and Stracchino are creamier, especially the latter which almost melts in the mouth. **6** Mozzarella is a different consistency, almost chewy, and is, of course, the famous pizza cheese. **7, 8, 9** Provolone, Parmesan and Pecorino Sardo are all hard, grating cheeses. Parmesan is particularly loved by cooks because it does not turn stringy when it is melted. **10.** Ricotta is like a curd cheese and is used in both savoury and sweet dishes, especially with pasta.

Above: *Italian medium-grain risotto rice is essential for making risottos. More round than long, it can absorb a lot of liquid without becoming soft or sticky.*

For example, a rich meat or vegetable broth could be used to cook the pasta, which might then be served with the sauce in which the meat was cooked. Any leftover meat could be used in meatballs, meatloaf, a sauce for another pasta or a stuffing for cannelloni or ravioli. Even the leftover pasta could be used, in a pasta soup.

Much of Italian cooking is home-made. Most families preserve their own tomatoes, and many preserve their own olives. They make their own pasta and bread and often their own wine and olive oil as well.

Ingredients
Like the techniques, the ingredients used in Italian cooking vary from region to region. Here is a brief survey of widely used ingredients which you may not be familiar with. Where an ingredient could be difficult to obtain, an alternative is suggested.

Amaretti Hard almond macaroons served after meals with coffee or a liqueur.

Amaretto Liqueur made from almonds. Medium sherry plus 1 tsp almond essence can be substituted.

Basil A herb invariably used with tomato, it should ideally be fresh, not dry.

Capers Unopened buds of a Mediterranean shrub, pickled and used in sauces.

Marsala A fortified dessert wine used extensively in Italian cooking. You could substitute a medium sherry.

Mortadella A distinctive sausage from Bologna.

Olive oil This is important in Italian cooking, and you should use a good quality one. Extra Vergine is the best.

Home-made Ricotta
If you cannot find Ricotta in the shops, you can substitute cottage cheese, or make your own. Follow these instructions to make 100 g/4 oz Ricotta. Bring 500 ml/18 fl oz very creamy milk to the boil with 1/2 tsp salt. Add 2 tsps lemon juice and simmer very gently for 15 minutes, stirring frequently. Line a nylon sieve with a linen cloth and pour the milk into it. Tie up the cloth, and hang it to drip into a bowl for about 1 hour.

Pancetta A short, thick, fatty sausage that can be eaten raw or cooked. Use unsmoked streaky bacon as a substitute.

Pine nuts Little nuts with a delicious flavour, often used in Italian cooking. They are obtainable from delicatessens.

Prosciutto The most popular cured meat in Italy, it is a salted and air-dried fresh ham which is eaten raw.

Other frequently used ingredients include anchovies, artichokes, aubergines, chillies, peppers, olives and tomatoes. Widely used herbs, apart from basil, are marjoram, oregano, rosemary and parsley. Butter, which is used mainly in the north, is always unsalted.

Types of pasta
Pasta is the Italian word for dough or paste. There are two basic types, *pasta all'uovo*, or egg pasta, which is made with eggs and is always flat, and *pasta secca*, or dry pasta, which is prepared by machines that force the dough through drums with specially perforated discs, giving the pasta its many shapes.

There are over 600 different pasta shapes; names for the same shape often vary from one region of Italy to another. The best-known are described below and over the page.

Strands *Spaghetti*, probably the most popular and famous shape, is a thin, solid rod 25–30 cm/10–12 in long. *Bucatini* strands are slightly thicker and hollow – the name means pierced. *Linguini* are narrow, like spaghetti but are flat rather than round. These are all served with a sauce. Very much thinner are *vermicelli* ('little worms') which are very fine strands, sold in bundles. *Capellini* are the finest of all. Both of these are used in clear soups.

Left: *Moulded desserts, like this classic* Zuccotto *(page 314), are popular in Italy.*

Boiling pasta

1 Bring to a rolling boil a large pan of salted water with a little oil in it. Add the pasta a handful at a time to keep the water boiling. Feed long pasta in gradually so it will coil round the pan as it softens.

2 Stir, then lower the heat and simmer uncovered for the specified time, stirring once or twice. Towards the end of the minimum recommended cooking time, begin testing by biting or pinching a strand to see if it is done.

3 Drain the pasta in a large colander as soon as it is done. Rinse in hot (not boiling) water only if it is sticky. For a glossy finish, heat some olive oil or butter in the rinsed out pan, add the drained pasta and toss. Serve at once.

Tubes Macaroni (*maccheroni* in Italy) is sold in several sizes, always with a smooth surface. Big fat tubes are served with sauce for a substantial main course. 'Elbow' macaroni is curved; 'short-cut' macaroni is straight. *Cresti di gallo* are tubes which are shaped like decorative cock's combs. All can be served with a sauce, or used in baked dishes of different kinds. *Rigatoni* are fairly large tubes with a ribbed surface: the name means striped. *Penne* (quills) are tubes, cut diagonally to give a nib-shaped end. They come in various widths and lengths. Serve them with a sauce. *Ditali* are very short tubes which look rather like children's beads, sold in various sizes. Use them in vegetable soups. *Ditalini* are the miniature size.

Patterns There are several types of spiral pasta; *bucatini* tubes are short and thickish. *Tortiglione* are thinner than *bucatini* and have a more twisted, corkscrew shape. *Fusilli* (spindles) are similar. *Cappelletti* are shaped like hats. Serve all with a sauce.

Shells, *conchiglie*, come in small, medium and large sizes. Use small shells in soups, medium shells with sauces. Large shells can be filled after cooking with any soft mixture. Snails, *lumache*, are also sold in various sizes.

Butterflies, *farfalle*, are shaped like bows with a frilly edge. *Fiochette* and *fiochelli* are small bow shapes. Wheels, *ruoti*, and rings, *anelli*, are also sold in various sizes. The larger ones are served in sauces, the smaller in soups.

Pastini is a general name for small pasta cooked in soups, but these will be described in Italy by the shape they bear.

Left: Pasta all'uovo, *or egg pasta (clockwise, from bottom left): cannelloni, lasagnetti, tagliatelle, ravioli, lasagne*

Some shapes are better suited than others to particular purposes: twisted and curved shapes are best for holding the sauce, making it easier to eat. Tiny shapes (pastini, miniature rings, etc.) and fine strands (like vermicelli) are unsuccessful with sauces; they are used to add texture and body to soups, broths and stews. Long rods and ribbons, medium-sized tubes and round shapes are for a main course served with a sauce.

Egg pasta This is traditionally used for layered and stuffed shapes. *Cannelloni* tubes are filled with stuffing then served with a topping of sauce. *Lasagne*, available *verde* (green, from the addition of spinach) and plain, is layered with a meat or cheese filling or used to make cannelloni. *Ravioli* envelopes enclose a cream cheese and spinach or a meat filling and are served with a sauce. *Tagliatelle* is sometimes sold in bundles, and is available *verde* or plain. *Lasagnetti* is used like other flat ribbon noodles. Frilly edges help to hold a runny sauce.

Fresh egg pasta is available from delicatessens, or you can make your own (see page 276). It has a flavour that dry pasta simply cannot match.

Cooking pasta
Quantities Pasta almost trebles in bulk when cooked. Allow 25–50 g/1–2 oz pasta (dry weight) per person for a first course and 50–100 g/2–4 oz for a main course, depending on appetites, the type of sauce used and the other dishes you are serving. Always use a large quantity of salted water, with a little oil in it to prevent the pasta pieces from sticking together. You will need at least 1 L/2 pt water plus 1 tsp salt and 1 tbls oil to each 100 g/4 oz pasta.

Cooking time This varies according to shape, size and thickness: 6–9 minutes for small shapes and thin strands; 10–15 minutes for long rods and large shapes. Fresh pasta usually requires less time. But the secret of cooking any pasta is to test it frequently during cooking. Perfectly cooked pasta looks creamy and opaque. Italians describe this as *al dente* – just resistant to the bite but neither hard at the core, nor soft.

Keeping it hot Never cook pasta too far in advance. But if you have to keep it hot for a little while before serving, set the colander over a saucepan containing 25 mm/1 in of boiling water and cover with a damp cloth until ready to serve.

Storing Cooked pasta will keep for up to 3 days in a covered container in the refrigerator – drain and cool quickly under running cold water before storing; before using, rinse briefly in freshly boiled water to separate the pieces, and drain well. Heat in butter or oil. Pasta can be frozen if it forms part of another dish, such as soup; but there is little point in freezing plain cooked pasta.

Sauces for pasta
In Italy, pasta is often served with a very simple sauce – no more than a dressing of olive oil, a little softened butter or cream, generously seasoned. It can be flavoured with chopped fresh herbs, garlic, grated Parmesan or strips of bacon or ham. For more elaborate sauces for pasta, see pages 276-279.

Eating pasta
The correct way to eat spaghetti and other long thin pasta is to catch a couple of strands between the prongs of a fork and, keeping the end of the fork on the plate, wind the pasta round it. If you find that difficult, place the end of the fork against a spoon held in your other hand as you wind it.

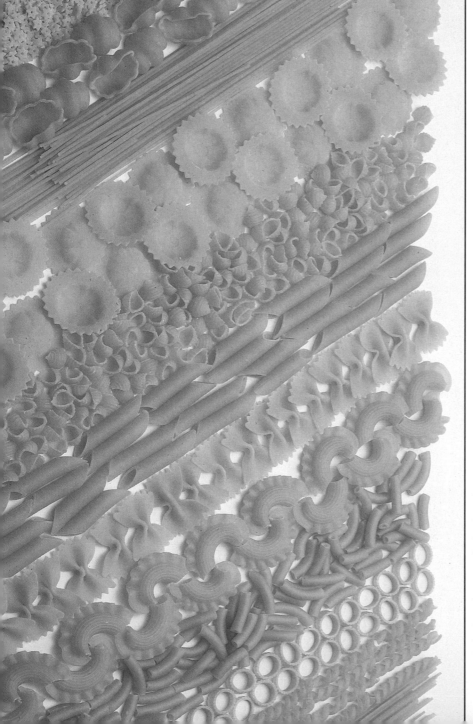

Left: *A selection of* pasta secca, *or dry pasta (from the top): rigatoni, stellete, conchiglie, spaghetti, cappelletti, conchiglie, penne, farfalle, cresti di gallo, macaroni, anelli, fusilli, linguini and conchiglie*

Regional Cooking and Wines

Italy only became one nation in the 19th century – and 2,000 years of history preceded this. It's no wonder, then, that Italian cooking remains fundamentally regional. Each area has its own ingredients and specialities, cooking styles and flavour preferences, even its own pastas and its own wines.

Northern Italy

In **Piemonte** the hearty alpine cooking of Val d'Aosta is juxtaposed with the more refined fare of Turin, further south. The greatest delicacy of Piemonte is its truffles, and another speciality is the long, narrow, crusty bread sticks known as *grissini*. Other specialities include Potato Dumplings (page 279), Chicken Marengo (page 300), Piemonte Meat Roll (page 296), *Bagna Cauda* (page 271), Turin Walnut Cake (page 318) and *Zabaglione* (page 314).

Milan is the original capital of **Lombardy** and also its gastronomic centre. It is justly famed for *Minestrone* (page 272), for boiled, stewed and braised meat dishes such as *Ossobuco* (page 295) and for other specialities flavoured with Gorgonzola and Bel Paese cheese, which are made in the region. Lombardy is the rice bowl of Italy, and here risottos, such as the famous *Risotto alla Milanese* (page 282) are more popular than pasta.

Food is all-important in **Veneto**, particularly in Venice itself. Unlike most of the rest of Italy, spices are commonly used, especially cinnamon. Pasta does not feature heavily here, but rice is cooked with seafood as well as many other ingredients. Venetians devote the largest share of their culinary skill to fish, as in Sole in Sweet and Sour Sauce (page 289). The people also have a partiality for sweets, such as their Coffee and Brandy Trifle (page 315).

Bologna, nicknamed *Bologna la Grassa* – 'fat Bologna' – is the main city of **Emilia-Romagne,** Italy's richest gastronomic region. Cream is used lavishly, and meat plays a central role. This is the region most noted for its varied ways with pork, such as Coriander Pork in Creamy Sauce (page 298). Bologna's mortadella sausage is enjoyed the world over. The neighbouring town of Parma is the centre of the region's version of haute cuisine, and this is where Italy's best prosciutto, also known as Parma ham, comes from. Parmesan cheese is also made around the town of Parma. Emilia-Romagna is famous for its pasta.

Deliciously simple as well as elaborate dishes are found in **Liguria**. Basil is used extensively, as in the famous sauce *Pesto* (page 278), created here centuries ago. Ravioli was also invented in Liguria. One of the finest fish recipes is *Cappon magro* (page 288), and another famous dish to originate in Liguria is *Vitello tonnato* (page 294).

Central and southern Italy

Since the Renaissance, **Tuscany** has enjoyed a tradition of simple, beautifully cooked fish, meat, game and above all vegetables. Despite the fantastic banquets for which the Medicis' Florence was famous, basic Tuscan cooking was, and is, very simple. The home of Italian cattle farming, Tuscany can offer the very best ingredients, such as huge steaks. These are often served with haricot beans, as in Tuscan Baked Beans (page 306). The great fish dish *Cacciucco* (page 290) comes from this region, and the stunning dessert *Zuccotto* (page 314).

Roman cooking is renowned throughout the world, though the region of **Lazio**, which surrounds the capital, is a poor one. Milk-fed spring lamb is a Roman speciality, as in the Lamb Casserole on page 299, since there is not enough grass for a shepherd to keep a large herd. Veal is eaten more often than beef for the same reason. Romans take particular care in the cooking of vegetables, and Stuffed Artichokes (page 270) is a typical dish. Herbs too are an important part of the cooking. Romans think of pasta as a winter dish, so Roman pasta sauces are rich and satisfying.

Although generally poor, the central area of Italy – **the Marches, Abruzzi, Molise** and **Umbria** – has a wealth of local ingredients. All four regions are noted for the quality of their pork and their olive oil, and Umbria is famous for the simplicity and high quality of its food. Umbrian Onion and Tomato Soup (page 272) is a good example. Umbria and the Marches also boast the finest truffles. Some of the best fish in Italy are found in the Marches, while lamb is a feature of the cooking of Abruzzi and Molise.

Southern Italy begins in **Campania**, the region surrounding the city of Naples. Pizza and pasta have made Naples famous throughout the world. Some of the best pasta in Italy is made in Naples, and the region is also the home of Mozzarella cheese. Typical Neapolitan

Left: *Typical Roman dishes – Lamb casserole (page 299), Roman beef stew (page 297) and Roman peas (page 305).*

recipes are Long Pasta with Garlic and Oil (page 279) and Cannelloni with Ham and Tomatoes (page 281). Fish and shell-fish are almost as important as tomato sauce in Naples, as in Spaghetti with Mussels and Tomatoes (page 280). Deep-fried Fish and Shellfish (page 291) is one of the great classics of Italian cooking.

Apulia and **Basilicata** share a diet based on vegetables and fruit, pastas and breads. Apulia's coastline provides a rich variety of fish, but there is little meat. Mountainous Basilicata is the poorest region of Italy, and simplicity is the keynote. Aubergines and peppers are favourites, as in Aubergine and Egg Pie (page 304). Chilli is used a lot, and excellent sausages and salamis are also produced.

The dishes of sunny **Sicily** and **Calabria** are simple and wholesome, based mainly on fish, pasta and beautiful fresh vegetables and citrus fruits. Typical dishes from Calabria include Calabrian Egg and Anchovy Antipasto (page 270) and Pasta with Oregano and Bread-crumbs (page 279). Many of Sicily's rich desserts are world-famous, in particular *Cassata Siciliana* (page 318).

In **Sardinia** meat is flavoured with wild herbs and roasted over an open fire.

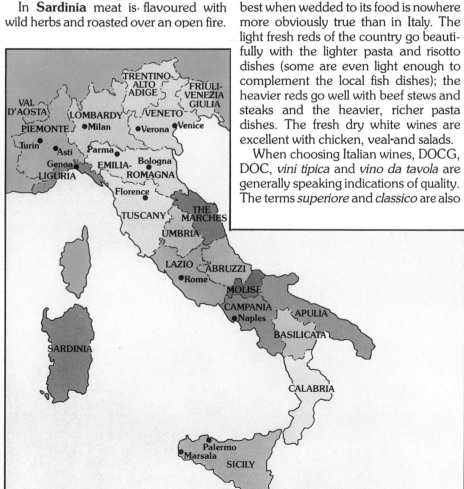

Often several animals are roasted one within another. Locally caught fish find their way into tasty soups.

Italy's wines
Most areas of Italy produce wine. In fact, Italy now produces more wine annually than any other country in the world. The adage that the wines of a country are best when wedded to its food is nowhere more obviously true than in Italy. The light fresh reds of the country go beautifully with the lighter pasta and risotto dishes (some are even light enough to complement the local fish dishes); the heavier reds go well with beef stews and steaks and the heavier, richer pasta dishes. The fresh dry white wines are excellent with chicken, veal and salads.

When choosing Italian wines, DOCG, DOC, *vini tipica* and *vino da tavola* are generally speaking indications of quality. The terms *superiore* and *classico* are also

Above: *Three famous dishes with their origins in Bologna and neighbouring Parma – Chicken Parmesan-style (page 300), Spaghetti Bolognese (page 280) and Parma ham with melon (page 270).*

usually marks of quality. The following are some of Italy's best known wines.
White wines *Soave,* from the hills around Verona, is a pale white wine, fresh and crisp, smooth and slightly flowery. It goes well with deep-fried fish, and is also a popular party wine. *Corvo Bianco* is Sicily's best known table wine. Dry and gentle, it makes an excellent aperitif and goes well with antipasti. *Verdicchio* comes from the Marches and is a delicate white; it goes well with fish or poultry. *Orvieto,* from Umbria, is a delicately scented, smooth, rich, golden wine, either dry or semi-sweet. *Frascati,* from Lazio, is a golden white wine with a strong grape flavour; it is usually dry. *Asti Spumante,* a sparkling slightly sweetish white wine, comes from Piemonte: other regions also produce Spumantes. *Marsala* is a fortified dessert wine.

Red wines *Bardolino* and *Valpolicella* are two popular light red wines made in Veneto. They are perfect for cold meats, salads, picnic lunches, as well as light pasta dishes and risottos. *Corvo Rosso*, from Sicily, is a dry, fruity red that goes as well with red meat roasts as with veal and chicken. Italy's most famous wine, *Chianti*, comes from Tuscany. It goes with all kinds of not too elaborate food – any meal that requires a vigorous red. The finest Italian wine is the heavy, full-bodied *Barolo*, made in Piemonte. Another of that region's best known wines is *Barbaresco,* also a full-bodied red. Both go well with beef stews, steaks and heavier pasta dishes.

Antipasti and Soups

*Antipasti – which means 'before the meal' – are colourful,
attractively arranged hors d'oeuvres designed to stimulate the
appetite. A wide range of ingredients is used, including
preserved meats like mortadella, salami and especially
prosciutto; hard-boiled eggs; seafood such as anchovies,
mussels, clams, prawns, etc; figs, melons, artichokes, peppers,
olives, tomatoes – the list is endless, and the selection of recipes
given in this section is very typical.*

*Soup is served after the antipasto in an Italian meal, as an
alternative to pasta, but you could just as easily serve it instead
of an antipasto, or before a pasta dish, or simply as a snack.*

Antipasti

Tomato and salami salad

Insalata di pomodori e salame
(in-sah-lah-tah dee pom-oh-dohr-ee eh sah-lah-may)

Illustrated on pages 268-269
Serves 6
450 g/1 lb tomatoes, thinly sliced
175 g/ 6 oz salami, thinly sliced
6 black olives, chopped
6 tbls olive oil
3 tbls white wine vinegar
1 tsp lemon juice
1 large garlic clove, crushed
salt and freshly ground black pepper
1 tbls chopped fresh basil

1 Arrange the tomato and salami slices in a serving dish. Separate the rows with the chopped olives.
2 Combine all the remaining ingredients, except the basil, in a screw-top jar and shake well to blend. Pour the dressing over the tomato mixture.
3 Refrigerate for 15 minutes. Sprinkle over the basil before serving.

Stuffed artichokes

Carciofi ripieni alla Romana
(kar-choh-fee rip-yeh-nay ah-lah ro-mahn-ah)

Illustrated on pages 268-269
Serves 4
4 medium-sized artichokes
100 g/4 oz dried breadcrumbs
2 garlic cloves, finely chopped
2 tsps mint leaves, finely chopped
1/4 tsp nutmeg, freshly grated
1/2 tsp salt
1/2 tsp freshly ground pepper
100 ml/4 fl oz olive oil

1 Heat the oven to 180° C/350° F/gas 4. Holding the artichokes upside-down firmly, strike them one at a time against a table surface to make the leaves open easily. Cut off the stems evenly at the base so the artichokes will stand upright. Remove tough outer leaves. Trim 25 mm/1 in from tips of remaining leaves.

2 Mix breadcrumbs, garlic, mint, nutmeg, salt, pepper and oil. Pull the outer leaves back and cut away the inner purple leaves.

3 Remove the prickly choke above the base with a knife or spoon. Spoon in the breadcrumb mixture and reshape the artichokes.

4 Place the artichokes in a casserole in one layer and pour round water to a depth of 25 mm/1 in. Cover the pan and place in the oven for 1 hour or until tender.

● To eat, pull off the leaves and eat the soft flesh at the base. Then eat the stuffing and heart together with a fork.

Parma ham with melon

Prosciutto e melone
(pro-shoo-toh eh mel-ohn-ay)

Illustrated on page 267
Serves 4
1 large melon, honeydew if possible
12 paper-thin slices Parma ham
freshly ground black pepper

1 Cut the melon in half and take out the seeds. Cut the flesh into 12 thin crescents and remove the rind.

2 Arrange 3 melon crescents on each plate with 3 pieces of ham. Season with freshly ground black pepper.

Parma ham with figs Replace the melon with thin slices of fresh green or dark figs.

Calabrian egg and anchovy antipasto

Antipasto di Reggio Calabria
(an-tee-pass-toh dee re-joh kah-lah-bree-ah)

Serves 4
4 large yellow or red peppers
4 medium-sized hard-boiled eggs
8 anchovy fillets
4 tbls olive oil
1 garlic clove, very finely chopped
salt and freshly ground black pepper
flat-leaved parsley, to garnish

1 Spear each of the peppers securely with a fork, through their stem ends. Heat the grill to high. When hot, turn the peppers over and over under the grill until their outer skin is burned and charred. When the peppers are cool enough to handle, peel off their skins.

2 Cut each pepper into quarters, remove and discard the seeds, white ribs and core. Cut the flesh into thin strips.

3 Shell each egg, cut in half and arrange them with the peppers and anchovy fillets on a dish.

4 Mix the oil, garlic, parsley, salt and plenty of pepper together well. Spoon the sauce over the eggs, peppers and anchovies and let the dish stand at least 30 minutes. Garnish with flat-leaved parsley and serve.

Hot anchovy dip

Bagna cauda
(bahn-yah cow-dah)

Serves 4
**6 anchovies in brine, filleted and
  rinsed, or 12 canned anchovy
  fillets, drained**
175 ml/6 fl oz olive oil
4 garlic cloves, crushed
75 g/3 oz butter, in small pieces
To serve
**stalks of 1 cardoon and/or celery
  sticks, carrot sticks, cauliflower
  florets, strips of red and green
  pepper, and button mushrooms**

1 If using cardoon, use only the soft inner stalks. Trim away the leaves and any stringy pieces of stalk, as well as the thin skin from the insides of the stalks. Cut the cardoon stalks into 7.5 cm/3 in lengths.

2 Finely chop the anchovies. Heat the oil in a saucepan over a medium heat. Add the garlic and cook until it begins to sizzle. Stir in the anchovies and cook for 2 minutes, stirring, then remove the pan from the heat.

3 Beat in the butter, then continue beating until the sauce thickens slightly. Pour the sauce into 4 small, very hot dishes, or one large dish placed over a spirit burner. Serve at once.

● To eat, dip the pieces of vegetable into the sauce with a fork or your fingers.

Above right: *Calabrian egg and
anchovy antipasto*
Right: *Hot anchovy dip*

Soups

Vegetable soup Milanese-style

Minestrone alla Milanese
(me-ne-stroh-nee ah-lah me-lan-eh-say)

Serves 6–8
50 g/2 oz butter
50 g/2 oz pancetta or unsmoked
 streaky bacon, chopped
3 medium-sized onions, sliced
4 medium-sized carrots, diced
2 celery stalks, diced
350 g/12 oz potatoes, diced
150 g/5 oz borlotti beans, soaked, or
 400 g/14 oz canned cannellini
 beans
2 medium-sized courgettes, diced
125 g/4 oz French beans, trimmed
 and diced
125 g/4 oz shelled peas
200 g/7 oz Savoy or other green,
 leafy cabbage, shredded
1.5–1.7 L/2½–3 pt meat stock or
 3 stock cubes dissolved in the
 same quantity of water
200 g/7 oz fresh tomatoes,
 blanched and peeled, or canned
 plum tomatoes, drained
salt and freshly ground black
 pepper
175 g/6 oz Italian rice
40 g/1½ oz freshly grated
 Parmesan cheese

1 Melt the butter in a saucepan large enough to hold all the ingredients. Add the pancetta and the onion, and sauté them over low heat until soft.
2 Add the carrots and celery to the pan and, after 2–3 minutes, stir in the potatoes and fresh beans, if using. After another 2–3 minutes, stir in the courgettes, French beans and the peas. After

Below: *Vegetable soup Milanese-style*

5 minutes, stir in the cabbage. Cook for 5 minutes, stirring.
3 Add the stock, tomatoes and salt and pepper to taste. Cover and cook over very low heat for about 3 hours.
4 Add the rice, stir, and then add the canned beans (if you are using them instead of fresh ones).
5 When the rice has cooked about 10–12 minutes, stir in the Parmesan, taste and adjust the seasoning. Serve hot.

● *Minestrone* is even better when made a day ahead.

Umbrian onion and tomato soup

Cipollata
(cheep-poh-lah-tah)

Illustrated on pages 268-269
Serves 4
50 g/2 oz pancetta or unsmoked
 streaky bacon, cut in half
2 tbls olive oil
800 g/1 lb 12 oz onions, thinly sliced
1 L/1¾ pt chicken stock or
 2 chicken stock cubes dissolved
 in the same quantity of water
400 g/14 oz canned tomatoes,
 drained
½ dried chilli, crumbled
salt and freshly ground black
 pepper
6–7 basil leaves, roughly chopped
3 tbls freshly grated Parmesan
8 thick slices of stale French bread,
 toasted
1 garlic clove, cut in half

1 Fry the chopped pancetta or bacon in the oil in a large saucepan over medium low heat. Add the onion, cover and cook at the lowest heat for one hour or until the onion has disintegrated.
2 Add the stock, tomatoes, chilli and a little salt and pepper. Cover and cook for 30 minutes.
3 Add the basil and the grated cheese. Taste and adjust the seasoning.
4 Rub the toasted bread with the cut garlic. Put the slices in a soup tureen or individual bowls and pour the soup over.

Soup Romano

Minestra alla Romana
(me-nes-trah ah-lah ro-mahn-ah)

Serves 4
1 tbls olive oil
1 medium-sized onion, chopped
4 small carrots, sliced
3 stalks celery, sliced
**2 large tomatoes, blanched,
    skinned, seeded and chopped**
50 g/2 oz mushrooms, chopped
1.5 L/2½ pt bacon stock
100 g/4 oz boiled bacon, chopped
75 g/3 oz small pasta shells
½ tsp oregano
**salt and freshly ground black
    pepper**

1   Heat the oil in a large saucepan and gently sweat the onions, carrots and celery for 5 minutes.
2   Add the tomatoes, mushrooms and stock, bring to the boil and simmer for 20 minutes.
3   Stir in the cooked bacon, pasta shells, oregano, salt and freshly ground black pepper, and simmer for a further 15 minutes. Serve immediately.

Lacy egg soup

Stracciatella
(strah-cha-tell-ah)

Illustrated on pages 268-269
Serves 4
1.25 L/2 pt stock
2 medium-sized eggs
2 tbls semolina
2 tbls Pecorino or Parmesan, grated
1 tbls finely chopped parsley
**1 fresh basil leaf, finely chopped
    (optional)**
pinch of salt
pinch of sugar
**small pinch of freshly ground
    nutmeg**

1   Heat the stock to boiling. Mix the other ingredients together and pour into the boiling liquid. Stir for 4 minutes and serve immediately.

● The name of this soup means 'little rags', as the cheese and eggs in the soup give a lacy effect. It is a simple, light and elegant soup which can be made very quickly with chicken, beef or lamb stock, or canned chicken consommé.

Above: *Soup Romano*

Pasta and tomato soup

Minestra coi pomodori
(me-nes-trah koy-ee poh-moh-dor-ee)

Serves 4
75 ml/3 fl oz olive oil
2 garlic cloves, crushed
**450 g/1 lb ripe tomatoes, blanched,
    skinned and coarsely chopped**
**2 medium-sized onions, thinly
    sliced**
3 tbls chopped parsley
**salt and freshly ground black
    pepper**
**150 g/5 oz ditalini, or other small
    short tubular pasta for soup**
**2 tbls freshly grated Parmesan
    cheese**

1   Put the oil in a saucepan over medium heat, add the garlic and sauté until the garlic is just coloured, about 3–4 minutes. Remove the garlic with a slotted spoon.
2   Add the chopped tomatoes, onion and half the parsley. Fry gently for 10 minutes, stirring frequently.
3   Pour into the saucepan 1.5 L/2½ pt water, season generously with salt and freshly ground black pepper, and simmer, covered, for 20 minutes.
4   Raise the heat and drop in the pasta. Cook, covered, for about 10 minutes, stirring occasionally, until the pasta is *al dente*.
5   Just before serving, add the remaining parsley and the Parmesan cheese. Mix well, pour into a warmed tureen and serve.

Below: *Pasta and tomato soup*

Pasta, Rice and Pizzas

Although in Italy pasta is always eaten before the main course, the main course is sometimes less substantial than the pasta dish itself. Outside Italy pasta dishes can also be served as informal main courses, side dishes or snacks. But the beauty of pasta is that it can be eaten whenever and however you like.

Rice is generally served in Italy as an alternative to pasta before the main course, but the recipes here also make excellent accompaniments to main courses. Pizza has been eaten in southern Italy since ancient times; in ancient Pompeii, the citizens ate pizza for breakfast. Nowadays it is eaten as a snack or as a meal.

Light Pasta Dishes

Home-made pasta

Pasta casalinga
(pass-tah kas-ah-ling-ah)

Serves 3–4
175–225 g/6–8 oz plain white flour
2 large eggs

1   Pour the flour in a mound on a clean working surface. Make a well in the centre and break the eggs into it. Start beating the eggs with a fork, gradually drawing the flour from the inside of the well. As the dough thickens mix in the rest of the flour with your hands, working quickly until the mixture forms a mass. If it is too sticky and moist add a little more flour (but do not overdo it).

2   Set the mixture aside and clean the surface, using a knife to scrape off the crumbs. Wash your hands, removing every trace of dough, and dry them properly.

3   Lightly flour the working surface and your hands and start kneading the dough, pushing it away from you with the heels of your hands then folding it back into a ball. Continue kneading for about 10 minutes or until the dough is elastic. Wrap the dough in cling film and let it rest in the refrigerator for a minimum of 20 minutes and a maximum of 3 hours.

4   To roll out the pasta prepared dough, lightly flour the working surface and the rolling pin. Pat the dough into a flattish shape and start gently rolling away from you. After each roll give the

dough a quarter turn so that it remains circular. Repeat until the dough is about 3 mm/⅛ in thick.

5   The final rolling process is slightly tricky, but once you have mastered it you will never have much trouble again. You need a long, thin rolling pin about 4 cm/1½ in in diameter and 80 cm/32 in long. Dust the surface and the rolling pin lightly with flour. Curl the far end of the dough around the middle of the rolling pin and roll it towards you.

6   As you do this, work over the dough on top of the rolling pin: quickly move your hands towards the ends of the pin, gently pressing the dough in each new position stretching it away from the centre while you roll the pin backwards and forwards very rapidly.

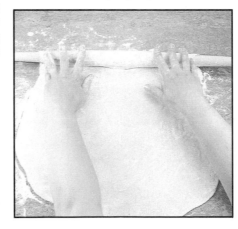

7   Continue with this movement, stretching the dough with your hands, not pressing down on it. Move the position of the pin until you have rolled up

nearly the whole circle of dough. While it is still wrapped around the pin lift and shift the circle around a quarter turn before unrolling the sheet. Repeat this rolling and stretching process making sure that the sheet is even, smooth, and has no holes or creases. If the dough is a little sticky, dust the surface again with flour. Keep rolling until the sheet becomes nearly paper thin or about 1 mm/1/16 in, but try not to take longer than 10 minutes or the dough will become dry and lose elasticity.

8   If you are making stuffed pasta (ravioli, tortellini or cannelloni) the sheet of dough must not be allowed to dry. If you are making flat pasta (tagliatelle, lasagne, etc.), place a clean dry towel on the table and lay the sheet of dough on it, letting one-third of the sheet hang over the edge of the table. The dough is ready to cut when it is dry to the touch and begins to look leathery – this will take about 30 minutes, depending on the temperature of the room.

Rolling pasta dough with a machine
1   Make up the dough as in the basic recipe. Knead the dough with the heels of your hands for 7–8 minutes. Divide the dough into 4 equal parts and work on one piece at a time, leaving the others wrapped in cling film.

2   Set the rollers of the machine at the maximum opening. Run the dough through 5 or 6 times, folding it over and turning it after each time. Do not fold it the last time. If it sticks add a bit more flour. Close the opening one notch at a time and feed the dough through the rollers once each time. Stop when you have reached the desired thinness. Leave the strip of dough between two clean cloths while you repeat the process with the remaining three balls of pasta dough.

3   If you are making stuffed pasta, proceed immediately with the recipe. If you are making flat pasta, leave it to dry as instructed in step 8, and, when ready, pass the sheet of dough through the broad cutting blades. Unroll the noodles and leave them to dry for at least 10 minutes.

Right: *Baked pasta with aubergines*

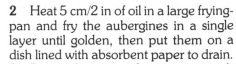

Quick home-made pasta

Pasta rapida casalinga
(pass-tah rah-pee-dah kas-ah-ling-ah)

Serves 2
225 g/8 oz plain flour
salt
75–100 ml/3–3½ fl oz cold water

1   Sift the flour and ¼ tsp salt into the goblet of a blender or food processor. Work for a few seconds, gradually adding enough water for a dough to be formed which has the consistency of fine breadcrumbs, but forms into a ball when it is pressed together.
2   Remove the dough, press it into a ball, then place on a lightly floured surface and cut the dough into two equal halves.
3   Roll out 1 piece of dough very thinly so that the board can just be seen through the dough – it should measure 30 × 25 cm/12 × 10 in. Trim off any dry edges of the dough with a sharp knife.
4   Fold and cut the dough to make long narrow ribbons. Let the pasta dry for 2–3 minutes while rolling, folding and cutting the second piece of dough. Allow this batch of the pasta to dry for 2–3 minutes before cooking.
5   Bring a large pan of well salted water to boil and plunge all the pasta into it. Bring back to the boil and cook for 30 seconds. Drain and serve at once.

● Fresh pasta freezes well: do not pull the ribbons apart after cutting dough. Wrap cut 'sausage' in foil, seal, label and freeze for 2–3 months. To serve: thaw overnight in refrigerator or cook straight from frozen for an additional 2 minutes, stirring constantly to pull the dough ribbons apart as they soften.

● If you wish to make pasta for 4, double the quantities here, then cut dough into 4 pieces, as large quantities of pasta dry out and become difficult to handle.

● Add 1 egg to dough for tastier pasta.

● Dough cut into very thin ribbons is ideal for serving in soup.

Baked pasta with aubergines

Pasticcio di penne e melanzane
(pass-tee-choh dee pen-nay eh mel-ahn-zahn-ay)

Serves 6
500 g/18 oz glossy aubergines
salt
vegetable oil for frying
400 g/14 oz canned plum tomatoes, with their juice
4 tbls olive oil
1 garlic clove, crushed
freshly ground black pepper
400 g/14 oz cut tubular pasta
25 g/ 1 oz butter
2 tbls dry breadcrumbs
75 g/3 oz Mozzarella, thinly sliced
1 tbls oregano
50 g/2 oz freshly grated Parmesan cheese

1   Peel and slice the aubergines into 5 mm/¼ in thick rounds. Put the slices in a colander, sprinkle with salt and leave them to drain for 1 hour. Pat them dry with absorbent paper.

2   Heat 5 cm/2 in of oil in a large frying-pan and fry the aubergines in a single layer until golden, then put them on a dish lined with absorbent paper to drain.
3   Purée the canned tomatoes with their juices in a blender, or pass through a food mill. Transfer to a small saucepan. Add the olive oil, garlic, salt and pepper and cook for 10 minutes over medium heat, then reserve.
4   Heat the oven to 200° C/400° F/gas 6. Cook the pasta in rapidly boiling salted water for 10 minutes or until *al dente* – firm yet tender to the bite.
5   Meanwhile butter an ovenproof dish and sprinkle with half of the breadcrumbs and cover with half the aubergine slices. Drain the pasta and toss with the butter and tomato sauce.
6   Pour half of the pasta into the dish and cover it with half the Mozzarella slices. Add half the oregano and a little black pepper and repeat the layers. Cover with the remaining pasta and sprinkle with the Parmesan and the rest of the breadcrumbs.
7   Dot the top of the pasta with a little butter and bake for 10–15 minutes. Remove from the oven and let the dish stand for 5 minutes before serving.

Green tagliatelle with Gorgonzola sauce

Tagliatelle verdi al Gorgonzola
(tahl-yee-ah-tell-ay ver-dee ahl gor-gon-zole-ah)

Illustrated on pages 274-275
Serves 4–6
100 g/4 oz Gorgonzola cheese, cut into small pieces
150 ml/¼ pt milk
50 g/2 oz butter
50 ml/2 fl oz double cream
freshly ground black pepper
finely chopped parsley to garnish
500–750 g/1–1½ lb tagliatelle verde

1   Cook the tagliatelle as directed on page 264, for about 8–10 minutes.
2   Meanwhile, pour the milk into a heavy-based saucepan and heat gently until hot but not simmering. Add the cheese and butter and stir gently with a wooden spoon until smooth.
3   Add the cream to the pan with pepper to taste and heat through gently. Do not allow the sauce to simmer. Serve at once with the pasta, garnished with chopped parsley.

Pirates' spaghetti

Spaghetti alla bucaniere
(spah-get-tee ah-lah buck-an-yer-ay)

Serves 8
**100 g/4 oz shelled clams (or shelled
cockles or mussels)**
100 g/4 oz small squid
100 g/4 oz shrimps
3 garlic cloves, chopped
1 tbls olive oil
450 g/1 lb spaghetti
**50 g/2 oz canned anchovy fillets,
drained**
**400 g/14 oz canned tomatoes,
drained**
**salt and freshly ground black
pepper**
2 tbls parsley, finely chopped
1 tbls fresh basil, finely chopped

1   Prepare the squid (*see* steps 2–3 of
Seafood stew, page 290). Slice into 25
mm/1 in rounds. In a saucepan, cook the
garlic in 1 tsp of the oil. When golden,
add the clams, squid and shrimps and
cook over low heat for 10 minutes.
2   Cook the spaghetti as directed on
page 264, for 12–14 minutes. Meanwhile,
add the anchovies, tomatoes, salt and
pepper to the seafood and continue
cooking for 10 minutes.
3   Place the drained spaghetti in a large
warmed serving dish and toss in the remaining olive oil. Pour the sauce on to
the spaghetti and mix again. Sprinkle
with parsley and basil and serve.

Tagliatelle with pesto sauce

Tagliatelle al pesto
(tahl-yee-ah-tell-ay ahl pes-toh)

Illustrated on pages 274-275
Serves 4–6
50 g/2 oz fresh basil leaves
bunch of fresh parsley
40 g/1½ oz pine nuts
2 cloves garlic
225 ml/8 fl oz olive oil
**75 g/3 oz Parmesan cheese, freshly
grated**
**50 g/2 oz butter, softened and cut
into small pieces**
¼ tsp sugar
¼ tsp salt
freshly ground black pepper
500–750 g/1–1½ lb tagliatelle

1   Put the basil, parsley, pine nuts and

garlic in a blender or food processor and
work until finely chopped.
2   With machine running, slowly pour
in the olive oil, then add the Parmesan
followed by the butter, sugar and salt.
Season to taste with pepper, then transfer to a pan or bowl.
3   Cook the tagliatelle as directed on
page 264, for about 8–10 minutes.
4   Add 1 tbls pasta cooking water, stir
well and serve at once with the pasta.

●   Pesto freezes very well, so it can be
made in quantity while basil is in season.
Omit the cheese and the garlic and add
after the sauce is thawed.

Tagliatelle with walnut sauce Grind
100 g/4 oz shelled walnuts to a paste in a
blender with 4–6 sprigs fresh marjorám
or 6–8 sprigs fresh parsley, chopped
finely. Blend in 125 ml/4 fl oz double
cream. Work in a little olive oil to make
the sauce like a soft purée, and season
with salt and pepper. Cook the tagliatelle,
and toss in 50 g/2 oz butter. Spoon the
sauce over the pasta. Serves 4.

Spaghetti with ham sauce

Spaghetti con pancetta e pomodori
(spah-get-tee kon pan-chet-ah eh
pom-oh-dohr-ee)

Illustrated on pages 274-275
Serves 4–6
1 tbls olive oil
15 g/½ oz butter
**100 g/4 oz pancetta or unsmoked
streaky bacon, finely diced**
1 onion, sliced

1 clove garlic, thinly sliced
**600 g/1 lb 5 oz canned tomatoes,
drained**
1 tbls tomato purée
1 tsp dried mixed herbs
½ tsp freshly ground black pepper
salt
500–750 g/1–1½ lb spaghetti

1   Heat the oil and butter in a large frying-pan. Add the bacon and fry for 2 minutes. Add the onion and garlic and fry
for a further 3 minutes until soft.
2   Stir in the tomatoes, tomato purée,
herb seasoning and pepper. Bring to the
boil, then lower the heat, cover the pan
and simmer for 20 minutes.
3   Meanwhile, cook the spaghetti as directed on page 264, for about 12 minutes.
4   Season the sauce to taste with salt
and serve with the spaghetti.

**Spaghetti with anchovy and mush-
room sauce** Sauté 100 g/4 oz sliced
button mushrooms and 12 chopped anchovy fillets in butter. Stir in 125 ml/4 fl
oz single cream. Pour over 450 g/1 lb
cooked spaghetti. Serves 4.
Spaghetti with cream sauce Beat 150
ml/¼ pt double cream with 1 large egg
yolk, salt and pepper. Pour over 450 g/
1 lb freshly cooked spaghetti. Serves 4.
Spaghetti with tomato sauce Sauté 2
crushed garlic cloves in 3 tbls olive oil.
Add 900 g/2 lb tomatoes which have
been chopped and sieved, 3–4 basil
leaves, roughly chopped, and salt to
taste. Simmer for 10 minutes and pour
over 450 g/1 lb freshly cooked spaghetti.
Serves 4.

Below: *Pirates' spaghetti*

Long pasta with garlic and oil

Linguine con aglio e olio
(lin-gwee-nay kon ahl-yoh eh ohl-yoh)

Serves 4
350 g/12 oz linguine, spaghetti or
  vermicelli
125 ml/4 fl oz olive oil
3 garlic cloves, very finely chopped
3 tbls chopped parsley
1 dry chilli, crushed
salt

1   Cook the pasta as directed on page 264. Do not overdrain it.
2   Meanwhile, heat the oil in a large frying-pan over medium heat, add the garlic, parsley and chilli and cook for 2 minutes, stirring constantly. Add the pasta to the frying-pan and cook it over medium-low heat for 12 minutes, stirring continually. Serve at once, straight from the frying-pan.

Pasta bows with grilled peppers Char the skin of 2 yellow and 2 red peppers under a hot grill, turning constantly; wrap in absorbent paper and leave to cool, then peel and cut into strips. Fry the garlic, chilli and parsley in the olive oil for 4 minutes along with the pepper strips. Replace the long pasta with pasta bows and fry for 1 minute more.

Pasta shells with pizza sauce (Illustrated on front cover) Cook 400 g/14 oz shell pasta, drain well and serve topped with the pizza sauce (page 299). Accompany with Parmesan cheese and a salad of radicchio, endive, peppers and olives.

Pasta with oregano and breadcrumbs Cook 400 g/14 oz short tubular pasta. Fry 2 thinly sliced garlic cloves in 75 ml/3 fl oz olive oil for 30 seconds, then add 1½ tsps oregano, 75 g/3 oz stale white breadcrumbs, salt and a lot of black pepper. Mix thoroughly, add the drained pasta and sauté for 2 minutes. Serves 4.

Potato dumplings

Gnocchi di patate
(nee-oh-kee dee pah-tah-tay)

Illustrated on page 297
Serves 4
450 g/1 lb floury potatoes
salt and freshly ground black
  pepper
65 g/2½ oz butter
100 g/4 oz flour, plus flour for
  flouring hands
1 small egg, beaten
freshly grated nutmeg
50 g/2 oz freshly grated Parmesan

Above: *Long pasta with garlic and oil*

1   Drop the potatoes into lightly salted boiling water and simmer for about 20 minutes or until tender. Drain, peel, mash and sieve them.
2   Mix the potatoes with 15 g/½ oz butter and the flour, egg, salt, pepper and nutmeg to taste. Work the mixture to a firm dough, adding a little extra flour if the dough is wet. Chill for 1 hour.
3   Form into small cylindrical shapes with floured hands.
4   Bring a very large pan of lightly salted water to the boil. Gently lower the dumplings into the water and simmer for about 5 minutes, or until they rise to the surface.
5   Melt the remaining butter. Place the dumplings on a heated serving dish, pour the melted butter over the top, sprinkle with Parmesan and serve.

● Serve this classic Italian first course with Pesto (page 278) or a tomato or meat sauce instead of melted butter, if wished.

Substantial Pasta Dishes

Spaghetti Bolognese

Spaghetti con ragú
(spah-get-tee kon rah-goo)

Illustrated on page 267
Serves 4–6
225–350 g/8–12 oz spaghetti
1½ tbls salt
1 tbls olive oil
freshly grated Parmesan cheese
For the bolognese sauce
1 medium-sized onion, finely
**   chopped**
1 medium-sized carrot, finely
**   chopped**
1 medium-sized celery stalk, finely
**   chopped**
100 g/4 oz pancetta or unsmoked
**   streaky bacon, finely chopped**
50 g/2 oz butter
2 tbls vegetable oil
150 g/5 oz minced pork
200 g/7 oz minced beef
225 ml/8 fl oz dry white wine
salt and freshly ground black
**   pepper**
1 bay leaf
1 tbls tomato purée
225 ml/8 fl oz stock
3 tbls single cream

1 Sauté the onion, carrot, celery and pancetta or bacon in the butter and oil in a saucepan over low heat. When they begin to colour, add the pork and beef and crumble with a fork.

2 When the meat has barely lost its raw colour – 2–3 minutes – add the wine. Raise the heat to medium-high and cook until the wine has nearly evaporated. Add seasoning, the bay leaf and the tomato purée diluted with half of the stock. Stir thoroughly and simmer, covered, over very low heat for 1½ hours, adding a little more stock as necessary, if the sauce is too dry. It should be of a thick but moist consistency.
3 Add the cream and simmer another hour, adding more stock as necessary. Remove the bay leaf.
4 Cook the spaghetti as directed on page 264, for about 12 minutes.
5 Put the drained pasta in a large, warmed serving dish. Pour over the bolognese sauce, and serve immediately with the freshly grated Parmesan.

Spaghetti with chicken livers Omit the minced pork and substitute 100 g/4 oz chopped chicken livers.
Spaghetti with mussels and tomatoes Prepare 1 kg/2 lb mussels in their shells (see steps 1–5 of Stuffed Mussels, page 290). Remove mussels from shells. Boil the strained liquid over high heat to reduce it. Sauté 2 finely chopped garlic cloves in 4 tbls olive oil for 1–2 minutes. Add 450 g/1 lb blanched and peeled fresh tomatoes or drained canned tomatoes with the reduced mussel liquid. Adjust seasoning and cook over medium heat while cooking 350 g/12 oz spaghetti. Add the mussels to the tomato sauce with 1 tbls chopped parsley, and cook over low heat for 5 minutes. Cover the hot cooked spaghetti with sauce.

Baked lasagne

Lasagne al forno
(lah-sahn-yeh ahl for-noh)

Serves 4–6
Bolognese sauce (see recipe for
**   Spaghetti Bolognese, this page)**
25 g/1 oz butter plus butter for
**   greasing**
75 g/3 oz freshly grated Parmesan
**   cheese**
225 g/8 oz plain or green lasagne

For the white sauce
700 ml/1¼ pt milk
90 g/3½ oz butter
75 g/3 oz flour
freshly grated nutmeg
salt and freshly ground black
**   pepper**

1 To make the white sauce, bring the milk to simmering point in a pan; remove from heat.
2 Meanwhile, melt the butter over very low heat in a heavy-bottomed saucepan. When melted, add the flour, stirring well. Cook for 1 minute.
3 Remove the pan from the heat and add the hot milk, a little at a time, stirring constantly, until all the milk has been incorporated and the sauce is smooth. Season with nutmeg, salt and pepper.
4 Return the saucepan to the heat, and slowly bring the sauce to the boil, stirring constantly. Boil for 2 minutes and remove from the heat. The sauce should

have the consistency of double cream.

5 Cook the lasagne as directed on page 264, for only 5 minutes. Plunge them into a bowl of cold water. Lift them out and spread them on tea-towels. Repeat until all the pasta has been blanched in this way. Gently pat the pasta dry on top.

6 Heat the oven to 200° C/400° F/gas 6. Butter an oven dish measuring 20 × 28 cm/8 × 11 in and 6.5 cm/2¾ in deep. Spread 2 tbls of the bolognese sauce on the bottom. Cover with a layer of lasagne and spread over a little bolognese, some white sauce and sprinkle

with grated cheese. Cover with another layer of pasta and repeat until all ingredients are used up, coating the top layer with white sauce, then sprinkling with cheese. Dot with butter.

7 Bake the lasagne for 20–25 minutes or until the top is golden brown. If necessary raise the heat and bake for another 5 minutes or put it briefly under the grill. Allow the dish to stand for at least 5 minutes before serving.

Cannelloni with ham and tomatoes

Cannelloni alla moda di Partenopea
(kan-ehl-ohn-ee ah-lah mo-dah dee par-ten-oh-pee-ah)

Serves 4
16 cannelloni tubes
1 tbls oil
225 g/8 oz Mozzarella cheese, diced
225 g/8 oz sieved Ricotta or cottage cheese
75 g/3 oz lean cooked ham, diced
2 large eggs, beaten till frothy
salt and freshly ground black pepper
700 ml/1¼ pt white sauce (see recipe Baked lasagne, opposite)

For the topping
400 g/14 oz canned tomatoes, drained and roughly chopped
75 g/3 oz butter, plus butter for greasing
salt and freshly ground black pepper
1 tsp freshly chopped basil or ½ tsp dried basil
25 g/1 oz butter
25 g/1 oz grated Parmesan cheese

1 Mix the Mozzarella and Ricotta cheeses and add the diced ham. Stir the eggs into the cheese mixture. Season to taste with salt and pepper.

2 Melt 75 g/3 oz of the butter in a frying pan. Add the tomatoes, salt and pepper and basil. Cook for 7–8 minutes, stirring from time to time to prevent mixture sticking.

3 Pre-heat the oven to 200° C/400° F/gas 6. Grease an ovenproof dish.

4 Cook the cannelloni as directed on page 264, for 13–15 minutes.

5 Wring out a large, clean tea cloth in cold water. Drain the tubes and lay them in rows on the cloth, without touching. Allow to cool slightly.

6 Holding the edges of a tube apart, push the filling in with a teaspoon. You will need about 5 tsps filling per tube. Leave room at the ends for expansion.

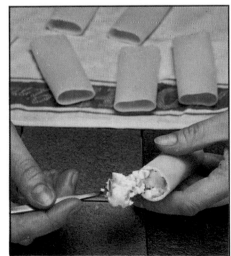

7 As the tubes are filled, place in the greased dish side by side in one layer.

8 Make the white sauce as outlined opposite. Pour over the cannelloni, then top with the tomato mixture. Sprinkle with the Parmesan and dot with butter.

9 Bake for 15–20 minutes until the cheese is browned.

Left: *Cannelloni with ham and tomatoes*

Rice with four cheeses

Riso al quattro formaggi
(ree-zo ahl kwa-troh for-mah-gee)

Serves 4
175 g/6 oz Italian rice
1 tsp salt
50 g/2 oz cooked ham or tongue
25 g/1 oz Provolone
25 g/1 oz Bel Paese
50 g/2 oz Gruyère
50 g/2 oz butter
50 g/2 oz grated Parmesan

1 To boil the rice, place it in a saucepan with twice its volume of cold water, plus 1 tsp salt. Set the pan over medium heat, stir once and bring the water to the boil. Cover the pan, reduce the heat and leave to simmer for 15 minutes, without lifting the lid or stirring.
2 When the cooking time is up, remove the lid; almost all the water will have gone and the rice will be tender. Either tip the rice into a colander to drain then rinse well with boiling water, or turn off the heat and leave the lid on the pan for 5 minutes. Turn into a serving dish and fluff the rice with a fork to separate the grains and prevent them sticking.
3 Dice the solid cheeses and the meat, and mix the cubes together.
4 Heat the oven to 200° C/400° F/ gas 6.
5 Place one-third of the rice in an ovenproof dish. Sprinkle with half of the diced meat and cheese mixture. Dot with butter and sprinkle with one-third of the grated Parmesan. Make another layer in the same way with one-third of the rice and the remaining meat and cheese. Dot with butter and one-third of the Parmesan. Add the top layer of rice. Sprinkle with remaining Parmesan and dot with remaining butter.
6 Place the dish in a dish of hot water in the centre of the oven and cook for 30 minutes until the top is golden.

● This dish is best made with four cheeses as suggested, but failing this you could use just Gruyère and Parmesan. Although Gruyère is a Swiss cheese, it is used in Italy for this dish.

Risotto Milanese-style

Risotto alla Milanese
(ree-soh-toh ah-lah me-lan-ay-seh)

Illustrated on pages 258-259
Serves 6
1 medium-sized Spanish onion, finely chopped
25 g/1 oz beef marrow
50 g/2 oz butter
350 g/12 oz Italian rice
125 ml/4 fl oz dry white wine
1.2 L/2¼ pt chicken stock
2 saffron strands (or ¼ tsp powdered saffron)
25 g/1 oz grated Parmesan cheese
25 g/1 oz butter

1 Scoop the beef marrow out of the bones, chop and weigh.

2 Heat the butter in a large saucepan over medium heat and gently sauté the onion for about 4 minutes.
3 Add the beef marrow and cook until melted, about 3 minutes.
4 Add the rice and cook over medium heat for 3 minutes, stirring continuously with a wooden spoon.
5 Add the wine and cook for 1 minute, stirring, then add about 75 ml/3 fl oz of the hot stock and stir well.
6 When the stock has been absorbed add another 75 ml/3 fl oz. Continue adding stock in this way, setting 75 ml/3 fl oz aside for the saffron strands.

7 Infuse the saffron strands for 10–15 minutes in the reserved stock, and then strain. (Or dissolve the powdered saffron in the reserved stock.) Use this stock last.

8 When all the stock has been added, test a grain of rice. It should be soft and creamy.

9 Stir the cheese and butter into the rice. When the cheese has melted, serve immediately.

● This dish is traditionally served with *Ossobuco* (page 295).

Vegetable risotto Omit the beef marrow and saffron and add vegetables in season, such as sliced courgettes.

Risotto with peas Sauté 1 chopped small onion in 25 g/1 oz butter till soft, add 50 g/2 oz chopped prosciutto ham and sauté 1 minute, stirring. Add 350 g/12 oz shelled fresh peas and stir gently until coated with butter. From 1 L/1¾ pt hot chicken stock, add about 150 ml/¼ pt and bring to the boil. Add 175 g/6 oz Italian rice then cook as above, using about 675 ml/23 fl oz more of the stock, until the rice is very tender. Stir in 25 g/1 oz butter and 50 g/2 oz Parmesan, then add enough of the remaining stock for a slightly soupy consistency. Serve in bowls with Parmesan. Serves 4.

Rice and cheese balls

Suppli al telefono
(soo-plee ahl tel-eh-fon-oh)

Serves 4–5
225 g/8 oz Italian or long-grain rice
salt
50 g/2 oz melted butter
freshly ground black pepper
100 g/4 oz ham, thinly sliced
100 g/4 oz Mozzarella cheese in
**   12 mm/½ in cubes**
2 medium-sized eggs, lightly beaten
75 g/3 oz breadcrumbs
oil for deep frying

1 Cook the rice in boiling salted water for 15 minutes. Drain, rinse and fluff. Stir in the melted butter and leave to get completely cold.

2 Cut the ham into 20 mm/¾ in squares. Cube the cheese and beat the eggs, salt and pepper into the rice.

3 Place 1 tbls of the rice mixture in the palm of your hand and flatten it into a small circle. Lay a square of ham on top and then a cube of cheese. Top with another 1 tbls rice.

4 Gently roll the mixture between your hands to make a neat ball. Make about

20 balls in the same way, using up all the ingredients.

5 Heat the oil for deep frying until it reaches 180° C/350° F or until a small cube of stale bread dropped into the oil turns golden in 50 seconds.

6 Meanwhile roll each ball in breadcrumbs on a plate or sheet of greaseproof paper, to coat them all over. Shake off any excess crumbs.

7 Deep fry the balls, a few at a time, for 5 minutes or until golden brown. Remove them from the oil and drain on absorbent paper. Keep the balls hot while you fry the others. Drain and serve.

● The Roman name for these rice balls means 'telephone wires', because, when the balls are broken open, the melted cheese stretches like wires between the two pieces. Serve them as a first course or with home-made Tomato Sauce (page 278) as a main course for 3–4 people.

● This is a good way of using up a large quantity of cold, cooked, left-over rice: you need 700 g/1½ lb. In Italy this dish is often made with left-over *Risotto alla Milanese* (page 282), made with 225 g/8 oz raw rice. Omit the melted butter.

Below: *Front, Rice and cheese balls;*
Back, Rice with four cheeses

Pizzas

Quick salami pizza

Pizza con salame
(peet-zah kon sah-lah-may)

Serves 4
For the tomato sauce
1 medium-sized onion, sliced
1 clove garlic, crushed
800 g/1¾ lb canned tomatoes, with
  their juice
2 tsps dried oregano
1 tsp caster sugar
salt and freshly ground black
  pepper
For the pizza base
225 g/8 oz self-raising flour
1 tsp baking powder

Below: *Quick salami pizza*

1 tsp salt
25 g/1 oz butter, softened
freshly ground black pepper
½ tsp dried mixed herbs
150 ml/¼ pt milk
For the topping
175 g/6 oz Cheddar cheese, grated
100 g/4 oz salami, sliced
1 red pepper, seeded and cut in
  rings
1 green pepper, seeded and cut in
  rings
50 g/2 oz stuffed olives, sliced
50 g/2 oz mushrooms, sliced
salt and freshly ground black
  pepper
2 tsps chopped oregano or 1 tsp
  dried oregano

1   To make the tomato sauce for the

topping, put the onion and garlic in a small saucepan with the tomatoes, and their juice, and the oregano and sugar. Season with salt and pepper. Cook over a moderate heat, stirring occasionally, for 30 minutes, or until thick. Remove from the heat and leave to cool while you prepare the dough.

2   Heat the oven to 200° C/400° F/gas 6. To make the pizza base, sift the flour, baking powder and salt together into a mixing bowl. Rub in the butter until the mixture resembles fine breadcrumbs, season with pepper and stir in the dried herbs. Mix to a soft dough with the milk.

3   Turn the dough on to a lightly floured board and roll out to a 25 cm/10 in circle. Transfer to a greased baking sheet.

4   Spread the tomato sauce over the pizza base to within 25 mm/1 in of the edge and sprinkle with three-quarters of the cheese.

5   Arrange the slices of salami over the tomato and cheese topping, in overlapping circles. Arrange rings of red and green pepper on top of the salami, then arrange olive and mushroom slices inside the rings. Season with salt, pepper and the oregano. Sprinkle the remaining grated cheese on top, and garnish with mushroom slices.

6   Bake in the oven for 30–40 minutes, until the base is well risen and the topping brown and bubbling. Serve hot.

Chorizo pizza Heat the oven to 180° C/350° F/gas 4. Cover the pizza base with 400 g/14 oz canned tomatoes, drained and coarsely chopped, then overlap 16 thin slices of chorizo, quartered, with 2 red peppers cut into rings. Scatter slices of 12 large green olives over the top. Season with paprika, salt and pepper, and bake for 20–25 minutes.

Garlic salami and ham pizza Heat the oven to 200° C/400° F/gas 6. On the pizza base lay 12 thin slices of Italian garlic salami, quartered, and 160 g/6 oz sliced Mozzarella cheese, overlapping them slightly. Scatter over 4 thin slices of ham cut into strips and 4 tbls sultanas, then arrange 2 small green peppers cut into rings on top. Season with cayenne, salt and pepper, and bake for 20–25 minutes.

Chicken and pine nuts pizza Heat the oven to 180° C/350° F/gas 4. Sauté 2 finely chopped small Spanish onions in 60 g/2 oz butter until transparent. Over the pizza base spread 400 g/14 oz canned tomatoes, drained and coarsely chopped, then cover with 160 g/6 oz sliced Mozzarella cheese. Mix the onion with 200 g/8 oz chopped cooked chicken and place on top. Sprinkle with tarragon and 4 tsps pine nuts sautéed in 60 g/2 oz butter. Top with 16 anchovy-stuffed olives, cut in half. Season with salt and pepper. Bake for 20–25 minutes.

Prawn and spinach pizza Heat the oven to 200° C/400° F/gas 6. On the pizza base overlap 160 g/6 oz sliced Mozzarella cheese. Spread 100 g/4 oz spinach purée and 75 g/3 oz chopped cooked peeled prawns on top. Season with ginger, nutmeg, salt and pepper, and bake for 20–25 minutes.

Ham and mushroom pizza Heat the oven to 200° C/400° F/gas 6. Over the pizza base, spread 400 g/14 oz canned tomatoes, drained and coarsely chopped. Cover with 160 g/6 oz Mozzarella cheese in overlapping slices, then sprinkle over 4 thin slices of ham, diced, and 60 g/2 oz finely sliced button mushrooms. Sprinkle with oregano, and dot with 8 large black olives, stoned and diced. Season lightly with salt and pepper, and bake for 20–25 minutes.

Mussel and fennel pizza Heat the oven to 180° C/350° F/gas 4. On the pizza base lay 160 g/6 oz sliced Mozzarella cheese, and spread over 400 g/14 oz canned tomatoes, drained and coarsely chopped. Distribute 900 g/2 lb (or 2 pt) mussels, steamed and shelled, over the tomatoes. Mix ½ tsp ground saffron into 125 ml/4 fl oz double cream, and distribute over the mussels. Scatter 4 tbls finely chopped fennel fronds over the top. Season with salt and pepper, and bake for 20–25 minutes.

Courgette and prosciutto pizza Heat the oven to 180° C/350° F/ gas 4. Sauté 2 finely chopped Spanish onions in 60 g/ 6 oz butter till transparent. On the pizza base lay 160 g/6 oz sliced Mozzarella cheese, overlapping the slices slightly. Mix together 100 g/4 oz sliced, simmered and drained courgettes, the onion and 400 g/14 oz canned tomatoes, drained and coarsely chopped. Spread them over the cheese. Make a lattice pattern on top of the courgette mixture with 4 thin slices of prosciutto ham cut in thin strips. Decorate with 16 stuffed olives sliced across, and season with oregano, salt and pepper. Bake for 20–25 minutes.

Neapolitan pizza

Pizza Napoletana
(peet-zah nap-ohl-eh-tah-nah)

Illustrated on pages 260-261
Serves 4
15 g/½ oz fresh yeast or 1½ tsps dried yeast and ½ tsp sugar
250 g/8 oz flour
1 tsp salt
4 tbls olive oil
For the filling
400 g/14 oz canned tomatoes, drained
1 tsp dried oregano
salt and freshly ground black pepper
175 g/6 oz Mozzarella cheese, sliced
50 g/2 oz canned anchovy fillets, drained and cut into strips
about 15 black olives

1 To make the pizza base, dissolve the fresh yeast in 175 ml/6 fl oz warm water. If you are using dried yeast, dissolve the sugar in 175 ml/6 fl oz warm water, add the dried yeast and leave in a warm place for 10–15 minutes until frothy.

2 Put the flour on to a board, make a well in the centre and pour in the yeast mixture, salt and 1 tbls oil. Work with your fingers to form a pliable dough, then turn on to a floured surface. Knead for 5–10 minutes until the dough is smooth and elastic. Transfer to a large clean bowl, cover with a cloth and leave in a warm place for about 1 hour, until the dough has doubled in size.

3 Heat the oven to 220° C/425° F/gas 7 and grease a baking sheet with oil. Knock back the risen dough, then roll out to a 30 cm /12 in round, 6 mm/¼ in thick. Place the round on the greased baking sheet and brush with oil.

4 Break up the drained tomatoes, and spoon on to the pizza base. Season with oregano and salt and pepper to taste. Cover the tomatoes with the Mozzarella slices.

5 Next, arrange the anchovy strips in a lattice pattern over the cheese. Top with olives.

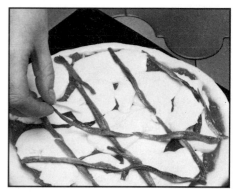

6 Spoon over the remaining oil and bake for 20 minutes.

Pizza toppings

Any of the following can be used as pizza toppings.
Meat: ham, salami, sausages
Fish and shellfish: tuna, prawns, mussels, anchovy fillets
Cheese: sliced Mozzarella, sliced Bel Paese, grated Gruyère, grated Cheddar
Vegetables: onion rings, chopped red and green peppers, chopped fennel, sliced mushrooms, canned pimientos, canned artichoke hearts
Tomatoes: sliced tomatoes, puréed canned tomatoes, skinned, seeded and chopped tomatoes
Other: freshly chopped herbs, garlic, capers, green and black olives, pine nuts

Fish and Seafood

Fish and Seafood are very important in Italian cooking, especially along the coastline, and Venice is known as the Queen of the Sea. As the fish are so fresh, they are often cooked very simply, and served with a salad rather than anything more elaborate. A variety of sauces are also sometimes used, however, particular favourites being the sweet-and-sour sauces.

The recipes in this chapter represent a wide selection of the many different Italian ways of cooking fish, including the classic dishes Cacciucco (Seafood Stew) and Fritto Misto di Mare (Deep-fried Fish and Shellfish).

Fish and Seafood

Celebration salad

Cappon magro
(kah-pon mah-groh)

Serves 10–12
**750 g/1½ lb hake or any large,
    firm, white fish in one piece**
**1 small lobster, about 450 g/1 lb,
    boiled**
12 large, boiled peeled prawns
10–12 cream crackers
200 g/7 oz French beans
200 g/7 oz potatoes
4 medium-sized carrots
1 small cauliflower
200 g/7 oz salsify (in season)
1 medium-sized beetroot
75 ml/3 fl oz olive oil
juice of ½ lemon
4 tbls wine vinegar
2 hard-boiled eggs, sliced
50 g/2 oz green olives
For the piquant sauce
1 tbls capers
**1 tbls Italian pickled mixed
    vegetables, giardiniera, or
    gherkins, chopped**
12 black olives, stoned
4 anchovy fillets
25 g/1 oz crustless white bread
50 g/2 oz pine nuts
large bunch of parsley, chopped
1 garlic clove
2 medium-sized egg yolks
125 ml/4 fl oz olive oil
4 tbls wine vinegar
**salt and freshly ground black
    pepper**

1 Put the piece of fish into a large saucepan of boiling salted water, reduce the heat and simmer, half-covered, for 20 minutes.
2 Meanwhile, make the sauce by puréeing the capers, mixed vegetables or gherkins, black olives, anchovy fillets, bread, pine nuts, parsley, garlic and egg yolks for 1 minute.
3 Blend the sauce mixture again, adding the olive oil and vinegar gradually, drop by drop at first like a mayonnaise, until the sauce is quite thick. Add more oil to thin it if necessary. Correct the seasoning and reserve.

4 Remove the fish from the heat, let the fish cool in the water, then remove the fish. Cut the fish into bite-sized pieces, discarding any skin or bone, then sprinkle 2 tbls oil over it.
5 Boil the beans, potatoes, carrots, cauliflower and salsify, if using, separately until just tender. Refresh each one in cold water. When cool, peel the salsify. Cut the cauliflower florets and beans into bite size pieces and the carrots, potatoes, salsify and beetroot into thin slices. Reserve separately.
6 Mix together the remaining olive oil, the lemon juice and 3 tbls of the vinegar and season with salt and pepper. Divide the mixture between the vegetables, tossing to coat.
7 Mix together the rest of the vinegar and 1 tbls water. Dip the crackers into this and cover the bottom of a large round dish to serve as the base layer.
8 Spread over a thick layer of the sauce. Cover with a layer of the beetroot slices, then a layer of the French beans, followed by a layer of the potato slices, a layer of carrot slices and a layer of salsify, if using, making each layer slightly less wide than the previous one.
9 On top of the vegetables put the fish pieces in a layer covered by a little sauce. On top put the floret of cauliflower.
10 Retain the lobster claws but shell the rest. To do this, first cut the lobster horizontally across where the carapace joins the tail.

11 Cut away the soft undershell of the tail with sharp scissors and lift out the meat in one piece.

12 Cut the tail meat into thick slices.

13 Cut along the centre of the head. Remove and discard the dark cord and the stomach sac. Leave the creamy grey-green liver around the stomach sac. Remove and reserve the coral, if any. Remove the meat.
14 Crack the 4 pairs of legs with the handle of a knife and pull out the meat.

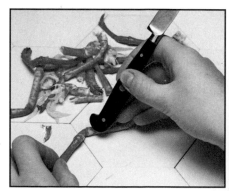

15 Decorate the top and sides of the cone with the lobster meat, claws and prawns. Garnish with the eggs and olives, dotting over any remaining sauce.

Sole in sweet and sour sauce

Sogliole in saor
(soh-lee-oh-ley in sah-ohr)

Illustrated on page 291
Serves 4
600 g/1 lb 6 oz fresh sole (or plaice) fillets, cut in half lengthways
flour for coating
salt and freshly ground black pepper
150 ml/¼ pt olive oil
1 medium-sized carrot, very finely sliced
1 medium-sized onion, very finely sliced
1 celery stalk, thinly sliced
50 ml/2 fl oz white wine vinegar
50 ml/2 fl oz dry white wine
50 g/2 oz sultanas
½ tsp cinnamon
2 cloves
2 bay leaves

1 Mix the flour with salt and pepper and lightly coat each sole fillet. Shake the fillets to remove the excess flour.

Below: *Celebration salad*

2 Heat 100 ml/3½ fl oz of the oil in a frying-pan over high heat. When the oil is very hot, slide in the fillets so they do not overlap. Fry them on both sides until a golden crust is formed, 4–5 minutes. Drain the fillets on absorbent paper and put them in a dish large enough to hold them all without overlapping.
3 Sauté the sliced vegetables in the remaining oil in a small frying-pan over medium heat, stirring often until they are soft and slightly coloured, about 15 minutes. Season with salt and pepper, add the vinegar and wine, raise the heat and reduce the liquid by half.
4 Pour the liquid and vegetables over the fish and sprinkle with the sultanas, cinnamon, cloves and bay leaves. Cover the dish with cling film and refrigerate for at least 48 hours. Serve the fillets at room temperature.

● This is the most famous of the Italian marinated fish dishes and is very popular in Venice.

● This dish must be prepared at least 48 hours before eating and can be served as a first course, a summer luncheon dish or an elegant buffet dish. If served as a main course, precede it with hot thick soup and serve the sole with a green salad.

Scampi with capers and lemon juice

Scampi al terrazzo
(skam-pee ahl ter-aht-zoh)

Illustrated on pages 286-287
Serves 4
1 kg/2 lb frozen peeled scampi, thawed and drained
4 tbls olive oil
2 garlic cloves, finely chopped
3–4 tsps lemon juice
6 tbls freshly chopped parsley
2 tbls capers, drained
boiled rice to serve
lemon slices to garnish

1 Pat the scampi dry with absorbent paper. Heat the oil in a large heavy-based frying-pan and cook the scampi very gently over low heat, turning them now and then, for 7–8 minutes, until almost cooked.
2 Stir the garlic, lemon juice, parsley and capers into the frying-pan and cook, stirring, for a further 1–2 minutes.
3 Spoon the scampi and cooking juices over a bed of plainly boiled rice arranged on a large serving platter. Garnish with lemon slices. Serve immediately.

Stuffed mussels

Cozze ripiene
(koht-say rip-yeh-nee)

Serves 4
1 kg/2 lb or 2 pts mussels
10 tbls dried breadcrumbs
10 tbls chopped parsley
2 garlic cloves, finely chopped
salt and freshly ground black
  pepper
125 ml/4 fl oz olive oil
1½ tbls freshly grated Parmesan
yellow pepper and flat-leafed
  parsley, to garnish

1 Wash the mussels in plenty of fresh
water, scrubbing them thoroughly with a
hard brush and scraping off any bar-
nacles with a stout-bladed knife.

2 Pull away the dark frond-like beards.
Place them in a colander under cold running water for 30 minutes.

3 Discard any mussels which are open,
put the rest in a large saucepan. Cover
the pan with a tight-fitting lid and cook
the mussels over a high heat about 3 minutes or until they open, stirring the top
mussels to the bottom once or twice.
4 Discard any mussels that have not
opened and the empty half shells. Keep
the other half shells, gently detaching the
mussels from the shells but keeping them
in the shell.
5 Strain the liquid left in the pan
through a sieve lined with muslin or absorbent paper.
6 In a bowl mix together the breadcrumbs, parsley and garlic. Season
generously with freshly ground black
pepper.
7 Add the oil and 4 tbls of the strained

mussel liquid. Blend everything together
well and add some salt if necessary.
8 Heat the oven to 230° C/450° F/
gas 8.
9 Place the mussels in their shells in a
single layer on a baking sheet. Fill each
shell with the breadcrumb mixture and
press it down so it is slightly mounded.
10 Sprinkle the mussels with the
Parmesan and bake in the oven for 10
minutes, turning the baking sheet round
after 5 minutes. Garnish and serve immediately as an hors d'oeuvre.

Seafood stew

Cacciucco
(kah-chook-oh)

Serves 4
125 ml/4 fl oz olive oil
2 garlic cloves, chopped
1 red chilli
225 g/8 oz shelled shrimps
225 g/8 oz squid
125 ml/4 fl oz dry white wine
3 tbls tomato purée
½ tsp salt
225 g/8 oz cod fillet, cut into pieces
225 g/8 oz haddock, cut into pieces
4 slices Italian or French bread,
  toasted
1 garlic clove, halved
2 tbls chopped pimiento

1 Scrape out the chilli seeds with a
knife, taking care not to handle the
seeds. Rinse the pods to remove any remaining seeds.
2 To clean the squid, hold the sac in
one hand and with the other pull off the
tentacles. As you pull them, the internal
organs should come out of the sac. Cut
off the head and discard it and the organs. Reserve the tentacles.

Left: *Stuffed mussels*

Right: *Left, Fresh anchovies au gratin; Centre, Deep-fried fish and shellfish; Right, Sole in sweet and sour sauce (page 289); Back, Seafood stew*

3 Remove the transparent spine from the sac and peel off the violet 'skin' under running water. Wash the sac and tentacles thoroughly. Chop the squid.

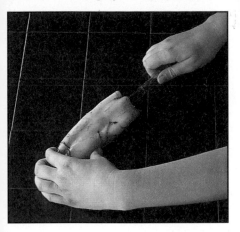

4 Heat the oil in a large saucepan. Add the chopped garlic and chilli and fry until the garlic is lightly browned. Stir in the shrimps and squid, reduce the heat to low and cover. Simmer for 30 minutes, stirring occasionally.

5 Pour in the wine and simmer, uncovered, for a further 15 minutes. Stir in the tomato purée, 450 ml/3/4 pt water and salt, and bring to the boil. Stir in the cod and haddock pieces, cover, reduce the heat to low again and simmer for 15 minutes, or until the fish flakes easily.

6 Meanwhile, rub the toasted bread slices with the garlic halves, then arrange a slice on the bottom of four individual soup bowls. Pour over the hot stew, sprinkle with the pimiento and serve.

Deep-fried fish and shellfish

Fritto misto di mare
(free-toh mee-stoh dee mar-ay)

Serves 4–6
oil for deep-frying
2 plaice fillets, skinned and cut into strips
2 whiting fillets, skinned and cut into strips
4 small scallops
225 g/8 oz large frozen prawns or shrimps, thawed and shelled but with the tails left on
8 sprigs parsley
1 lemon, quartered

For the batter
125 g/4 oz flour
1/4 tsp salt
1 egg yolk
1 tbls vegetable oil
250 ml/8 fl oz milk
2 egg whites

1 To prepare the batter, sift the flour and salt into a bowl. Make a well in the centre and put in the egg yolk and oil. Mix the egg yolk and oil together, gradually incorporating the flour, then add the milk, a little at a time. Cover the bowl and set it aside in a cool place for 30 minutes.

2 Beat the egg whites until they form stiff peaks. Quickly fold into the batter.

3 Fill a large deep-frying pan about one-third full with oil and heat until it reaches 190° C/375° F on a deep-fat thermometer, or until a small cube of stale bread dropped into the oil turns light brown in 40 seconds.

4 Using tongs, dip the fish pieces first into the batter, then into the oil. Fry them for 3–4 minutes or until they are crisp and golden brown. As each piece is cooked, remove from the pan and drain on absorbent paper then transfer to a warmed serving dish and keep hot.

5 Garnish with parsley sprigs and lemon quarters and serve at once.

Fresh anchovies au gratin

Alici ammollicate
(ah-lee-chee ah-mol-ee-kah-tay)

Serves 6
1 kg/2 lb fresh anchovies (or fresh sardines or small herrings)
150 ml/1/4 pt olive oil
3 garlic cloves, finely chopped
2 sprigs of parsley, chopped
4 tbls soft breadcrumbs
salt and freshly ground black pepper

1 Heat the oven to 220° C/425° F/gas 7. Wash and gut the fish. Remove their heads, tails and backbones. Arrange them in a shallow, oiled oven dish and pour most of the olive oil over them. Reserve a little olive oil for later use. Sprinkle with finely chopped garlic and the seasoning.

2 Mix the parsley with the breadcrumbs and moisten with the remaining olive oil. Distribute the mixture evenly over the fish and bake for 15 minutes. Serve hot.

Anchovies with oregano Sprinkle with chopped garlic and parsley, salt and pepper and oregano before baking.

Meat and Poultry

Italians cook meat and poultry in innumerable delicious ways. Veal is the meat most associated with Italian cooking, and Scaloppine and Ossobuco are the two most celebrated veal dishes. Vitello Tonnato is a popular summer dish eaten all over Italy. Meat is cooked so as to retain the natural juices, and Italian beef pot roasts and stews are good examples of this. Pork is cooked in a variety of ways, in particular in a creamy sauce and in a pizzaiola sauce, while lamb is also frequently eaten, with baby lamb being a great delicacy.

All kinds of poultry and game are popular in Italy, and the recipes included here are amongst the most famous examples of the Italian way with chicken dishes.

Veal

Veal escalopes with lemon sauce

Scaloppine al limone
(skah-law-pee-nay ahl lee-moh-nay)

Serves 6
**6 veal escalopes, each weighing
  100 g/4 oz
6 tbls lemon juice
salt and freshly ground black
  pepper
75 g/3 oz butter
275 ml/9 fl oz dry white wine or
  chicken stock
1½ tsps butter mixed to a paste
  with 1 tbls flour
2 tbls finely chopped fresh parsley**

1   Place each escalope between pieces
of wet greaseproof paper.

Below: *Veal escalopes with lemon
sauce*

2   Beat firmly but not too heavily with a
rolling pin or cutlet bat until each is twice
its original size.

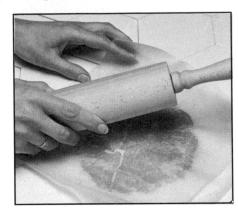

3   In a large, shallow dish, marinate the
escalopes in 3 tbls of lemon juice for 30
minutes, basting occasionally.
4   Remove the escalopes from the dish
and pat dry with absorbent paper. Rub
them all over with salt and pepper.

5   In a large frying pan, melt 75 g/3 oz
butter over moderate heat. When the
foam subsides, fry the escalopes for 3 to
4 minutes on each side or until they are
lightly browned. Transfer to a dish and
keep them warm.
6   Pour the remaining lemon juice and
the wine or stock into the pan and bring
to the boil, stirring. Boil for 5 minutes or
until the liquid has reduced slightly.
7   Reduce the heat to moderate and return the escalopes to the pan. Cook for 1
minute. Add the butter-and-flour paste
to the pan a little at a time and cook for a
further 1 minute, stirring constantly.
8   Remove the pan from the heat and
transfer to a warmed serving dish. Garnish with the parsley and serve.

Veal escalopes with Marsala Coat the
escalopes with seasoned flour and cook
as above, substituting Marsala for the dry
white wine.

Veal escalopes with Gorgonzola Coat
the escalopes with seasoned flour and fry
in 4 tbls olive oil. Remove the meat, add
175 ml/6 fl oz brandy and sprinkle with 2
tsps flour. Stir, then boil rapidly to reduce
the sauce by half. Add 100 g/4 oz chilled
unsalted butter, cut into small pieces,
and cook, stirring, till the butter melts.
Stir in 150 g/6 oz chopped Gorgonzola
cheese (without rind) and 175 ml/6 fl oz
double cream. Cook, stirring, till the
cheese is melted. Coat the meat with the
sauce, and serve.

Veal with tuna sauce

Vitello tonnato
(vee-tehl-oh tohn-ah-toh)

Serves 4–6
**1 kg/2 lb loin of veal, boned, rolled
  and tied
70 cl/1¼ pt bottle dry white Italian
  wine
1 carrot, sliced
1 onion, sliced
1 celery stalk, sliced
2 cloves
2 bay leaves
salt and freshly ground black
  pepper
chicken stock**

Shin of veal Milanese-style

Ossobuco alla Milanese
(oh-soh-boo-koh ah-lah me-lan-ay-seh)

Illustrated on pages 258-259
Serves 6
65 g/2½ oz butter
1 tbls vegetable oil
1 medium-sized onion, very finely chopped
6–7 pieces shin of veal, 5 cm/2 in thick, tied securely together with string (about 1.5–1.6 kg/3¼– 3½ lb)
2 tbls flour
salt and freshly ground black pepper
150 ml/¼ pt dry white wine
250 ml/9 fl oz hot beef stock
For the topping
1 tsp grated lemon zest
½ garlic clove, very finely chopped
1 tbls finely chopped parsley

1 Heat the butter and oil over medium-low heat in a large heavy frying-pan. When hot, add the onion and cook until it is translucent.
2 Dredge the bundle of veal in the flour, shaking off any excess. Brown the meat well on all sides in the pan and season with salt and pepper.
3 Add the wine and boil briskly for 5 minutes, turning the bundle over and over.
4 Add 175 ml/6 fl oz of the hot stock, cover the pan tightly and cook over very low heat for about 2 hours. Turn and baste the bundle every 15 minutes. If the sauce becomes dry, add more of the hot stock or water during the cooking. If the sauce is too thin when the veal is done, remove the meat and boil the sauce briskly over high heat to reduce and thicken it.
5 Cut the string and arrange the pieces of veal on a warmed serving dish and pour over the sauce. Mix together the ingredients for the topping and sprinkle it over the meat. Mix well and serve piping hot.

● *Ossobuco* is traditionally served with Risotto Milanese-style (page 282).

● In Italy, some restaurants provide a special marrow fork or spoon to scoop out every last bit of marrow from the centre of the bones.

For the sauce
2 egg yolks, at room temperature
150 ml/¼ pt olive oil
1 tbls lemon juice
200 g/7 oz can tuna in oil
1 tsp capers, drained, rinsed and finely chopped
To garnish
lemon slices
parsley sprigs

1 Put the veal in a large saucepan. Pour in the wine and add the carrot, onion, celery, cloves and bay leaves. Season with salt and pepper. Add some chicken stock if necessary, just to cover the meat.
2 Cover the pan, bring to the boil, lower the heat and simmer for about 1¼ hours or until the veal is cooked right through when tested with a fine skewer.
3 Remove the pan from the heat and leave until the veal is just cool enough to handle. Untie the veal and replace in the cooking liquid to cool completely (about 2 hours). Do not refrigerate.
4 While the veal is cooling, make the sauce: put the egg yolks in a bowl and beat with a wooden spoon until thoroughly blended. Very vigorously beat in the olive oil, drop by drop. (Should the mayonnaise curdle, whisk

Above: *Veal with tuna sauce*

another egg yolk in a clean bowl and beat the curdled mayonnaise into it, drop by drop.) When the mayonnaise begins to thicken, add a few drops of lemon juice to dilute the mixture. Continue to beat vigorously, adding the oil in the same way, drop by drop, adding a few drops of lemon juice each time the mayonnaise becomes very thick. Continue in the same way until half the oil has been absorbed and the mayonnaise is very thick and pale. Still beating constantly, add the remaining oil in a steady trickle, and the remaining lemon juice, scraping down the sides of the bowl occasionally. Season with salt and pepper.
5 When the veal has cooled completely, remove it from the cooking liquid and drain well. Skim the cooking liquid and measure out 5 tbls.
6 Pass the tuna with its oil through a fine metal sieve and mix it into the mayonnaise. Add the capers and the 5 tbls cooking liquid. Mix well to make a thin sauce of coating consistency.
7 Carve the veal into very thin slices. Arrange the slices on a serving platter and pour the tuna mayonnaise sauce evenly over them. Garnish with lemon slices and parsley sprigs and serve.

Beef

Piemonte meat roll

Polpettone casalingo
(pohl-peh-tohn-ay kas-ah-ling-oh)

Serves 6
**250 g/9 oz good quality beef,
    minced**
**250 g/9 oz boneless lean pork,
    minced**
**250 g/9 oz boneless chicken,
    minced**
4 medium-sized eggs
**100 g/4 oz freshly grated Parmesan
    cheese**
2 tbls chopped parsley
125 g/4 oz dry breadcrumbs
**salt and freshly ground black
    pepper**
75 ml/3 fl oz vegetable oil
**a sprig of fresh rosemary or ½ tsp
    dried rosemary**
150 ml/¼ pt strong meat stock
3 tbls dry red wine
15 g/½ oz butter
1 tbls flour
parsley, to garnish

1   Put the minced meats in a bowl with
3 whole eggs and the yolk of the fourth,
reserving the egg white. Add the Parmesan, parsley, 5 tbls breadcrumbs, salt
and pepper to taste and mix thoroughly
with your hands.
2   Shape the mixture into a firmly
packed ball and put it on a work surface.
Roll the mixture into a long round loaf,
about 8 cm/3 in in diameter, then pat the
roll with the palm of your hand to drive
out any air bubbles.
3   Put the remaining egg white into a
dish as long as the meat roll. Slide the
meat into the dish, turning in the egg to
coat. Slide it on to a tray or wooden
board and sprinkle over the remaining
breadcrumbs, turning the roll to coat it
evenly. Refrigerate the roll for at least 30
minutes.
4   Heat the oil in a large frying-pan or a
shallow oval casserole over high heat,
add the rosemary, slide in the meat roll
and brown it briskly on all sides until a
rich dark crust is formed.
5   Pour over the stock, cover the saucepan and cook over low heat for 1 hour or

until done. Baste the meat frequently
and give the roll a quarter turn every 15
minutes, taking care not to break it.
6   Heat the oven to 170° C/325° F/gas
3. Lift out the cooked meat roll and put it
on a cutting surface to cool about 10 minutes to make it easier to carve. Cut the
roll into 10 mm/⅓ in slices and arrange
them, slightly overlapping, on a heated
dish.
7   Strain the cooking liquid into a
saucepan and heat the mixture gently
over low heat. Pour 2 tbls of the warm
liquid on to the meat, cover the dish with
foil and put it in the oven.
8   Heat the remaining liquid and when
it is bubbling, add the dry red wine and
boil for 1 minute.

Below: *Piemonte meat roll*

9   Meanwhile, make the sauce by
mashing the butter and flour together
with a fork. Add this mixture a little at a
time to the gently bubbling liquid, stirring
until the sauce thickens. Pour the sauce
into a warmed gravy boat and serve it
separately with the meat. Garnish the
meat with parsley.

Braised beef in wine

Stracotto di manzo
(strah-koh-toh dee mahn-zoh)

Serves 6
1.5 kg/3 lb top rump joint
3 tbls oil
**25 g/1 oz ham or bacon fat, finely
    chopped**

1 large onion, finely chopped
2 medium-sized carrots, finely
    chopped
1 celery stalk, finely chopped
1 garlic clove, finely chopped
300 ml/½ pt young red wine
1 bay leaf
400 g/14 oz canned tomatoes, with
    their juice
salt and freshly ground black
    pepper
chopped parsley to garnish

1   Heat the oven to 160° C/325° F/gas
3. Tie the beef joint into a compact
shape.
2   Heat the oil in a deep flameproof casserole into which the joint fits fairly
tightly. When the oil is hot, fry the meat
briskly, turning, to seal all surfaces.
Transfer to a plate.
3   Add the ham or bacon fat, onion,
carrots, celery and garlic and fry over
moderate heat stirring frequently, for 5
minutes, or until slightly coloured.
4   Add the wine, bay leaf and the tomatoes and their juice. Bring to the boil
and allow to bubble for a minute or so.
Season with salt and pepper, return the
meat to the casserole and cover tightly.
(If necessary line the lid with foil to improve the seal.)
5   Transfer the casserole to the centre

of the oven and simmer gently for 3
hours or until very tender, turning the
meat halfway through the cooking time.
6   Remove the meat from the casserole, slice thickly and arrange on a hot
dish. Keep warm.
7   Remove the bay leaf from the
casserole and purée the remaining
vegetables and juices in a blender or by
pressing through a sieve. Reheat, skim
off any surplus fat, check the seasoning
and pour over the sliced meat.

● Serve with Tuscan Baked Beans (page
306) and Potato Dumplings (page 279)
or creamed potatoes.

Roman beef stew

Stufatino alla Romana
(stoo-fah-tee-noh ah-lah ro-mahn-ah)

Illustrated on page 266
Serves 4–6
1 kg/2 lb top rump of beef, cubed
50 g/2 oz seasoned flour
1 tbls olive oil
175 g/6 oz streaky bacon, chopped
1 medium onion, thinly sliced into
    rings
2 garlic cloves, crushed
2 celery stalks, thinly sliced

Above: *Front, Braised beef in wine; Left
back, Potato dumplings (page 279); Right
back, Tuscan baked beans (page 306).*

1 tbls fresh marjoram
250 ml/8 fl oz red wine
125 ml/4 fl oz beef stock
2 tbls tomato purée

1   Coat the cubes in the seasoned flour,
shaking off any excess.
2   Heat the oil in a large flameproof casserole. Add the bacon pieces and fry
until they are crisp and have rendered all
of their fat. Drain on absorbent paper.
3   Add the onion, garlic and celery to
the casserole and fry until the onion is
soft. Add the beef cubes and fry until
they are evenly browned. Stir in the marjoram and reserved bacon, and pour
over the wine and stock.
4   Bring to the boil, reduce the heat to
low and simmer the stew, uncovered, for
30 minutes, or until the liquid has reduced by about half. Stir in the tomato
purée and continue to simmer for a
further 30 minutes, moistening the meat
with a little more stock if it becomes too
dry. It should be very tender and the
sauce very thick and dark by the time the
stew is cooked. Serve at once.

● Serve with potatoes and courgettes.

Pork and Lamb

Coriander pork in creamy sauce

Maiale al latte
(my-yah-lay ahl lah-tay)

Serves 4

**700 g/1½ lb rindless loin of pork,
boned weight**
1 garlic clove
**2 tbls coriander seeds, crushed or
ground**
pinch of freshly grated nutmeg
**salt and freshly ground black
pepper**
1 onion, peeled and thinly sliced
2 celery sticks, finely sliced
**225 g/8 oz young carrots, sliced in
half lengthways**
**2 rashers streaky bacon, cut into
thin strips**
25 g/1 oz butter
850 ml/1 pt milk
**700 g/1½ lb potatoes, peeled and
cut into chunks**

1 Lay the meat flat on a board. Peel the garlic clove and cut into slivers. Make small incisions in the flesh and push in the slivers of garlic.
2 Sprinkle three-quarters of the crushed coriander seeds over the meat. Season with salt, pepper and nutmeg.

3 Roll up the meat and tie at intervals with string to make a neat bolster. Roll the bolster in the remaining coriander, with more salt and pepper. Set aside.
4 Melt the butter in a large heavy-based casserole or saucepan into which

the meat and vegetables will fit snugly over low heat, taking care not to let it sizzle and burn. Increase the heat to medium and add the bacon and prepared vegetables. Cook, stirring until lightly browned.
5 Add the meat and brown it on all sides, turning it so that browning is even.
6 Scald the milk and pour it over the

meat and vegetables, stirring once. Reduce the heat as low as possible.
7 Cook gently, uncovered, without stirring for 1¼ hours. A creamy skin will gradually form across the top of the meat. When the 1¼ hours are up, stir the skin into the casserole. Scrape down the sides and base of the dish and stir meaty deposits into the liquid.
8 Increase heat slightly and add potatoes and remaining carrots. Continue cooking uncovered for 25–30 minutes, stirring in skin as it forms.
9 Just before serving, lift the meat on to a heated plate, cut away the string and carve into thick slices. Surround with vegetables and pour over the sauce.

Below: *Coriander pork in creamy sauce*

Right: *Pork chops in pizza sauce*

Pork chops in pizza sauce

Costoletta di maiale alla pizzaiola
(koh-stoh-let-ah dee my-yah-lay ah-lah peet-zah-oh-lah)

Serves 6
6 centre-cut pork loin chops, cut about 20 mm/¾ in thick
salt and freshly ground black pepper
50 ml/2 fl oz vegetable oil
2 garlic cloves, crushed
1 tsp dried basil
1 tsp dried thyme
1 bay leaf
75 ml/3 oz dry red wine
400 g/14 oz canned tomatoes, drained and chopped
3 tbls tomato purée
40 g/1½ oz butter
3 medium green peppers, pith and seeds removed, chopped
1 medium onion, sliced
225 g/8 oz button mushrooms, quartered if large
1½ tbls cornflour blended with 1 tbls water
1 tbls chopped parsley

1 Rub the chops with salt and pepper.
2 Heat the oil in a large frying-pan. Add the chops to the pan, a few at a time, and fry until they are evenly browned. Transfer them to a plate.
3 Pour off all but a thin film of oil from the pan. Add the garlic and herbs, and stir to mix. Pour over the wine and bring to the boil. Stir in the tomatoes and tomato purée.
4 Return the chops to the pan and baste thoroughly with the sauce. Reduce the heat to low, cover the pan and simmer for 40 minutes, basting occasionally.
5 About 10 minutes before the chops are cooked melt the butter in a frying-pan. Add the peppers and onion and fry until they are soft. Stir in the mushrooms and cook for a further 3 minutes.
6 Transfer the vegetables to the frying-pan containing the meat. Simmer, uncovered, for 15 minutes, or until the chops are cooked through and tender. Transfer the chops to a warmed serving dish. Stir the cornflour mixture into the sauce and cook, stirring constantly, for 2 minutes, or until it has thickened. Remove the bay leaf.
7 Pour the sauce over the chops, and sprinkle over the parsley. Serve at once.

● Serve with green tagliatelle and a mixed salad.

● This is one of the most popular sauces in Italy and can also be used for other meat or for fish or pasta.

Lamb casserole Roman-style

Abbacchio alla Romana
(ah-bah-kee-oh ah-lah ro-mahn-ah)

Illustrated on page 266
Serves 6
1 kg/2¼ lb shoulder or leg of lamb, cut into 25 mm/1 in cubes
3 garlic cloves, finely chopped
4 anchovy fillets, chopped
100 ml/4 fl oz distilled or wine vinegar
sprig of fresh rosemary or ¼ tsp dried rosemary
50 ml/2 fl oz olive oil
salt and freshly ground black pepper
4 tbls flour
2 lemons, cut into wedges

1 Pound the garlic and anchovies with a pestle and mortar (or mash to a smooth paste) and mix in the vinegar.
2 Cook the rosemary in the oil for 5 minutes in a large flameproof casserole over medium heat. Meanwhile coat the lamb cubes with seasoned flour. Remove the rosemary sprig from the pan.
3 Sauté the lamb, in two batches, in the oil over medium-high heat until all the surfaces are sealed and brown. Reduce the heat and add the anchovy mixture to the lamb. Cover and cook 15 minutes, stirring frequently. Season and serve immediately, garnished with lemon wedges.

Chicken casserole Roman-style Substitute poussin (a small chicken) for the shoulder or leg of lamb.

Chicken

Chicken Marengo

Pollo alla Marengo
(poh-loh ah-lah mar-en-goh)

Illustrated on pages 292-293
Serves 4
**1.6 kg/3½ lb chicken, cut into
serving pieces (see steps 2–4 of
Chicken Parmesan-style, this page)**
1 lemon, quartered
50 g/2 oz flour
50 ml/2 fl oz vegetable oil
40 g/1½ oz butter
50 ml/2 fl oz brandy
**salt and freshly ground black
pepper**
flat-leafed parsley, to garnish
For the sauce
**450 g/1 lb fresh tomatoes, blanched
and skinned or 400 g/14 oz
canned tomatoes, drained and
roughly chopped**
1 garlic clove, chopped
125 ml/4 fl oz good meat stock
100 g/4 oz button mushrooms
**4 slices of good quality white bread,
cut in half**
2 tbls parsley, chopped

1 Wash and dry the chicken, rub with
the lemon, then coat lightly with flour.
2 Fry the chicken in the oil over
medium-high heat until rich brown. Reserving the oil, transfer the chicken to a
casserole. Add half the butter and the
brandy, salt and pepper and lay pieces
skin side down.
3 Add the tomatoes, garlic and the
stock to the casserole, cover and cook
slowly until the chicken is ready, about
40 minutes. Test by pricking the thickest
part of the leg: the meat is done when its
juice runs out clear.
4 Ten minutes before the chicken is
done, melt the rest of the butter in a frying-pan over medium heat and add the
mushrooms. Cook them briskly for 5 minutes, stirring, then add to the chicken.
5 Heat the reserved oil and when very
hot, slip in the bread slices. Fry until
golden on both sides. Keep them warm.
6 Add the parsley to the chicken and
turn the pieces over. Transfer to a heated
serving dish. Boil the sauce quickly to

reduce if necessary, spoon it over the
chicken, garnish and serve.

● Marengo is an area in southern
Piemonte where Napoleon won one of
his fiercest battles against the Austrians.
There his chef created this dish from the
ingredients at hand.

Chicken Parmesan-style

Pollo Parmigiana
(poh-loh par-me-jan-ah)

Illustrated on page 267
Serves 4–6
2 kg/4 lb chicken
**salt and freshly ground black
pepper**
125 ml/4 fl oz olive oil
1 medium green pepper, sliced
125 g/4 oz mushrooms, sliced
3 medium onions, sliced
2 garlic cloves, crushed
1 tsp dried oregano
**400 g/14 oz canned tomatoes, with
their juice**
4 tbls dry white wine or sherry
**75 g/3 oz Parmesan cheese, freshly
grated**

1 Preheat the oven to 180° C/350° F/
gas 4.
2 To cut the chicken into serving portions, pull one leg towards you and cut
through the pink, moist part of this joint.
Cut off the other leg. If desired divide
each leg into thigh and drumstick by cutting through the centre joint.

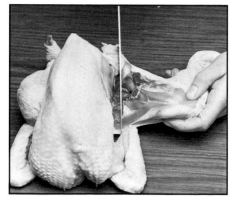

3 To remove each wing, first slice into
the white breast meat to make a better
portion. Pull the wing away and cut
through the exposed joint.

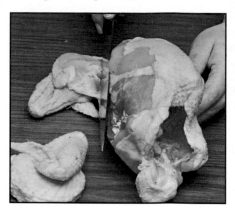

4 Separate the whole breast from the
back by cutting through the rib bones
along the side of the body. Then cut
down the centre of the breastbone to
divide the breast into two.

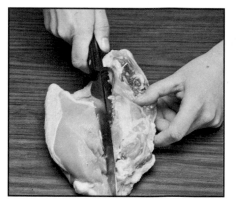

5 Rub with salt and pepper.
6 Heat the olive oil in a large flameproof casserole. Add the chicken pieces
and fry until they are evenly browned.
7 Chop the tomatoes, reserving the
juice.
8 Add the vegetables, oregano, juice
from the can of tomatoes and the wine or
sherry to the chicken, and bring to the
boil, stirring occasionally.
9 Cover the casserole and transfer it to
the oven. Bake for 1½ to 1¾ hours, or
until the chicken is cooked through.
10 Sprinkle one-third of the grated
cheese over the top and serve at once
with the remaining grated cheese.

Chicken hunter's-style

Pollo alla cacciatora
(poh-loh ah-lah kah-cha-tor-ah)

Serves 4–6
15 g/½ oz butter
2 tbls olive oil
2 garlic cloves, crushed
2 spring onions, finely chopped
175 g/6 oz mushrooms, sliced
2 kg/4 lb chicken, cut into 8 serving
   pieces (see steps 2–4 of Chicken
   Parmesan-style, page 300)
salt and freshly ground black
   pepper
175 ml/6 fl oz dry white wine
50 ml/2 fl oz chicken stock
6 medium tomatoes, blanched,
   peeled, seeded and coarsely
   chopped
1 large bay leaf
¾ tsp butter and 1¼ tsp flour,
   blended to a paste
1 tbls chopped fresh parsley

1 Melt the butter with the oil in a flameproof casserole. Add the garlic and spring onions and fry until they are soft. Add the mushrooms and fry for a further 3 minutes. Transfer to a plate.

2 Add the chicken pieces to the casserole and fry until they are lightly and evenly browned.

3 Stir in the salt, pepper, wine, stock, tomatoes, bay leaf and the mushroom and onion mixture. Bring the liquid to the boil, stirring constantly. Reduce the heat to low, cover and simmer for 40 to 50 minutes or until the chicken pieces are cooked through and tender. Remove from the heat and transfer the chicken pieces to a warmed serving dish. Keep warm.

4 Return the casserole to moderate heat and boil the sauce, stirring frequently, for 3 to 5 minutes or until it has reduced slightly. Stir in the butter-and-flour paste, a little at a time, and cook for a further 3 minutes or until the sauce is smooth and fairly thick. Remove from the heat and discard the bay leaf.

5 Pour the sauce over the chicken pieces, sprinkle over the parsley and serve immediately.

● This dish may be served with potatoes and green beans or broccoli.

Right: *Front, Chicken hunter's-style;*
Back, Chicken Bolognese-style

Chicken Bolognese-style

Pollo alla Bolognese
(poh-loh ahl-lah bol-ohn-yeh-say)

Serves 4
4 chicken breasts, skinned and
   boned
2 tbls seasoned flour
50 g/2 oz butter
8 slices smoked ham, thinly sliced
   and cut a little smaller than the
   chicken breasts
50 g/2 oz Parmesan cheese,
   grated

1 Cut each chicken breast in half, crosswise. Place each piece between two sheets of greaseproof or waxed paper and with a mallet or rolling pin pound to flatten. Remove paper.

2 Coat chicken with the seasoned flour, shaking off any excess.

3 Melt half the butter in a large frying-pan. Add the chicken pieces and fry for 10 to 15 minutes or until they are lightly and evenly browned and cooked through. Remove from the heat.

4 Meanwhile, melt the remaining butter. Remove from the heat.

5 Place a slice of ham on each chicken piece and sprinkle over about one-quarter of the grated cheese. Pour over the melted butter. Return the frying-pan to moderate heat, cover and cook for 3 to 4 minutes or until the ham is hot and the cheese has melted.

6 Transfer to a warmed serving dish and serve with the remaining Parmesan cheese.

● This is delicious served with sautéed potatoes and creamed spinach.

Vegetables and Salads

Vegetables are an important and fundamental part of Italian cooking. As accompaniments to a main course, they are fairly simple, but vegetables appear in Italian cooking in many other guises as well – as appetizers, as soups, in pasta dishes and in main course dishes. By the same token, many of the vegetable recipes given here would be just as suitable for appetizers or snacks as for side dishes.

Salads are eaten the year round. Like the vegetable dishes, they can be served not only as accompaniments to a main course but also as appetizers and even main courses.

Vegetables

Cheese-stuffed peppers

Peperoni ripieni
(pep-ehr-ohn-ee rip-yeh-nee)

Serves 4–5
4–5 plump peppers
25 g/1 oz butter
2 tbls olive oil
175–225 g/6–8 oz onions, chopped
1 garlic clove, chopped
175–225 g/6–8 oz easy-cook Italian rice
300 ml/11 fl oz stock
2 hard-boiled eggs
125 g/4 oz Cheshire or Lancashire cheese, chopped
100 g/4 oz walnuts, chopped
3 tbls grated Parmesan cheese
2 tbls chopped parsley
1 tsp oregano
salt and freshly ground black pepper
100 g/4 oz Mozzarella (or Cheddar) cheese, sliced in 4

1 Heat the oven to 180° C/350° F/gas 4. Heat the butter and oil in a large pan over medium heat and fry the onions

Below: *Cheese-stuffed peppers*

and garlic until soft. Add the rice and cook, stirring, for about 2 minutes.

2 Meanwhile slice the lids from the peppers and seed them. Parboil the peppers for 10 minutes. Then drain them and turn them upside down until needed.

3 Meanwhile, chop the uncooked trimmings from the lids and add these to the rice. Add the stock to the rice, stir once, cover and cook for 12 minutes, adding more stock as necessary for the larger quantity of rice.

4 Peel and chop the eggs and add

these, plus the chopped Cheshire cheese, walnuts, freshly grated Parmesan, parsley and oregano to the rice and season to taste.

5 Arrange the peppers in a greased baking dish in which they fit snugly. Fill with the stuffing and top with the slices of Mozzarella. Bake for 30 minutes.

Aubergine and egg pie

Tortino di melanzane e uova sode
(tohr-tee-noh dee me-lahn-zahn-ay eh woh-vah soh-day)

Serves 4
900 g/2 lbs aubergines
salt
vegetable oil for frying
400 g/14 oz canned tomatoes, drained
24 fresh basil leaves, roughly torn
1 tbls oregano
2 garlic cloves, very finely chopped
3 large eggs, hard-boiled and peeled
1 tbls finely chopped parsley
freshly ground black pepper
75 ml/3 fl oz olive oil
50 g/2 oz freshly grated Parmesan cheese
15 g/½ oz butter

1 Peel the aubergines, unless very young and fresh, then slice them into 5 mm/¼ in thick rounds.

2 Put the slices in a colander, sprinkle with salt and leave to drain for 1 hour.

1 Plunge the tomatoes into boiling water for 5 seconds, remove and drop into cold water. Cut out the blossom ends, make a nick in the skin then peel and chop.

2 Remove the pith and seeds from the red peppers and cut into strips.
3 Melt the butter with the oil in a large saucepan. Add the onion and garlic and fry until the onion is soft. Stir in the red peppers, reduce the heat to low and cover. Simmer for 15 minutes.
4 Stir in the tomatoes, seasoning and bay leaf, and simmer, uncovered, for a further 20 minutes. If there is too much liquid in the pan, increase the heat to moderately high and cook for 5 minutes, or until the mixture is thick and some liquid has evaporated.
5 Remove from the heat and discard the bay leaf. Serve at once, if serving hot. (It is equally good served cold.)

● This goes well with veal escalopes, sliced liver, lamb or chicken.

3 Rinse the aubergine slices under cold water and dry with absorbent paper.

Above: *Aubergine and egg pie*

4 Pour vegetable oil into a large frying-pan to a depth of 25 mm/1 in and put over medium heat. When hot, fry the aubergine slices in a single layer, turning until golden on both sides. Transfer each batch onto absorbent paper to drain.
5 Heat the oven to 180° C/350° F/ gas 4.
6 Purée the tomatoes in a food mill or through a sieve. Put into a bowl and mix with the basil, oregano and garlic.
7 Spread 2 tbls of the tomato and herb mixture over the bottom of a shallow ovenproof dish, about 25 cm/10 in square. Cover with a layer of the aubergines and a few slices of the hard-boiled egg. Sprinkle with some of the tomato and herb mixture, a little parsley and salt and a generous amount of freshly ground black pepper. Pour over 1½ tbls of the olive oil and repeat these layers until all the ingredients are used, finishing with the tomato and herb mixture.
8 Sprinkle with the Parmesan and the remaining oil. Dot with the butter and cook in the oven for 20 minutes.
9 Remove the pie from the oven and let it cool slightly, as the dish should be served warm rather than piping hot.

Red pepper and tomato stew

Peperonata
(pep-ehr-ohn-ah-tah)

Illustrated on pages 302-303
Serves 4–6
25 g/1 oz butter
2 tbls olive oil
1 large onion, thinly sliced
1 garlic clove, crushed
450 g/1 lb red peppers
450 g/1 lb tomatoes
salt and freshly ground black pepper to taste
1 bay leaf

Roman peas

Piselli alla Romana
(pee-zell-ee ah-lah ro-mahn-ah)

Illustrated on page 266
Serves 4
2 tbls olive oil
1 medium-sized onion, chopped
6 bacon rashers, finely chopped
450 g/1 lb frozen peas
salt and freshly ground black pepper
pinch of sugar

1 Heat the oil in a saucepan and gently brown the onion. Add the bacon and cook over medium heat for 10 minutes.
2 Add the peas, salt, pepper and sugar, cover and cook over low heat for 10 minutes. Serve immediately.

● This dish can be served as a light lunch with poached eggs.

305

Stuffed mushrooms

Funghi ripieni
(foon-ghee rip-yeh-nee)

Serves 4
16 large mushrooms
100 g/4 oz frozen chopped spinach,
 cooked and drained
1 tbls olive oil
50 g/2 oz margarine or butter
1 small onion, finely chopped
1 clove garlic, crushed (optional)
100 g/4 oz Ricotta cheese (or plain
 sieved cottage cheese)
4 tbls grated Parmesan cheese
4 tbls fresh white breadcrumbs
salt and freshly ground black
 pepper
parsley sprigs, to garnish

1 Heat the oven to 180° C/350° F/
gas 4.
2 Meanwhile, remove the stalks from
the mushrooms and set aside. Heat the
oil and half the margarine in a frying-
pan, add the onion and garlic, if using,
and fry gently for 5 minutes until the
onion is soft and lightly coloured.
3 Put the cooked spinach in a bowl
with the Ricotta, Parmesan and breadcrumbs. Stir in the onion and garlic, together with the buttery juices left in the
pan, and season to taste with salt and
pepper.
4 Place the mushrooms, gills uppermost, in an ovenproof dish and divide
the stuffing equally between them. Dot
with the remaining margarine and bake
in the oven for 15 minutes.
5 Transfer the mushrooms to 4 warmed
individual serving plates, garnish with
sprigs of parsley and serve at once.

Tuscan baked beans

Fagioli al forno
(fah-jol-ee ahl for-noh)

Illustrated on page 297
Serves 6
450 g/1 lb dried white haricot
 beans, soaked overnight and
 drained
3 garlic cloves, crushed
3 tbls chopped fresh basil, plus
 extra to garnish
salt and freshly ground black
 pepper to taste
½ tsp ground cinnamon
8 slices streaky bacon, coarsely
 chopped

1 Preheat the oven to 140° C/275° F/
gas 1.
2 Place the beans, garlic, basil, seasoning, cinnamon and bacon in a large
ovenproof casserole. Stir and add just
enough water to cover the mixture.
Cover and put the casserole into the
oven. Bake for 3 to 3½ hours, or until
the beans are very tender but still firm.
3 Remove from the oven, strain off any
excess liquid and serve at once, garnished with chopped basil.

Asparagus Milanese-style

Asparagi alla Milanese
(ahs-par-ah-jee ah-lah me-lan-eh-say)

Serves 4
900 g/2 lb fresh or frozen asparagus
salt
50 g/2 oz butter
50 g/2 oz Parmesan cheese, freshly
 grated

1 For fresh asparagus, wash, scrape
and trim it, cutting off any woody ends.

2 Sort into spears of equal thickness,

and tie in a bundle with the tips level. Use
soft string and tie in two places, just
below the tips and towards the bottom.
Trim the cut ends so that the stalks are of
similar length and the bundle will stand
firmly in the cooking pan.
3 To cook the asparagus, stand the
bundle upright in simmering salted water
to reach two-thirds up the stalks. If you
do not have a saucepan that is deep
enough, improvise with a domed 'lid' of
foil, making it high enough to stand
above the tips. Crimp it well at the pan
edge to hold in the steam.
4 If your pan is too wide, prevent the

stalks from keeling over by standing the loose stalks in a tall, straight-sided jar and fill to just below the tips with boiling salted water. Set the jar in a covered pan of simmering water, or cover the jar itself with foil.

5 Cook the asparagus until tender, allowing from 12–20 minutes for green asparagus and up to 30–45 minutes for large blanched spears. If you are using frozen asparagus, cook it from frozen in a small quantity of boiling salted water for 5–6 minutes. The asparagus is cooked when the thick part of the stalk feels tender when pierced with a sharp knife.

6 Drain thoroughly and lay on a clean, folded tea towel.

7 Arrange the cooked spears on a buttered flameproof dish and sprinkle with the grated Parmesan cheese.

8 Melt the butter to the *noisette* stage, when it is just beginning to turn brown and smell nutty. Pour the butter over the asparagus.

9 Slip the asparagus under a hot grill for a minute or two, until the Parmesan cheese begins to melt, and serve immediately.

● This is a delicious accompaniment to veal or chicken. In Italy it is frequently served with fried eggs for a light meal.

Below: *Left, Asparagus Milanese-style; Right, Sweet-sour onions; Top, Stuffed mushrooms*

Courgettes gratin

Tortino di zucchini
(tohr-tee-noh dee zoo-kee-nee)

Illustrated on pages 302-303
Serves 5–6
1 kg/2¼ lb small, firm courgettes
25 g/1 oz butter and butter for greasing
3 tbls vegetable oil
salt and freshly ground black pepper
For the cheese sauce
1 L/1¾ pt milk
75 g/3 oz butter
75 g/3 oz flour
salt and freshly ground black pepper
pinch of freshly grated nutmeg
3 tbls freshly grated Parmesan
2 medium-sized egg yolks

1 Carefully wash the courgettes, scrubbing them thoroughly under cold water. If the skin is not smooth after this operation, scrape or peel lightly with a potato peeler. Cut off and discard both ends, then cut the courgettes into rounds 10 mm/½ in thick.

2 Sauté the courgettes in the butter and oil. Season with salt and pepper and cook for 15 minutes, stirring from time to time.

3 Heat the oven to 200° C/400° F/gas

6. Meanwhile prepare the cheese sauce. Bring the milk to simmering point and remove from the heat. Melt the butter in a saucepan over very low heat, add the flour and stir well with a wooden spoon. Cook for 1 minute, stirring constantly. Remove from the heat and add the hot milk, a little at a time, stirring constantly until all the milk has been incorporated and the sauce is glossy and smooth. Season with salt, pepper and nutmeg.

4 Put the saucepan over medium-low heat and slowly bring the sauce to the boil, stirring constantly. Boil for 4 minutes. The sauce should be rather thick.

5 Remove the sauce from the heat and stir in the grated cheese and then the egg yolks, one at a time. Adjust seasoning.

6 Transfer the courgettes into a buttered oven dish and cover with sauce. Bake on the upper shelf of the oven for 10–15 minutes or until a golden crust has formed. Cool the dish for 5 minutes before serving.

Sweet-sour onions

Cipolle agrodolce
(chee-poh-lay ah-groh-dol-chay)

Serves 4
450 g/1 lb frozen pickling onions
2 tbls olive oil
2 tbls red wine vinegar
2 tbls stock
1 tbls brown sugar
25 g/1 oz raisins, soaked 10 minutes
2 cloves
1 bay leaf
salt

1 Heat the olive oil in a heavy-bottomed pan over low heat. Add the frozen onions, and cook gently over a low heat for 10 minutes, shaking the pan regularly, until browned on the outside.

2 Add the vinegar, stock, brown sugar, raisins, cloves and bay leaf. Cover and simmer for 10 minutes, checking regularly that they are not dry. The liquid should reduce to a coating syrup.

● Serve with roast or grilled meat, especially lamb and game.

● To freeze onions, blanch for 3 minutes. Cut off the tops and roots and slip off the skins. Cool 1 minute in iced water and blot dry then chill. Open freeze them on trays then bag and label when firm. Do not keep them more than 3 months, as they sometimes develop 'off' tastes.

Salads

Tomato and Mozzarella salad

Insalata di pomodori e mozzarella
(in-sah-lah-tah dee pom-oh-dohr-ee eh mot-zah-rel-ah)

Serves 6
450 g/1 lb firm ripe tomatoes, cut into 5 mm/¼ in slices
2 tbls chopped fresh parsley
2 tbls chopped fresh basil or ½ tsp dried basil
pinch of sugar
salt and freshly ground black pepper
175 g/6 oz Mozzarella cheese, cut into 5 mm/¼ inch slices
3 tbls black olives
4 tbls olive oil
1 tsp lemon juice

1 Arrange the tomato slices in an overlapping circular pattern around a flat serving dish. Sprinkle over the herbs and sugar and season with salt and freshly ground black pepper to taste. Cover the dish loosely with foil and chill in the refrigerator for 30 minutes.
2 Remove the foil and arrange the cheese slices in the centre of the tomatoes. Scatter the olives over.
3 Just before serving, pour over the olive oil and lemon juice. Using a fork, gently lift up the tomato slices so that the oil drains through to them.

● This classic Italian salad makes a good accompaniment to roast and grilled meats. Well chilled, it also makes a refreshing first course.

Below: *Tomato and Mozzarella salad*

Mushroom salad

Insalata di funghi
(in-sah-lah-tah dee foon-ghee)

Illustrated on pages 302-303
Serves 4
3 tbls olive oil
1 tbls fresh lemon juice
¼ tsp salt
pinch of black pepper
225 g/8 oz button mushrooms, wiped clean and thinly sliced
50 g/2 oz cooked peas
1 crisp lettuce, outer leaves removed, washed and shredded

1 In a screw-top jar, combine the oil, lemon juice, salt and pepper. Shake the dressing well.
2 Place the mushrooms and peas in a

Right: *Salami and pasta salad*

mixing bowl and pour over the dressing. Toss well and chill for 30 minutes.

3   Line a medium-sized serving dish with the lettuce. Remove the mushroom and pea mixture from the refrigerator and pile it into the centre of the leaves. Serve at once.

Salami and pasta salad

Ruote in insalata
(roo-oht-ay in in-sah-lah-tah)

Serves 4
250 g/9 oz pasta shells or wheels
salt
1 tsp vegetable oil
175 g/6 oz salami, cut into strips
    4 cm/1½ in long and 1 cm/½ in
    wide
8 spring onions, each cut into
    4 lengths
400 g/14 oz can artichoke hearts,
    drained, rinsed and halved
50 g/2 oz black olives
2 tomatoes, each cut into 8 wedges
lettuce leaves, to serve
For the dressing
3 tbls vegetable oil
1 tbls white wine vinegar
½ tsp sugar
½ tsp mustard powder
freshly ground black pepper

1   Bring a large pan of salted water to the boil, swirl in the oil and add the pasta. Cook for 7–10 minutes or until tender yet firm. Rinse under cold running water and drain.

2   Put the pasta wheels in a large bowl and mix in the salami, spring onions, artichoke halves, black olives and tomato wedges.

3   Make the dressing: put all the ingredients in a screw-top jar, adding salt and pepper to taste, and shake well to mix.

4   Pour the dressing over the pasta mixture and toss until coated.

5   Arrange lettuce leaves around the edge of a serving dish, then spoon the pasta mixture into the centre.

Asparagus, salami and pasta salad
Use drained canned asparagus instead of artichoke hearts.
Hearty salami and pasta salad Add sliced button mushrooms or cooked whole green beans.
Cheese, salami and pasta salad Add crumbled Feta cheese.

Orange salad

Insalata d'arancia
(in-sah-lah-tah dah-ran-cha)

Illustrated on pages 302-303
Serves 4
1 crisp lettuce, outer leaves
    removed and washed
2 oranges
1 large tomato, thinly sliced
juice of ½ lemon
1 tbls vegetable oil
1 tsp chopped fresh chives
½ tsp salt
¼ tsp white pepper

1   Shred the lettuce and place it on a flat serving dish.

2   Peel the oranges, remove the pith and separate the segments.

3   Place the orange segments and tomato slices in a bowl.

4   In a screw-top jar, combine the lemon juice, oil, chives, salt and pepper and shake well to blend.

5   Pour over the fruit and toss well. Arrange the mixture on the lettuce and chill for 15 minutes before serving.

● This colourful salad makes a refreshing accompaniment to roast chicken, or it may be served as a first course.

Desserts

Desserts in the Italian household tend to be fairly simple. Often they are based on fruit, which is so bountiful in Italy. Frozen desserts are favourites, and the layered desserts known as cassatas are well known outside Italy. Moulded custard and cream desserts are also popular, as are sweets made from Ricotta.

The queen of Italian desserts is, of course, the simple but elegant Zabaglione. Italy's elaborate pastries have been famous for centuries, but these are most often eaten in the morning and afternoon, and their preparation is generally left to the professional pastry cooks.

Fruit-based Sweets

Fruit cake pudding

Dolce tota frutto
(dol-chay toh-tah froo-toh)

Illustrated on pages 310-311
Serves 4
4 slices any rich fruit cake
8–12 tbls whisky
2 large oranges
2 large eggs, separated
4 tbls caster sugar
150 ml/¼ pt double cream
4 tbls sweet white wine
grated zest ½ large lemon

1   Place the cake slices on 4 individual dessert plates. Carefully spoon some whisky over each, allowing it to soak in.
2   Peel the oranges, dividing them into segments, and remove all the pith. Arrange a quarter of the segments on each slice. Chill for at least 2 hours.
3   Place the egg yolks and caster sugar

in the top pan of a double boiler and whisk over hot water until thick.
4   Whisk the egg whites until thick and whip the cream until it stands in soft peaks.
5   Fold the wine, lemon zest, egg whites and cream into the yolks. Spoon over the oranges and either serve immediately or place under a very hot grill until glazed.

Caramelized oranges

Arance al caramello
(ar-an-chay ahl kar-am-ehl-oh)

Serves 4
4 large oranges
175 g/6 oz sugar

1   Using a potato peeler, remove very thin strips of zest from 2 of the oranges and reserve. Cut 2 strips from a third orange. Put all the oranges into the

freezer compartment of the refrigerator to firm up for 10 minutes. Meanwhile reserve 2 strips of zest and cut all the rest into thin julienne strips. Simmer the strips in boiling water for 5 minutes. Drain and pour cold water over them.

2   Put the sugar, 125 ml/4 fl oz water and 2 orange strips into a small saucepan. Stir over medium heat to dissolve, then boil for 5 minutes to form a syrup. Remove from heat.
3   Take the oranges from the freezer and peel them with a very sharp knife, removing the peel and every trace of pith. Slice one orange into neat rings. Reassemble into an orange and hold in shape by sticking a cocktail stick down through the rings. Prepare the other oranges in the same way and arrange in a shallow dish.
4   Remove and discard the orange strips. Spoon the syrup over the oranges, coating each orange 2–3 times.
5   Transfer the oranges to a serving plate and pour the syrup back into the saucepan. Add the julienne strips, bring to the boil and boil for 2 minutes or until the syrup begins to turn brown round the edges of the pan. Remove the pan from the heat, stir once, then spoon a little heap of strips on top of each orange. Chill 2 hours before serving.

●   If desired, add 2 tbls of Marsala or Grand Marnier to the syrup before pouring it over the reassembled oranges.

Left: *Caramelized oranges*

Cherries in Marsala

Ciliege al Marsala
(chee-led-jeh ahl mar-sah-lah)

Serves 4
1 kg/2 lb canned stoned Morello cherries, drained
150 ml/¼ pt Marsala
½ tsp grated nutmeg
1 tbls sugar
150 ml/¼ pt double cream, stiffly whipped

1 Put the cherries, Marsala, nutmeg and sugar in a saucepan and bring to the boil over moderate heat, stirring to dissolve the sugar. Reduce the heat to low and simmer gently for 10 minutes. Remove from the heat and transfer to a serving dish.
2 Return the pan to the heat and boil the liquid for 3 to 4 minutes, or until it is thick and syrupy. Pour the syrup over the cherries.
3 Chill the dish in the refrigerator for at least 1 hour. Top the cherries with the stiffly whipped double cream before serving.

Below: *Cherries in Marsala*

Orange salad Do not reassemble the rings. Simply place them in a bowl and pour syrup over them. Decorate with julienne strips or a scattering of flaked, toasted nuts.

Above: *Stuffed peaches*

4 Divide equally between the peach halves. Arrange peaches in prepared dish. Bake for about 30 minutes, until stuffing is set. Serve hot, with cream.

Stuffed peaches

Pesche ripiene
(pes-kay rip-yeh-nay)

Serves 4
4 large, ripe peaches, halved and stoned
25 g/1 oz butter, softened, plus butter for greasing
50 g/2 oz caster sugar
1 egg yolk
100 g/4 oz amaretti (or ratafias or macaroons), finely crushed
1 tsp Amaretto liqueur, optional
pouring cream or custard, to serve

1 Heat the oven to 180° C/350° F/gas 4. Lightly butter a shallow ovenproof dish large enough to hold the peach halves in a single layer.
2 Using a teaspoon, scoop out about one-third of the peach flesh from each peach and put it into a bowl, then mash to a pulp.
3 Beat butter and sugar until pale and fluffy. Add the egg yolk and continue beating until blended. Stir in crushed amaretti, peach pulp and the Amaretto liqueur, if using.

Puddings

Egg yolk and wine dessert

Zabaglione
(zah-bal-yohn-ay)

Serves 2
2 large egg yolks
2 tbls caster sugar
3 tbls Marsala (or sweet sherry)
1 tsp finely grated lemon zest

1 Place the egg yolks and sugar in the top of a double boiler and beat for 1 minute.

2 Set over low heat so the water does not boil, and whisk until the mixture begins to thicken – about 2 minutes.
3 Add the Marsala and whisk until thick and pale in colour. If wished, add the finely grated lemon zest.
4 Continue whisking the mixture until it doubles in bulk – about 3–5 minutes. Pour into glasses which have been rinsed with warm water and serve immediately with sponge fingers, langues de chat or cigarettes russes.

Lemon zabaglione Replace the Marsala with lemon juice.

Cold zabaglione Soak 1 tsp powdered gelatine in 2 tbls cold water for 5 minutes, dissolve over low heat, cool, then whisk into the zabaglione. Place the bowl in a bowl containing ice cubes and stir gently until beginning to set. Stir in 150 ml/¼ pt whipped cream and 2 tbls chopped pistachio nuts or flaked almonds. Pour into dishes and leave to set in a cool place for 1 hour.
Strawberry zabaglione Follow the instructions for Cold Zabaglione, but place strawberries in the base and sprinkle with a few drops of brandy. Decorate with sliced strawberries.
Orange zabaglione Follow the instructions for Cold Zabaglione, but place mandarin orange segments in the base and sprinkle with curaçao.

Moulded cream pudding

Zuccotto
(zoo-koh-toh)

Illustrated on page 263
Serves 6–8
50 g/2 oz almonds, blanched
50 g/2 oz hazelnuts in their skins
butter for greasing
350 g/12 oz rectangular, bought
    Madeira cake
30 ml/2 fl oz brandy
2 tbls Cointreau
2 tbls maraschino or other sweet
    cherry liqueur
150 g/5 oz bitter chocolate
500 ml/18 fl oz double cream
100 g/4 oz icing sugar, sifted
For the decoration
sifted icing sugar for sprinkling,
    plus an extra 2 tbls
1 tbls cocoa, sifted

1 Heat the oven to 200° C/400° F/gas 6. When hot, put the almonds and the hazelnuts on to two baking sheets and put them in the oven for 5 minutes.
2 Rub off as much of the skin of the hazelnuts as possible and chop them with the almonds. Reserve the nuts.

Left: *Egg yolk and wine dessert*

3 Grease a 1½ L/2½ pt bowl thoroughly with butter, then line it with cling film, pressing it in place. Generously butter the cling film.

4 Cut the Madeira cake into 10 mm/½ in thick slices. Moisten the slices with the brandy and liqueurs and line the mould: arrange 3 slices in the bowl from the rim to the centre, cutting them to a point where they fit together. Cut 3 more pieces slightly larger than the remaining gaps, shaping them to fit. Press them tightly in place. Reserve the rest.

5 Cut the chocolate into small pieces. Melt 25 g/1 oz chocolate in a small bowl over barely simmering water.

6 Whip the cream until just stiff and fold in the sugar. Mix the chopped nuts and 100 g/4 oz chocolate pieces into the cream. Spoon one half of the cream into the cake-lined mould, spreading it out over the entire lining in a thick layer.

7 Add the melted chocolate to the remaining cream mixture and mix thoroughly. Spoon it into the mould to fill the cavity and level the top.

8 Moisten the reserved cake, if necessary, with brandy and liqueurs. Cover the top of the mould with the smaller pieces of cake, filling any gaps. Cover the mould with cling film and weight with a plate. Refrigerate at least 12 hours.

9 Up to 30 minutes before serving, invert a round serving dish over the mould and turn out the dessert. Remove the cling film.

10 Cut out a circle of greaseproof paper 26 cm/10½ in in diameter. Fold the circle in half and then in half twice more, to make eighths. Open the paper and cut out each alternate section, without cutting through the centre where they join.

11 Sift icing sugar all over the *Zuccotto*. Mix 2 tbls icing sugar with the cocoa. Arrange the pattern over the *Zuccotto* and sprinkle the cocoa and sugar in the cut-out sections. Serve immediately.

Coffee and brandy trifle

Tiramesu
(teer-ah-meh-zoo)

Serves 8
450 g/1 lb sponge cake
200 ml/7 fl oz strong Italian coffee
2 tsps coffee essence
100 ml/3½ fl oz brandy
For the custard
3 medium-sized egg yolks
100 g/4 oz caster sugar
3 tbls flour
500 ml/18 fl oz milk
½ tsp vanilla essence
For the decoration
275 ml/½ pt double cream, whipped
2 tbls finely ground Italian coffee

1 To make the custard, put the egg yolks and sugar in a heavy saucepan. Beat the mixture with a wooden spoon until it is pale and creamy and add the flour, 1 tbls at a time, beating constantly.

2 In another saucepan bring the milk to simmering point. Pour the milk on to the egg mixture, stirring all the time. Put the pan over very low heat and cook for 3 minutes or until an occasional bubble breaks through the surface. Remove from heat, add vanilla essence and stir well. Leave to cool completely.

3 Cut the cake vertically into 15 mm/½ in thick slices and cover the bottom of a 15 × 20 cm/6 × 8 in deep cake tin with one layer of cake, patching if necessary for a good fit.

4 Mix together the coffee, coffee essence and brandy in a small bowl. Brush some of this mixture over the cake slices in the tin. Cover the cake with some of the custard, place another layer of cake slices on top of the custard and repeat the operation until the ingredients are used up, finishing with a layer of cake.

5 Refrigerate the trifle for at least 6 hours. Turn it out on to a serving dish, pipe whipped cream around the base and, at the last minute, sprinkle the top with the ground coffee and pipe with the remaining cream.

● The name of this pudding in Venetian dialect means 'pull me up' because the coffee and brandy have an invigorating effect.

Below: *Coffee and brandy trifle*

Frozen Desserts

Pistachio ice cream

Gelato di pistacchio
(jehl-ah-toh dee pee-stah-kee-oh)

Illustrated on pages 310-311
Serves 4
250 ml/8 fl oz single cream
125 g/4 oz pistachio nuts, shelled,
  chopped and blanched
250 ml/8 fl oz double cream
1/2 tsp almond essence
3 egg yolks, well beaten
50 g/2 oz sugar
3 egg whites, stiffly beaten

1 Put the single cream and nuts in a blender and blend until the nuts are puréed. Spoon the mixture into a small saucepan and stir in the double cream. Place over low heat and simmer gently until the mixture is hot. Remove from the heat, cover and set aside to cool.
2 Pour into a medium-sized bowl and beat in the almond essence.
3 Dissolve the sugar in 75 ml/3 fl oz water over low heat, stirring constantly. Increase the heat to moderate and boil the syrup until the temperature reaches 140° C/220° F on a sugar thermometer or until a little of the syrup spooned out of the pan and cooled will form a short thread when drawn out between your index finger and thumb. Remove from the heat and leave the syrup to stand for 1 minute.

4 Pour the syrup over the egg yolks in a steady stream, whisking constantly. Continue whisking until the mixture is thick and fluffy. Mix in the cooled cream mixture, then lightly fold in the beaten egg whites.

5 Pour into an ice-cream container equipped with paddles or into a hand-propelled ice cream churn, and freeze according to the manufacturer's instructions. Store in the freezer until required.

Neapolitan cassata

Cassata Napoletana
(kah-sah-tah nap-ohl-eh-tah-nah)

Serves 8
450 ml/16 fl oz vanilla ice cream
350 ml/12 fl oz chocolate ice cream
150 ml/5 fl oz double cream
50 g/2 oz icing sugar, sifted
100 g/4 oz mixed crystallized fruit,
  cut into small pieces
1 egg white

1 With a metal spoon dipped in hot water, line the inside of a chilled 1.4 L/ 2½ pt pudding basin with the vanilla ice cream. Cover the basin with foil and freeze for 1½ hours.
2 Cover the vanilla ice cream with a layer of chocolate ice cream, leaving a well in the centre for the cassata mixture.

Above: *Neapolitan cassata*

Cover and freeze for about 1½ hours.
3 Meanwhile, make the cassata mixture: whip the cream until it forms soft peaks. Fold in the sugar and fruit. Whisk the egg white until fairly stiff and fold it in gently but thoroughly.
4 Spoon the mixture into the basin, tapping the basin to eliminate any air bubbles. Smooth the top, cover and freeze until firm, about 3–4 hours.
5 To serve, dip the basin briefly into hot water and turn the cassata out onto a serving dish. Smooth the surface with a palette knife, if necessary. Cut into wedges to serve.

Strawberry and lemon cassata Line a 1.4 L/2½ pt pudding basin with 200 ml/ 7 fl oz strawberry ice cream and freeze. Then make a second layer using 200 ml/ 7 fl oz lemon sorbet and freeze again. Make the cassata mixture from 75 ml/3 fl oz double cream, flavoured with a little orange juice, 1/2 tsp sifted icing sugar, 25 g/1 oz each chopped angelica and glacé cherries and 40 g/1½ oz chopped pistachio nuts.

Brazil nut cassata Use vanilla and coffee ice creams. Flavour basic cassata mixture with 75 g/3 oz chopped Brazil nuts and 2 tsps rum. Decorate the unmoulded cassata with caraque chocolate and Brazil nuts.

Pineapple and praline cassata Use praline ice cream and pineapple sorbet. Flavour basic cassata mixture with 50 g/2 oz each of raisins plumped up in rum and crystallized pineapple which has first been rinsed and dried and then chopped.

Honeymoon cassata Use chocolate ice cream, tangerine sorbet and basic cassata mixture flavoured with chopped mandarins and hazelnuts.

Perfect pink cassata Use vanilla ice cream and raspberry and redcurrant sorbet. The cassata mixture is flavoured with chopped fresh strawberries sprinkled with orange juice and with grated orange zest.

Below: *Coffee granita*

Coffee granita

Granita di caffè
(gran-ee-tah dee kah-fay)

Serves 6
100 g/4 oz coarsely ground coffee
75 g/3 oz caster sugar
150 ml/¼ pt double cream, whipped
powdered drinking chocolate

1   If using the freezing compartment of your refrigerator, turn it down to its lowest temperature an hour beforehand.
2   Gently dissolve the sugar in 1 L/2 pt water, stirring, then boil rapidly for 3 minutes. Remove from the heat, stir in the coffee and leave for 15 minutes.
3   Strain into a jug. Cool, then chill. Pour into a shallow freezerproof container. Cover and freeze for 30 minutes.
4   Remove from the freezer and stir well with a metal spoon until evenly blended. Return to the freezer. Repeat this operation twice more at 30-minute intervals until a granular slush is formed.
5   Spoon the granita into individual tall glasses, and top each with whipped cream sprinkled with drinking chocolate.

Lemon granita Make the syrup from 600 ml/1 pt water and 175 g/6 oz sugar, boiling for 5 minutes. When cold, add the juice of 6 large lemons and proceed as above, freezing for 4 hours and stirring every 30 minutes. Decorate with lemon twists and mint. Serves 4–6.

Black grape granita Make the syrup with 175 g/6 oz caster sugar and 150 ml/¼ pt water, boiling for 1 minute before cooling. Purée 700 g/1½ lb black grapes (reserving 9–12 grapes for decoration) in a blender. Stir in syrup and 275 ml/½ pt dry white wine. Freeze for 2 hours, then proceed as above. Transfer to the refrigerator about 15 minutes before serving, and spoon into serving glasses. Garnish with the peeled, halved and deseeded grapes. Serves 6–8.

Cakes and Pastries

Sicilian cassata

Cassata Siciliana
(kah-sah-tah see-cheel-ee-ahn-ah)

Serves 8
400 g/14 oz Ricotta or cottage cheese
175 g/6 oz caster sugar
pinch of ground cinnamon
200 g/7 oz best quality crystallized fruit
75 g/3 oz bitter chocolate, cut into small pieces
25 g/1 oz pistachio nuts, blanched, peeled and chopped
100 ml/4 fl oz Maraschino or another sweet liqueur such as curaçao or Drambuie
450 g/1 lb Madeira cake
For the icing
600 g/1¼ lb icing sugar, sifted
1 tbls lemon juice

1   Press the Ricotta cheese through a fine-mesh sieve and set on one side. Simmer the caster sugar and 150 ml/¼ pt water in a heavy saucepan over very low heat until the syrup is clear but not coloured. Do not stir the mixture during cooking.
2   Meanwhile, cut 100 g/4 oz of the crystallized fruit into small pieces, reserving the best pieces for decoration.
3   When the sugar has dissolved, pour it over the Ricotta and stir hard until the mixture is glossy and smooth. Add the cinnamon, chocolate, chopped crystallized fruit, pistachios and half the liqueur, and mix thoroughly.
4   Line an 18 cm/7 in round cake tin with greaseproof paper. Cut the Madeira cake into thin slices and use these to line the bottom and the sides of the tin. Use the trimming to fill in any gaps. Moisten

the cake by sprinkling over some of the liqueur.
5   Spoon in the Ricotta mixture and cover it with a layer of sliced cake. Moisten the top layer with the remaining liqueur. Cover with cling film and chill for at least 3 hours.
6   To make the icing, melt the icing sugar with 100 ml/3½ fl oz water and the lemon juice in a heavy saucepan over low heat. Do not let the icing get too hot. When it evenly coats the back of a spoon turn the cake out on to a flat plate or cake board and pour the icing over the cake, letting it run down the sides. Smooth the icing with a palette knife.
7   Put the cake back into the refrigerator for at least 5 minutes to allow the icing to set. Transfer the cake to a serving plate and decorate with the reserved crystallized fruit. Serve chilled.

Below: *Sicilian cassata*

Turin walnut cake

Torta di noci
(tohr-tah dee noh-chee)

Illustrated on pages 310-311
Serves 8
6 medium-sized eggs, separated
250 g/9 oz sugar
3 drops vanilla essence
50 g/2 oz butter, melted
250 g/9 oz walnut kernels, finely chopped
1 tbls flour
icing sugar for sprinkling
single cream, to serve (optional)

1   Heat the oven to 180° C/350° F/gas 4. Whisk the egg yolks with the sugar until they are pale yellow and creamy. Add the vanilla essence, melted butter, walnuts and flour, mixing very thoroughly.
2   Whisk the egg whites until stiff peaks form, then gently fold them into the walnut mixture.
3   Grease a 23 cm/9 in square cake tin, line the bottom with greaseproof paper and grease the paper. Pour the cake mixture into the tin and bake for about 50 minutes or until a skewer inserted in the middle comes out clean.

4 Remove the cake from the tin to cool. When cold, sprinkle over icing sugar and serve, if wished, with single cream.

Italian cake frosting

Ghiaccia
(ghee-ah-cha)

*Covers a 20 cm/8 in
sandwich cake*
225 g/8 oz granulated sugar
4 large egg whites

1 Put the sugar in a heavy-based saucepan with 75 ml/3 fl oz water. Heat gently, stirring, until the sugar is dissolved.
2 Turn up the heat and boil the syrup to 130° C/260° F; at this temperature a sample in cold water will make a hard ball. Whisk the egg whites until softly peaked.

3 Pour the syrup on to the beaten egg whites a little at a time, whisking all the time. Continue until the meringue is smooth and shiny. Leave to cool.
4 To use, spread it over the top and sides of the cake with a palette knife, using the tip to make a pattern.

Coffee icing Dissolve 1 tbls instant coffee in the water.

Sicilian chocolate pie

Crostata di ricotta e cioccolata
(kroh-stah-tah dee ree-koh-tah eh choh-koh-lah-tah)

Serves 6–8
325 g/12 oz Ricotta or low-fat curd cheese

Above: *Italian cake frosting*

125 g/4 oz cottage cheese
pinch of salt
3 tbls cognac or rum
75 g/3 oz caster sugar
50 g/2 oz bitter chocolate, grated
**50 g/2 oz preserved orange peel,
 plus extra to decorate**
22 cm/8½ in baked pastry case
**3 tbls apricot jam for brushing
grated chocolate to decorate**

1 Sieve the cheeses and salt into a bowl. Stir in the cognac or rum lightly. Stir or fold in the sugar and chocolate.
2 Chop the peel finely and stir into the cheese mixture. Chill for at least 1 hour.
3 Heat the apricot jam in a small pan until liquid, then brush over the inside of the pastry case. Fill the case with the cheese mixture. Chill until needed.
4 Scatter grated chocolate and chopped peel over the pie before serving.

Left: *Sicilian chocolate pie*

Cook Chinese

Introduction

You can enjoy Chinese cooking without needing to track down exotic ingredients or learn complicated cooking techniques. What makes dishes distinctively Chinese is largely the cooking time, the way that foods are cut and the use of a few specialist ingredients and seasonings. Nor does it all have to be prepared at the last minute. The ingredients for stir-fried dishes are cut up beforehand then quickly fried in just a few moments; and other dishes, such as cold starters and slow-cooked recipes, can be prepared well in advance.

Chinese Meals

Rice is regarded as the main course of a Chinese meal (except in the north of China). Savoury dishes are seen as the flavourings to or accompaniments for rice – quite the reverse of the Western idea that meat or fish forms the main dish of a meal.

There is no set order of courses for Chinese meals. The soup may be served first, but people can help themselves to more during the meal. Each person has a bowl, rather than a plate, which is used for eating a little of one dish at a time, along with the rice. Chopsticks are used for picking up the food. These were invented by the civilized Chinese centuries before Europeans first thought of using the fork.

If something like spare ribs is served, which has to be picked up in the fingers, finger bowls of water for washing may be needed. These look pretty with a flower, or a slice of lemon floating in them. You may need extra napkins for drying your fingers afterwards. In China steamed towels may be brought to you in a restaurant but these are difficult to organize in a Western home.

In Chinese restaurants, food is always kept warm at the table on a small warmer. If you don't have one of these available, you can improvise by placing two night-lights in a shallow dish and standing a wire cake rack on the top to support dishes of food.

In Chinese homes the meal is usually eaten fast – and silently. After the meal China tea – without milk, sugar or lemon of course – is served, when the company will relax and chat. Tea is drunk in small handleless cups. The correct way to hold these is with the thumb underneath the ring at the bottom and the index finger on the rim, so that you do not burn your fingers.

Menu planning
Obviously, there is no need to make an entire meal of only Chinese food; many Chinese dishes blend very successfully with European food. But once you become proficient at Chinese cooking, you will probably want to plan your own full-scale Chinese meals. Ideally, you should aim to include a balance of each of the following:
- colour, texture, flavour and aroma
- different types of dish (soup; rice or noodles; plus one each of meat, fish, poultry, vegetable and made-up dishes)
- different cooking techniques (perhaps two cold dishes or hors d'oeuvres, followed by two or three stir-fried dishes; followed by two or three braised, steamed or roasted dishes; together with rice and soup).

Using chopsticks

Hold one chopstick between thumb and index finger, against middle and ring fingers. Place the second under thumb against index finger like a pencil. To pick food up, move the second chopstick and support the food with the first.

Growing beansprouts

The most popular kind of beansprout is grown from the small, green mung bean. Put 45 ml/3 tbls mung beans into a 1 kg/2 lb jam jar. Cover the top of the jar with muslin anchored with an elastic band. Pour warm water into the jar, rinse it round and pour it out. Pour in enough warm water to cover the beans and leave them to soak for 24 hours in a warm place. Pour away the water, rinse the beans again and drain well.

Place the jar on its side in a flat dish and put the dish into a brown paper bag. Leave the dish in a warm place for 3-6 days, rinsing the beans

twice a day with warm water, then draining well. Eat the sprouts when they have grown to a length of 3-5 cm/1¼-2 in; they should weigh 225-300 g/8-11 oz in total.

Ingredients

Genuine Chinese ingredients will help to make your dishes authentic, but it is often possible to substitute more commonly available ingredients, and these are suggested in the recipes in this section. The Chinese ingredients shown in the photograph are abalone (1), star anise (2), bamboo shoots (3), beancurd (4), bean paste (5), salted black beans (6), beansprouts (7), 'bird's nest' (8), beancurd 'cheese' (9), 'dragon's eyes' (10), 'hundred year old' egg (11), five-spice powder (12), ginger root (13), hoisin sauce (14), lichee (15), lotus leaves (16), monosodium glutamate (17), Chinese dried black mushrooms (18), Chinese noodles (19), oyster sauce (20), Chinese sausage (21), sea cucumber (22), shark's fin (23), shrimp sauce (24), soy sauce (25), soy paste (26), water chestnuts (27) and wontun skins (28).

Note that monosodium glutamate, or MSG, which is a white powder that can be added to savoury dishes to bring out their flavour, may be harmful if it is consumed continually or in large amounts. It is already present in soy sauce, and the powder itself should be used only very sparingly.

Flavourings

Many people have the impression that to cook Chinese dishes you need an enormous range of Chinese herbs, seasonings and other flavouring ingredients. The truth is that you can cook a good range of Chinese dishes with hardly any specifically Chinese ingredients. In fact, with soy sauce supplemented only by common flavouring ingredients such as salt and freshly ground pepper, you should be able to cook 70-80% of all Chinese dishes.

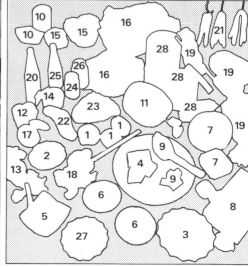

Equipment and Techniques

The Chinese either cook their food quickly at very high heat or they cook it slowly at very low heat. The many traditional methods of cooking in China and by Chinese throughout the world are variations of these two basic principles.

Tender fresh food is usually cooked in a matter of minutes or even seconds by the stir-fried method in order to retain its natural flavour and juiciness. Tougher ingredients, especially some cuts of meat, are cooked slowly for some hours to extract all the goodness from the food and make it very tender. This results in a dish rich in flavour and full of extremely tasty gravy or sauce that is perfect to eat with plain boiled rice.

Equipment
The principal piece of equipment used for Chinese cooking is the wok, a large, thin frying pan with a curved bottom and wooden (or heatproof) handles. Used on a modern stove, it has a ring to support it.

If you plan to buy a wok, choose an iron one about 35 cm/14 in across, with sides that are not too shallow. If you do not want to buy a wok specially, you can use a frying-pan instead.

Woks are used for deep-frying, brais-ing, steaming and boiling, as well as for stir-frying, and many come with a dome-shaped lid. You can also buy a wok scoop, which is used for scooping and tossing food; alternatively, use a metal spatula or a long-handled spoon. Chopsticks are used for stirring the food, but two forks will work as well. Stiff bamboo brushes are used for cleaning the surface afterwards – or use a soft washing-up brush instead.

For steaming, you can use either the traditional straw (or metal) baskets with tight-fitting lids, which are placed over boiling water in a wok or pan; or a trivet or steamer tray that stands inside a lidded pan or wok to hold the food above boiling water.

Finally, for preparing ingredients you'll need a good, medium-weight cleaver and a solid wood chopping board.

Preparing ingredients
In Chinese cookery, the way the ingredients are cut is very important and is determined by the method of cooking and how long each ingredient takes to cook.

Below: *Hunan stuffed peppers (page 334)*

Traditional techniques include: **slicing** – cutting straight down into thin slices; **shredding** – cutting slices lengthways into thin shreds like matchsticks; **dicing** – cutting shreds crossways into cubes; **diagonal cutting** – cutting at an angle; **roll cutting** – making diagonal cuts in opposite directions; **mincing** – using two cleavers at the same time to chop finely from side to side.

Stir-frying
The most popular style of cooking in China and also the one which most attracts the West is quick stir-frying. Food is added a little at a time to the centre of a wok for quick cooking and it is moved up the sides where it keeps warm but without cooking further. Very small amounts of oil are used, compared with Western frying, just enough to prevent the food sticking to the pan.

Preparing the ingredients for stir-frying can be time consuming. But once prepared, they can then be cooked very quickly by tossing them in the hot oil.

Traditionally, cooks aim for what is known as 'wok fragrance' when stir-frying. This is achieved by following a four-fold process in quick succession.

First the wok is heated until a wisp of smoke rises; a small amount of oil is poured in and swirled around and the spring onion, ginger and garlic are usually added. As these sizzle in the hot oil and release their fragrance, they 'arouse the wok'. The main ingredients of the dish – already prepared – come next. The strips are added in rapid succession and are turned for a short time, until partially cooked. Third, a dash of rice wine is splashed along the wok rim, just above the ingredients. The sizzling of the alcohol interacts with the other ingredients, enhancing the fragrance. Last, a small amount of sauce, containing a thickening agent, is poured into the wok, and stirred in to bind the mixture.

Deep-frying

For deep-frying, Chinese cooks use a wok, placed on its stand so it is completely secure, but you may find a deep-fat frier easier to use.

If you have a cooking thermometer, use this to ensure the oil is the exact temperature specified in the recipe (placing it in the oil before heating). Otherwise, test the temperature by timing how long a cube of stale bread takes to brown, as indicated in the recipe.

Use wooden chopsticks or tongs to place the food in the oil, and a slotted spoon or frying basket to remove it.

Braising

With this technique, the food is first browned and then simmered gently in a

Cleaning a wok

After use, wash under hot water; do not use detergent. Brush or scour with soapless scourer, then dry thoroughly over moderate heat to prevent rusting.

Always season a new wok before use: wash in hot water, dry over moderate heat and wipe inside with a pad of absorbent paper soaked in vegetable oil.

sauce. When the sauce contains soy sauce, Chinese yellow wine or sherry and a little sugar, the method is known as red-cooking.

Steaming

In Chinese kitchens an enormous amount of steam is usually generated. Sensibly, this steam is used for cooking. Quick-steamed dishes use fish, seafood and tender cuts of meat which do not require lengthy cooking. Steaming is also used for slow-cooked dishes; food is steamed in a tightly covered pan for a good many hours. Many of the inexpensive ingredients taste best when slow-cooked, and there are several dishes in the Chinese repertoire which use this method.

Roasting

Most Chinese kitchens do not have or need ovens, and roasting is generally confined to restaurants. The meat is roasted in large ovens, in which it is hung on hooks, but you can achieve a similar effect by placing the food on a rack in the roasting pan.

Other techniques

There are actually about 40-50 traditional methods of Chinese cooking, including shallow-frying, boiling, simmering, blanching, poaching and barbecuing. Sometimes a combination of two methods is used for one dish. This is known as twice-cooking or double-cooking.

Stir-frying

Prepare all the ingredients in advance by cutting the meat and vegetables into pieces the size and shape required, and place them on individual plates near the stove.

After heating the wok and then adding oil, add the ingredients. Stir with wooden chopsticks or two forks, pushing food away from the centre of the pan as it becomes cooked.

Add additional raw ingredients a little at a time, according to their required cooking time, putting them in the centre of the wok, where the heat is concentrated.

Regional Cooking Styles

Cooking styles do not vary fundamentally throughout China, but some regions emphasize certain flavourings, ingredients or cooking techniques more than others. And of course each locality has become famous for its own particular specialities. Traditionally, Chinese cuisine is divided into four main regions.

Peking and the northern region

Peking's most famous dish is Peking Duck, a spectacular dish which is part of the city's Imperial heritage. The dishes once made in the kitchen of the Imperial Palace can be very refined and elaborate. On the whole, however, the food and dishes of northern China, with its harsh climate and Mongolian influence, are heavier and coarser than those produced in the south.

More mutton and lamb are eaten in Peking than anywhere else in China, while the province of Shantung, well to the south of Peking, is renowned for its chickens and its fat prawns.

A copious use of garlic and other strong-tasting vegetables and spices, such as onions, spring onions, leeks and ginger, is typical of this region. Coriander leaves are used in many of its dishes.

Soy paste is extensively used in stir-fry cooking in these northern provinces. It is a solid paste which is simmered briefly with fat or oil and seasonings to give a creamy, bubbling mixture. The Chinese term for this technique is 'explosion' frying, because that is the effect of adding wet ingredients to a hot pan of fat.

Everyone associates rice with China, but in Peking and the northern provinces people just as often eat noodles, steamed buns or dumplings.
Characteristic dishes: Peking Duck (page 367), Lamb and Leeks (page 347), Chicken and Shrimps (page 348).

Canton and the southern region

Cantonese is the most versatile, diversified, innovative and best known of all Chinese regional cuisines. This vast rich region has never lacked fine raw materials for use in delicious dishes.

Cantonese cooking is a tradition that has grown in sophistication over more than 700 years. Beef is eaten more here than in other Chinese provinces. Besides pork, chicken, duck and goose, the Cantonese also enjoy crab, clams, conger eel, crayfish, prawns, squid, scallops and oysters, not to mention an enormous array of fish and various exotic delicacies. The lichee is only one of the many native tropical fruits.

There is a seemingly inexhaustible list of dishes to go with plain rice, which is eaten at every meal. While the preparation of dishes runs the gamut of Chinese culinary techniques, stir-frying is the Cantonese speciality. The region is also famous for its sweet and sour dishes and the use of soy, hoisin and oyster sauces.

On the whole, Cantonese dishes are neither highly seasoned nor peppery-hot. Rather, a harmonious blending of different flavours is the rule of thumb. Because fresh ingredients are plentiful, there is no need to use many spices.

Dim sum deserves special mention because even outside of Canton and Hong

Kong, this Cantonese speciality has become a household word. Westerners might consider these morsels as hot hors d'oeuvres or snacks.

Characteristic dishes: Sweet and Sour Pork (page 340), Tea Eggs (page 378), Pork Chow Mein (page 375), Chicken and Mushroom Soup (page 337).

Shanghai and the eastern region

Once called the Paris of the East, Shanghai continues to be the gastronomic centre of eastern China.

The food reflects the wide variety of

Below: *Back, Quick-fried mixed vegetables (page 354); Centre, Hot and sour soup (page 336); Right, 'Ants in the tree' savoury noodles (page 374); Front, Double-cooked pork (page 341).*

produce. Pork is eaten by everybody; little beef is eaten, if any. There are many dishes made with chicken, duck, freshwater fish, shrimp and crab. Chinese cabbage is cooked in numerous ways.

The food is both rich and sweet but not peppery hot. Although many dishes are stir-fried, the method of red cooking is special to the region.

Ginger and spring onion are used generously, but garlic less often. Many dishes are laced with sugar and vinegar, especially the dark vinegar from Chinkiang. The combination of marinating and deep-frying gives a 'smoked' effect.

Yangchow is another city in the region which boasts a fine cuisine. In the neighbouring province of Chekiang, the market town of Shaohsing makes China's best rice wine, while another market centre, Chin-hau produces a very special ham. But it is Hangchow which rivals Shanghai in representing eastern regional cuisine.

The cuisine of another province, Fukien, is just as distinctive. Unusual seafood is a special feature, and Fukien dishes are both decorative in appearance and subtly flavoured. Sugar is used to season savoury dishes. Coriander leaves feature as a garnish, sesame oil adds a finishing touch to even a deep-fried dish, and five-spice powder is widely used.

Characteristic dishes: Crystal Sugar Pork (page 363), 'Smoked' Fish Shanghai-style (page 332), Yangchow Fried Rice (page 373), 'Lion's Head' Pork (page 363), Stir-fried Sweet and sour Cabbage (page 355), Deep-fried Five-spice Rolls (page 334).

Szechuan and the western region

Szechuan cooking is hot and spicy, but it is claimed that instead of burning the taste-buds, the widespread use of chilli actually makes them more sensitive to other flavours.

The people of Szechuan have a preference for multi-flavoured dishes: they like them sour, salty, hot and sweet all at the same time, creating a sophisticated range of flavours.

The sauce most widely used is 'toupan jian', a hot sauce that is used mostly in stir-frying. Szechuan peppercorns are also frequently used, and mustard and sesame regularly feature in sauces which are served with simply cooked food.

Preserving food is important in this isolated region. One of the best-known pickled vegetables is 'ja ts'ai'. It is an easy way of giving dishes a typical Szechuan flavour, and is used throughout China.

There is a strong tradition of peasant cooking in Szechuan. Typical are the savoury meat puddings and noodle dishes. They favour multiple cooking processes, such as double-cooking.

The cooking of a neighbouring western province, Hunan, is similar and also has its devoted admirers, but it has been largely overshadowed by Szechuan cuisine.

Characteristic dishes: Hot and Sour Soup (page 336), Long-steamed Pork Pudding (page 362), 'Ants in the Tree' Savoury Noodles (page 374), Double-cooked Pork (page 341), Hunan Fish Steaks (page 369).

Starters and Soups

The Chinese do not make a feature of starters in the same way as we do in the West. For family meals, all the dishes are set out at once, though at banquets each dish is brought out individually. Then, and at dinner parties, the meal may begin with one or two seasonal delicacies, cold dishes or hors d'oeuvres. Nor is soup treated as a starter. Although it may be served at the beginning, it is drunk instead of any other beverage along with the meal. At banquets it is served between courses and at the end of the meal to clear the palate. The recipes included in this chapter are therefore suitable for beginning a meal, either in the Chinese manner or Western-style as a separate course.

Starters

Spicy meat dip

Illustrated on pages 330-331

Serves 2
1 slice fresh root ginger, peeled
100 g/4 oz boneless chicken
breasts, skinned
1 spring onion
100 g/4 oz unpeeled prawns
100 g/4 oz piece lean cooked ham,
cut into strips
¼ cucumber to garnish
1 tomato to garnish (optional)
For the dip
1 tbls mustard powder
1 tbls light soy sauce
1 tbls wine vinegar
1 tbls sesame oil

1 Peel and slice the root ginger. Put the chicken into a pan, cover with cold water and add the ginger and spring onion. Cover, bring to the boil, then lower the heat slightly and simmer for 10 minutes until the chicken is tender. Remove from the heat and leave the chicken to cool in the liquid.

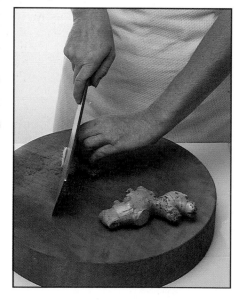

2 While the chicken is cooling, make the dip. Put the mustard powder into a small serving bowl and mix with a little cold water to form a thin, smooth paste. Stir in the soy sauce, wine vinegar and sesame oil until they are thoroughly blended.

Place the bowl in the centre of a serving plate.

3 Drain the chicken and discard the ginger and spring onion. Cut the chicken into strips.

4 Arrange the chicken, prawns and ham on the serving plate, radiating out from the bowl.

5 Garnish the platter of chicken, ham and prawns with cucumber and tomato slices, if liked, and serve at once with the dip and with Chinese prawn crackers (available from many supermarkets and from Chinese grocers).

'Smoked' fish Shanghai-style

Serves 8
1 kg/2¼ lb hake or cod steaks,
from the tail, cut into
20 mm/¾ in thick, round pieces
oil for deep-frying
flat-leafed parsley to garnish
For the marinade
4 cm/1½ in piece of root ginger
3 tbls thin soy sauce
1 tbls Shaohsing wine or medium
sherry
For the sauce
1 whole star anise or 8 star anise
segments
25 mm/1 in cinnamon stick
1 piece preserved mandarin
orange peel, ¼ of the whole
orange
1 tsp black peppercorns
2 large spring onions
4 thick slices root ginger
3 tbls Chinkiang or 2 tbls red wine
vinegar
4 tbls sugar

1 Pat the fish dry and put the steaks into a large flat dish. Pierce the fish all over with the tip of a sharp knife to ensure better absorption of the marinade.

2 Chop the root ginger. Using a garlic press, squeeze out the juice on to the fish and discard the pulp. Add the soy sauce and wine or sherry. Set the fish aside and leave to marinate for 2 hours, turning the fish occasionally.

3 Meanwhile prepare the sauce. Put 600 ml/1 pt water in a large saucepan, add the whole star anise or segments, cinnamon, mandarin orange peel, black peppercorns, spring onions and root ginger. Bring the liquid to the boil, lower the heat and simmer for 25-30 minutes or until the liquid is reduced to about 425 ml/15 fl oz. Strain and discard the solids. Return the sauce to the pan. Add the vinegar and sugar.

4 Pour enough oil into a wok so that it is just under half-full or, if using a deep-fat frier or a heavy saucepan, until the oil is

Below: *'Smoked' fish Shanghai-style*

about 5 cm/2 in deep. Heat the oil to 200° C/400° F or until a cube of stale bread browns in 40 seconds.

5 Five minutes before you are ready to cook, put the fish on a wire rack to drain.

6 Handling the fish carefully, put in half the steaks and deep-fry for 10 minutes, turning them over at half-time, until brown. Lift with a slotted spoon or frying basket and drain on absorbent paper.

7 Reheat the oil to 200° C/400° F before deep-frying the rest of the fish.

8 Bring the reduced sauce slowly to the boil again, stirring to make sure that the sugar has dissolved. Put the fish into the sauce and spoon the boiling sauce over the fish repeatedly for 3-4 minutes. Transfer the fish to a large dish.

9 Continue to boil the sauce until it thickens and becomes a syrupy glaze. Use this to glaze the fish. When cold, refrigerate, covered, for at least a few hours.

10 Serve cold or at room temperature, garnished with flat-leafed parsley.

Crisp stir-fried shrimps

Serves 6
500 g/18 oz raw peeled shrimps, fresh or frozen and thoroughly defrosted
¾ tsp salt
6 tsps cornflour
1 large egg white
1 L/1¾ pt groundnut or corn oil
4 tbls chicken stock
¼ tsp sugar
1 tbls Shaohsing wine or medium-dry sherry

1 Wash the peeled shrimps in cold water twice, rubbing them gently with fingers. Drain them well and put them into a large bowl.

2 Sprinkle the shrimps with the salt and mix. Stir in 5 tsp cornflour, then the egg white and stir again to coat evenly and

thoroughly. Cover the bowl and leave it in the refrigerator for a minimum of 5 hours, overnight or up to 3 days. (This technique is known as 'velveting'.)

3 Heat the oil in a wok or deep-fat frier until it reaches barely 150° C/300° F or until a cube of stale bread will brown in 90 seconds. Tip in the shrimps and deep-fry them for about 30-45 seconds, separating them with a long pair of chopsticks or a wooden spoon. The shrimps will turn pink and will be almost cooked by now.

4 Remove the shrimps with a frying basket or a slotted spoon. Mix together the remaining cornflour, chicken stock and sugar and reserve.

5 If you were cooking in a wok, pour out all the oil. Return 2 tbls oil to the wok and reheat this for shallow frying. If you were cooking in a deep-fat frier, set this aside. Heat 3 tbls oil in a large frying-pan until the first sign of smoke appears. Add the shrimps to the wok or pan, stir a few times and splash in the Shaohsing wine or sherry along the rim. When the sizzling subsides, dribble in the thickening mixture, turning and tossing the shrimps with a wok scoop or a metal spatula. As soon as the thickening is cooked, add salt to taste.

6 Pour the mixture on to a warm serving plate and serve immediately for the 'wok fragrance' to be at its peak.

✿ If freshwater shrimps are used, use 1 tsp salt. If raw shrimps are not available raw prawns can be used as a substitute. Cut them into 2 cm/¾ in pieces.

Deep-fried five-spice rolls

Illustrated on pages 320-321

Serves 12

1 packet (225 g/8 oz) dried
   beancurd sheets, 33 x 15 cm/
   13 x 6 in
600 g/1¼ lb pork with some fat in
   it, chopped into rice-sized bits
the white part of 12 spring onions,
   cut into small rounds
175 g/6 oz canned or fresh, peeled,
   water chestnuts, chopped into
   rice-sized bits
3 tbls tapioca flour or potato flour
2 medium-sized egg yolks
vegetable oil for deep-frying
tomato ketchup to serve
chilli sauce to serve
1 tbls thick soy sauce mixed with
   1 tsp prepared hot mustard
   to serve

For the marinade

1 tsp salt
2 tsps thin soy sauce
2½ tsps sugar
5 tsps Shaohsing wine or medium-
   dry sherry
2 tsps sesame oil
1 tsp five-spice powder
1½ medium-sized egg whites

1 Soak the beancurd sheets in cold water for about 4 minutes or until the sheets are soft and pliable. Lift each sheet carefully with both hands to drain, blot them with absorbent paper and put them flat on a large tea-towel, one on top of another. Cover them with another tea-towel to keep them just moist.

2 Put the finely chopped pork into a big bowl. Add the ingredients for the marinade, stir and leave for 5 minutes.

3 Add the spring onions and the water chestnuts to the mixture. Stir in the tapioca flour or potato flour, 1 tbls at a time, to ensure smooth mixing. Divide the mixture into 16 portions.

4 Take one beancurd sheet from the covered pile and put it on a flat surface with the long side next to you. Cut the sheet in half crossways.

5 Scoop up one portion of the filling and roll it between your palms into the shape of a sausage. Place the filling near the edge of the beancurd sheet and roll it away from you as tightly as possible.

6 Using either your fingers or a pastry brush, smear some egg yolk on the opposite edge and seal the roll. Leave the two ends open like a cigarette and place

the roll on a tray, sealed side down. Cover the tray with a damp cloth. Repeat until all the sheets are filled.

7 If you are using a wok for deep-frying, half-fill it with vegetable oil. If you are using a deep-fat frier the oil should be 6-8 cm/2½-3 in deep. Heat the oil to 190° C/375° F, at which temperature a cube of stale bread will brown in 50 seconds.

8 Put in 8 rolls or however many will float freely in the oil and deep-fry for 8 minutes or until milk chocolate-brown in colour. Remove them with a slotted spoon and drain on absorbent paper. Keep them warm. Repeat until all the rolls are done.

9 Cut each roll into 5 pieces and put them on a large platter. Serve with the ketchup, chilli sauce and soy-mustard dips arranged on the table or in the middle of the platter.

Hunan stuffed peppers

Illustrated on page 326

Serves 6-8 with other dishes

1½ tbls dried shrimps
8 medium-sized dried Chinese
   black mushrooms
8 small red peppers
175-200 g/6-7 oz lean pork
1½ tsps salt
2 tbls soy sauce
2 tbls cornflour
vegetable oil for deep-frying

For the sauce

15 g/½ oz lard
125 ml/4 fl oz good stock
2 tbls soy sauce
½ tsp monosodium glutamate
4 tsps oyster sauce
2 tbls cornflour mixed with 3 tbls
   water

1 Soak the dried shrimps and mushrooms for 20 minutes in a bowl of warm water.

2 Meanwhile, remove the stems, all the seeds and any pith carefully from the

Above: *Spring rolls*

peppers through the hole at the top, making sure you keep the peppers whole.

3 Finely chop the pork. Drain and chop the shrimps and mushrooms (discarding the hard stem tips) and add to the pork. Stir in the salt and soy sauce. Stuff the mixture in each pepper through the stem-hole, filling each one completely. Make a paste from the cornflour mixed with 2 tbls water. Seal the stuffing at the top of the peppers by spreading the paste over the hole.

4 Heat the oil in a wok or deep-fat frier to 180° C/350° F; at this temperature a cube of stale bread will brown in 60 seconds. Lower the peppers, pasted-side down, into the oil one by one. Turn the heat to low and fry the peppers for

3-4½ minutes or until the skins are softened and are slightly blistered.
5 Remove the peppers from the oil and drain them. Arrange them, pasted-end upward, in a heatproof dish. Stand the dish on a trivet in a steamer and bring the water beneath to the boil. Cover and steam steadily for 15 minutes.

6 Meanwhile heat the lard in a wok or frying-pan over medium-low heat and add the rest of the sauce ingredients. Stir them, over high heat, for 1½-2 minutes until the sauce thickens. Pour the sauce over the stuffed peppers and serve immediately, from the heatproof dish.

Spring rolls

Makes 6
3 tbls vegetable oil
300 g/10 oz beansprouts
8 spring onions, cut into matchstick strips
1 red pepper, deseeded, quartered and thinly sliced
100 g/4 oz mushrooms, sliced
1 slice fresh root ginger, finely chopped
1 tbls soy sauce
1 tbls dry sherry
freshly ground black pepper
vegetable oil for deep-frying
spring onion flowers to garnish (see page 345)
For the pastry
200 g/7 oz plain flour
½ tsp salt
125 ml/4 fl oz warm water

1 To make the pastry sift the flour and salt into a bowl, then make a well in the centre and pour in the water. Mix with a wooden spoon until well blended, then knead well until the dough is soft and pliable. Wrap in cling film and put in the refrigerator for 30 minutes to chill.
2 Heat the oil in a large frying-pan or wok and add the beansprouts, the spring onions, red pepper, mushrooms and ginger. Stir-fry for 2 minutes, then add the soy sauce, sherry, and pepper to taste. Cook for 1 further minute and remove from the heat.
3 Roll out the pastry on a lightly floured surface as thinly as possible to a neat rectangle, 45 × 30 cm/18 × 12in. Cut the pastry into six 15 cm/6 in squares.

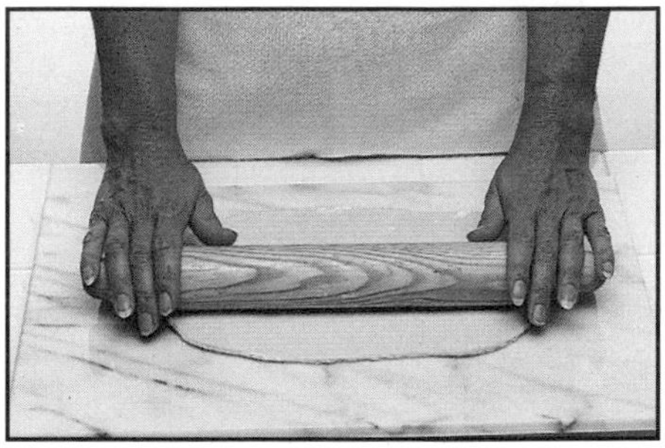

4 Place 2 tbls of the vegetable mixture in the centre of each pastry square.

5 Fold in the sides, brush with a little water then carefully roll up. Dampen underside of pastry ends and press to seal.

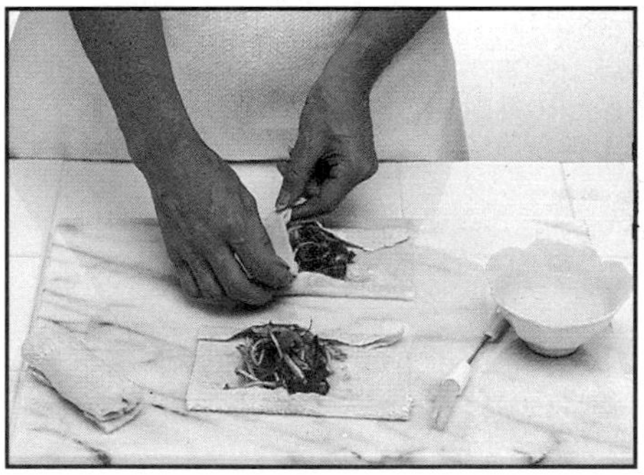

6 Heat the oven to 110° C/225° F/gas ¼.
7 Heat the oil in a deep-fat frier to 190° C/375° F or until a cube of stale bread browns in 50 seconds.
8 Using a slotted spoon lower 3 rolls into the oil and fry for about 5 minutes until crisp and golden. Remove with a slotted spoon and drain. Keep warm while frying the remainder.

The rolls may be made a few hours in advance, allowed to cool, then reheated in a 170° C/325° F/gas 3 oven just before serving.

Soups

Shredded pork and pickle soup

Serves 5-6
4-6 dried Chinese mushrooms
**75 g/3 oz transparent pea-starch
  noodles**
1.1 L/2 pt good chicken stock
**100 g/4 oz loin of pork, cut in
  matchstick strips**
**75 g/3 oz ja ts'ai pickle, cut into
  matchstick strips, or pickled
  cucumber plus 1 tsp chilli powder**
**75 g/3 oz bamboo shoots,
  drained**
3 spring onions, chopped
**2 tbls distilled or white wine
  vinegar**
2 tbls soy sauce
1 chicken stock cube

1 Soak the mushrooms in warm water
to cover for 2 minutes, drain and cut into
shreds. Soak the noodles in water to
cover for about 5 minutes and drain very
thoroughly.

2 Heat the stock in a saucepan over
high heat. When simmering add the pork
and all the other ingredients. Bring the
liquid back to the boil, lower the heat and
simmer gently for 15 minutes before
serving.

Shredded meat and vegetable soup

Serves 4-5
**7.5 cm/3 in piece bamboo shoot,
  cabbage heart or cauliflower,
  cut into matchstick strips**
1.2 L/2 pt good stock
1 chicken stock cube
**75 g/3 oz chicken breast in
  5-7.5 cm/2-3 in strips**
**100 g/4 oz ham in 5-7.5 cm/2-3 in
  strips**
**7.5 cm/3 in piece of cucumber, in
  matchsticks**
**2 small young carrots, cut into
  matchstick strips**
**salt and freshly ground black
  pepper**
1 tsp sesame oil

1 Blanch the cabbage or cauliflower
strips, covering them with boiling water
for 3 minutes to remove the bitterness.
2 Heat the stock and dissolve the stock
cube in it. Add the shredded ingredients
and simmer for 5-6 minutes. Season
with salt and pepper.
3 Just before serving, add the sesame
oil to the soup and serve either in heated
bowls or in a heated terrine, placed in the
centre of the table so that people can
help themselves throughout the meal.

Hot and sour soup

Illustrated on pages 328-329

Serves 5-6
**5-6 large dried Chinese
  mushrooms**
2 stalks dried lily buds (optional)
1-2 cakes beancurd
1 L/1¾ pt good stock
**100 g/4 oz pork tenderloin, cut into
  thin 5 cm/2 in strips**
2 tbls dried shrimps
1 chicken stock cube
8 tsps soy sauce
4 tbls distilled or wine vinegar
½ tsp freshly ground black pepper
8 tsps cornflour
1 medium-sized egg, beaten
2 tsps sesame oil

1 Soak the mushrooms and lily buds, if
using, in warm water to cover for 20
minutes.
2 Discard the stems and cut the mushrooms into thin slices. Cut the lily buds
into 25 mm/1 in sections and cut the
beancurd into 10 mm/½ in cubes.

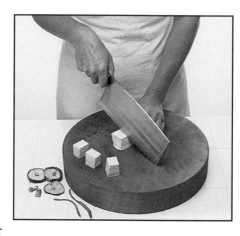

3 Bring the stock to the boil in a large
saucepan. Add the pork, mushrooms,
dried shrimps, lily buds, stock cube and
soy sauce and simmer gently for 10
minutes.
4 Add the beancurd, vinegar and pepper to the pan. Blend the cornflour into
100 ml/3½ fl oz cold water and stir it into
the simmering stock.
5 Cook, stirring, until the soup has thickened, then turn off the heat. Pour the
beaten egg in a very thin stream along
the prongs of a fork, trailing it over the
surface of the soup. Add the sesame oil
and serve immediately.

Chicken and mushroom soup

Serves 4-6
50 g/2 oz dried Chinese mushrooms, sliced, or 4 button mushrooms, thinly sliced
125 g/5 oz cooked chicken breast
1.15 L/2 pt chicken stock
salt and freshly ground black pepper
sprigs of watercress to garnish

1 Reconstitute the dried mushrooms by soaking in hot water for 20 minutes or until swollen.
2 Skin the chicken breast and cut into slivers.
3 Bring the stock to the boil. Add the drained mushrooms and chicken.
4 Simmer for 5 minutes. Season to taste and garnish with watercress.

For a luxurious version of chicken and mushroom soup, add 4 tbls dry sherry just before serving.

Instead of chicken meat use turkey or pork. Just before the end of cooking, add a few slices of cucumber.

Leafy noodle soup

Above: *Leafy noodle soup*

Serves 4
850 ml/1½ pt chicken stock
1 bunch spring onions, finely shredded diagonally including the green tops
1 tsp finely grated fresh root ginger
2 tsps lemon juice
2 tsps soy sauce
salt and freshly ground black pepper
50 g/2 oz Chinese fine egg noodles
2-3 lettuce leaves, finely shredded and chopped
½ bunch watercress, chopped

1 Heat the stock until on the point of boiling, then add just over half of the spring onions together with the grated ginger, lemon juice and soy sauce. Half cover with a lid and simmer gently for 5 minutes.
2 Meanwhile, bring a pan of salted water to the boil and add the egg noodles. Cook for 6 minutes until the noodles are tender.
3 Add the lettuce and watercress to the chicken stock and simmer for a further 5 minutes. Adjust seasoning, if necessary, transfer to a warmed serving bowl and garnish with the remaining shredded spring onions.
4 Drain the noodles thoroughly, then divide them equally between 4 warmed individual soup bowls. Spoon the soup into the bowls of noodles and serve immediately.

If desired, add a little chopped cooked chicken or some chopped, peeled prawns a few minutes before the end of cooking time.

Quick-fried Dishes

Not only is stir-frying quick and easy, but it is also a remarkably healthy way of cooking food, preserving its flavour, texture and goodness while cooking in the minimum of oil. Because of the varying cooking times, temperatures and ingredients, there is an almost infinite number of possible stir-fried dishes. And it is economical in using up small quantities of raw food and cooked left-overs. No wonder stir-frying is becoming so popular in the West. Deep-frying, although not so widely associated with Chinese food as stir-frying, is also an important Chinese cooking method and is used in a wide variety of interesting and delicious dishes.

Pork

Sweet and sour pork

Serves 4
750 g/1½ lb pork fillet
1 tbls cornflour
salt
vegetable oil for deep-frying
For the sauce
1 tsp cornflour
4 tbls water
2 tbls wine or cider vinegar
2 tbls brown sugar
2 tbls orange juice
1 tbls tomato purée
2 tbls soy sauce
pinch of cayenne pepper
1 small onion, finely
   chopped
1 tbls vegetable oil
½ green pepper, deseeded and cut
   into thin strips
½ red pepper, deseeded and cut
   into thin strips

1 To make the sauce, put the cornflour into a bowl and then gradually pour on the water, stirring all the time to form a smooth mixture. Stir in the vinegar, sugar, orange juice, tomato purée, soy sauce, cayenne pepper and half the chopped onion.
2 Trim away any excess fat from the pork and cut into 2.5 cm/1 in cubes. Season the cornflour with a pinch of salt and put it into a greaseproof or polythene bag. Toss the meat cubes in it, a few at a time, to coat them thoroughly. Remove the meat and shake off any excess cornflour.
3 Heat the oil in a wok or deep-fat frier to a temperature of 190° C/375° F or until a cube of stale bread browns in 50 seconds. Fry half the meat for about 6-8 minutes, until it is crisp and golden brown. (Do not try to cook it all together in a small pan of oil because the meat will lower the temperature of the oil too much, and it will not cook to the characteristic crispness that is important in this dish.) Remove the meat from the oil with a slotted spoon or frying basket, drain it on crumpled absorbent paper and keep it warm while you fry the remainder of the floured meat.

4 Heat the vegetable oil in a wok or frying-pan, add the remaining chopped onion and strips of green and red pepper. Fry over high heat for 1 minute, lower the heat to moderate, then pour in the sauce. Stir for a few minutes until the sauce is bubbling and thickened. Add the cooked cubes of pork and stir carefully. Cook for 1 minute only, to blend the flavours. Turn the meat and sauce into a warmed dish and serve at once.

Cubes of lamb or chicken can be cooked and stirred into the sauce in the same way. Small cubes of chicken will deep-fry in 5-6 minutes.

Chop suey

Serves 4
250 g/9 oz pork fillet, trimmed of
   excess fat
2 tsps cornflour
1 tbls dry sherry
2 tbls soy sauce
2 spring onions
2 slices fresh root ginger
½ cauliflower
2 carrots
1 small green pepper
100 g/4 oz fresh beansprouts
3 tomatoes
5 tbls vegetable oil
1 tsp salt
1 tsp sugar
a little chicken stock (optional)

1 Cut the pork lengthways into four 2.5 cm/1½ in slices, then cut each into slices about 5 mm/¼ in thick. Place in a shallow dish.

2 In a small bowl, blend together the cornflour, sherry and soy sauce to make a smooth paste. Pour the mixture over the pork, stir well to mix, then cover and leave to marinate while you prepare the vegetables.
3 Cut the spring onions into 1 cm/½ in strips. Peel and finely chop the root ginger. Break the cauliflower into florets, discarding the leaves and any thick fibrous stalks. Thinly slice the carrots. Deseed and finely shred the green pepper. Trim the beansprouts of any husks. Slice the tomatoes.

4 Heat 3 tbls oil in a wok or large frying-pan until it is just smoking. Add the sliced pork and stir with a long-handled spoon or spatula for 2-3 minutes until each slice is coated with oil. Transfer the pork slices to a plate with a slotted spoon.

5 Heat the remaining oil in the wok and add the spring onions and slices of fresh root ginger to flavour the oil.

6 Add the cauliflower florets and sliced carrots to the wok and stir-fry for 1 minute.

7 Add the green pepper, beansprouts and tomatoes and stir-fry for 1 further minute. Season with salt and sugar and stir a few more times until heated through.

8 Add the pork slices, moisten with a little stock if necessary and stir-fry for 30 seconds. Taste and adjust seasoning, transfer to a warmed dish and serve at once.

弎 Chicken breast or lean rump or frying steak are good replacements for pork.

Home-made hoisin sauce

Makes 150 ml/5 fl oz sauce
3 garlic cloves, finely chopped
1 spring onion, finely chopped
4 tbls soy paste
5 tsps Chinese plum sauce, plum chutney or plum jam
2 tbls tomato purée
1 tbls corn oil
5 tsps chilli sauce

1 Stir all the ingredients together until well blended.

Double-cooked pork

Illustrated on pages 328-329

Serves 5-6 with other dishes
4 tbls vegetable oil
1 medium-sized onion, thinly sliced
1 medium-sized red pepper, seeded and cut into 4 x 5 cm/1½ x 2 in pieces
1 green pepper, prepared as for red pepper
2 tbls lard
2 tbls chilli sauce or chilli paste
3 tbls soy sauce
2 tbls hoisin sauce (see recipe on this page) or soy paste
3 tbls tomato purée
1 tbls sugar
350 g/12 oz left-over boiled or roast pork cut into 4 x 4 x 5cm/ 1½ x 1½ x 2 in pieces

1 Heat the oil in a wok or large frying-pan over high heat. When the oil is hot, add the onion slices and stir-fry for 1½ minutes. Add the peppers and stir-fry for

Above: *Chop suey*

1 minute and push the onions and peppers to the side of the pan.

2 Melt the lard in the middle of the pan, then add the chilli sauce or paste, the soy sauce, hoisin sauce or soy paste, tomato purée and sugar. Stir them together into a thick sauce.

3 Mix the pork pieces into the sauce and bring the pepper and onions into the centre of the pan. Stir over high heat for 1½ minutes and serve hot with rice.

弎 To use fresh belly of pork, boil the meat for 30 minutes, drain, cool and cut it into 4 x 4 x 5 cm/1½ x 1½ x 2 in pieces, then proceed as above.

Pork with cucumber

Serves 4-6

**1 kg/2 lb streaky pork rashers
    (belly of pork)**
1 medium cucumber
2 tbls cornflour
2 tbls dry sherry
2 tbls soy sauce
300 ml/½ pt chicken stock
2 tbls vegetable oil
1 clove garlic, finely chopped
1 large onion, finely chopped
**1 tsp ground ginger, or ½ tsp
    finely chopped fresh root ginger**

1 Trim the rinds, bones and any excess fat from the pork rashers. Cut the rashers into thin strips about 5 cm/2 in long.
2 Wipe but do not peel the cucumber, then cut into quarters lengthways, trimming off the ends. Scoop out the seeds with a teaspoon. Cut the quarters lengthways again and cut the pieces into 2.5 cm/1 in lengths.

3 Mix the cornflour to a paste in a bowl with a little of the sherry or soy sauce, then stir in the remainder with the stock.
4 Put the oil and garlic into a wok or frying-pan and heat quickly until the garlic is sizzling.

Above: *Pork with cucumber*

5 Add the pork and stir-fry over high heat for about 15 minutes until all the pieces are crisp and well browned.
6 Pour all but about 1 tablespoon of the fat from the wok and then set it back over low heat.
7 Stir in the cucumber, onion and ginger and stir-fry for about 5 minutes until the onion is translucent.
8 Give the cornflour mixture a stir and pour it into the pan. Increase the heat and bring the mixture to the boil. Cook over high heat for 3 minutes until a thick, translucent sauce is formed.

9 Transfer to a warmed serving dish and serve at once.

Shredded pork

Illustrated on pages 338-339

Serves 2-4

**250 g/9 oz pork fillet, trimmed of
    excess fat**
1 small cucumber, unpeeled
2-3 spring onions
3 tbls vegetable oil
1 tbls thin soy sauce
1 tbls dry sherry
1 tsp salt
1 tsp sesame oil

1 Cut the pork into matchstick strips and finely shred the cucumber and spring onions.
2 Heat the wok over a high heat for 35-40 seconds. Pour in the oil and heat it until smoking. Swirl the wok so that most of the surface is well coated with a layer of oil.
3 Add the pork and stir-fry until the colour of the meat changes. This should take less than 45 seconds. Add the soy sauce and the dry sherry and stir a few more times.

4 Add the cucumber and spring onions, stir and season with salt. Continue until done to your taste. Mix in the sesame oil and serve at once.

Pork with lettuce

Serves 4 with other dishes
350 g/12 oz pork fillet, trimmed of excess fat
2 oranges
2 tbls vegetable oil
1 red pepper, deseeded and cut into 5 mm/¼ in strips
1 clove garlic, crushed (optional)
4 spring onions, thinly sliced
1 tsp cornflour
2 tbls soy sauce
1 tsp white wine vinegar
15 g/½ oz light soft brown sugar
½ tsp ground ginger
100 g/4 oz beansprouts
salt and freshly ground black pepper
8 leaves Chinese lettuce, cut into 5 cm/2 in strips

1 Cut the pork fillets into 2 cm/¾ in slices.
2 Working on a board or holding the oranges over a bowl, cut all the peel and white pith from the oranges with a sharp knife.

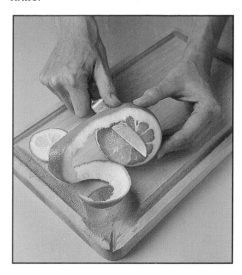

3 Cut the fruit into segments. Remove any membranes and pips and reserve any juice.

4 Heat the oil in a wok or large frying-pan. Add the pork, red pepper and garlic, if using, and fry over high heat, stirring occasionally, for 5-8 minutes.
5 Add the spring onions and oranges (including any juice). Blend the cornflour with the soy sauce in a cup and stir into the pan, followed by the vinegar, sugar, ginger and beansprouts. Season with salt and pepper to taste and cook, stirring for 2 minutes.
6 Add the lettuce and cook for 1 minute only, stirring the mixture all the time.
7 Transfer to a warmed serving dish and serve at once.

Instead of pork fillet, you can use thinly sliced topside of beef.

Left: Pork with lettuce

Beef and Lamb

Beef with mange-tout peas

Serves 4

**350 g/12 oz frying steak, cut across
grain into 4 x 2.5 cm x 5 mm/
1½ x 1 x ¼ in strips**
1 tbls cornflour
1 tbls dry sherry
2 tbls light soy sauce
1 tsp salt
1½ tsps sugar
4 tbls vegetable oil
**250 g/9 oz mange-tout peas,
topped and tailed**
1 tbls chicken stock (optional)
2 spring onions, finely chopped
2 slices fresh root ginger, chopped

1 Beat the steak between 2 sheets of greaseproof paper to tenderize as well as flatten it to the required thickness before cutting into strips.

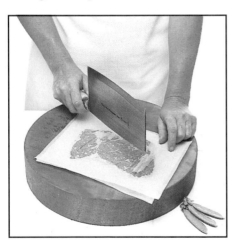

2 If the mange-tout peas are small, leave them whole – if they are large, it is better to cut them in half.
3 In a large bowl, blend the cornflour with the sherry and soy sauce to a smooth paste. Add a pinch of the salt and 1 tsp of the sugar. Stir in the beef strips, then cover and leave to marinate for about 30 minutes, stirring once.
4 Heat a wok or frying-pan for 1½ minutes. Heat half the oil in the wok. When it is smoking, add the mange-tout peas, stir over brisk heat until evenly

coated with oil, then add the remaining salt and sugar and stir-fry for 1-1½ minutes, adding a little chicken stock if the peas show signs of sticking. Transfer the mange-tout peas to a warmed serving dish, cover and keep in a warm place (but not in the oven, or they will lose their bright green colour).
5 Wash and dry the wok, heat it again,

Below: *Beef with mange-tout peas,
Fried rice with egg (page 373)*

then add the remaining oil. Heat until smoking, then add the spring onions and root ginger and stir once.
6 Using a slotted spoon, lift the beef strips from the marinade, draining off any excess, and add to the wok. Stir over brisk heat until evenly coated with oil, then stir-fry for 1 minute, adding a little chicken stock if the beef shows any signs of sticking. Spoon the beef over the mange-tout and serve at once, accompanied by fried rice with egg.

Above: *Beef with cashews*

Beef with cashews

Serves 4

**500 g/1 lb rump steak or flash-fry
steak, cut no more than 1 cm/
½ in thick and all fat removed**
3 tbls vegetable oil
1 clove garlic, crushed (optional)
**4 spring onions, cut into 2.5 cm/
1 in pieces**
1 large onion, chopped
50 g/2 oz unsalted cashew nuts
**1 small green or red pepper,
deseeded and cut into thin strips**
1 tsp ground ginger
1 tbls cornflour
150 ml/¼ pt chicken stock
2 tsps medium sherry
2 tsps soy sauce
**salt and freshly ground black
pepper**
**1 spring onion flower to garnish
(see recipe).**

1 Dry the beef on absorbent paper.
Place it between 2 sheets of greaseproof
paper and beat to flatten, with a wooden
rolling pin. Using kitchen scissors, snip
the beef into thin strips about 5 cm/2 in
long.
2 Heat 1 tbls of oil in a wok or large frying-pan, add half the beef strips, stir-fry

for about 1 minute until browned on all
sides, remove from the pan with a slotted
spoon and reserve. Heat 1 further tbls of
oil in the pan, add the remaining beef
strips, stir-fry in the same way and reserve.
3 Heat the remaining oil in the pan, add
the garlic, if using, spring onions, onion,
cashew nuts and pepper strips and stir-
fry gently for 3-4 minutes, until the vegetables are tender and the nuts lightly
browned. Remove the pan from the heat
and stir in the ginger.
4 Blend the cornflour with the chicken
stock, sherry and soy sauce to make a
smooth paste, and stir into the pan.
5 Return to the heat, bring to the boil,
lower heat and simmer gently for 1
minute, stirring constantly. Season to
taste with salt and pepper.
6 Return the reserved cooked beef
strips to the pan and stir over gentle heat
until heated through. Serve at once in
individual bowls.
7 To make a spring onion flower garnish, trim the spring onion of most of the
green top and remove the thin skin and
the bulb end. With a small sharp knife,
make several slits close together from the
top to about three-quarters of the way
towards the bulb end of the onion.

8 Place the onion in a bowl of iced water
for 1 hour. The top will curl back to make
an attractive 'flower'. Drain thoroughly.

Beef with corn

Serves 4-6
1 tbls dry sherry
1 tbls soy sauce
1½ tsps cornflour
**500 g/1 lb rump steak, thinly sliced
    across the grain**
1 tbls oil
1 small onion, quartered
125 g/4 oz mange-tout peas
1 tsp salt
**400 g/14 oz canned miniature corn
    cobs, rinsed and drained**
**400 g/14 oz canned straw
    mushrooms, drained**
2 tsps sugar

1 In a bowl, blend the sherry and soy sauce into the cornflour. Add the beef and turn it so that it is thoroughly coated.

2 Heat the oil in a wok or frying-pan. Fry the onion for 2 minutes over a high heat. Remove the beef from the cornflour mixture with a slotted spoon, reserving the liquid. Add the beef to the frying-pan and stir-fry until lightly browned. Add the mange-tout peas and the salt and stir-fry for another 30 seconds.

3 Add the baby corn cobs and the straw mushrooms and stir-fry for 1 minute. Add the sugar and blend well.
4 Blend the remaining cornflour liquid with 2 tsps cold water and stir into the pan. Cook for 1 minute until thick. Serve the stir-fried beef and vegetables with rice or noodles.

Beef with bamboo shoots

Serves 4
700 g/1½ lb top rump steak
**450 g/1 lb canned bamboo shoots,
    drained**
4 tbls oil
1 garlic clove, finely chopped
125 g/4 oz carrots, thinly sliced
1 large onion, finely chopped
1 tsp ground ginger
¼ tsp cayenne pepper
juice of 1 lemon
2 tbls soy sauce

1 Cut the steak into small, thin slivers. Slice the bamboo shoots.
2 Put the oil and garlic into a wok or a large frying-pan and set it over a high heat. When the garlic begins to sizzle, add the beef and carrots. Stir-fry them until the meat has browned.
3 Lower the heat and add the onion, bamboo shoots, ginger and cayenne pepper. Stir-fry for a further 2 minutes.
4 Pour in the lemon juice and soy sauce. Bring to the boil, stirring, and remove the pan from the heat. Turn it into a heated serving dish and serve immediately with boiled rice, boiled Chinese noodles or fried rice.

Lamb and leeks

Serves 4-6
500 g/1 lb leg of lamb without bone
4-5 young leeks
1 garlic clove
**3 thin slices from 25 mm/1 in fresh
    root ginger**
½ tsp salt
3 tbls vegetable oil
25 g/1 oz lard
2 tbls soy sauce
**3 tbls Chinese yellow wine or dry
    sherry**
freshly ground black pepper

1 Cut the lamb into 2 x 4 cm/¾ x 1½ in thin slices. Wash the leeks thoroughly and cut into 25 mm/1 in sections. Cut the garlic into thin slices and the ginger into short matchsticks. Rub the slices of lamb with the salt.

2 Heat the oil and lard in a frying-pan. When hot, add the lamb, garlic, and ginger. Stir 2-3 times and add the leeks. Continue stirring over high heat for 2-3 minutes. Sprinkle with soy sauce, wine and pepper. Serve immediately.

Left: *Lamb and leeks*; Opposite page: *Beef with corn*

Chicken and Duck

Sliced sweet and sour chicken

Serves 4
225 g/8 oz chicken breasts
½ tsp salt
½ tsp cornflour
3 tbls corn oil
25 g/1 oz bamboo shoots
1 green pepper
1 small onion
1 slice root ginger
1 garlic clove
For the sweet and sour sauce
1 tbls soy sauce
1 tbls red wine vinegar
1 tbls soft brown sugar
1 tbls tomato purée
4 tbls chicken stock

1 Remove the skin and any small rib bones from the chicken breasts.
2 Slice the breasts with the grain of the meat, into oblique slices, about 12 mm/½ in thick.

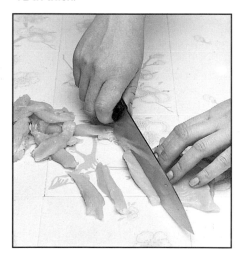

3 Mix together the salt and the cornflour and rub into the sliced chicken.
4 Heat the oil in a wok or frying-pan over moderate heat.
5 Place the sliced chicken in the wok, spreading it out in a single layer. Stir-fry for about 4 minutes until the chicken is cooked.
6 Remove the chicken from the pan, drain on absorbent paper and set aside in a warm place.

7 Slice the bamboo shoots. Deseed and thinly slice the green pepper.

8 Peel and chop the onion. Chop the slice of root ginger finely. Skin the garlic clove and chop finely.
9 Mix together all the sauce ingredients.
10 Return the wok to the heat. Add the bamboo shoots, pepper, onion, garlic and ginger and stir-fry over moderate heat for 1 minute.
11 Return the chicken to the wok and mix well with the sauce to coat each piece. Cook for 1 minute then serve.

Chicken and shrimps

Serves 4-6
250 g/8 oz boiled peeled shrimps
250 g/8 oz boned, skinned chicken breast
½ tsp salt
10 cm/4 in piece of cucumber
2 spring onions
2 tbls vegetable oil
100 g/4 oz small button mushrooms
thin cucumber slices to garnish
For the sauce
25 g/1 oz lard
4 tsps soy paste
2 tsps soy sauce
2 tsps tomato purée
2 tsps hoisin sauce (see page 341)
1 tbls sherry
1 tsp chilli sauce
2 tsps sesame oil

1 Rub the shrimps with salt. Cut the chicken into 10 mm/½ in cubes and cut

the cucumber into cubes slightly larger. Clean the mushrooms thoroughly and cut the spring onions into 10 mm/½ in sections.

2 Heat the oil in a wok or frying-pan over high heat. When hot, add the mushrooms and stir-fry for 1 minute. Add the chicken and stir-fry for 3 minutes. Add the shrimps, spring onions and cucumber. Stir-fry over high heat for 1½ minutes and remove from the wok with a slotted spoon.
3 Add the lard to the wok. When melted, add the remaining sauce ingredients and stir them over high heat until the ingredients have blended into a bubbling sauce. Add the chicken, shrimps, mushrooms, cucumber and spring onions. Stir

over high heat for 1 minute. Serve immediately in a warmed serving dish, garnished with cucumber slices. Accompany with plain noodles if wished.

Chicken and pineapple

Serves 4-6
1.5 kg/3½ lb chicken, jointed
1 medium-sized onion, sliced
salt and freshly ground black
    pepper
3 tbls oil
100 g/4 oz Chinese celery cabbage
    (Chinese leaves) or white
    cabbage, shredded
2 stalks celery, diced
100 g/4 oz Brazil or cashew nuts,
    chopped
2 tbls soy sauce
1 tsp sugar
250 g/9 oz fresh or drained canned
    unsweetened pineapple chunks

1 Put the chicken pieces into a deep saucepan and add 600 ml/1 pt water, the sliced onion, and salt and freshly ground black pepper to taste. Bring the water to the boil, cover the pan and simmer for 1 hour or until the chicken is tender. Remove the chicken and strain and reserve 275 ml/½ pt of the cooking liquid.
2 When it is cool enough to handle, skin and bone the chicken and cut the meat into bite-sized pieces.
3 Heat the oil in a wok or large saucepan. Add the shredded cabbage, diced celery, and pieces of chicken. Sauté, stirring constantly, for 5 minutes. Then stir in the nuts, soy sauce, sugar and the reserved chicken cooking liquid. Cook, stirring, until the liquid boils.
4 Add the pineapple, bring the liquid back to the boil and cook for another 3 minutes. Serve with plain boiled rice or Chinese egg noodles.

If you substitute pineapple in syrup for unsweetened pineapple, omit sugar.

Above: *Chicken and shrimps*   Below: *Chicken and pineapple*

Chicken and beansprouts

Serves 4
3 tbls vegetable oil
250 g/9 oz fresh beansprouts
1½ tsps cornflour
1 tbls water
150 ml/¼ pt chicken stock
350 g/12 oz boneless cooked
    chicken, skin removed and cubed
1 large onion, thinly sliced
2 carrots, coarsely grated
1 small green pepper, deseeded
    and finely diced
1 clove garlic, crushed (optional)
2.5 cm/1 in piece fresh root
    ginger, finely chopped
1 tbls dry sherry
2 tsps soy sauce
salt and freshly ground black
    pepper

1 Heat 2 tbls of the oil in a wok or large frying-pan, add the beansprouts and stir-fry briskly for 1 minute.
2 Remove the beansprouts with a slotted spoon and set aside. In a jug, blend the cornflour with the water to make a smooth paste. Stir in the chicken stock.
3 Heat the remaining oil in the pan, add the chicken, onion, carrots, green pepper, garlic, if using, and ginger and stir-fry for 2-3 minutes.
4 Stir the thickened stock into the pan together with the sherry and soy sauce. Stir well to mix. Bring to the boil, stirring, and cook for 2 minutes. Taste and adjust the seasoning.
5 Return the beansprouts to the pan and heat through gently, stirring carefully.
6 Pile the mixture into a warmed serving dish, or serve straight from the pan. Serve at once.

Below: *Duck with ginger and leeks*

If fresh beansprouts are not available, use a 400 g/14 oz can. Drain and omit the initial frying.

Duck with ginger and leeks

Serves 5-6 with other dishes
4 tsps salted black beans
4 tbls vegetable oil
3 garlic cloves, roughly chopped
4 slices root ginger, cut into thin
    slivers
1 small red pepper, cut into
    matchstick strips
2 medium-sized leeks, cut into
    matchstick strips
2 tbls lard
500 g/1 lb boned smoked or cold
    roast duck, cut into matchstick
    strips
4 tbls good stock
2 tbls soy sauce
2 tbls distilled or white wine vinegar
2 tsps sugar
2 tsps chilli sauce

1 Soak the black beans in water to cover for 10 minutes and drain.

2 Heat the oil in a wok or a large frying-pan over high heat. Add the beans, garlic, ginger, pepper and leeks; stir-fry for 2 minutes, then push to sides of pan.
3 Melt the lard in the centre of the pan and add the duck and all the other ingredients and stir-fry vigorously for 2

minutes. Bring the pepper and leek mixture back into the centre of the pan and stir-fry them with the duck mixture for 1 1/2 minutes. Serve immediately with boiled rice.

Duck and walnut stir-fry

Serves 4
2 large duckling pieces
salt
1 tbls cornflour
300 ml/1/2 pt chicken stock
2 tsps soy sauce
1 tbls dry sherry
1 tbls vegetable oil
4 small onions, thinly sliced
1 clove garlic, crushed (optional)
1 large carrot, thinly sliced
2 celery stalks, sliced
4 tbls cooked peas
50 g/2 oz walnut pieces

1 Heat the oven to 180° C/350° F/ gas 4.
2 Pat the duckling pieces dry with absorbent paper, prick the skin with a fork and sprinkle with salt.
3 Roast skin side up on a rack in a roasting tin for 1 1/4 hours until cooked through (the juices run clear when pierced in the thickest part of flesh with a skewer). Remove from the oven and set aside.
4 Heat the grill to high. Strip the skin from the cooked duckling and place the skin under the hot grill until it is very crisp and deep golden brown. Remove from the grill pan and reserve.
5 Remove the duckling meat from the bones, if necessary, and cut it into matchstick strips. Set aside.
6 To make the sauce: blend the cornflour in a saucepan with a little of the stock then stir in the remaining stock, soy sauce and sherry. Bring to the boil, then simmer for 2 minutes, stirring. Cover and set aside.
7 Heat the oil in a wok or frying-pan over gentle heat. Add onions, garlic, if using, carrot and celery, and stir-fry for 3-5 minutes until lightly cooked but still crisp.
8 Stir in the peas, walnut pieces and duckling strips and cook until heated through. Stir in the prepared sauce and stir until heated through.
9 Transfer the duckling and sauce to a warmed serving dish. Crush the crisped duckling skin between your fingers or snip it with scissors and sprinkle over the duckling. Serve at once, with rice.

Above: *Duck and walnut stir-fry*

Fish and Shellfish

Crispy fish with pork and black beans

Serves 5-8 with other dishes
1 kg/2½ lb whole firm white fish,
   such as grey mullet, sea bass,
   sea trout, bream, hake, brill,
   carp or turbot
2 tbls cornflour
vegetable oil for deep-frying
5 tbls lard
100 g/4 oz fat pork, cut into 5 mm/
   ¼ in cubes
3 tbls salted black beans
2 garlic cloves, roughly chopped
3 thin slices root ginger, roughly
   chopped
3 tbls soy sauce
3 tbls tomato purée
4 tsps chilli sauce
4 tsps sugar
4 tbls good stock
5 tbls Chinese yellow wine or dry
   sherry
2 spring onions, roughly chopped

1 Scale and clean the fish thoroughly if necessary. Slash each side of the fish 6 times with a sharp knife. Mix the cornflour with 4 tbls cold water and reserve.
2 Heat 5 cm/2 in of vegetable oil in a deep frying-pan large enough to hold the fish over medium heat. Fry the whole fish for 12-13 minutes until head, tail and protruding bones are crisp and golden on both sides. Drain the fish on absorbent paper.
3 Heat the lard in a wok or a large frying-pan over high heat. When hot, add the pork and stir-fry it for 3 minutes. Add the black beans, garlic, ginger, soy sauce, tomato purée, chilli sauce, sugar, stock, wine and spring onions, stir-fry for 2 minutes or till liquid has reduced by a quarter.
4 Put the fish in the pan, spooning over sauce. Put the fish on a heated serving dish.
5 Stir the cornflour mixture with the rest of the sauce for 1½ minutes or until the sauce has reduced by one-third.
6 Pour the sauce over the fish; serve.

Stir-fried prawns in tomato sauce

Serves 2 with 1 other dish
225 g/8 oz medium-sized raw
   prawns in the shells, heads
   removed, completely defrosted
   if frozen
½ tsp salt
225 g/8 oz ripe tomatoes
5 tbls peanut or vegetable oil
4-5 garlic cloves, finely chopped
4 spring onions, cut into 25 mm/
   1 in sections, white and green
   parts reserved separately
2 tsps thin soy sauce
½ tsp sugar
½ tsp potato or tapioca flour

1 Shell the prawns.

2 Devein prawns, pat them dry with absorbent paper and sprinkle with half of the salt; this will firm them up. Leave them for about 15 minutes.

3 Put the tomatoes in very hot water for 5-10 seconds. Peel off the skin and cut them into slices.
4 Heat a wok until a wisp of smoke rises. Add the oil, and swirl it around until it is very hot. Add the garlic and half of the white part of the spring onions, stirring.
5 Add the prawns. Flip and turn them rapidly from the bottom of the wok with a wok scoop or metal spatula for 1 minute or until the prawns have curled up and turned pink. Scoop them on to a warm plate, leaving behind as much oil as possible.

6 Add the remaining white of the spring onions to the wok. Add the tomato slices and stir to incorporate the oil. Season with the rest of the salt, the soy sauce and sugar. Cover and cook over medium heat for 7-8 minutes.
7 Mix the potato or tapioca flour with 1 tbls water. Remove the cover and add the flour mixture, stirring well.
8 Return the prawns to the wok and add the green of the spring onions. Turn up the heat, stir and turn until the prawns are very hot. Scoop everything on to a warm serving plate. Serve immediately while the fragrance is at its best.

When all the flour is incorporated, beat well. Whisk in the ginger and pepper.

4 Fill a wok or frying-pan with oil to a depth of 2 cm/¾ in and put over moderate heat. When the oil is on the point of smoking, dip a few prawns in the batter: coat with batter, then drop into the oil.

5 Fry the prawns for 1 minute on each side, until the batter turns golden brown. Transfer with a slotted spoon to a serving platter; keep hot while frying the rest. Serve hot, accompanied by dips.

Fish with pepper and celery heart

Serves 2
300 g/10 oz sole or plaice fillet, skinned and cut into fairly large pieces
2 tbls dry sherry
1 tsp salt
1 tbls cornflour
2 tbls water
300 ml/½ pt vegetable oil for deep-frying
1 red pepper, deseeded and thinly sliced
1 celery heart, sliced
2 slices fresh root ginger, peeled and finely chopped
2 spring onions, finely chopped
1 tsp sugar
1 tbls light soy sauce
1 tsp chilli sauce (optional)

1 Put the fish pieces into a bowl. Pour over half the sherry, add a pinch of salt and leave to marinate at room temperature for at least 10 minutes.

2 Drain the marinade off the fish slices. Blend the cornflour and water.

3 Heat the oil in a wok or deep-fat frier to 170° C/325° F or until a cube of stale bread browns in 75 seconds. Dip the fish pieces, one at a time, into the cornflour mixture to coat well, then fry in the oil for 1-2 minutes. Drain on absorbent paper.

4 Pour off enough oil to leave about 1 tbls in the wok or pan. Place over moderate heat, then add the red pepper, celery, ginger and spring onions and stir until well coated with oil. Add the remaining salt and the sugar and continue to stir-fry for a further minute, adding a little water, if the mixture seems dry.

5 Add the reserved fish pieces, together with the soy sauce and the remaining sherry. Bring to the boil, then lower the heat and cook gently until the pan juices have almost evaporated. Stir in the chilli sauce, if using. Serve hot with noodles.

Above: *Fish with pepper and celery heart;* Below: *Stir-fried prawns in tomato sauce*

Gingered deep-fried prawns with dips

Serves 6
500 g/1 lb large prawns, fresh or frozen and defrosted
vegetable oil, for deep-frying
50 g/2 oz plain flour
¼ tsp salt
1 egg
150 ml/¼ pt water
1 tsp chopped root ginger
¼ tsp freshly ground black pepper
For the dips
tomato sauce
soy sauce
chilli sauce
English mustard

1 First make the dips. For soy-tomato dip, mix together equal quantities of tomato sauce and soy sauce. To spice it up, add a dash of chilli sauce. For soy-mustard dip, mix 1 part English mustard with 2 parts soy sauce.

2 Peel the prawns, then make a shallow cut down the centre back of each prawn and gently scrape away the black vein with a knife. Rinse prawns well, then pat dry.

3 To make the batter, sift the flour with the salt into a bowl and make a well in the centre. Beat the egg with the water, pour into the well and, using a wire whisk, gradually draw the flour into the liquid.

Vegetables

Quick-fried mixed vegetables

Illustrated on pages 328-329

Serves 4-6
6-8 large dried Chinese mushrooms
75 g/3 oz bamboo shoots, drained
1 medium-sized aubergine
vegetable oil for deep-frying
350 g/12 oz French beans, topped and tailed
3 tbls lard
2 garlic cloves, roughly chopped
4 tsps black bean paste
2 tbls soy sauce
4 tbls good stock
2 tsps sugar
1 tbls sesame oil

1 Soak the mushrooms in warm water to cover for 20 minutes. Drain the mushrooms and discard the stems. Cut the bamboo shoots and aubergine into thin 4 cm/1½ in triangular pieces.
2 Fill a small saucepan with vegetable oil about 5 cm/2 in deep and place the pan over medium heat. When the oil is hot, deep-fry the beans, aubergines, bamboo shoots and mushrooms, a few at a time, for 2½ minutes and drain thoroughly on absorbent paper.
3 Heat the lard in a wok or a large frying-pan. When hot, add the beans, mushrooms, bamboo shoots and aubergines and stir-fry them for 1½ minutes. Add the remaining ingredients and stir-fry for 2 minutes. Serve the mixture in a well-heated dish with or without rice.

Stir-fried beansprouts

Serves 2
250 g/8 oz beansprouts
2 tbls peanut or vegetable oil
1-2 spring onions, cut into 25 mm/ 1 in sections, white and green parts reserved separately
2 thin slices of fresh root ginger, peeled
¼ tsp salt
1 tbls oyster sauce

1 Do not wash the beansprouts if they are commercially sealed in a plastic container, but do refrigerate them until they are cooked. (Chilling helps assure they remain crunchy when cooked.) If the beans have to be washed, make sure you drain them well and refrigerate for 2-3 hours before cooking them.
2 Heat a wok or frying-pan over high heat until it starts to smoke. Add the oil and swirl it around. Put in the white part of the spring onion and as soon as they sizzle, add the ginger slices.
3 Add the beansprouts. Leaving the heat on high, stir-fry by sliding the wok scoop or metal spatula to the bottom of the wok and then flip and toss the beansprouts evenly and vigorously for about 2 minutes.
4 Sprinkle the beansprouts with salt towards the end of the cooking time; add the green parts of the spring onion. The beansprouts should still be crisp and crunchy, having lost only a minimum of water. Transfer them to a warm serving plate.
5 Pour the oyster sauce over, mix lightly with a pair of chopsticks or a fork and serve immediately.

Leeks with walnut and celery

Serves 4-6
25 g/1 oz margarine
250 g/9 oz leeks, cut into 5 cm/2 in lengths
1 onion, sliced
50 g/2 oz walnut pieces
4 celery stalks, chopped
250 g/9 oz Chinese celery cabbage (Chinese leaves), sliced
salt and freshly ground black pepper
a few dashes of soy sauce

1 Melt the margarine in a wok or frying-pan, add the leeks and onion and fry gently for 5 minutes until the onion is soft and lightly coloured.
2 Add the walnuts, together with the celery, and stir-fry over moderate heat for 3 minutes.
3 Stir the Chinese leaves into the pan

Below: *Mushrooms with mange-tout peas and cashews*

and cook for a further 2 minutes until the Chinese leaves begin to soften.

4 Season to taste with salt and pepper, stir in a few dashes of soy sauce and cook for a further minute. Turn into a warmed serving dish and serve at once.

Mushrooms with mange-tout peas and cashews

Serves 4
250 g/8 oz mange-tout peas
salt
250 g/8 oz button mushrooms
1 small red pepper
1 tbls soy sauce
1 tbls dry sherry
1 tsp clear honey
4 tbls sunflower oil
1 garlic clove, chopped
50 g/2 oz cashews

1 Top and tail the mange-tout peas, string if necessary and cut into 25 mm/1 in pieces. Blanch them in a large pan of boiling, lightly salted water for 1½ minutes; drain and refresh them in cold water and drain thoroughly again.
2 Trim, wipe and slice the mushrooms. Core and seed the red pepper and cut the flesh into matchstick strips. In a small bowl, combine the soy sauce, sherry and honey.
3 Heat the oil and garlic in a wok or

large frying-pan over a moderate heat. When the garlic begins to sizzle, add the sliced mushrooms and strips of pepper and stir-fry for 2 minutes. Add the cashews and stir-fry for 1 minute more.
4 Add a good pinch of salt and 4 tbls water and boil over high heat until the liquid has almost entirely evaporated. Give the soy sauce mixture a good stir and pour into the pan. Toss the vegetables and nuts in the sauce, then add the mange-tout peas and stir-fry for 1 minute. Serve immediately.

Stir-fried sweet and sour cabbage

Illustrated on pages 320-321

Serves 4-6
700-900 g/1½-2 lb Chinese celery cabbage (Chinese leaves)
4-6 tsps rice or wine vinegar
4-6 tsps sugar
4-6 tsps thin soy sauce
large pinch salt
1-1½ tsps tapioca or potato flour
4-5 tbls groundnut or corn oil
1 large or 2 small chillies, seeded and cut into thread-like strips
2-3 tsps sesame oil for sprinkling

1 Remove any tough leaves, halve the rest lengthways and slice across into 5 cm/2 in strips. Mix the vinegar, sugar, soy sauce, salt and tapioca or potato flour; reserve.

2 Heat a wok or frying-pan until hot. Add 2-3 tbls of the groundnut or corn oil and swirl it around. Add the cabbage. Going to the bottom of the wok with a wok scoop or a metal spatula, stir and

toss the cabbage continuously for 5-6 minutes. If the pieces begin to burn, lower the heat. The cabbage bulk will decrease. Transfer the cabbage to a colander and drain.
3 Wipe the wok dry and reheat it. Add the rest of the oil, swirl it around, then the chilli, stirring twice, and then the sauce. When the sauce bubbles, add the cabbage.

4 Stir and toss to let the cabbage absorb the sauce. When thoroughly hot, transfer it to a warmed serving dish. Sprinkle the sesame oil over the cabbage and serve immediately.

Stir-fried spinach

Illustrated on pages 322-323

Serves 4
500 g/1 lb young spinach
2 spring onions
3 tbls vegetable oil
3 garlic cloves
½ tsp salt
3 tbls soy sauce
20 g/¾ oz lard
3 tbls dry sherry

1 Wash the spinach thoroughly, removing any discoloured leaves and tough stalks. Cut the spring onions into 10 mm/½ in sections and the garlic into thin slices.
2 Heat the oil in a large saucepan and stir the spring onion and garlic in hot oil for 30 seconds. Add the spinach, sprinkle with salt and stir over medium heat for 2½ minutes. Add the soy sauce, lard and sherry and continue stirring for 3 minutes. Serve immediately with rice.

Foo-Yung

Prawn foo-yung

Serves 4
8 medium-sized eggs, well beaten
4 tbls soy sauce
4 tbls oil
16 spring onions, in 25 mm/1 in lengths
300 g/11 oz beansprouts
350 g/12 oz boiled shelled prawns, defrosted if frozen
spring onion flowers to garnish (see page 345)
tomato wedges to garnish
flat-leaved parsley to garnish (optional)

1 Beat the eggs with the soy sauce.
2 Heat the oil in a wok or a large frying-pan over a high heat. Add the spring onions and beansprouts and stir-fry them until the onions begin to wilt, about 2 minutes.
3 Stir in the prawns, then add the well-beaten eggs. Stir until the eggs set, then serve immediately, garnished with the spring onion flowers, tomato wedges and flat-leaved parsley, if desired.

Ham and beansprout foo-yung

Serves 4
6 eggs, well beaten
100 g/4 oz cooked ham
100 g/4 oz beansprouts
2 spring onions
1 slice root ginger
3 tbls sesame oil or corn oil
1 tbls dry sherry
1 tbls soy sauce

1 Prepare the ingredients for the filling, slicing or shredding finely.

2 Heat 2 tsps of the oil in a wok or frying-pan over fierce heat.
3 Place the filling, flavouring and liquid in the pan and stir-fry for 1 minute. Remove from heat.
4 Mix the filling with the beaten eggs. Heat the remaining oil in a pan. To make individual portions, pour one-quarter of the egg mixture at a time into a 12.5 cm/5 in pan and stir once. Or, to make one large foo-yung, pour all the egg mixture into a 25 cm/10 in pan.
5 Leave over the heat for 1 minute to allow the bottom of the foo-yung to set.

6 Place a dinner plate over the pan, and invert so the foo-yung falls on to the plate.

7 Slide the foo-yung back into the pan. Cook for a further minute.

8 To turn out, invert on to a plate. Stand the plate over boiling water to keep the foo-yung warm.

手 For spring foo-yung, fill with 50 g/2 oz beansprouts, 25 g/1 oz finely sliced button mushrooms, 2 chopped spring onions and 25 g/1 oz finely shredded lettuce.

手 For crab and ginger foo-yung, fill with 100 g/4 oz canned crabmeat, 2 chopped spring onions and 1 slice root ginger, finely chopped.

Far left: *Ham and beansprout foo-yung*; Right: *Prawn foo-yung*

Braised, Steamed and Roasted Dishes

Whereas quick-frying is used to make the most of tender cuts of meat, there are many less expensive cuts which benefit from slower cooking. This can range from quick-braising in a sauce for, say, ten minutes, to gentle, slow braising for two or three hours. The technique of steaming offers equal flexibility, according to the ingredients used. And roasting, though not used much in Chinese homes, is responsible for some of China's most succulent restaurant dishes.

Pork

Red-cooked pork with chestnuts

Illustrated on pages 322-323

Serves 4
500 g/1 lb belly of pork with skin
250 g/8 oz dried chestnuts, or
 350 g/12 oz shelled and skinned
 fresh chestnuts
125 ml/4 fl oz stock
3 tbls soy sauce
2 tsps sugar
1-2 drops red food colouring
2 tbls vegetable oil
50 ml/2 fl oz dry sherry
spring onion flowers to garnish
 (see page 345)

1 Heat the oven to 170° C/325° F/gas 3. Cut the pork into 2.5 x 5 cm/1 x 2 in pieces, retaining the skin. Drop the dried chestnuts into a saucepan of boiling water, boil for 3 minutes and drain. Mix the stock, soy sauce, sugar and food colouring together.

2 Heat the oil in a medium-sized flameproof casserole over high heat. Add the pork and cook on all sides for 3-4 minutes. Add the prepared dried or fresh chestnuts and stir them with the pork for 3-4 minutes more. Pour in the stock mixture, bring to the boil, lower the heat and simmer for 10 minutes stirring occasionally.

3 Cover and place the casserole in the oven for 1 hour. Remove the casserole from the oven, add the sherry, stir, cover and continue cooking for 1¼ hours. Serve immediately, garnished with spring onion flowers.

Streaky pork with mandarin sauce

Serves 4
1 tbls vegetable oil
500 g/1 lb lean belly of pork
 rashers (streaky pork rashers),
 rind, bones and excess fat
 removed, and cut in half across
1 large onion, sliced
300 g/11 oz can mandarin orange
 segments, drained with juice
 reserved
about 150 ml/¼ pt chicken stock
¼ tsp ground ginger
1 tbls lemon juice or vinegar
1 green pepper, deseeded and
 chopped
salt and freshly ground black
 pepper
1 tbls cornflour
2 tbls water

1 Heat the oil in a wok or large frying-pan. Add the pork and fry over moderate heat for 5 minutes, turning, until brown.
2 Add the onion to the pan and fry for a

further 5 minutes until the onion is soft. Pour off excess fat from the pan.
3 Make up the reserved fruit juice to 300 ml/½ pt with the chicken stock and pour into the pan. Add the ginger, lemon juice and green pepper and season to taste with salt and pepper. Bring to the boil, then lower the heat, cover, and simmer for 30-40 minutes until the pork is cooked (the juices run clear when the meat is pierced with a skewer).
4 Remove from the heat. Blend the cornflour with the water, then stir in a little of the liquid from the pan. Pour back into the pan and bring to the boil, stirring constantly, then simmer for 3 minutes until the liquid is thick and has a smooth consistency. Add the mandarin orange segments and stir carefully to coat in sauce.
5 Turn into a warmed serving dish and serve at once with a mixed salad and plain boiled rice.

Below: *Streaky pork with mandarin sauce*

Chinese spare ribs

Serves 4
1 kg/2 lb American-cut or Chinese
  pork spare ribs
1 tsp salt
2 garlic cloves
half a small onion
2 thin slices root ginger
4 tbls corn oil
1 tbls caster sugar
4 tbls soy sauce
3 tbls sherry
freshly ground black pepper
150 ml/¼ pt chicken stock

1 Cut the spare ribs into individual ribs by cutting between each bone with a sharp knife. Rub the ribs with salt. This will help the skin to crisp.

2 Skin and crush the garlic cloves. Peel and finely chop the onion. Chop the root ginger finely.

3 Heat the oil in a wok or frying-pan over fierce heat. Place the garlic, onion and ginger in the pan and stir-fry for a minute.

4 Add the ribs, lower the heat slightly and stir-fry for a further 5 minutes. Remove the ribs.

5 Add the sugar, soy sauce, sherry and pepper and stir-fry for 2 minutes. Return the ribs to pan.

6 Now pour in the chicken stock. Turn the ribs in the sauce until all sides are coated. Lower the heat so the liquid is just simmering. Cover the wok or, if you have used a frying-pan, turn into a heavy-based saucepan. Leave to cook gently for 20 minutes.

7 Remove the lid, turn the ribs, cover and cook for a further 10 minutes.

8 Heat the oven to 190° C/375° F/gas 5. Arrange the ribs in a roasting tin and spoon over any remaining sauce. Leave in the oven for 5-10 minutes until the surface of the ribs is dry.

卐 The spare ribs can be made as far as step 7 the day before and reheated and dried in the oven for 15 minutes just before the meal.

Marinated roast pork

Serves 6
1.4 kg/3 lb pork fillet, cut into
  5 cm/6 in lengths
3 tbls sunflower or groundnut oil
3 tbls clear honey
shredded lettuce to garnish
For the marinade
5 tbls soy sauce
3 tbls medium-dry sherry
1½ tbls brown sugar
2 cloves garlic, crushed
½ tsp freshly ground black
  pepper
½ tsp salt
½ tsp mixed dried sage and thyme
¼ tsp ground cinnamon

1 Place the pork fillet lengths in a single layer in a deep dish.

2 Beat the marinade ingredients together until thoroughly combined.

3 Pour the marinade over the pork and leave to marinate for at least 2½ hours, turning occasionally

4 Heat the oven to 220° C/425° F/gas 7. Remove the pork from the marinade with a slotted spoon, reserving the marinade. Place the pork on a rack in a roasting tin.

5 Roast the pork in the oven for 15 minutes, then remove from the oven and reduce the oven temperature to 180° C/ 350° F/gas 4. Brush the pork with the reserved marinade and the oil to coat thoroughly, then return to the oven for a further 10 minutes.

6 Just before the end of the cooking time, warm the honey in a small pan over low heat. Remove the pork from the oven, brush with the warmed honey, then return to the oven to roast for a further 5 minutes.

7 Cut the fillets into 5 mm/¼ in slices. Serve hot, garnished with lettuce.

Long-steamed pork pudding

Serves 6-8
350 g/12 oz belly of pork with the
  skin attached
350 g/12 oz minced pork
150 g/5 oz turnips
1 small aubergine
200 g/7 oz potato
1 medium-sized egg, beaten
2 tsps salt
2 tbls cornflour
2-3 fresh or dried chillies, seeded
  and chopped
2 tbls sesame sauce
2 spring onions, chopped
40 g/1½ oz lard, softened
1 tsp sugar
5 tbls soy sauce
1 medium-sized onion, thinly
  sliced
2 tbls chopped coriander

1 Cut the belly of pork into 12-16 pieces
so that each piece has skin attached. Cut
the turnips, aubergine and potato into 25
mm/1 in triangle shapes, about 10 mm/
½ in thick.
2 Add the egg, salt and cornflour to the
minced pork and mix well. Divide the
mixture in half and mix the chilli
thoroughly into one part and the sesame
sauce and spring onions into the other
part.
3 Use the lard to generously grease the
inside of a 2 L/3½ pt metal bowl or
round casserole. Put in the belly of pork
pieces, skin-side down and sprinkle the
pork with the sugar and 2 tbls of the soy
sauce.
4 Cover the pork evenly with the onion
slices and pack the potato pieces evenly
on top. Pack the pork-chilli mixture
evenly over the potato. Cover with the
turnip pieces; sprinkle with 2 tbls soy
sauce.
5 Pack the pork and sesame sauce mixture evenly on top of the turnip layer and
press down firmly. Put the aubergine
pieces on top, sprinkle with the coriander
and then the rest of the soy sauce.
6 Cover the bowl or casserole with foil
and tie it with string. Put the bowl or casserole in a wok or large, deep saucepan
and pour in water to come one-third of
the way up the pudding. Bring to the boil
and simmer for 3 hours, adding water as
necessary.
7 Turn the pudding on to a warmed
serving dish and serve with boiled rice.

Crystal sugar pork

Serves 6

1 pork knuckle or hand weighing
  about 1.4-1.6 kg/3-3½ lb
4 thick slices root ginger
2-3 spring onions, halved
  crossways
4 tbls thick soy sauce
3 tbls Shaohsing wine or
  medium-dry sherry
25 g/1 oz crystal sugar (or
  granulated sugar if
  unobtainable)

1 Pluck any hair off the hand or knuckle skin. Cut through the skin on the tender, fleshy side along the length of the bone and right down to it. This helps to keep the knuckle in shape, as well as absorbing the sauce better as the knuckle cooks.

2 Put the knuckle in a thick saucepan or an enamelled casserole and add cold water to cover. Bring the water to a boil and cook, uncovered, for 4-5 minutes so that the scum collects on the surface. Pour off the water and rinse the skin free of scum, if necessary.

3 Return the knuckle to the saucepan or casserole. (In Shanghai the knuckle is placed on a thin latticed bamboo mat inside the saucepan, which prevents the rind from sticking to the pot.)

4 Add the ginger, spring onions, soy sauce, Shaohsing wine or sherry and crystal sugar to the pot. Pour in 1 L/1¾ pt water, bring the liquid to a boil, reduce the heat and let it simmer, tightly covered, for 1 hour, loosening the knuckle skin from the bottom of the pot once during cooking.

5 Turn the pork over, checking the water level to make sure it is about one-third of the way up the pork. Replace the lid and continue to cook for another 1¼-1½ hours, moving the knuckle 2-3 times to make sure the skin is not sticking to the pot. The juice should by now be reduced to about 225 ml/8 fl oz or a little less.

6 Turn up the heat and boil to reduce the sauce for 5 minutes or until it is thick and glossy. Spoon the sauce over the knuckle several times with a long spoon.

7 Transfer the knuckle to a warmed serving dish. Discard the ginger and spring onion and pour the sauce over the pork. Serve with rice.

Left: Long-steamed pork pudding

'Lion's head' pork

Serves 4 with other dishes

450 g/1 lb Chinese celery cabbage
  (Chinese leaves)
4-5 water chestnuts, fresh or
  canned
375 g/13 oz lean pork, and 75 g/
  3 oz pork fat, coarsely minced
  together
2 tbls thick soy sauce
1 tbls Shaohsing wine or medium
  sherry
1 tsp brown sugar
2½ tbls cornflour
3 tbls groundnut or corn oil
300 ml/½ pt chicken stock
2-3 tsps potato flour

1 Wash the cabbage and shake off the water. Cut it across into 5 cm/2 in pieces and separate the crisp bottom pieces from the leafier, more delicate, top pieces.

2 If using fresh water chestnuts, wash and peel them. Chop fairly finely.

3 Put the pork in a large bowl. Add 3 tbls water and, using one hand, stir in one direction for 1-2 minutes or until the meat is smooth and gelatinous to the touch.

4 Scoop up the whole mass in your hand and throw it back into the bowl about 20 times. The stirring and throwing action makes the pork light and tender.

5 Add the soy sauce, Shaohsing wine or sherry and sugar to the meat and mix well. Stir in the chopped water chestnuts. Divide the mixture into 4 equal portions, shaping them into thick, round cakes which will be the 'lions' heads'.

6 Mix the cornflour with enough water to form a thin paste in a deep plate. Roll the 'lions' heads' in the paste to coat all over.

7 Heat a wok or frying-pan over moder-

ate heat and add the oil. As soon as the first sign of smoke appears put in the meat cakes, 2 at a time, to cook until golden-brown on all sides. Put the meat cakes on a plate, leaving the oil in the wok.

8 Add the bottom pieces of the cabbage to the oil and stir-fry them for about 30 seconds, then add the leafy pieces and continue to stir-fry them together for 1 minute. Remove from heat.

9 Transfer half of the cabbage to the bottom of a large, flameproof casserole. Place the meat cakes on top, then cover them with the remaining cabbage, scraping over the oil from the wok as well. Add the stock.

10 To cook, bring to the boil, lower the heat and simmer, covered, for 2 hours.

11 To serve, arrange the cabbage underneath and around each meat cake to give the visual effect of the lion's head with its mane. To thicken the sauce, mix the potato flour with a little water and stir into the sauce until thickened. Pour over the pork.

This dish is traditionally thought to endow those who eat it with the four things most desired by the Chinese: good fortune, prosperity, longevity and happiness.

363

Beef and Lamb

Lamb casserole

Illustrated on pages 320-321

Serves 6-8
1.75 kg/4 lb leg of lamb, boned and trimmed of fat
8 large spring onions, cut in half crossways
50 g/2 oz ginger root
1 L/1¾ pt beef or veal stock, unseasoned
3 tbls Shaohsing wine or medium-dry sherry
2 whole star anise
4 cm/1½ in piece of cinnamon stick
2 tbls thick soy sauce
1 tbls thin soy sauce
1½ tbls Demerara or light brown sugar
sesame oil to taste

1 Cut the meat into 4 cm/1½ in cubes and put them into a large, heavy sauce-pan or an enamelled casserole with the onion halves.
2 Peel the ginger root, cut it into several chunks and bang them on a board with the flat side of a meat cleaver or a rolling pin and add them to the lamb and onions in the casserole.
3 Add the stock with the Shaohsing wine or sherry, the star anise and the cin-namon stick to the lamb and bring it to a brisk boil. Remove any scum from the surface, then lower the heat and cook slowly for 1¾-2 hours. Check the liquid level occasionally and add more stock or water if necessary to ensure the meat re-mains covered.
4 Add the soy sauces and sugar and cook for another 20-30 minutes. There should be ample sauce, about 275 ml/½ pt, at the end of the cooking.
5 Remove and discard the star anise and the cinnamon. Sprinkle sesame oil on the lamb and serve warm.

Below: *Ginger beef and vegetables*

Peking beef

Serves 4
1 tbls French mustard
500 g/1 lb frying steak, trimmed of excess fat and cut into 5 x 1 cm/ 2 x ½ in slices
3 tbls plain flour
salt and freshly ground black pepper
2 tbls vegetable oil
225 ml/8 fl oz water
2 tbls soy sauce
1½ tbls light soft brown sugar
2 tsps Worcestershire sauce
1½ tbls tomato purée
1 onion, chopped
1 celery stalk, finely chopped

1 Heat the oven to 150° C/300° F/gas 2.
2 Put the mustard in a bowl, add the beef slices and stir until they are well coated.
3 Spread the flour out on a flat plate and

Above: *Peking beef*

season with salt and pepper. Dip each piece of beef in the seasoned flour until thoroughly and evenly coated.

4 Heat the oil in a wok or large frying-pan, add the beef slices and stir-fry over brisk heat for about 2 minutes, until browned on all sides. Remove from the pan with a slotted spoon and place in a shallow ovenproof dish or casserole.

5 Stir all the remaining ingredients into the fat in the pan, bring to the boil, then pour over the beef slices.

6 Stir once, cover the dish and cook in the oven for 1 hour. Remove from the oven and stir again. Return to the oven, uncovered, and cook for a further 1½ hours, stirring every 30 minutes. Serve hot, straight from the dish, with boiled rice or noodles.

✦ Instead of frying steak you can use rump steak, cooked in the oven at 170° C/325° F/gas 3 for a total time of 1½-1¾ hours. Substitute 125 ml/4 fl oz red wine for half the water. Serve with noodles.

Ginger beef and vegetables

Serves 4

25 g/1 oz margarine or butter
2 tbls vegetable oil
500 g/1 lb rump steak, fat removed, cut into 1 cm/½ in strips
1 onion, thinly sliced
250 g/9 oz carrots, thinly sliced
100 g/4 oz French beans, cut into 2.5 cm/1 in pieces
350 g/12 oz courgettes, thinly sliced
150 ml/¼ pt water
50 g/2 oz dark soft brown sugar
2 tbls cornflour
4 tbls malt vinegar
4 tbls soy sauce
1 tsp ground ginger

1 Melt the margarine with the oil in a wok or frying-pan, preferably one with a lid. Add the steak strips and fry over moderate heat for about 1 minute until

browned on all sides. Do this in batches so the meat browns evenly. Remove the steak from the pan with a slotted spoon and drain on absorbent paper.

2 Reduce the heat slightly, then add the vegetables and water and stir well. Cover with the lid or foil and cook for about 10 minutes or until the vegetables are just tender, stirring occasionally.

3 Meanwhile mix together the remaining ingredients. When the vegetables are tender, increase the heat to moderate and add the cornflour mixture to the pan. Simmer for a few minutes, stirring until thickened.

4 Return the reserved steak strips to the pan. Stir to mix with the vegetables and sauce, then heat through for 1-2 minutes. Serve at once with rice.

✦ Instead of beef you can use strips of pork or chicken, and instead of onion slices you can use spring onions, halved lengthways stand cut into 2.5 cm/1 in lengths.

Chicken and Duck

Soy-glazed chicken

Serves 6
**2 whole or 16 segments of star
  anise**
1 tsp Szechuan peppercorns
3-4 tbls corn or vegetable oil
**6 large garlic cloves, peeled and
  bruised**
**6 chicken drumsticks, 6 chicken
  wings**
225 ml/8 fl oz thick soy sauce
5 tbls soft brown sugar
**2 tbls Shaohsing wine or medium-
  dry sherry**

1 Put the star anise and peppercorns in a small saucepan. Add about 350 ml/12 fl oz water; bring to the boil. Reduce the heat and simmer for 15 minutes or until reduced by half. Strain and reserve the liquid.
2 Heat a wok or frying-pan over high heat until very hot. Add 2 tbls of the oil and swirl it around. Add 3 of the garlic cloves. When they sizzle and begin to colour, add the drumsticks. Brown for about 2 minutes, turning occasionally. Transfer to a plate and reserve. Discard the garlic.

Below: *Soy-glazed chicken*

3 Add the remaining oil to the wok, swirl around and add the remaining garlic. Put in the chicken wings and brown for 1 minute per side. Transfer to the plate, discard the garlic.
4 Lower the heat. Pour the spiced liquid into the wok, then add the soy sauce, sugar and wine or sherry. Bring the mixture slowly to the boil, stirring.
5 Return the drumsticks and wings to the wok and gradually bring the liquid to the boil. Spoon the hot sauce mixture over the chicken pieces for about 10 minutes, turning the pieces occasionally.
6 Cover the wok and simmer for about 25 minutes or until the meat is cooked, turning the pieces over halfway through. Transfer them to a warm serving platter. Serve hot, accompanied by the remaining sauce and boiled rice.

Bang bang chicken

Serves 6-8
1.7 kg/4 lb chicken
4 tbls vegetable oil
**4 tsps dried chillies, seeded and
  finely chopped**
**4 tbls sesame sauce or peanut
  butter**
4 tsps sugar
2 tbls sesame oil
4 tsps soy sauce

1 Put the chicken in a large saucepan with water to cover, bring to the boil and boil for 5 minutes.
2 Remove the skum and add 150 ml/5 fl oz water, bring back to the boil and boil for 5 minutes. Do this 2 more times adding water to cover, remove the pan from the heat and leave the chicken in the water for 10 minutes.
3 Remove the chicken from the water and insert a metal skewer deep into the flesh. If the juices do not run clear, simmer the chicken in the water for 10 minutes or until its juices run clear when tested. Reserve the stock for another recipe.
4 Cut the wings and legs from the chicken and cut the body into 4 pieces.
5 Gently strike the chicken pieces several times with a rolling pin to loosen the

meat. Remove the meat from the bones and cut it into long thin strips or shreds and arrange them on a large serving dish.

6 Heat a small dry frying-pan over low heat. Add the vegetable oil and chopped chilli and stir for 3-4 minutes.

7 Strain the oil into a small bowl and stir in the pepper, sesame sauce, or peanut butter, sesame oil, sugar and soy sauce until the mixture is well blended. Pour the sauce evenly over the shredded chicken to serve.

Peking duck

Illustrated on pages 358-359

Serves 5-6
2 kg/5 lb oven-ready duck
1 tbls sugar or clear honey
1½ tbls soy sauce
20 cm/8 in piece of cucumber
5 spring onions
Peking pancakes (see recipe on this page)
For the sauce
6 tbls soy paste
3 tbls Chinese plum sauce or plum chutney, or 2 tbls plum jam
3 tbls sugar
2 tbls sesame oil

1 Slowly pour 1 L/1¾ pt boiling water over the duck until the skin becomes almost white. Wipe the duck with kitchen paper and hang it up to dry in an airy place for 4-5 hours or overnight.

2 Heat the oven to 200° C/400° F/gas 6. When hot, place the duck on a wire rack in a roasting pan. Roast for 1 hour; do not open the oven door while the duck is cooking.

3 Mix together the sugar or honey, soy sauce and 200 ml/7 fl oz water. Remove the duck from the oven and brush with the soy sauce mixture. Return to the oven for another 20-25 minutes.

4 Slice the spring onions into 5-7 cm/2-3 in long matchstick slivers. Slice the cucumber into pieces the same length, but about three times as thick. Place the spring onion and cucumber slices on separate plates.

5 Stir the sauce ingredients together in a small saucepan over low heat until well blended and pour into a bowl. Peel the skin from the duck using the blade of a sharp knife and your thumb, as if peeling an apple. Place the skin on a serving plate. Carve the meat and place the slices on another serving plate.

6 To eat, each person takes a portion of duck skin and meat and puts it on a pancake with sliced cucumber, spring onion and sauce. The pancake is then rolled and eaten with the fingers. Provide finger bowls if wished.

Peking pancakes

Serves 5-6
250 ml/8 fl oz boiling water
250 g/8 oz flour
1 tbls sesame oil

1 Add the water to the flour; mix well, transfer the dough to a floured board

and knead. Cover with a damp cloth and leave for 30 minutes.

2 Roll the dough into a long cylinder 25 mm/1 in wide. Cut off 25 mm/1 in pieces and roll each piece into a ball. Flatten each ball into a 6-7.5 cm/2½-3 in disc.

3 Brush one side of each pancake with sesame oil and place it against the brushed side of a second pancake. Lightly dust with flour and roll out the pairs into 12 cm/5 in pancakes.

4 Heat a frying-pan over medium heat for 45 seconds. Place a pair of pancakes in the pan. When the dough begins to bubble turn over and cook for 1½ minutes.

5 Remove the pair of pancakes from the pan, gently tear them apart and pile them on a small dish. Continue until all the pancakes are cooked.

6 Before serving, place the pancakes in a steamer. Cover and steam for 5 minutes until hot.

Fish

Fish with spring onions and mushrooms

Serves 4

1 kg/2 lb red trout (or bream or mullet), cleaned and scaled, with head and tail left on
salt and freshly ground black pepper
1 tbls vegetable oil
1 bunch spring onions, halved lengthways and cut into 2.5 cm/ 1 in pieces
1 small piece fresh root ginger, finely shredded (optional)
1 small green pepper, deseeded and finely sliced
100 g/4 oz button mushrooms, very thinly sliced
2 tbls light soy sauce
2 tbls dry sherry
spring onion flowers to garnish (see page 345)
vegetable oil for greasing

1 Heat the oven to 180° C/350° F/gas 4.

Cut a piece of foil large enough to contain the fish. Grease with oil.
2 Pat the fish dry inside and out with absorbent paper and season with salt and pepper. Place on foil.
3 Heat the oil in a wok or frying-pan, add the spring onions, ginger if using, green pepper and mushrooms and stir-fry for 1 minute. Stir in the soy sauce and sherry and cook, stirring, for 1 minute.
4 Spread the mixture evenly over the fish, then seal the foil edges securely to make a neat parcel.

5 Place on a baking sheet and bake in the oven for 45 minutes or until the fish is cooked (the flesh flakes easily when pierced with the point of a sharp knife).

6 Carefully remove the trout to a warmed serving dish. Garnish the dish with spring onion flowers and spoon the mushrooms and juices alongside.

Below: *Fish with spring onions and mushrooms*

Alternatively, after transferring the fish to a warmed serving dish, pour the juices into a small saucepan, add 3 tbls fresh orange juice and 1 tbls tomato purée and heat through until bubbling, stirring constantly. Pour over the prepared fish, then garnish and serve as above.

Hunan fish steaks

Serves 4-5
700-900 g/1½-2 lb firm white fish
    such as cod, sea bass or
    haddock, skinned
2 tbls thick soy sauce
vegetable oil for deep-frying
2½ tbls chopped spring onions
2 tsps sesame oil
For the sauce
4 medium-sized dried Chinese
    black mushrooms
2 medium-sized onions, chopped
2 slices of bacon, rind removed
3 slices of root ginger, chopped
2 garlic cloves, chopped
1-2½ tbls chopped ja ts'ai (radish
    pickle)
3-4 dried red chillies
150 ml/¼ pt good stock
2½ tbls thick soy sauce
50 g/2 oz sugar
2½ tsps salt
4 tbls rice wine or dry sherry

1 Soak the mushrooms for the sauce in warm water for 30 minutes, drain and reserve them.
2 Meanwhile, clean the fish and cut into 25 mm-4 cm/1-1½ in thick steaks. Rub them with the soy sauce and leave for 15 minutes.

3 Chop the onions, bacon, ginger, garlic, soaked mushrooms (discarding the

Above: *Hunan fish steaks*

stem tips), pickle and chillies for the sauce and reserve them separately.

4 Heat the oil in a wok or deep-fat frier to 180° C/350° F; at this temperature a cube of stale bread will brown in 60 seconds. Lower the fish steaks into the hot oil, a few at a time, to fry for 2½ minutes, giving the oil time to reheat before frying the next batch. Drain the fish on absorbent paper and reserve.
5 Heat 2½ tbls vegetable oil in a wok or saucepan. Add the chopped sauce ingredients with the stock and soy sauce and

stir-fry them together for 2 minutes. Add the rest of the sauce ingredients and stir until the sauce thickens.
6 Add the fish and baste the steaks with the sauce. Cover and cook over high heat for 4-5 minutes. The sauce should be reduced by half.

7 Transfer the fish to a large serving dish and pour the sauce over it, finally sprinkling the dish with the chopped spring onions and the sesame oil. Serve immediately accompanied by a large bowl of plain boiled rice.

369

Rice and Noodles

Plain boiled or steamed white rice is the main course in a Chinese meal and provides the perfect foil to the flavours and variety of the meat, poultry, fish and vegetable dishes. Fried rice is not served as an alternative to boiled or steamed rice, but at the end of the meal or as a snack. In the north of China, where rice does not grow, noodles are an alternative to rice. In fact, all over China noodles are served at birthdays and the Chinese New Year, as the length of the noodles is said to represent long life. Like many rice dishes, noodles can form the basis of a substantial snack.

Rice

Fried rice

Serves 6
5 tbls vegetable oil
1 large onion, chopped
50 g/2 oz frozen peas
½ green pepper, deseeded and diced
50 g/2 oz lettuce, shredded
350 g/12 oz long grain rice, boiled
1 tbls soy sauce
salt and freshly ground black pepper

1 Heat 3 tbls of the oil in a wok or large frying-pan, add the onion and fry gently for 5 minutes until soft and lightly coloured.
2 Add the peas, green pepper and lettuce, stir for 1 minute, then push to the side of the pan.
3 Pour the remaining oil into the centre of the pan, heat gently, then add the rice and fry for 1 minute, stirring. Draw the vegetables from the sides of the pan into the rice and stir together.
4 Stir in the soy sauce, then add salt and pepper to taste. Remove the pan from the heat and continue to stir for a further minute off the heat. Transfer to a warmed dish.

Special fried rice with foo-yung

Serves 4
225 g/8 oz pre-fluffed long grain rice
1 tsp salt
2 medium onions
50 g/2 oz button mushrooms
5 tbls oil
4 tbls cooked peas
100 g/4 oz peeled shrimps
50 g/2 oz cooked ham
For the foo-yung
2 large eggs
1 tbls soy sauce
salt
freshly ground black pepper
15 g/½ oz unsalted butter

Above: *Special fried rice with foo-yung*

1 Put rice, salt and 550 ml/1 pt cold water into a large saucepan. Place over medium heat, bring to the boil and stir once. Cover.
2 Reduce the heat to as low as possible. Simmer for 15 minutes without removing the lid or stirring.
3 Test the rice by biting a grain. If it is not quite tender, or if the liquid is not quite absorbed, cook for a few minutes longer.
4 Remove the pan from the heat and turn the rice into a dish. Leave until cold. If cooking in advance, cover and leave in the refrigerator until needed.
5 Peel and finely chop the onions. Wipe and thinly slice the mushrooms.

6 Heat the oil in a wok or frying-pan over medium heat. Add the onions, mushrooms, peas and shrimps and stir-fry for a minute.
7 Cut the ham into small strips and add to the pan. Stir-fry for a minute to mix the ingredients. Add the rice to the pan. Stir-fry for 2 minutes, mixing well.
8 Mound the rice in a serving dish and place in a low oven to keep warm.
9 Break the eggs into a bowl. Add the soy sauce and seasonings. Beat with a fork until frothy.
10 Heat the butter in a 25 cm/10 in omelette pan over fierce heat. When it has stopped foaming, add the eggs. Stir the eggs twice and then leave to set. Heat the grill to medium.
11 When the bottom of the foo-yung

has set (after about 2 minutes), remove from the heat and place under the grill for a minute to set the top.

12 Tip the foo-yung out on to a warmed plate. Cut into strips and use to decorate the rice with a lattice pattern.

Yangchow fried rice

Illustrated on pages 370-371

Serves 4 as a main course
300-350 g/11-12 oz long-grain rice
225 g/8 oz raw prawns in their shells, fresh or frozen and thoroughly defrosted
8 tbls groundnut or corn oil
2 garlic cloves, finely chopped
1 tbls Shaohsing wine or medium-dry sherry
salt and freshly ground black pepper
4 spring onions
2 large eggs
225 g/8 oz petits pois or peas, fresh or frozen and thoroughly defrosted
225 g/8 oz cooked ham, cut into small dice
1½ tbls thick soy sauce
2-3 tbls chicken stock
1 tsp extra thick soy sauce (optional)
For the marinade
scant ½ tsp salt
2½ tsps cornflour
1 tbls egg white

1 Start a day ahead or on the morning of the day in which you intend to cook the dish. Measure the volume of the rice in a measuring jug and then use 1½ times the volume of water to cook it. Add 2 tsps oil to the water and bring to the boil. Stir thoroughly with a wooden spoon and continue to boil until all the water is absorbed, leaving only tiny droplets around the rice.
2 Reduce the heat to a minimum. Put a metal heat diffuser or an asbestos mat under the saucepan and leave the rice to

cook with the lid on for 13-15 minutes. Turn off the heat and leave the rice until ready to use.
3 Peel and devein the prawns. Rinse and drain thoroughly, then cut them into 2 cm/1¾ in pieces, if necessary. Mix the marinade ingredients together in a bowl and stir in the prawns, making sure they are evenly coated. Refrigerate them, covered, for a minimum of 3 hours.
4 Heat a wok or frying-pan over high heat until a wisp of smoke rises. Add 2 tbls oil and swirl it around. Add in the chopped garlic to the oil and, as soon as it takes on colour, add the prawns. Separate them, stirring and tossing with a metal spatula for about 30-45 seconds or until they are almost cooked and turning pinkish.
5 Splash the Shaohsing wine or sherry along the rim of the wok; as soon as the sizzling dies down, remove the prawns from the wok and reserve them. Wash and dry the wok.
6 Chop the spring onions across into thin rounds, separating the white rounds from the green ones.
7 Beat the eggs lightly with 1 tbls of the oil and a little salt. Heat a large, flat frying pan until moderately hot, add 1 tbls oil and swirl it around to cover the whole surface.
8 Pour in half of the beaten egg, reserving the rest, and tip the pan to spread the egg evenly to the edges. When firm, turn the foo-yung over with a fish slice and fry the other side for a few seconds. Put the foo-yung on a plate and slice into narrow strips.
9 Stir the cooked rice to loosen it as much as possible. Blanch the petits pois or peas in boiling salted water for 3 minutes and drain.
10 Reheat the wok over high heat until a wisp of smoke is visible. Add the remaining oil and swirl it around. Add the white rounds of spring onion to the oil. Stir twice with the spatula.
11 Pour in the remaining beaten egg, then immediately tip in all the rice. Going to the bottom of the wok where the runny egg is, turn and toss the rice, separating any lumps.
12 When the rice is thoroughly hot, add the ham, stir, then add the petits pois, stir, and add the prawns. Still stirring, add the soy sauce and the stock. Stir in the extra thick soy to give a more pronounced reddish colour, if you wish. Finally, stir in half of the foo-yung strips. Serve on a warm serving plate, with the remaining foo-yung strips and the green spring onion on top for garnish.

Fried rice with egg

Illustrated on page 344

Serves 4
350 g/12 oz long-grain rice
425 ml/¾ pt water
2 eggs
1 tsp salt
2 spring onions, finely chopped
2 tbls vegetable oil
1 tbls light soy sauce

1 Put the rice with the water in a large saucepan. Bring to the boil, stir once, then turn heat to very low and cook gently, covered, for 15 minutes or until the rice is just tender and all the liquid has been absorbed. Transfer the rice to a large plate and stir it through to separate the grains. Leave to cool 15 minutes.

2 Beat the eggs with a pinch of the salt and stir in half the spring onions.
3 Heat a wok or frying-pan for 1½ minutes. Heat about 1 tablespoon of the oil in the wok, add the egg mixture and cook over brisk heat, stirring, until very lightly scrambled. Transfer the eggs to a plate and set aside.

4 Heat the remaining oil in the wok, add the cooked rice and stir to separate the grains. Add the remaining salt with the soy sauce and the scrambled eggs, breaking the eggs up into small pieces. Stir until well blended. Pile into a warmed serving bowl, sprinkle with remaining spring onions.

Noodles

Fried rice sticks

Serves 6
450 g/1 lb rice sticks (rice noodles)
225 g/8 oz lean pork, cut into matchstick strips
225 g/8 oz raw medium-sized prawns in the shell, with the heads removed
700 ml/1¼ pt clear chicken stock
275 ml/½ pt groundnut or corn oil
100 g/4 oz spring onion, cut into 25 mm/1 in sections, the white and green parts reserved separately
50 g/2 oz Chinese chives (optional), cut into 25 mm/ 1 in sections
300 g/12 oz cucumber, cut into matchstick strips
2½ tbls thick (dark) soy sauce
For the pork marinade
¼ tsp salt
1 tsp sugar
1 tbls thick (dark) soy sauce
2 tsps Shaohsing wine or medium-dry sherry
1 tsp tapioca flour or potato flour
2 tsps sesame oil
For the prawn marinade
¼ tsp salt
½ tsp sugar
2 tsps sesame oil

1 Soak the dried rice sticks in warm water to cover for 30-45 minutes.

2 Put the pork strips into a bowl and add the salt, sugar, thick soy sauce and Shaohsing wine or sherry for the marinade. Mix the tapioca flour or potato flour with 2 tbls of water into the marinade. Leave at room temperature

for about 15 minutes, then stir in the sesame oil.
3 Wash the shells of the prawns very well before shelling them; reserve the shells.
4 Divide each prawn into 8 strips on a cutting board: hold it between the thumb and the index finger of one hand and slit it along the back in half lengthways with a knife, then quarter each of the halves. Put the prawns in a bowl and stir in the prawn marinade ingredients.

5 Bring the stock to a boil, add the prawn shells, lower the heat and simmer gently for 5 minutes. Remove all the shells with a slotted spoon and discard. Season the stock with a little salt, if wished.
6 Drain the rice sticks very well and reserve. Heat a wok or frying-pan over high heat until you see smoke rising. Pour in the oil and swirl it around. Add the white part of spring onion, stir a few times with a wok scoop or spatula and then add the pork. Turn and toss the pork in the wok for about 30 seconds, partially cooking it.
7 Add the prawns to the wok and then continue to turn and toss the mixture for another 20 seconds. Add the green part of spring onion, the Chinese chives and the cucumber. Pour in the soy sauce. Stir a few more times, then pour in the hot stock.
8 Bring everything to the boil, then add the rice sticks using a wok scoop and spatula or 2 spatulas. Return everything to the boil, then remove from the heat. The rice sticks will have absorbed most of the stock by now but will still be tender yet firm to the bite.
9 Scoop everything immediately into a

deep, warmed serving dish and serve.
✿ You can double the quantity of prawns and prawn marinade if wished.

'Ants in the tree' savoury noodles

Illustrated on pages 328-329

Serves 5-6 with other dishes
3 tbls dried shrimps
100 g/4 oz pea-starch or wheat noodles
100 g/4 oz minced pork
1 tbls sugar
2 tsps cornflour
4 tsps chilli sauce or paste
275 ml/½ pt good stock
3 tbls lard
1 chicken stock cube
3 tbls soy sauce
2 spring onions, roughly chopped

1 Soak the dried shrimps in water to cover for 20 minutes and drain well. Soak the noodles in water to cover for 10

minutes and drain well. Blend the pork with the sugar, cornflour, chilli sauce or paste and 4 tbls of the stock.

2 Heat the lard in a wok or a large frying-pan over high heat. When hot, add the shrimps and pork; stir-fry for 3-4 minutes. Add the remaining stock, the stock cube and soy sauce; bring to the boil and stir-fry for 3-4 minutes.

3 Add the noodles and spring onions, lower the heat and stir for 5 minutes.

Pork chow mein

Serves 4
225 g/8 oz Chinese noodles or spaghetti
100 g/4 oz large boiled prawns, peeled
salt and freshly ground black pepper
4 tbls vegetable oil
2 medium-sized onions, halved and sliced thinly
100 g/4 oz streaky pork, or leftover roast pork or lamb, cut into matchstick strips
3-4 large button mushrooms, cut into thick matchstick strips
3½ tbls soy sauce
3 tbls dry sherry
2 tbls butter or lard
3 large lettuce leaves, shredded

1 Boil the noodles or spaghetti in salted water for 6-12 minutes or until just tender, then drain and rinse under cold water to separate the strands. Sprinkle the prawns with salt and pepper to taste, and rub this seasoning in.

2 Heat the oil in a wok or large saucepan over high heat. Add the onion and stir-fry for 1 minute. Add the pork and mushroom matchsticks and stir-fry with the onion for 1½ minutes. Sprinkle over two-thirds of the soy sauce and stir-fry for another 1½ minutes. Turn the heat to medium.

3 Add the noodles or spaghetti to the pan and stir until all the ingredients are well mixed. Sprinkle in the rest of the soy sauce and half the sherry, reduce the heat and simmer for 2-3 minutes.

4 Heat the butter or lard in a small frying-pan over medium heat. When it just melts, add the prawns and stir-fry them for 1½ minutes. Add the lettuce and stir-fry for 30 seconds. Place the mixture from the wok in a large, deep, well heated serving dish. Put the prawns and lettuce on top and sprinkle with the remaining sherry to serve.

Above: *Fried rice sticks*   Below: *Pork chow mein*

Snacks and Sweets

The Chinese have long specialized in irresistible savoury and sweet snacks, and the Cantonese delicacies known as 'dim sum' represent the ultimate in this type of cooking. These are eaten as a light lunch anytime between mid-morning and late afternoon. The Snacks recipes in this chapter are popular examples of 'dim sum', but they are equally suited to Western eating habits. Some of the recipes in the other chapters, especially the Starters, Rice and Noodles, also make excellent snacks. The Chinese do not as a rule have desserts, but the Sweets recipes given here are typically Chinese dishes and are a good way to end a meal.

Snacks

Shanghai sweet dumplings

Illustrated on pages 376-377

Makes about 32 dumplings
225 g/8 oz glutinous rice flour
225 g/8 oz canned red bean paste
corn or vegetable oil (optional)

1 Stir 225 ml/8 fl oz cold water gradually into the flour and work it into a smooth dough. There is no need to knead.
2 Take a small piece of dough about the

size of a chestnut and shape it into a round. Press a thumb into the round.
3 Insert 1 tsp bean paste and work the

dough over the bean paste completely. Roll the dumpling between the palms to make it round. Repeat until all the dough and bean paste are used.

4 Bring 1.4 L/2½ pt of water to the boil in a large saucepan. Add about half of the dumplings, one by one, and let the water come back to the boil. Move the dumplings once or twice with a wooden spoon to prevent them from sticking to the pan.
5 Reduce the heat but continue to boil for 5-6 minutes or until the dough looks transparent.
6 Lift out the dumplings with a slotted spoon, drain them, and put them on to a warmed serving plate. Cook the rest of the dumplings in the same way, draining them thoroughly and putting them on the serving plate.
7 Serve hot as they are or, if wished, when they are drained, fry them in a little oil over medium low heat, gently stirring, until they begin to brown; this gives the sticky dumplings a delicious crisp outer coating.

The dumplings can be frozen after step 3. It takes 8-9 minutes to cook them from frozen in boiling water and, again, they can be fried if wished.

Chinese leaf salad

Serves 4
100 g/4 oz mushrooms, sliced
4 large spring onions, chopped
250 g/9 oz Chinese celery cabbage (Chinese leaves), shredded
For the dressing
4 tbls corn oil
2 tbls wine vinegar
1 tbls soy sauce

1 First make the dressing: put the oil, vinegar and soy sauce in a large bowl and beat together with a fork until well mixed.
2 Add the mushrooms and onions and toss well so that they are thoroughly coated in dressing. Cover and leave to marinate for at least 15 minutes.
3 Turn the mushroom mixture into a large salad bowl and surround with the shredded Chinese leaves. Toss together thoroughly just before serving.

Above: *Chinese leaf salad*

Tea eggs

Illustrated on pages 376-377

Serves 6
2 tbls tea leaves, either Oolong, Keemun, Orange Pekoe or Iron Goddess of Mercy
12 small eggs
spring onion flower to garnish (see page 345)
For the sauce
2 tbls thick soy sauce
¾ tsp salt
1½ tsps sugar (optional)
1 tbls medium-dry sherry
1 whole or 8 segments of star anise
25 mm/1 in cinnamon stick

1 Boil the tea in 275 ml/½ pt water for 5 minutes. Strain, discard the leaves and reserve the tea.
2 Wash the eggs carefully. Pierce each one on its rounded end with a pin to prevent it cracking.
3 Put the eggs into a large saucepan, cover them with plenty of cold water, slowly bring to the boil and boil gently for 10 minutes.
4 Drain the eggs, then submerge them in cold running water for 5 minutes.
5 Gently crack the egg shells by tapping

them with the back of a spoon or by rolling the eggs on a flat surface.

6 Put the sauce ingredients and the eggs into a large saucepan. Pour in the tea and add enough water just to cover. Bring to the boil, then simmer, covered, for 1½ hours.

7 Check the sauce occasionally and, if necessary, add more water. There should be about 150 ml/¼ pt of sauce left at the end.

8 Remove the eggs. Do not shell them until ready to serve, then garnish and accompany with the remaining sauce.

The eggs will keep in a covered container in the refrigerator for up to 2 weeks.

Lettuce parcels

Serves 6
6 large crisp lettuce leaves
2 tbls vegetable oil
4 spring onions, finely chopped
1 tsp ground ginger
1 celery stalk, finely chopped
75 g/3 oz mushrooms, finely chopped
50 g/2 oz canned water chestnuts, drained and finely sliced
100 g/4 oz long-grain rice, cooked
100 g/4 oz frozen peas, cooked and drained
1½ tbls soy sauce
1 egg, beaten
extra soy sauce, to serve

Below: *Lettuce parcels*

1 Soften the lettuce leaves by dipping in boiling water for 10 seconds. Drain on absorbent paper.

2 Heat the oil in a wok or large frying-pan. Add the spring onions and ginger and fry gently for 2-3 minutes until soft.
3 Add the celery, mushrooms and water chestnuts and fry for a further 5 minutes.
4 Stir in the rice, peas and soy sauce. Remove the pan from the heat and stir in the egg.

5 Lay the lettuce leaves out flat on a work surface. Put about 2 generous tablespoons of the mixture at the base of each lettuce leaf. Fold the leaf around the mixture and roll up to form neat parcels. Secure firmly with cocktail sticks, if necessary.

6 Place the parcels in a steamer. If you do not have a steamer, use a metal colander which fits neatly inside a saucepan (the base must not touch water). Fill the pan with boiling water, place the parcels in the colander and place the colander in the pan. Cover with foil or lid of steamer and steam for 5 minutes.
7 Remove the cocktail sticks from the parcels, if using, then place the parcels on a warmed serving dish. Serve at once, with extra soy sauce handed separately.

Sweets

Toffee fruits

Serves 4
3 bananas
1 dessert apple
1 tbls lemon juice
100 g/4 oz rice flour
75 g/3 oz plain flour
1 tbls baking powder
1 tbls semolina
1 tbls peanut oil
225 g/8 oz sugar
oil for deep-frying
1 tbls sesame seeds

Above: *Toffee fruits*
Right: *Oriental fruit salad*

1 Peel the bananas and apple and cut them into chunks. Mix the lemon juice with 1 tbls water and pour over.

3 Remove the apples and bananas from the bowl with a slotted spoon. Drain them on kitchen paper to remove excess moisture.

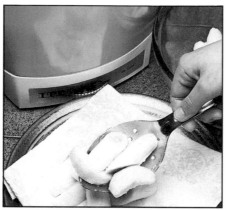

2 To make the batter, sift the rice flour, plain flour, baking powder and semolina into a bowl. Make a well in the centre, pour in 200 ml/7 fl oz water and blend to a coating consistency.

4 Combine the peanut oil, sugar and 125 ml/¼ pt water in a saucepan. Dissolve over gentle heat, and bring to the boil. Boil until pale golden. Remove the pan from the heat.

5 Heat the oil in a deep-fat frier or wok to 180-190° C/350-375° F, or until a cube of stale bread browns in 50-60 seconds. Dip the fruits in the batter and place them in the oil a few at a time. Fry for 2 minutes until golden.

6 Off the heat, add the sesame seeds to the peanut syrup. Dip the fruit fritters in the syrup, then immediately into a bowl of iced water, using two oiled spoons. Arrange the fruits on a serving platter and serve at once.

Oriental fruit salad

Serves 6
1 small honeydew or ogen melon
300 g/11 oz can mandarins, drained
50 ml/2 fl oz medium-dry sherry
600 g/1½ lb can lichees

1 Cut the melon in half and scoop out the seeds. Cut the flesh into balls using a melon baller, then put in a glass bowl.

2 Add the drained mandarins and sherry to the melon, then pour the lichees, together with their juice, into the bowl.

3 Stir the fruit gently, cover and refrigerate for 2 hours before serving.

Fresh mandarins and lichees may be used when in season, substituting the canned lichee juice with a sugar syrup: dissolve 50 g/2 oz sugar in 150 ml/¼ pt water, add the sherry, then boil for 2-3 minutes. Leave the syrup to cool completely before mixing with the fruit. The sherry in the salad may be replaced by dry white wine, or, for added zing, by an orange liqueur, such as Cointreau.

Cake Craft

Introduction

Cake making is a very satisfying occupation. It's not difficult to produce a cake that looks wonderful and tastes delicious too. You can bake a cake to suit a special occasion – or make an occasion special by serving a super cake!

Ideas for all sorts of occasions are included in this section, but if you're imaginative you'll just use them as starting points. However, do remember that while you can be as inventive as you like when it comes to decorating cakes, successful baking requires strict recipe-following and precise measurements.

This chapter tells you all you need to know about preparing and baking a variety of sponges and fruit cakes.

The Basics

Equipment

Choosing cake tins

For cakes that turn out perfectly every time, always choose the correct tin.

Most cake tins are made of aluminium or tin, as these are good heat conductors. Non-stick silicone-coated tins cost more, but they reduce the risk of the cake sticking, are easy to clean and long lasting. Some tins have loose bases, and these make the baked cake easier to remove. Heavy tins are less likely to dent or overheat.

The tin must be large enough to hold the cake mixture and allow it to rise, but not so big that the rising process is prevented. Most tins should be between half and two-thirds full before baking.

For the best results, use the size of tin specified in the recipe. But if you have a square tin and the recipe calls for a round tin, or vice versa, remember that provided the depth is the same, a square tin will hold the same amount as a round tin measuring 2.5 cm/1 in more — for example, an 18 cm/7 in square tin can be used instead of a 20 cm/8 in round tin, if preferred.

Basic bakeware

Sandwich tins are shallow and round, and are used for sandwich and layer cakes and some gâteaux. Straight-sided ones give the best results. The 18 or 20 cm/7 or 8 in sizes are the most useful – buy a pair. *Deep round and square tins* are used for rich fruit and other large cakes, and are usually about 7.5 cm/3 in deep. *Swiss roll tins* are used for cakes rolled up with a filling inside, small fancy cakes cut into shapes, and slab cakes. *Flan tins* are for baking sponge cases with raised edges which are filled with fruit and cream, for example. *Patty and bun tins* can be used for small cakes. They come in 6, 9 and 12 mould sizes, and are best lined with small paper cases so the cake mixture doesn't spread during cooking. *Small paper and foil cases* are also used for small cakes, though the cakes will hold their shape better if the cases are placed in patty tins before baking. These cases need no preparation as they peel off easily after baking. *Dariole moulds*, small flowerpot-shaped metal moulds, are used for making madeleines, as well as jellies and castle puddings. *Moules à manqué* are shallow round tins with sloping sides; the icing will thus run quickly down the sides of the turned-out cake. They are traditional for genoise sponges, but ordinary sandwich tins can be substituted.

Other equipment

Accurate measuring equipment is vital. You'll need a set of scales, a measuring jug and spoons. *Scales*: traditional balance scales with weights are, in general, the most accurate and longest lasting ones you can buy, but they are rather expensive and some people find them fiddly to use. Plastic spring balance scales with clearly marked gradations will do perfectly well; some have a mixing bowl instead of the usual pan, and an adjustable measure which is useful for weighing out mixtures of ingredients or sticky things like syrup and honey. *Measuring jug*: choose a heat-resistant one of clear rigid plastic or toughened glass with a well-defined lip. *Measuring spoons* are made of rigid plastic or stainless steel and come in sets – 15 ml/ 1 tbls, 5 ml/1 tsp, 2.5 ml/½ tsp and 1.5 ml/¼ tsp. Measuring spoons should always be used for measuring, rather than ordinary spoons, as they are more accurate.

You will also need large and small mixing bowls, one or two wooden spoons for beating and stirring, a fine sieve for sifting dry ingredients, a rubber or plastic spatula to ensure you don't waste any cake mixture when you transfer it from the bowl to the tin, a palette knife to smooth the surface of the unbaked mixture and to loosen the baked cake from the tin, a fine skewer for testing the baked cake, kitchen scissors for cutting lining paper – greaseproof

Below: *Always use the correct size tin*

paper or non-stick silicone paper – and a pastry brush for greasing tins and trays. You'll also need a wire rack for cooling.

Going electric

Although a wooden spoon will do the job accurately, a hand-held *electric whisk* is better for creaming fat and sugar, whisking egg yolks and whites and whipping cream – and also easier on the cook. Electric whisks can be used with any size bowl, and are especially handy for mixtures such as whisked sponges which are whisked over heat – but remember to keep the flex away from the hot ring or flame.

Table mixers are useful for making large cakes, royal icing and for whipping cream, but are not designed for small quantities, and you must be careful not to overbeat your mixture. With both electric whisks and table mixers, it is im-portant to have cake-making ingredients at room temperature and to warm the mixing bowl.

A *food processor* can also cream fat and sugar, mix, whisk and whip, though unless you have a special whisk attachment or a round, tilted bowl, it will not be as effective as a hand-held mixer at whisking as it doesn't get as much air in. A processor is great for all-in-one sponges, though, and is also useful for grating chocolate or citrus peel and making breadcrumbs.

Blenders can make granulated sugar into caster or icing sugar, grind or chop nuts or chop candied peel.

Microwave ovens: microwaved cakes cook in minutes rather than hours. If you are an avid microwave user, by all means adapt the recipes in this volume, following the instructions on pages 14-25 for reference. Alternatively, use the recipes on pages 58-61.

Above: *Basic equipment needn't be expensive*

Preparing cake tins

Greasing: use a pastry brush and vegetable oil or melted butter or margarine to coat the base and sides lightly and evenly. This will prevent sticking. Before using a new non-stick tin, season the tin according to the manufacturer's instructions.

Lining prevents the base and sides of the cake overbrowning, and makes turning out easier. Greaseproof paper is usually used, but it must be lightly greased first. Non-stick silicone paper doesn't need to be greased and is ideal for whisked sponges and other cake mixtures which are prone to sticking. Alternatively, whisked sponges can be baked in unlined tins which are greased, then dredged with a half-and-half mixture of caster sugar and plain flour.

Sandwich tins

1 Place the tin on a piece of lining paper and outline the base in pencil. Cut out the circle with scissors, just inside the pencil line.

2 Grease the base and sides of the tin. Position the lining paper in the tin, then grease the paper.

Deep round tins

1 Cut a paper lining for the base as for a sandwich tin. Cut a strip of paper 6 cm/2½ in deeper than the tin and allow a 2.5 cm/1 in overlap.
2 Make a 1 cm/½ in fold along one of the longer edges and crease firmly. Unfold it, then make diagonal snips to the crease at 1 cm/½ in intervals.

3 Grease the base and sides of the tin. Arrange the strip in the tin with the snipped edge flat on the base, then put the paper circle in the tin and grease it.

4 Rich fruit cakes take a long time to bake so need extra protection. Line the tin, then tie a double thickness of brown paper around the outside of the tin and stand the tin on two or three layers of brown paper on a baking sheet.

Square tins

1 Cut a paper lining for the base as for a sandwich tin. Cut a strip of paper for each side of the tin, making each strip 6 cm/2½ in deeper and 2.5 cm/1 in longer than the sides of the tin.

2 Make a 1 cm/½ in fold along one of the long edges of each strip and crease firmly. Unfold, then make diagonal snips to the crease at 1 cm/½ in intervals.
3 Grease the base and sides of the tin. Position the strips with the snipped edges flat on the base, then position the base lining paper and grease that.

Swiss roll tins

1 Place the tin on a piece of lining paper and outline the base in pencil, then cut the paper 2.5 cm/1 in out from the drawn line. Crease the paper on the line.

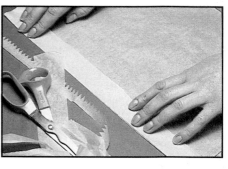

2 Grease the tin and press down the lining paper to fit. In each corner, make a cut from the corner of the paper to the corner of the crease.
3 Position the paper in the tin so that the corners overlap, then grease the paper.

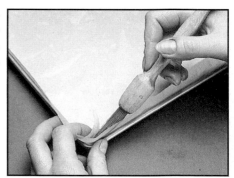

Flan tins

1 Grease the tin. Cut a circle of lining paper to fit the raised base.
2 Place the base in the tin and grease the paper.

Basic ingredients

Flour: soft plain or self-raising flour is most commonly used for cakes. If a recipe calls for self-raising and you only have plain, add 2½ tsp baking powder to each 225 g/8 oz plain flour. Always sift flour before using it – it will be easier to incorporate.

Fat: butter and block margarine are interchangeable in most cake mixtures, though butter does give a better flavour and improve keeping qualities. As a rule, these fats should be at room temperature. For a genoise sponge, however, melted, unsalted butter is a necessity. For all-in-one sponges, chilled soft tub margarine is essential for success.

Sugar: caster sugar is used in most cake recipes as its fine crystals dissolve easily. Using granulated sugar in a creamed cake won't be a disaster, but the cake will turn out slightly gritty and speckled. Soft brown sugar adds colour and a rich flavour to fruit cakes, and it can be used in all-in-ones too. Icing sugar is, as its name suggests, used in most icing recipes as its fine texture makes for smoothness.

Eggs bind cake mixtures, add colour and act as raising agents. Eggs should be at room temperature – cold eggs might make your cake mixture curdle.

Baking powder: this raising agent consists of bicarbonate of soda and cream of tartar. It reacts with liquid and heat to produce a gas which expands, making the cake rise; if you use too much, your cake will rise quickly, then collapse.

Dried fruit adds colour, flavour, texture and sweetness to fruit cakes. The traditional cake fruits are currants, sultanas, raisins, candied citrus peel and glacé cherries. Packaged fruit is usually already washed, but if you buy fruit that does need cleaning, or glacé cherries that are very syrupy, make sure you dry them thoroughly before adding them to your cake mixture – wet fruit tends to sink. Buying large pieces of candied peel and chopping them yourself will give your cake a better flavour than if you use the ready-chopped variety.

Nuts are used for flavour and texture in rich fruit cakes, and for decorating. Almonds, the most usual variety, are used whole, chopped, sliced or ground, while walnuts, hazelnuts and Brazil nuts are usually whole or chopped.

Chocolate is a favourite flavouring for both cakes and icings. Both cocoa powder and plain chocolate are used, according to the recipe, but make sure

you use a good-quality chocolate, preferably bitter or cooking chocolate. 'Cake coverings' are less expensive, but don't have the same taste.

Spices, essences and other flavourings: powdered spices are essential ingredients in rich fruit cakes. Ready-ground spices are easiest to use, though you might prefer to grind them yourself for a stronger flavour.

Vanilla, almond and other essences should always be the natural sort, usually labelled 'essence' or 'extract'. 'Flavourings' are artificial, and don't have as good a taste.

Other common flavouring ingredients for cakes and icings include grated lemon and orange zests (remember to include only the coloured, outer part – the white pith below is bitter), coffee (usually instant coffee dissolved in a little boiling water, then cooled, or coffee and chicory essence), and spirits and liqueurs. Spirits such as brandy and rum help to preserve rich fruit cakes, while liqueurs add flavour to butter creams and whipped cream for finishing a cake.

Techniques

Beat: to mix vigorously with a hand or

Above: *Ingredients for a rich fruit cake*

electric whisk, fork or spoon to incorporate air into a mixture.

Cream: to beat fat, or fat and sugar, until light coloured and fluffy.

Dredge: to sprinkle heavily with sifted flour or sugar.

Dust: to sprinkle lightly with sifted flour or sugar.

Feather: to make a pattern by piping parallel lines across an icing-topped cake, then drawing a skewer or knife through them, first in one direction, then another.

Fold in: to add one mixture to another which already has air incorporated in it by cutting in with a spatula or metal spoon, making a figure-of-eight motion and working very lightly.

Glaze: to give a shiny appearance by brushing with liquid – sieved apricot jam is often used for glazing cakes.

Rub in: to mix fat into flour by rubbing them together between cool fingertips, lifting the mixture while rubbing to incorporate as much air as possible.

Sift: to shake flour, icing sugar, etc., through a sieve to remove lumps and add air.

Whip: to beat air into a substance with a hand or electric whisk.

Steps to a perfect cake

Before you begin
1 Read through the recipe carefully.
2 Assemble all the equipment you'll need and prepare the tin or tins so there won't be any delay between mixing and baking.
3 Decide whether you are working in metric or imperial measures, then stick to that system. Don't mix the two, as they are not exact equivalents and proportions will differ.
4 Assemble all your ingredients and weigh and measure them accurately (extra important in baking!). If necessary, remove eggs and fat from the refrigerator beforehand, to allow them to come to room temperature.
5 Before you start mixing the cake, heat the oven to the recommended temperature.

Baking the cake
1 Put the cake into the oven as soon as possible after it has been mixed, otherwise it will not rise properly.
2 Place the pans as near the centre of the oven as possible (unless the recipe states otherwise). If necessary, place the pans on two shelves, but not directly over each other – and don't let them touch each other or the sides of the oven. If you have to use two shelves, switch the tins over once the cakes have set, about two-thirds of the way through baking.
3 Don't open the oven door unless it's absolutely necessary. If you do, close it carefully – don't slam it.

Testing for doneness
Test for doneness at the end of the minimum recommended time. If you open the oven door too early, before the cake is set, the sudden draught of cold air may make it sink.
Small cakes and shallow sponges: press the top lightly in the centre. The cake should feel springy and there should remain no impression when you lift your fingertips.
Large, deep cakes: check that the cake is just shrinking from the sides of the tin, then insert a warmed, thin skewer into the centre. If the cake is done, the skewer will come out clean, with no uncooked mixture clinging to it.
Rich fruit cakes: use the skewer test, and also lift the cake close to your ear. A continuous sizzling sound means that it is not yet cooked.

Cooling the cake
1 Leave the cooked cake in the tin for a few minutes so that it can shrink slightly from the tin and make turning out easier. Leave whisked, creamed and genoise sponges 1 minute, all-in-ones and other large cakes 3-5 minutes, rich fruit cakes 30 minutes, unless the recipe specifies otherwise. If the cake shows signs of sticking, run a narrow palette knife around the sides of the tin to loosen it.
2 After turning out, peel off the lining paper carefully and turn the cake right side up. Leave it to cool on a wire rack so the air can circulate freely; this will prevent the cake from becoming soggy.

Storing the cake
1 Don't store a cake until it is completely cold, or condensation will make it soggy.
2 Keep cakes which are filled or decorated with cream in the refrigerator.
3 Keep other cakes in an airtight container in a cool place. A piece of apple in the container with an unwrapped cake will help keep the cake moist.
4 Wrap rich fruit cakes in foil before storing.
5 Never store cakes in the same container as biscuits, or the biscuits will soften.
Storage times: cakes stored according to these rules should keep as follows:
Fatless whisked sponges: best eaten the same day
All-in-one sponges: 3 days

Above: *A sponge flan case filled with fresh fruit and whipped cream*

Creamed sponges: 3-4 days
Genoise sponges: 2-3 days
Rich fruit cakes: several months.

Freezing
1 Most cakes – especially undecorated ones – freeze very well, though rich fruit cakes keep so well at cool room temperature that freezing is usually not necessary.
2 Swiss rolls should be rolled in cornflour, not sugar, if they are to be frozen without filling.
3 Don't fill cakes with jam before freezing – it will soak into the cake.
4 Wrap plain cakes with freezer film or foil between the layers.
5 Open-freeze iced cakes until the icing has set, then wrap airtight and pack in rigid containers to protect the icing.
6 Pack small cakes in one layer in a rigid container, then overwrap with foil.
7 Freeze plain cakes for up to 3 months, iced cakes for 2 months.

Defrosting
1 Defrost plain cakes in their wrappings at room temperature for 1-2 hours for layers, 3-4 hours for large, deep cakes. Let them defrost completely before icing and decorating.
2 Unwrap iced cakes before defrosting, then defrost at room temperature for up to 4 hours.

Using the recipes

- All spoon measurements level.

- Use size 3 (medium) eggs unless the recipe states otherwise.

- Use either the metric or the imperial measures when following a recipe; don't mix the two.

- When a cake recipe refers back to one of the basic recipes in Chapter 1, method, size of tin and baking time and temperature remain the same unless otherwise stated.

- Read Chapters 1 and 2 before you begin baking.

Basic all-in-one sponge

Makes a 20 cm/8 in cake
225 g/8 oz self-raising flour
1½ tsp baking powder
225 g/8 oz caster sugar
225 g/8 oz soft tub margarine, chilled
4 eggs

1 Heat the oven to 170°C/325°F/gas 3 Prepare a deep 20 cm/8 in round tin.
2 Sift the flour and baking powder into a large, warmed bowl. Add the remaining ingredients. Using a wooden spoon, beat for 2 minutes until slightly glossy and lighter in colour.

3 Scrape the mixture into the prepared tin with a spatula, level the top and bake for 1-1½ hours or until the cake tests done.
4 Allow the cake to cool in the tin for 3 minutes, then turn out on to a wire rack. Remove the tin, peel off the lining paper and leave the cake to cool completely.

Simple all-in-one fruit cake

Makes an 18 cm/7 in cake
350 g/12 oz self-raising flour
175 g/6 oz soft tub margarine, chilled
175 g/6 oz soft brown sugar
3 eggs
100 g/4 oz dried apricots, chopped
175 g/6 oz sultanas
100 g/4 oz glacé cherries, halved

1 Heat the oven to 170°C/325°F/gas 3. Prepare a deep 18 cm/7 in round tin.
2 Sift the flour into a large, warmed bowl. Add the remaining ingredients. Using a wooden spoon, beat for 2-3 minutes until slightly glossy and lighter in colour.
3 Scrape the mixture into the prepared tin with a spatula, level the top and bake for 1½ hours or until the cake tests done.
4 Allow the cake to cool in the tin for 3 minutes, then turn out on to a wire rack. Remove the tin, peel off the lining paper and leave the cake to cool completely. This cake is ready to eat at once.

Genoise sponge

Makes a 22 cm/8½ in cake
50 g/2 oz butter
100 g/4 oz plain flour
3 large eggs
2 large egg yolks
100 g/4 oz caster sugar
1 tsp vanilla essence

1 Heat the oven to 180°C/350°F/gas 4. Prepare a 22 cm/8½ in sandwich tin by brushing with melted butter, lining the base and greasing the paper, then lightly dusting the base and sides of the tin with flour.
2 Clarify the butter: put it in a small, heavy-based saucepan and melt it over very low heat. When the butter foams, allow the foam to fall gently to the bottom of the pan. Then pour off the clear oil from the top into a small bowl, being careful not to disturb the white sediment.
3 Sift the flour three times on to greaseproof paper.
4 Choose a bowl of 1.4 L/2½ pt or larger capacity in which to whisk up the cake and a large saucepan over which it will fit firmly. Pour 5 cm/2 in water into the pan and bring to the boil. Reduce the heat until the water is barely simmering.
5 Add the eggs and egg yolks, sugar and vanilla to the bowl, set it over the simmering water and whisk until very thick, light and lukewarm (10 minutes if using an electric mixer at high speed, longer if you are using a hand whisk).

Below: *Basic all-in-one sponge*

6 Remove the bowl from the heat. Stand it on a cool surface and continue to whisk until the mixture leaves a distinct trail on the surface when the beaters are lifted and the mixture has cooled (5 minutes if using an electric mixer at high speed, longer with a hand whisk).

7 Resift the flour a little at a time over the egg mixture, folding it in lightly but thoroughly with a large metal spoon.

8 Add the cool clarified butter to the batter, a spoonful at a time, continuing with the folding motion until it has been completely absorbed. Work as lightly as you can.

9 Pour the batter into the prepared tin and bake for 25-30 minutes or until the cake tests done.

10 Allow the cake to cool in the tin for 1 minute, then turn out on to a wire rack. Remove the tin, peel off the lining paper very carefully and leave the cake to cool.

Creamed sponge

Makes two 18 cm/7 in layers
175 g/6 oz self-raising flour
175 g/6 oz butter or block
margarine, at room temperature
175 g/6 oz caster sugar
3 eggs
about 2 tbls milk, if necessary

1 Place the shelf above the centre and heat the oven to 180°C/350°F/gas 4. Prepare two 18 cm/7 in sandwich tins.

2 Sift the flour into a bowl and reserve.

3 Place the fat and sugar in a large bowl and cream with an electric whisk until light and fluffy. Alternatively, cream the fat until light with a wooden spoon, then add the sugar and continue creaming until light and fluffy.

4 Whisk the eggs lightly, then beat into the mixture, a little at a time, beating well after each addition. If the mixture shows signs of curdling, add a spoonful of flour and beat it in.

5 Fold in the flour, a third at a time, adding milk if necessary to make a soft dropping consistency. Divide the mixture equally between the prepared tins and level the tops with a palette knife.

6 Bake for 25-30 minutes or until the cakes test done.

7 Allow the cakes to cool in the tins for 1 minute, then turn out on to a wire rack. Remove the tins, peel off the paper and leave the cakes to cool completely.

Whisked sponge

Makes two 20 cm/8 in layers
75 g/3 oz plain flour
3 large eggs
75 g/3 oz caster sugar

1 Heat the oven to 180°C/350°F/gas 4 and prepare two 20 cm/8 in sandwich tins. Half fill a large saucepan with water, bring to the boil, then remove from the heat.

2 Sift the flour twice and reserve. Place the eggs and sugar in a large bowl over, but not touching, the hot water.

3 Whisk the eggs and sugar together with a balloon, rotary or electric whisk until the mixture is very thick, light in colour and lukewarm.

4 Remove the bowl to a cool surface and continue whisking until the mixture leaves a distinct trail when the beaters are lifted.

5 Quickly but carefully fold in the flour, a quarter at a time, until it has all been incorporated.

6 Pour the mixture into the prepared tins and bake for 25-30 minutes or until the cakes test done.

7 Allow the cakes to cool in the tins for 1 minute, then turn out on to a wire rack. Remove the tins, peel off the paper and leave the cakes to cool completely.

Rich fruit cake

Makes a 20 cm/8 in cake
450 g/1 lb currants
200 g/7 oz sultanas
200 g/7 oz raisins
150 g/5 oz glacé cherries
75 g/3 oz mixed candied peel
75 g/3 oz blanched almonds
350 g/12 oz plain flour
pinch of salt
½ tsp ground mixed spice
½ tsp ground cinnamon
275 g/10 oz butter or block
margarine, at room temperature
275 g/10 oz soft brown sugar
5 large eggs
1-2 tbls brandy or rum
brandy, rum or sherry, for
enriching (optional)

1 Prepare a deep 20 cm/8 in round tin. Heat the oven to 150°C/300°F/gas 2.

2 Wash and dry the currants, sultanas and raisins, if necessary. Wash, dry and halve the cherries. Scrape the sugar from the candied peel caps and snip the peel (or use ready-chopped mixed peel).

together, then add to the creamed mixture alternately with the flour mixture, beating well after each addition.

3 Chop the almonds. Sift the flour, salt and spices into a bowl.

4 Place the fat and sugar in a large bowl and cream with an electric whisk until light and fluffy. Alternatively, cream the fat with a wooden spoon, then add the sugar and continue creaming until light and fluffy.

5 Beat the eggs and brandy or rum

Below: Making a rich fruit cake

6 Beat in the fruits and nuts. Transfer the mixture to the prepared tin. Level the top with a palette knife and make a slight hollow in the centre to prevent the cooked cake forming a peak.

7 Stand the tin on two or three layers of greaseproof or newspaper on a baking sheet and bake for 3½ hours or until the cake tests done, covering the top with

greaseproof paper or foil to prevent overbrowning.

8 Allow the cake to cool in the tin for 30 minutes, then turn out on to a wire rack. Remove the tin and leave the cake to cool completely in its lining paper.

9 The cake is best left to mature for 2-3 months before eating. Leave in its lining paper, wrap in foil and store in an airtight tin. To enrich the cake, prick the surface and brush with a little brandy, rum or sherry every week until the cake is needed for icing.

The Finishing Touches

*Almost all cakes look better for being decorated in some way.
There are many ways to finish a cake; adding a dusting of icing
sugar or a generous dab of whipped cream will only take a
minute but can make all the difference.*

*When you're feeling more ambitious, or for a special
occasion, make up a batch or two of icing, flavoured and
coloured to match or contrast with your cake. Simply spread it
over your cake and add a few bought decorations, or try your
hand at piping an attractive design.*

Decorating your Cake

Now that you've mastered the art of cake baking, it's time to learn how to add the finishing touches.

Preparing a cake for decorating

An extra bit of care in preparing the cake before you fill and decorate it makes all the difference between an adequate result and a simply splendid one.

The first rule is to make sure that the cake is completely cold. Any icing applied to a warm cake will melt. Bear in mind that it is not advisable to decorate a cake which is only just cold, because it tends to be too soft to handle. Purists insist that the cake should be at least 12 hours old, but this is a matter of convenience – and won't apply if you're decorating a whisked sponge.

The second rule is that the surface of the cake for icing must be level. It's difficult to ice a cake with a peaked surface; it also looks unsightly. For large cakes, place the cake on a level surface. Slice the 'peak' from the surface of the cake horizontally with a long-bladed sharp knife, using a sawing motion. Brush away any loose cake crumbs using a pastry brush. Repeat, if there is still a peak, until the cake is level.

Cakes baked in sandwich tins can simply be turned upside down. If they are very peaked, though, follow the procedure for larger cakes.

Place the cake on a wire rack before you ice and decorate it, so you can move it easily once it's finished.

Fillings

Unless your cake is a particularly buttery one, you'll probably want to give extra flavour and moistness to a large basic sponge by adding a filling. You can use either two sandwich layers or one deep cake, cut in half:

1 Place the cake on a wooden board and crouch down so your eye is level with the cake. Insert the tip of a large knife with a serrated edge into the

centre. Turn the cake, keeping the knife straight and steady, and cut with a sawing action.

2 Separate the halves, inverting the bottom half so the cut side is on the plate. Spread with filling and replace the top half.

Jam is probably the most popular filling (you'll need about 3 tbls for an 18 cm/7 in cake), but there are lots of exciting and equally quick alternatives. Try some of the following:

● thick honey, marmalade or lemon curd
● any soft thick fruit purée, such as apple
● cream or curd cheese mixed with chopped pineapple or grated orange or lemon zest
● two parts chocolate to one part butter, melted together
● whipped cream on its own, or spread on top of jam, or mixed with orange or grapefruit segments, or flavoured with a little rum
● any of the butter creams in this chapter make excellent fillings, as does Fudge icing (page 402).

Above: A pretty pattern made with icing sugar and a wire rack

Decorating with icing sugar

Perhaps the simplest way to decorate a sponge is to dust it evenly with icing sugar. Or make the icing sugar look like

lace by placing a doily on top of the cake and sifting icing sugar over it. Then gently lift the doily from the cake.

Decorating with cream

Whipped cream – sweetened and flavoured, if you like – makes a simple but delicious cake topping or filling. It can also be piped. It should be whipped until it is stiff enough to leave a trail and will slowly drop off the whisk.

Above: *A sponge decorated with apricot halves, cream and angelica*

Decorating with almond paste

Almond paste is traditionally used to cover rich fruit cakes before applying royal icing. It makes a smooth base on which to apply the icing, and also adds richness and flavour to the cake. It can be bought, but the homemade version will taste better and is easy to make – the important thing is not to overwork it or it will become oily. It must be applied over a thin layer of apricot glaze.

Coating a cake with almond paste

1   With a piece of string, measure the outside edge of the cake. With another piece, measure its depth.
2   Cut the top of the cake level, if necessary. Turn it over.
3   Cut off two-thirds of the almond paste and roll it to a rectangle half the length of the string and twice the depth of the cake. Halve it lengthways.
4   Brush each strip with warm apricot glaze, then roll the cake on the strips to cover the sides. Neaten the joins.
5   Roll out the remaining piece of almond paste to fit the top of the cake. Brush the cake top with glaze, then place the almond paste on top, lifting it with a rolling pin. Trim away any surplus.
6   Brush the rolling pin with icing sugar and roll it gently over the top of the cake to smooth the surface and help the almond paste to adhere.
7   Run a straight-sided jam jar around the edges of the cake. Leave the cake to dry out, lightly covered, for at least 24 hours – a week is better – before icing it.

Making almond paste decorations

Use food colourings to make leaves, flowers, fruit, letters, etc., from leftover almond paste. Divide the paste into appropriate amounts and colour each by working in small amounts of colouring with your fingers, until you reach the desired shade – deep colours look best.

1   For holly leaves, draw a leaf on a card, cut it out and use it as a template to

cut shapes from green paste. Mark veins with a knife. Alternatively, cut out small rounds with a plain cutter, then cut away the edges with a smaller cutter. For holly

berries, roll small balls of red paste between your fingers.
2   For candles, cut candle shapes from red paste and use yellow for the flames.

3   For bells, cut out templates from a card. Assemble small bells in bunches: large ones can be used on their own.

Icing your Cake

Glacé icing

Glacé icing is simple to make and very useful. Use it on large and small sponge cakes for a crisp, smooth glaze.

Covering a cake with glacé icing
1   Place the cake on a wire rack with a plate underneath to collect any drips.
2   Pour the icing on to the centre of the cake and spread it to the edges with a palette knife, allowing it to run down the sides. Fill any spaces with surplus icing from the bowl or plate, making sure you don't include any crumbs.
3   Add decorations such as nuts and silver cake balls when the icing has stopped flowing and it has a slight skin, but before it has set completely. Leave for 1-2 hours to set.

Glacé icing decorations
Using two contrasting colours, you can make easy but very effective decorations. Cover the top and sides of a cake in one colour. Working quickly so the icing doesn't have time to harden, pipe lines of contrasting, slightly thinner icing as below.
For feather icing, pipe parallel lines across the cake, then turn the cake and draw a thin skewer across the lines in alternate directions, wiping the skewer clean each time.

For a cobweb, pipe glacé icing in a spiral on the top of the iced cake in a contrasting colour, starting in the centre, then draw a skewer into and out from the centre alternately to form the pattern of a spider's web.

Butter icing and Crème au beurre

Butter icing and Crème au beurre are richer and softer than glacé icing, and easy to spread. Crème au beurre has a mousse-like texture and is even richer than butter icing, though the simpler butter icing can be substituted for it. Both are used for covering and filling cakes and for piping.

Covering a cake with butter icing or crème au beurre
1   First apply icing to the sides. Spread it fairly thickly with a palette knife, moving it backwards and forwards to eliminate any air bubbles, then smooth the surface, if wished, or use the knife or the tines of a fork to make patterns.
2   Apply the remaining icing to the top and finish in the same way.

Decorating the sides of a cake
1   Sprinkle chopped nuts, chocolate vermicelli, grated chocolate or desiccated coconut on a large sheet of greaseproof paper.
2   Ice the sides of the cake, or brush them with apricot glaze, then roll in the decorations, holding the top and bottom of the cake. For a square cake, press one side at a time into the decorations.

Fudge icing and Royal icing

Fudge icing makes a delicious cake covering and filling that sets to a glossy finish.
   Royal icing is traditionally used, over a layer of almond paste, for rich fruit cakes for weddings, Christmas and other special occasions. It makes an ideal surface for piping and other decorations as it sets very hard.

Rough icing a cake
1   Anchor the cake to a board with a dab of icing, making sure it's centred. Put all the icing on top of the cake, then spread it over the top and sides with a palette knife, working backwards and forwards to burst any air bubbles and making sure the almond paste is completely covered.
2   Using the flat side of the knife blade or the back of a small metal spoon, pull

the icing up in peaks. Leave it to set for at least 24 hours before adding decorations and cutting, though the peaks may be topped with silver cake balls when still wet, to add sparkle to the cake.

Flat icing a cake
Flat icing takes time and practice but is very rewarding to achieve. Keep the

icing covered so it doesn't dry out.

1 Anchor the cake to a board with a dab of icing, centring the cake on the board. Put about half the icing on top of the cake. Using an icing ruler or palette knife, spread the icing over the surface, working backwards and forwards to burst any air bubbles.

2 With a palette knife, scrape away any icing that has run down the sides, being careful not to get crumbs in it. Return the surplus icing to the bowl.

3 Holding your ruler at an angle of 30°, draw it steadily towards you so it scrapes across the icing, leaving a smooth surface. Repeat if the icing is not perfectly smooth, turning the cake through 90° and adding a little more icing, if necessary. Scrape any icing off the sides and leave the cake to dry overnight.

4 Place the cake and board on a turntable. Spread the remaining icing round the sides of the cake, working it back and forth. When there are no more air bubbles, hold a plain-edged scraper or palette knife in one hand against the side of the cake and revolve the turntable away from you to smooth the surface. Lift the scraper away carefully. Remove any surplus icing at top and bottom with a palette knife and leave to dry out for at least 24 hours.

Below: *A rough-iced Christmas cake*

5 Smooth out any imperfections and rough edges with fine sandpaper, then brush with a clean pastry brush to remove any icing dust.

6 For a really professional finish, re-ice the cake with a second batch of icing with an extra egg white added for a thinner coating (it should be a thick pouring consistency that will leave a trail). Leave to set for 1-2 days.

All about piping

Piping equipment

The only special tools you need are a piping bag and a selection of nozzles. *Piping bags* can be made at home from greaseproof paper.

1 Cut a 25 cm/10 in square of paper and fold diagonally. Holding the triangle so the base line is facing away from you, bring the left-hand corner of the base up to meet the top of the triangle, twisting it.

2 Holding the two points at the top together, wrap the right-hand corner up and around the back so it meets the top of the triangle to form a cone.

3 Fold the three corners towards the inside of the cone.

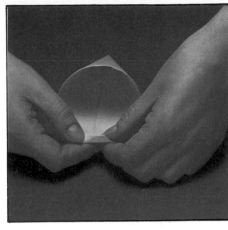

4 Cut off the point of the bag to fit the chosen nozzle, then slip this into the bag so it points out of the bottom.

5 To fill the bag, hold it in one hand at an angle, then fill with a teaspoon, not more than half full. Fold the top of the bag down to secure it.

You can also buy nylon, cotton or plastic piping bags. To fill one of these:

1 Slip the chosen nozzle into the bag, so that it projects through the hole at the point of the bag.

2 Place the assembled bag inside a tall jar, nozzle end first. Fold the rim of the bag over the rim of the jar and half fill the bag with icing.

3 Fold over the top of the bag and twist, to force out any trapped air.

The main difference between a bought piping bag and a greaseproof paper one (which is equally as good and less expensive) is that a paper piping bag takes slightly less icing and can only be used once, for one batch of icing.

If you are using different coloured icings for one cake, you must make several greaseproof paper piping bags. It is essential to make them all before you start, though, making sure that you have the correct size of nozzle in each. Bought piping bags can be washed and dried if more than one colour icing is being used. This can, however, be a time-consuming process.

Icing pump: instead of a piping bag you may prefer to use an icing pump. This resembles a syringe and is much cleaner to use than a bag once you have acquired the knack; follow the manufacturer's instructions for assembly and use. However, a pump is suitable only for thick icings.

Nozzles: a greaseproof paper piping bag can be used without a metal nozzle for simple designs – simply snip off the pointed end of the bag. How much you cut off from the tip of the bag will determine the size of the thread of icing. Always cut away a little less than you think you need, to be on the safe side. If the hole is not big enough, you can always cut off more.

For any other bag a nozzle is essential. There are numerous shapes of nozzle available but, to begin with, three basic shapes are adequate. Choose two plain (or writing) nozzles, two star nozzles and a shell nozzle. With these three you can produce a wide range of designs. Make sure you clean your nozzles carefully every time you use them.

Other equipment you may need for piping includes small bowls for holding small quantities of different coloured icings, a spatula for scraping all the icing out of a bowl, and a damp cloth to cover the bowl of icing to prevent it from drying out while you work.

How to pipe

Piping requires a light yet firm hold and a very steady touch. It's a good idea to practise on a sheet of greaseproof paper first.

Hold the bag so that one hand secures the twist at the top of the bag ready for squeezing. Leave the other free for guiding the bag as you work – start by practising the simple designs then gradually progress to more complicated patterns. The same technique applies to all forms of piping whether you are using icing or cream.

Piping with a plain nozzle

Plain nozzles are used for straight lines, wavy lines, writing, dots and outlining run-outs. They come in many sizes, but a fairly fine and a medium size are good ones to start with, then as you become more adept at the art of piping you can increase your stock of plain nozzles.

To pipe straight lines, hold the bag at a 45° angle. Squeeze out just enough icing to touch the surface of the cake. Raise the nozzle slightly from the cake.

Keeping the pressure on the bag even, direct the sagging line of icing in the direction you want it to go. To finish the line, touch the surface gently with the nozzle and release the pressure.

For writing, try piping capital letters first. Once this has been mastered, you can progress to script. Before writing on the cake, write the words on a piece of greaseproof paper, the same size as the top of the cake.

Lay the paper on top of the cake. Using a pin, prick through the paper into the icing so that you can see the design on the surface of the cake.

With a medium nozzle, follow the pinpricks, using the same technique as for straight lines.

For wavy lines, work as for straight lines, moving the nozzle to and fro.

Dots make an effective border around the top or sides of a cake (*see illustration page 403*). The size of the dot depends on the width of the nozzle. To pipe a dot, place the tip of the nozzle on the surface of the cake and hold the bag upright.

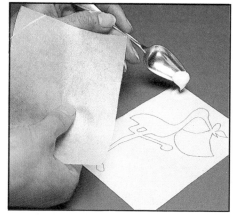

Squeeze the bag gently and at the same time lift the nozzle slightly. Use a quick down and up movement.

Run-out designs are made from royal icing. First draw the shape, letter or number you want on a piece of card, keeping it fairly simple with clean lines. Cut a piece of non-stick silicone paper to cover the card and stick in place with a spot of icing at each corner.

Trace the outline of the design in royal icing using a plain nozzle.

Thin the remaining icing slightly with beaten egg white; you might want to add a little food colouring too. Put this into a greaseproof paper piping bag without a

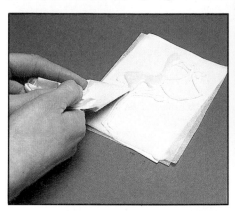

nozzle. Cut off the tip and flood the icing into the outline – it will run smoothly into place. Leave to set for 2-3 days.

Carefully remove the paper from the card. Very cautiously peel the paper

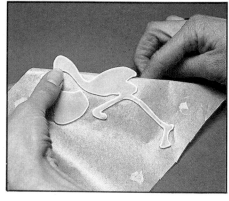

away from the shape and stick it on the cake with a little thin icing. (Run-outs can be stored, wrapped in tissue paper in an airtight container, for several months.)

Piping with a star nozzle

This nozzle is used for stars, rosettes and shells, among other decorations. The number of points to the star may vary but this will not affect the way you use the nozzle.

For stars, hold the bag vertically, just above the surface of the cake. Using short squeezes, press out icing until a star is formed, then lift off quickly.

Rosettes are formed in the same way as stars, but the nozzle is moved in a circular movement as you squeeze the bag, gradually releasing pressure as you move. Lift the tip up and away gently.

Piping with a shell nozzle

This is used to make a shell border around the top edge of a cake, or the bottom edge where it meets the cake board. It will make a fatter shell than the star nozzle, as it has more ridges.

Hold the bag at a 45° angle with the nozzle close to the cake. Press a blob of icing on to the surface.

Pull the nozzle down and away sharply to taper the end of the blob.

Pipe the next shell on the pointed end of the previous shell, and continue piping to form a border.

About chocolate

Either plain or milk chocolate can be used for cake decorations.

To melt chocolate: the simplest way to melt chocolate is to break it into a heatproof bowl and place it over a pan of barely simmering water. The bowl should not touch the water. Heat gently until melted. Alternatively, use a double boiler.

It is best not to stir until the chocolate has almost melted and then only gently as it can become granular.

Decorating with chocolate

Chocolate rose leaves: melt chocolate in a heatproof bowl. Choose even-sized rose leaves and wash and dry them gently. Using fingers or tweezers, put one leaf at a time, shiny side up, on top of the melted chocolate. Press very lightly into the chocolate to coat the underside only. Carefully move the leaf to the side of the plate and draw it across the edge to

remove excess chocolate. Place the coated leaves, chocolate sides up, on greaseproof paper. Put in a cool place to set – not the refrigerator as this will give the leaves a 'bloom'. Once the chocolate has set, carefully peel off the leaves.

Caraque or scrolls: spread melted chocolate thinly on an oiled, smooth surface (marble is best). Leave until hard, then shave away from you with a sharp knife

held lengthways at an angle. The long curls look spectacular arranged on top of

a gâteau, radiating from the centre and dusted with a little icing sugar before serving.

Whole shapes: place a piece of greaseproof paper on a work surface. Carefully spread over a thin, even layer of melted chocolate. Allow the melted chocolate to set. Cut the sheet of chocolate into shapes with a knife or metal biscuit cutters.

Piping chocolate: put a little melted chocolate into a paper piping bag and cut a small hole at the tip end. Melted chocolate sets quite quickly, so make a few small piping bags and use only a little chocolate at a time, keeping the rest over a pan of hot water. Place greaseproof paper over a drawing of the shape then pipe around the outline and/or fill in the centre.

Straight, criss-cross or curly lines can be piped directly on to all types of cakes.

To make shell or star borders, thicken the chocolate slightly with 1-2 drops of glycerine so that it will hold its shape. Stir until the chocolate thickens, then spoon it carefully into a piping bag which has been fitted with the correct nozzle and pipe the border in the normal way.

Chocolate curls: pull a vegetable peeler along one long edge of a block of chocolate. Use in the same way as grated chocolate (see below).

Grated chocolate: grate the chocolate on either the fine, medium or coarse side of

a grater. The finer sides will produce a more powdered effect, while the coarser side will produce tiny curls or curved shavings. Use for sprinkling over or coating the sides of cakes.

Chocolate vermicelli: pure chocolate vermicelli is harder to find than the more commonly available chocolate-coated sugar strands. Use either to coat sides and tops of cakes.

Glacé icing

Makes 225 g/8 oz
225 g/8 oz icing sugar
4 tbls warm water or liquid
flavouring (see below)
colouring (optional)

1 Sift the icing sugar into a bowl through a fine sieve.
2 Gradually beat in the warm water or other liquid (see below), and beat vigorously with a wooden spoon for 3 minutes or until smooth and shiny. Add colouring, if using, and beat in.
3 Pour the icing on to the cake and spread with a palette knife.

Flavourings
● Liquid flavourings must be used in place of water and not in addition.
Vanilla: use 1 tsp vanilla essence to replace 1 tsp water.
Chocolate: replace 2 tbls icing sugar with 2 tbls cocoa powder, sifted.
Coffee: use 1 tbls instant coffee dissolved in 1 tsp boiling water to replace 1 tsp water. Cool before adding to the icing.
Liqueur: use 1 tbls liqueur to replace 1 tbls water. Add colouring if wished.
Fruit: replace the water with lemon, orange, pineapple or other fresh or canned fruit juice. Add colouring if wished.
● Use slightly less liquid to make an icing which is stiff enough for piping.
● The chart on page 405 shows you how much icing you need for different cake sizes. Always use 2 tbls liquid to each 100 g/4 oz icing sugar.

Butter icing

Makes 225 g/8 oz
100 g/4 oz butter, at room
temperature
225 g/8 oz icing sugar, sifted
flavouring (see below)
colouring (optional)

1 Beat the butter with a wooden spoon or whisk it with an electric mixer until it is light and fluffy.
2 Gradually beat in the icing sugar, a few spoonfuls at a time.
3 Add flavouring and colouring (see below), if wished.

Flavourings for Butter icing and Crème au beurre
Vanilla: use 1-2 tsp vanilla essence.

Lemon: use 1 tsp grated lemon zest and 2-3 tbls lemon juice.
Orange: use 1 tsp grated orange zest and 2-3 tbls orange juice. Add orange colouring, if you wish.
Chocolate: use 100 g/4 oz plain chocolate, melted and cooled slightly, or 4 tbls cocoa powder, sifted.
Coffee: use 2 tbls instant coffee dissolved in 1 tbls boiling water and then cooled.
Strawberry, raspberry or blackcurrant: use 125 ml/4 fl oz fruit purée, made from 225 g/8 oz fresh fruit, sieved.
Liqueur: use 2 tbls liqueur; add colouring if you wish. Liqueurs can also be used with dry flavourings, for instance use Cointreau to replace orange juice in orange-flavoured Butter icing or Crème au beurre.
Peppermint: use 1-2 tsp peppermint essence. Add green food colouring.
Honey and nut: use 25 g/1 oz chopped walnuts and 125 ml/4 fl oz clear honey, instead of the sugar.
● If you wish to make Butter icing or Crème au beurre a day or two in advance, keep it in the refrigerator and bring it out to soften before use.
● The chart on page 405 shows you how much icing you need for different cake sizes. The proportions remain the same.

Crème au beurre

Makes 175 g/6 oz
3 large egg yolks
60 g/2½ oz granulated sugar
175 g/6 oz unsalted butter, at
room temperature
flavouring (see Butter icing recipe)
colouring (optional)

1 Lightly whisk the egg yolks in a bowl.
2 In a small pan, heat the sugar with 50 ml/2 fl oz water until dissolved. Bring to the boil and boil for a few minutes until the temperature on a sugar thermometer reaches 115°C/240°F. At this temperature a sample dropped into cold water will form a soft ball between your fingers which will not hold its shape when pressed. The syrup must not be allowed to heat above this temperature, so start testing it early rather than too late.
3 As soon as the syrup is ready, remove it from the heat and immediately pour it all at once on to the egg yolks, whisking continuously, preferably with an electric whisk. Continue whisking until the mixture is pale in colour, cool and of a very thick consistency.

4 In another bowl, cream the butter until very soft and the same consistency as the egg yolk mixture. Gradually beat the creamed butter into the egg yolk mixture, a very small amount at time to begin with until the mixture thickens, then more quickly. When all the butter is beaten in, add flavouring and colouring.

Fudge icing

Fills and covers the top
of a 20 cm/8 in sandwich cake
225 g/8 oz caster sugar
50 ml/2 fl oz evaporated milk
75 ml/3 fl oz single cream
100 g/4 oz unsalted butter
flavouring (see below)

1 In a medium-sized, heavy-based saucepan stir the sugar, milk and cream with a wooden spoon. Place over low heat and stir until the sugar has dissolved.
2 Increase the heat slightly and boil the mixture, stirring constantly with a wooden spoon, for about 9 minutes or until it reaches 115°C/240°F on a sugar thermometer. At this temperature a sample dropped into cold water will form a soft ball. Allow the syrup to cool for 5 minutes.
3 Cut the butter into small pieces and stir them into the fudge mixture, followed by the flavouring. Beat the icing until it becomes thick and smooth, about 3 minutes.
4 Fill and cover the cake immediately, using a palette knife to spread the icing. Allow the icing to run down the sides, rather than spreading it with a palette knife, because overworking it will make it granular.

Flavourings
Vanilla: use 2 tsp vanilla essence.
Coffee: use 2 tbls coffee dissolved in 1 tbls boiling water and then cooled.
Almond: use 2 tsp almond essence.

Royal icing

Makes 900 g/2 lb
900 g/2 lb icing sugar
4 large egg whites
1 tbls lemon juice
2 tsp glycerine

1 Sift the icing sugar twice, to make sure your icing will have no lumps.

sugar syrup to make it soft and flowing. To make this, dissolve 50 g/2 oz sugar in 125 ml/4 fl oz water in a small pan over a low heat. Bring it to the boil and boil until the temperature reaches 105°C/220°F, about 10 minutes. At this stage, an even bubbling appears on the surface, and if you dip the back of two small spoons into the syrup and pull them apart gently, a thick thread forms.

8 Warm the fondant in the top pan of a double boiler, adding 2-3 tbls sugar syrup. Heat, stirring, until the icing is the consistency of thick cream. (If the icing becomes too runny, add a little sifted icing sugar to correct it.) Finally, add colouring if you wish.

9 Pour the fondant icing over the top of an apricot-glazed cake and smooth it to the edge with a palette knife.

Almond paste

Makes 450 g/l lb
100 g/4 oz icing sugar
100 g/4 oz caster sugar
225 g/8 oz ground almonds
1 tsp lemon juice
few drops of almond essence
1 small egg, beaten

1 Sift the sugars and the almonds into a bowl. Make a well in the centre.
2 Add the lemon juice, almond essence and some of the egg. Mix well to a smooth paste, adding more egg if necessary to bind.
3 Turn out on to a board sprinkled lightly with icing sugar. Knead for 3 minutes, until it is completely smooth and free from cracks. Do not overwork.
● The chart on page 25 shows you how much almond paste you'll need to cover different sizes of cake; quantities refer to the total weight of the made-up almond paste.

Apricot glaze

Covers a
20-23 cm/8-9 in cake
3 tbls apricot jam

1 Sieve the jam into a small saucepan. Add 1 tbls water and heat gently, stirring, until the jam has melted completely.
2 Let the glaze stand a moment or two, then brush the warm glaze over the cake and leave to cool.

2 Place the egg whites in a large bowl. Whisk until just frothy. Beat the sugar into the whites, a tablespoon at a time.
3 When half the sugar has been added, beat in the lemon juice. Add the remaining sugar as before.
4 Beat in the glycerine. Cover with a damp cloth, place in a covered container and leave for at least 24 hours so it can stiffen to the correct texture for icing the cake.
● The chart on page 405 shows you how much icing you need for different sizes of cake. The quantity is based on the amount of icing sugar used; proportions of the other ingredients remain the same.

Fondant

Makes 450 g/1 lb

450 g/1 lb granulated sugar
25 ml/1 fl oz liquid glucose or
   ½ tsp cream of tartar
icing sugar, for dusting
To make Fondant icing
50 g/2 oz granulated sugar
sifted icing sugar, if necessary
colouring (optional)

1 Put 450 g/1 lb sugar and 150 ml/5 fl oz water in a large, heavy-based saucepan and dissolve the sugar over low

Above: *Royal icing is used both for covering and piping on this special-occasion cake*

heat. You may find that you get a rim of sugar round the pan above the level of the liquid. If so, dip a pastry brush in cold water and wipe any sugar crystals not dissolved back down into the syrup.
2 Bring the syrup to the boil. Meanwhile, add the glucose (or the cream of tartar dissolved in 1 tsp water) to the syrup. Boil steadily for 10-15 minutes until it reaches 115°C/240°F. At this temperature a teaspoonful dropped into cold water will form a soft ball.
3 Remove the pan from the heat, let the bubbles subside, then pour the syrup slowly into a heatproof bowl. Leave for about 1 minute, until a skin forms.
4 Using a wooden spoon, work the fondant with a figure-of-eight movement until it becomes white and firm.
5 Dust your hands with icing sugar and knead the fondant until it is smooth.
6 Pack the fondant into a small bowl, cover with a damp cloth and leave for 1 hour. Then either use immediately, or wrap the fondant in waxed paper and keep in an airtight container until needed. It will keep for up to a year. This is the fondant you use for making moulded cake decorations.
7 To make the fondant into an icing for coating a cake, you need to add a little

Cake and Icing Charts

Guide to cake tins for rich fruit cakes

Size of tin*	15 cm/6 in round	15 cm/6 in square 18 cm/7 in round	18 cm/7 in square 20 cm/8 in round	20 cm/8 in square 23 cm/9 in round	23 cm/9 in square 25 cm/10 in round	25 cm/10 in square 28 cm/11 in round
Ingredients						
Currants	225 g/8 oz	350 g/12 oz	450 g/1 lb	625 g/1 lb 6 oz	800 g/1¾ lb	1.15 kg/2½ lb
Sultanas	90 g/3½ oz	140 g/4½ oz	200 g/7 oz	225 g/8 oz	375 g/13 oz	400 g/14 oz
Raisins	90 g/3½ oz	140 g/4½ oz	200 g/7 oz	225 g/8 oz	375 g/13 oz	400 g/14 oz
Glacé cherries	50 g/2 oz	75 g/3 oz	150 g/5 oz	175 g/6 oz	250 g/9 oz	275 g/10 oz
Mixed candied peel	25 g/1 oz	50 g/2 oz	75 g/3 oz	100 g/4 oz	150 g/5 oz	200 g/7 oz
Blanched almonds	25 g/1 oz	50 g/2 oz	75 g/3 oz	100 g/4 oz	150 g/5 oz	200 g/7 oz
Plain flour	175 g/6 oz	215 g/7½ oz	350 g/12 oz	400 g/14 oz	600 g/1 lb 5 oz	700 g/1½ lb
Salt	pinch	pinch	pinch	pinch	pinch	pinch
Mixed spice	¼ tsp	½ tsp	½ tsp	1 tsp	1 tsp	2 tsp
Cinnamon	¼ tsp	½ tsp	½ tsp	1 tsp	1 tsp	2 tsp
Butter/margarine	150 g/5 oz	175 g/6 oz	275 g/10 oz	350 g/12 oz	500 g/1 lb 2 oz	600 g/1 lb 5 oz
Soft brown sugar	150 g/5 oz	175 g/6 oz	275 g/10 oz	350 g/12 oz	500 g/1 lb 2 oz	600 g/1 lb 5 oz
Eggs	2½ large	3 large	5 large	6 large	9 large	11 large
Brandy or rum	1 tbls	1 tbls	1-2 tbls	2 tbls	2-3 tbls	3 tbls
Oven temperature*	150°C/300°F/gas 2	150°C/300°F/gas 2	150°C/300°F/gas 2	150°C/300°F/gas 2	150°C/300°F/gas 2	150°C/300°F/gas 2
Approximate cooking time	2½-3 hours	3½ hours	3½ hours	4 hours	6 hours	7 hours
Weight of cooked cake	1.15 kg/2½ lb	1.45 kg/3¼ lb	2.2 kg/4¾ lb	2.7 kg/6 lb	4 kg/9 lb	5.2 kg/11½ lb

*Quantities given are for tins at least 7.5 cm/3 in deep
For cakes 25 cm/10 in and over reduce oven temperature to 130°C/250°F/gas ½ after ⅔ cooking time

Guide to cake tins for whisked sponges

Recipe ingredients	Size of cake tin	Oven temperature	Baking time	Serves
50 g/2 oz flour	two 18 cm/7 in sandwich	180°C/350°F/gas 4	20-25 minutes	6-8
2 large eggs	one 20 cm/8 in sandwich	180°C/350°F/gas 4	25-30 minutes	6-8
50 g/2 oz sugar	one 27 × 18 cm/11 × 7 in Swiss roll	200°C/400°F/gas 6	8-10 minutes	4-6
	one 20 cm/8 in flan	180°C/350°F/gas 4	25-30 minutes	6-8
75 g/3 oz flour	three 18 cm/7 in sandwich	180°C/350°F/gas 4	20-25 minutes	8-12
3 large eggs	two 20 cm/8 in sandwich	180°C/350°F/gas 4	25-30 minutes	8-10
75 g/3 oz sugar	one 33 × 23 cm/13 × 9 in Swiss roll	200°C/400°F/gas 6	8-10 minutes	6-8

	one deep 15 cm/6 in round	180°C/350°F/gas 4, then
		  170°C/325°F/gas 3
			25 minutes, then
			  40 minutes
				4-6

28 cm/11 in square	30 cm/12 in square
30 cm/12 in round	
1.5 kg/3 lb 2 oz	1.7 kg/3¾ lb
525 g/1 lb 3 oz	625 g/1 lb 6 oz
525 g/1 lb 3 oz	625 g/1 lb 6 oz
350 g/12 oz	425 g/15 oz
250 g/9 oz	275 g/10 oz
250 g/9 oz	275 g/10 oz
825 g/1 lb 13 oz	1 kg/2 lb 3 oz
pinch	pinch
2½ tsp	2½ tsp
2½ tsp	2½ tsp
800 g/1¾ lb	950 g/2 lb 2 oz
800 g/1¾ lb	950 g/2 lb 2 oz
14 large	17 large
4 tbls	6 tbls
150°C/300°F/gas 2	150°C/300°F/gas 2
8 hours	8½ hours
6.7 kg/14¾ lb	7.7 kg/17 lb

Guide to cake tins for all-in-ones

Recipe ingredients	Size of cake tin	Oven temperature	Baking time	Serves
100 g/4 oz flour 1 tsp baking powder 100 g/4 oz sugar 100 g/4 oz fat 2 eggs	one deep 15 cm/6 in round	170°C/325°F/ gas 3	40-45 minutes	4-6
	one shallow 18 cm/ 7 in square	170°C/325°F/ gas 3	35-40 minutes	4-8
	two 18 cm/7 in sandwich	170°C/325°F/ gas 3	25-35 minutes	6-8
	18 patty tins or paper cases	180°C/350°F/ gas 4	20-30 minutes	
175 g/6 oz flour 1½ tsp baking powder 175 g/6 oz sugar 175 g/6 oz fat 3 eggs	one deep 15 cm/6 in square	170°C/325°F/ gas 3	50-60 minutes	6-8
	one deep 18 cm/7 in round	170°C/325°F/ gas 3	50-60 minutes	6-8
	two 20 cm/8 in sandwich	170°C/325°F/ gas 3	30-40 minutes	8-10
	shallow 28 × 18 cm/ 11 × 7 in oblong	170°C/325°F/ gas 3	30-40 minutes	8-12
	24-30 patty tins or paper cases	180°C/350°F/ gas 4	20-30 minutes	
225 g/8 oz flour 1½ tsp baking powder 225 g/8 oz sugar 225 g/8 oz fat 4 eggs	one deep 18 cm/7 in square	170°C/325°F/ gas 3	1-1½ hours	8-14
	one deep 20 cm/8 in round	170°C/325°F/ gas 3	1-1½ hours	8-12
	one 23 cm/9 in ring	170°C/325°F/ gas 3	50-60 minutes	10-16
	36 patty tins or paper cases	180°C/350°F/ gas 4	20-30 minutes	

Quantities of butter icing

Quantity of icing sugar used	Size of cake covered
75 g/3 oz	15 cm/6 in round
100 g/4 oz	18 cm/7 in round 18 cm/7 in square
175 g/6 oz	20 cm/8 in round 20 cm/8 in square
225 g/8 oz	23 cm/9 in round 23 cm/9 in square

Quantities of glacé icing

Quantity of icing sugar used	Size of cake covered
100 g/4 oz	15 cm/6 in round 18 cm/7 in round 18 cup cakes
175 g/6 oz	18 cm/7 in square 20 cm/8 in round
225 g/8 oz	23 cm/9 in round 23 cm/9 in square

Quantities of almond paste and royal icing

Tin size: round	15 cm/6 in	18 cm/7 in	20 cm/8 in	23 cm/9 in	25 cm/10 in	28 cm/11 in	30 cm/12 in	–
square	–	15 cm/6 in	18 cm/7 in	20 cm/8 in	23 cm/9 in	25 cm/10 in	28 cm/11 in	30 cm/12 in
Almond paste	350 g/12 oz	450 g/1 lb	550 g/1¼ lb	800 g/1¾ lb	900 g/2 lb	1 kg/2¼ lb	1.1 kg/2½ lb	1.4 kg/3 lb
Royal icing	450 g/1 lb	550 g/1¼ lb	700 g/1½ lb	900 g/2 lb	1 kg/2¼ lb	1.1 kg/2½ lb	1.4 kg/3 lb	1.6 kg/3½ lb

Tea-time Specials

Next tea-time, whip up one – or two or even three – of these delicious cakes. Some of them, like Madeleines and Butterfly cakes, will appeal especially to the younger members of the family, while others, like Chocolate boxes and the Coffee and almond cake, are rather more sophisticated.

The cakes vary in difficulty, too: Tea-time lemon cake, based on the so-simple all-in-one sponge, takes minutes to prepare and decorate, though the results are as pretty as a picture. On the other hand, Battenburg cake is slightly fiddly to put together – but it tastes so much better than the bought version that it's definitely worth it!

Cakes for Family and Friends

Orange pineapple sandwich

Serves 8-10
ingredients for Basic all-in-one sponge (page 391)
grated zest of 1 orange
For the filling and decoration
275 ml/10 fl oz double or whipping cream
50 g/2 oz chopped fresh or canned pineapple
pineapple chunks and orange slices, cut into wedges

1 Mix and bake the sponge as directed on page 391, adding the orange zest with the sugar, margarine and eggs. When it is cold, cut in half.

2 Whip the cream until it forms soft peaks. Spread half on the bottom layer of sponge and scatter with the chopped pineapple.
3 Top with the second layer and spread with most of the remaining cream. Pipe the reserved cream into a border and decorate the top of the cake with pineapple and orange.

Banana sandwich Make the sponge with soft light brown sugar instead of caster sugar. Mash 2 large bananas with brown sugar and lemon juice to taste and use to sandwich the layers together. Top with 175 g/6 oz lemon-flavoured Glacé icing (page 402).
Lemon sandwich Add the grated zest of one lemon to the basic sponge mixture. Sandwich the layers together with 3-4 tbls lemon curd.

Above: *Orange pineapple sandwich*

Coffee marble sandwich Divide the sponge mixture in half. Dissolve 1½ tsp instant coffee in 1½ tsp hot water and cool, then add to one portion of the mixture. Put the mixtures into the tin in alternate tablespoonfuls for a marbled effect. Fill and top with 175 g/6 oz coffee-flavoured Butter icing (page 402), and decorate with mock coffee beans.

Madeleines

Illustrated on pages 406-407

Makes 9
100 g/4 oz self-raising flour
100 g/4 oz butter or block margarine

408

100 g/4 oz caster sugar
2 eggs
To finish
175 g/6 oz red jam
50 g/2 oz desiccated coconut
5 glacé cherries, halved

1 Heat the oven to 190°C/375°F/gas 5. Grease nine dariole moulds and stand them on a baking tray.
2 Make the cake mixture following the method for Creamed sponge (page 392). Two-thirds fill the tins with the mixture. Bake just above the centre of the oven for 20 minutes or until done. Cool in the moulds for 5 minutes before turning out.
3 Using a small, sharp knife, cut the risen tops to form flat bases.
4 Place the jam and 4 tbls water in a small saucepan over low heat until the jam has melted. Remove from the heat.
5 Sprinkle the coconut on a large sheet of greaseproof paper. Insert a skewer into the cut end of a madeleine and brush the entire surface with jam, then roll it in the coconut. Repeat with the

Below: *Coffee and almond cake*

remaining cakes. Top each cake with a halved cherry.

Coffee and almond cake

Serves 8-10
75 g/3 oz plain flour
pinch of baking powder
3 large eggs
150 g/5 oz caster sugar
½ tsp almond essence

For the filling and decoration
225 g/8 oz coffee-flavoured Butter icing (page 402)
25 g/1 oz flaked almonds, toasted
25 g/1 oz plain chocolate, melted

1 Heat the oven to 180°C/350°F/gas 4. Prepare a deep 20 cm/8 in round tin, then sift in a little flour, tilt the tin until evenly coated inside, and tip out any excess flour.
2 Make the cake mixture following the method for Whisked sponge (page 392), whisking the essence with the eggs and sugar and sifting the flour with the baking powder.
3 Pour the mixture into the prepared tin and tilt gently to spread evenly. Bake for 35 minutes or until done.
4 Cut the cold cake into three equal layers, then sandwich together with some of the icing. Spread the remaining icing over the top. Press the almonds into the topping.
5 Put the melted chocolate into a greaseproof paper piping bag. Snip off the tip of the bag and pipe the chocolate across the top of the cake. Leave to set.

Battenburg cake

Serves 6

100 g/4 oz butter or block margarine
100 g/4 oz caster sugar
2 eggs, lightly beaten
1 tsp vanilla essence
100 g/4 oz self-raising flour, sifted
few drops of red food colouring
To finish
5 tbls apricot jam, sieved and melted
225 g/8 oz almond paste (page 403) ·
caster sugar, for dredging

1 Heat the oven to 190°C/375°F/gas 5. Prepare a deep 18 cm/7 in square tin with a loose base.

2 Cut a rectangle of foil measuring 40 × 30 cm/16 × 12 in. Fold across in half, then across again in quarters to make a strip of four thicknesses, 30 × 10 cm/12 × 4 in.

3 Place the foil strip across the centre of the tin, to divide it in half, and fold both ends flush with the sides of the tin. Secure the ends in place with paper clips, then grease the foil.

4 Make the cake mixture following the method for Creamed sponge (page 392), beating in the vanilla after the eggs.

5 Turn half the mixture into one half of the prepared tin and level the surface.

Tint the remaining mixture pink with food colouring, then turn into the other half and level the surface.

6 Bake just above the centre of the oven for 30 minutes or until done. Leave to cool in the tin. If the cakes have domed slightly, press them gently with a clean tea-towel while hot to give a flat surface.

7 Remove the paper clips. Remove the cakes from the tin. Slide a palette knife underneath each cake to loosen it from the lining paper, then carefully separate the cakes by easing them away from the foil.

8 Using a sharp serrated knife, trim the cakes so that they are exactly the same size. Cut each cake in half lengthways to make four strips.

9 Place one pink and one plain strip

side by side. Brush the adjacent sides with jam, then press the cakes together. Brush the top with jam.

10 Use the remaining strips to make a second layer. Arrange in a chequerboard pattern and brush with jam. Press firmly to stick.

11 Sprinkle your work surface generously with caster sugar, then roll out the almond paste to a 28 × 16 cm/11 × 6½ in rectangle. Trim the edges with a sharp knife.

12 Brush the top of the cake with jam, place the cake, jam side down, across one short end of the almond paste, then brush remaining three sides with jam.

13 Carefully roll the cake up in the almond paste, then press the join firmly to seal. Trim both ends of the cake to neaten.

14 Place the cake, seam side down, on a serving plate. Crimp each long top edge of almond paste to decorate, then use a knife to mark a diamond pattern on the top of the cake. Sprinkle with a little caster sugar.

Iced cup cakes

Makes 20
150 g/5 oz self-raising flour
100 g/4 oz soft tub margarine
100 g/4 oz caster sugar
2 eggs
2-3 drops of vanilla essence
For the icing and decoration
225 g/8 oz vanilla-flavoured Glacé icing (page 402)
pink, blue, yellow and orange food colourings
sugar strands, hundreds and thousands, sugared flowers, angelica and other cake decorations

1 Heat the oven to 180°C/350°F/gas 4. Stand 20 paper cup cake cases in bun tins.
2 Make the cake mixture following the method for Basic all-in-one sponge (page 391), creaming the vanilla with the margarine, sugar and eggs.
3 Divide the mixture between the paper cases. Bake in the centre and just above the centre of the oven for 15 minutes or until done, swapping the tins round halfway through baking time so the cakes cook evenly. Remove from the tins to cool.

Above: *Iced cup cakes*

4 Divide the icing into five portions. Leave one batch plain and tint the others pink, blue, yellow and orange. Using a small palette knife, spread the icing over the tops of the cakes. Decorate while the icing is still soft, then leave to set.

Below: *Battenburg cake*

Chocolate cream sandwich

Serves 6-8

**ingredients for Creamed sponge
    (page 392), replacing 3 tbls flour
    with 3 tbls cocoa powder**
To finish
**150 ml/5 fl oz double or whipping
    cream, whipped
icing sugar, to decorate**

1   Mix and bake the sponge mixture as
directed on page 392, blending the cocoa
to a thick paste with a little warm water
and adding it with the eggs.
2   Sandwich the cold sponges with the
cream and decorate by sifting icing sugar
through a doily (see page 396).

Chocolate boxes

Illustrated on pages 406-407

Makes 16
**90 g/3½ oz self-raising flour
15 g/½ oz cocoa powder
2 eggs
100 g/4 oz butter or block
    margarine
100 g/4 oz caster sugar
a little milk, if necessary**

Below: *Chocolate cream sandwich*

To finish
**450 g/1 lb plain chocolate
175 g/6 oz vanilla-flavoured
    Crème au beurre (page 402)**

1   Melt the chocolate and pour it on to a
large sheet of waxed or non-stick silicone
paper, spreading it evenly with a palette
knife until it is about 5 mm/¼ in thick.
Leave until almost set.
2   Heat the oven to 190°C/375°F/gas 5.
Prepare a shallow 18 cm/7 in square tin.
3   Make the cake mixture following the
method for Creamed sponge (page 392),
sifting the flour and cocoa together. Bake
for 25-30 minutes or until done.
4   When the cake is cold, cut it into four
strips, 4.5 cm/1¾ in wide, then cut each
strip into four to make 16 squares.
5   Using two-thirds of the crème au
beurre, ice the sides of the cakes. Place
the remaining icing in a piping bag fitted
with a star nozzle and reserve.

6   Using a sharp, long-bladed knife, cut
the chocolate into 80 rectangles, each
4.5 × 3 cm/1¾ × 1¼ in. Press a rectangle against each of the four sides of
each cake.
7   Pipe stars of crème au beurre to
cover the top of each cake. Then place a

chocolate rectangle at an angle on top of
each cake, so that the piped icing shows.

Chocolate arctic roll

Illustrated on page 383

Serves 6-8
ingredients for Whisked sponge (page 392) replacing 15 g/½ oz flour with cocoa powder
To finish
caster sugar
150 ml/5 fl oz soft-scoop vanilla ice cream

1 Heat the oven to 200°C/400°F/gas 6 and prepare a 33 × 23 cm/13 × 9 in Swiss roll tin (see page 388).
2 Prepare the sponge mixture as directed on page 392, sifting the cocoa with the flour twice. Pour the mixture into the tin and bake for 8-10 minutes or until done.
3 While the sponge is baking, cut two sheets of greaseproof paper slightly larger than the Swiss roll. Sprinkle one sheet with 2 tbls sugar. Invert the baked sponge on to the sugared paper.
4 Peel off the lining paper and trim off any crusty edges with a sharp knife, then make a cut, halfway through the cake, about 2.5 cm/1 in away from a short end.
5 Place the second sheet of paper on top. Starting at the cut end, roll up the cake with the paper inside and leave to cool on a rack, seam side down.
6 When the cake is cold, unroll it and remove the top paper. Spread the cake evenly with ice cream and roll it up again with the aid of the bottom sheet of greaseproof paper.
7 Sprinkle with caster sugar and serve at once.

Chocolate and coffee log Omit the ice cream filling. Make 175 g/6 oz coffee-flavoured Butter icing (page 402). Use a quarter of the icing to fill the cold roll. Re-roll and ice the cake with the remaining icing. Chill to firm.
Chocolate and walnut roll Omit the ice cream filling. Make 100 g/4 oz vanilla-flavoured Butter icing (page 402) and beat in 25-50 g/1-2 oz chopped walnuts. Use this to fill the cold roll. Decorate with butter icing and walnut halves.
Christmas log Omit the ice cream filling. Fill with 100 g/4 oz vanilla-flavoured Butter icing (page 402) and cover with 100 g/4 oz chocolate-flavoured Butter icing, swirling and marking it with a fork to resemble the bark of a tree. Finish with a dusting of icing sugar and decorate with holly, if liked.

Above: *Swiss roll*

Swiss roll

Serves 6-8
ingredients for Whisked sponge (page 392)
To finish
2 tbls caster sugar
5-6 tbls jam
225 ml/8 fl oz double or whipping cream, whipped
icing sugar, for dredging

1 Heat the oven to 200°C/400°F/gas 6 and prepare a 33 × 23 cm/13 × 9 in Swiss roll tin (see page 388).
2 Prepare the sponge mixture as directed on page 392 pour it into the tin and bake for 8-10 minutes or until done.
3 While the sponge is baking, cut two sheets of greaseproof paper slightly larger than the Swiss roll. Sprinkle one sheet with caster sugar. Invert the baked sponge on to the sugared paper.
4 Peel off the lining paper and trim off any crusty edges with a sharp knife, then make a cut, halfway through the cake, 2.5 cm/1 in away from a short end.
5 Place the second sheet of paper on top. Starting at the cut end, roll up the cake with the paper inside and leave to

cool on a rack, seam side down.
6 When the cake is cold, unroll it and remove the top paper. Spread the cake evenly with jam and whipped cream and roll it up again with the aid of the bottom sheet of paper. Dredge with icing sugar.

Honey spiced roll Sift 1½ tsp ground mixed spice with the flour and fold in 1 tbls hot water after the flour. For the filling, cream 100 g/4 oz butter until very soft, then gradually beat in 4 tbls honey. When thoroughly blended, add 1 tbls water and beat until very smooth.

413

Walnut and chocolate marble cake

Illustrated on pages 382-383

Serves 10-12
225 g/8 oz self-raising flour
pinch of salt
175 g/6 oz butter or block
 margarine
175 g/6 oz caster sugar
4 eggs
50 g/2 oz chopped walnuts
50 g/2 oz cocoa powder, sifted
For the icing and decoration
225 g/8 oz chocolate-flavoured
 Butter icing (page 402)
4 tbls chocolate vermicelli
8 walnut halves

1   Heat the oven to 180°C/350°F/gas 4. Prepare a deep 18 cm/7 in round tin.
2   Make the cake mixture following the method for Creamed sponge (page 392), sifting the flour with the salt. Transfer half the mixture to another bowl and stir in the chopped nuts.
3   Mix the cocoa to a thick paste with a little hot water and beat this into the plain cake mixture.

4   Place the two mixtures in the tin in alternate heaped teaspoonfuls, swirl through the mixture with a skewer, briefly and with a light hand, then smooth over the surface with a palette knife. Bake above the centre of the oven for 45-50 minutes or until done. Turn out and leave to cool on a wire rack.
5   Place a generous third of the icing in a piping bag fitted with a shell or star nozzle.
6   Spread the sides of the cake with half the remaining icing and smooth with a palette knife, then coat with chocolate vermicelli (see page 401).
7   Spread the remaining icing from the bowl smoothly over the top. Pipe a border of shells or stars around the top edge of the cake and decorate with the walnut halves.

Tea-time lemon sponge

Serves 6-8
ingredients for Basic all-in-one
 sponge based on 175 g/6 oz
 flour (page 391)
finely grated zest of 1 lemon
1 tbls lemon juice

Above: *Tea-time lemon sponge*

For the icing and decoration
225 g/8 oz lemon-flavoured Glacé
 icing (page 402)
crystallized lemon slices and
 angelica shapes

1   Mix and bake the sponge in a prepared deep 18 cm/7 in round tin as directed on page 391, adding the lemon zest and juice with the sugar, margarine and eggs.
2   Pour the icing over the cold cake, letting it trickle down the sides. Decorate with the lemon slices and angelica shapes and leave to set.

Butterfly cakes

Makes 12
**150 g/5 oz self-raising flour, sifted
  with a pinch of salt**
**75 g/3 oz butter or block
  margarine**
75 g/3 oz caster sugar
grated zest of 1 large orange
1 egg
2 tbls orange juice
To finish
**225 g/8 oz orange-flavoured
  Butter icing (page 402)**
icing sugar, for dusting

1   Heat the oven to 200°C/400°F/gas 6. Stand 12 paper cup cake cases in bun tins.
2   Make the cake mixture following the method for Creamed sponge (page 392), creaming the orange zest with the fat and sugar, and mixing in the orange juice after folding in the flour.
3   Divide the mixture equally between the paper cases. Bake above the centre of the oven for 15 minutes or until done. Remove from the tins to cool.
4   Cut a slice from the top of each cake. Cut the slices in half and reserve.
5   Put the icing into a piping bag fitted with a star nozzle. Pipe a large rosette of icing on each cake, then replace the cake slices at an angle on the icing to resemble butterflies' wings. Sift icing sugar over the tops.

Frosted walnut layer cake

Illustrated on pages 406-407

Serves 8
**ingredients for Creamed sponge
  (page 392), using soft brown
  sugar instead of caster sugar**
2 tsp coffee and chicory essence
50 g/2 oz walnuts, chopped
For the filling and decoration
1 egg white
175 g/6 oz caster sugar
pinch of cream of tartar
8 walnut halves

1   Make the sponge as directed on page 392, using soft brown instead of caster sugar, beating in the coffee and chicory essence before the eggs, and folding in the chopped walnuts after the flour has been incorporated.
2   Bake in a prepared deep 15 cm/6 in round tin for 1-1¼ hours or until done. Cut the cold cake into three equal layers.
3   Make the frosting: put the egg white, sugar, cream of tartar and 2 tbls cold water in a large bowl and beat lightly together until mixed.
4   Place the bowl over a pan of hot, but not boiling, water. Beat for 7-10 minutes if using a hand whisk, or 2-3 minutes if using an electric whisk, until the frosting stands in soft peaks.
5   Spread a scant quarter of the frosting over the bottom layer of cake, then place the middle layer on top. Spread a further scant quarter of the frosting over the centre layer and top with the remaining cake layer.
6   Quickly spread the remaining frosting on the top of the cake, using a small palette knife, and spread down the sides, swirling it decoratively. Decorate the top with walnut halves.

Frosting variations
● For a coffee frosting, add 1 tsp coffee and chicory essence to the mixture while it is being beaten but before it is placed over the pan of hot water to thicken.
● For caramel frosting, use Demerara instead of caster sugar.
● For orange frosting, add a few drops of orange essence and a few drops of orange food colouring before beating over hot water.

Below: Butterfly cakes

White fruit cake

Serves 12-15
100 g/4 oz plain flour
100 g/4 oz self-raising flour
50 g/2 oz cornflour
100 g/4 oz glacé pineapple
175 g/6 oz glacé cherries
100 g/4 oz mixed glacé fruit
50 g/2 oz mixed candied peel
50 g/2 oz angelica
50 g/2 oz crystallized ginger
50 g/2 oz blanched almonds
50 g/2 oz walnuts
**225 g/8 oz butter or block
   margarine**
150 g/5 oz caster sugar
4 large eggs
1 tbls lemon juice
3 tbls milk
For the decoration
3 tbls clear honey
22 shelled Brazil nuts
22 pieces glacé pineapple
8 glacé cherries, halved
10 blanched almonds
5 walnut halves

1   Prepare a deep 20 cm/8 in round cake tin and tie a double thickness of brown paper around the outside of the tin to prevent overbrowning. Heat the oven to 160°C/325°F/gas 3.
2   Sift together the flours and the cornflour.
3   Wash the glacé fruit and pat dry with absorbent paper. Scrape the sugar from the candied peel caps and chop the peel roughly. Soak the angelica and crystallized ginger in warm water for about 2 minutes, then pat dry and chop. Chop the almonds and walnuts.
4   Mix all the fruits and nuts together and toss them in a little of the flour.
5   In a large bowl, cream the fat and sugar with an electric whisk or wooden spoon until light and fluffy.
6   Beat the eggs with the lemon juice and milk. Beat the eggs and flour alternately into the creamed mixture, then beat in the fruits and nuts.
7   Turn the cake mixture into the prepared tin. Level the top and make a hollow in the centre.
8   Place a thick layer of newspaper on a baking sheet. Place the tin on the paper and bake for 2½ hours or until done. Cool in the tin for 15 minutes before turning out.
9   Brush the top of the cold cake with honey. Arrange the nuts and fruits in concentric circles, first the Brazil nuts, then the pineapple, then the cherries, then the almonds, then the walnuts. Finish with a cherry.
10   Heat the remaining honey in a small, heavy-based pan. When it is liquid, brush it liberally over the fruits and nuts on top of the cake. Leave to set for at least 24 hours before cutting.

Genoa cake

Serves 8-10
100 g/4 oz glacé cherries
50 g/2 oz mixed candied peel
40 g/1½ oz blanched almonds
225 g/8 oz plain flour
**175 g/6 oz butter or block
   margarine**
175 g/6 oz caster sugar
3 large eggs
1 tbls milk
1 tsp baking powder
grated zest of 1 lemon
**50 g/2 oz flaked almonds or
   chopped walnuts, to decorate**

1   Prepare a deep 18 cm/7 in square or 20 cm/8 in round tin and tie a double thickness of brown paper around the outside of the tin to prevent overbrowning. Heat the oven to 150°C/300°F/gas 2.
2   Wash the glacé cherries and dry them well. Cut them in half. Scoop the sugar out of the candied peel caps and chop the peel roughly. Chop the almonds. Toss the fruits and nuts in a little of the flour.
3   In a large bowl, cream the fat and sugar with an electric whisk or wooden spoon until light and fluffy.
4   Beat the eggs with the milk. Sift the flour and baking powder together and add the lemon zest.
5   Add the eggs and flour alternately to the creamed mixture, beating well after each addition. Beat in the fruits and nuts.
6   Transfer the mixture to the prepared tin. Level the top, then make a hollow in the centre. Scatter with the flaked almonds or chopped walnuts.
7   Place a thick layer of newspaper on a baking sheet. Place the tin on the paper and bake the cake for 3-3¾ hours or until done.
8   Let the cake mature for at least 24 hours before cutting.

Right: White fruit cake, Genoa cake (top)

Something to Celebrate

When there's something to celebrate, what better way to do it than by baking a beautiful cake?

The traditional choice is a rich fruit cake, jam-packed with fruits and spices and other good things. These cakes keep well – in fact they need time to mature – and taste delicious; they make a great base for simple or elaborate decorations, whether you're celebrating a Christening, Easter, a birthday or a wedding. There's a choice of Christmas cakes too, including an economical, but still very good to eat, version which you can ice or not, as you prefer.

For an engagement party, a buttery Genoise sponge, cut into a heart shape and topped with pink fondant, roses and ribbons, makes a truly romantic centrepiece.

Cakes for Special Occasions

Engagement cake

Serves 24
**1½ × ingredients for Genoise
  sponge (page 391)**
For the filling and decoration
**275 ml/10 fl oz double cream,
  whipped**
2 × Apricot glaze (page 403)
700 g/1½ lb Fondant (page 403)
  plus ingredients for Fondant icing
icing sugar, sifted
few drops of pink food colouring
½ tsp rose water

1 Heat the oven to 180°C/350°F/gas 4. Prepare a deep 23 cm/9 in square tin.
2 Make the cake mixture and bake for 40 minutes or until done. Mark a diagonal line across one corner of the cold cake, about 5 cm/2 in from the centre. Using a saucer with a 16 cm/6½ in diameter as a guide, cut out the two rounded tops of the heart from the smaller portion. Trim the sides and corners, as necessary, to form a heart shape. Leave the cake overnight in an airtight container to settle before filling and icing.
3 Cut the cake in half horizontally and sandwich with half the whipped cream.

Brush the apricot glaze over the top and sides of the cake.
4 Knead 75 g/3 oz of the fondant with a little sifted icing sugar until smooth. Divide in half and tint one section pink. Roll each section out on a sugared surface and cut out two 7.5 cm/3 in hearts. Leave in a cool place to dry and harden.
5 Return any leftover fondant to the fondant in the pan and thin it to a pouring consistency with sugar syrup (see recipe). Add a few drops of pink colouring and the rose water and mix well.
6 Stand the cake on a wire rack over a tray. Pour the pink fondant over it,

spreading it with a warmed, wet palette knife to cover the top and sides evenly. Leave to set.

7 Scoop up any icing from the tray. Thin it, if necessary, with warm water, and coat the cake again. Leave to set.

8 Transfer the cake carefully to a 35 cm/14 in round silver board or cake plate. Place the two fondant hearts, just touching, on top of the cake and arrange a tiny bunch of flowers tied with pink and white satin ribbons.

9 Fit a piping bag with a small star nozzle and spoon in the remaining whipped cream. Pipe stars or shells around the bottom edges of the cake for a neat finish. Refrigerate until needed, but not longer than 24 hours.

● You could tint the fondant yellow and decorate with narcissi or primroses.

Below: *Engagement cake*

Holly Christmas cake

Illustrated on pages 418-419

Serves 25-30
25 cm/10 in square Rich fruit cake (page 392)
For the icing and decoration
1½ × Apricot glaze (page 403)
1 kg/2 lb Almond paste (page 403)
1.1 kg/2½ lb Royal icing (page 402)
red and green food colourings

1 Brush the square rich fruit cake with apricot glaze, then cover it with the almond paste, reserving all the trimmings.

2 Flat ice the top and sides of the cake with royal icing. When set, spread extra royal icing over the sides of the cake, roughen up with a knife and then leave to set.

3 Colour most of the remaining almond paste green and the rest red, and make green holly leaves and red berries (see page 397). Stick the leaves and red berries to the top of the cake with a little royal icing, arranging them in a circle or as liked.

Birthday cake

Illustrated on pages 418-419

Serves 16-20
23 cm/9 in round Rich fruit cake (page 392)
For the icing and decoration
Apricot glaze (page 403)
800 g/1¾ lb Almond paste (page 403)
900 g/2 lb Royal icing (page 402)
food colouring
bought cake decorations and ribbons

1 Brush the rich fruit cake with apricot glaze, then cover it with the almond paste.

2 Tint most of the royal icing pink, or whatever colour you may prefer, and then flat ice the cake with the coloured icing.

3 Make a run-out in white icing of the number or numbers you want on the cake and stick in place on top (see page 400).

4 In white icing, using a star or shell nozzle, pipe a shell border around the bottom and top edges of the cake. Finish with bought cake decorations and ribbons.

Simnel cake

Illustrated on pages 418-419

Serves 16
350 g/12 oz currants
175 g/6 oz sultanas
100 g/4 oz mixed candied peel, chopped
225 g/8 oz plain flour
1 tsp ground cinnamon
1 tsp ground mixed spice
½ tsp grated nutmeg
pinch of salt
175 g/6 oz butter
175 g/6 oz soft dark brown sugar
3 large eggs, lightly beaten
For the filling and decoration
icing sugar, for dusting
700 g/1½ lb Almond paste (page 403)
2 tbls apricot jam, sieved and warmed
a little Glacé icing (page 402)
bought cake decorations

1 Heat the oven to 150°C/300°F/gas 2. Prepare a deep 18 cm/7 in round tin.

2 Make the cake mixture following the method for Rich fruit cake (page 392).

3 Dust your work surface with a little icing sugar, then roll out one-third of the almond paste to an 18 cm/7 in circle.

4 Put half the cake mixture into the tin and level the surface. Press the almond paste circle on top. Spoon over the remaining cake mixture. Bake for 3 hours or until done.

5 Wrap the cooled cake in cling film or foil and store in an airtight container in a cool place for at least 1 week before decorating.

6 Roll out half the remaining almond paste on a surface sprinkled with icing sugar to an 18 cm/7 in circle. Brush the top of the cake with jam, then cover with the almond paste circle and press in place. Flute the edges of the almond paste with your fingertips.

7 Use the remaining almond paste to make 11 equal-sized balls and stick them around the top edge of the cake with a little apricot jam. Place the cake under a hot grill to brown the balls, watching constantly and turning the cake as necessary so the balls are evenly browned. Leave to cool.

8 Spread a circle of glacé icing in the centre of the cake and arrange some bought decorations, such as chicks and wrapped chocolate eggs, in the icing before it sets.

Snowy Christmas cake

Serves 16-20
**23 cm/9 in round Rich fruit cake
  (page 392)**
For the icing and decoration
Apricot glaze (page 403)
**700 g/1¹/₂ lb Almond paste (page
  403)**
900 g/2 lb Royal icing (page 402)

1 Brush the cake with apricot glaze,
then cover it with almond paste.
2 Rough ice the cake with royal icing.
3 To decorate, place a gold candle in a
small ball of modelling paste, then
arrange some gold paper leaves and
gold-sprayed holly leaves around the
candle, securing them in the paste. Add
a few artificial holly berries and loops of
gold ribbon. Cover the modelling paste
with foil before placing the decoration on
the cake.

Christening cake

Illustrated on pages 418-419

Serves 16-20
**23 cm/9 in round Rich fruit cake
  (page 392)**

Above: Snowy Christmas cake

For the icing and decoration
Apricot glaze (page 403)
**800 g/1³/₄ lb Almond paste (page
  403)**
900 g/2 lb Royal icing (page 402)
blue or pink food colouring

1 Brush the cake with apricot glaze,
then cover it with almond paste.
2 Flat ice the cake with most of the
royal icing. Tint a quarter of the remaining icing pale blue or pink.
3 In white icing, using a small star or
shell nozzle, pipe a shell border around

the bottom of the cake where it joins the board.

4 In white and blue or pink, using a small plain nozzle, pipe straight lines – first two white lines, then one coloured line, then repeat as necessary – across half of the cake, then pipe the baby's name on the other half.

5 Pipe large dots all around the edge of the cake to neaten the top and the ends of the straight lines, and pipe one white and one coloured curving line inside the dots on the plain half of the cake. Using the same nozzle, pipe white and coloured dots in the shape of flowers (*see illustration*).

6 Add a bought Christening cake decoration and attach a lace ribbon around the sides of the cake with a little icing.

Economical Christmas cake

Serves 10-12
225 g/8 oz sultanas
225 g/8 oz raisins
100 g/4 oz currants
275 g/10 oz plain flour
½ tsp bicarbonate of soda
1 tsp ground mixed spice
pinch of grated nutmeg
the grated zest of ½ lemon
225 g/8 oz block margarine
225 g/8 oz soft brown
  sugar
4 large eggs
few drops of vanilla
  essence
few drops of almond essence
1 tbls marmalade

1 Mix and bake the cake mixture following the method for Rich fruit cake (page 392), sifting the bicarbonate of soda with the flour and spices and adding the lemon zest to this, tossing the fruit in a little of the flour mixture, and beating the vanilla and almond essences and the marmalade into the eggs. Bake for 4 hours or until done.

2 The cold cake can be covered with almond paste and royal icing in the traditional way (*see pages 398-399 and 402-403*), or simply decorated with holly leaves, different coloured ribbons and snipped crêpe paper.

Below: Economical Christmas cake

Posy wedding cake

Serves 100-150

18 cm/7 in round Rich fruit cake
  (page 392)
23 cm/9 in round Rich fruit cake
28 cm/11 in round Rich fruit cake
For the icing and decoration
4 × Apricot glaze (page 403)
2.3 kg/5 lb Almond paste (page
  403)
2.3 kg/5 lb Royal icing (page 402),
  tinted yellow
1 egg white, to thin icing
450 g/1 lb Royal icing

1 Brush each of the cakes with apricot glaze.

2 Divide the almond paste into three pieces weighing 450 g/1 lb, 800 g/1¾ lb, and 1 kg/2¼ lb and use to cover each of the cakes. As you finish each cake, place it in the centre of the appropriate cake board – you will need one 20 cm/8 in board, one 25 cm/10 in, and one 33 cm/13 in. Leave all the cakes to dry, lightly covered, for 1 week.

3 Flat ice each of the cakes with yellow icing, allow to set, then cover and dry for 1 week.

4 Use some of the remaining yellow icing to coat two thin 15 cm/6 in cake boards. Spread the icing thinly and evenly over the cards and smooth with an icing ruler.

5 While the icing is still soft, mentally quarter each card, then make four symmetrical marks about 4 cm/1½ in in from the circumference. Press a 7.5 cm/3 in high round plaster pillar into the soft icing over each mark (you will need a total of eight pillars). Leave to dry, then cover and store.

6 Smooth any imperfections from the cakes and brush with a pastry brush. Thin the remaining yellow icing with lightly beaten egg white and re-ice each cake. Remove any excess icing from the top and bottom edges of the cakes and clean the exposed areas of all of the cake boards with a clean cloth wrung out in hot water.

7 Allow to dry, cover when set and leave for 1 week.

8 Fill a piping bag fitted with a small shell or star nozzle with a small amount of white royal icing and pipe a shell border around the top and bottom edge of each cake.

9 Pipe a shell border around the edge

Left: Posy wedding cake

of each of the thin cake boards holding the pillars.

10 Attach white and yellow ribbons and lace to the sides of the cakes (see illustration) securing them with a little icing.

11 Place the biggest cake on a cake stand, if using. Arrange a few flowers among the pillars on one of the thin cake boards. Place it in the centre of the cake.

12 Place the middle cake in position. Decorate the second thin cake board in the same way and put it in place. Top it with the third cake.

13 Arrange the posy of flowers in place on the top.

Wedding cake countdown

Four months before the wedding
(Takes 2 days.) Make the two smaller cakes the first day. The next day make the largest cake. When cold, wrap them in foil and store in airtight containers. Once every 14 days, prick the cakes with a skewer and feed them with a few spoonfuls of brandy, rum or sherry.

Two months before the wedding
Buy cake boards, pillars and ribbons and order fresh flowers. Make the almond paste and store it in a cool place. Order the cake stand and knife, if necessary.

Four weeks before the wedding
(Takes 1½ hours.) Cover the cakes with apricot glaze and almond paste. Place on

cake boards. Cover loosely with foil and leave in a cool, airy place for 1 week.

Three weeks before the wedding
(Takes 1½ hours on each of 2 days.) Make the yellow royal icing and allow to stand for 24 hours. The next day, flat ice the cakes. Allow the icing to dry before you cover with greaseproof paper. Immediately after icing the cakes, coat the two thin cake boards with icing and stick the pillars on. Leave iced cakes and boards separately in a cool airy place. Cover the remaining icing with a damp cloth and cling film.

Two weeks before the wedding
(Takes 1 hour.) Using a sharp knife, remove any uneven edges from the icing. Use the royal icing thinned with egg white to coat the cakes a second time. Cover with greaseproof paper and allow to dry for 1 week.

One week before the wedding
(Takes 1½ hours.) Make fresh, royal icing. Pipe shells of icing around the top and base of each cake and around the edge of the cake boards on which the pillars are standing. Attach lace and ribbons to the cakes.

On the day of the wedding
Assemble the cake on the cake stand, if using, placing a few flowers on each of the thin cake boards. Place the posy on the smallest cake.

Below: *The iced cake, ready to assemble*

IT'S YOUR BIRTHDAY!

Fun Cakes

Make your child's next birthday really special by baking a cake he or she will always remember.

Our Rainbow cake is made bright and colourful with rows of sugar-coated chocolate sweets, and is bound to delight children of all ages, while the Gingersnap house, in true Hansel and Gretel fashion, is designed to be nibbled away! In Sweden and Germany, biscuit houses are baked at Christmas time, but our house would make a perfect children's party cake at any time of year.

There are many other gaily decorated cakes to add sparkle and magic to a party. All children love to be surprised, and the unveiling of one of these cakes will be the highlight of the day.

Cakes for Kids

Clown cake

Serves 16-20
**20 cm/8 in round Rich fruit cake
(page 392)**
For the icing and decoration
Apricot glaze (page 403)
**550 g/1¼ lb Almond paste (page
403)**
700 g/1½ lb Royal icing (page 402)
**pink, red and brown food
colouring**
350 g/12 oz Fondant (page 403)
icing sugar, for dusting
red and pink sugar flowers
100 g/4 oz Glacé icing (page 402)

1 Brush the cake with apricot glaze, then cover it with almond paste. Place it on a cake board or serving plate.
2 Flat ice the cake with most of the royal icing. Tint most of the remaining royal icing deep pink and, with a plain nozzle, pipe a line all around the top edge of the cake, and a decorative border inside that.
3 Knead the fondant until it is smooth. Divide it into three equal sections, then halve one section. Tint one small section red and the other brown; tint one large section deep pink; leave the remaining fondant white. Roll out the pink fondant on a surface dusted with icing sugar. Cut out a 12.5 cm/5 in circle for the face, and two ears.
4 Roll out the white fondant and cut out two eyes and one mouth shape, plus six dots for the clown's bow-tie. Make 28 balls from the remaining white fondant to decorate the bottom edge of the cake.
5 Roll out the red fondant and cut out lips and two pieces for the bow-tie (see illustration). Roll a large ball of red fon- dant between your palms for the nose.
6 Roll two brown fondant balls for *eyes* between your palms. Make the clown's hat from a large brown ball surrounded by a rope of brown fondant, also rolled between your palms.
7 Place the shapes on the top of the cake and mark lines on the lips and ears with a skewer. Paint eyelashes with a paint brush dipped in brown colouring. Attach the sugar flowers to the hat.
8 Tint a small amount of glacé icing brown; tint the rest deep pink. Using greaseproof paper piping bags, pipe brown and pink hair.
9 Place the balls of white fondant around the base of the cake, then pipe pink glacé icing in a fine line around the outer edge of the balls. Make large pink dots between the white balls.

Below: Clown cake

Spinning top cake

Serves 12-16
**ingredients for Basic all-in-one
   sponge (page 391)**
For the icing and decoration
**pink, green and orange food
   colouring**
4-5 tbls raspberry jam
450 g/1 lb Butter icing (page 402)
25 g/1 oz desiccated coconut

1   Heat the oven to 180°C/350°F/gas 4.
Prepare two 20 cm/8 in sandwich tins.
2   Make the cake mixture as directed on
page 391, then divide it in half and stir a
few drops of pink colouring into one half.
Put the mixture into the prepared tins in
alternate spoonfuls for a marbled effect.
Bake the cakes for 30-35 minutes or

until done. Leave to cool in the tins for 3
minutes, then cool on a wire rack.
3   Sandwich the cold cakes together
with jam.

Above: *Spinning top cake*

4   Place a third of the icing in a bowl,
soften it with a little warm water and
spread it around the sides of the cake,
then roll the cake in the desiccated
coconut (see page 398) to coat the sides.
Place the cake on a cake board or serving plate.
5   Put 4 tbls icing in a separate bowl
and add a few drops of pink colouring.
Repeat with the green and orange
colourings. Leave the rest of the icing
plain.
6   Mark the top of the cake into eight
sections and rough ice them in different
colours. Put the remaining plain icing in
a piping bag fitted with a medium star or
shell nozzle and pipe a shell border
around the top and base of the cake.
Add candles if appropriate.

429

Tanker lorry

Serves 8-12

200 g/7 oz self-raising flour
25 g/1 oz cocoa powder
225 g/8 oz butter or block
margarine
225 g/8 oz caster sugar
4 eggs
about 2 tbls milk, if necessary
For the icing and decoration
225 g/8 oz red Butter icing
(page 402)
2 × Apricot glaze (page 403)
6 liquorice wheels
100 g/4 oz granulated sugar
coloured chocolate buttons
small silver cake balls
liquorice strips
icing sugar, for dusting
175 g/6 oz Fondant (page 403)
100 g/4 oz Glacé icing
(page 402)
red and blue food colouring

1 Heat the oven to 170°C/325°F/gas 3. Grease and flour two 400 g/14 oz cans. Prepare a 28 × 18 cm/11 × 7 in tin.

2 Make the cake mixture following the method for Creamed sponge (page 392), sifting the cocoa with the flour. Half-fill the two cans and put the remaining mixture in the baking tin. Bake for 25-40 minutes or until done. Let the cakes settle for 2 minutes, then turn out.

3 When they are cold, cut off and discard the rounded tops of the two cylindrical cakes. Stick the two cylinders together, end to end, with butter icing to make the tank.

4 Cut a strip 2.5 cm/1 in wide off the end of the rectangular cake (**1** on diagram, right), then cut the rest of the cake in half lengthways. Reserve one half (**2**) and cut two 7.5 cm/3 in pieces (**3**) from the other half. Discard the remaining piece. Sandwich the two equal pieces with butter icing to form the cab.

5 Brush the apricot glaze over the top

Above: *Tanker lorry*

and sides of the cab and the two remaining rectangles.

6 Cover these sections with butter icing. Lay the 2.5 cm/1 in strip in the centre of a foil-covered board with the flat piece on top (see diagram). Put the cab in position and smooth the icing.

7 Using a little of the butter icing, attach three liquorice wheels on each side.

8 In a small, heavy-based pan, dissolve the sugar in 2 tbls water and boil over medium heat until it is golden. Turn the caramel on to an oiled baking sheet. When it just begins to set, cut it into three window shapes. Allow to cool, then position them with butter icing.

9 Put a little butter icing into a piping bag fitted with a small plain nozzle and pipe around the edges of the cake and windows. Pipe in a radiator grid, doors and hubcaps.

10 Position yellow chocolate buttons

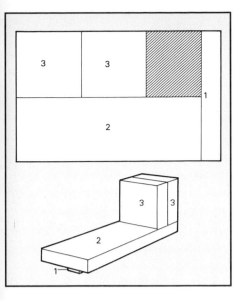

on the cake as lig^l.ts. Put the silver balls over the windscreen. Cut liquorice strips for the bumpers and attach. Use small bits of liquorice for steps and door handles.

11 Brush the cylindrical cakes with apricot glaze. On a flat surface dusted with icing sugar, roll the fondant out thinly. Cut a rectangle of fondant measuring 23 × 11.5 cm/9 × 4½ in and roll it round the cakes.

12 Cut two 7.5 cm/3 in circles from the fondant and position them at each end of the cylinder. Dip your fingers in icing sugar and mould the fondant to the cake by rubbing it lightly with a circular movement. Mould the fondant joins together in the same way.

13 Colour half the glacé icing red and the other half blue.

14 Using a small piping bag fitted with a small plain nozzle, pipe a blue circle on each side. With another bag and red icing, pipe 'Esso' or another name in the circle and two stripes down each side of the tank.

15 Lay the tank in position on the chassis, wedging it with coloured chocolate buttons. Attach coloured chocolate buttons to the top of the tank and the back of the cab with butter icing.

16 Make a licence plate from a bit of white fondant. Pipe letters on it with butter icing and attach to the strip of cake beneath the lorry.

Butterfly cake

Serves 10-12
ingredients for Basic all-in-one sponge (page 391)

For the icing and decoration
Apricot glaze (page 403)
175 g/6 oz Glacé icing (page 402)
pink food colouring
2 small silver cake balls
1 chocolate finger biscuit

1 Mix and bake the sponge as directed on page 391 in a prepared deep 20 cm/8 in square cake tin for 1½ hours or until done.

2 Trim the top level, then cut the cake

Above: 'Feather' icing the Butterfly cake

in half diagonally. Cut off the two corners opposite the cut sides.

3 Place the cakes on a work surface, trimmed sides down and with the cut corners facing each other. Spread the cut corners with apricot glaze and push together to make a butterfly shape. Cut out a semicircle from each long cut side (see illustration, left). Brush the top of the cake with glaze.

4 Put 3 tbls of the icing into a paper piping bag without a nozzle. Tint the remaining icing pink and use to cover the top of the cake.

5 Working quickly, stick the silver cake balls on one end of the biscuit with glaze. Place the biscuit on the top of the cake, where the wings meet, to make the butterfly's body.

6 While the pink icing is still soft, snip off the tip of the bag and pipe parallel lines of white icing, 1-2 cm/½-¾ in apart, down the top of the cake. Draw a skewer through, in one direction only, to give a feathered effect (see page 398). Let the icing set.

Rainbow cake

Illustrated on pages 426-427

Serves 8
175 g/6 oz self-raising flour
1½ tsp baking powder
175 g/6 oz caster sugar
175 g/6 oz soft tub margarine
finely grated zest of 1 lemon
3 eggs
For the icing and decoration
2-3 tbls apricot jam, sieved and
warmed
150 g/5 oz lemon-flavoured Glacé
icing (page 402)
blue food colouring
purple, green, yellow, orange and
red chocolate buttons (2 ×
125 g/4.4 oz packets)

1   Heat the oven to 190°C/375°F/gas 5. Prepare a deep 18 cm/7 in round cake tin.
2   Make the cake mixture following the method for Basic all-in-one sponge (page 391), creaming the lemon zest with the sugar and margarine.
3   Bake for 45-60 minutes or until done.
4   Trim the top of the cold cake level, if necessary, then turn it upside down so the flat base is uppermost. Using a 5 cm/ 2 in plain cutter, cut a circle from the centre of the cake.

5   Cut the cake in half to make two arches. Using a little jam, sandwich the arches together into a rainbow shape.
6   Lay the cake face down. Colour the glacé icing pale blue. Using a palette knife, ice the surface of the cake, includ-

ing the sides and the small inner arch, but not the cut ends at the bottom of the arch. Leave the icing to set.
7   Stand the cake upright, with the un-iced side facing you. Spread the un-iced side of the cake with most of the remaining jam. Starting at the top edge, make rows of purple, green, yellow, orange and, finally, red chocolate buttons, pressing them in place. To secure

firmly, use small amounts of glacé icing for each sweet.
8   Stand the cake on a 23 cm/9 in cake board, securing it in position with jam. Press candles firmly into holders and arrange them on the rainbow.

Maypole cake

Serves 12
175 g/6 oz self-raising flour
1½ tsp baking powder
175 g/6 oz caster sugar
175 g/6 oz soft tub margarine
3 eggs
For the icing and decoration
3-4 tbls apricot jam
Apricot glaze (page 403)
175 g/6 oz orange-flavoured
Butter icing (page 402)

Above: Maypole cake

small pink, green and gold cake balls
pink and yellow sugar flowers
striped candy stick
red, green and yellow jelly babies

1   Make the cake mixture following the method for Basic all-in-one sponge (page 391), baking it in two prepared 19 cm/7½ in round tins, each 4 cm/1½ in deep, for 25-30 minutes or until done.

2   Sandwich the cold cakes together with the jam and place on a 23 cm/9 in cake board or serving plate.

3   Brush the cake with glaze, then spread with butter icing, reserving about a quarter of it in a piping bag fitted with a large shell or star nozzle. Pipe a border around the bottom edge of the cake.

4   Stud the top of the cake with coloured cake balls and sugar flowers. Push the candy stick firmly into the centre. Arrange the jelly babies and candles on top of the cake, then tape thin red, green and gold ribbons to the top of the maypole. (Wrap them tightly around a pencil if you want them to curl.) You can, if wished, top the maypole with a primrose or other small fresh flower. Remember to remove the ribbons before you light the candles.

Gingersnap house

Illustrated on page 434

Serves 15-20
75 g/3 oz butter
4 tbls black treacle
4 tbls golden syrup or honey
100 g/4 oz soft brown sugar
450 g/1 lb flour
1½ tbls ground ginger
1 tbls ground mixed spice
1 tbls bicarbonate of soda
finely grated zest of 1 small lemon
1 egg, beaten
For the icing and decoration
1 egg yolk
red, yellow and green food colouring
small silver cake balls
coloured sugar hundreds and thousands
450 g/1 lb Royal icing (page 402)
350 g/12 oz marshmallows, in two colours
100 g/4 oz coloured chocolate buttons
225 g/8 oz small liquorice sweets in assorted colours and shapes
25-50 g/1-2 oz fruit gums

1   Make cardboard templates (see overleaf) and prepare three or four baking sheets, lining them with non-stick silicone paper. Heat the oven to 190°C/375°F/gas 5.

2   Put the butter into a large pan, add the treacle, syrup or honey and sugar. Stir over low heat until the sugar dissolves and the butter melts. Remove from the heat and leave for a few minutes. Sift the flour, ginger and spice.

3   Mix the bicarbonate of soda and 2 tbls cold water in a bowl and stir it into the melted mixture. Add the lemon zest. Then gradually mix in the flour and spices alternately with the beaten egg. Mix thoroughly until a dough is formed.

4   Gather the dough into a ball by hand. It should be pliable but firm. If not, leave it for 10-15 minutes to settle, knead again and, if still too soft, work in a little more sifted flour.

5   Assemble cutters: a 2.5 cm/1 in round fluted one, and people or animal shapes, if wished.

6   Divide the dough into four portions, one slightly larger than the others. Roll each out on non-stick paper to about 3 mm/⅛ in thick, as follows.

7   Roll out one smaller ball. Arrange the templates for one end wall and one side wall on the dough. Hold them in place and cut round the edges with a sharp knife. Lift each shape, on the rolling pin, on to one lined baking sheet. Trim if necessary. Bake for 8-10 minutes, until the dough has puffed up and feels dry. Cool on a wire rack. Repeat with a second small portion of dough for the remaining walls, then bake.

8   Cut the largest portion of dough in half, roll out each piece and cut two roof sections, using a template of 18 × 20 cm/7 × 8 in. Bake for 8-10 minutes.

9   Roll out the last ball of dough and cut six individual shutters. Bake for 2-3 minutes, mark lines across each shutter with a sharp knife and bake for 4-5 minutes.

10   From the remaining dough cut two chimney shapes. For the doorstep, cut a 5 × 2 cm/2 × ¾ in rectangle. Bake on the lower shelf for 5-8 minutes.

11   Gather up all the trimmings and knead briefly. Cut out four trees, then cut two of them in half lengthways. Trim the bases so the trees will stand firm when arranged. To glaze and colour them, mix a quarter of the egg yolk in a small dish with green colouring and brush it over the trees. Bake on a lower shelf for 5-8 minutes.

12   Cut out 24 little biscuits to decorate the roof and garden, using the round fluted cutter. To colour them, mix a quarter of the egg yolk with red and another quarter of the egg yolk with yellow colouring. Paint red and yellow lines alternately on 12 biscuits for the roof. Press a silver cake ball in the middle of each. Brush some biscuits with red colouring. Brush the other biscuits with the remaining egg yolk and dip them into a dish of hundreds and thousands. Bake on a lower shelf for about 5 minutes.

13   For the door frame and the round-topped windows at each end of the house, roll pencil-thin strips of dough. Shape one round the pattern of the door and join the ends neatly. Make more strips and form three windows.

14   For the fencing, roll 15 cm/6 in

433

long strips of dough. Attach them in pairs by 2.5 cm/1 in long strips which form the posts. Make several fences.

15 For the gate, roll two strips 4 cm/ 1½ in long and join with two strips 2.5 cm/1 in long.

16 Use up any remaining dough for logs, garden stepping-stones, animals and people. Bake all these shapes for 5-8 minutes.

17 Let the biscuits become completely cold before assembling. They can be kept in an airtight container for several weeks.

18 Make the royal icing and keep most

of it covered with a damp cloth in the bowl while working with a small portion. Prepare a base for the house 35-40 cm/ 14-16 in across: use a round cake board or a tray inverted and covered with foil. Assemble some cans or jars to prop the house up while it sets.

19 Using your fingertip, smear some icing along the edges of each wall and join an end wall and a side wall together. Stand them on the board, propping with a jar inside. Remove the jar when set and attach the other walls.

20 Spread a 2.5 cm/1 in wide border of icing on the surface which will be the

Above: *Gingersnap house*

underside of the roof. The border should be 2.5 cm/1 in from the lower edge and 1 cm/½ in from the front and back edges. To seal the top of the roof, spread the icing along the top outside edges.

21 Place one roof section in position, resting on the walls, using the icing border to fix it. Support the roof at the lower edge with a jar or a can. Place the other section in place. Secure the top joint with extra icing, if necessary. With your fingertips, feel along the other joins and put in more icing if there are any

Gingersnap house templates

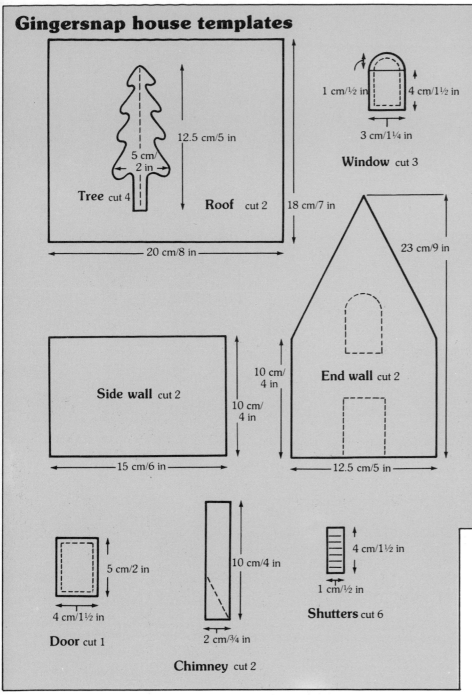

Tree cut 4

12.5 cm/5 in
5 cm/2 in

Roof cut 2

20 cm/8 in

18 cm/7 in

1 cm/½ in   4 cm/1½ in

3 cm/1¼ in

Window cut 3

23 cm/9 in

Side wall cut 2

15 cm/6 in

10 cm/4 in

10 cm/4 in

End wall cut 2

12.5 cm/5 in

5 cm/2 in

4 cm/1½ in

Door cut 1

10 cm/4 in

2 cm/¾ in

Chimney cut 2

4 cm/1½ in

1 cm/½ in

Shutters cut 6

Roof
Cut two rectangular roof sections of dough, each 20 × 18 cm/8 × 7 in.

Door and end windows
Using the cardboard shape as a marker, make pencil-thin rolls of dough. Model these round the edge of the door. Make three window frames the same way.

Chimney
Cut two rectangular shapes 10 × 2 cm/4 × ¾ in. Sandwich them together with icing.

Shutters
Cut six shutters of dough. Half-bake them, then make cut lines on them before baking completely.

Trees
After cutting other shapes, use rolled out dough trimmings to make the trees.

Fencing and gate
Make from pencil-thin rolled strips attached together by shorter strips.

Side walls
Cut two rectangular side wall sections of dough, each 15 × 10 cm/6 × 4 in.

End walls
Cut two each of these shapes, as shown.

gaps. Support the second roof side with a jar or can at the lower edge and leave to set for 30 minutes.

22 Sandwich the chimney pieces together with icing. Use a sharp knife to shave off a corner from the base of the chimney so that it fits snugly against the roof. Spread icing all over the roof. Use more to fix the chimney in place.

23 Now decorate the roof. Cut the marshmallows (which will be the tiles) in half. Attach them to the roof, alternating the colours. If any do not stick, dab them with more icing.

24 If necessary, add a little water to the

icing to make it stickier. Spread some along the ridge of the roof and attach the decorated round biscuits as shown.

25 Ice the back of the door and end window frames and attach them, two windows to one end wall, a door and window to the other. Put more icing on the back of the shutters and attach them to the side walls in pairs. Arrange them so there is one long window on one side of the house and two narrower windows on the other.

26 Fit a piping bag with a fine plain nozzle and spoon in some icing. Pipe lines to represent window panes

between the shutters on the side walls.

27 Using a round-bladed knife, spread some icing along the front and back roof edges to make icicles, and decorate with the coloured chocolate buttons.

28 Ice the front window frame and door and decorate with liquorice sweets and coloured chocolate buttons. Put coated biscuits on either side of the door and lay the doorstep in front. Decorate the bottom edge of the house and chimney top with liquorice sweets and fruit gums.

29 For the trees, spread icing along the cut edge of the half trees and pipe a line of icing down the centre of whole trees. Join the cut sides of the half trees to the icing on the whole trees.

30 Spread any remaining icing over the base around the house. Arrange the fences and gate and support them with pieces of marshmallow stuck in the icing. Put the trees and any figures in position, secure them with icing and support them until set. The completed house will keep under cling film for 1-2 weeks.

Gorgeous Gâteaux

This chapter gives you a selection of cakes for those special occasions which call for a gâteau rather than just a cake! Serve them to accompany mid-morning coffee when you've guests you want to impress, for a special tea or as the sensational end to a dinner party.

There are some luscious chocolate gâteaux, including the classic German Black Forest torte with whipped cream, cherries and kirsch, and a pretty summertime sponge sandwiched with strawberries and decorated with chocolate.

Genoise fruit flan can be filled with various fruits to suit the season, while the rich-tasting Orange flower gâteau will give you a chance to show off your cake-decorating skills.

Cakes to Impress

Cream and custard sponge

Serves 8-10
dried breadcrumbs, for sprinkling
5 eggs
100 g/4 oz caster sugar
100 g/4 oz plain flour, sifted
¼ tsp baking powder
For the filling and decoration
5 tsp custard powder
2 tsp granulated sugar
200 ml/7 fl oz milk
600 ml/1 pt double or whipping
  cream
few drops of almond essence
4-5 tbls Morello cherry or other
  red jam
few drops of vanilla essence
25 g/1 oz flaked almonds, toasted
8-10 drained maraschino cherries
fresh or drained canned peach
  slices

1 Heat the oven to 170°C/325°F/gas 3. Grease a deep 18 cm/7 in round tin and dust it thickly with breadcrumbs.
2 Beat the eggs and sugar together until thick enough to retain the impression of the whisk for 3 seconds when the beaters are lifted. Fold in the flour and baking powder. Bake for 40-50 minutes or until done. Cool in the tin for 30 seconds, then turn out.
3 Meanwhile, put the custard powder and sugar into a small saucepan. Gradually stir in the milk. Bring slowly to the boil over low heat and simmer for 2 minutes, stirring constantly. Remove from the heat and stir in 50 ml/2 fl oz cream and the almond essence. Pour into a bowl, cover with cling film and leave until cold.
4 Slice the cake into three layers. Put the bottom layer on to a serving plate and spread with jam. Cover with the middle layer and spread with custard. Top with the remaining layer.

5 Whip the remaining cream with the vanilla until thick. Spread some over the top. Put the rest into a piping bag fitted with a large star nozzle. Pipe vertical lines down the sides of the cake and top each with a piped star.
6 Stud the top of the cake with the toasted almonds and arrange the fruits in the centre. Keep cool and serve within 2 hours.

Orange flower gâteau

Serves 8-10
50 g/2 oz unsalted butter
100 g/4 oz plain flour
4 large eggs
100 g/4 oz caster sugar
1 tsp orange oil or 2 tsp orange
  essence

Below: Cream and custard sponge

For the filling and decoration
**175 g/6 oz Crème au beurre
(page 402)
2 tbls orange flower water
few drops of orange oil or orange
essence
orange food colouring
50 g/2 oz flaked almonds, toasted
175 g/6 oz icing sugar, sifted**

1 Heat the oven to 180°C/350°F/gas 4. Grease and line a deep 20 cm/8 in round cake tin with a loose base, then grease and lightly flour the lining paper.
2 Make the cake mixture following the method for Genoise sponge (page 391) adding the orange oil or essence to the cooled melted butter. Bake for 45 minutes or until done.
3 Beat 1 tbls orange flower water and 1-2 drops of orange oil or essence into the crème au beurre, and tint it pale orange with the food colouring.
4 Split the cake in half horizontally and use a third of the crème au beurre to sandwich the two layers together. Use half the remaining crème to cover the sides of the cake. Coat the sides in toasted almonds (see page 398).
5 Make the glacé icing by mixing the

icing sugar with 1 tbls orange flower water and sufficient hot water to give a fairly thick consistency. Add 1-2 drops orange oil or 2-3 drops orange essence to flavour and tint with a few drops of orange food colouring. Use this icing to cover the top of the cake. Leave to set.
6 Fill a piping bag fitted with a large shell nozzle with the remaining crème au beurre. Pipe a shell border around the top edge of the cake.

Chocolate and cream gâteau

Illustrated on pages 436-437

Serves 12
**200 g/7 oz self-raising flour
225 g/8 oz butter or block
margarine
225 g/8 oz caster sugar
3 tbls cocoa powder blended with
2 tbls hot water
4 eggs**
For the filling and decoration
**4 tbls apricot jam, sieved and
warmed**

Above: Orange flower gâteau

**425 ml/15 fl oz double cream,
whipped to soft peak stage
15 g/½ oz grated chocolate (page 401)**

1 Make the cake mixture following the method for Creamed sponge (page 392), beating the cocoa paste into the creamed fat and sugar.
2 Spoon the mixture into a prepared deep 20 cm/8 in round tin with a loose base. Make a small hollow in the centre and bake for 40-50 minutes or until done.
3 Cut the cake in three. Spread half the jam over the bottom layer and place this on a serving plate.
4 Place about a quarter of the whipped cream in a piping bag fitted with a large star nozzle and reserve. Spread two spoonfuls of the remaining cream over the jam and top with the middle cake layer. Spread this with jam and cream and top with the remaining layer.
5 Spread the remaining cream thickly on top of the cake. Pipe a star border around the top edge and sprinkle grated chocolate in the centre. Keep cool and serve within 2 hours.

Chocolate and strawberry gâteau

Serves 8-10
200 g/7 oz self-raising flour
25 g/1 oz cocoa powder
175 g/6 oz butter
175 g/6 oz soft light brown sugar
3 eggs
100 g/4 oz plain chocolate, melted
with 5 tbls milk
For the filling and decoration
425 ml/15 fl oz double cream
225 g/8 oz plain chocolate
100 g/4 oz strawberries, hulled
and sliced
100 g/4 oz plain chocolate
caraque (page 401)

1   Heat the oven to 180°C/350°F/gas 4.
Prepare two 20 cm/8 in sandwich tins.
2   Make the cake mixture following the
method of Creamed sponge (page 392),
sifting the flour with the cocoa and beating in the melted chocolate after the
eggs. Bake for 25-30 minutes or until
done.
3   Put a third of the cream into a pan
with the chocolate and heat gently, stirring, until melted. Cool, then whisk until

Above: *Chocolate and strawberry
gâteau*

thick and glossy. Whip the remaining
cream and fold half into the chocolate
mixture. Spoon the remaining cream
into a piping bag fitted with a star nozzle
and reserve.
4   Use half the chocolate cream,
topped with most of the strawberries, to
sandwich the cakes together. Spread the
remaining chocolate cream on top and
decorate with rosettes of whipped
cream, caraque and the remaining berries. Keep cool and serve within 2 hours.

Black Forest torte

Serves 8-10
150 g/5 oz plain flour
2 tsp bicarbonate of soda
1 tsp coffee powder
1 tbls cocoa powder
6 eggs, separated
150 g/5 oz caster sugar
1 tsp lemon juice
75 g/3 oz plain chocolate, finely
grated
pinch of salt

For the filling and decoration
800 g/1¾ lb canned black
cherries, stoned
150 ml/5 fl oz kirsch
425 ml/15 fl oz double cream
3 tbls caster sugar
25 g/1 oz plain chocolate, coarsely
grated

1   Heat the oven to 180°C/350°F/gas 4.
Grease the base and sides of two 23 cm/
9 in loose-bottomed tins. Line the bases
with greaseproof paper and grease the
paper. Mix together 1 tbls each plain
flour and caster sugar, sprinkle over the
insides of the tins, then shake to coat
evenly. Shake out any excess.
2   Sift the flour three times with the
bicarbonate of soda, coffee and cocoa.
3   In a bowl set over a pan half full of
simmering water, whisk the egg yolks
and sugar until thick enough to hold the
trail of the whisk for 3 seconds when the
beaters are lifted. Mix in the lemon juice
and grated chocolate.
4   Whisk the egg whites and salt until
they form soft peaks. Stir 2 tbls of the
whisked whites into the egg yolk mixture
then, using a large metal spoon, fold a
quarter of the remaining whites into the
mixture. Sift over 2 tbls flour and fold in.
Repeat until all the egg whites and all the
flour has been added.
5   Divide the mixture between the tins.
Bake for 25 minutes or until done.
6   Drain the cherries, reserving 75 ml/
3 fl oz syrup. Pat them dry with absorbent paper and reserve eight for decoration. Add 125 ml/4 fl oz kirsch to the
reserved syrup.
7   Whip the cream until it forms soft
peaks and beat in the sugar. Fold in the
remaining kirsch. Put 4 tbls of the cream
into a piping bag fitted with a large star
nozzle and reserve.
8   Split each cake in two. Sprinkle one-
third of the syrup over one bottom layer,
cover with about a quarter of the cream
and press half the fruit into the cream.
Cover with a second sponge, sprinkle
with more syrup, a layer of cream and
the rest of the cherries. Lay the third
sponge on top, sprinkle with the last of
the syrup and cover with more whipped
cream. Top with the last sponge layer
and spread the remaining cream over
the top and sides.
9   Scatter grated chocolate over the top
and pipe rosettes of cream around the
edge. Stud every other one with a
cherry. Chill for 1 hour before serving.

Right: *Black Forest torte*

Genoise fruit flan

Serves 6
50 g/2 oz plain flour
2 large eggs
1 large egg yolk
50 g/2 oz caster sugar
½ tsp vanilla essence
25 g/1 oz unsalted butter
For the filling
**150 ml/5 fl oz double or whipping
cream**
icing sugar, sifted (optional)
**2 red plums, sliced, and a few
raspberries**

1   Prepare a 20 cm/8 in flan tin by greasing well and dusting with flour. Make the cake mixture following the method for Genoise sponge (page 391).

Turn the mixture into the tin and bake for 20-25 minutes or until done.
2   Whip the cream until it forms soft peaks, sweetening it to taste with icing sugar, if wished.
3   Fill the cold flan case with whipped

Above: *Genoise fruit flan*

cream and arrange the fruit attractively on top.

Variation
Almost any sort of fruit can be used in this flan. Fresh fruit is nicest, though frozen or canned fruits can also be used successfully.

Rose marble cake

Serves 12
**ingredients for Basic all-in-one
sponge (page 391), using 2 tsp
baking powder**
2 tbls rose water
**few drops of red food
colouring**
½ tsp vanilla essence

For the icing and decoration
100 g/4 oz icing sugar, sifted
1 tbls rose water
crystallized rose petals

1 Heat the oven to 180°C/350°F/gas 4. Generously grease a 1.5 L/2½ pt plain ring mould.
2 Prepare the sponge mixture as directed on page 391. Turn half the mixture into a second bowl. Stir the rose water into one half and tint it pink with a few drops of food colouring. Stir the vanilla essence into the other half.
3 Place alternate spoonfuls of the two mixtures in the mould. Draw the blade of a knife through the mixture, first in one direction, then the other, but be careful not to 'over-swirl'. Bake for 45 minutes or until done.
4 To make the icing, blend the sifted icing sugar with the rose water and enough warm water to give a smooth, runny consistency. Spoon the icing over the top of the cooled cake and let it trickle down the sides.
5 Finish with crystallized rose petals and leave to set.

Chestnut cream gâteau

Serves 8-10
Whisked sponge, baked in two
**   20 cm/8 in sandwich tins**
**   (page 392)**
For the filling and decoration
275 ml/10 fl oz double cream
250 g/9 oz can chestnut spread
1 tbls brandy
sliced marrons glacés

1 Cut each cake in half horizontally.
2 Whip the cream until it stands in soft peaks, then fold in the chestnut spread and the brandy. Use a third of the cream mixture to sandwich the layers together.
3 Spread half the remaining cream mixture over the top and sides of the cake. Spoon the remaining cream mixture into a piping bag fitted with a star nozzle and pipe a shell design on the top of the cake, with series of shells radiating into the centre of the gâteau. Decorate with marrons glacés. Refrigerate for up to 3 hours before serving.

Chestnut cherry gâteau Use rum instead of brandy in the cream mixture, and decorate the gâteau with halved maraschino cherries.

Below: Chestnut cream gâteau

Party
Planner

Introduction

It's partytime—so take the guesswork out of entertaining, and follow our guidelines and recipes to put on parties you can be proud of. It's not impossible to entertain a crowd yet still be able to enjoy the food and relax with your guests. With careful planning and the right menu, you can serve delicious, imaginative food and drinks whatever the occasion. And the beauty of the menus in this section is that they can be adapted to suit the number of people and type of occasion you are catering for. Plan a party soon, and show your friends just how easy entertaining can be.

Carefully planned food and drinks can make all the difference to the success of a party, whether it is a drinks party or a buffet, a children's party or a wedding reception.

Finger food

When planning the eats for a drinks party remember that the food should all be bite-sized finger food. The party will probably be a stand-up affair, so guests must be able to take the food directly and comfortably from the serving platter and eat it in one bite.

To estimate how much food you will need, allow roughly 12 'bites' per person; people with large appetites will probably eat 16–18 'bites', while slimmers will only eat 7–8 'bites'.

● Choose the food so that it is varied in appearance, flavour and texture.

● Make dishes that can be prepared in advance. The cold fare must keep well in the refrigerator or a cool kitchen. Soggy biscuits or wet pastry are out. The hot food should be quick to reheat.

● If possible, provide a choice of meat, fish, cheese and vegetables for variety.

● Avoid any deep-fried food; it is impracticable since it has to be cooked immediately before serving, and the smell lingers.

● Try not to make the food too salty as this encourages people to drink more.

● Make full use of your freezer for cooking ahead.

Small cocktail savouries, consisting of a crisp base covered with a spread and topped with a savoury garnish, are known as canapés.

The most sophisticated canapés are made on a pastry base, often a savoury cheese or almond pastry. For simpler versions, small savoury biscuits make perfect bases.

● For toast canapés, cut rounds from white or wholemeal bread and toast on both sides.

● For fried bread canapés, fry white bread rounds in oil or butter until crisp, drain on absorbent paper and cool.

● For baked bread canapés, bake white bread rounds in a hot 200° C/400° F/gas 6 oven for 10 minutes until browned.

When making up the canapés, leave those with a moist topping until last, so that the bases do not have time to go soggy. Those made with drier ingredients can be made further ahead, but the toppings can become dry, which makes them look unappetizing. To prevent this, make a quick aspic by dissolving aspic granules or crystals in water,

Below: *Bar equipment, including ice bucket, tongs, strainer, spirit measures, cocktail shaker, cocktail glass, swizzle sticks, mixing jug and spoon*

leave until syrupy and almost set, then brush a little over each canapé.

Providing hot finger food for a crowd is no easy job. Choose carefully, so that nearly all the work can be done well ahead, leaving you with only last-minute reheating and garnishing.

Shallow ovenproof serving dishes which you can use to pass the food round save a lot of time and effort. Allow a few minutes' cooling to prevent the first guest burning himself, and put the dish on a heatproof tray to protect your hands.

Generally, it is better to pass round one thing at a time, rather than make up trays or platters of assorted food.

Apart from specially prepared eats, you may like to provide extra nibbles that require the minimum of preparation, as illustrated on pages 446-447.

Nuts: peanuts, cashews, almonds or, in fact, any nuts, are suitable. Try mixing them with muscatel raisins. You can also salt your own nuts – fry the shelled nuts in a little oil until they begin to brown, then drain well and toss in a little salt. For your own variations, try garlic salt or celery salt. Almonds are particularly good salted.

Sausages: buy thin chipolata sausages and twist each one in the centre to make small cocktail sausages. Grill or put in a moderate oven until golden. These are

st served hot, speared on cocktail
cks.

egetable ideas: cut celery, cucumber
nd carrots into sticks, cauliflower into
small florets, and serve with a tasty dip.
Sautéed mushroom caps are lovely filled
with liver pâté. Small tomato halves can
be seeded and filled with cottage cheese
and chives. Button mushrooms, marinated in a well-flavoured dressing, can
be speared on cocktail sticks.

Pickles: rather than serving plain olives,
try mixing stuffed and black olives with
cocktail-sized gherkins, silverskin onions
and any other pickles. Delicatessens
usually stock a wide variety of pickles.

Cocktails and other drinks

Cocktails are ideal for entertaining a
small group of friends. In the late morning, in the evening before dinner, sitting
around in hot weather or late at night –
all of these occasions call for a really in-
spired social drink.

Make the drinks in front of your
guests, like a barman does, because part
of the fun of cocktail drinking is seeing
the drink assembled. Generally speaking, it is not practical to make more than
four cocktails at once.

Don't try to serve mixed drinks to a
large crowd, unless you have several
professional waiters and barmen. Stick
to wine or simple punches, which are

Above: *Tomato tartlets (page 465)*

easier to assemble and serve in large
quantities.

Many cocktails include a cordial that
will not blend instantly with spirits. The
traditional way to make this type of
cocktail is to shake the ingredients together with lots of ice, in a cocktail
shaker. A strainer is usually built into the
shaker, so that the drink is strained as
you pour it into the glass. When using a
shaker, it is always a good idea to wrap it
in a tea-cloth so that you will avoid any
spillages.

If you do not have a shaker, use the
stirring method with a mixing jug and
long spoon. Simply stir the ingredients
with plenty of ice then pass through a
strainer (the best one is a Hawthorn
strainer) into the serving glass. A particularly useful method for cocktails that
blend easily, it can be used for all
cocktails not made on-the-rocks.

For a cocktail mixed on-the-rocks,
simply pour the ingredients over ice in a
serving glass or tumbler and stir – the ice
is left in the drink.

Crushed ice is often a vital ingredient
of the drink – to prepare the ice, either
crush ice cubes in a strong blender or
food processor, or put ice in a heavy
polythene bag and crush with a wooden
mallet or rolling pin.

A proper cocktail measure is very
helpful, but a standard measuring jug
and spoon can be used if ingredients are
kept in the proportions given in the
recipes. As a useful guide remember that
30 ml/1¼ fl oz equals 2 tablespoons.

When serving the drinks, bear in mind
that short cocktails are served in
stemmed glasses, while long ones are
served in tall glasses, large wine goblets
or tumblers.

To give your cocktails a decorative
effect, frost the rims of the glasses. First
dip the rim into iced water or lemon
juice, and then dip it into caster sugar,
turning the glass to give an even coating.

When using citrus fruit, remember to
wash the fruit thoroughly if you intend to
use the peel in a drink.

Champagne cocktails create an especially festive atmosphere. For a party
lasting about two hours, you should
allow about three or four cocktails per
person. One bottle of champagne makes
about eight champagne cocktails, so for
a party of, say, twelve people, you will
need five or six bottles of champagne altogether. To cut costs, you could use a
good dry sparkling wine instead, such as
a *méthode champenoise* sparkling wine.

Wine cups are an easy and inexpensive alternative to cocktails. Laced with
spirits and liqueurs for added zing, and
topped up with refreshing fizzy drink,

there are wine cups to suit every taste. Use cheap, non-vintage sparkling wines or champagne, well chilled. Add soda water only at the last moment; for sweet wine cups use fizzy lemonade.

Brandy, curaçao, maraschino, grenadine, chartreuse and crème de menthe are the most commonly used additives. Gin may also be used, but never add too much.

Remember, a big block of ice melts more slowly than cubes. Ice cubes will be clearer if you boil the water first, then cool and freeze. Make decorative cubes by freezing small pieces of fruit or sprigs of mint in each.

Garnish with fruit, but remember you are making a wine cup, not an alcoholic dessert! Use herbs – lemon balm, sweet verbena, bergamot, mint and borage – or try rose petals, to garnish.

Hot punches are not only great ice-breakers at a party, they also make perfect pick-me-ups for when you feel tired and chilly, and are marvellous as nightcaps, too!

The wine or spirit used as the base does not have to be very expensive, but you must use fresh fruit and juices. Do not boil the drink, as this will spoil the flavour. Make the punch the centre of attention and serve it from a punch bowl or large Victorian jug. You will need a ladle that pours well, and glasses with handles or mugs.

There are many strange names for hot mixed drinks, but the most common is punch. Nowadays, most wine- or spirit-based mixed drinks are loosely called punches.

Mulls are similar to punches in that they are made with warmed wine, beer or cider, but they are not quite as alcoholic. Possets are always made up of milk curdled with wine, ale or other alcohol. Traditionally, possets were used as cures for colds and other ailments, but they are now mainly drunk for pleasure.

Toddies and grogs are both made from spirits, and are usually prepared individually. Nogs must always include eggs. They are popular in the United States during cold weather.

Non-alcoholic drinks can be made to look as exotic as real cocktails. Serve the drinks in a punch bowl or in jugs, or present them in glasses. Use different shapes, colours and sizes of glasses and raid the cocktail cupboard for a variety of exotic garnishes.

Put a few drops of food colouring into the water when you fill the ice trays. Or you could freeze strawberries or melon

Above: *Left to right, Ham and potato scallop (page 480), Melon and orange salad (page 481), Scrambled eggs and olives in toast cones (pages 478)*

balls in the ice trays to make fruity ice cubes. For an extra dimension in ice, try freezing water in a household glove, a balloon or even fish and star shapes from sandpit sets, to make shaped ice blocks for punch bowls.

Decorate the rims of the glasses with orange, lemon, lime or cucumber slices.

Buffets

Your buffet party could be on the small side – around a dozen – and this number will probably be within the capacity of the plates, glasses and cutlery that you own. On the other hand, once you have got down to cooking, it is almost as much work to give a party for 12 as it is for 20, and the larger number will help create the party atmosphere. The basic menus are likely to be the same for 20 or 30 guests, and catering problems don't greatly increase with the extra numbers.

Here are some tips to remember that will make your buffets memorable for your guests and labour-saving for you.
● A cold buffet is acceptable at any time of year – your guests will quickly warm a cold room. But if you are giving a mid-

winter party it is a good idea to include at least one hot item.
● If the guests are going to eat standing up, the food should be easy to eat with just a fork. If the food requires knives, you should provide places for the guests to sit to cut the food.
● Avoid very complicated or very expensive food when entertaining a larger number of guests. Avoid dishes that are too rich.
● Use seasonal ingredients and fresh herbs.
● Avoid dishes which will be affected by heat: ice cream and aspic could melt.
● Select dishes which are easy to serve and do not crumble or disintegrate. Carve or divide meat and poultry ahead.
● If possible, divide each item between two serving dishes to help reduce hold-ups during serving.
● When planning the menu, select items that will complement and contrast with each other in colour, texture and flavour. Use different dressings for each salad.
● Select items which can be prepared in advance: avoid too much last minute detail.
● Choose a starter that can be eaten on the same plate as the main course, for example a pâté, quiche or salad.
● Avoid dishes with sauces: if you serve fruit salad, provide bowls, not flat plates.

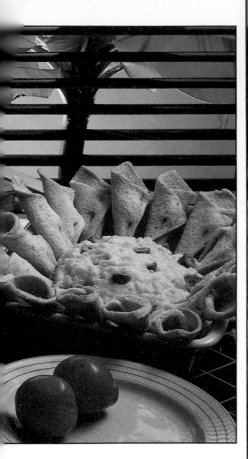

Right: *Kid's kooler (page 494)*

● If you are serving cream, several small jugs of pouring cream, discreetly replenished, are better than a rich-looking mound of whipped cream, because the first guests tend to over-help themselves, leaving nothing for later, however generously you have catered. Better still, serve a dessert where cream is generous but already portioned: meringues sandwiched with cream, trifles and jellies with piped swirls on top.

Brunches

Brunches usually start at about 11 a.m. with drinks in the living room, but the buffet table can be in the dining room, or out on the patio if it is warm. If the guests are going to stand, choose food that can be eaten with the fingers or a fork.

Limit the choice of pre-brunch drinks. Tomato juice or a mixed vegetable juice, offered in a large jug with ice, can be drunk as it is with Worcestershire sauce and a slice of lemon. To make it an alcoholic cocktail spike it with vodka and present it with a celery stick as a swizzler. Orange juice is another good idea. The children can drink it straight or it can be combined with sparkling white wine.

Bread is usually provided. Serve croissants or hot rolls or scones in a basket lined with a napkin, or a selection of different types of bread on a board. Arrange butter curls nearby.

On the main table, have the cooked dishes. These should be the kind you would expect for a particularly fancy breakfast but that are also suitable for lunch. Make sure that not all of them involve last-minute cooking. Tea, coffee, cups and saucers are best on a separate table.

Special celebrations

A family celebration needs to be special, and you must serve something to remember. Whether you are entertaining a large group or a relatively small number of people, the menu needs to have a touch of luxury and elegance.

It is also more important than ever to choose food that requires minimal last-minute attention. You will certainly want to be enjoying celebratory drinks with the guests rather than seeing to frantic preparations in the kitchen.

Children's parties

The birthday cake is the star at a children's party. The trick is to choose a design that looks spectacular, yet is relatively quick and easy to create.

There is a vast choice of bought foods that children adore, so buy a supply of crisps and savoury snacks and nuts, plus chocolate biscuits. Keep the food in bite-sized portions. Do not make too many sandwiches but try to provide savouries as well as sweet cakes.

Serve home-made lemonade in the summer, fizz up squashes with soda water or make a fruit punch with colourful fruit to garnish.

Drinks Parties

At a truly successful drinks party there is always plenty of food as well. Ready-made snack food is popular, but with a little effort you can provide your own home-made finger food to make the party a memorable affair. As regards drink, don't waste money on classic wines—serve exotic cocktails, wine cups and punches instead. Cocktails make a perfect start to a party and are delicious sipped in the early hours of the evening. Ice-cool wine cups are an ideal way to relax on hot summer days, while spicy, hot drinks, packed with alcoholic punch, will liven up any party. For thirsty teenagers, you can make thirst-quenching, non-alcoholic 'mocktails', using fruit, vegetables, fruit juices and fizzy drinks.

Cocktail Party

Black Russian

Makes 1 drink
50 ml/2 fl oz vodka
50 ml/2 fl oz Kahlua or, if not
available, Tia Maria

1 Mix the vodka and Kahlua or Tia Maria on-the-rocks.

Summertime

Makes 1 drink
25 ml/1 fl oz vodka
25 ml/1 fl oz dry vermouth
75 ml/3 fl oz grapefruit juice
tonic water

1 In a tall glass, mix the vodka, vermouth and grapefruit juice on-the-rocks. Fill up the glass to the top with tonic water.

Screwdriver

Makes 1 drink
50 ml/2 fl oz vodka
25 ml/1 fl oz fresh orange juice
2.5 ml/¹/₂ tsp caster sugar
(optional)

1 Shake and strain into a cocktail glass.

🍸As an alternative version, mix on-the-rocks – fill a tumbler with ice and pour over the vodka and orange juice.

Tequila sunrise

Makes 1 drink
25 ml/1 fl oz tequila
2 tsps Galliano
2 tsps crème de banane
2 tsps grenadine
2 tsps lemon juice

1 Shake and strain into a glass.

🍸If you have difficulty in obtaining crème de banane, try this light variation: mix 50 ml/2 fl oz orange juice with 25 ml/

1 fl oz tequila and strain into a glass. Pour in 10 ml/2 tsps grenadine.

Margarita

Makes 1 drink
50 ml/2 fl oz tequila
25 ml/1 fl oz Cointreau
25 ml/1 fl oz fresh lemon juice
lemon rind
salt

1 Frost the rim of a cocktail glass by rubbing with lemon rind and dipping lightly in salt.

2 Stir the tequila, Cointreau and fresh lemon juice together and strain into the frosted glass.

Daiquiri

Makes 1 drink
25 ml/1 fl oz white rum
15 ml/¹/₂ fl oz fresh lime juice
15 ml/¹/₂ fl oz grenadine syrup

1 Shake until very cold then strain into a cocktail glass.

🍸There are many variations of the daiquiri made with fruit juice syrups in place of grenadine.

🍸Frozen daiquiri is made with crushed ice in a blender.

🍸If limes are unavailable, substitute 25 ml/1 fl oz lemon juice for the lime juice.

Dry martini

Makes 1 drink
50 ml/2 fl oz dry gin
a few drops of extra dry vermouth
slice of lemon
1 green olive (optional)

1 Stir the gin and vermouth together, and strain into a chilled cocktail glass.
2 Squeeze the lemon over the drink. Add a green olive on a stick, if you wish.

🍸For a Gibson, serve with a pearl onion.

Whisky sour

Makes 1 drink
75 ml/3 fl oz whisky
juice of ¹/₂ lemon
1¹/₂ tsps sugar
ice
soda water
**slice of orange and a cocktail
    cherry**

1 Crush the ice, shake the first four ingredients together then strain into a small tumbler. Add a dash of soda water.
2 Serve, garnished with the orange slice and the cherry on a stick.

Horse's neck

Makes 1 drink
spiral of lemon zest
50 ml/2 fl oz gin
ginger ale

1 Cut the lemon spiral and hang from the rim of a tall glass. Pour the gin into the glass on-the-rocks. Top with ginger ale to taste.

Substitute any other spirit for the gin; try whisky, brandy or light rum. Made with brandy, it was traditionally offered to passengers on long sea voyages.

Chilli nibbles

Makes 30
225 g/8 oz lean minced beef
1 tsp butter
**6 spring onions, trimmed and
    finely chopped**
1 garlic clove, crushed
2 tsps chilli sauce
1 tbls finely chopped parsley
2 tsps chopped capers
1 tbls tomato ketchup
**8 slices of white or wholemeal
    bread**
50 g/2 oz butter, melted
**chopped capers, to garnish
    (optional)**

1 Put the minced beef into a food processor and switch on for about 30 seconds or until the beef is very finely ground.
2 Melt the butter in a small frying pan and quickly fry the spring onions and garlic. Add to the beef in a mixing bowl, then add the chilli sauce, parsley, capers and tomato ketchup. Mix until well combined.

Below: *Left to right, Margarita, Daiquiri, Summertime, Tequila sunrise, Black Russian, Screwdriver*

3 Using a 4 cm/1½ in plain round cutter, cut out 30 rounds from the slices of bread. Coat them in the melted butter and place them on a baking tray. Mound them with the meat mixture and bake at 200° C/400° F/gas 6 for about 6 minutes, or until the bread is golden and the meat mixture is cooked.
4 Garnish with capers and serve hot or cold.

🍸 To serve at a drinks party, arrange Chilli nibbles on a platter with Nutty pork rounds, Watercress wheels and German cheese snacks.

Hot cheese and crab dip

Illustrated on pages 452-453

Serves 12
175 g/6 oz mature Cheddar cheese, grated
50 g/2 oz margarine or butter
50 g/2 oz plain flour
425 ml/¾ pt milk
1 tbls lemon juice
1 tsp Worcestershire sauce
1 tsp French mustard
salt and freshly ground white pepper
2-3 tbls finely chopped canned pimiento
2-3 tbls finely chopped green pepper
6 black olives, stoned and finely chopped
4 tbls dry white wine
175 g/6 oz canned crabmeat, drained and all cartilage removed

1 Melt the margarine in a saucepan, sprinkle in the flour and stir over low heat for 1-2 minutes until straw-coloured. Remove from the heat and gradually stir in the milk. Return to the heat and simmer, stirring continuously, until thick and smooth.
2 Remove from the heat and stir in the cheese until melted and smooth. Add the lemon juice, Worcestershire sauce, mustard and salt and pepper to taste and mix well.
3 Stir in the pimiento, green pepper, olives, wine and crabmeat, then heat through gently, stirring.
4 Pour into a warmed serving dish. Serve at once with small Melba toast squares, cubes of French bread and savoury biscuits.

Chilli meat balls

Illustrated on pages 452-453

Makes 36-40
500 g/1 lb lean minced beef
2 tbls tomato ketchup
2 tbls mild chilli sauce
1 tbls Worcestershire sauce
25 g/1 oz cornflakes, finely crushed
125 ml/4 fl oz canned evaporated milk
salt and freshly ground black pepper
vegetable oil, for greasing
For the dipping sauce
5 tbls tomato ketchup
3 tbls mild chilli sauce
1 tbls lemon juice
¾ tsp creamed horseradish
¾ tsp Worcestershire sauce
few drops of Tabasco

1 Heat the oven to 200° C/400° F/gas 6. Grease 2 baking trays with oil.
2 Place the beef in a large bowl together with the tomato ketchup, chilli sauce, Worcestershire sauce, cornflakes and evaporated milk. Season with salt and pepper to taste, then mix well together with your fingers.
3 Shape the beef mixture into about 40 bite-sized meat balls and arrange on the greased baking trays. Cook in the oven for 15-20 minutes or until the meat balls are browned.
4 Meanwhile, make the sauce. Put the tomato ketchup in a small serving bowl and stir in the rest of the sauce ingredients. Place the bowl of sauce in the centre of a large platter.
5 Serve the meat balls on a warmed serving dish accompanied by the sauce and cocktail sticks for dipping.

Nutty pork rounds

Makes 12
400-450 g/14-16 oz roast or smoked loin of pork
4 tbls curd cheese
1 tsp tomato purée
1 tsp French mustard
50 g/2 oz walnuts, finely chopped
½ sachet aspic
12 cocktail gherkins fans, to garnish

1 Cut the loin of pork into 12 equal slices. Using a 5 cm/2 in plain round

cutter, cut a round from each slice. Place the rounds on a wire rack and refrigerate.
2 Mince the pork trimmings in a food processor until finely divided, then add the curd cheese, tomato purée and mustard. Process again for a short time until all the ingredients are combined. Turn the mixture out on to a board and form into a log 15 cm/6 in long and 4.5 cm/1¾ in in diameter. Wrap in foil and chill in the refrigerator for about 30 minutes.
3 Unwrap the log and coat thoroughly with the chopped walnuts. Slice into 12 rounds.
4 Place a round on top of each slice of pork and top with a gherkin fan. Chill.
5 Make the aspic according to the directions on the sachet. Chill until quite cold, then spoon over the rounds until thoroughly coated. Chill again until set, then serve.

Watercress wheels

Makes 14
75 g/3 oz watercress
4 spring onions
3 eggs
pinch of freshly grated nutmeg
**salt and freshly ground black
    pepper**
vegetable oil, for greasing
**4 tbls freshly grated Parmesan
    cheese**
For the filling
100 g/4 oz Ricotta cheese
1 tbls single cream
1 tbls lemon juice
**salt and freshly ground black
    pepper**
pinch of cayenne pepper

1 Remove the stalks from the water-cress and discard. Chop the leaves finely. In a food processor, combine the spring onions, eggs, nutmeg and seasoning. Add the watercress and process for a few seconds.
2 Lightly grease an 18 cm/7 in square tin and heat over a medium heat. Pour in the egg mixture and heat until the omelette is cooked. If preferred, a large omelette pan may be used and the sides of the omelette squared off after cooking.
3 Spread the grated Parmesan on a sheet of greaseproof paper and turn the omelette out on to it. Roll up, leaving the paper inside. Set aside and leave to cool.
4 To make the filling, beat together all the ingredients in a bowl. When the omelette is cool, unroll, remove the greaseproof paper and spread the omelette with the cheese mixture, then reroll and chill in the refrigerator. Cut into 14 slices and serve.

German cheese snacks

Makes 24
225 g/8 oz Cambozola blue Brie
2 celery stalks, finely chopped
2 tbls medium dry sherry
2 tbls single cream
**4 slices pumpernickel, each cut
    into 6 pieces**
**thinly sliced vegetables, to
    garnish, e.g. peppers, carrots,
    cucumber**

1 Combine the blue Brie and the celery in a bowl and mix until a smooth consistency is obtained. Add the sherry and cream and beat together until well mixed.
2 Spread over the pumpernickel pieces and garnish with small slices of vegetable.

Creamy kipper pâté

Serves 4-6
**227 g/8 oz packet frozen kipper
    fillets, thawed**
cayenne pepper
3 tsps lemon juice
knob of butter
100 g/4 oz full-fat soft cheese
1 tbls creamed horseradish
freshly ground black pepper
**stuffed olives and red pepper
    strips, to garnish**

1 Heat the grill to moderate.
2 Place fish in a shallow heatproof dish, sprinkle them to taste with cayenne and 1 tsp of the lemon juice, then top the kippers with the knob of butter.
3 Cover with foil to keep moist and place under the grill for 10 minutes, until the fish fillets are cooked through. Leave to cool.
4 Flake the kipper flesh into a bowl, removing the skin and any bones. Add the juices from the dish together with all the remaining ingredients, including the rest of the lemon juice and pepper to taste. Beat with a fork or work in a blender or food processor until smooth. Taste, adjust seasoning, if necessary, then refrigerate for at least 1 hour. Spread over the top of cocktail biscuits and garnish with cayenne pepper, stuffed olive slices or red pepper.

Below: *Creamy kipper pâté*

Champagne Cocktail Party

Champagne cocktail

Makes 1 drink
1 lump sugar
Angostura bitters
1 tbls brandy
chilled champagne

1 Place the sugar in a saucer-shaped champagne glass and sprinkle with 3-4 drops Angostura bitters. Leave for at least 1 hour until the sugar lump has dissolved.
2 Add 1 tbls brandy and top up with chilled champagne.

Buck's fizz

Makes 1 drink
chilled freshly squeezed orange juice
chilled champagne

1 Fill a champagne flute one-third full with chilled orange juice.
2 Carefully top up the glass with chilled champagne.

Black velvet

Makes 1 drink
chilled Irish stout
chilled champagne

1 Half-fill a 300 ml/½ pt lager or balloon glass with chilled Irish stout.
2 Top up with chilled champagne.

Champagne Framboise

Makes 1 drink
1 tbls Framboise (French raspberry-flavoured liqueur)
chilled champagne

1 Pour 1 tbls Framboise into a champagne flute.
2 Top up with chilled champagne.

Below: *Clockwise from top left, Crispy chicken bites, Anchovy puffs, Devils on horseback, Crab vol-au-vents; Drinks, clockwise from top, Black velvet, Champagne cocktail, Buck's fizz, Champagne Framboise*

Crispy chicken bites

Makes 50-60
4 large boned chicken breasts, each weighing about 250 g/9 oz, skinned
75 g/3 oz fresh white breadcrumbs
finely grated zest of 1 lemon
3 tsps garam masala
1 egg
4 tbls plain flour
salt and freshly ground black pepper
3 tbls vegetable oil
25 g/1 oz butter

1 Cut the chicken into bite-sized pieces, discarding any fat.
2 Mix the breadcrumbs with the lemon zest and garam masala in a shallow bowl. Beat the egg in another shallow bowl.
3 Put the flour in a polythene bag and season with salt and pepper to taste. Add the chicken cubes and shake to coat well. Dip the chicken pieces first in the beaten egg, then in the breadcrumb mixture, to coat thoroughly on all sides.
4 Heat the oil and butter in a large

frying-pan, add the coated chicken pieces and fry for 5-6 minutes, turning occasionally, until golden brown and crisp. Drain the chicken pieces well.

5 To serve, spear each chicken piece on a cocktail stick. Arrange pieces on a large serving platter and serve the chicken bites at once.

♥ Serve with dip made from 150 ml/¼ pt mayonnaise, 75 g/3 oz grated cucumber and a dash of Worcestershire sauce.

Anchovy puffs

Makes about 30
500 g/1 lb frozen puff pastry, defrosted
2 × 45 g/1¾ oz cans anchovy fillets, drained
2 tbls freshly grated Parmesan cheese
1 egg, beaten, to glaze

1 Heat the oven to 220° C/425° F/gas 7.
2 Cut pastry in half and roll out each piece thinly on a lightly floured surface to a 28 cm/11 in square.
3 Arrange the strips of anchovies head to tail on 1 square of pastry, in rows spaced about 1 cm/½ in apart. Sprinkle lightly with 1 tbls Parmesan cheese.
4 Brush the remaining pastry with half the beaten egg, then carefully place, glazed side down, over the rows of anchovies.

5 Press the pastry firmly together along the edges and between the ridges formed by the anchovies. Brush the top with beaten egg and sprinkle with remaining Parmesan. Slice into strips, cutting between the ridges formed by the anchovies, then cut each strip into fingers.
6 Arrange the fingers on dampened baking sheets and bake above the centre of the oven for about 12 minutes or until risen and golden brown.

Devils on horseback

Makes 32-34
350 g/12 oz lean streaky bacon rashers, rinds removed
250 g/9 oz packet no-need-to-soak prunes

1 Stretch bacon rashers with the back of a knife, then cut in half.
2 Heat the grill to moderate.
3 Wrap a half bacon rasher around each prune, then grill half for 10-15 minutes, turning occasionally, until bacon is crisp. Grill the remainder. Serve on cocktail sticks.

Crab vol-au-vents

Makes 40
40 frozen cocktail-sized plain or fluted vol-au-vents
a little beaten egg, to glaze
For the filling
25 g/1 oz butter
25 g/1 oz plain flour
300 ml/½ pt creamy milk
75 g/3 oz fresh or frozen crabmeat, defrosted
1-2 tsps lemon juice
salt and freshly ground black pepper
freshly grated nutmeg
small diamonds of green and red pepper, to garnish

1 Heat the oven to 220° C/425° F/gas 7.
2 Place vol-au-vents on dampened baking sheets, 1 cm/½ in apart, and brush the rims with beaten egg.
3 Bake them for about 15 minutes, turning the sheets round after 8 minutes, until golden and well risen.
4 Meanwhile, make the filling: melt the butter in a small saucepan, sprinkle in the flour and stir over low heat for 1-2 minutes until straw-coloured.
5 Remove pan from the heat and

gradually stir in the milk. Return to heat, bring to boil and simmer for 2 minutes,

stirring, until the sauce is thick and smooth. Remove from heat and beat in the crabmeat. Season to taste with lemon juice, salt, pepper and grated nutmeg.

6 Remove the lids from the vol-au-vents and reserve.

7 Fill each case with a teaspoon of the crab sauce. Garnish each with a pepper diamond, then replace the pastry lids, if wished. Serve hot.

Summer Cooler

Sangria

Makes 8-10 drinks
75 cl bottle red wine, chilled
2 oranges, sliced thinly
2 lemons, sliced thinly
150 ml/5 fl oz brandy
block of ice
600 ml/1 pt soda water, chilled

1 Marinate the orange and lemon slices in the brandy for 1 hour in the refrigerator.
2 Put a block of ice into a large jug, add the marinated fruit and brandy and stir in the wine. Top up with soda water and serve in wine glasses.

Champagne cup

Makes 14-16 drinks
2 × 75 cl bottles non-vintage dry champagne, chilled
75 ml/3 fl oz brandy
75 ml/3 fl oz curaçao
25 ml/1 fl oz lemon juice
5 tsps icing sugar
700 ml/1¼ pt soda water, chilled
crushed ice
2 nectarines, sliced
225 g/8 oz raspberries
sprigs of mint

1 Stand a punch bowl in a larger bowl filled with crushed ice. Mix all the liquid ingredients together in the punch bowl, adding the soda water last.

2 Stir in the sugar: be careful the liquid does not spill over – it will be very effervescent.

3 Add the nectarines and raspberries, garnish with the mint and serve immediately in champagne glasses.

Loving cup

Makes 10-12 drinks
75 cl bottle light red wine
75 cl bottle non-vintage dry champagne
150 ml/5 fl oz curaçao
100 g/4 oz icing sugar
zest of a lemon, cut thinly in a long twist
zest of 1 orange, cut thinly in a long twist
ice cubes
225 g/8 oz sweet black grapes, skinned, cut in half and deseeded
handful of crystallized violets (optional)

1 Put all the ingredients, except the grapes and crystallized violets, into a large punch bowl and allow to stand for 1 hour in the refrigerator.
2 Add plenty of ice cubes, garnish with the grapes, and violets, if wished, and serve immediately.

Right: *From left to right, Sangria, Loving cup, Pineapple cooler, Champagne cup, Rothschild cup*

Rothschild cup

Makes 10-12 drinks
75 cl bottle non-vintage dry champagne, chilled
225 g/8 oz strawberries, hulled and washed
100 g/4 oz icing sugar
crushed ice

1 Put the strawberries and icing sugar into a blender and purée.

2 Half-fill long glasses with crushed ice and pour a little strawberry purée over the ice in each glass. Top up each long glass with the chilled champagne, stir and serve immediately.

Pineapple cooler

Makes 12-14 drinks
700 ml/1¼ pt pineapple juice, chilled
75 cl bottle dry white wine, chilled
crushed ice
50 g/2 oz icing sugar
1.4 L/2½ pt soda water, chilled
zest of 1 orange, cut thinly in a long twist
zest of 1 lemon, cut thinly in a long twist
sprigs of eau-de-cologne mint

1 Half-fill a large jug with crushed ice and pour in the pineapple juice and white wine. Add the sugar and stir well.
2 Top up with soda water, stir again and add the orange and lemon zest. Float the mint on top. Serve in tall glasses with a lump of ice in each glass.

York fingers

Illustrated on pages 444-445

Makes 48
375 g/12 oz frozen puff pastry, defrosted
1 tbls made mustard
175 g/6 oz Cheddar cheese, grated
175 g/6 oz ham, thinly sliced
beaten egg or milk to glaze

1 Heat the oven to 200° C/400° F/gas 6.

Roll out the pastry on a lightly floured surface to a 30 cm/12 in square.
2 Spread the mustard thinly on half the pastry, leaving a narrow border all round the edge. Cover with cheese, then ham.
3 Damp the narrow border with cold water then fold the bare pastry over and press the edges together. Transfer carefully to a baking tray. Brush the top with egg or milk, to glaze. Using a sharp knife, mark across the parcel into 24 fingers. Mark lengthways down the middle, making 48 fingers.
4 Bake in the oven for 20-30 minutes or until well risen and cooked underneath.
5 Cool the fingers slightly on the baking tray, then cut through to separate.
6 Serve as soon as possible or reheat in a hot oven for 10 minutes to crisp.

Piped cream cheese canapés

Illustrated on pages 444-445

Makes 40 canapés
500 g/1 lb cream cheese
100 g/4 oz butter
½ tsp curry powder
salt and freshly ground black pepper
milk
40 crisp biscuits or fried bread rounds
10 walnut halves
5 black grapes, halved and pipped
10 slices button mushrooms
10 rolled anchovy fillets

1 Beat the cream cheese, butter and curry powder together, adding salt and pepper to taste and a little milk if necessary to make a piping consistency.
2 Using a piping bag fitted with a star nozzle, pipe rosettes on to the crisp biscuits or fried bread rounds.
3 Top each canapé with a walnut half, grape half, mushroom slice or anchovy.

Opening Champagne

First remove the wire from the top of the bottle by untwisting the loop. Cover the top with a cloth and hold the cork with one hand and the bottle with the other. With the bottle at a 45° angle, twist the bottle, not the cork, and ease the cork gently out.

Crudités and dip

Serves 6
For the crudités
6 carrots, cut into sticks
6 celery stalks, cut into sticks
**6 small tomatoes, left whole, or 3
  large tomatoes, quartered**
**½ cucumber, peeled (if desired)
  and cut into 16 long strips**
**8 radishes (optional), topped and
  tailed**
**1 small cauliflower, separated into
  florets**
For the dip
225 g/8 oz cottage cheese
2 tbls natural yoghurt
**2 spring onions or ½ onion,
  trimmed and chopped finely**
4 gherkins, finely chopped
**salt and freshly ground black
  pepper**
dash of Tabasco sauce (optional)
**chopped spring onion and gherkin,
  to garnish**

1 Arrange the crudités in groups around
the edge of a tray, shallow basket or dish.
2 Sieve or blend the cottage cheese
until smooth. Add the yoghurt and mix.

Above: *Crudités and dip*

3 Add the spring onions and gherkins to
the mixture.
4 Season to taste and add Tabasco, if
using. Give a final mixing.
5 Transfer to a serving bowl and place in
centre of crudités.

Sweetcorn and pepper canapés

Illustrated on pages 444-445

Makes 60 canapés
**1 fresh, medium-sized, thinly
  sliced white loaf**
300 g/10 oz cream cheese
1 red pepper, finely chopped
**1 green pepper, deseeded and
  finely chopped**
1 small can sweetcorn, drained

1 Toast the slices of bread, cut off the
crusts and cool the slices, pressed under
a heavy board to keep them flat.
2 Spread each slice of cold toast thickly
with cream cheese.
3 Mix the chopped red and green pepper together, and press over half of each

slice. Press the sweetcorn over the other
half of each slice.
4 Cutting across the pepper and sweetcorn, cut each slice in three.

Swiss prawn tartlets

Illustrated on pages 444-445

Makes 40
**Rich shortcrust pastry, made with
  350 g/12 oz flour, or 575 g/21 oz
  made weight pastry, defrosted**
25 g/1 oz butter
1 medium-sized onion, grated
450 g/1 lb boiled, peeled prawns
100 g/4 oz Gruyère cheese
150 ml/5 fl oz milk
**6 tbls natural yoghurt or soured
  cream**
25 g/1 oz flour
2 medium-sized egg yolks
½ tsp ground nutmeg
few drops of anchovy essence
**salt and freshly ground black
  pepper**
1 medium-sized egg white
butter for greasing

1 Heat the oven to 190° C/375° F/gas 5.
Roll out the pastry on a lightly floured

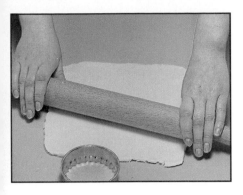

surface, very thinly. Using a 7.5 cm/3 in cutter, cut out 40 rounds.

2 Grease forty 5 cm/2 in tartlet tins, then line with the pastry.

3 Melt the butter in a small saucepan and cook the onion until softened.

4 Reserve 40 of the best prawns for garnish. Stir the remaining prawns into the onion. Divide the prawn and onion mixture between the lined tartlet tins.

5 Divide the cheese equally between the pastry cases, sprinkling it over the prawn and onion mixture.

6 Whisk together the milk, yoghurt or soured cream, flour, egg yolks, nutmeg,

anchovy essence and salt and pepper to taste. Lightly whisk the egg white until frothy but not too stiff. Fold into the milk mixture. Divide it between the tartlets.

7 Bake the tartlets in the oven for 30 minutes or until golden brown on top and the pastry is cooked and crisp. Serve warm, garnished with the reserved prawns.

Smoked salmon and watercress pinwheels

Illustrated on pages 444-445

Makes about 60
1 fresh, medium-sized uncut white loaf
175 g/6 oz butter, softened
1 tbls lemon juice
2 tbls finely chopped watercress leaves
350 g/12 oz smoked salmon, thinly sliced

1 Remove the top and bottom crusts from the loaf then cut the loaf into 8 slices, lengthways. An electric carving knife makes this job easier.

2 Remove the remaining crusts from each slice of bread and roll each slice lightly with a rolling pin.

3 Beat the softened butter with the lemon juice and watercress. Spread the slices with the watercress butter then arrange the smoked salmon on top.

4 Roll up each slice lengthways. Wrap the rolls firmly in cling film, to hold them in shape.

5 Either store the rolls in the refrigerator until later or, if you are preparing well in advance, freeze them.

6 To serve, cut each roll into thin rounds. If the rolls have been frozen, cut them while they are only partially thawed, using an electric carving knife if possible. This helps to keep the pinwheels in a good shape.

7 Arrange the pinwheels on serving plates and cover until ready to serve.

Left: *Smoked salmon and watercress pinwheels*

Winter Warmer

Negus

Makes 12-14 drinks
**2 × 75 cl bottles port (or 1
    bottle red wine and 1 bottle
    port)**
125 ml/4 fl oz brandy (optional)
1 large lemon
12 cloves
peel of 3 lemons
2 tsps freshly grated nutmeg
2 tbls soft brown sugar
4 cinnamon sticks
300 ml/11 fl oz boiling water

1 Stick the cloves into the lemon and
place in a large pan. Add the rest of the
ingredients and heat slowly, testing to
see if more sugar is needed.

English bishop

Makes 6-8 drinks
75 cl bottle port
75 ml/3 fl oz dark rum
75 ml/3 fl oz brandy
12 cloves
1 medium-sized orange
1 tsp allspice
1 tsp freshly grated nutmeg
soft brown sugar to taste

1 Stick the cloves into the orange and
bake until brown. Meanwhile heat the
port in a pan.
2 Cut the browned orange into quarters
and place in a warmed bowl. Pour the
warmed port on top and stir in the spices,
rum and brandy. Sweeten with sugar if
necessary.

Dr Johnson's
special punch

Makes 14-16 drinks
2 × 75 cl bottles red wine
200 ml/7 fl oz brandy
200 ml/7 fl oz Cointreau
12 cubes of sugar
1 medium-sized orange
freshly grated nutmeg

1 Rub the sugar cubes on the orange.
Slice the orange and place in a pan. Add
the wine and heat slowly, stirring in the
flavoured sugar.
2 When hot, remove from heat and add
the brandy and Cointreau. Ladle into
punch cups and sprinkle with nutmeg.

Stuffed mushrooms
on croûtons

Makes 12
**15 medium-sized cup mushrooms,
    about 5 cm/2 in in diameter**
9-10 tbls olive oil
**3 large garlic cloves, finely
    chopped**
100 g/4 oz finely chopped onion
½ tsp dried thyme
**salt and freshly ground black
    pepper**
4 tbls finely chopped parsley
25-50 g/1-2 oz butter
**3 tbls white breadcrumbs, made
    with day-old bread**
**bouquets of watercress, to garnish
    (optional)**
For the croûtons
**4 slices white bread, 5 mm/¼ in
    thick**
oil for frying the croûtons

1 Wipe the mushrooms clean with a
damp cloth. Remove the stalks from 12
of the mushrooms, leaving the caps
whole.

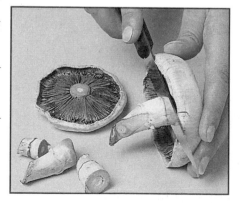

2 Put the mushroom caps in a bowl,
dribble over about 5 tbls oil and toss the

caps in the oil until well coated. Set the
bowl aside, leaving the caps to absorb
the oil. Chop the mushroom stalks and
the three whole mushrooms finely.

3 Over medium heat, sauté the garlic
and onion in the remaining oil until soft
but not brown. Add the chopped mushroom mixture and dried thyme. Turn up
the heat and cook, stirring continuously
until the liquid from the mushrooms has
evaporated. Lower the heat, and season
with salt and freshly ground black pepper to taste. Remove the mixture from
the pan, stir in the chopped parsley and
leave to get cold.
4 Using a plain 5 cm/2 in biscuit cutter,
cut 12 rounds from the bread.
5 In a large frying-pan, heat the oil and
sauté the bread rounds in three batches

Above: *Negus, garnished with fruits*

until they have turned a very pale gold on both sides.

6 Drain well on absorbent paper. When cool and dry, arrange on a baking sheet.

7 Remove the mushroom caps from the bowl. Put a tiny knob of butter inside each cap, then spoon in the prepared mixture, mounding it slightly in the centre. Put some breadcrumbs and a tiny knob of butter on top, then arrange each cap on a croûton, hollow side up. Cover with cling film. Put the baking sheet in the refrigerator or in a cool place until required.

8 Heat the oven to 200° C/400° F/gas 6.

9 About 30 minutes before serving, transfer the baking sheet to the oven and bake for 25 minutes, or until the caps are tender and the croûtons gold. Transfer to a serving platter and serve immediately, garnished with bouquets of watercress, if wished.

Tomato tartlets

Illustrated on page 449

Makes 25
**400 g/13 oz shortcrust pastry,
    defrosted if frozen**
4 garlic cloves, finely chopped
175 g/6 oz finely chopped onion
**5 tbls olive oil, plus extra for
    brushing**
**750 g/1½ lb ripe tomatoes,
    blanched, skinned, seeded and
    chopped**
**2-3 tsps finely crushed coriander
    seeds**
1 tsp sugar
**salt and freshly ground black
    pepper**
5-6 tbls finely chopped parsley
**1 large red pepper, halved and
    seeded**
50 black olives, stoned and halved
sprigs of parsley, to garnish

1 Heat the oven to 200° C/400° F/gas 6. Grease 25 × 6.5 cm/2½ in tartlet tins.

2 On a floured surface, roll out the dough to 5 mm/¼ in thick and line the tins. Prick them inside with a fork. Chill for 30 minutes. Line with greaseproof paper, weight with rice, and bake blind for 20 minutes. Remove the paper and rice, return to the oven for 5-10 minutes, or until pale gold. Leave to get cold, then remove from the tins.

3 In a heavy-based frying-pan, sauté the garlic and onion in the oil until soft but not brown, stirring frequently. Add the tomatoes, coriander and sugar. Cook over fairly high heat, stirring occasionally, for about 20 minutes, or until the tomatoes have reduced to a very thick pulp. Season with salt and pepper to taste. Stir in the parsley and leave to get cold.

4 Heat the grill to high. Grill the red pepper halves, skin side up. When the skin blisters, remove and wrap in a damp cloth, to loosen the skin. When cool enough to handle, peel off the skin and discard it. Cut the pepper into thin strips.

5 Spoon the cold tomato filling into the cold tartlet cases. Transfer to a baking sheet and arrange the red pepper strips in a criss-cross pattern on top. Garnish each tartlet with 4 slices of black olive. Cover with cling film and chill.

6 Heat the oven to 200° C/400° F/gas 6.

7 Brush the tartlets lightly with oil and bake in the oven for about 20 minutes.

8 Serve hot, garnished with parsley.

Below: *Stuffed mushrooms on croûtons*

Mocktail Party

Cola cup

Makes 1 L/1¾ pt
2 bananas
1 orange
1 lemon
1 L/1¾ pt cola, chilled

1 Pour water into a household glove, seal it with a freezer tie and put in the freezer compartment of the refrigerator until solid.
2 Slice the bananas, oranges and lemons. Place them in the jug or bowl and pour over the cola.
3 Remove the glove from the freezer compartment. Peel off the glove. Add the shaped ice block to the jug or bowl and serve.

Strawberry froth

Makes 500 ml/18 fl oz
225 g/8 oz strawberries, defrosted if frozen
275 ml/10 fl oz fresh orange juice
sugar to taste
To garnish
extra strawberries, or strawberry ice cubes (optional)

1 Blend together the strawberries, orange juice and sugar. Place in a jug or bowl and chill in the refrigerator.
2 Make strawberry ice cubes or slice the strawberries for a garnish.
3 When ready to serve, add the strawberry ice cubes or sliced strawberries. Each person should get some slices of fruit with their drink.

Ginger and melon cup

Makes 700 ml/1¼ pt
1 medium-sized Spanish melon
575 ml/1 pt ginger ale, chilled
green food colouring (optional)
ice cubes, to serve (optional)

1 Quarter the melon, scoop out the seeds and, using a melon baller, scoop out the flesh of one of the quarters.

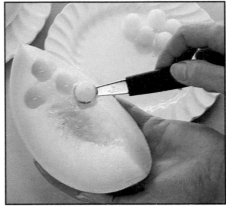

2 Place the melon balls into the sections of an ice tray. Fill the ice tray with water with a few drops of green food colouring added, if wished. Freeze.

3 Scoop out the rest of the flesh of the melon and blend it until smooth.
4 When ready to serve, add the puréed melon to the chilled ginger ale. Remove the melon ice cubes from the freezer, add them to the mixture, stir well and serve in novelty glasses or with decorative straws.

Tropical special

Makes 1.6 l/2¾ pt
425 g/15 oz canned guavas, drained
425 g/15 oz canned sliced mangoes, drained
425 g/15 oz canned kiwi fruit, drained
575 ml/1 pt pineapple juice
275 ml/10 fl oz fresh orange juice
ice cubes, to serve

1 Blend together the guavas, mangoes and kiwi fruit. Pass them through a fine sieve over a glass serving jug or punch bowl.
2 Pour in the pineapple and orange juice, stir to mix and chill in the refrigerator. Serve with ice cubes.

Fruit cocktail

Makes 1 L/1¾ pt
425 ml/15 fl oz mixed fruit drink, chilled
275 ml/10 fl oz bitter lemon, chilled
275 ml/10 fl oz apple juice, chilled
ice cubes, to serve
2 lemons, quartered and sliced
2 oranges, quartered and sliced

Quick sardine pizza

Serves 4
**2 × 90 g/3½ oz cans sardines in
    oil, drained**
250 g/9 oz self-raising flour
pinch of salt
50 g/2 oz soft tub margarine
1 egg, beaten
4 tbls milk
**180 g/6½ oz can pizza topping
    sauce**
50 g/2 oz Cheddar cheese, grated

1 Heat the oven to 220° C/425° F/gas 7.
2 Sift the flour and salt into a bowl and
rub in the margarine. Stir in the egg and
milk to make a soft, but not sticky dough.
3 Roll out the dough on a floured surface to a circle and use to line a 20 cm/8
in loose-bottomed flan tin or flan ring
placed on a baking sheet.
4 Spoon over the sauce to within 1 cm/
½ in of the edge. Arrange the sardines
on top then sprinkle over the cheese.
5 Bake in the oven for 15 minutes.
Remove from the tin or ring and serve.

1 Pour the mixed fruit drink, bitter
lemon, and apple juice into a glass jug or
punch bowl.
2 Pour into glasses, add ice and garnish
with slices of lemon and orange.

Vegetable cocktail

Makes 1 L/1¾ pt
2 celery stalks, roughly chopped
½ cucumber, roughly chopped
1 carrot, roughly chopped
1 clove garlic, roughly chopped
2 × 425 g/15 oz cans tomato juice
**100 g/4 oz beetroot, cooked and
    chopped**
2 tsps Worcestershire sauce
**salt and freshly ground black
    pepper**
ice cubes, to serve

1 Blend half of the celery, cucumber,
carrot and garlic together with a little of
the tomato juice. Add the rest of the vegetables and blend again.
2 Pass the mixture through a fine sieve
into a glass jug or punch bowl. Add the
remaining tomato juice, Worcestershire
sauce and salt and pepper to taste. Stir.
3 Chill. Serve with ice in tall glasses.

Ψ Serve with celery or carrot sticks as
edible cocktail swizzles.

Above: *Top, Fruit Cocktail, Tropical special; Middle row, Ginger and melon cup,
Strawberry froth, Cola cup, Vegetable cocktail; Below: Quick sardine pizza cut in
wedges to serve with 'Mocktails'*

Buffets and Brunches

A buffet is the ideal way to entertain a crowd. In fact, buffet parties often start when the number you wish to entertain exceeds the number your dining table will hold. And an occasion when guests help themselves to the food is sure to be a relaxed affair. Another way to entertain a large group in a stylish but informal way is Sunday brunch. A happy combination of breakfast and lunch, it is perfectly suited to a lazy Sunday.

Summer Buffet

Fish and vegetable salad

Serves 12
800 g/1¾ lb haddock fillets
1.25 L/2 pt cold water
150 ml/¼ pt dry white wine
1 bay leaf
1 onion, finely chopped
bouquet garni
6 black peppercorns
salt
500 g/1 lb French beans, cut into
 5 cm/2 in lengths
500 g/1 lb baby carrots, cut into
 5 mm/¼ in slices
2 large green peppers, deseeded
 and cut into 5 cm/2 in strips
2 large red peppers, deseeded and
 cut into 5 cm/2 in strips
1 large head celery, cut into
 5 mm/¼ in slices
1 kg/2 lb unpeeled prawns
2 × 200 g/7 oz cans tuna fish
250 g/9 oz black olives, to garnish
For the oil and vinegar dressing
12 tbls olive oil
4 tbls white wine vinegar
1 tsp mustard
salt and freshly ground black
 pepper
For the mayonnaise dressing
225 ml/8 fl oz thick bottled
 mayonnaise
2 tsps chopped fresh parsley
2 tsps chopped fresh dill
1 garlic clove, crushed (optional)

1 Put the water in a large saucepan with the white wine, bay leaf, onion, bouquet garni and peppercorns. Bring to the boil then simmer for 30 minutes.
2 Strain the cooking liquid, cool and return to the rinsed-out pan. Add the haddock fillets, bring to the boil, then reduce the heat and simmer for 10 minutes or until the fish flakes easily. Remove the fish with a slotted spoon and set aside to cool. Discard the cooking liquid.
3 Rinse out the pan and fill two-thirds with cold salted water. Bring to the boil, add the French beans and boil for 5 minutes to blanch them. Remove with a

slotted spoon and put beans into a bowl.
4 Shake the ingredients for the oil and vinegar dressing together in a screwtop jar. Pour over 3 tbls of the dressing while the beans are still warm.
5 Put the carrots into the same boiling water and cook for 3 minutes. Remove with a slotted spoon, put in a separate bowl and pour over 3 tbls of the oil and vinegar dressing.
6 Put the pepper strips into a bowl and pour 6 tbls of the oil and vinegar dressing over them. Mix well. Put the celery pieces into another bowl and pour over

the remaining oil and vinegar dressing.
7 Skin and flake the cooled fish fillets. Make the mayonnaise dressing: mix the mayonnaise with the chopped parsley, dill and crushed garlic, if using. Carefully stir in the fish to coat it evenly.
8 Reserve 14 unpeeled prawns for the garnish and peel the rest.

Below: Clockwise from top, Strawberry Charlotte, Red fruit salad, Fish and vegetable salad served with a salad of pasta, apple, watercress and spring onion mixed in a vinaigrette dressing

9 Put the tuna fish with its oil into a large bowl and then flake it with a fork so fish and oil are combined.

10 To assemble the salad, spread the French beans all over the surface of a large platter. Cover the French beans with a layer of carrots, leaving about 5 cm/2 in of the beans exposed around the edge. Lightly season the celery pieces with salt and layer them on top of the carrots, leaving some carrots exposed. Cover with the pepper strips.

11 Pile the white fish mixture on top of the layer of peppers. Place the tuna fish along the top of the white fish.

12 Cover the exposed white fish mixture with the peeled prawns and arrange the unpeeled ones around the edge of the dish. Garnish with the black olives.

Ⓨ Prepare ingredients up to step 9, cover and chill until needed.

Red fruit salad

Serves 12
500 g/1 lb Ogen melon, seeds removed
75 g/3 oz light soft brown sugar
425 ml/³⁄₄ pt water
thinly pared rind of 1 lemon
4 tbls port
250 g/9 oz raspberries
250 g/9 oz redcurrants, stalks removed
100 g/4 oz strawberries, hulled
500 g/1 lb black cherries, stoned
25 g/1 oz flaked almonds (optional)

1 Put the sugar, water and lemon rind into a pan over a low heat until the sugar has melted, then simmer gently for 5 minutes.

2 Remove from the heat and allow to cool. Discard the lemon rind and stir in the port.

3 Put all the fruit into a glass serving dish, pour over the port syrup and chill for 2 hours.

4 Sprinkle with the flaked almonds before serving, if wished.

Strawberry Charlotte

Serves 12
350 g/12 oz fresh strawberries, hulled
175 g/6 oz unsalted butter, softened
100 g/4 oz caster sugar
grated zest and juice of 1 orange
¹⁄₄ tsp almond flavouring
100 g/4 oz ground almonds
300 ml/¹⁄₂ pt dry white wine
450 ml/³⁄₄ pt double cream
2 packets sponge fingers
butter, for greasing

1 Grease the base of an 18 cm/7 in deep round cake tin and line with greaseproof paper; grease the lining paper.

2 In a large mixing bowl, beat the butter, sugar, orange zest and almond flavouring together until light and fluffy. Gradually beat in the ground almonds alternately with 100 ml/3¹⁄₂ fl oz of the wine. Do not add the wine too quickly to the mixture, otherwise it may curdle.

3 Whip 300 ml/¹⁄₂ pt of the cream until it forms soft peaks, then fold into the almond mixture.

4 Mix the remaining wine with the orange juice in a large bowl. Trim the

sponge fingers so that they are the same height as the tin. Reserve the trimmings. Dip each sponge finger quickly into the

wine and orange mixture, and use to line the sides of the cake tin in a single layer, placing the rounded untrimmed end upwards and the sugar-coated side outwards.

5 Quickly soak any remaining sponge fingers, together with the reserved trimmed ends in the wine and orange mixture. Reserve 100 g/4 oz strawberries, and slice the rest.

6 Spread one-third of the almond mixture over the base of the prepared tin. Cover with half the sliced strawberries and half the remaining sponge fingers

and trimmed ends. Repeat these layers once more, finishing with the remaining third of almond mixture.

7 Place a piece of greased greaseproof paper over the top. Cover with a small plate and place a weight on top to press it down.

8 Refrigerate for at least 4 hours, or preferably overnight, until the mixture is quite firm.

9 Remove the weight and paper. Place an inverted plate on top of the tin. Holding the tin and plate firmly, invert, giving a sharp shake. Lift off the tin.

10 Slice all but one of the reserved strawberries. Arrange the slices over the top and around the bottom edge of the Charlotte; place the whole one in the centre. Whip the remaining cream until it forms soft peaks and pipe decoratively around the top and bottom edges. Chill until ready to serve.

Pâté Party

Smoked haddock pâté

Serves 10-12

500 g/1 lb smoked haddock fillets, skinned and cut into small cubes
2 egg whites
300 ml/½ pt double cream
freshly ground white pepper
softened butter, for greasing
1 lettuce, leaves separated
tomato and cucumber slices, to garnish

1 Pound the haddock to a smooth purée with a pestle and mortar, then pound in the egg whites. Alternatively, blend the haddock with the egg whites in a food processor until smooth.
2 Transfer the mixture to a large bowl and gradually beat in the double cream until it is well incorporated. Season with pepper, then cover and refrigerate.
3 Thoroughly grease a loaf tin or ovenproof dish, measuring about 18 × 9 cm/ 7 × 3½ in and 7.5 cm/3 in deep.
4 Bring a large pan of water to the boil, then plunge in the lettuce leaves for a few seconds until they soften. Drain and immediately plunge into cold water, to retain the colour. Drain the lettuce leaves on a clean tea-towel.
5 Line the buttered tin with lettuce leaves, reserving some for the top.
6 Heat the oven to 180° C/350° F/gas 4.
7 Spoon the haddock mixture into the lined tin and smooth the top. Fold any overhanging lettuce leaves over the fish mixture, then cover the top with the reserved leaves. Butter a piece of greaseproof paper and lay it buttered side down, on top of the lettuce.
8 Stand loaf tin in a roasting tin, pour in hot water to come halfway up the sides of the loaf tin, then cook in the oven for 40-45 minutes, until the pâté is firm to the touch.
9 Remove the pâté from the oven, cool, then refrigerate overnight.
10 To serve, remove the greaseproof paper, place a serving plate on top of the tin, then invert and turn out. Wipe away excess liquid. Garnish with tomato and cucumber and serve cut into slices.

Pâté in puff pastry

Serves 10-12

500 g/1 lb lean pork
25 g/1 oz butter
1 onion, chopped
2 tbls brandy
350 g/12 oz fatty pork belly rashers
250 g/9 oz pig liver, washed
1 large egg, beaten
50 g/2 oz fresh white breadcrumbs
finely grated zest of 1 orange
3 tbls finely chopped fresh parsley
2 cloves garlic, crushed
¼ tsp ground allspice
salt and freshly ground black pepper
50 g/2 oz black olives, quartered and stoned
250 g/9 oz piece lean cooked ham, cut into 1 cm/½ in cubes
350 g/12 oz frozen puff pastry, defrosted
vegetable oil, for greasing
plain flour, for dusting
1 small egg, beaten, for sealing
mustard and cress, to garnish
tomato wedges, to garnish

1 Melt the butter in a frying-pan, add the onion and fry gently for 5 minutes until soft and lightly coloured. Add the brandy, bring to boil and boil for 1 minute, until reduced by half, then cool.
2 Meanwhile, carefully trim and remove any skin from the lean pork, pork belly and liver and coarsely mince them twice. This is best done in a food processor.

3 Put the minced meats into a large bowl together with the contents of the frying-pan. Add the large egg, breadcrumbs, orange zest, parsley, garlic and allspice. Season generously with salt and pepper, then beat well together. Cover and stand in a cool place for 2 hours.
4 Heat the oven to 180° C/350° F/gas 4. Grease a 1.5 L/2½ pt oval ovenproof dish, line the base with foil and grease.
5 Gently mix the olives and ham into the pork mixture, then spoon into the dish and cover.

472

flaps to enclose the pâté completely. Press all joins firmly to seal.

13 Dampen a baking tray, put the pâté on it join side down, and brush with beaten egg. Make leaves with the pastry trimmings, brush the undersides with egg and place on top of the pâté. Brush with beaten egg and make a small hole in the centre.

14 Bake in the oven for 40-45 minutes until the pastry is well risen and golden brown. Immediately loosen from the baking sheet with a palette knife, cool and refrigerate.

15 To serve, place the pâté on a platter, garnish with mustard and cress and tomato wedges and serve cut into neat slices.

Cheese pâté

Serves 10
350 g/12 oz cream cheese
2 cloves garlic, crushed
1 tbls snipped chives
salt and freshly ground black
 pepper
25 g/1 oz black peppercorns,
 crushed, or chopped parsley
vegetable oil, for greasing

1 Grease a 425 ml/¾ pt straight-sided casserole or soufflé dish with vegetable oil.

2 Put the cheese in a bowl and beat until very soft, then beat in the garlic and chives until well blended. Season with salt and freshly ground black pepper to taste.

3 Spoon the cheese mixture into the prepared dish and smooth the top. Cover with a lid or foil and freeze for 30 minutes.

4 Remove the pâté from the freezer and remove the lid or foil. Place a small flat serving plate on top of the pâté, then invert and carefully turn the pâté out on to the plate.

5 Using a palette knife, press the crushed peppercorns or chopped parsley on to the pâté to coat the top and sides completely. Brush away any excess and then wipe the plate clean.

6 Defrost in the refrigerator for 30 minutes, then stand at room temperature for 15 minutes. Serve with a spoon, to scoop out individual portions. Serve with French bread or Melba toast.

Above: *From left to right, Pâté in puff pastry, Smoked haddock pâté, Cheese pâté, served with a mixed salad and Melba toast*

6 Stand the dish in a roasting tin, and pour in boiling water to come halfway up the sides of the dish. Cook for 2 hours, or until a skewer inserted in the centre of the pâté feels very hot when removed.

7 Allow the pâté to cool, then refrigerate overnight.

8 Run a knife around sides of the pâté to loosen it, place a serving plate on top, then turn out.

9 Heat the oven to 220° C/425° F/gas 7.

10 Roll out the pastry on a lightly floured surface to a square large enough to enclose the pâté. Trim the edges, reserving trimmings.

11 Place the pâté in the centre of pastry and cut out a small square from each corner of the pastry.

12 To enclose pâté, brush flaps of pastry well with beaten egg then fold the top and bottom flaps over the ends of the pâté, pressing them neatly round the shape of the pâté. Fold over the 2 side

🍸 For a sophisticated finish, try garnishing the cheese pâté with small bunches of either green or black grapes.

Winter Buffet

Rice salad

Serves 10
500 g/1 lb long-grain rice
1 cucumber, cut into 1 cm/½ in
  dice
salt
4 tomatoes, deseeded and diced
1 red or green pepper, deseeded
  and diced
50 g/2 oz flaked almonds
75 g/3 oz seedless raisins
about 20 black olives, halved and
  stoned, to garnish (optional)
¼-½ cucumber, halved
  lengthways and thinly sliced, to
  garnish (optional)
For the dressing
4 tbls vegetable oil
4 tsps lemon juice
¾ tsp ground ginger
freshly ground black pepper

1 Put the diced cucumber into a colander set on a tray or large plate. Sprinkle with salt and leave to stand for 30 minutes, to allow the cucumber to drain.

Below: *Quiche quartet, Rice salad, Courgette and carrot vinaigrette, with a choice of winter fruit salads for dessert*

2 Meanwhile, cook the rice in plenty of boiling salted water for 12-15 minutes until tender, then rinse well under hot running water to separate the grains.
3 Put the drained rice while it is still warm into a large bowl and add the tomatoes, red pepper, almonds and raisins. Pat the cucumber dry with absorbent paper and add to the salad, then fold gently to mix.
4 Put all the dressing ingredients into a screw-top jar with salt and pepper to taste. Shake to mix thoroughly. Pour over the warm rice salad and stir in gently. Leave the salad to cool, then cover and keep in a cool place.
5 Transfer to a large shallow serving dish. Arrange the halved olives around the edge and scatter the cucumber slices on top, if wished.

Courgette and carrot vinaigrette

Serves 10
1 kg/2 lb small carrots, cut into
  matchstick strips
salt
1 kg/2 lb small courgettes, cut into
  matchstick strips

For the dressing
5 tbls vegetable oil or olive oil
2 tbls white wine vinegar
2-3 tbls finely chopped parsley
freshly ground black pepper
½ tsp ground coriander
  (optional)

1 Put the carrots into a pan of boiling salted water, return to boiling point and simmer for 8 minutes, or until just tender. Drain in a colander, rinse under cold running water and drain again thoroughly.
2 Meanwhile, plunge the courgettes into a pan of boiling salted water. Return to boiling point and simmer for about 3 minutes, or until just tender.
3 Drain the courgettes well in a colander, rinse under cold running water and drain thoroughly. Transfer the courgettes and the carrots to a large flat dish.
4 Put all the dressing ingredients into a screw-top jar with salt and pepper to taste and the coriander, if using. Shake thoroughly to mix.
5 Pour the dressing over the vegetables while they are still warm, then turn with a large metal spoon until evenly coated with dressing. Leave to cool.
6 To serve, spoon the courgettes and carrots into 1 or 2 serving dishes, then pour over any remaining dressing.

Quiche quartet

Makes 4 x 20 cm/8 in quiches
For the basic quiches
750 g/1½ lb shortcrust pastry,
    defrosted if frozen
8 eggs
600 ml/1 pt milk
lightly beaten egg white, to seal
For the chicken and walnut filling
250 g/9 oz cooked chicken, finely
    chopped
50 g/2 oz shelled walnuts, roughly
    chopped
100 g/4 oz Gruyère cheese, finely
    grated
large pinch of freshly grated
    nutmeg
salt and freshly ground black
    pepper
watercress sprigs, to garnish
    (optional)
For the bacon, mushroom and
parsley filling
100 g/4 oz unsmoked streaky
    bacon, rinds removed, cut into
    strips
100 g/4 oz button mushrooms,
    thinly sliced
1-2 tbls chopped fresh parsley
salt and freshly ground black·
    pepper
75 ml/3 fl oz milk
tomato wedges and parsley sprigs,
    to garnish (optional)
For the spicy sausage and tomato
filling
100 g/4 oz thin smoked sausages
    (e.g. kabanos or chorizo), sliced
4 tomatoes, skinned, deseeded and
    finely chopped
¼ tsp dried marjoram
pinch of chilli powder (optional)
salt and freshly ground black
    pepper
2 tbls tomato purée
4 black olives, to garnish (optional)
For the prawn and sweetcorn filling
100 g/4 oz peeled prawns,
    defrosted if frozen
200 g/7 oz can sweetcorn, drained
½ tsp dillweed
grated zest of ½ lemon
salt and freshly ground black
    pepper
fresh dill, to garnish (optional)
whole prawns, to garnish
    (optional)

1 Heat the oven to 200° C/400° F/gas 6.
2 Roll out the pastry on a floured surface and use it to line four 20 cm/8 in

ceramic flan dishes or flan rings set on baking sheets. Prick each base with a

fork. Place a large circle of greaseproof paper or foil in each pastry case and weight it down with baking beans.

3 Bake in the oven for 10 minutes. Remove the paper and beans and brush the insides of the pastry cases with beaten egg white.
4 Return to the oven for a further 5 minutes.

5 To make the chicken and walnut filling, mix the chicken with the walnuts and half the cheese. Add nutmeg, and season with salt and pepper.
6 To make the bacon, mushroom and parsley filling, heat a frying-pan without fat over low heat. Add the bacon and fry over moderate heat, stirring, for 2

minutes. Add the mushrooms and fry for a further 1-2 minutes until slightly softened. Remove the pan from the heat and stir in the parsley. Season to taste with salt and pepper. Set aside to cool slightly.
7 To make the spicy sausage and tomato filling, mix the sliced sausage in a bowl with the chopped tomatoes, dried marjoram and chilli powder, if using. Season to taste with salt and pepper.
8 To make the prawn and sweetcorn filling, combine the prawns, sweetcorn, dill and lemon zest in a bowl. Season to taste with salt and pepper.
9 Spoon the chosen fillings into the pastry cases, distributing them evenly.
10 In a large bowl, beat together the eggs and the milk with a fork. Pour one-quarter of the egg and milk mixture evenly over each filling.

11 Return to the oven and bake for about 35 minutes until set and golden. A skewer inserted in the centre should come out clean.

12 Serve warm or cold, cut into wedges and garnished with the watercress, tomato and parsley, olives or dill and prawns, if liked.

Chicken pie

Serves 6
**1.6 kg/3½ lb oven-ready chicken,
  plus the giblets
1.1 L/2 pt water
1 onion, quartered
1 carrot, roughly sliced
1 bay leaf
6 peppercorns
1 tsp salt
2 sprigs fresh thyme (optional)
50 g/2 oz margarine or butter
50 g/2 oz plain flour
3 tbls chopped fresh parsley
pinch of freshly grated nutmeg
freshly ground black pepper
350 g/12 oz frozen puff pastry,
  defrosted
margarine or butter, for greasing
milk, for glazing**

1 Put the chicken and giblets in a large saucepan, pour over the water and bring to the boil. Skim the fat from the surface with a slotted spoon, then add the onion, carrot, bay leaf, peppercorns, salt and thyme, if using. Lower the heat, cover and simmer for about 1½ hours, until the chicken is tender.
2 Remove from the heat and, when the chicken is cool enough to handle, remove from the cooking liquid. Strain off 600 ml/1 pt of the liquid and reserve, then slice the flesh into chunks.
3 Heat the oven to 220° C/425° F/gas 7 and grease a 1 L/2 pt pie dish.
4 Melt the margarine in a saucepan, sprinkle in the flour and stir over low heat for 1-2 minutes until straw-coloured. Remove from the heat and gradually stir in the reserved stock. Return to the heat and simmer, stirring, until thick and smooth. Stir in the parsley and nutmeg, then season to taste with salt and pepper. Gently stir the chicken pieces into the sauce to mix well.
5 Pour the chicken sauce mixture into the prepared dish. Cool.
6 Roll out the pastry on a floured surface to a shape slightly larger than the circumference of the pie dish. Cut off a long narrow strip all around the edge and reserve all the trimmings. Brush the rim of the dish with water and press the strip of pastry on to the rim. Brush the strip with a little more water, then place the large piece of pastry on top. Trim the edge, then knock up and flute.
7 Make leaves with the pastry trimmings, brush the undersides with water and press on top of the pie. Make a small hole in the centre of the pie, then brush the pastry all over with milk. Transfer pie to oven and bake for 30 minutes until the top is puffed up and golden brown.
8 Remove from the oven, allow to cool, then refrigerate until required.

Mushroom and pepper salad

Serves 6
**500 g/1 lb button mushrooms,
  thickly sliced
15 g/½ oz margarine or butter
5 rashers streaky bacon, rinds
  removed
1 red pepper, deseeded and cut
  into small strips
1 green pepper, deseeded and cut
  into small strips
chopped fresh parsley, to garnish**
For the dressing
**6 tbls olive oil
juice of 1 lemon
salt and freshly ground black
  pepper**

1 Melt the margarine in a frying-pan, add the bacon and fry until it is thoroughly cooked and crisp.
2 Meanwhile, bring a pan of water to the boil, add the red and green pepper strips and blanch for 1 minute. Drain and rinse under cold running water.
3 Chop the bacon into small pieces and combine with the mushrooms and peppers in a serving dish.
4 To make the dressing, put the oil in a small bowl with the lemon juice and salt and pepper to taste. Mix well with a fork and pour over the salad. Refrigerate, covered, until required.
5 Just before serving, toss the salad and garnish with parsley.

Blackberry mousse

Serves 6
**750 g/1½ lb blackberries, fresh or
  frozen
75 g/3 oz caster sugar
4 tbls water
1½ rounded tbls (1½ sachets)
  gelatine
300 ml/½ pt double cream
2 egg whites**

1 Reserve a few whole blackberries for decoration, then put the remainder in a saucepan. Add the sugar, cover and

cook gently until soft and mushy, stirring occasionally.
2 Press the cooked blackberries

through a nylon sieve to remove all pips and form a smooth purée.
3 Put the water in a small bowl, sprinkle the gelatine over the top and leave to soak for about 5 minutes until spongy. Stand the bowl in a pan of gently simmering water and stir until the gelatine has dissolved and the liquid is clear.

Above: *Blackberry mousse*

Pork stroganoff

Illustrated on pages 468-469

Serves 18
3.2 kg/7 lb pork fillet
100 g/4 oz butter
8 tbls oil
4 garlic cloves, crushed
225 g/8 oz onions, sliced
1 tbls ground coriander
2 tsps salt
2 tsps freshly ground pepper
2 tbls flour
600 ml/1 pt reduced chicken stock
1 tbls lemon juice
225 g/8 oz button mushrooms,
   sliced
275 ml/10 fl oz soured cream
4 tbls finely chopped parsley

1 Trim the pork and cut into 25 mm/1 in thick slices. Pat the pork slices on absorbent paper. In a large frying-pan or saucepan, melt 25 g/1 oz butter and 3 tbls oil. When it is hot, add a single layer of pork and fry over a moderate heat until browned. Turn and brown the other side. Remove the meat to a large casserole (or divide between 2 casseroles). Add a little more butter and oil as needed, and fry the rest of the pork in batches.
2 Add the remaining oil to the pan and fry the garlic and onions over moderate heat for 4-5 minutes, stirring frequently. Stir in the coriander, salt and freshly ground black pepper and fry for 2 minutes, stirring. Stir in the flour and cook for 2-3 minutes, stirring continuously, to form a pale roux.
3 Pour on the stock gradually, stirring all the time, and bring to the boil. Simmer for 3 minutes and stir in the lemon juice.
4 Pour the sauce over the meat, stir well and cover. Lower the heat and simmer for 30 minutes, stirring occasionally.
5 Heat the remaining butter in a pan and fry the mushrooms for 3 minutes, stirring.
6 Stir the mushrooms, soured cream and half the parsley into the casserole. Taste and adjust the seasoning if necessary. Serve garnished with parsley.

As an alternative to the cold chicken pie, pork stroganoff makes an excellent hot dish for a large group. It can be made a day in advance, then just re-heated gently; the flavours improve with keeping. Serve with mixed pepper salad and with plain boiled rice or buttered noodles.

4 Remove the bowl from the pan and cool slightly. Pour the gelatine solution in a thin stream on to the sieved blackberries, stirring constantly. Allow to cool

in stiff peaks and fold into the mixture. Pour into a serving dish, or into 6 individual glasses, and refrigerate for at least 4 hours until set.

then refrigerate until beginning to set.
5 Whip the cream until thick and fold half into the cooled purée.
6 Whisk the egg whites until they stand

7 Just before serving, spoon the remaining whipped cream into a piping bag and use to decorate the mousse. Finish with the reserved blackberries. Serve with sponge fingers or shortbread biscuits.

Sunday Brunch

Scrambled eggs and olives in toast cones

Illustrated on pages 450-451

Serves 8
8 medium-sized eggs
salt and freshly ground black pepper
40 g/1½ oz butter
16 stuffed green olives, halved
For the toast cones
16 large thin slices of white bread
75 g/3 oz butter, melted
butter for greasing

1 First make the toast cones. Heat the oven to 190° C/375° F/gas 5. Trim the crusts from each slice of bread then flatten lightly with a rolling pin.
2 Brush each piece of bread on one side with melted butter, then roll them up to form cones with the buttered surfaces inside. Secure with wooden cocktail sticks or place the cones in cream horn tins to hold them in shape.

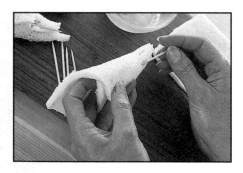

3 Arrange the cones on a greased baking sheet and brush them with the remaining butter. Bake for about 15 minutes, or until they are golden brown. Cool on a wire rack.
4 Beat the eggs with seasoning to taste. Melt the butter in a pan over medium heat, add the egg mixture and stir until thickened and just creamy. Do not allow the eggs to overcook and become too firm.
5 Stir in the halved olives and transfer the mixture to a heatproof bowl and cover tightly. Place this over a pan of hot but not boiling water; the eggs will keep warm for 30 minutes without spoiling.
6 To serve, put the egg in a warm shal-

low bowl set in a larger bowl, piling the toast cones round. To give your guests the right idea, fill a few of the cones with egg, topping each with half an olive.

Smoked haddock risotto

Serves 12
1.5 kg/3-3½ lb whole smoked haddock
1 large bunch parsley, weighing about 100 g/4 oz, stalks and tops separated
1 bay leaf
1 lemon, sliced
8 black peppercorns
100 g/4 oz butter
4 bacon rashers, rinds removed, cut into 1 cm/½ in strips
2 onions, finely chopped
1 green pepper, deseeded and cut into thin strips
1 red pepper, deseeded and cut into thin strips
500 g/1 lb long-grain rice
4 eggs
juice of 1½ lemons
freshly ground black pepper
5 tbls single cream
1-2 tsps sweet paprika, to garnish

1 Wash the haddock and cut each fish into 3-4 pieces. Place in a large saucepan and cover with cold water. Add the stalks of the parsley, bay leaf, lemon slices and black peppercorns. Bring to the boil and simmer gently for about 10 minutes, or until the flesh flakes easily with a fork. Transfer to a plate with a fish slice and leave to cool. Strain the stock into a large measuring jug and measure 1 L/2 pt,

making up the volume with water if necessary.
2 Melt half the butter in a large saucepan and fry the bacon, onions and green and red pepper strips until the onions are soft and lightly coloured. Stir in the rice.

3 Add the measured fish stock to the rice mixture and bring to the boil, stirring. Lower the heat, cover with a tight-fitting lid and simmer gently for 30 minutes, or until all the stock has been absorbed.
4 Meanwhile, remove all the skin and bones from the fish and flake the flesh.

Hard-boil the eggs for 7-8 minutes, cool rapidly under cold running water, then shell and cut into quarters. Chop the parsley tops finely, reserving a few of them for garnish.
5 When the rice is cooked, gently fold in the flaked haddock, parsley, lemon juice and pepper to taste. Over low heat, fork in the cream and remaining butter until the risotto is heated all through. Transfer to a warmed serving dish and, if necessary, keep hot until ready to serve.
6 To serve: garnish with the quartered hard-boiled eggs and reserved parsley and sprinkle with a little paprika.

Devilled kidneys

Serves 12

24 lamb kidneys, halved, with
   membranes and cores removed
100 g/4 oz margarine or butter
2 large onions, finely chopped
2 tbls mustard powder
2 tbls Worcestershire sauce
2 tbls mustard ketchup
pinch of cayenne pepper
salt and freshly ground black
   pepper
1-2 tbls finely chopped parsley

Above: *Left, Smoked haddock risotto;
Right, Devilled kidneys; Back, Buck's
fizz (page 458)*

1 Melt half the margarine in a saucepan,
add the onions and fry over gentle heat
until just translucent.

2 In a bowl, blend the mustard powder
with the Worcestershire sauce to form a
smooth paste. Stir in the mustard
ketchup, then add this mixture to the
onions. Stir thoroughly and bring to a
slow simmer. Turn down the heat and
allow the mixture to simmer, uncovered,
while you cook the kidneys separately.

3 Melt the remaining margarine in a
large frying-pan, add the kidneys and fry
over moderate heat until browned on all
sides. When they are lightly browned,
transfer the kidneys, with their pan
juices, to a shallow flameproof dish.

4 Heat the grill to high.

5 Remove the sauce from the heat, add
the cayenne and salt and pepper to taste,
then pour over the kidneys. Place under
the grill for 1-2 minutes until the sauce is
bubbling. If necessary, keep hot until
ready to serve. Sprinkle the kidneys with
a little finely chopped parsley just before
serving on slices of hot buttered toast.

Breakfast lamb cutlets

Right: *Back, Tropical fruit cup; Right, Breakfast lamb cutlets served with chutney and bread rolls*

Serves 4-6
450 g/1 lb very thin 'breakfast' lamb cutlets (12-16 cutlets)
6 tbls redcurrant jelly
1 tbls Dijon mustard
3 tbls dry white breadcrumbs
salt and freshly ground black pepper
6 tbls finely chopped parsley
75 g/3 oz butter
lemon slices, to garnish
parsley sprigs, to garnish

1 Melt the redcurrant jelly in a small saucepan over moderate heat. Combine it with the mustard and breadcrumbs and season with salt and pepper.
2 Coat the cutlets on both sides with this mixture. Roll them in parsley, then place on a plate, cover loosely, and refrigerate overnight.
3 Melt half the butter in a large, heavy-based frying-pan and, when sizzling, add as many chops as will fit in 1 layer. Sauté for 3 minutes each side, then remove to a warmed serving platter. Keep warm while you cook the remaining chops, adding more butter as necessary.
4 Garnish the cutlets with slices of lemon, sprigs of parsley and an extra sprinkling of pepper and serve at once.

Tropical fruit cup

Serves 8
½ medium-sized watermelon or 1 large Ogen melon
1 small pineapple, peeled, cored and diced
8 lichees, peeled, halved and stoned
8 ripe apricots, peeled, halved and stoned
1 papaya, peeled, seeded and diced
4 kiwi fruit or 4 fresh figs, peeled and thinly sliced
175 g/6 oz cape gooseberries, dehusked, or 175 g/6 oz seedless white grapes
2 large, sweet oranges, peeled, pith removed and thinly sliced
150 ml/5 fl oz clear honey
juice of 1 lime

1 If you are using an Ogen melon, cut a slice off the top. Scoop out the flesh of the watermelon or Ogen, being careful not to pierce the shell, and remove all the seeds. Chop the Ogen or watermelon flesh coarsely and put it into a large bowl with its juice. Reserve the melon shell, wrapped in cling film.

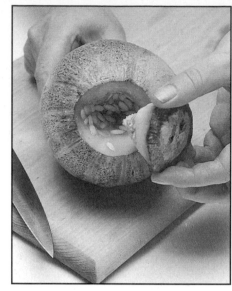

2 Prepare the pineapple, lichees, apricots, papaya, kiwi fruit or figs, cape gooseberries or grapes, and the oranges, and add to the melon flesh together with their juices.

3 Heat the honey gently in a small saucepan until it is liquid, then pour it over the fruit. Put the bowl in the refrigerator to macerate overnight.
4 Just before serving, pile the fruit into the melon shell and pour over the lime juice. If there is any fruit left over, pile it around the melon shell on a serving dish.

Ham and potato scallop

Illustrated on pages 450-451

Serves 8
8 medium-sized potatoes (about 1.1 kg/2½ lb)
750 g/1½ lb sweet-cured gammon joint
75 g/3 oz butter
1 small onion, finely chopped
1 tsp dry mustard
40 g/1½ oz flour
400 ml/14 fl oz milk
¼ tsp salt
¼ tsp freshly ground white pepper
For the topping
100 g/4 oz butter
100 g/4 oz fresh white breadcrumbs

1 Cut the potatoes into 3 mm/⅛ in slices and reserve. Cut the gammon joint

into 20 mm/³⁄₄ in cubes and put them in a 2 L/3½ pt shallow ovenproof dish. Heat the oven to 180° C/350° F/gas 4.

2 Melt the butter in a large saucepan over medium-low heat, add the onion and fry gently until it is soft but not coloured. Stir in the mustard and flour and, when blended, cook for 1 minute, stirring. Gradually add the milk and bring to the boil, stirring constantly, until the sauce is thick. Add the salt and pepper, then the reserved potato slices and mix thoroughly.

3 Transfer this mixture to the ovenproof dish, covering the gammon evenly. Cover and cook in the oven for about 1½ hours or until the potato slices are tender.

4 Meanwhile, melt the butter for the topping in a large pan over medium-high heat. Add the breadcrumbs and cook, stirring frequently, until the crumbs are golden brown.

5 Take the dish from the oven, and sprinkle the surface evenly with the fried breadcrumbs.

6 Take the dish to the brunch table and serve; or cover, reduce the oven to the lowest setting and keep the scallop warm until needed.

Melon and orange salad in lemon syrup

Illustrated on pages 450-451

Serves 8
1 small honeydew melon
1 Ogen, canteloupe or Charentais melon
3 oranges
For the syrup
75 g/3 oz sugar
4 tbls lemon juice
¼ tsp ground ginger (optional)

1 For the syrup, put the sugar in a small pan with the lemon juice and 4 tbls water. Heat gently until the sugar has dissolved. Add the ginger, if using, and bring to boiling point. Remove the pan from the heat immediately and let the syrup stand until warm.

2 Meanwhile, prepare the fruit. Scoop out all the seeds from the melons. Slice the melon flesh away from the rind using a curved grapefruit knife. Cut the flesh into bite-sized pieces. Peel and segment the oranges, removing pith and membrane.

3 Put the melon and orange in a serving bowl, pour the warm syrup over and turn the fruits gently until coated with syrup. Cover and chill for at least 1 hour, then stir again gently before serving.

Ⴤ Instead of the oranges, you can use a large wedge of watermelon.

Special Celebrations

A family celebration, such as a christening, silver wedding anniversary or wedding reception, calls for a rather special party. This is the time when elegant and delicious dishes are called for, dishes with a touch of luxury. Pride of place in such celebrations usually goes, of course, to a spectacular decorated cake. Whether you are catering for a christening or a coming-of-age party, an engagement or a golden wedding anniversary, the recipes in this chapter will help to make it an occasion that will be remembered by everyone.

Christening

Open sandwich platters

Makes 60

**30 slices wheatmeal, wholemeal or
  rye bread, crusts removed,
  halved and buttered**
For the egg tartare topping
18 eggs, hard-boiled and chopped
300 ml/½ pt thick mayonnaise
2 tbls capers, drained and chopped
6 small gherkins, finely chopped
**12 small stuffed olives, thinly
  sliced**
4 tbls chopped parsley
**salt and freshly ground black
  pepper**
½ cucumber, thinly sliced
slices of stuffed olive, to garnish
For the liver pâté topping
**500 g/1 lb soft liver pâté or liver
  sausage**
**8 tbls snipped chives or spring
  onion tops**
**salt and freshly ground black
  pepper**
3-4 large tomatoes, sliced
1 bunch watercress
3-4 gherkins, sliced
For the smoked salmon topping
500 g/1 lb full-fat soft cheese
freshly ground black pepper
½ cucumber, thinly sliced
250 g/9 oz salmon, thinly sliced
**1 carton mustard and cress
  (optional)**
25 g/1 oz lumpfish roe (optional)
To garnish (optional)
lettuce leaves
parsley sprigs
2 lemons, cut into thin wedges

1 To make the egg tartare topping, put
the chopped eggs in a bowl with the
mayonnaise, capers, gherkins, olives
and parsley. Season to taste with salt and
pepper and mix well. Spread on to 20 of
the bread slices and top each with a twist
of cucumber or a slice of stuffed olive.
2 To make the liver pâté topping, mash
the liver pâté in a bowl, then beat in the
chives and season with salt and pepper
to taste. Spread on to another 20 bread
slices. Top each of the open sandwiches
with a half slice of tomato and gherkin.

Arrange on a serving platter and garnish
with watercress.
3 To make the smoked salmon topping,
spread the remaining bread slices with
the cheese and sprinkle with pepper.
Place a cucumber slice on each
sandwich, followed by a roll of smoked
salmon. Top each with a little mustard
and cress and lumpfish roe, if using.
4 To serve, arrange the sandwiches
decoratively on several large platters and
garnish with lettuce leaves and parsley
sprigs if wished. Lemon wedges may be
passed round separately for squeezing
over smoked salmon.

The bread can be cut into as many
different shapes as possible – fingers,
triangles or even circles cut out with a
plain or fluted biscuit cutter. Crackers
and savoury biscuits can also be used as
a base for toppings, for a crisper texture
which contrasts well with the soft bread.

Christening cake

Illustrated on pages 482-483

Makes 20 slices
**⅓ × Celebration Cake recipe,
  without the covering or the icing
  (see pages 486-487)**
For the almond paste
225 g/8 oz ground almonds
100 g/4 oz caster sugar
100 g/4 oz icing sugar
2 egg yolks or 1 whole egg
2 tsps lemon juice
For the glaze
1 tbls apricot jam
1 tbls lemon juice
For the royal icing
1 egg white
225 g/8 oz icing sugar, sifted
1 tsp glycerine
For the decoration
1 egg white
225 g/8 oz icing sugar
**few drops blue or pink food
  colouring**

1 Make the cake as directed on pages
486-487, using ⅓ quantity of ingredients and baking the cake in a 15 cm/6
in deep round cake tin at 150° C/300° F/
gas 2 for 2-2½ hours. If the cake starts to
rise in the centre or overbrowns, cover
with greaseproof or foil and lower oven
temperature to 140° C/275° F/gas 1.
2 After at least 2 months, mix the almonds, caster and icing sugars together
in a bowl. Stir in egg yolks and lemon
juice to make a firm paste and knead
lightly until smooth.
3 Heat the jam and lemon juice in a
small saucepan until melted, then sieve.
Turn the cake upside down on a silver
cake board and brush with half the glaze.
4 Sift a little icing sugar over work surface and roll out half the almond paste to
a circle to fit the cake top. Press on top of
the cake and smooth with a rolling pin.
5 Measure depth and circumference of
the cake with pieces of string. Roll out remaining almond paste into a strip. Trim
to the measurements taken with the
string.
6 Brush the sides of the cake with the remaining glaze. Press strip of paste

Florentine flapjacks

Makes 48
350 g/12 oz margarine or butter
350 g/12 oz light soft brown sugar
8 tbls clear honey
350 g/12 oz rolled oats
100 g/4 oz blanched almonds,
  chopped
100 g/4 oz glacé cherries, chopped
100 g/4 oz chopped mixed peel
100 g/4 oz sultanas
400 g/14 oz plain dessert
  chocolate
vegetable oil, for greasing

1 Heat the oven to 180° C/350° F/gas 4. Line two 33 × 23 cm/13 × 9 in Swiss roll tins with non-stick baking parchment or greased greaseproof paper, so that it stands about 1 cm/½ in above the rim.
2 Put the margarine, sugar and honey into a saucepan and heat gently, stirring until melted and well mixed. Remove from the heat and stir in the rolled oats. Add the almonds, cherries, peel and sultanas and stir well.
3 Spoon the mixture into the prepared tins. Flatten with the back of a spoon and spread with a palette knife to level the surface. Bake in the oven for 15-20 minutes until golden brown all over, swapping the tins over after 10 minutes.
4 Remove the tins from the oven and leave to cool for 5 minutes then, with a long, sharp knife, mark 2 lines lengthways to make 3 sections. Mark 7 lines crossways to make 24 rectangles in each tin (do not cut right through). Leave to cool for a further 10-15 minutes, then turn out upside down on to 2 clean sheets of greaseproof paper so that the flapjacks stay in one whole block. Peel off the lining paper.
5 While the flapjacks are cooling, melt the chocolate in a basin over a pan of simmering water, stirring once or twice until melted. Pour the hot melted chocolate on to the block of flapjacks and spread evenly all over.
6 Leave the chocolate to cool for 5-10 minutes, then drag a fork across the chocolate to make straight or wavy lines all over.
7 Leave to cool until the chocolate is completely set. Turn the flapjacks over on to a clean board or paper and cut through lines to separate.

Y These flapjacks will keep for up to 1 week in an airtight tin.

---

around the cake, pressing ends together with a palette knife.
7 Leave to dry at room temperature for a minimum of 2-3 days before icing; it can be left for as long as 3 weeks.
8 To make the royal icing, beat the egg white until frothy. Stir in the sugar, 1 tbls at a time, beating well after each. When half the sugar has been added, stir in the lemon juice then beat in the remaining sugar. Beat till the icing forms soft peaks. Cover with a damp cloth for 2-3 hours.
9 Spoon half the icing on top of the cake, keeping the rest covered. Spread the icing over the top of the cake with a palette knife. To give a flat surface, draw a metal ruler across the top of the cake towards you, holding it at a slight angle. Remove surplus icing from the edges and smooth again with the ruler. Leave for 1 hour.
10 Spread the remaining icing over the sides. Smooth with a palette knife held at an angle. Leave to dry for 2-3 days then trim off rough edges with a sharp knife or fine sandpaper. Brush off loose icing.
11 Make up the same quantity of icing again and apply another layer in the same way. Leave to dry for 2-3 days.
12 For the decoration, make up the icing in the same way but omit the lemon juice and glycerine.
13 Transfer the name to the top of the cake as for the Clown Cake on page 498 (step 11).
14 Stir the colouring into half the icing a few drops at a time, adding a few drops

Above: *Left, Florentine flapjacks; Right, Open sandwich platters*

of water if necessary. Using a small plain nozzle, pipe the name in icing on the top of the cake.
15 Using a small star nozzle, and holding the piping bag upright just above the surface of the edge of the cake, pipe stars in the white icing close together round the edge, carefully turning the cake as you work.
16 Holding the piping bag at an angle just above the bottom edge of the cake, pipe a border round the bottom. Small

blue or pink stars may be piped around the edge of the board.
17 Leave to dry, then tie 1.5 m/1¼ yd of ribbon round the cake.

Anniversary

Ham mousse

Serves 12
500 g/1 lb cooked ham, minced
4¹/₂ tsps powdered gelatine
425 ml/³/₄ pt cold chicken stock
425 ml/³/₄ pt thick bottled
    mayonnaise
1 tsp made English mustard
salt and freshly ground black
    pepper
4 egg whites
vegetable oil for greasing
halved cucumber slices and twists,
    to garnish
radish waterlilies, to garnish

1 Grease a 2 L/3¹/₂ pt soufflé dish, line the base with greaseproof paper, then lightly grease the paper.
2 Sprinkle the gelatine over half the stock in a small pan and leave for 1-2 minutes to soften and become spongy. Set the pan over very gentle heat without allowing it to boil, until the gelatine is completely dissolved (the liquid should be absolutely clear). Leave to cool.
3 Meanwhile, put the mayonnaise in a bowl, then mix in the remaining cold chicken stock, the cooked minced ham and mustard.
4 Stir the gelatine slowly into the mayonnaise mixture and season carefully with salt and pepper.
5 Whisk the egg whites until they stand in stiff peaks, then fold into the mayonnaise mixture. Pour into the prepared soufflé dish and refrigerate for 3 hours until set.

6 Dip the base of the dish in very hot water for 1-2 seconds, then invert a serving plate on top of the dish. Hold firmly together and invert the dish, giving a sharp shake halfway round. Lift off the dish and carefully peel off greaseproof paper.
7 Surround the mousse with cucumber slices, and garnish with cucumber twists and radish waterlilies.

Coriander chicken

Serves 12
2 × 2 kg/4¹/₂ lb oven-ready
    chickens
50 g/2 oz butter, softened
1 tbls coriander seeds,
    crushed
salt and freshly ground black
    pepper
300 ml/¹/₂ pt chicken stock
4 tbls vegetable oil
1 tsp lemon juice
lettuce and watercress, to garnish

1 Heat the oven to 190° C/375° F/gas 5. Rub the butter all over the chickens, then sprinkle inside and out with 2 tsps crushed coriander and salt and pepper to taste. Put the chickens in a large roasting tin and pour the stock around them.
2 Roast in the oven for 1¹/₂ hours until the chickens are tender and the juices run clear when the thickest part of the thigh is pierced with a skewer. Baste frequently during the cooking time.
3 Remove the chickens from the tin, strain the juices into a jug and reserve.

Allow the chickens to cool, then slice off the meat. Cover and refrigerate until required.
4 To make the dressing for the chicken, put 4 tbls of reserved juices in a bowl and whisk in the oil, lemon juice and salt and pepper to taste.
5 Arrange the sliced chicken on a serving platter and sprinkle with the remaining coriander. Garnish with lettuce leaves and watercress, then pour the prepared dressing over the top.

Celebration cake

Makes 35-40 slices
1.5 kg/3 lb 4 oz mixed dried fruit
100 g/4 oz glacé cherries, halved
100 g/4 oz shelled walnuts,
    chopped
500 g/1 lb plain flour
1 tbls ground mixed spice
pinch of salt
350 g/12 oz margarine or butter
350 g/12 oz light soft brown sugar
7 eggs
grated zest and juice of 1 lemon
grated zest and juice of 1 orange
3 tbls brandy
For the covering
750 g/1¹/₂ lb almond paste
4 tbls apricot jam, sieved and
    warmed
margarine, for greasing
For the fondant icing
1 egg white
2 tbls liquid glucose
1 tsp lemon juice
500 g/1 lb icing sugar, sifted
few drops of yellow food colouring
extra icing sugar and a little
    cornflour, for dusting
For the decorative icing
1 egg white
225 g/8 oz icing sugar, sifted
few drops of yellow food colouring

1 Heat the oven to 170° C/325° F/gas 3. Grease and line the sides and base of a 23 cm/9 in square cake tin with a double thickness of greaseproof paper. Grease the paper.
2 Mix the dried fruit, glacé cherries and walnuts in a bowl. Sift the flour with the

spice and salt into a separate bowl, then add half the flour to the fruit and mix well.

3 Beat margarine and sugar until pale. Gradually beat in eggs adding a little flour with each. Fold in remaining flour.

4 Stir in fruits, citrus zest and juice. Turn into tin, level and make shallow hollow in centre.

5 Bake in oven for 3½-4 hours or until a warmed fine skewer inserted in centre comes out clean. Leave to cool for 30 minutes. Prick top and spoon on brandy. Leave until cold.

6 Turn out, peel off the greaseproof paper, wrap in foil and store in an airtight tin for at least 2 months.

7 8 days before the cake is required, prepare the almond paste covering: brush the cake all over with warm apricot jam. Sift a little icing sugar over a work surface and roll out half the almond paste to a 24 cm/9½ in square. Press on to cake top and trim edges.

8 Roll the remaining almond paste to a 30 × 23 cm/12 × 9 in rectangle. Cut into 4 strips across and press a piece on to each side of the cake. Trim and work edges together.

9 Lift on to a 28 cm/11 in square cake board. Leave for 7 days.

10 The day before the cake is required, make the fondant icing. Put the egg white, glucose and lemon juice in a bowl. Beat in the sugar, a tablespoon at a time, until it is too stiff to stir, then knead to a smooth paste, adding more sugar as necessary. Work in food colouring.

11 Sift a little icing sugar over a work surface and roll out icing to a 30 cm/12 in square. Place on the cake and, using hands dusted with cornflour, ease down the sides.

Below: *Left, Ham mousse; Right, Celebration cake; Front, Coriander chicken served with potato salad and a salad of avocados, tomatoes, green pepper and pineapple cubes in an oil and vinegar dressing*

12 While the icing is still soft, mark a line 1 cm/½ in in from the edge all the way round the top. Mark another line along the sides 1 cm/½ in down from the edge, and another line 1 cm/½ in up from the base. Set aside.

13 To make the decorative icing, beat the egg white until frothy, then stir in the icing sugar, a tablespoon at a time. Beat until the icing forms soft peaks. Stir in food colouring.

14 Spoon the icing into a piping bag fitted with a small plain nozzle. Using the marked lines as a guide, pipe lines vertically over the edge of each side and more lines down to the base and out on to the board.

15 Pipe a dot on both ends of each line. Squeeze a dot of icing on to the back of cake decorations and fit on to each corner and in centre, then pipe 2 lines at right angles in each corner. Decorate with more dots on top of cake and on board. Leave to dry overnight, before fixing ribbon round the cake.

Wedding Reception

Party sandwich loaf

Illustrated on page 490

Serves 10-12
1 large white loaf, 1 day old
6 tbls thick mayonnaise
1 tbls tomato ketchup
pinch of cayenne pepper
dash of Worcestershire sauce
100 g/4 oz cream cheese
1 tbls finely snipped fresh chives
salt
1 tbls lemon juice
½ tsp paprika
3 tomatoes, blanched, skinned and
thinly sliced
2 large eggs, hard boiled and
sliced
8 lettuce leaves, shredded
150 g/5 oz canned white crabmeat
(drained weight), finely shredded
For the watercress mayonnaise
1 bunch watercress, finely
chopped
150 ml/4 fl oz thick mayonnaise
green food colouring (optional)
For the cheese coating
250 g/9 oz cream cheese
salt
juice of ½ lemon
paprika
6 tbls double cream
For the garnish
stuffed olives, sliced
sprigs of watercress
freshly snipped chives
lettuce leaves
tomato wedges

1 First make the watercress mayonnaise: blend the watercress with the mayonnaise. Tint green, if wished, and reserve.
2 Trim the crusts from the loaf, cutting it into a neat rectangle. Cut it lengthways into 6 even horizontal slices.
3 In a small bowl, blend the mayonnaise and tomato ketchup. Season to taste with cayenne pepper and Worcestershire sauce.
4 In another bowl, combine the cream cheese with the chives and season to taste with salt, lemon juice and paprika. Stir and spread over 1 slice of bread.

5 Spread a second slice of bread with half the watercress mayonnaise. Using half the sliced tomatoes and 1 egg, cover with alternate slices of tomato and egg.
6 Spread a third slice with half of the ketchup-flavoured mayonnaise. Cover with half the shredded lettuce, followed by half the crabmeat. Repeat with a fourth slice.
7 Spread a fifth slice with the remaining watercress mayonnaise, sliced tomatoes and egg as for the second slice.
8 Neatly layer the slices in the order given, then top with the remaining plain slice. Wrap the loaf in aluminium foil and chill for 2 hours or until firm.
9 Meanwhile prepare the cheese coating. In a large bowl, combine the cream cheese, salt, lemon juice and paprika. Beat together until smooth, adding enough cream for an easy spreading consistency.
10 Spread the top and sides of the loaf with the coating, smoothing it with a palette knife. Garnish with sliced olives, sprigs of watercress and chives, and serve on a bed of lettuce leaves, surrounded by tomatoes.

Cold loin of pork with courgette stuffing

Serves 20
4.3-4.5 kg/9½-10 lb loin of pork,
boned weight (bones and rind
reserved)
125 g/4 oz smoked back bacon,
finely chopped
450 g/1 lb small courgettes,
coarsely grated
225 g/8 oz Ricotta cheese
2 tbls finely chopped fresh basil
1 tbls crushed fresh thyme
1 tbls coriander seeds, crushed
1 garlic clove, crushed
salt and freshly ground black
pepper
2 medium-sized eggs, beaten
50 g/2 oz almonds
oil, for frying
sea salt
275 ml/10 fl oz dry white wine
slices of lime, to garnish
sprigs of fresh thyme, to garnish

1 Ask your butcher to bone the loin and remove the rind, then cut it into 2 joints, leaving it unrolled and untied.
2 Fry the almonds in a little oil and coat them with fine sea salt; leave to cool.
3 Put the chopped bacon into a large heavy-based saucepan over a moderate heat and cook for 3-4 minutes, stirring, until the fat begins to run. Add the courgettes and cook for 4 minutes, stirring.
4 Transfer the courgettes and bacon to a large bowl. Add the Ricotta cheese, basil, thyme, coriander and garlic. Mash well, season with salt and pepper and bind with the beaten eggs.
5 Lay the pork joints out flat, fat sides down, and divide the stuffing between them, spreading it evenly. Roll up the joints very carefully, enclosing the stuffing as much as possible, then tie in several places with string. Heat the oven to 180° C/350° F/gas 4.

6 With the tip of a sharp knife, make little incisions in the fat side of the pork. Insert a salted almond into each, pushing in well. Sprinkle the joints with pepper.
(continued on page 490)

Right: *Cold loin of pork with courgette stuffing served with a selection of salads*

7 Put the joints into 1 or 2 large oven-proof dishes. Surround with the bones and rind so that the joints fit snugly. Cover with the wine and 1.7 L/3 pt water and cook uncovered in the oven for 30 minutes or until the fat has taken on colour.

8 Lower the heat to 150°C/300° F/gas 2. Cover the meat with a double thickness of foil and cook for a further 2½ hours.
9 Remove the meat from the oven and discard the bones and rind. Leave the joints, covered, in a cool place overnight.
10 Remove the jellied juices from around the joints and chop finely. Reserve.
11 Carve the pork into 5 mm/¼ in slices and arrange on 1 or 2 serving platters. Garnish the pork with the chopped jelly, slices of lime and sprigs of thyme and serve.

Above: *Party sandwich loaf (page 488)*

Raspberry meringue tower

Serves 8 or more
8 large egg whites
2 pinches of salt or cream of tartar
450 g/1 lb caster sugar
600 ml/1 pt thick cream
350 g/12 oz fresh raspberries
angelica leaves, to decorate

1 The meringue is made in two batches. Start by preparing 2 baking sheets: cover them with foil or greaseproof paper and grease well. Draw a circle 23 cm/9 in in diameter on one sheet and two circles, one 12 cm/5 in and one 7.5 cm/3 in on the other sheet. Put a large plain nozzle into a piping bag, stand it upright in a tumbler and turn back the top of the bag, like a cuff, ready for filling. Heat the oven to 110° C/225° F/gas ¼.

2 Prepare the first batch of meringue: whisk 4 egg whites with 1 pinch of salt or cream of tartar until stiff peaks are formed. Whisk in 100 g/4 oz caster sugar then gently fold in 100 g/4 oz more sugar.

3 Fill the piping bag with half the meringue and pipe around the 23 cm/9 in circle, just inside the guideline. Work inwards in circles until the bag is empty. Refill the bag with the remaining meringue, complete the first meringue circle then pipe in the other two circles in the same way.

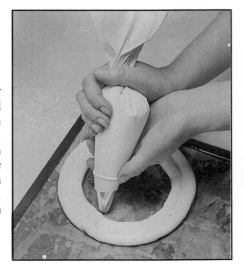

4 Place the sheets in the oven and bake for 2½-3 hours (the bottom sheet will need a little longer). Set aside to cool.
5 For the second batch, line and grease two baking sheets, as before. Draw an 18 cm/7 in circle on one sheet. Put a large plain nozzle into a piping bag. Make up more meringue with the remaining egg white and sugar, in the same way as the first batch. Put half in the bag; pipe the 18 cm/7 in circle.
6 Clean the piping bag and change the

nozzle to a medium star nozzle. Fill the bag with the remaining meringue and pipe 24 rosettes 25 mm/1 in across on to the baking sheets. Bake for 2½-3 hours.

7 Assemble the gateau not more than 1 hour before eating. Whip the cream and mix half with half of the raspberries.
8 Put the 23 cm/9 in meringue layer on a flat serving plate or cake stand. Arrange 10 meringue rosettes around the edge, 25 mm/1 in from the rim. Spread some raspberry cream in the centre.
9 Gently place the 18 cm/7 in meringue

layer on top and spread some raspberry cream in the centre. Place 8 meringue rosettes around the edge.
10 Position the 12 cm/5 in layer on top, fill the centre and place 6 meringue rosettes around the edge. Top with the smaller layer.
11 Fit a piping bag with a medium star nozzle and fill with the remaining whipped cream. Pipe rosettes of cream, one on the top layer then one in between each meringue rosette. Place a raspberry and angelica 'leaves' on each cream rosette.

Muscat jelly

Serves 12-16
75 cl bottle Muscat de Beaumes de Venise
200 g/7 oz sugar
300 ml/10 fl oz lemon juice
grated zest of 2 lemons
50 g/2 oz gelatine
300 ml/10 fl oz thick cream
2 tbls icing sugar
seedless white grapes, to garnish

1 Put the sugar, lemon juice and zest into a saucepan with 700 ml/1¼ pt water. Bring to the boil and then simmer for 10 minutes to dissolve sugar. Cool, then add the wine.
2 Sprinkle the gelatine over 5 tbls cold water, in a small bowl. Put the bowl into a pan of simmering water until the gelatine has dissolved. Stir the gelatine into the wine mixture and mix well.
3 Pour the liquid into a wetted 2 L/3½ pt ring mould and put in the refrigerator to set.
4 About 20 minutes before serving, turn out the jelly by putting a cloth dipped in very hot water over the bottom of the mould. Put the plate over the mould, invert the two together, then tap the mould sharply and the jelly should slip out on to the plate.
5 Whip the cream with the icing sugar until soft peaks form. Pile some in the centre of the jelly and pipe the rest round the edge, using a small rose nozzle. Garnish the jelly with the seedless white grapes and serve.

Below: *Raspberry meringue tower*

Children's Parties

Children love asking their friends home to tea, and birthday parties are always popular. Choosing a particular theme, like 'the circus' or 'outer space', is a great way of organizing a birthday party, and gives you plenty of scope for originality. It is also a good chance to provide food that looks fun but is made with ingredients that children love. Food, decorations and games can all follow the basic theme, and the children could even come in appropriate fancy dress. No children's party is complete without an exciting cake as a centrepiece, and the eye-catching cakes in this chapter are sure to be greeted with shouts of delight.

Tea Party

Fun cakes

Makes 20
150 g/5 oz self-raising flour
**100 g/4 oz block margarine,
    softened**
100 g/4 oz caster sugar
finely grated zest of ¹/₂ orange
2 eggs
vegetable oil, for greasing
For the icing and decoration
500 g/1 lb icing sugar
2 tbls lemon juice
5-6 tbls hot water
**few drops of pink and green food
    colouring**
**100 g/4 oz vanilla flavour fondant
    icing**
**25 g/1 oz plain chocolate, broken
    into pieces**
**marshmallows, liquorice sweets
    and sugar-coated chocolate
    buttons, to finish**
little extra icing sugar, for dusting

1 Heat the oven to 180° C/350° F/gas 4 and grease 20 individual bun tins.
2 Sift the flour into a large bowl. In another bowl, beat the margarine and sugar with a wooden spoon or a hand-held electric whisk, until pale and fluffy. Beat in the orange zest, then add the eggs, one at a time, beating thoroughly after each addition. Fold in the flour.
3 Divide the mixture equally between the tins and bake just above the centre of the oven for 15 minutes, until golden and springy.
4 Leave the cakes in their tins for 30 seconds, then turn out on to a wire rack. Leave to cool completely.
5 Meanwhile, make the icing. Sift the icing sugar into a bowl, then stir in the lemon juice and water to give a thick coating consistency.
6 Pour a tablespoon of icing over 10 cakes, to cover completely. Tint the remaining icing pink and use to coat rest of cakes. Leave for 1 hour.
7 To decorate, knead a few drops of pink food colouring into half the fondant icing and a few drops of green food colouring into the other half. Lightly dust a work surface with icing sugar, then roll

out the fondant. Cut out hat shapes, hair, ears and faces as in photograph.
8 Put the chocolate in a heatproof bowl. Set the bowl over a pan half full of simmering water and leave, stirring occasionally, until the chocolate has melted. Spoon the melted chocolate into a piping bag fitted with a small plain nozzle.
9 Cut 4 marshmallows in half to use as ears for the 'bunny' faces.
10 Fix the fondant shapes and sweets on to the cakes by piping a dot of chocolate on to the back of each. Pipe chocolate details on to the sweets, place each cake in a paper cup cake case and leave to set for at least 1 hour.

Kids' kooler

Illustrated on page 451

Serves 4
12 ice cubes
**350 ml/12 fl oz unsweetened
    pineapple juice, chilled**
few drops of fresh lime juice
**350 ml/12 fl oz unsweetened
    orange juice, chilled**
**2 tbls grenadine syrup
    (non-alcoholic type)**
To garnish (optional)
**¹/₂ slice fresh pineapple with skin,
    or 4 canned pineapple pieces,
    drained**
2 slices lime
2 small slices orange
8 maraschino or glacé cherries

1 Prepare the garnish, if using: cut the pineapple slice into quarters to make 4 triangular wedges. Cut each slice of citrus fruit into halves. On each of 4 cocktail sticks, spear 1 cherry followed by 1 piece of lime, pineapple and orange, then another cherry.
2 Make the drinks: put 3 ice cubes into the bottom of 4 highball glasses or tall 225 ml/8 fl oz tumblers. Pour 75 ml/3 fl oz pineapple juice into each glass, add a squeeze of lime, then 75 ml/3 fl oz orange juice.
3 Pour a thin stream of grenadine, in a circle around the edge of each drink. (The grenadine will sink to form a rosy layer at the bottom of the glass.)

4 Garnish the drinks with the prepared fruits, by balancing a cocktail stick across the top of each glass. Put 1-2 long straws into each drink and serve at once.

Fruit 'n' nut snacks

Serves 4
4 slices white bread
**4 slices wholemeal or granary
    bread**
40 g/1¹/₂ oz soft tub margarine
1-2 tbls chocolate spread
50 g/2 oz stoned dates, chopped
**50 g/2 oz fresh skinned peanuts,
    chopped**
1 dessert apple

1 Put the margarine in a bowl and stir in the chocolate spread, dates and peanuts. Core and finely chop the apple, leaving the skin on, then add it to the bowl. Mix well to combine all the ingredients.
2 If wished, remove crusts from bread. Divide the mixture equally between the slices of white bread, spread it on evenly, then cover with the brown slices.
3 Cut each of the sandwiches into 4 triangles, then arrange them on a serving

cutter, cut into rounds and place on a greased baking sheet.

5 Bake in the oven for about 15-20 minutes or until the biscuits are a golden brown. Remove from the baking sheet and cool on a wire rack.

6 Squeeze the juice from the remaining half of the lemon, strain into the icing

plate – half with the brown bread uppermost and the other half with the white bread on top.

If desired, extra margarine with chocolate spread mixed into it can be piped in small swirls on each sandwich and decorated with peanuts or dates.

Above: *Fun cakes*

and squeeze the juice from one half. Add the zest and juice to the creamed mixture; gradually work in the sifted flour to form a dough. Knead until the dough is smooth. Chill in the refrigerator for 10 minutes.

sugar and blend to make a thick glacé icing, adding a little cold water if necessary to make it a spreading consistency.

7 Beat the icing, then spread over the biscuits, stopping just short of the edges.

8 Before the icing sets, decorate the biscuits. Use the dolly mixture sweets for half of them, making eyes with the round two-tone sweets cut in half, noses with the jelly sweets, and mouths with the square two-tone sweets cut into 3. On the remaining biscuits, use the diamond-shaped cake decorations for eyes, a small piece of glacé cherry for the nose and half a mint ring for each smile.

Funny face biscuits

Illustrated on pages 492-493

Makes 16 biscuits
175 g/6 oz margarine, softened, plus extra for greasing
75 g/3 oz caster sugar
1 small lemon
175 g/6 oz flour, sifted
225 g/8 oz icing sugar, sieved
1 packet dolly mixture sweets
16 diamond-shaped cake decorations
1 glacé cherry
4 mint rings

1 Heat the oven to 170° C/325° F/gas 3.
2 In a bowl, cream together the margarine and sugar until light and fluffy.
3 Finely grate the zest from the lemon

4 On a lightly floured surface roll out to 5 mm/¼ in thick. Using a 6.5 cm/2½ in

Castle cake

Makes 12-14 slices
melted butter and flour for tins
300 g/12 oz self-raising flour
3 tsps baking powder
300 g/12 oz soft margarine
300 g/12 oz caster sugar
6 large eggs
9 drops of vanilla essence
green food colouring
pink food colouring
6 tbls red jam
200 g/7 oz chocolate hazelnut
   spread
8 chocolate-covered mini Swiss
   rolls
To finish
2 lime jelly tablets
3 chocolate-covered wafer
   fingers
jelly diamond-shaped cake
   decorations
coloured dragées
3 x 50 g/2 oz milk chocolate
   Toblerones
candles and candle holders
   (optional)
toy knights and flags (optional)

1 Heat the oven to 170° C/325° F/gas 3.
2 Brush the bases and sides of two deep, 16 cm/6½ in square tins with melted butter. Line the base of each tin with a neat square of greaseproof paper and brush that with melted butter as well. Lightly dust the bases and sides of the tins with flour, knocking the tins against the side of the table to shake off the surplus.
3 Sift the flour with the baking powder into the mixing bowl of your electric mixer and add the margarine, caster sugar, eggs and vanilla essence. Whisk until well mixed (1-2 minutes). Divide the mixture in half, colouring half with the green food colouring and half with the pink. Pour into each of the prepared tins. Place them in the hot oven and bake for 25-30 minutes. The cakes are cooked when they shrink away slightly from the sides of the tins and when they spring back into shape when pressed lightly with a fingertip.
4 Remove the cakes from the oven and leave for 1-2 minutes to settle. Then turn them out on to a clean tea-towel. Peel off the greaseproof paper and invert the cakes on to a wire rack to cool right side up. It is usual for the cakes to have a wrinkled surface but this may be trimmed level, if liked.

5 Trim the cakes, if necessary, and cut each in half horizontally. Sandwich together with jam, then trim off each corner. Place on a 30 cm/12 in cake board.

6 Use most of the chocolate hazelnut spread to cover the cake. Press 1 mini roll against each of the trimmed corners. Trim one end of the remaining rolls level,

if necessary, and spread with a little chocolate hazelnut spread. Place on top of the first set of rolls to make 4 turrets. (Fill in any gaps with more spread.)
7 Make up the jellies according to the manufacturer's instructions, pour into shallow trays and leave to set.
8 Put chocolate hazelnut spread on the underside and one end of the wafer fingers; place on the cake board, in the centre of the base of the front side of the cake, to represent the drawbridge. Use jelly diamonds to make the portcullis, then use dragées to mark an arched gateway around the portcullis.
9 Make the battlements on the top edges of the cake, between the turrets,

using the triangular chocolate bars. Trim the bars to size (use the trimmings on the back edge).

10 Arrange jelly diamonds around the sides of the cake to represent windows, then stick 3 more down the front of each turret with chocolate hazelnut spread. Put a little spread on the top of each turret and decorate with a ring of dragées. Place candles on cake.
11 Just before serving, break up the jelly with a fork and spoon around the

castle to represent the moat. Place the knights and flags in position, if using.

Sausage-pastry twizzlers

Illustrated on pages 492-493

Serves 8
200 g/7 oz frozen puff pastry,
 defrosted
8 pork sausages
1 medium-sized egg, beaten
tomato ketchup and cucumber
 relish, to serve

1 Heat the oven to 220° C/425° F/gas 7.
2 Roll out the pastry into a rectangle 30 x 20 cm/12 x 8 in, and then cut it into eight 30 cm/12 in long strips.
3 Moisten one edge of each strip with water and roll round each sausage, overlapping the moistened edge of each strip very slightly; leave the sausage ends uncovered.
4 Place on a baking sheet and brush the pastry with the beaten egg. Bake for 20-25 minutes until the pastry is golden brown.
5 Spear with lollipop sticks if wished. Serve immediately, with tomato ketchup and cucumber relish.

Traffic light jellies

Illustrated on pages 492-493

Serves 8
100 g/4 oz tablet lime jelly
100 g/4 oz tablet orange jelly
100 g/4 oz tablet raspberry jelly

Above: *Castle cake*

1 Dissolve the lime jelly in 150 ml/5 fl oz hot water, cool quickly with a few ice cubes then add cold water to make the jelly up to 600 ml/1 pt.
2 Divide the liquid between 8 deep glasses, approximately 225 ml/8 fl oz in capacity. Put the glasses in the refrigerator and leave for 1-2 hours until the jelly has set.
3 When the lime jelly has set, dissolve the orange jelly in the same way and divide the orange jelly between the glasses and return to the refrigerator to set.
4 Repeat the procedure with the raspberry jelly.
5 About 20 minutes before serving, take the glasses out of the refrigerator to let the jelly come to room temperature.

♈ For extra appeal, top the jellies with a swirl of whipped cream and decorate with hundreds and thousands or coloured jelly sweets.

Circus Party

Gingersnap clowns

Makes 8
75 g/3 oz margarine
100 g/4 oz caster sugar
2 tbls golden syrup
175 g/6 oz plain flour
2 tsps ground ginger
½ tsp bicarbonate of soda
margarine for greasing
For the icing
50 g/2 oz icing sugar
about 2 tsps water

1 Heat the oven to 180° C/350° F/gas 4 and grease 2 large baking sheets.
2 Put the margarine, sugar and syrup into a heavy-based saucepan and heat very gently, stirring, until melted. (Keep the heat low and do not allow to boil or it will turn into toffee.) Cool slightly.
3 Meanwhile, sift the flour, ginger and bicarbonate of soda into a large bowl, then make a well in centre.
4 Add the melted mixture to the dry ingredients and mix with a wooden spoon to a firm dough.
5 Turn the dough out on to a lightly floured surface, divide into 8 and roll out each piece to 5 mm/¼ in thickness, then cut each into a clown shape. Use a gingerbread man biscuit cutter to cut out the clowns. If you do not have one, draw a clown shape on a piece of cardboard and cut out. Lay shape on rolled-out dough and cut round it with a knife.
6 Using a fish slice, carefully lift the biscuits on to the prepared baking sheets and bake for 10-12 minutes, swapping baking sheets halfway through so that all the biscuits will brown evenly. Cool for 5 minutes then transfer to a wire rack. Leave until cold.

Below: Clown cake

7 Meanwhile, make the icing. Sift the icing sugar into a bowl and beat in the water. Spoon into a piping bag fitted with a plain writing nozzle.
8 Pipe a face and clothes on to the clowns as shown below, and leave to set for 1 hour.

Clown cake

Serves 12
250 g/9 oz plain flour
3 tbls cocoa powder
1 tsp bicarbonate of soda
1 tsp baking powder
200 g/7 oz caster sugar
2 tbls golden syrup
3 eggs, lightly beaten
150 ml/¼ pt milk
150 ml/¼ pt corn oil
vegetable oil, for greasing
For the fondant icing
1 egg white
2 tbls liquid glucose
1 tsp lemon juice
500 g/1 lb icing sugar, sifted
few drops of pink food colouring
For the filling and decoration
250 g/9 oz chocolate spread
red and blue glossy decorating gel
1 round red lollipop
2 tbls apricot jam, for sticking
red liquorice sticks
sugar-coated chocolate buttons
1 white marshmallow
few drops of red food colouring
250 g/9 oz almond paste
50 g/2 oz icing sugar
2 tsps water

1 Heat the oven to 170° C/325° F/gas 3. Grease a deep 18 cm/7 in round cake tin and a deep 18 cm/7 in square tin. Line bases of tins with greased greaseproof paper.

2 Sift the flour, cocoa, bicarbonate of soda and baking powder into a large bowl. Make a well in the centre and add the sugar, syrup, eggs, milk and corn oil. Using a wooden spoon, gradually draw the flour into the liquid ingredients, then beat for 2-3 minutes.

3 Divide the mixture between the cake tins and level surfaces, then bake for about 45 minutes until firm.

4 Cool the cakes in the tins for 5 minutes, then turn out on to a wire rack and peel off the lining paper. Leave to cool completely.

5 Starting at one corner of the square cake, cut out the sides of the hat. Using the empty round tin as a guide, cut out the curved base of the hat so that it fits closely to the round cake, which will be the face.

6 Slice both the cakes horizontally. Sandwich the cake layers together with the chocolate spread.

7 Make the fondant icing. Put the egg white, glucose and lemon juice in a bowl. Beat in the icing sugar, a tablespoon at a time, then knead to a smooth paste, adding more sugar as necessary.

8 Cut the fondant in half and knead pink colouring into one half; cover.

9 Roll out the uncoloured fondant on a surface lightly dusted with icing sugar and cut out a round 5 cm/2 in larger than the diameter of the round cake. Lift on to the round cake and mould over the top and sides.

10 Roll out the pink fondant and cut out a triangle 5 cm/2 in larger than the triangular cake. Lift on to the triangular cake and mould over the top and sides to cover, trimming as necessary. Leave to set for 4 hours. Make a bow tie with the remaining fondant, and reserve.

11 Draw an exact plan of the clown's face on a piece of greaseproof paper, then, using a pin, prick guide lines through the paper plan on to the top of the round cake.

12 Transfer both cakes to a 40 cm/16 in round cake board and slot together. Paint on eyes, mouth and cheeks with decorating gel. Press lollipop stick into centre for nose. Use jam to stick liquorice hair in place and sugar-coated buttons on eyes. Stick marshmallow on top of hat and press lines of sugar-coated chocolate buttons down on hat.

13 Knead red food colouring into the almond paste to colour it bright red, then roll out into a 10 cm/4 in wide strip. Trim and curl around one side of the round cake to make a ruffle collar. Place the fondant bow tie in position.

14 Sift the icing sugar into a bowl, then beat in the water until smooth. Spoon into a piping bag fitted with a plain writing nozzle, then pipe 2 hands and 3 juggling balls on to the cake board on either side of the cake and fill in coloured balls with decorating gel.

Above: *Lion and tiger cheesies*

Lion and tiger cheesies

Makes 26 biscuits
150 g/5 oz packet round wheatgerm crackers
225 g/8 oz full-fat soft cheese
225 g/8 oz packet cheese savoury shapes
75 g/3 oz packet potato chip sticks currants, for eyes

1 Carefully spread each cracker with the cheese, making sure that the cracker is completely covered.

2 Decorate half the cheese-covered crackers to make lion faces; for each cracker use 2 oval savoury shapes to make ears, and a diamond and 2 rounds to make nose and mouth. Press chip sticks all round the edge for the mane, then make the lion's eyes with 2 currants.

3 Decorate the remaining cheese-covered crackers to make tiger faces; for each cracker use 2 ovals to make the ears, and a diamond and 2 ovals to make the nose and mouth. Press on 3 triangles to represent the tiger's stripes, then press 3 chip sticks on either side for whiskers. Press on 2 currants to make the eyes.

Ⓨ Make the cheesies no more than 1 hour in advance, otherwise the biscuit base will go soggy.

Outer Space Party

Flying saucer

Serves 12
**175 g/6 oz block margarine,
    softened**
175 g/6 oz caster sugar
3 eggs
175 g/6 oz self-raising flour, sifted
3 tbls jam
vegetable oil, for greasing
For the butter cream
75 g/3 oz butter
175 g/6 oz icing sugar, sifted
1 tbls lemon juice
For the decoration
**5 x 225 g/8 oz packets vanilla
    flavour fondant icing**
few drops of blue food colouring
150 g/5 oz chewy square sweets
225 g/8 oz box liquorice allsorts
icing sugar, for dusting

1 Heat the oven to 180° C/350° F/gas 4. Lightly grease two 23 cm/9 in pie plates, line the bases with greaseproof paper, then lightly grease the paper. Grease 1 individual bun tin.

2 Beat the margarine and sugar until pale and fluffy. Add the eggs one at a time, beating thoroughly after each addition. Using a large metal spoon, fold in the flour.

3 Spoon 1 tbls of the mixture into the bun tin, then divide the remainder between the 2 pie plates and level the surfaces.

4 Bake the large cakes in the oven for 25 minutes, the bun for 15 minutes. Turn them out on to a wire rack, peel off the lining paper and leave until cold.

5 Meanwhile, make the butter cream, beating the butter, the icing sugar and lemon juice together until pale and fluffy. Cover and set aside.

6 To prepare the decoration, put the fondant icing into a bowl and knead in the blue food colouring for a pale blue effect.

7 To assemble the cake, spread the jam on the top side of one cake and half the butter cream on the top side of the other cake. Sandwich the two together and spread butter cream around the edges to fill any gaps. Refrigerate for 1 hour until

firm. Cover the remaining butter cream and refrigerate.

8 Roll 225 g/8 oz fondant into a 1 cm/½ in thick rope, then place around circumference of the cake.

9 Stand the bun upside down and lightly roll out 225 g/8 oz fondant on a work surface dusted with icing sugar.

Place fondant on top of bun. Gently press the fondant down the sides of bun to make top of the flying saucer. Roll a small extra piece of fondant into a ball, flatten and put on top of bun. Put aside and leave to set.

10 Lightly roll out half the remaining fondant. Using an empty pie plate as a guide, cut out a round 23 cm/9 in in diameter. Lift fondant on to the cake with a fish slice and mould over cake, pressing gently until the fondant meets the 'rope'. Leave in a cool place for about 1½ hours to set. Wrap remaining fondant in cling film.

11 When the fondant has set, place a 15 cm/6 in silver board on the top, hold together and invert, so that the cake is standing on the board. Roll out remaining fondant, cut into 23 cm/9 in round and place on top of cake. Mould as before. Place the bun in centre.

12 Spoon some of the butter cream into a piping bag fitted with a small plain nozzle, then pipe a little on to the back of the square sweets and stick them round the edge of the flying saucer. Stick the liquorice allsorts on the bun centrepiece with more butter cream, then place candles on top. Leave to set for 2 hours.

Y To raise the flying saucer off the board, colour an extra packet of fondant icing yellow and mould into 4 'stands' 2 days in advance.

Right: *Flying saucer*

Spaceship cake

Serves 6-8
melted butter and flour
225 g/8 oz softened butter
225 g/8 oz caster sugar
½ tsp vanilla essence
½ tsp finely grated lemon zest
4 large eggs
225 g/8 oz flour
2 tsps baking powder
For the filling and decoration
225 g/8 oz chocolate Butter cream
   (see page 500)
100 g/4 oz green Butter cream
   (see page 500)
100-150 g/4-5 oz icing sugar
4 chocolate discs, about 25 mm/
   1 in across
8 long mint-flavoured chocolate
   sticks
1 ice cream cone
1 green liquorice comfit
1 packet oblong ice cream wafers
coloured chocolate buttons
spearmint sweets, quartered
1 mint-chocolate wafer
1 model spaceman (optional)

1 Heat the oven to 170° C/325° F/gas 3.
2 Brush the bases and sides of a 400 g/
14 oz size empty can and 2 x 1 L/1¾ pt
ovenproof bowls with melted butter.
Lightly dust the bases and sides with
flour, knocking them against the side of
the table to shake off the surplus.
3 In a large mixing bowl, combine the
butter with the caster sugar, vanilla essence and finely grated lemon zest.
Cream them together with a wooden
spoon until light and fluffy. In another
bowl, whisk the eggs until light and
frothy.
4 Beat the eggs, a few spoonfuls at a

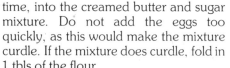

time, into the creamed butter and sugar
mixture. Do not add the eggs too
quickly, as this would make the mixture
curdle. If the mixture does curdle, fold in
1 tbls of the flour.

Above: *Spaceship cake*

5 Sift the flour and baking powder together, then add it to the creamed mixture a little at a time, folding it in lightly

but thoroughly with a large metal spoon.

6 Fill the can a quarter full and divide the remaining mixture evenly between the bowls. Bake the can for 30-35 minutes and the bowls for 1-1¼ hours. Cool the cakes for 10 minutes before turning out on to a wire rack. Leave the cakes until cold, preferably 24 hours.

7 Sandwich the bowl cakes together with some of the chocolate butter cream to make a globe.

8 Cut the rounded top off the cylindrical cake, ice its cut surface and stick it on top of the globe to form a dome.

9 Cover the domed and the cylindrical cakes with chocolate butter cream, smoothing it evenly with a palette knife.

10 Stand the cylindrical 'base' cake on a cake board and put the body of the spaceship on top. Surround the base with unsifted icing sugar 'snow'. Position the 4 chocolate discs around the edge of the board. Prop the spaceship with 2 mint chocolate sticks at each quarter point, resting the bottoms on the chocolate discs.

11 Cut the middle section out of the ice cream cone and stand it inside the base of the cone. Put the pointed end on top, attaching it with green butter cream.

12 Cut 6 'fins' from the oblong wafers (see picture). Make 6 cuts in the base of the cone with a sharp knife and insert the fins. Stand this on top of the spaceship. Break off the pointed tip of the cone and insert the liquorice comfit.

13 Cut enough 25 x 15 mm/1 x ½ in strips of wafer to stick in the icing around the body of the cake to form a ledge about halfway down. Cut more fins from other wafers and insert them beneath the ledge at each intersection (see picture).

14 Put a second ledge 25 mm/1 in below the base of the cone on top of the cake.

15 Arrange coloured chocolate buttons around the cake below the cone and at the top of the cylindrical cake. Arrange spearmint sweets around the cake above and below the main ledge to resemble lights. Edge the wafers with green butter cream.

16 Position the mint-chocolate wafer to form a ramp. If wished, stand a model spaceman next to the ramp.

Right: Space-age gingermen can be made from the mixture on page 498. Use a gingerbread woman cutter, then remove the heads and split the ends of the arms to make 'probes'. Decorate them with glacé cherries, nuts, raisins and angelica.

Cheesy stars

Makes about 17
100 g/4 oz potato, boiled
25 g/1 oz Cheddar cheese, grated
75 g/3 oz plain flour
pinch of mustard powder
pinch of cayenne
pinch of salt
25 g/1 oz margarine, diced
25 g/1 oz lard, diced
vegetable oil, for greasing

1 Heat the oven to 200° C/400° F/gas 6 and lightly grease 2 baking sheets.

2 Mash the potato, allow to cool, then press through a sieve.

3 Sift the flour, mustard, cayenne and salt into a bowl. Add the margarine and lard and rub in with your fingertips until the mixture resembles fine bread-crumbs. Stir in the potato and cheese, then knead the mixture to form a fairly stiff dough.

4 On a lightly floured surface roll out the mixture to a square 5 mm/¼ in thick. Cut into star shapes.

5 Transfer shapes to baking sheets. Bake above and below centre of oven for 15 minutes until golden brown, swapping the sheets halfway through baking. Cool on wire racks.

Animal Party

Animal cheese biscuits

Makes 50
225 g/8 oz plain flour
pinch of salt
¼ tsp mustard powder
100 g/4 oz margarine or butter
75 g/3 oz strong Cheddar cheese,
   finely grated
1 egg yolk
2 tbls water
little milk, for glazing
sesame seeds and/or poppy seeds
margarine, for greasing

1 Sift the flour, salt and mustard powder into a a large bowl. Rub in the margarine until mixture resembles fine breadcrumbs, then add the cheese. Mix in the egg yolk and water with a knife, then gather up the pastry in your hands to make a firm dough.
2 Turn the dough on to a lightly floured surface and knead briefly until smooth. Place in a polythene bag and leave to rest in the refrigerator for 30 minutes.
3 Heat the oven to 200° C/400° F/gas 6 and grease 2 baking sheets.
4 Roll out the pastry on a floured surface until it is about 2 mm/⅛ in thick. Using different-shaped animal biscuit cutters, cut out shapes and place on the greased baking sheets, spacing them apart to allow for them spreading during baking. Brush all over with milk. Using a skewer or the point of a knife, make holes for the animals' eyes, mouths, noses, etc.

Below: Butterfly birthday cake, Animal cheese biscuits, Cucumber caterpillar

5 Decorate the biscuits with sesame seeds and/or poppy seeds.
6 Bake in the oven in 2 batches for 15-20 minutes each until golden brown. Remove from the oven, allow to settle for 1-2 minutes, then place on a wire rack and leave to cool before serving.

Cucumber caterpillar

Serves 12
1 large cucumber, preferably
   slightly curved
2 glacé cherries
500 g/1 lb cocktail sausages
6 rashers streaky bacon, rinds
   removed and cut in half
   crossways
225 g/8 oz can pineapple pieces,
   drained

1 Cutting at a slant, slice off the thicker end of the cucumber. To make the eyes, spear each cherry on to the end of half a cocktail stick; press sticks in cut end of cucumber.

2 At the other end, with a sharp knife, make a few small cuts across the cucumber, about 2 mm/1/8 in apart, for the 'tail'.

3 Heat the grill to high.

4 Prick the sausages with a fork and fry over gentle heat until they are golden brown on all sides.

5 Meanwhile, wrap each half bacon rasher around a piece of pineapple and secure with a wooden cocktail stick. Grill the bacon and pineapple rolls for 3-4 minutes until the bacon is crisp. Drain on absorbent paper.

6 Drain the sausages and spear a cocktail stick into each one. Stick the sausages in a ridge down the centre of the cucumber and the bacon rolls on either side and serve at once.

Y If you have difficulty buying cocktail sausages, buy chipolatas and cut each in half by twisting the skin in the middle then cutting it.

Butterfly birthday cake

Makes 24 slices
225 g/8 oz self-raising flour
2 tsps baking powder
225 g/8 oz soft tub margarine
225 g/8 oz caster sugar
grated zest of 2 oranges
4 large eggs
margarine, for greasing
For the filling and decoration
225 g/8 oz apricot jam
25-50 g/1-2 oz desiccated coconut
225 g/8 oz icing sugar
2-3 tbls water
gravy browning
To finish
30 cm/12 in silver cake-board
3 chocolate flake bars
candles and candle-holders
3 small packets of sugar-coated
   chocolate buttons
2 liquorice 'pipes'

1 Heat the oven to 170° C/325° F/gas 3. Grease a deep 23 cm/9 in square cake tin. Line the sides and base of the tin with greaseproof paper, then grease the paper.

2 Sift the flour and baking powder into a large bowl. Add the margarine, caster sugar, orange zest and eggs. Mix well,

then beat with a wooden spoon for 2-3 minutes, or with a hand-held electric whisk for 1 minute, until blended and glossy.

3 Turn the mixture into the prepared tin and level the surface, then make a slight hollow in the centre. Bake in the oven for about 65 minutes, until the top of the cake is golden and springy to the touch.

4 Cool the cake in the tin for 5 minutes, then turn out on to a wire rack and peel off the lining paper. Leave the cake upside down to cool completely.

5 Trim the cake to level it off, if necessary. Slice the cold cake in half horizontally and sandwich together with 5 tbls of the apricot jam. Cut the cake in half diagonally to make 2 triangles, then trim off the triangle tips opposite the cut edge.

6 Sieve all but 1 tbls of the remaining jam into a small, heavy-based saucepan and stir over low heat until melted. Brush the sides of the cakes, except the trimmed corners, with some melted jam.

7 Spread a thick layer of coconut on a large plate. Press the jam-coated sides of cake into the coconut one at a time until evenly coated. (Add more coconut to plate if needed.)

8 Brush the trimmed corner of each cake with melted jam. Place the 2 pieces of cake on the cake-board, with the trimmed corners almost touching to make a butterfly shape. Place the chocolate flakes in the gap, one on top of another, then push the 2 'wings' together.

9 To make the glacé icing, sift the icing sugar into a bowl, then beat in enough water to give a thick coating consistency.

10 Put 2 tbls of the icing into a small bowl. Add several drops of gravy browning, stirring well, to make a fairly dark brown icing. Spoon this icing into a small piping bag fitted with a writing nozzle.

11 Brush the top of the cakes with the remaining melted jam. Spread the white glacé icing smoothly and evenly over the

top with a knife. Immediately, before the icing starts to set, pipe parallel lines of brown icing down the 'wings'.

12 Draw a skewer through the brown lines to give a 'feather' effect.

13 Neaten edges, removing surplus icing, then arrange the candles in their holders on top. Leave to set.

14 Two hours before the party, melt the remaining tablespoon of jam. Brush a little jam on each chocolate button and

stick them round the edges of the cake. Stick in 2 pieces of liquorice for the 'antennae' and curl them round slightly.

Y Very fresh cake is difficult to cut and ice neatly, so bake the cake a day before decorating. You can assemble and ice the cake on the evening before the party, but not before, otherwise the icing will dry out and crack.

Index

Acknowledgements

COLOUR PHOTOGRAPHS: Bryce Atwell 147(b), 184(b), 236, 391, 428; Rex Bamber 496; Tom Belshaw 240-241; Theo Bergstrom 171, 177, 183(t),280-281, 295, 313(t), 489; Martin Brigdale 22-23, 28, 31, 37, 38-39, 44-45, 46, 50-51, 62-63, 69, 71, 105(t), 146(bl), 148(b), 192(t), 214(t), 224, 234, 238, 239(t), 247, 274-275, 332-333, 401, 409, 458-459, 465; Paul Bussell 67, 106(t), 117(t), 130-131, 154, 173(b), 195(b), 200, 219, 228-229, 242, 252, 253, 254-255, 263(b), 271(t), 272, 273(t), 279, 286-287, 289, 292-293, 315(b), 319(b), 365, 432-433, 438, 439, 448-449, 450, 494-495, 499; Nick Carman 166, 178-179; Ken Copsey 353; Chris Crofton 255, 436-437; Alan Duns 18, 23(l), 41, 56-57, 87, 88, 99(t), 101, 112, 114, 148(t), 149(b), 150(bl), 152-153, 158, 159, 167(b), 172, 176(t), 187(t), 216-217, 223, 226, 251, 254, 270(r), 305(tr), 312(r), 334-335, 338, 363, 468, 484-485; Ray Duns 21, 35, 40, 48, 53, 57, 58, 70, 79(t); John Elliott 143; Laurie Evans 104, 318, 378, 379, 414(t), 430, 440, 477, 493; Paul Forrester 42, 192(b), 232; Edmund Goldspink 128-129, 144-145, 227, 475; Paul Grater 392, 394-395, 406-407, 412(t), 414(b), 426-427, 432, 442(b); Melvin Grey 209, 264(b), 367; Christine Hanscombe 316(b), 319(t); Tony Hurley 62, 68-69; James Jackson 33, 34, 49, 65, 84-85, 85, 100, 121(t), 123, 160, 163, 169, 174(t), 213, 214-215, 250, 256, 271(b), 296, 297, 309, 325, 344-345, 358-359, 360-361, 366, 374(t), 380, 390, 454-455, 476-477, 489-490; Michael Kay 109(r), 115; Paul Kemp 52-53, 480; Chris King 138, 139(t), 186, 266, 267, 268-269, 291(tr), 302-303, 306-307, 310-311, 389, 422; Dave King 387, 408; Chris Knaggs 17, 23, 59, 92, 98, 105(b), 109(l), 120-121, 212(b), 221, 239(b), 265, 273(b), 276, 342-343, 386, 396, 397(bl), 398-399, 403, 412(b), 413, 456-457; Bob Komar 36, 103, 107, 141; Don Last 47, 61, 92-93, 181(t), 191(t), 211, 218-219, 231(t), 243, 245, 308, 343, 429, 461, 502, 503; David Levin 89, 244, 257, 388, 369(b), 397, 399, 400, 401, 471, 473, 504(t), 504-505; Fred Mancini 53, 78-79(b), 90-91, 106(b), 109(l), 120-121, 161(tr), 170, 173(t), 181(b), 183(b), 202, 231(b); Peter Myers 44, 102, 148(t), 157(b), 191(l), 193, 194, 210, 215, 218, 220, 232-233, 233, 237, 290(br), 291(tl), 305(tl), 317, 324-325, 326-327, 330-331, 356-357, 372-373, 374(b), 415, 420-421, 434, 443, 469, 470, 481, 486, 490, 500-501; Roger Phillips 60-61, 162, 184(t), 301, 350; Iain Reid 299; Peter Reilly 411; Grant Symon 80-81, 82-83, 94-95, 96-97, 110-111, 117(b), 142(b), 164-165, 188-189, 206-207, 248-249, 482-483; Roger Tuff 348-349; Paul Webster 30, 54, 113, 122, 147(t), 151(t), 156, 167(t), 168, 180(b), 185(t), 230, 235, 244, 327, 346-347, 355, 370-371, 375, 377, 441, 462-463, 467, 472-473; Andrew Whittuck 86, 284; Paul Williams 55, 66, 90, 124-125, 176(b), 190, 195(t), 270(l), 277, 278-279, 304(bl), 314, 336-337, 341, 368-369, 388, 393, 398, 404, 416-417, 418-419, 423, 424, 425, 431, 442(t), 448, 466-467, 474, 478-479; Paul Windsor 29, 46-47, 225; George Wright 262, 290(t), 289(br); Graham Young 32, 99(r), 174(b), 182, 234-235, 246, 488.

STEP BY STEP PHOTOGRAPHS: Martin Brigdale 415(t); Ken Copsey 330, 331(r), 336, 339, 342, 347, 348, 349, 352, 353, 354, 364, 372, 373; Alan Duns 15, 16(tr), 351, 469, 497; Paul Grater 138-195, 200-257; Melvin Grey 340; Tony Hurley 15(t), 16(tc), 16(b), 17, 20, 22(l), 25, 28, 29, 30, 31, 34, 35, 40, 44, 46, 47, 48, 52, 54, 57, 58, 61, 64, 67, 68, 71, 456, 457, 458, 459, 460, 464, 466, 468, 471, 473, 474, 476, 479, 484, 487, 489, 491, 492, 493, 498, 502, 503; James Jackson 123, 381; Paul Kemp 341, 480; David Levin 331(l), 335, 351, 366, 367, 371, 378, 451(b), 472, 485, 504, 505(t); Fred Mancini 116; Peter Myers 374-375; Nick Powell 91; Grant Symon 84, 87, 88, 93, 94, 99, 100, 103, 104, 105, 107, 108, 113, 115, 119, 127, 130; Paul Webster 376, 467, 505(r); Paul Williams 371, 449.

ILLUSTRATIONS: Alan Suttie 14; Simon Roulstone 452.

The publishers would also like to thank Belling & Co. Ltd. for providing photographs, Elizabeth David Ltd. and David Mellor for lending props for photography, and Sharp Electronics (UK) Ltd. for lending ovens for photography.